Frontispiece

Lord Keynes, Lord Halifax, Mr. Byrnes and Mr. Vinson at the signing of the Anglo-American loan agreement at the Department of State on 6 December 1945. Standing behind from left to right are Mr. R.H. Brand, Sir Henry Self, Sir Edward Bridges, Professor Robbins, Sir Percivale Liesching, Mr. Dean Acheson, Mr. W.L. Clayton and Mr. Thomas B. McCabe.

DOCUMENTS ON
BRITISH POLICY OVERSEAS

EDITED BY

ROGER BULLEN, Ph.D.
(London School of Economics)

AND

M.E. PELLY, M.A.

ASSISTED BY

H.J. YASAMEE, M.A. AND G. BENNETT, M.A.

SERIES I

Volume III

LONDON

HER MAJESTY'S STATIONERY OFFICE

ISBN 0 11 591684 9

Printed for Her Majesty's Stationery Office by Hobbs the Printers
Dd 716937 C13 11/86

DOCUMENTS ON BRITISH POLICY OVERSEAS

Series I, Volume III

Britain and America: Negotiation of the United States loan
3 August – 7 December 1945

PREFACE

VOLUMES I and II concentrated on Britain as one of the Big Three. Volumes III and IV are focused on Britain's bilateral relationship with the biggest of the Big Three, the United States of America, from August 1945 to July 1946. A full coverage would extend globally as the relations between two world-wide powers were conducted in exchanges of views and overlapping of interests in virtually all corners of the earth. Transatlantic issues only are treated in this volume but the unseen effects on the Anglo-American relationship of developments in other areas must be borne in mind.

In this first year after the War it began to appear that for Britain, the weakest of the Three, to maintain her position as a world power would over-extend her resources. In most situations she was unable to impose her views on the American Government, but could only seek to modify the details of policies pursued by a United States very conscious of the world supremacy earned by her war effort, and from 6 August 1945 by her possession of the atomic bomb. Volume III takes the story up to December 1945.

Two papers, Nos. 1 and 3, written in early August by Mr. Hall-Patch in the Foreign Office and Mr. John Balfour in Washington from the economic and political standpoints respectively, highlight the problems. To begin with an exhausted Britain required urgent financial aid for reconstruction from the United States, with the alternative being, as Lord Keynes, the eminent adviser to the Treasury, saw it, isolation, which meant 'Starvation Corner' or 'Austerity' (see No. 1). The urgent need for financial aid arose because since July Lend-Lease had been limited to supplies for the war against Japan, and that war was about to end. On 10 August, the very day of the Japanese offer to surrender, British Treasury representatives in Washington were warned that 'it would be impossible to justify continued shipment on credit Lend-lease to United Kingdom for more than very short time after V.J. day' (message from Mr. Lee in No. 4).

At the same time the Americans would now be seeking British redemption of the pledge in Article 7 of the Mutual Aid Agreement of 1942 that as the 'consideration' for Lend-Lease all forms of discriminatory treatment in international commerce should be eliminated. This struck at the life blood of the British Commonwealth, the system of Imperial Preference, and at the trading and banking system of the Sterling Area, centred in London, where payments outside the area were controlled, as described by Lord Keynes in No. 98. Mr. Hall-Patch suggested that in forthcoming talks with Mr. W.L. Clayton, U.S. Assistant Secretary of State for Economic Affairs, a leading protagonist of a multilateral approach to international trade, British acquiescence regarding commercial policy might well influence the attitude of the U.S. Administration to financial aid. Furthermore 'at a time when America was ready and eager to enter into broad international commitments' it would be damaging politically as well as economically to Britain if she pursued a contrary policy, and the United States again retreated into isolation (No. 1).

On the political side Mr. Balfour discussed the implications of the American public's perception of Britain as a junior partner, even, in an extreme case, as 'of no more significance than Costa Rica' (No. 3). By contrast American opinion saw Soviet Russia emerging from the war as 'the only world power comparable in stature to the United States'. Responsible official circles, wrote Mr. Balfour, believed that the United States, as the major Western Power, should 'take the initiative in determining the shape of things on the periphery of the Soviet orbit no less than elsewhere'. Although there was a deep seated conviction that 'a strong and prosperous Britain is an essential U.S. interest', there were also fears that on this Soviet periphery British foreign policy could 'embark on ill-advised courses which in the last analysis might constitute a threat to United States' security'.

Concern for security as well as idealism and hard business instinct were, in Mr. Balfour's view, factors encouraging American expansionism in such fields as trade, shipping, aviation, telecommunications and oil exploitation. It was not Soviet interests which confronted such pressure but those of the rambling British Commonwealth, and Anglo-American discussions on all these issues are considered in this volume. Thus, while the Conferences at Potsdam, London and Moscow documented in Volumes I and II show a general Western alignment against the U.S.S.R., American support for Britain was far from automatic, and as the negotiations documented in the present volume develop a picture of a Britain on the defensive against stronger American interests emerges.

On 14 August an authoritative survey of 'Our Overseas Financial Prospects' by Lord Keynes (see No. 6), circulated to the Cabinet by Mr. Hugh Dalton, Chancellor of the Exchequer, spelt out the problems outlined by Mr. Hall-Patch. Lord Keynes argued that $5 billions were required from the United States to meet British commitments. He hoped for a grant-in-aid, even if described as a credit, since 'payment of interest and stipulated terms of repayment' could not be undertaken 'in addition to our existing obligations with any confidence that we can fulfil the obligations'. Lord Keynes' views were in line with Mr. Hall-Patch's arguments in No. 1, but he added that 'the most persuasive argument we can use for obtaining the desired aid is that only by this means will it lie within our power to enter into international co-operation in the economic field on the general principle of non-discrimination . . . In my opinion we need not despair of obtaining an agreement which provides sufficient safeguards and will not seriously hamper the future development of our economy along lines freely determined by our own policies. Bases, islands, air facilities and the like may conceivably come into the picture.'

With the United Kingdom 'virtually bankrupt', Lord Keynes concluded that '(*a*) an intense concentration on the expansion of exports, (*b*) drastic and immediate economies in our overseas expenditure, and (*c*) substantial aid from the United States on terms which we can accept' were required to avoid 'a financial Dunkirk' leading to acceptance of the position of a second-class power and austerity at home for about five years. For the future Lord Keynes predicted an age of abundance and believed that advance into it should not be endangered as the time would come 'when the sums which now overwhelm us may seem chicken-feed'.

While believing that a free grant from the United States would constitute 'Justice' (see No. 1), Lord Keynes was aware of the possibility that the Americans might require interest and attach other conditions to any financial assistance to the U.K. In particular they would press for early British adherence to the agreements reached at Bretton Woods in 1944, including those sections of the Articles of Agreement of the International Monetary Fund which provided for the removal of currency discrimination and for the convertibility of foreign held balances during a transitional period of 3–5 years after the war, provisions which were of special importance to the U.K. in view of her indebtedness to the Sterling Area countries (the accumulated sterling balances). It was clear to Lord Keynes from the outset that while American financial aid might make possible the early convertibility of current sterling earnings, it was vital for the U.K. to retain her rights under the transitional period to modify more gradually the basis of her financial and trading relations with the Sterling Area.

The Foreign Secretary, Mr. Bevin, however, was 'anxious to be able to isolate us if there is a major economic recession in the U.S.A. which he fears. He is not at all sure that we shall be able to do this if we take Bretton Woods as it stands. On this point he will see Lord Keynes next week and go over the ground with him' (minute of 9 August by Mr. Hall-Patch – No. 1, note 12). As Lord Keynes recorded on 15 August, Mr. Bevin preferred not to 'agree to commit ourselves to any monetary or commercial arrangements . . . until we could see our way more clearly', though he accepted that financial facilities to cover the transitional period should be sought from the Americans (No. 9). While sympathising with Mr. Bevin's view, Lord Keynes believed that the Bretton Woods agreements contained 'sufficient safeguards to be safe' and that the advantages of the commercial arrangements proposed by the Americans (see No. 2) outweighed the disadvantages. In a review of necessary action Lord Keynes argued that financial negotiations with the Americans should begin forthwith, with winding up Lend-Lease the first topic, while Cabinet decisions on commercial policy could be deferred.

On the following day in the Foreign Office Mr. John Coulson, Acting Head of Economic Relations Department, also considered the situation in a brief (No. 10) for Mr. Bevin for the second of a series of informal meetings which he had arranged with Mr. Dalton and Sir S. Cripps, President of the Board of Trade, to co-ordinate the economic aspects of foreign policy (see No. 6). While covering broadly similar ground to Lord Keynes, Mr. Coulson highlighted in particular that 'the U.S. Government will give us no financial support unless its repayment comes ahead of the repayment of our debts to the sterling area and unless we accept their proposals in regard to commercial and commodity policy, as well as ratifying the Bretton Woods Agreements', and he concluded that 'if we do not get from the U.S. the financial assistance we need, we shall ... be forced to take measures which would result in a serious deterioration of our relations with the U.S.'.

Within the week three high-level meetings on 20, 21 and 23 August (Nos. 12, 13 and 17) advanced the formulation of British policy both on the long-term financial need for American aid and the immediate situation caused by the termination of Lend-Lease, announced in a letter of 18 August from Mr. Crowley, U.S. Foreign Economic Administrator, and involving the stoppage of all food shipments to the United Kingdom as from that day (No. 11). The first meeting, between Mr. Bevin and Mr. Dalton and their advisers, agreed that the two Ministers should see Mr. Clayton before it could be decided whether a second British contribution of 1% of national income could be made to the United Nations Relief and Rehabilitation Administration, as proposed in a Resolution then under discussion by the U.N.R.R.A. Council.

The second meeting (No. 13), with Mr. Clayton on 21 August, was the first Ministerial discussion with a high American authority on the British financial predicament since 'this most grim problem' (No. 6) had been put to the Cabinet (v.ibid., note 2). Mr. Dalton apparently said nothing, even on the general British financial case, but left Mr. Bevin to expound his views in a development from those in No. 9. Mr. Bevin first voiced his doubts as to how to meet the commitment to U.N.R.R.A., a problem complicated by political bargaining introduced by the Russians in applying for aid themselves. His main concern was about being tied down by the interlocking American proposals on financial and economic policy during the restoration of a full peace-time economy in Britain, which might extend to five years. He also hoped that the 6 billion dollars of exchange which Britain had spent before Lend-Lease would be taken into account.

Mr. Clayton made it clear that the extra British contribution to U.N.R.R.A. was connected with his proposal to Lord Keynes that talks on Lend-Lease, financial and commercial policy should begin in Washington on 1 September, that financial aid was linked to a multilateral commercial policy, and that compensation for U.K. expenditure in 1940 would not be possible, 'the most that could be got would be credit on very liberal terms'. The immediate result was that the Americans agreed that the flow of supplies should be continued, on terms to be mutually agreed, and that Britain agreed to pay the extra 1% to U.N.R.R.A.

At the third meeting (No. 17), on 23 August, Lord Keynes set out for Ministers his ideas on handling the negotiations, notably that he thought that initially he should not be authorized to agree to anything except an out and out grant. If the Americans agreed to a sum of 4 or 5 billion dollars, as a *quid pro quo* it would be possible to ask the Sterling Area countries to cancel part of the British indebtedness to them and agree that the remainder should be made fully convertible by instalments. On Bretton Woods Lord Keynes repeated the views in No. 9 and, despite Mr. Clayton's warning, maintained that there would not be detailed discussions on commercial policy at this stage. Mr. R.H. Brand, Head of the Treasury Delegation in Washington, was less hopeful than Lord Keynes about a grant in aid.

The meeting concluded by entrusting the negotiations to Lord Halifax and Lord Keynes (the wording of the Parliamentary statement giving this precedence to H.M. Ambassador at Washington was presumably deliberate) and approving the latter's proposals for their conduct. A suggestion by Mr. Bevin, Mr. Dalton and Sir S. Cripps in a minute of 22 August to Mr. Attlee for 'a careful study of alternative sources of supply both in food and raw materials' to provide a 'bargaining counter' in the negotiations produced nothing useful (No. 17, note 2). These four Ministers and Mr. H. Morrison, Lord President of the Council, met informally on weekday evenings to direct the Whitehall response to the Delegation (see No. 18, note 2, also No. 22, note 4).

In the event Lord Keynes was wrong about commercial policy on which the Americans, while disavowing any intention of linking the 'financial and commercial discussions tactically in a spirit which would exploit the U.K. financial situation', persuaded Whitehall to overrule Lord Keynes and 'send out our Commercial Policy first eleven, headed by Sir Percivale Liesching' of the Board of Trade (Nos. 27, 30–2). This was the first British concession.

The meeting also approved a Parliamentary statement in which the Prime Minister would express regret at the sudden termination of Lend-Lease. According to a letter from Mr. Brand on his return to Washington, Mr. Truman and Mr. Byrnes were 'furious . . . very largely from a bad conscience' (cf. No. 17). Some softening of the American rigidity on Lend-Lease followed a personal appeal (No. 20) from Mr. Attlee to the President, who agreed that supplies to the United Kingdom should continue and the terms of payment be settled by the Financial Mission (see No. 23).

On arriving in Washington on 7 September Lord Keynes telegraphed that the Mission were anxious not to make heavy weather of Lend-Lease, where the Americans were unlikely to concede much, in view of the 'much more important main negotiations' (No. 24). Private conversations indicated that the American War Department had 'very moderate' views (No. 33) and Lord Keynes was able to agree with Mr. Crowley on 20 September that future British requirements would in the interim be financed either by cash payments or by a 30-year credit at $2\frac{3}{8}$ per cent interest (Nos. 37–8). This was acceptable to the Treasury, though they feared that large sums might be owed before Congress approved the major settlement (No. 40). At this stage in the negotiations the Treasury felt they could not urge Ministers to cut food rations (No. 36), a view which was justified by the increasing likelihood of a global settlement on Lend-Lease at a reasonable level.

Meanwhile Lord Keynes had prepared a final version (see No. 22) of his paper of 14 August (No. 6). This paper identified two main problems: the treatment of the accumulated sterling balances and the running adverse balance. Though the latter was the most immediately serious, the former had wider consequences because Britain owed it to the Sterling Area countries, many of them poor, to begin to release these balances which comprised substantially their reserves which they had entrusted to Britain during the war. This liability could neither be repudiated nor subordinated to other debts.

Lord Keynes suggested alternative courses of action. The first was a development of the Sterling Area, with full convertibility within the Sterling Area and with countries linked to it by Payments agreements, which would be the best that Britain could do on her own: an 'essay in cunctation' which would postpone any final settlement of the U.K.'s financial position until after the transitional period.

The second alternative was a liquidation of the financial consequences of the war, in which Britain accepted a unique burden of external indebtedness to her Allies amounting to $16–18 billions. For the $12–14 billions from this total which were owed to the other countries of the Sterling Area, Lord Keynes set out a plan which centred on negotiations with each country for writing off about $4 billions, together with a gradual release of about $8 billions: current earnings would also be released. To help solve the question of British wartime indebtedness the United States should place at Britain's disposal $5 billions over three years. Lord Keynes felt that with less 'we could not accept the responsibility of the obligation to make sterling available on the scale suggested . . . or of relaxing the existing Sterling Area arrangements so soon as the end of 1946'. Lord Keynes did not, however, use the word 'convertibility'.

After a few days in Ottawa, where his Canadian hosts were 'so jolly and truly warm in their approach' (No. 28), Lord Keynes found the atmosphere in Washington on 7 September 'rather too good', with indications that the U.S. Treasury were thinking of a 50–year loan without interest, but that a disturbing plan by Dr. Harry White, Assistant Secretary of the U.S. Treasury, for the United States to take over a certain part of the sterling balances was in the air.

Chapter II, which covers the introductory period of the negotiations when the two sides were each probing the other's intentions, begins with the first high level meeting on 11 September (No. 29). The wide-ranging scrutiny to which the Americans would subject British affairs was soon apparent in the 'keen interest' they took in 'our vast Middle East expenditure' (Mr. Hall-Patch, No. 34). In the same letter Mr. Hall-Patch warned that the Americans seemed unlikely to accept Lord Keynes' plan to reach a settlement with them first and then to deal with the Sterling Area creditors. He disliked their approach 'as commercial bankers' expecting priority over all other creditors, and advised breaking off the negotiations if they developed in this way.

On 21 September Lord Keynes reported pressure in this direction from Mr. Clayton and his colleagues, but remained hopeful that 'a fair settlement all round' could be achieved (No. 39). His request, however, for authority to present in writing his proposals, covering not only the amount of assistance required but also sterling, gave 'serious grounds for hesitation' in London as leakages could cause 'serious trouble with Dominions and India', and, tactically, it was suggested, with Mr. Attlee's agreement, that it would be desirable to get the Americans to indicate, 'in a form which could be used if necessary', that an adjustment of the sterling balances would be part of the deal for assistance (No. 41). Lord Keynes reported on 29 September, in connexion with Mr. Clayton's emphatic statement that 'we must expect special treatment of the sterling balances to be part of any settlement', that he had 'indicated to the Americans that the new system would come into operation not later than the end of 1946' (No. 49).

With Lord Keynes having completed his exposition of the British case on 20 September (see No. 39) the next move, on American initiative, was to invite Lord Halifax and Lord Keynes for the first of a series of private talks with Mr. Vinson, U.S. Secretary of the Treasury, and Mr. Clayton. From this talk, on 25 September, it became clear that the proposals on sterling were acceptable to the Americans (No. 44) but '(a) *no* grant in aid, (b) no loan *without* interest' (Mr. Hall-Patch, No. 45). Mr. Hall-Patch gloomily suggested that it might be better to withdraw for a few months in the hope that the Americans might come to a better appreciation of British difficulties.

At the second meeting *à quatre* on 27 September, however, it appeared that there was a possibility of American consideration of a combination of a grant-in-aid with a credit at a low rate of interest and an escape clause (No. 46), especially if accompanied by 'some sweetener' such as extending the leases for American bases in the West Indies to 999 years (No. 47). American pressure was increased at the next such meeting on 5 October, when it appeared that the American airlines were lobbying to make an agreement on civil aviation, on which negotiations had been deadlocked since the Chicago Conference of 1944, a condition of financial assistance (No. 58).

Meanwhile on 1 October Lord Keynes sought further guidance on the basis of his belief that 'a non-interest loan, repayment of which begins ten years hence, represents the very best terms we have any hope of getting' (No. 51), adding three days later, however, that 'nothing nearly so good as this is yet in sight' (No. 57). He pointed out that the £25 millions ($100 millions) annual repayment on a loan of $5 billions was little more than the cost of importing American films, while the alternative was the austerity he had described in No. 6. Sir W. Eady in the Treasury, however, preferred the idea mooted on 27 September (Nos. 46 and 57, note 4), commenting also that the 'adjustment of our relations with the Sterling Area is going to be very much more difficult than Keynes has ever been willing to admit' (*ibid.*).

The Ministerial instructions sent to Lord Halifax and Lord Keynes on 8 October (No. 62), while still hoping that there were ways of dressing up a grant to appear as a repayment, in effect accepted that a gift was not obtainable and assistance must be in the form of a loan. This was the second British retreat from the plan of 23 August. Ministerial concern focused on avoiding obligations which Britain could not be certain of discharging, with the £25 millions postulated by Lord Keynes regarded as a maximum. Furthermore conditions relating to trading terms and exchange rates were put forward, especially the possibility of a world shortage of dollars, and the sensitivity of the sterling question stressed. American desiderata in respect of civil aviation and bases in the British Empire (see No. 61) were to be considered on their merits and not under the pressure of the talks.

At the same time the commercial negotiations, on which the first British concession had been made, were proceeding (Nos. 54, 59–60, 63–5). The fundamental problem was American determination to secure the elimination of Imperial Preference in return for what appeared to the British negotiators to be inadequate assurances on tariff reductions, with the possibility still that the American intention was to make this elimination a condition for financial assistance. The 'idea of using a financial pistol to obtain preference concessions' was repudiated by Mr. Vinson, who referred to the English blood flowing through his own veins (No. 69), and despite some misgivings in Whitehall and among the Dominions (Nos. 70 and 83) about compromise proposals suggested by the British negotiating team (No. 65), on 6 November Sir S. Cripps was able to circulate to his Cabinet colleagues a memorandum (No. 95) announcing that agreement with the Americans on a revised version of the proposals put forward in August by Mr. Clayton was near. In particular all the Dominions and India would be invited to attend the preliminary conference on the proposed International Trade Organisation, and a new formula on preferences linked their elimination with 'substantial reduction of tariffs . . . in conjunction with adequate measures for the substantial reduction of barriers to world trade' (Annex A, *ibid.*). Sir S. Cripps sent his 'best thanks' to Sir P. Liesching and his colleagues for their 'magnificent fight' (*ibid.*, note 1), and on 29 November told the Cabinet that 'our negotiators had obtained satisfaction on all the points which they had raised' (No. 132).

When the two British negotiators put the financial proposals in No. 62 to Mr. Clayton and Mr. Vinson on 9 October they remained 'outwardly adamant that neither a grant nor a loan free of interest was practical politics . . . in the present mood of Congress and the public', even though the financial concessions involved were 'only peanuts'. Mr. Clayton now, for the first time, made a proposal. It was for a loan of 5 billion dollars repayable after five years with interest by annuities of 150 million dollars. This worked out at interest of more than 1 per cent. (No. 67: 1.7% in the calculation in No. 74). After the very real British anxieties about possible currency difficulties in meeting these payments (see No. 62) had been explained the Americans accepted the principle of escape clauses on the lines put to Mr. Dalton in No. 68. None of this was acceptable to Ministers: 'in the circumstances in which our need to borrow has arisen' it lacked 'the sweet breath of justice' (No. 71); and an annuity of 150 million dollars was not peanuts. But the Americans were not to be shifted (No. 72).

On 18 October, six weeks after his arrival in Washington, Lord Keynes took stock of the situation in consultation with others in the Delegation (No. 74). The 'grand gesture of unforgetting regard' represented by the solution that he had put to the Americans on the basis of No. 22, 'which would enable us to share world responsibilities with them free from undue financial pre-occupation and to join them in shaping the pattern of world commerce and currency on lines which would favour expansion and general prosperity', and which might have interested President Roosevelt, appeared 'out of character with the general lines' followed by President Truman's Administration. Therefore 'substituting prose for poetry' must be considered. Mr. Clayton was willing to find an acceptable solution, but it would have to 'escape notice wearing a business suit'.

Lord Keynes accordingly recommended accepting the proposal in No. 67. He argued that with a form of escape clause or waiver, which provided a safeguard in years when exports did not reach £750 millions at prewar prices, Britain could almost certainly afford the extra $50 millions over the Ministerial limit of $100 millions. He also submitted a waiver relating to a breakdown of multilateral clearing, a world depression and scarcity of dollars: the slightly revised version subsequently presented to the Americans (No. 97) was not well received (No. 96), and the final agreement included only a very generalised formula. The possibility that the powerful American economy would not import from Britain, thus making it very difficult to pay off the debt, was, however, a justified concern to British Ministers.

Meanwhile, on 20 October, Mr. Vinson and Mr. Clayton put to the British Delegation the best offer which they could make which was likely to be acceptable to Congress (No. 78). This was less favourable than the already-rejected offer of 9 October in that the loan would be for $3.5 billions at 2 per cent. interest, plus the sum required to settle Lend-Lease at 2⅜ per cent. repayable over thirty years. Eventually Lord Keynes persuaded the Americans to consider a figure of $4 billions plus the clean-up of Lend-Lease, repayable in fifty equal annual instalments, beginning after 5 years, with annual interest payments equivalent to 2 per cent. over the whole period, which would be payable only when British exports and net invisible income exceeded £875 millions at prewar prices.

The Delegation were convinced that nothing better was now attainable: a further departure from the hopes of August.

There followed a week's pause, and Chapter III opens on 27 October with a 'definite' British proposal (No. 81, ultimately presented to the Americans in No. 97). In No. 81 Alternative A was for a loan of $2½ billions for 50 years at 1 per cent. with a waiver condition, plus an option on a further $2 billions interest-free to help free current expenditure outside the Sterling Area of members of the Area. If this were acceptable Britain would seek a contribution from her sterling creditors towards rehabilitating the whole situation, sponsor the proposed International Trade Conference and adhere to the Bretton Woods Agreements. Alternative B for borrowing on commercial terms without these three commitments was ruled out by the Delegation as being 'quite beyond any practical possibility' (No. 85), though Mr. Bevin had seen advantages in the independence of a commercial loan and Mr. Coulson supported the Treasury's 'rather rigid line' (No. 81.i–ii).

Comment in No. 82 on the British proposal showed once again how difficult it was for Ministers, 'reluctant to admit' any dependence on the United States (Sir W. Eady, No. 71, note 7), to accept that the American attitude was business-like rather than altruistic. Yet they had reason to complain that they were borrowing money in order to enable countries which were 'valuable markets of our own to turn to dollar goods in the immediate future' and 'probably making sterling convertible earlier than we should like', though the move towards this would, by this plan, be regulated and on the lines set out by Lord Keynes in No. 22. At the same time, however, Mr. Dalton, who mentioned the 'risk of deep misunderstanding with the Americans' about sterling balances, informed the Mission that 'we could not at any time have been bound by advance arithmetic on this matter' (No. 82). This question was further discussed by Lord Keynes in No. 88, where he pointed out that he had emphasized repeatedly to the Americans that the contemplated arrangements with the Sterling Area would not be 'a unilateral imposition of a cut-and-dried settlement'. Some countries, such as India, might stand out, in which case their postwar earnings would be available for current transactions, but their wartime accumulations would only be repaid after Britain had met her other obligations.

Ministers also disliked the form of waiver proposed by Lord Keynes, who appreciated their misgivings about possible Congressional interference, but argued that the British position after accepting a plan approved by the American Administration would be 'immensely stronger' (Nos. 85 and 87). In the Foreign Office, where Mr. Coulson considered the waiver 'a very valuable safeguard', Mr. Hall-Patch noted on 3 November that Mr. Bevin 'does not like waivers in principle. Nevertheless if they were necessary in order to enable us to obtain the financial assistance we need he would be prepared to accept them on the distinct understanding that ... they do not admit of any prying into our affairs ...' (No. 87, note 9).

This marked an increasing conviction by Mr. Bevin that the loan was essential to Britain for domestic and foreign policy reasons.

Mr. Bevin appears to have followed the course of the negotiations more closely, and to have been more alive to their implications, than most of his officials. Indeed, during Mr. Hall-Patch's absence in Washington Mr. Coulson was almost alone in keeping abreast of developments in Washington, crucial though their outcome would be for the future conduct of British foreign policy. Thus Sir A. Cadogan, the Permanent Under Secretary of State, was 'afraid I, too, have been unable to follow the Keynes talks' (No. 84, note 8). Interest in the Foreign Office was largely limited to the question of possible 'sweeteners' (see No. 73), although Mr. N. Butler, an Assistant Under Secretary of State, noted on 27 October that Lord Halifax and he 'consistently believed that no solution will be possible . . . if the issue is treated as a purely financial one, which it is not'. He urged that it would be 'most unfortunate if an irreparable breakdown now occurred because the Americans were not aware' that concessions in regard to bases, on which Mr. Bevin was trying to 'get from U.S. what they want', were contemplated (No. 84). Mr. Bevin, while unwilling to be browbeaten by American airline interests on a matter of great potential for British invisible earnings, was also anxious about 'the strain which the continued absence of any decision on . . . questions of principle [on civil aviation] is imposing on our relations with the United States' (No. 91). Fortunately Mr. Clayton wished to keep this issue, and that of telecommunications, separate from the financial negotiations (No. 93).

Some ten days after the despatch of No. 81, and following two Cabinet meetings on 6 November, Lord Halifax and Lord Keynes were authorised to present the British proposal (No. 97) to the Americans, which they did that afternoon. This was the first written paper to emerge from the negotiations which had already lasted almost two months. The Delegation reported next day that Mr. Vinson and Mr. Clayton 'took the whole paper quietly', but the waiver based on sufficient U.K. exports was the only point taken as 'definitely acceptable': on this matter they were optimistic about avoiding Congressional interference. On the negative side Mr. Vinson recalled that his approved offer was limited to $3½ billions. Worse, he and Mr. Clayton now denied that 'any part of the proposed credit was for the purpose of bailing out the Sterling area. At the same [time] that they regard our proposals for liberalising the area as a necessary condition of the credit, they reject the idea of definitely associating the two things' (No. 96). Nevertheless on 7 November Lord Keynes sent to Dr. Harry White the full statement on the proposed arrangements of the Sterling Area (No. 98), which had been carefully drafted in consultation with the Treasury.

A period of nearly two weeks ensued when only scanty reports emerged from a form of negotiation described on 15 November by a 'steadily more worried' Mr. Hall-Patch as 'the "smoke-filled room" technique with no witnesses and no record' (No. 104). He had already written on 9

November (No. 100) that 'the Americans apparently want us to give sterling full Bretton Woods convertibility by June 1946 as a counterpart of *any* financial assistance. This is a bitter pill, and quite impossible for us to swallow.' 'This is news', commented Mr. Coulson in the Foreign Office (*ibid.*) It was, however, certain by 11 November that the British proposals of 6 November were 'finally rejected' – yet another backward step – though there was still the possibility of a loan of $4½ billions plus a settlement of Lend-Lease on the same terms. These were 'a five years moratorium followed by a fifty years annuity of 31,800 dollars for each 1,000,000 dollars of the original amount of the loan'. The Americans described this as a 2 per cent loan, but allowing for the moratorium it worked out at 1.6 per cent, which still compared favourably with Mr. Dalton's cheap money policy at home. But 'several tiresome and difficult points have been raised and some matters have been re-opened' (No. 101).

While the Washington negotiators were thus engaged, on 8 November Mr. Bevin was considering 'The Foreign Situation' in a survey of 'the developments that are taking place as a whole', notably what he termed 'three great Monroes', namely the spheres of influence of the United States in the Western hemisphere under the Monroe Doctrine (cf. No. 3, note 6), the Soviet sphere from Lubeck to Port Arthur, and Britain 'between the two with the western world all divided up, with the French and British colonial empire[s] separated and with a very weak position in what is called the western group'. It seemed to him that 'we are dealing with power politics naked and unashamed . . . therefore the only safe course for this country is to stand firm behind the United Nations Organisation', and 'within the conception of the United Nations' to maintain the security of the British Commonwealth and develop good relations with near neighbours (No. 99). This pessimistic assessment, with its unusually harsh criticism of the Americans, illustrates Mr. Bevin's appreciation of Western Europe's weak position in relation to the two superpowers, but was justifiably queried by Lord Halifax who did not see American policy as designed to divide the world in the manner described (No. 99.i). Mr. Bevin was almost certainly influenced by the unsatisfactory outcome of the London Conference of Foreign Ministers in the previous month, and probably also by the adverse turn which the financial negotiations appeared to be taking.

In Mr. Bevin's survey another underlying consideration may have been the American desire for bases. Secretary of State James F. Byrnes informed Lord Halifax on 7 November that the United States sought British support in negotiations for bases in Iceland and the Portuguese Atlantic islands (see Nos. 48, 61 and 90), the grant of military bases in 9 British Commonwealth administered islands in the Pacific and in Ascension Island, abandonment of the British claim to sovereignty over 25 disputed islands in the Pacific and joint negotiations with the Indian Government for the United States to share with the U.K. rights to the military use of two air bases in India. In view of the constitutional status of

India Lord Halifax told Mr. Byrnes that this last suggestion would present 'great difficulty' (No. 102, note 2). On these sweeping requests Mr. Bevin sought the views of Mr. Winston Churchill.

The notion of joint Anglo-American occupation of bases was one which appealed to Mr. Churchill's grandiose vision and to his fervent belief, as he wrote to Mr. Bevin on 13 November (No. 102), that 'a special and privileged relationship between Great Britain and the United States makes us both safe for ourselves and more influential as regards building up the safety of others through the international machine'. Such a relationship would mean that 'we should be able to achieve more friendly and trustful relations with Soviet Russia' and 'build up the United Nations organization around us and above us with greater speed and success'. Mr. Churchill urged Mr. Bevin to seize 'this sublime opportunity'.

Mr. Bevin set out his views in his report of 29 November to the Defence Committee (No. 135), after he had sought further clarifications from Mr. Byrnes (Nos. 103 and 127–8). He believed that it was 'on broad grounds of the highest importance, to take advantage of Mr. Byrnes' move to tie up the United States to the maximum extent in the defence of the British Commonwealth', but he saw 'very serious objection' in Mr. Byrnes contemplating the suggested arrangements before the establishment of the international system of security under the Security Council, thus giving the Russians 'gratuitous and justifiable cause for suspicion'. Privately, he told Lord Halifax that 'many people in this country are getting frightfully worried about the push of the United States right around us with bases which, it appears from their claim, are to be a purely United States affair'. For himself he disclaimed 'fear of any difficulty with the United States in the future', and in a Churchillian phrase concluded: 'I want partnership, which will give us a sense of fairness and security' (No. 128). Mr. Churchill himself was to return to the theme with remarkable effect in his Fulton Speech of 5 March 1946.

The opening of a new phase in the financial negotiations in Washington was signalled on 18 November by the arrival of a clutch of telegrams (see Nos. 106–110) from the Mission in Washington discussing proposals likely to be forthcoming from the Americans and forecasting 'further troubles ahead' (see No. 106). On the waiver, for instance, 'the technicians and lawyers got to work, in elaborating complicated provisions which were clearly incompatible with your fundamental conditions for accepting a waiver clause' (*ibid.*).

No comment had been sent from London before the Mission reported on 21 November that an American text, dated 18 November (No. 113), had been presented at the meeting of the Combined Finance Committee on 19 November. This text, which included both amendments suggested by the British and 'novel provisions' prepared by American experts, was described as 'provisional' by the Mission, who made suggestions themselves and sought further instructions from Mr. Dalton (No. 111). They did, however, suggest, perhaps only too prophetically, that the only convenient course would be to treat the text as 'a final or formal proposal'. In the event over two further weeks of negotiation produced few changes of substance in this American draft memorandum of understanding, which the Americans persisted in retaining as the text under negotiation. This marked a further backward step for the British negotiators.

The main points in the American draft of 18 November were:

(1) The amount of the credit was unfixed.

(2) The purposes of the credit were to assist British purchases in the United States, to meet deficits in the British balance of payments, to help Britain maintain adequate reserves and to assume the obligations of multilateral trade. The understanding that the credit was not to be used to settle obligations to other countries was important to the Americans to avert Congressional objections.

(3) The interest was to be 2 per cent. paid in 50 instalments beginning on 31 December 1951 (cf. No. 101).

(4) The provisions on waiver were: firstly an elaboration of the formula for waiving of interest based on average annual U.K. imports of £866 millions in 1936–8 (see Nos. 74, 96–7), with the addition of a complicated formula about British reserves against which the Mission argued in No. 106; secondly a waiver would not be allowed unless accompanied by corresponding waivers of payments on new British loans and sterling balances for release after 1950.

(5) On accelerated repayment it was stipulated that in the case of early repayment, above a ceiling of $175 millions, of the loans and balances mentioned in (4), corresponding early repayment of the American credit would be made. The Mission regarded this stipulation and the corresponding second provision in (4) as 'quite inacceptable' (No. 111).

The Mission had pointed out, however, that Mr. Clayton 'began by being very insistent that the American credit, being new money, was to have absolute priority over repayment of accumulated Sterling balances'. What was now proposed was therefore 'a concession from his point of view' (No. 109), and Mr. Clayton needed to be able to tell Congress that he had protected the position of the United States. A redraft was accordingly suggested (No. 112).

(6) On Sterling Area exchange arrangements the British Government would complete arrangements as early as practicable and in any case not later than the end of 1946 for full convertibility of sterling receipts from current transactions of all sterling area countries. The wording of this American proposal was identical to that in No. 107 which the Delegation had described as 'much more satisfactory than ... we would have ventured to hope'. It closely followed that of Lord Keynes' statement in No. 98, except that No. 98 committed the British Government to 'proceed not later than the end of 1946 to make arrangements' rather than to 'complete' them.

(7) The two Governments agreed that after the end of 1946 they would impose no restrictions on payments and transfers for current

international transactions, except in relation to foreign owned balances accumulated before the end of 1946. This provision was directed against payments agreements and the effect was the general convertibility of sterling.

(8) The two Governments agreed that from the end of 1946 at latest they would impose no exchange restrictions on permitted imports and that if either Government imposed quantitative restrictions they should be administered so as not to discriminate against the other country.

Points (7) and (8) were not only serious new restraints on Britain but also effectively constituted the abrogation of British rights under the Bretton Woods agreement whereby Members would be permitted to 'maintain and adapt to changing circumstances' exchange restrictions during the post war transitional period of 3 to 5 years.

(9) On the accumulated sterling balances the American proposal again followed closely Lord Keynes' statement in No. 98 in setting out the British intention to make individual settlements with the holders of such balances on the basis of dividing them into three categories; balances to be released at once and convertible into any currency for current transactions, balances to be released in instalments and balances to be written off as a contribution to the general settlement. This was on the general lines set out by Lord Keynes in September in No. 22.

While waiting for Whitehall's reaction Lord Keynes expressed vividly to the Governor of the Bank of England anxieties already communicated to the Treasury that 'the long delays have caused a steady deterioration of the position . . . the consequences were that the initial atmosphere was completely lost. The American side now seem convinced that they can get nothing past Congress which they cannot represent as hard trading' (No. 116: see also No. 117).

Summarising Mr. Dalton's objections to the provisions in No. 113 regarding British monetary reserves (4), convertibility of sterling (6), which would make 'our negotiations with our sterling creditors impossible', and payments agreements (7), Mr. Coulson in the Foreign Office added his agreement with the Mission's objections in No. 111 to the linking of British payments to sterling creditors with those to the United States. He supported the Treasury's recommendation to make 'an attempt to revert to an agreement on simple lines' and 'not be afraid of breaking off the negotiations for a little'. He still felt that British acceptance of the American plan for liberalising world trade was so important to the Americans that 'we can afford to be tough' (No. 117). This attitude seemed 'crazy' to Mr. Fleming of the Lord President's staff, in particular because 'we cannot do without the money' and 'no alternative supplies of the necessary finance are in sight' (ibid., note 6). Behind this difference of opinion lay the fact that wartime conditions had made Britain heavily dependent on imports from the United States. If the loan fell through British consumers would suffer, but so also might American exporters.

Ministers considered the situation on 23 November, when Mr. Bevin disagreed with Mr. Dalton and suggested a personal approach from Mr. Attlee to Mr. Truman who, he thought, would 'not wish to jeopardise the whole position . . . A breakdown would be misunderstood by the peoples of the two countries, by the Empire, by the rest of the world' (No. 118.i). When consulted on this point Lord Halifax, however, advised deferring an approach to the President (No. 120, note 5).

The instructions to Lord Halifax authorised by Ministers took up the points mentioned by Mr. Coulson and, in particular, objected to the 'abrogation at the end of 1946 of our transitional rights under Bretton Woods', while accepting the liberalisation of the Sterling Area on the lines set out in No. 98. Lord Halifax was also informed of British willingness to accept only $4 billions, including Lend-Lease, at 2 per cent. When he put the British proposal (No. 121) for a 'change in the general approach' to Mr. Vinson and Mr. Clayton on 25 November they 'did not react too violently' (No. 120).

On the following day, however, Mr. Dalton telegraphed that while he found No. 121 'admirable in tone' he was disturbed to find that 'we shall release all current earnings throughout the whole of the Sterling Area as from the end of 1946' (No. 124). The Delegation in their turn were 'gravely disturbed' at this reaction and, distinguishing between liberalising newly earned sterling receipts of Sterling Area countries by the end of 1946 and the separate issue of the accumulated balances, listed the occasions on which they had understood that the former had been approved, whereas on the latter they had reserved the British position on completing a settlement by that date (No. 125). This may have been a misunderstanding at the highest level by Ministers (see No. 130) deeply involved in launching the peacetime programme of a new Government with many reforms to implement, but Sir W. Eady minuted in the Treasury on 1 December that it had 'obviously always been in all our minds that the £ area negotiations must deal with old & new balances at same time . . . & the "time-limit" has become a question of how much vagueness we can get away with' (No. 125, note 11).

Also on 26 November, at a meeting of the Top Finance Committee (No. 126), Mr. Vinson spoke 'in the most generous and sympathetic language we have yet heard from him' in withdrawing the provision about British reserves in the waiver clause (4) in No. 113. In the light of this meeting Lord Keynes reported that the three central unresolved questions were convertibility of sterling, other exchange arrangements, on which he saw the general lines of settlement, and exchange restrictions and import controls which was becoming the largest difficulty (see No. 113, paras. (6)–(8)). This latter issue was of 'very great and perhaps justifiable importance' to the State Department, whereas for the British 'to forego the right to discriminate against the United States during the transition [cf. Article XIV of the I.M.F. agreement] will certainly cost us something, particularly in the case of oil. But if it is only the right to discriminate against the United States which we give away we do not believe it will cost us much.' Lord Keynes accordingly proposed a new draft and sought authority to offer this concession in return for satisfaction on all other outstanding matters, especially fixing the amount of the loan at $4½ billions including Lend-Lease, on which a satisfactory agreement was emerging.

Both he and Mr. Brand telegraphed on 27 November urging that this 'most favourable opportunity . . . to settle whole business' should not be lost (No. 126, note 12). The progress made on Lend-Lease gave some support to their point, the final settlement for a net British payment of $650 millions on the same terms as the main loan being described by the Mission as 'a fair one', and indeed generous, as they went on to indicate (No. 143, see also Nos. 114, 126, 129, 160 and 163).

After considering No. 126 Mr. Dalton presented to the Cabinet on 29 November (No. 132) a revision (No. 134) of the American draft in No. 113 which incorporated Lord Keynes' suggestions and a few other modifications. This revision in particular toned down the American proposals on completing the liberalisation of current sterling receipts and arrangements for the accumulated balances, omitted any provision for *pari passu* treatment of other loans and used Lord Keynes' new draft on exchange arrangements. In a long discussion some Ministers felt strongly against accepting even these proposals, but the views of Mr. Bevin, who had had initial doubts about a loan from the United States, that it was essential to decide at once and that, without American assistance, it would be impossible to revive trade with Europe, evidently carried weight. The Cabinet accordingly agreed that No. 134 should be presented to the Americans, and when the Mission made representations about their instructions on sterling and treatment of other loans (Nos. 136–8, see also No. 141) insisted on 30 November that the text in No. 134 should be presented (No. 140).

At this stage Mr. Dalton decided to send the senior Civil Servant, Sir E. Bridges, to Washington to pull things together, especially since Lord Keynes, who had earlier suggested that Sir Edward should come out (No. 72, note 5), was evidently exhausted (Nos. 111, note 13, and 141, note 5). His arrival in Washington on 1 December marks the beginning of the final phase of the negotiations. On the following day, 2 December, the two sides met for six hours and exchanged draft agreements. The Americans did not look with favour on the British text in No. 134, while Sir W. Eady in London noted that the American text 'sharpened the case against us, particularly on certain aspects of the Sterling Area arrangements and the transitional period' (Nos. 142 and 147).

As a result of the second meeting between the two sides on 2 December a modification of the American text was sent to London on 3 December (No. 144). The main differences in substance between this text and that in No. 113 were as follows. The objectionable clause about British reserves in regard to the waiver was replaced by an anodyne formula, but the Americans insisted on a provision on proportionate reduction of other external obligations. On Sterling Area arrangements the Americans were persuaded to defer the date for completion to a year after the agreement became effective. Paragraph 7 on other exchange arrangements was a much elaborated text which represented a significant stiffening of the terms set out in paras. (7) and (8) of No. 113, widening the scope of the restraint on the imposition of restrictions on payments and transfers. It included a provision to ensure that the British Government could not invoke Article XIV of the I.M.F. agreement on the transitional period to impose exchange restrictions, but it would appear that it preserved the right to apply them to non-members set out in Article XI of that agreement (No. 146, note 6).

The Delegation also reported that the Americans had now made a firm offer of a loan of $3.75 billions which, with the $650 millions for Lend-Lease, made a total of $4.4 billions (No. 145), which was more than the sum Ministers had been willing to accept on 23 November. On balance Sir E. Bridges felt that 'there is not much left to argue about' (No. 147).

Ministers in London agreed, subject to one important exception, namely the loss of the main safeguards of Bretton Woods, which meant that Britain 'alone among all the other signatories' was deprived of the full five-year transitional period, of the provisions relating to scarce currencies, and of the right to resign from the I.M.F. (Nos. 148–9).

The Mission sought to persuade the Americans to relent, but though Mr. Vinson and Mr. Clayton yielded on the points about scarce currencies and resigning from the I.M.F., they 'made it perfectly clear that they would break off the negotiations rather than concede the point about the transitional period' (No. 152). In a further effort to escape, the Prime Minister informed Sir E. Bridges on 5 December that in his view Parliament would reject Bretton Woods shorn of the transitional period, which had been 'put forward to justify our acceptance, and by no one more strongly than by Keynes'. Sir E. Bridges was instructed to suggest to the Americans either that the date 'on which we voluntarily abandon our transitional rights' should be deferred to the end of 1948 or that restrictions imposed under the transition could be continued after consultation (No. 153). Neither was acceptable to the Americans (No. 154).

Lord Halifax 'most earnestly' advised the Cabinet that he could not think that 'the practical disadvantage of accepting the American Draft comes anywhere near the grave mischief' to Anglo-American relations of a rupture (No. 155), while the whole Mission telegraphed its explanation that the Americans considered, evidently with some plausibility, that their financial aid no longer justified the British capability to discriminate against American exporters which would have been available under the transition. The Mission themselves sought to argue, not altogether convincingly, that the effects of its loss would be limited (No. 156).

These considerations may have had some influence on Mr. Bevin who, when the Cabinet met on 5 December, opposed 'breaking off the negotiations on the narrow issue of the length of the transitional period' (No. 161.ii). Nevertheless, in accepting the agreement, the Cabinet sought to delay the operative date for general convertibility of sterling to the end of 1947. This request was rejected, though with regret, by the Americans in a final imposition of their will (Nos. 161–2), and the Financial Agreement was signed on the following morning, 6 December 1945.

The documentation in this volume is preponderantly concerned with British relations with the United States, by far the greatest Power in the Western hemisphere, with the negotiation of the loan of overwhelming importance in these relations in the last months of 1945. Even atomic energy, treated in Volume II, appeared of secondary importance in comparison. Britain was, however, also interested in Latin America, especially, and traditionally, in Argentina. A few documents have been included to illustrate these British interests and how they were affected by United States policy in the area. The relaxed nature of Anglo-Argentine relations, and the possibility of British representations being taken in good part, are shown in Mr. Bevin's talk with the Argentine Ambassador on 1 November (No. 92), which followed the communication of a British note on the Falkland Islands (No. 79).

Britain had important investments in Argentina, as well as longstanding trade links, which she was anxious to maintain, with the aims of obtaining meat and cereals for herself and for relief purposes and of regaining export markets there, including those for arms. American policy was, however, actively unfavourable to the Argentine regime, already under the influence of Colonel Juan Perón and not acceptably anti-Nazi. Mr. Bevin sought to persuade Mr. Byrnes to soften this policy which was blocking the British aims (Nos. 14, 25, 66). A 'Gentleman's Agreement' of 23 October on restraint in arms sales was accepted by H.M. Government, but it was not clear how binding it was considered by the State Department, representations to whom had been toned down by the Embassy in Washington, to the regret of South American Department in the Foreign Office (No. 77).

In respect of wheat supplies Mr. Bevin made a direct approach on 30 October to the Argentine Government, which was 'most anxious to help in supply of foodstuffs to Europe' (No. 89), but his further appeal to Mr. Byrnes to allow coal and fuel exports to Argentina to secure the despatch of these foodstuffs (No. 115) remained unanswered in mid December. At the same time, however, the United States, where food rationing had virtually ended the previous month, agreed to the urgently needed further contributions to U.N.R.R.A., which was heavily dependent on American financing (Nos. 76, 122).

For the diplomatic historian the documentation in this volume, though of fundamental importance for British foreign policy, to a large extent lies outside the normal channels of diplomacy because it relates to matters of finance. Indeed the negotiation which is central to the coverage was almost entirely uninfluenced by the Foreign Office itself, though it seems likely that Mr. Bevin played an important part at Ministerial meetings, having become convinced that the loan was essential both for the Government's domestic programme and for underpinning his policy of maintaining the world-wide strength of the British Commonwealth. It is not for the diplomatic historian to assess the economic effects of the loan, still less to speculate on what might have happened if it had been rejected.

It is, however, the task of the diplomatic historian to try to assess how effectively policy was conducted. In general Mr. Bevin remained on target in his aims of defending British interests and keeping on good terms with the United States. Neither he nor Mr. Churchill seem, however, to have realised how little leverage was left to an impoverished Britain in the partnership with the United States which they sought. In this respect acceptance of the loan, together with American possession of atomic know-how, increasingly cast Britain as an American client, and thus unable to function with the complete independence of a power of the first rank on the world stage.

As for the negotiations themselves, though there had been long preparation in Whitehall for the post-war 'consideration' on Lend-Lease, yet when the time came there seems to have been both an inadequate perception of American determination to open up markets hitherto protected by Imperial Preference and control of sterling, and a failure to clarify for Ministers what were the implications. Thus it was only at a crucial stage in the negotiations that the Chancellor of the Exchequer appreciated how far convertibility would have to go, which was further than Lord Keynes had originally proposed.

After the failure of Lord Keynes' plan not to negotiate on commercial policy until a financial settlement had been reached, talks on the projected International Trade Organisation were quickly successful in ensuring that the phasing out of Imperial Preference went hand in hand with lowering of tariffs. At the same time the outlines of an agreement on winding up Lend-Lease soon became clear and in the final settlement the Americans were generous. The financial talks, however, dragged on: perhaps Lord Keynes explained too much, perhaps Whitehall was too busy to push them on. The possible chance of a quick settlement on 27 September, on better terms than were eventually accepted, was missed because Ministers, intent on 'Justice' and conceivably a little misled by Lord Keynes, still sought at least an interest-free loan.

Far from the two sides drawing closer by mutual concessions, as the talks proceeded the American proposals became tougher on important points relating to British renunciation of exchange restrictions and import controls, which were outside the strictly financial ambit. In effect Mr. Clayton's first formal proposal on 9 October was for a larger loan but on broadly similar monetary lines to the final agreement. Its rejection may have been a further British error; though it would appear that it was when the American lawyers were brought in that the going became hard for the British negotiators. In perspective the financial terms were not ungenerous, especially when the deferred starting date and long period of repayment are considered.

Ultimately the Cabinet had to decide between two risks. Either they shied at taking down the defensive mechanisms of the Sterling Area and opted for an austere independence, or they accepted multilateralism, with all the dangers of American competition for markets, as the price for financial backing for their ambitious policies at home and abroad. They had not seriously studied alternatives, such as consultations with other West European countries, to the loan as proposed by the Americans, and it is understandable that the risk backed by money was the more attractive.

The documentation in this volume is unusually concentrated on one major theme, and the Editors have decided to make it the first of a number of more compact volumes. In matters of editorial practice the volume continues to follow the principles explained in Volume II of this Series, pp. xxi–xxii, and amplified in the Introduction to Series II, Volume I, pp. v–viii.

The main sources of documentation for this volume have been the archives of the Foreign and Commonwealth Office at the Public Record Office, especially the Foreign Office political files (F.O. 371). Within this class documents have been selected mainly from those of the following Departments: Economic Relations (UE 53 – Economic; UE 71 – Supplies); General (W 58 – Shipping; W 801 – Telecommunications; W 802 – Civil Aviation); Northern (N 27 – Iceland); North American (AN 45 – United States); Refugee (WR 48); South American (AS 2 – Argentina; AS 51 – General); Supply and Relief (UR 850 – General; UR 851 – Supplies; UR 852 – Finance); Western (Z 36 – Portugal). For further guidance see Public Record Handbooks No. 13, *The Records of the Foreign Office 1782–1939* (H.M.S.O., 1969) and No. 15, *The Second World War . . .* (H.M.S.O., 1972).

Additional documentation has been drawn from the Private Office papers of Mr. Ernest Bevin (F.O. 800/443–513 *passim*), Dominions Office records (D.O. 35/1216), and also from the files of the Cabinet Office and the Treasury, and of the Prime Minister (PREM). I am grateful to Associated Press for permission to reproduce the photograph in the frontispiece. This signed copy belonged to a member of the British staff in Washington and is in the possession of the Foreign and Commonwealth Office.

A more technical account of the negotiation of the American loan is given in Professor L.S. Pressnell's forthcoming authoritative work, *External Economic Policy since the War*, vol. i (H.M.S.O.), which he has kindly allowed the Editors to consult in proof; see also Donald Moggridge (ed.), *The Collected Writings of John Maynard Keynes*, vol. xxiv (Cambridge, 1979). Cross references to these and to other official publications or primary sources have been given where relevant.

In accordance with the Parliamentary announcement cited in Volume I the Editors have had the customary freedom in the selection and arrangement of documents, including access to material which, as in the case of some of the private papers, may not yet be fully listed, but will be included in the archives of the Foreign and Commonwealth Office. The Editors also enjoy reference to special categories of material such as records retained in the Department under Section 3(4) of the Public Records Act of 1958, but they have followed customary practice in not consulting personnel files or specifically intelligence material. No exceptional case of restriction on security grounds of the availability of a particular document editorially selected in accordance with regular practice has arisen in the present volume.

I should like to thank both the present Head of the Library and Records Department, Miss P.M. Barnes, and her predecessor, Miss E.C. Blayney, and their staff for all facilities in the preparation of this volume. Kind assistance has also been received from the Records Branches of the Cabinet Office and of the Treasury, and from the staff of H.M. Stationery Office and of the Public Record Office. To Mrs. H.J. Yasamee, M.A., Miss K.E. Crowe, B.A., Miss K.L. Jones, B.A., and Mrs. S. Desmond I am grateful for valuable help at various stages in the preparation of the volume. Once again, I am pleased to record my especial thanks to the Assistant Editor, Mrs. Gillian Bennett, M.A., who has co-operated in all stages of the editing of the volume with technical skill, enthusiasm and historical judgment.

July 1986   M.E. PELLY

CONTENTS

ABBREVIATIONS FOR PRINTED SOURCES

B.F.S.P.   *British and Foreign State Papers* (London, 1841–1977).

Cmd.   Command Paper (London).

D.B.F.P.   *Documents on British Foreign Policy 1919–1939* (H.M.S.O., London, 1946–86).

D.S.B.   *Department of State Bulletin* (Washington).

F.R.U.S.   *Foreign Relations of the United States: Diplomatic Papers* (Washington, 1861f.)

Moggridge   Donald Moggridge (ed.), *The Collected Writings of John Maynard Keynes*, Volume XXIV (1979).

Parl. Debs.,   *Parliamentary Debates (Hansard), Fifth Series, House of*
5th ser.,   *Commons, Official Report* (London).
H. of C.

Parl. Debs.,   *Parliamentary Debates (Hansard), Fifth Series, House of*
5th ser.,   *Lords, Official Report* (London).
H. of L.

Pressnell   L. S. Pressnell, *External Economic Policy since the War,* Volume I (H.M.S.O.).

Public Papers: *Public Papers of the Presidents of the United States: Harry S.*
Truman 1945   *Truman: Containing the Public Messages, Speeches, and Statements of the President April 12 to December 31, 1945* (Washington, 1961).

ABBREVIATED DESIGNATIONS

ASKEW	Board of Trade Telegram series.
BABOON/ NABOB	Telegram series on Keynes mission exchanged between Cabinet Offices (London) and J.S.M. (Washington).
B.F.M.	British Food Mission (Washington).
B.S.C.	British Supply Council in North America.
C.F.B.	Combined Food Board.
C.O.S.	Chiefs of Staff.
F.A.O.	United Nations Food and Agriculture Organisation.
F.E.A.	American Foreign Economic Administration.
G.M.T.	Greenwich Mean Time.
I.A.T.A.	International Air Transport Association.
I.M.F.	International Monetary Fund.
J.A.S.	Joint American Secretariat (London).

J.S.M.	British Joint Staff Mission (Washington).
MIN/PROD	Telegram series to and from Ministry of Production.
M.W.T.	Ministry of War Transport.
P.C.S.C.	Principal Commonwealth Supply Committee.
RAFDEL	R.A.F. Delegation in Washington.
REMAC/ CAMER	Telegram series to and from H.M. Treasury.
SEVER	Telegram series to and from J.A.S.
U.K.T.D.	United Kingdom Treasury Delegation in Washington.
U.N.R.R.A.	United Nations Relief and Rehabilitation Administration.
USLON/ LONUS	Telegram series between Washington and London transmitted through Air Ministry Channels.

CHAPTER SUMMARIES

CHAPTER I

The End of Lend–Lease
3 August–10 September 1945

CHAPTER II

Preliminary consideration of terms of U.S. loan:
Imperial Preference
11 September–21 October 1945

CHAPTER III

Negotiations leading to financial and commercial agreements of 6 December: convertibility of sterling
27 October–7 December 1945

xl

CHAPTER I

The End of Lend-Lease

3 August – 10 September 1945

No. 1

Memorandum by Mr. Hall-Patch[1]

[*UE 3595/1094/53*]

FOREIGN OFFICE, *3 August 1945*

Mr. Clayton is arriving in London this week.[2] He is the Assistant Secretary of State specially charged with economic questions. He wishes to discuss:

(*a*) Commercial policy in the light of the unofficial and exploratory talks which have been conducted by Mr. Hawkins of the American Embassy with the Treasury and the Board of Trade.[3]

---

[1] This minute was the result of a discussion between Sir O.G. Sargent, senior Deputy Under Secretary of State, Sir R.I. Campbell, Acting Under Secretary of State and designated Deputy to the Secretary of State on the Council of Foreign Ministers, and Mr. N.M. Butler and Mr. E.L. Hall-Patch, Assistant Under Secretaries of State superintending Departments dealing with American and economic affairs respectively. The discussion related to the minute by Sir R. Campbell, 'American Economic Policy and Economic Policy of H.M.'s new Government', printed in Volume I as No. 554.

[2] Mr. William L. Clayton had already arrived in London to attend, as principal U.S. delegate, the third council meeting of the United Nations Relief and Rehabilitation Administration (U.N.R.R.A.), opening on 7 August. On 3 August with Mr. H.C. Hawkins, Economic Counsellor to the U.S. Embassy in London, and Mr. E.G. Collado, Director of the U.S. Office of Financial and Development Policy, he had a general discussion with Lord Keynes, the distinguished economist and adviser to H.M. Treasury, Sir W. Eady, Joint Second Secretary in H.M. Treasury, and Mr. R.H. Brand, Head of the United Kingdom Treasury Delegation in Washington (U.K.T.D.) and Chairman of the British Supply Council in North America (B.S.C.). A memorandum of their conversation is printed in *F.R.U.S. 1945*, vol. vi. pp. 79–87, but no British record has been traced.

[3] For Anglo-American talks on commercial policy in 1945 see L.S. Pressnell, *External Economic Policy since the War*, vol. i (H.M.S.O.), Chapter 8, and *F.R.U.S., ibid.*, pp. 1–60 *passim*. A summary of the 9th meeting in the series of informal exploratory talks between British and American officials, attended by Mr. Clayton on 4 August, is printed as No. 2 below.

(b) The terms, duration and size of any financial aid required by the United Kingdom after the end of Lease-Lend (Stage III).[4]
He will, in the first instance, discuss these questions with officials of the Treasury and the Board of Trade, and subsequently with Ministers.

2. In the exploratory talks on commercial policy, it has not so far been possible to give any firm indications of the views of H.M.G., as everything turns upon the interpretation to be given to Article VII of the Mutual Aid Agreement,[5] upon which there were divergent views in the Coalition Government. We have been stalling with the Americans on this subject for a long time on the ground that a Coalition Government was in power, and we could not be expected, in these circumstances, and in the middle of a war, to enter into commitments on a long term commercial policy.

3. Now that a new Government with a large majority is in power,[6] and

---

[4] The Lend-Lease system of pooled resources and mutual aid derived from the Act to Promote the Defense of the United States (the Lend-Lease Act) of 11 March 1941 (printed in H. Duncan Hall, *North American Supply* (London, 1955), pp. 505–7) and the Anglo-American Agreement of 23 February 1942 on Principles applying to Mutual Aid in the Prosecution of the War against Aggression (printed in *B.F.S.P.*, vol. 144, pp. 1041–4). Stage III was the period of military and economic demobilisation following the defeat of Japan and the restoration of an economy of peace. Mr. Clayton had been instructed by President H.S. Truman to discuss these matters in London, in anticipation of the visit of a British delegation to Washington in September to discuss post-war economic arrangements, as suggested by the then Prime Minister, Mr. Winston S. Churchill, in his letter to President Truman of 24 July 1945: see Volume I, Annex I to No. 251, and No. 458.
    The question of financial problems in the Stage III period had been under detailed consideration in the Treasury, in consultation with the Board of Trade and the Bank of England, since 1944: see Pressnell, *op. cit.*, Chapter 9.(6)–(9). Since the spring of 1945 discussion had centred on a memorandum of 18 March 1945 by Lord Keynes, 'Overseas Financial Arrangements in Stage III'. This paper was circulated in a revised form to the War Cabinet in May, printed in Donald Moggridge (ed.), *The Collected Writings of John Maynard Keynes*, vol. XXIV (Cambridge, 1979), pp. 256–95. Lord Keynes set out the alternatives for British post-war economic policy as isolation ('Starvation Corner'— 'Austerity' in the first draft) or borrowing from the United States ('Temptation'), and went on to advocate a general settlement based on a free grant of financial aid from the U.S., with contributions from the sterling area, and the convertibility of sterling within a year from the end of the war ('Justice'). Discussions within the Treasury on these proposals can be followed in the papers of Lord Keynes (T 247/49–50) and Sir W. Eady (T 236/437) and in correspondence between Lord Keynes and Mr. Brand printed in Moggridge, *ibid.*, pp. 299–376. A minute of 20 July to Lord Keynes and Sir W. Eady, written on Mr. Brand's return to London, in which he argued against appealing 'merely to the generosity of the United States' and set out the basis on which a request for American aid should be made, is reproduced at i below. Cf. also Pressnell, *op. cit.*, Chapter 9.(10), and Sir R. Clarke, *Anglo-American Economic Collaboration in War and Peace 1942–49* (Oxford, 1982), pp. 52–9.
    [5] This article, which provided, in particular, for action 'directed to the expansion, by appropriate international and domestic measures, of production, employment, and the exchange and consumption of goods . . . to the elimination of all forms of discriminatory treatment in international commerce, and to the reduction of tariffs and other trade barriers', represented 'the consideration' for Lend-Lease. For its negotiation and consequences see R.S. Sayers, *Financial Policy 1939–45* (London, 1956), pp. 405–13, and Pressnell, Chapter 3.
    [6] In the result of the British general election, declared on 26 July 1945, the Labour Party

the war in Germany over, Mr. Clayton will press hard for some clear indication of our future intentions.

4. He will press the harder as he, himself, is one of the leading protagonists of a multilateral approach to international trade. What we say to him may well influence the attitude of the U.S. Administration to the help we shall require in Stage III. This is the most difficult external problem we shall have to face immediately after the end of the war with Japan. Caution in handling the talks on commercial policy is therefore very desirable.

5. The general trend of American economic policy is, at present, away from their old heresies which hit us so hard, and towards what our own economic policy had been until the 1930's when we were forced to abandon it under pressure of the exorbitant American tariff, and the world wide increase in economic nationalism.

6. But the situation has changed since 1930. While at that time, we might have been willing and able to continue our traditional policy, we are less able to do so now. We are now the world's greatest debtor nation, and we are committed to a policy of full employment. These are both new factors with wide implications. Moreover, we have learned the advantages of bulk purchases, which are an anathema in America, and we may now wish to maintain, or possibly to extend, these practices.

7. There is already in America a lively interest in the domestic programme of the new Government. There is a feeling that it can only be realised by shielding the domestic economy behind currency and commercial controls. Such a policy, in the American mind, is in direct conflict with Article VII of the Mutual Aid Agreement. The Americans are convinced that full employment in their own country is an indispensable condition to the recovery of the world. To Mr. Clayton has been assigned the duty of finding very large numbers of 'jobs from the export trade'. He is likely to tell us with a good deal of force that if our commercial policy seems designed to exclude imports from the U.S., which has helped us so generously with Lease-Lend, it will be politically impossible to persuade Congress to give us further financial easement.

8. It would do us great harm if a current of opinion were formed that, at a time when America was ready and eager to enter into broad international commitments, we were intent on pursuing, what in American eyes, was a contrary policy. If this feeling became widespread, it would affect detrimentally the possibility of economic collaboration, e.g. in reparation and reconstruction on the continent of Europe, and also the degree and conditions of any direct help which the Americans may be disposed to give us. It might even affect the whole view the Americans take of us as partners in world affairs. 'Discrimination', 'Exclusiveness', 'Monopoly', 'Imperialist Economy'—all these unsavoury words will be

had secured an overall majority of 146 seats in the House of Commons. Mr. Churchill resigned and was succeeded by Mr. Clement Attlee. Mr. Ernest Bevin succeeded Mr. R.A. Eden as Secretary of State for Foreign Affairs.

freely used against us, and will gain spontaneous, and often unthinking response from the U.S. public.

9. We cannot ignore the gradual change of attitude which has been taking place in America towards international affairs. The first definite steps have now been taken by America at Hot Springs, Bretton Woods and San Francisco[7] to enter into international affairs as an active working partner. The passing of the Trade Agreements Act[8] shows a willingness to turn away from the high tariff policy which has caused such havoc in international trade. This tendency of America to assume international responsibilities, commensurate with its resources, is one of the most hopeful signs for the future. Any action on our part which might dam back this tendency would have the most unhappy results both for the world and for us. The World Organization would be disastrously weakened and this would weaken us. Even if the American tendency to participate fully in world affairs were not slowed down or reversed, any doubt of our value or respectability as partners in world affairs would be serious for us, since we can hardly afford to be ignored or looked upon askance by any of the Great Powers of the world Organization, least of all by the United states, whose support and co-operation we will need in so many ways.[9]

10. In this connexion, the recent leader in *The Times*, of which an extract is attached,[10] is of great interest. It expresses very clearly, in words to which nobody in the Foreign Office would dissent, the implications of the present trend in America, and it indicates that public opinion in this country is commencing to weigh these implications.

11. The position can be briefly summarised as follows. We are on the threshold of a great and beneficial change in America, and we should be chary of action which would hamper or arrest the present trend. It is to America we must look for that assistance in Stage III, without which our

[7] i.e. the United Nations Conferences of (i) 18 May—3 June 1943 (Final Act printed in Cmd. 6451 of 1944: cf. R.J. Hammond, *Food*, vol. i. (London, 1951), pp. 357–61) which recommended the establishment of a permanent organisation for Food and Agriculture; (ii) 1–22 July 1944 which provided for the establishment of an International Monetary Fund and International Bank for Reconstruction and Development (see Pressnell, *op. cit.*, Chapter 7: agreements annexed to the Final Act printed in Cmd. 6546 of 1944): (iii) 25 April–26 June 1945 on International Organisation which adopted the Charter of the United Nations (printed in *B.F.S.P.*, vol. 145, pp. 805–32: cf. Sir Llewellyn Woodward, *British Foreign Policy in the Second World War* (London, 1970f.), vol. v. pp. 308–12, 318–19).

[8] The reference was to the renewal on 5 July 1945 of the U.S. Trade Agreements Act of 1934 (An Act to Amend the Tariff Act of 1930). By this renewal the authority of the President was extended to permit the reduction (or increase) of any tariff by up to 50 per cent., although tariff cuts must be on a selective, not 'horizontal', basis. See *Documents on American Foreign Relations*, vol. vii (Princeton, 1947), pp. 506–7, and cf. vol. viii (1948), pp. 642–50. See also Pressnell, *op. cit.*, Chapter 8.(6).

[9] The three preceding sentences, beginning 'Any action', were included at the suggestion of Sir R. Campbell.

[10] This extract, comprising the last two paragraphs of the leading article, 'An American Lead', in *The Times*, 31 July 1945, p. 5, is not printed.

recovery from the effects of war will be almost intolerably protracted and painful. Indeed, without such assistance, the prospects of being able to maintain even our present standards are bleak. And, in the last analysis, if America feels we are pursuing a policy inimical to her own interests, she may demand consideration for the vast Lease-Lend deliveries we have received, which would threaten our liberty of action in both the economic and political fields.

12. As far as it is possible to judge these things, the Americans seem ready to accept the necessity for us to maintain controls, and all they imply, on a temporary basis i.e. during the transitional period, for which they are ready to admit a duration of three or possibly as much as five years after the end of hostilities.[11] During this period they may well be ready to continue to help us notwithstanding our maintenance of a policy contrary to their aims and beliefs. But this tolerance would be dependent upon an assurance that, after the transitional period—or even progressively during that period—we abandon our restrictive system and promote, and then fully adopt, a system of multilateralism and an expanding economy. The question of this assurance is likely to be the main hinge of the discussions with Mr. Clayton.

13. In these circumstances, it may be thought desirable to give a word of warning to those who will conduct these initial discussions with Mr. Clayton. We shall be playing for large stakes and these initial discussions may set the tone for the all important discussions on Stage III which are at present arranged to take place in Washington in the Autumn.[12]

E.L. HALL-PATCH

[11] Section 4 of Article XIV of the Articles of Agreement of the International Monetary Fund drawn up at Bretton Woods (see note 7) defined a post-war transitional period of 3–5 years for members of the Fund to remove any restrictions relating to Sections 2, 3 or 4 of Article VIII, i.e. those relating to current payments, discriminatory currency practices or the convertibility of foreign held balances. This period was generally referred to during Anglo-American financial negotiations as the 'Bretton Woods transitional period'. In his memorandum on Overseas Financial Arrangements (see note 4) Lord Keynes had stated that while the provision of U.S. financial aid might make possible the early convertibility of sterling, the U.K. should not surrender any of her rights under the transitional period: cf. Moggridge, op. cit., p. 281.

[12] This memorandum was initialled on 3 August by Sir A. Cadogan, Permanent Under Secretary of State for Foreign Affairs, and minuted as follows by Mr. Bevin: 'I will see Mr. Hall-Patch & discuss the matter in greater detail. Bretton Woods is of course involved. Reference closed economy, please read Blackpool Speech [by Mr. Bevin at the Labour Party Conference: see The Times, 24 May 1945, p. 2]. E.B.' Mr. Hall-Patch added on 9 August: 'Discussed with Secretary of State. He is anxious to be able to isolate us if there is a major economic recession in the U.S.A. which he fears. He is not at all sure that we shall be able to do this if we take Bretton Woods as it stands. On this point he will see Lord Keynes next week and go over the ground with him.

'On Commercial Policy discussions by officials with Mr. Clayton are proceeding. It looks as if the differences are such that the whole question will have to be put before Ministers very soon. We can then brief the Secy. of State in the light of what has taken place between officials and Mr. Clayton. E.L. Hall-Patch. 9/8/45.'

i *20 July 1945 Memo. by Mr. Brand* in response to criticism by Sir W. Eady of Lord Keynes' proposals (see note 4 above): it is essential to ask the U.S. for 'very considerable sums' but not only on grounds of 'Justice' and no distinction of principle should be drawn between a grant and a loan; immediate convertibility of sterling would be 'extremely risky' and 'we ought as far as possible to avoid borrowing dollars for account of other sterling countries'. Cf. Pressnell, *op. cit.*, Chapter 9.(10), and Clarke, *op. cit.*, p. 58 [T 247/49].

No. 2

Summary[1] of discussion held at the Board of Trade on 4 August 1945

A.S. (U.S.) (45) 9th Meeting [UE 3615/113/53]

Top secret

Article VII[2]

Present:
U.S.A.: Messrs. Clayton, Hawkins, Stinebower,[3] Fowler,[4] Penrose.[5]
U.K.: Sir P. Liesching,[6] Sir W. Eady, Professor Robbins,[7] Lord Keynes, the Hon. R.H. Brand, Mr. Hall-Patch, Mr. Helmore, Mr. Shackle.[8]

1. Mr. Clayton said that public opinion in the United States was now more solidly than ever before behind the Administration's programme for trade expansion, multilateralism and non-discrimination. He recognised this country's special difficulties, particularly in the early post-war years, and wished to help us to meet them; but there was in the United States much ill-informed apprehension and criticism of our 'Sterling–dollar pool' and 'blocked sterling balances'.[9]

---

[1] This summary, dated at foot 7 August, was communicated to the Foreign Office by the Board of Trade. A brief account of the discussion is printed in *F.R.U.S. 1945*, vol. vi, pp. 90–1.
[2] Of the Mutual Aid Agreement of 1942: see No. 1, note 5.
[3] Deputy Director of the Office of International Trade Policy in the State Department.
[4] First Secretary in the U.S. Embassy in London.
[5] Special Assistant to the U.S. Ambassador in London.
[6] Joint Second Secretary in the Board of Trade.
[7] Director of the Economic Section of the War Cabinet.
[8] Mr. Helmore and Mr. Shackle were Principal Assistant Secretaries in the Commercial Relations and Treaties Department of the Board of Trade.
[9] An analysis by Lord Keynes of the sterling area, including its definition as a trading and banking system which had evolved from 'the practice of British and other communities overseas to conduct most of their overseas transactions in sterling and to hold in sterling a substantial part of their external monetary reserves', is printed as No. 98. See also the explanation by Mr. Hugh Dalton, Chancellor of the Exchequer, in his parliamentary statement of 12 December (*Parl. Debs., 5th ser., H. of C.*, vol. 417, col. 425). On the pooling of sterling area countries' dollar and gold accruals and the American attitude towards the wartime accumulation of sterling balances, see Pressnell, *op. cit.*, Chapter 9, *passim*.

2. *Methods of tariff reduction.* Both the undertakings given to Congress in connection with the renewal and extension of the Reciprocal Trade Agreements Act[10] and the wording of the Act itself would prevent the United States from discussing any 'horizontal' all-round cut of tariffs; any such reductions must be selective, and must be preceded by the usual hearings of interested parties.

Personally, he thought a horizontal cut, even by as little as 20% would in any case be impossible: it would have to be submitted to the Senate, and would fail to get the necessary two-thirds majority.

He also felt that any horizontal cut that could be got through an international conference would have to be very modest—certainly not more than 25%; even so, many countries would be unlikely to ratify it.

Again he doubted the rightness of the method since it would unwarrantably assume that all rates were equally 'out of line' and too high.

He was convinced that, as regards tariffs the method of grouped or interlinked bilateral negotiations was the right one; the time required by it was a difficulty, but by suitable means this could be minimised. Some 10 or 12 bilateral tariff agreements could be concluded in a short period between the main countries, while an International Trade Conference was being arranged to deal with other aspects (quotas, exchange controls, discrimination, Cartels etc.).

3. Mr. Hawkins then outlined the contents of a revised paper[11] embodying the present form of the American proposals (this he handed to us). To a large extent these had now received the President's approval, but not all of them.

It was much the same as the paper he had handed us before, but a few passages had been added, particularly on tariffs and tariff preferences. A section on Employment had also been added though the Americans felt this subject to be proper not to the International Trade Organisation but to the Economic and Social Council.

The Americans had not been able to accept our agricultural proposals, though they had tried to meet us on them to some extent.[12]

4. The new section on tariffs and preferences in terms did little more than repeat Article VII; but the idea behind it was that, instead of a 'horizontal cut' of tariffs, a 'nuclear group' of 10 or 12 countries should be formed, who would agree at once to undertake bilateral negotiations among themselves on tariffs alone. Other aspects (quotas, exchange

[10] See No. 1, note 8.

[11] This document, 'Proposal to Establish an International Trade Organization', was the revised version of a paper submitted by Mr. Hawkins on 21 July, and represented the culmination of Anglo-American discussions on this subject over a period of months: see Pressnell, *op. cit.,* Chapter 8. The Board of Trade prepared a summary of this long paper for the 10th meeting of officials on 9 August (A.S. (U.S.) (45) 10th Meeting), which was annexed, following minor American amendments, to the record of the 11th meeting on 14 August: see No. 8.ii.

[12] For Anglo-American discussions on agriculture see Pressnell, *op. cit.,* Chapter 8.(2)–(3).

control etc.) would be dealt with by multilateral agreement between the nucleus countries.

The whole body of these agreements, bilateral and multilateral, would be treated as inter-dependent and would be brought into force simultaneously.

Other countries could later be brought in under suitable arrangements. (The whole scheme is outlined in a note which Mr. Hawkins handed to us: this forms the Annex to this paper [i]).

5. Answering questions by us, Mr. Hawkins said the Americans contemplated that the bilateral tariff negotiations and the multilateral negotiations on other aspects would proceed concurrently; for the Americans at least this would not involve serious personnel difficulties. We pointed out that as more or less the same persons would be involved in all of the negotiations the personnel difficulty would be serious for us. We also observed that even as between a nucleus group of 12 countries, 66 separate tariff agreements would be involved.

6. The Americans admitted that, if the negotiations on the 'general' or non-tariff aspects ran into difficulties, the tariff agreements, and indeed the whole Scheme, might have to be revised; but they regarded this as probably a less serious risk than that of the breakdown of an attempt at multilateral tariff reduction, and its attendant repercussions on the Scheme as a whole. At the worst, the bilateral tariff discussions could be extended to cover the non-tariff aspects, as in their pre-war bilateral negotiations.

7. There was some discussion on the question whether the Americans' constitutional difficulties really necessitated bilateral tariff negotiations, and whether their need to announce beforehand the imported commodities about which they would be negotiating, and to hold public hearings about them, might not be consistent with some form of multilateral negotiation between the 'nucleus' countries, (particularly since there would be a rule of most-favoured-nation treatment between those countries). They replied that such an arrangement might not be contrary to the provisions of the Reciprocal Trade Agreements Act, but it would be administratively unmanageable, owing to the complication of tariff Schedules. The various bilateral negotiations might all be held at two or three centres, thus facilitating contact. There might need to be certain preliminary discussions and agreements between certain of the 'nucleus' countries, e.g. an agreement among the Empire countries to 'unbind' preference margins.

8. From our side the criticism was made that even after such tariff negotiations, high tariffs would still tend to remain relatively high as compared with low ones. The Americans replied that in their view it would never be possible to get international flat rates for particular commodities. Tariff negotiations could seldom, if ever, be on a commodity-by-commodity basis; the method must be to strike a balance over the respective tariff schedules as wholes.

9. Discussion then turned to the number and composition of the 'nucleus' group of countries. The Americans had in mind the United States, the United Kingdom, with either 4 or 5 Dominions (if New Zealand were included) and India; France; the Dutch-Belgian customs union; also Czechoslovakia (their previous Agreement with her having been terminated); and among the South Americans, Cuba and possibly Brazil. Argentina would present political difficulties for them (we pointed out that from the trade point of view she is particularly important for us).

10. The Americans favoured as small a 'nucleus' as possible, so as to get quick results (indeed Mr. Clayton personally would have favoured the 'Big Five' Powers alone—including France and China). We on the other hand pointed out the risk of too narrow a limitation, which might lead to the formation of opposition blocs at the eventual Conference: we felt that there would have to be not less than 17 countries in the nucleus, while the Americans thought 15 should probably be the maximum.

11. On the question of opening up the subject of long term commercial policy with the European countries we said that the latter were finding our continued silence very baffling, and that it would be embarrassing for us to have to remain tongue-tied towards them much longer. It was very desirable to bring the Europeans in as quickly as possible, to prevent them falling back, in despair, into autarkic tendencies.

12. The suggestion was made, and met with a generally favourable reception on both sides, that there might be a preliminary unpublicised meeting of the 'nucleus' countries, to discuss the whole of the proposed programme and procedure, as regards both tariffs and other matters; a draft 'Statement of Principles' or 'White Paper' for general public issue might emerge from this meeting. The Americans said that in that event they would want to be sure in advance that they and we would generally see eye-to-eye on important issues. (We pointed out that we could not in any case speak for the Dominions).

13. Under this suggestion the 'nucleus' countries would first meet to discuss the general procedure, and also the general objectives and character of the solutions to be sought on non-tariff matters; this phase would end with the issue of the so-called 'White Paper'. Then at the Second stage, they would meet again to negotiate about tariffs. [It was not made quite clear whether bilaterally or multilaterally, but the Americans apparently adhered to their view that bilateral negotiations would be necessary on this aspect][13]: finally there would be a Conference to bring all the resultant agreements into force together.

14. As to the composition of the 'nucleus' group, the suggestion was made that the selection might be made generally on the basis of a minimum proportion of world trade, but that Russia would have to be included exceptionally. It was recognised however that probably the group would have to be selected more or less arbitrarily.

---

[13] Brackets as in original.

15. It was agreed that a further meeting or meetings should be held.[14] Mr. Clayton said that he was anxious to take back with him to Washington some definite measure of agreement, at least on the first steps to be taken.

BOARD OF TRADE

CALENDAR TO No. 2

i *4 Aug. 1945 Document No. 1 handed to U.K. officials by Mr. Clayton*: outline of nuclear scheme for tariff negotiations [UE 3615/113/53].

[14] Sir R. Clarke (*op. cit.*, pp. 58–9) refers to a meeting between Lord Keynes, Mr. Clayton and others on 6 August, when in addition to commercial policy issues wider questions relating to U.S. financial aid were apparently discussed. No record of this meeting has been traced in F.O. archives.

No. 3

Mr. Balfour[1](Washington) to Mr. Bevin (Received 23 August)

No. 1038 [AN 2560/22/45]

WASHINGTON, 9 August 1945

Sir,

During recent months the concept has steadily gained ground in this country that Great Britain has come to occupy a position on the world stage which in terms of power and influence is inferior to that of the U.S.A. and the U.S.S.R. The degree to which this concept has now implanted itself in the American mind was revealed in a recent five nation Gallup poll conducted in the United States, Canada, France, Denmark and Australia, on the question of which country would have most influence in the post-war world. Only 5% of the Americans questioned during this survey recorded their vote for Great Britain, as compared with respective percentages in favour of the United States and the Soviet Union of 63% and 24%. The United States easily headed the survey in the other four countries, although in France the margin was 43% in favour of the United States as compared with 41% for the U.S.S.R. In Canada 19% voted for Britain and in France no more than 4%.

2. In order that this idea of Britain's inferiority to her two associates in the Big Three partnership may be assessed in its true perspective, I propose in the present despatch to describe the various factors which have caused it to become prevalent amongst the American public, and to examine what effect it is likely to exercise on Anglo-American relations.

3. It is in the first place evident to every thinking American that the

[1] Minister in charge of H.M. Embassy in Washington during the absence of H.M. Ambassador, Lord Halifax, who was in England on leave.

contribution of his country on this occasion to the defeat of Germany is out of all proportion to that rendered during the first world war. Whereas in 1917–18 America was in process of transforming herself into the main arsenal of democracy and became, from the date of Russia's collapse, the principal source of Allied manpower reserves, she has emerged from the present European struggle as the one great power in the world whose population and metropolitan territories have suffered nothing from enemy action. Of the leading Western Allies in the former Armageddon, liberated France is no more than a shadow of her former self: a poor relation admitted on sufferance to the family of the Great Powers. Italy, thanks to her apostasy under Fascist rule, has but lately ceased to be a battle-ground and is a suppliant for the good graces of the conquerors. Great Britain alone, who won imperishable renown for herself in a year of single-handed resistance to Nazi aggression, has ridden out the storm to a triumphant finish. But in the course of a bitter struggle for existence she has been severely strained and her resources have been greatly depleted. For this and other reasons presently to be enumerated her star has ceased in American eyes to burn with quite the same accustomed radiance in the international firmament.

4. By contrast with the exhausted and devastated countries of Western Europe, the United States sees itself, as a result of the war, endowed with colossal productive and fighting capacity. Ever since the inception of lend-lease in March, 1941, it has been plain to the average American that other nations, beginning with Great Britain, have been largely dependent upon U.S. bounty for their ability to wage effective warfare. Although there is a widespread feeling that recompense of one sort or another ought eventually to be forthcoming for lend-lease aid, it is generally recognised that on this occasion the U.S.A. has been constrained to make good the deficiencies of others rather than, as in the earlier war, to sustain them with loans which it was thought at the time would be repaid in full at some later date. In spite of constant efforts on our part at enlightenment, the general public still too often ignores all that Great Britain has done in the way of reverse lend-lease assistance.

5. Whilst the press and radio are apt with unstinted exuberance to dwell almost exclusively on American achievements in the common struggle, the war output which the United States has attained is in itself miraculous enough to inspire the most sober minded citizens with the liveliest satisfaction and patriotic pride. In three and a half years, moreover, of front line combat, and at the cost of casualties which now exceed one million, American fighting men have proved their valour in every major theatre of war. With however little justification, the idea is prevalent among the public that after D-Day American forces took the lion's share of fighting in the European theatre. In the Pacific Britain's role is popularly regarded as still more puny by comparison with that of the United States. Looking towards the future Americans see their own two-ocean Navy as mistress of the waves. If anything further were needed

to convince Americans that their country has become the amphibious Leviathan of modern times, it is the knowledge that its stupendous war output and mobilisation of manpower has been achieved without any substantial encroachment on normal activities. As Mr. J.A. Krug, Chairman of the War Production Board, put it in his report on war production in 1944, made public on the 14th June last, 'the important and astounding fact is that in 1944, the year in which the crescendo of war mounted to a thunderous climax, the American consumer was furnished with more goods and services than in any year since 1941.' The only shadow on the landscape, and it is a lengthening one, derives from the many complex problems of reconversion and redeployment which are even now putting a certain strain on the national economy.

6. Turning now to the light in which Americans view Great Britain: As already indicated, the prestige that we acquired for ourselves before the U.S.A. became a belligerent has since been largely eclipsed by the burden imposed upon us as a result of six years of warfare. Whilst thoughtful Americans were profoundly impressed by the analysis of the U.K. war effort recorded in the White Paper issued last November,[2] the extent of British sacrifices which it revealed stimulated their awareness that very onerous demands had been placed upon our resources, including manpower. To a people inclined to measure power in terms of monetary wealth our situation may well appear somewhat parlous. And it is widely felt that, quite apart from her domestic difficulties, a Britain heavily denuded of her overseas assets and of other sources of invisible exports, will find herself grievously handicapped in achieving equilibrium in her post-war balance of payments.

7. In the field of foreign relations the aggressively independent line followed by the Australian Minister for External Affairs throughout the San Francisco Conference demonstrated once and for all that there was no truth in the popular American fallacy that the British Commonwealth voted as a block at international gatherings under United Kingdom ægis. However salutary in this respect, Dr. Evatt's attitude, by demonstrating with equal clarity that Britain could not count in her international dealings on the steady support of her sister nations of the Commonwealth, also gave an added impetus to the belief that the influence of the mother country and of the Commonwealth in general as a unit of world power is now on the wane. Whilst Americans take small stock of an Eire which has maintained a stubbornly neutral position during the war, the recent cryptic announcement of Mr. de Valera[3] that his country is an independent republic served to lend its particle of colour to the picture of an enfeebled and isolated Britain. A threat to our lines of imperial communication is moreover seen in such current developments as the

[2] Cmd. 6564, *Statistics relating to the War Effort of the United Kingdom.*
[3] Head of the Irish Government and Minister for External Affairs. For his statement in the Dail on 17 July see *The Times*, 18 July 1945, p. 2.

Russian interest in Tangier and the Dardanelles, in the pressure of a Soviet-influenced Yugoslavia on the frontiers of Istria and western Thrace, and in the mounting nationalism of the Arab states. Although far from typical of the public attitude as a whole, the light in which we to-day appear on the lunatic fringe of American opinion may be illustrated by citing the recent remark of an anti-British U.S. General: 'Britain is nowadays of no more significance than Costa Rica'.

8. The war, which by one sided and incomplete comparison has somewhat dimmed the reputation of Britain as a world power, has placed the prestige of Soviet Russia well in the ascendant. Here, as earlier reports have indicated, American public opinion, according to the particular outlook of the groups or individuals concerned, is animated by a gamut of feelings ranging from unreasoning fear and hatred to genuine admiration. Almost all thoughtful Americans are however imbued with the belief that, by reason of her vast size, limitless resources in men and raw materials, and industrial potential, Soviet Russia is the only world power comparable in stature to the United States.

9. This Big Two concept derives in the first instance from the spectacle of Soviet Russia's newly-fledged military might spread athwart Central and South-Eastern Europe and now in at the death against the Japanese in Northern China. Anxiety on this score is however to some extent assuaged in moderate minded and liberal circles by those factors in her contemporary life which appear to provide a basis for the long term development of peaceful relations between herself and the United States. The most notable of many recent expositions of these factors was contained in two speeches delivered at New York on the 24th May and 4th June last by Mr. Henry Wallace, the Secretary of Commerce, and former Vice-President. In them Mr. Wallace developed the thesis that, having now emerged to the most powerful positions on the world stage, and occupying geographical situations which had never led to any essential conflict of interests, Russia and the United States could find common ground for permanent amity because the one symbolised economic democracy to backward peoples and the other was the great exponent of political democracy. Neither country, he pointed out, possessed colonies. Both of them were groping for a way of life which would enable the common man everywhere to derive the most good out of the maximum use of modern technology. In his earlier and more detailed address Mr. Wallace declared that Germany had supplanted England from 1900 onwards in the domination of world commerce; that the cultural and political over-lordship of western nations had now passed and that in the conditions of the world to-day there was no place for old-fashioned or economic imperialism.

10. When examining the effect which the Big Two concept is likely to exercise on Anglo-American relations it is important to recollect that many other attitudes of mind also determine the outlook of Americans towards foreign countries in general and Great Britain in particular. At

the risk of platitudinous repetition of what has been said in former reports from this Embassy, it cannot in the first place be too strongly emphasised that the events of the war have revolutionised American thinking on the subject of security. The new and deep-seated conviction that the United States must assume wider responsibilities to buttress its own and world security was aptly symbolised in the Senate on the 27th July when its members paid Senator George of Georgia, a former Chairman of the Foreign Relations Committee, the rare tribute of rising to their feet after he had eloquently appealed to them to ratify the United Nations Charter as a means of redeeming the promise of a better world for which the flower of American youth had given their lives.

11. In their search for security in a world that modern science has contracted, Americans may be counted upon to display the virtues and defects inherent in a people which, throughout the comparative short span of its history, has seen itself as dedicated to the advancement of human freedoms and blessed beyond the inhabitants of other lands with a moral and democratic way of life. Now that the full strength of their country has become manifest to them, Americans hold that they are bound to take a leading part in the readjustment of international relationships. Faith in the magic of large words; an enthusiastic belief that the mere enunciation of an abstract principle is equivalent to its concrete fulfilment; a tendency to overlook the practical difficulties that obstruct the easy solution of current problems: above all a constant disposition to prefer the emotional to the rational approach—these are amongst the salient traits that are likely in the future, no less than in the past, to provoke Americans to impatience with the more stolid, disillusioned and pragmatic British, and to give rise to current misunderstandings between our two Governments. Taken in the aggregate these traits, for all that they at times bear the stamp of arrogant self-righteousness, spring from a core of genuine idealism which requires to be handled with more generosity and imagination and, be it also said, in a less patronising spirit than it has always received. In the meantime increased contacts with other regions are causing many Americans to shed their ignorance of the outside world.

12. The fact that Americans now tend to rate Great Britain somewhat lower in the scale of power values than their own country and the U.S.S.R. does not mean that they have written her off as a negligible factor in the comity of nations. On the contrary, esteem for the sterling qualities of the British stands as high as it ever did. This esteem, fortified by the thousand and one strands of sentiment that derive from the background of a common Anglo-Saxon heritage, co-exists, as it always has done, with a keen sense of rivalry and with the apparently ineradicable idea that nature has endowed the British with a well-nigh inexhaustible store of superior cunning, of which they are only too prone to make the fullest possible use in international negotiations with the object of 'outsmarting' the more simple-minded Americans.

13. Whenever they find reason to complain of our actions Americans

do not fail to apply to us a number of ugly catch-words that owe much of their origin to the traditional mistrust of British policies and to the above-mentioned sense of rivalry—e.g. balance of power, Spheres of Influence, reactionary imperialist trends, colonial oppression, old-world guile, diplomatic double-talk, Uncle Sam the Santa Claus and sucker, and the like. Anti-British outbursts are as a rule the result of the propensity of Americans to over-simplify vexatious issues which lie beyond their immediate ken. They need not therefore unduly disturb us, provided always that our own conscience is clear and that we are able in any given instance to rebut the accusations levelled against us by reference to some yard-stick of readily understood first principle,—whether it be expressed in terms of moral responsibility, idealism, or leadership. It must in any case be borne in mind that criticism of Britain is something that is bound to recur in a country of the continental proportions of the United States which comprises so many hyphenated communities within its borders and elements that are either inveterately anti-British or self-impelled to advertise their genuine Americanism. This being so, we should beware of hastily attributing to Americans as a whole the anti-British sentiments of one section of them.

14. To return to the central theme of this despatch: Americans, to whom as a witty observer once remarked all facts are free and equal, attach particular importance to quantitative standards of value. It follows that they are bound on a basis of sheer statistics to draw unfavourable comparisons between the British Isles, with their static population and dependence upon imported goods and raw materials, and the U.S.S.R. with its huge untapped resources and conglomeration of peoples destined, according to expert forecasts, to expand in numbers far beyond the two hundred million mark. To an America which, on all reasonable showing, has ceased to believe that she can remain safely sheltered behind ocean barriers, the Soviet Union appears as the only country in the world now capable, if it feels so inclined, of measuring odds with her.

15. Much public uncertainty prevails as to how best to deal with this new international portent. Accustomed enough at home to the idea of bigger and better elephants, most Americans none the less find themselves filled with a sense of uneasy bewilderment when they contemplate an unfamiliar Russian bear which is barred off from the cakes and buns of alien propaganda and refuses to be coaxed into behaviour that approximates to Western notions of democratic propriety. In their fear of the unknown, the bulk of American commentators, who share the well nigh universal conviction of the public that armed conflict with the Soviet Union is an unthinkable expedient, have tended to relapse into a mood of baffled dismay whenever danger seems to threaten from unilateral Russian action. Their main theme on such occasions has been to bewail the ineffectiveness of their own diplomatic agents and, as often as not, to accuse them of allowing themselves to be dragged along in a campaign of bear-baiting 'at the tail of the British kite'. These aspersions, which were

particularly vocal early this summer at the time of the Polish and Trieste crises, began to subside after Mr. Stettinius in his speech at San Francisco on the 28th May[4] had declared that the United States, whose interests extended to the whole world, must mediate between other great powers when their interests conflicted amongst themselves. Much comfort is now derived from the belief that President Truman can be counted upon to pursue an independent American policy, and that Mr. Byrnes,[5] who is reputed to be a born mediator, will succeed in resolving Soviet and American differences on a basis of honourable compromise.

16. The uncertainty in American thinking where the Soviet Union is concerned is much less marked when it comes to questions that relate to the role of the United States in that segment of the world which lies outside the Russian orbit of power. Here a blend of idealism, hard business instinct, and motives of security is propelling the United States to a greater extent than ever before into international fields far beyond the limits traced by the time-honoured Monroe Doctrine[6] and notions of hemispheric defence. An America which has found her place in the sun is resolved that the more efficient units of her vastly augmented merchant fleet shall not be laid up in idleness as occurred with the bulk of her ocean-going commercial vessels after the last war. Federal regulated civil aviation lines can rely upon constant official support to secure the foreign bases and facilities necessary to enable them to girdle the globe. The weight of administrative backing can readily be mobilized for the establishment of American-controlled telecommunications systems in undeveloped regions, and for securing the maximum possible American share in the exploitation of Middle East oil resources.

17. As citizens of a country that has tended to acclaim rapidly acquired material success as proof of moral rectitude the leaders of the influential pressure groups that promote these activities may be pardoned if they regard them not merely as profit-making enterprises but also as the media for disseminating the blessings of the American way of life to other and less fortunate peoples. By the same token they are quick to suspect the use of a privileged position to exclude themselves whenever circumstances confront them with the older established competing rights of Great Britain in her imperial possessions or in other territories vital to her security where she has hitherto exercised a paramount influence. For the time being at any rate a Soviet Union rotating within its own orbit

---

[4] This radio address by Mr. Edward R. Stettinius (since 27 June U.S. representative to the United Nations) in his capacity as U.S. Secretary of State and Chairman of the U.S. Delegation to the San Francisco Conference, is printed in *D.S.B.*, vol. xii, pp. 1007–13.

[5] U.S. Secretary of State since 3 July 1945.

[6] The Monroe Doctrine, promulgated by U.S. President Monroe on 2 December 1823 with the intention of deterring European interference in the western hemisphere, contained the statement that 'the American continents, by the free and independent conditions which they have assumed and maintain, are henceforth not to be considered as subject for future colonization by any European Power'. Cf. also No. 99.

represents no comparable points of friction, with the exception of a nascent Russian interest in Middle Eastern affairs and the possiblity of future clashes of interest in the Far East, in regard to which speculation, long since manifest, is likely to become more acute now that the Red Army is sharing the credit for the coup de grace of the Japanese.

18. A world that rotates in two orbits of power. Enough has been said to show that this concept is beginning to crystallize in the American mind. At the same time, as already indicated, the fact that Americans have come to believe that the key to world peace lies in the relationship of their country with the Soviet Union does not mean that they have ceased to view Great Britain with a twin sense of esteem and rivalry. Along, moreover, with this familiar psychological pattern there is to be found a deep seated conviction amongst a wide range of Americans, and not least amongst persons prominent in the Administration and general staff, that, whether from the political economic or strategic point of view, a strong and prosperous Britain is an essential U.S. interest. Indeed, even if many of them would not acknowledge the fact to themselves, it is no exaggeration to say that the majority of those elements which give shape and purpose to all that is best in their country's mode of existence are aware in their heart of hearts that the continuity of her moral values is inseparably bound up with the welfare of Great Britain. Even these elements, however, would incline to distinguish in their thoughts between Britain and her Empire and to hold the view that in areas of Europe and the Middle East adjacent to the Soviet orbit of power British foreign policy is liable at times to embark on ill-advised courses which in the last analysis might constitute a threat to United States' security.

19. All in all, therefore, it begins to look as though we are witnessing a gradual American shift away from the pattern traced by President Roosevelt in his grand design which, at any rate when he first conceived it at the height of the war, envisaged the coequal collaboration of Great Britain, the Soviet Union and the United States with the object of defeating the enemy and of creating a United Nations Organisation for the maintenance of world peace. Victory in Europe is won. America has committed herself in spectacular fashion to the United Nations' Charter, in the elaboration of which at San Francisco she can justly claim to have played a leading part. But, unless appearances are deceptive, the United States is also now groping towards a new order of things in which Great Britain, whilst occupying a highly important position as the bastion of Western European security and as the focal point of a far-flung oceanic system, will nevertheless be expected to take her place as junior partner in an orbit of power predominantly under American ægis. This theory of a U.S.A. destined for the role of leadership was implicit in a passage of the speech delivered by President Truman at Kansas City on the 3rd of July [sic] where he stated: 'I am anxious to bring it home to you that the world is no longer county-size, no longer state-size, no longer nation-size—it is one world, as Willkie said. It is a world in which we must all get along. And

17

it is my opinion that this great Republic ought to lead the way.'[7]

20. On the economic side the U.S. Administration sees itself as destined to point the way to an era of economic liberalism which will promote the exchange of goods and services between nations and restore prosperity to a war stricken world. The renewal by Congress this summer of the Reciprocal Trade Agreement[s] Act and its approval of the Bretton Woods proposals are regarded as milestones that mark progress to this end. The next and most important stage on the road will be to complete the discussions with His Majesty's Government preparatory to the international conference on trade and employment planned for the early part of next year. It is the present hope of the United States Government that this conference will in its turn lay the basis for the expanding world economy contemplated in Article VII of the master lend-lease agreements.

21. Excepting in the Far East where the United States has plainly asserted its leadership, the outlines of the new dispensation in the political sphere are as yet somewhat imprecise. An Administration conscious of its country's stake in world security but sensitive to the movements of an immensely variegated public opinion that is by no means rid of isolationist phobias, still displays hesitancy as to the lengths to which it should go to dispel storm clouds in distant regions. It is of course true that, quite apart from collaborating in the manifold tasks connected with the liquidation of the European war and the preparation of peace settlements, the United States has given many other positive proofs that it recognises the need for sharing the burden of world responsibilities. Thus, American influence has been steadily exerted to secure an equitable solution of the Polish problem. It has also been brought to bear to mitigate the crisis which arose last autumn in Soviet-Persian relations and to support our intervention this summer in the Levant. In the Trieste affair the United States went further than mere diplomatic representations and, albeit somewhat reluctantly, joined us in action which might have resulted in an armed clash between American troops and Yugoslav Partisans. The United States stands ready to participate in the future Administration of Tangier and in supervising the Greek elections. America has sought to encourage a reconciliation between Chungking and the Yenan Communists.

22. The above mentioned occurrences do not, however, imply that the United States is invariably prepared to march on parallel lines to His Majesty's Government in resolving problems of immediate concern to ourselves and more particularly those that arise in our dealings with the Soviet Union. The late President Roosevelt himself, although a firm believer in Anglo-American collaboration and to some extent under the spell of the superior genius of Mr. Churchill, jealously preserved the appearance of independent manœuvre. Indeed, after the Moscow and Tehran conferences he was not averse to encouraging the idea that the

[7] Mr. Truman's address on 28 June 1945 is printed in *Public Papers: Truman 1945*, pp. 149–52.

United States occupied the position of mediator between the Soviet Union and Great Britain, and that his powers of conciliation had more than once averted a breach between Marshal Stalin and Mr. Churchill. After the Greek crisis in December last the view gained ground that Britain was concerned to perpetuate reactionary governments in Europe. It was felt that, unless the United States intervened to promote more liberal tendencies, that continent would relapse into anarchy from which only the Soviet Union could derive benefit.

23. Against this background the previously unannounced decision of President Truman to send Mr. Hopkins on his mission to Moscow at the end of May,[8] together with the concomitant visit of Mr. Davies to London,[9] is to be regarded as no mere move to demonstrate to the U.S. public and to the world at large that the new President was continuing the mediatory role of his predecessor at a time when differences over Poland and the veto dispute at San Francisco seemed to imperil inter-Allied relations. It must also be ascribed to the growing belief in responsible official circles, already noticeable under the late Administration, that it should devolve on the United States in the first instance as the major Western power to take the initiative in determining the shape of things on the periphery of the Soviet orbit no less than elsewhere. President Truman's decision to proceed direct from Washington to Potsdam without breaking his journey in Britain provided another sign of the same process of thought.

24. Out of the hubbub of emotional talk which the announcement this week about the atomic bomb[10] has unleashed throughout the country, it is already clear enough that America's consciousness of superior power, or as one columnist puts it 'her capacity for Promethean rule', is being vigorously stimulated by the fact that she alone, for the present at any rate, possesses the means to exploit this awe-inspiring and revolutionary invention.

25. Whilst the advent of a Labour Government in Great Britain should in no way alter the shrewd reckoning of the Americans that the pattern of world power has radically shifted in their country's favour, it has injected new and unexpected factors into their calculations. Even amongst the more conservative minded, who now see the U.S.A. as the last stronghold of capitalistic economy, there would be few if any supporters of the notion that a Britain about to embark on a Socialist experiment is in the least likely to gravitate towards Communism. At the same time warnings are

[8] See Volume I, No. 78. Mr. Harry Hopkins was Special Adviser and Assistant to President Truman.

[9] Mr. Joseph E. Davies, Special Adviser to President Truman during the Potsdam Conference (see Volume I), travelled to London in May 1945 on the President's instructions for talks with Mr. Churchill. For an account of these conversations see *F.R.U.S. 1945, The Conference of Berlin*, vol. i, pp. 63–81.

[10] President Truman's announcement on 6 August of the use of the atomic bomb at Hiroshima that day is printed in *Public Papers, op. cit.*, pp. 197–200.

heard in financial and business circles that America should beware of countenancing any proposal to grant extensive credits to a Britain which would be likely to employ them to underwrite State Socialism. Of even more importance than these vested interests, which are doubtless influenced by the knowledge that the British Labour victory will be attended by repercussions at home, is the attitude of official Washington. In this quarter the change has come as something of a shock from the standpoint of its probable effect upon the U.S. programme for fostering world revival through the international relaxation of restrictive financial and trade practices. The Administration is apprehensive lest Britain, for all her temperamental caution, will now commit herself to a thorough-going system of State trading with its attendant features of subsidies, bulk purchases and quotas which might effectively defeat any sound working of the reciprocal trade programme.

26. An event that has multiplied our critics on economic grounds has none the less served to appreciate our political stocks. By capturing the imagination of Americans the vivid dynamic personality of Mr. Churchill had hitherto somewhat obscured the extent of our economic plight which is now revealed in fuller nakedness. On the other hand, the Labour landslide should remove the hitherto persistent impression that Great Britain is concerned to encourage European reaction. No less than Left Wing pressure groups, middle-of-the-road and liberal opinion in general, which includes some of the most prominent newspaper and radio commentators with the widest audiences, has hailed the election results as a notable democratic achievement destined to usher in the era of the plain man. It is widely conceded that Britain, now further left of centre than America herself, is presented with a new opportunity to assume the leadership of all progressive forces and to arrest the drift in Europe towards anarchy and Communism.

27. During the months to come Britain promises to be the cynosure of American eyes. Our official pronouncements will be eagerly awaited: the development of our economic and foreign policies will be scrutinised with the utmost care. If in the former respect our position from the point of view of enlisting a sympathetic American attitude has become more complicated, in the latter respect there can be no question but that our credit has been sensibly improved. From now onwards we should be less exposed to captious criticism of our actions in Europe; the charge that it is we who are needlessly provoking the Soviet Union to display intran-sigeance should become void of content; our handling of vexatious problems in India and the Middle East should command a more receptive audience; there is a somewhat enlarged prospect of enlisting American support, whenever we feel so disposed, in the effort to resolve debatable issues.

28. In general, and this would seem to be of the first importance, we may expect the U.S. Administration to show a disposition to promote early reference to the World Organisation of all matters that seem likely to

occasion friction between the Anglo-American and Soviet orbits of power. Within the broad overall framework set up by the United Nations Charter, which has been resoundingly approved by the nation at large, the United States Government is free to move with the Governments of other like minded countries along firmer lines to secure what it considers to be just solutions than if it chooses to manœuvre on its own with the knowledge that whatever decisions it takes will have to answer on their independent merits at the bar of a highly temperamental public opinion. By adopting the former course the U.S. Administration is in any case far less exposed to the charge that it has shaped its policy in deference to the wishes of His Majesty's Government. Whenever negotiations are conducted on a purely Three Power basis United States domestic reasons, in the future as in the past, will undoubtedly play a certain part in causing the Administration to share our view that there should be no appearance of an Anglo-American attempt to 'gang up' on the Russians. So too we may anticipate an analogous reluctance to aligning American policy too closely with that of Britain in the adjustment of post-war relations with China where, as already indicated, the United States is in any event peculiarly concerned to avoid possible causes of friction with the U.S.S.R.

29. In our own bilateral dealings with the United States Government we should be careful to formulate requests for their support in such a manner as to avoid the appearance of teaching the Americans where their best interests lie. It is equally self-understood that in any instance where we have reason to protest against U.S. actions our ground should be well chosen and our complaint prompted by no mere shift of selfish expediency or passing mood of irritation. As men who themselves prefer the simple forthright approach, the Americans appreciate plain speaking in others. Nor will they take it amiss if we stand up for ourselves when our interests are well founded, or, conversely, interpret it as a sign of weakness if, whenever there is scope for the adjustment of conflicting Anglo-American views, we eschew methods of obstinate bargaining. In inter-governmental negotiations our case to the Americans should be presented not so much on grounds of sentiment as upon lucidly argued appeals to reason and the logic of hard fact.

30. Last, but not least, the progressive elements of America will test our every word and deed on the touchstone of broad democratic principle. The early ratification by His Majesty's Government of the San Francisco Charter will be greeted here as an earnest of our intention to place ourselves squarely behind the cause of world peace. Rapid approval of the Bretton Woods proposals may do something to ease the thorny path of our trade discussions with the United States Government. In our day-to-day dealings with the Administration on current problems of foreign policy the omens are favourable. In the course of the last two centuries we have twice stood alone and have saved ourselves by our exertions. We are now seen to be better placed than ever before to save Europe by our example.

31. I am forwarding copies of this despatch to the High Commissioner for the United Kingdom in Ottawa, His Majesty's Ambassador at Moscow and the Joint Staff Mission at Washington.[11]

I have, &c.,
(For the Ambassador)
JOHN BALFOUR

CALENDARS TO NO. 3

i   *21 Aug. 1945 Mr. Balfour (Washington) Despatch No. 1088* Comments on development of U.S. opinion in favour of United Nations, in which 'Americans as a whole are bound to feel a certain proprietary pride' [U 6649/12/70].

ii   *14 Sept.–22 Nov. 1945 Earl of Halifax (Washington) despatch No. 1185* Comments on implications of No. 3 for British policy in Latin America, enclosing memo. stressing importance of keeping 'Great Britain in the van of post-war trade with the Americas' in view of likely U.S. policy of fighting for 'political and economic hegemony of this hemisphere'; Lord Halifax's views agreed with by Sir D. Gainer, H.M. Ambassador in Rio de Janeiro, but queried by Mr. C.H. Bateman, H.M. Ambassador in Mexico City [AS 5328, 5549, 6434/317/51].

---

[11] Mr. Philip Noel-Baker, Minister of State in the Foreign Office, and Sir O. Sargent minuted as follows on this despatch: 'I am most interested in § 28. If the U.S.G. will, in fact, pursue the policy of using the U.N. institutions & standing on the principles of the Charter, we shall find cooperation easy, & dangerous conflicts with Russia will be more easily avoided. We should encourage this with all means in our power.

'2. I am not at all afraid that Americans will continue to regard us as a second-rate power. There are other things in leadership besides dollars & guns, & when the British Commonwealth nations together defend the principles of the Charter, they will be a very formidable force in the Assembly & the Councils of the U.N.

'3. I *hope* the U.S.G. will share in the leadership of these bodies; but if their share is to be effective, they will have to find some new method of selecting their representatives. Their constitution is a serious handicap, as both President Hoover & President Roosevelt found. P.J.N.B. 27/9.'

'This despatch describes the position of Lepidus in the triumvirate with Mark Antony and Augustus. The position is no easy one and it seems doubtful whether we shall get much support from the Dominions in the uphill task of maintaining ourselves as a world power in the face of the United States, who now for the first time is prepared to assume this position with the help of the almighty dollar, export surpluses (in other words the swamping of foreign markets with dumped U.S. goods), civil aviation, and all the other instruments which they can if necessary use in order to "penetrate" the world. If this is so it behoves us all the more to strengthen our own world position vis-à-vis of our own two great allied rivals by building up ourselves as *the* great European Power. This brings us back to the policy of collaboration with France with a view to our two countries establishing themselves politically as the leaders of all the Western European Powers and morally as the standard-bearers of European civilisation. Once we have acquired this position both the United States and the Soviet Union are more likely to respect us and therefore collaborate with us than they are at present. O.G. Sargent Oct. 1st, 1945.'

No. 4

Mr. Balfour (Washington) to Mr. Bevin
(Received 11 August, 2.35 p.m.)

REMAC 596 Telegraphic[1] [UE 3579/32/71]

Most immediate   WASHINGTON, 11 August 1945, 2.29 a.m.

For Harmer from Lee.[2]

McCurrach[3] and I had informal talk this morning[4] with Hammaford [sic][5] about the situation likely to arise as a result of latest development.[6]

2. Hammaford said that while legal position was that Lend-Lease could continue until June 30th 1946 or earlier passage of Congress resolution as provided in 3 (c) of Lend-Lease Act,[7] present special offering [sic] in F.E.A. was that in practice it would be impossible to justify continued shipment on credit Lend-lease to United Kingdom for more than very short time after V.J. day.[8] He reminds us that in case of Russia credit Lend-Lease shipments were suspended in less than week after their V.E. day.[9]

It was envisaged that Lend-Lease and reciprocal aid[10] would continue

[1] REMAC and CAMER were designations for telegrams sent to and from H.M. Treasury.
[2] Mr. F.E. Harmer was a Temporary Assistant Secretary in H.M. Treasury. Mr. F.G. Lee was Deputy Treasury Representative in Washington.
[3] Mr. D.F. McCurrach was a member of the U.K.T.D.
[4] This telegram was drafted on 10 August.
[5] Mr. Hannaford was an official of the U.S. Foreign Economic Administration (F.E.A.).
[6] The reference was presumably to the offer to surrender made by the Japanese Government on 10 August: see Sir L. Woodward, op. cit., vol. v, p. 525. For the financial implications see Pressnell, op. cit., Chapter 9.(12).
[7] Cf. No. 1, note 4. Article 3(c) of the Lend-Lease Act provided that the powers conferred by the Act for the supply of 'defense articles' by the U.S. Government were not to be exercised by the President 'nor the head of any department or agency' after 30 June 1943 (or earlier if Congress passed a resolution that such powers were no longer necessary to promote the defence of the United States), but that until 1 July 1946 'any of such powers may be exercised to the extent necessary to carry out a contract or agreement with such a foreign government made before July 1, 1943, or before the passage of such concurrent resolution, whichever is the earlier'. See further No. 13, note 5.
[8] i.e. the day of Japanese capitulation announced on 15 August and subsequently celebrated in the United States on 2 September 1945, the date of the signature of the formal Instrument of Surrender for Japan.
[9] i.e. Victory in Europe day, celebrated on 8 May 1945 in the United Kingdom and the United States but on 9 May in the U.S.S.R.: cf. Woodward, ibid., pp. 395–400. The American note of 12 May to the Soviet Government on the discontinuance of Lend-Lease is printed in F.R.U.S. 1945, vol. v, pp. 1000–1.
[10] The system of Reciprocal Aid, by which the U.K. supplied military stores and services to the U.S.A. free of charge, to be set against supplies received under Lend-Lease, had been formalized in an Exchange of Notes on 3 September 1942 between Lord Halifax and Mr. Cordell Hull (U.S. Secretary of State 1933–44), printed in B.F.S.P., vol. 144, pp. 1051–4. Lord Halifax's note contained a statement of the general principle that 'as large a portion as possible of the articles and services which each Government may authorise to be provided to the other shall be in the form of reciprocal aid so that the need of each Government for the

for longer period in respect of supplies going to or moving in Pacific area including requirements for service connected with redeployment of United States forces. He thought it might . . .[11] to justify continued credit Lend-Lease for at any rate substantial portion of our oil and shipping programmes on grounds that these would be balanced by reciprocal aid programmes of approximate equal magnitude. But he saw no (repeat no) hope of justifying any similar arrangement as regards food, raw materials and civilian goods supplies for United Kingdom.

3. As regards latter Hammaford recurred to idea of a three (c) board [sic ?loan] to cover:

(a) Materials in pipeline at the time of termination of credit Lend Lease shipments.

(b) Users of Lend-Lease stocks already in United Kingdom. By goods in pipeline he had in mind requirements in respect of which requisites had been agreed by F.E.A. not (repeat not) new demands coming forward during period in question. It would of course be open to us to indicate what portion of materials in pipeline we no longer wanted and these would be excluded from any 3(c) agreement. His own announcement.

(III) (sic) It was still not (repeat not) too late for us to conclude such an agreement. Although he emphasised that he was speaking only for himself. If we did not (repeat not) conclude such an agreement then Hammaford saw no alternative but for supplies in pipeline to be stopped except against full cash payment from us to suppliers, although it might still be possible to negotiate separate agreement to cover user of Lend-Lease stocks. He mentioned possibility of assistance from export and import bank but thought it very unlikely that present direction of bank would agree to use of Bank Deadweight to finance current requirements.

(VI) (sic) He made no (repeat no) reference to possible terms which would apply in any 3(c) agreement except to say that he did not (repeat not) know whether . . .[11] accorded to liberated countries (20 years credit, 2⅜% interest) would be regarded as applicable in United Kingdom in circumstances. He added that F.E.A. estimates of payments of goods in pipeline probable for British empire varied considerably between 300 and 9,000,000,000 dollars.

(sic) 5. Above is sent for your information. You will appreciate that Hammaford was speaking in confidence and we should not (repeat not) quote him in any discussions with Americans here or in London. We made it clear to him that we were not (repeat not) authorised to negotiate any

currency of the other may be reduced to a minimum'. For the development of the Reciprocal Aid system during the war see Sayers, op. cit., pp. 413–26.

[11] The text is here uncertain.

arrangement with F.E.A. but were awaiting instructions from London on general questions involved.

6. Present arrangement is that supply council[12] will meet on August 13th to take stock of position following which appreciation will be sent in Uslon series.[13] But you will no doubt be considering urgently how we are to finance present import requirements from United States of America on assumption that credit Lend-Lease shipments may terminate within short period. We frankly see virtually no (repeat no) hope of our being able to induce F.E.A. to continue shipments to United Kingdom on credit lend-lease for more that [sic] very limited period indeed having regard to explicit commitments given to Congress. If therefore, we are to negotiate three (repeat three) . . .[11] agreement immediate action may be necessary. Presumably just [sic? first] necessity will be to assess what our immediate requirements on a minimum basis are likely to be from United States of America for say just six months after V.J. day and extent to which they would be covered by demands in . . .[11] i.e. assuming unimpeded user of lend-lease stocks within United Kingdom. We will ask missions here whether they can make any estimates of this but assume that work will have mainly to be done at your end.

7. I am not giving this telegram any circulation here.

CALENDARS TO NO. 4

i *6–9 August 1945   RAFDEL (Washington) Tels. USLON 111–114, Mr. Balfour (Washington) Tel. REMAC 590* Consideration by B.S.C. on 5 Aug. of 'position created by exchange of correspondence between President and P.M. at Terminal [Potsdam] regarding Lend-Lease eligibility of our military requirements in Stage II' (Vol. I, Nos. 458 and 503): arrangements and briefing for meeting on 13 Aug. with Mr. Patterson, U.S. Under Secretary for War, to discuss interpretation of directive in Mr. Truman's letter. Further consideration by B.S.C. on 8 Aug.: cf. Duncan Hall, *op. cit.*, p. 460 [UE 3412, 3520/32/71].

ii *9 Aug. 1945   Tel. LONUS 77 to Washington* Service Departments are trying to avoid asking for munitions not eligible under Lend-Lease when preparing their requirements programmes: importance of sticking closely to the rules laid down in the P.M.'s letter, which the Americans breached by their unilateral exclusion of occupational forces [UE 3412/32/71].

iii *10 Aug. 1945   Mr. Balfour (Washington) Tel. ELFUNOCOP 753* (Ministry of Fuel & Power telegram series, not to be shown to the Americans) Discussion of oil requirements after V.J. day and possible removal of rationing in U.S. [UE 3577/32/71].

---

[12] i.e. the British Supply Council in North America (B.S.C.).
[13] The USLON/LONUS series of telegrams were transmitted through the R.A.F. Delegation in Washington (RAFDEL) and the Air Ministry for the Joint American Secretariat (J.A.S.) in London. The times of telegrams transmitted through these channels were Greenwich Mean Time. Where the time of despatch is not recorded the time of origin is given.

No. 5

Mr. Balfour (Washington) to Mr. Bevin
(Received 15 August, 3.30 p.m.)

REMAC 608 Telegraphic[1] [UE 3646/32/71]

Immediate. Top secret   WASHINGTON, *14 August 1945, 11.45 p.m.*

My telegram No. 605[2] from Goschen.[3]

I lunched with Cramer[4] today. He told me that the President saw Crowley[5] and Byrnes this morning to discuss future of Lend-Lease. Cox[6] and Cramer had endeavoured to brief Crowley on lines set out in paragraph 2 below and Byrnes was known to have received recent, and from our point of view, satisfactory recommendations from Clayton.

2. Policy proposed by Cox and Cramer for Lend-Lease after VJ Day was:

(a) Continuance of shipping and oil programmes on the assumption that there would be compensating reciprocal aid.

(b) Continuance of Lend-Lease food shipments to United Kingdom until possibly the end of the year.

(c) Discontinuance of Lend-Lease shipments of raw materials and civilian goods almost immediately with simultaneous reversion of reciprocal aid of raw materials (and possibly foodstuffs) to a cash basis. They had talked to Crowley about allowing supplies to go forward on Lend-Lease but Cramer thought this was unlikely.

3. I asked whether I could reassure you that there would be no sudden cutting off of Lend-Lease as in case of Russia. Cramer said he could not go so far as that and he thought the above proposals would 'need some selling' to the President but Byrnes was thought to be working hard on our behalf.

[1] Some corrupt passages in the original text of this telegram have been supplied from an amended copy dated 16 August.

[2] REMAC 605, despatched at 5.12 a.m. on 14 August, had reported information from the F.E.A. that 'the President has asked them to produce by a.m. tomorrow (Tuesday) statement showing quantities and value of Lend-Lease stocks on hand in United Kingdom ... they profess not (repeat not) to know reason for request.'

[3] Mr. H.K. Goschen was an Administrative Officer in the U.K.T.D.

[4] Mr. A.C. Cramer was Acting Director of the British Empire and Middle East branch of the F.E.A.

[5] Mr. Leo T. Crowley was Foreign Economic Administrator.

[6] Mr. O.S. Cox was Deputy Administrator, F.E.A.

4. I will endeavour to keep in touch and let you know as soon as result of talk with the President is available. Cramer thought probable no decision would be taken today. I would be grateful if every precaution could be taken to see that above is not referred to in any way in discussions with Americans. Impression created by 'grave cables' referred to in my telegram No. 603[7] has made everyone in United States departments cautious of giving us any information.

5. Cramer stated that Griffin[8] on telephone this morning had said estimate of reciprocal aid for next three months was £100,000,000. Can you confirm? We think this estimate may have considerable bearing on the Lend-Lease decisions.

6. In assessing weight to be given to above information you will of course make due allowance for level from which it comes. This telegram has been seen by Self[9] but except for Makins[10] given no circulation.

[7] In this telegram, despatched at 3.27 a.m. on 14 August, Mr. Balfour reported information from the State Department that Mr. Collado had telegraphed from London to the effect that 'British Government had received "grave cable" from Washington about future of Lend-Lease, as a result of which they had cancelled meeting arranged with Keynes': see No. 8. In response to Mr. Collado's urgent request for information 'State Department are replying after consultation with Crowley and Cox that there have as yet been no policy decisions on Lend-Lease'.

[8] Mr. W.V. Griffin, Director of the British Empire Branch of the F.E.A., was in London with Mr. Clayton to participate in discussions on Stage III: cf. No. 1, note 4.

[9] Sir Henry Self was Deputy Chairman of the B.S.C.

[10] Mr. R. Makins was a Minister in H.M. Embassy in Washington.

No. 6

Note by Mr. Dalton[1]

C.P. (45)112 [CAB 129/1]

Secret

TREASURY CHAMBERS, 14 August 1945

I circulate herewith an appreciation by Lord Keynes of 'Our Overseas Financial Prospects'.[2]

[1] Mr. Hugh Dalton was Chancellor of the Exchequer.

[2] The memorandum circulated in C.P. (45)112 formed the second part of a paper of 13 August by Lord Keynes, which he had circulated with a covering note stating that it was 'a first draft, following a series of discussions in the Treasury, of the substance of the argument and proposals which we might present to the Americans at the first stage of the proposed oral discussions in Washington in September': see Moggridge, op. cit., pp. 377–411.

The first part of the paper, 'The Present Overseas Financial Position of U.K.', formed the basis of the memorandum circulated on 17 August by Mr. Dalton as 'Proposals to the United States for Financial Assistance to follow after Lend Lease', reproduced at i below. In a covering note to Mr. Attlee Mr. Dalton stated that this memorandum had only been sent to the Foreign Secretary, the Lord President of the Council (Mr. H. Morrison) and the

I am anxious that my colleagues should be informed, without delay, of this most grim problem.³ I shall shortly submit proposals for action.

H.D.

ANNEX TO NO. 6

Our Overseas Financial Prospects

13 August 1945

1. Three sources of financial assistance have made it possible for us to mobilise our domestic man-power for war with an intensity not approached elsewhere, and to spend cash abroad, mainly in India and the Middle East, on a scale not even equalled by the Americans, *without having to export* in order to pay for the food and raw materials which we were using at home or to provide the cash which we were spending abroad.

2. The fact that the distribution of effort between ourselves and our Allies has been of this character leaves us far worse off, when the sources of assistance dry up, than if the rôles had been reversed. If we had been developing our exports so as to pay for our own current needs and in addition to provide a large surplus which we could furnish free of current charge to our Allies as Lend-Lease or Mutual Aid or on credit, we should,

President of the Board of Trade (Sir Stafford Cripps), and was intended for discussion at the Ministers' meeting on 23 August: see No. 17.

C.P.(45)112 was brought before the Cabinet on 16 August. In drawing his colleagues' attention to the paper, Mr. Attlee stressed the need for the 'utmost secrecy', pointing out that there were 'one or two striking phrases in the Memorandum (e.g. in paragraphs 27 and 28) which might have unfortunate consequences if used outside the circle of confidential Ministerial discussions' (CM(45)23rd conclusions, CAB 128/1).

For a comparison of the paper of 13 August with Lord Keynes' earlier memoranda (see No. 1, note 4) see Pressnell, *op. cit.*, Chapter 9.(10): the course of the intervening discussions and revisions can be followed in Treasury files T 247/49–50 and T 236/437.

³ Mr. Dalton had informed Mr. Bevin and Sir S. Cripps of his intention to submit 'a document on our financial position' when on 10 August he attended the first of a series of ministerial meetings arranged by Mr. Bevin for the discussion of financial and commercial policy. At this meeting, also attended by Mr. Hall-Patch, Sir W. Eady and Sir P. Liesching, which was chiefly concerned with European commercial relations, Mr. Bevin proposed that he, Mr. Dalton and Sir S. Cripps should meet regularly to 'enable the economic aspects of foreign policy to be considered and coordinated by the Departments mainly concerned rapidly and effectively' (UE 3683/3683/53).

In a 'Note of discussion with the Secretary of State' dated 10 August Mr. P. Dixon, Principal Private Secretary to Mr. Bevin, outlined the arrangements: 'The Secretary of State has agreed with the two Ministers that the three of them shall meet every Friday morning in the Foreign Office at 10.30 a.m. At this meeting any matters which the Departments consider useful for discussion should be taken up and discussed. The object of the meeting of the three Ministers is to ensure that our diplomatic action is shaped in accordance with our trade policy, and vice versa. The meetings would be of an entirely informal character. The Secretary of State does not wish them to develop into a machine. For this reason no formal minutes of the discussion should be kept or circulated. An informal note for the Secretary of State's own information would, however, be taken by a member of the Foreign Office staff. As the meetings develop it may be necessary to call in other Ministers, e.g. the Colonial Secretary' (UE 3660/113/53).

of course, find ourselves in a grand position when the period of providing the stuff free of current charge was brought suddenly to an end.

3. As it is, the more or less sudden drying up of these sources of assistance shortly after the end of the Japanese war will put us in an almost desperate plight, unless some other source of temporary assistance can be found to carry us over whilst we recover our breath—a plight far worse than most people, even in Government Departments, have yet appreciated.

4. The three sources of financial assistance have been

(a) Lend-Lease from the United States;

(b) Mutual Aid from Canada;

(c) Credits (supplemented by sales of our pre-war capital assets) from the Sterling Area (including credits under Payments Agreements with certain countries, especially in South America, which are outside the Area, but have made special agreements with it).

5. In the present year, 1945, these sources are enabling us to overspend our own income at the rate of about £2,100 millions a year, made up roughly as follows (these figures were compiled on the assumption that Lend-Lease and Mutual Aid would continue on the basis of recent provisions until the end of 1945):

	£ millions
Lend-Lease (munitions)	600
Lend-Lease (non-munitions)	500
Canadian Mutual Aid	250
Sterling Area, &c.	750
	2,100

(The Mutual Aid, amounting recently to about £500 millions a year, which we ourselves are according is here treated as part of our own domestic expenditure. From some, but not all, points of view this should be deducted from the above.)

6. This vast, but temporary, assistance allows us for the time being to over-play our own financial hand by just that amount. It means, conversely, that others are under-playing their hands correspondingly. How vividly do Departments and Ministers realise that the gay and successful fashion in which we undertake liabilities all over the world and slop money out to the importunate represents an over-playing of our hand, the possibility of which will come to an end quite suddenly and in the near future unless we obtain a new source of assistance? It may be that we are doing some things which are useless if we have to abandon them shortly after V–J, and that our external policies are very far from being adjusted to impending realities.

7. To sum up, the overseas balance in 1945 is estimated as follows:

29

£ million

Imports excl. munitions ...1,250		Exports 350
Munitions received under		Net invisible income and
Lend-Lease and Mutual Aid 850		sundry repayments, &c. ... 100
Other Government expendi-		Government receipts from
ture overseas ... 800		United States and
		Dominions for their forces
		and munitions 350
Total expenditure overseas 2,900		Total income overseas ... 800
		Deficit 2,100
		2,900

These estimates have been compiled on the assumption of a continuance of the Japanese war and Lend-Lease to the end of 1945. But the early termination of the Japanese war is likely to reduce Lend-Lease aid by more than it reduces our expenditure; so that, apart from some new sources of aid, the financial position is more likely to be worsened than improved in the short run.

8. What happens on the morrow of V-J day? We are led to expect that Lend-Lease and Mutual Aid (amounting this year to £1,350 millions altogether) will cease almost immediately. The Sterling Area arrangements in more or less their present form are, we hope, rather more durable, but they will become increasingly less productive of finance as supplies and shipping become available, and before long will become a burden instead of an aid—for the credits in our favour accrued on account of its being physically impossible for the Sterling Area countries to spend what they have been induced to lend us. I shall assume below that we can continue to expect substantial aid from the Sterling Area for a year after V-J, but no longer. We also have fair assurance of some subsequent assistance from Canada.

9. On the other hand, certain sources of expenditure will also dry up almost immediately, more particularly the munitions which we are obtaining from North America under Lend-Lease and Mutual Aid. We shall no longer need them and we are entitled to cease taking them. This will save us expenditure which is running currently at the rate of about £850 millions a year.

Nothing else will cease automatically or immediately on the morrow of V-J day. But there will, of course, be a further substantial economy in Government expenditure overseas which can be obtained more slowly, say in the course of a year. There is likely, however, to be a considerable time-lag in reducing such expenditure, for three reasons. In the first place, bills for much of the expenditure are received considerably in arrear, and we are responsible in India and Australia (as we are not in the case of Lend-Lease supplies) for winding up our munition contracts just as at home. In the second place the withdrawal of our forces will be protracted on account both of lack of transport and of the slowness of the administrative machine. In the third place (and above all) a substantial part of our existing Government expenditure overseas has no direct or obvious connection with the Japanese war and will not, therefore, come to an end merely because the Japs have packed up; retrenchment in these other directions will require quite a separate set of Cabinet decisions. Merely as a personal judgment, based on a general knowledge of the break-down of the expenditure in question, I should guess that without any change in policy good and energetic management might bring down the annual rate of £800 millions to (say) £300 millions by the end of 1946, although the cost during that year as a whole may be not much less than £450 millions. Any further substantial reduction will require drastic revisions of policy of a kind which do not automatically ensue on V-J.

10. Unfortunately there are also certain items of *income* which arise out of the war and will fade away with it. In reckoning the current overseas balance, credit has been taken (see §7) for income of £350 millions a year arising partly out of the personal expenditure of the American forces in this country (£115 millions in 1944 and probably as much as £60 millions in 1945) and mainly out of the contributions made by the Dominions towards the equipment and maintenance of their own divisions which has been provided by us in the first instance. These sources of income will have disappeared almost entirely within a year of V-J, but, allowing for time-lags in meeting old bills, and for possible repayments from the North-Western European allies, they may amount, on optimistic assumptions, to as much as £150 millions during that year.

11. We must next allow for possible economies after V-J in other overseas expenditure for goods and for increased earnings from our shipping and from the expansion of our exports in 1946. To correct for these factors we have to embark on difficult guesswork, and the range of reasonable estimating is very wide.

12. In the cost of imports of food and raw material an increase, rather than a reduction, is in sight, if the public are to be fed reasonably and employed fully and taking account of the fact that stocks are being currently drawn upon. We are budgeting (unless circumstances force us to restrict, as is quite possible) for more rather than less food in 1946 than in 1945. The raw materials required to provide employment, though not always the same in character as those we now import, are unlikely to be reduced in aggregate, since the numbers to be employed in industry will, after demobilisation, be more rather than less. On the other hand, some miscellaneous economies should be possible. One way and another our import programme might be kept down to £1,300 millions. Even this, assuming prices at double pre-war, means considerable austerity. For our pre-war imports were £850 millions, that is (say) £1,700 millions at the assumed post-war price level. Thus the above figure assumes a reduction

31

of 23 per cent. below the volume of our pre-war imports and therefore presumes strict controls, in the absence of which an appreciably higher figure is to be expected as soon as supplies are available.

13. As for exports there seems a reasonable hope of increasing them from an aggregate of £350 millions in 1945 to £600 millions in 1946. Extreme energy and concentration on this objective should do better still. Net invisible income in 1946, allowing for some recovery in commercial shipping receipts, might be put at £50 millions.

14. On the assumption of an export and import price level double pre-war, and no major changes in present policies, the position in 1946 can, therefore, be summed up as follows:

£ millions

Imports 1,300	Exports 600	
Government expenditure	Net invisible income 50	
overseas 450	Government receipts from	
———	Allies and Dominions ... 150	
1,750	———	
	800	
	Deficit 950	
	———	
	1,750	

15. When we come to subsequent years, we are in the realm of pure guesswork. If, to cheer ourselves up, we make bold to assume that by 1949 we have reached the goal of increasing the volume of exports by 50 per cent., the value of exports in that year, at double pre-war prices, would be £1,450 millions. If we suppose further that we can keep the further growth of imports within very moderate limits, if we can steadily curtail Government expenditure overseas, and if we can steadily increase our net invisible income, we can produce the following pipe-dream, showing an eventual equilibrium in the fourth year after V-J, namely 1949:

(£ millions)

—	Imports	Government Expenditure Overseas	Total	Exports	Net Invisible Income	Total	Deficit
1947 ...	1,400	250	1,650	1,000	100	1,100	550
1948 ...	1,400	200	1,600	1,300	100	1,400	200
1949 ...	1,450	150	1,600	1,450	150	1,600	Nil

It should be emphasised that imports can be kept down to this figure only by strict regulation.

16. Combining the above assumed deficits in 1947 and 1948 with the estimated deficit of £950 millions in 1946, we have a total deficit of £1,700 millions for the three years taken together.

17. Where, on earth, is all this money to come from? Our gold and dollar reserves at the end of 1945 will stand at about £500 millions. We might, if necessary, draw on this to the tune of £250 millions but certainly not more. In 1946 we might conceivably increase our net borrowing from the Sterling Area by (say) another £300 millions by stipulating that the further expenses in those countries strictly arising out of the war should be added to the War Debts. But there will be chaos in the trade relations of the Sterling Area and a break-down of the whole system unless we are prepared to release at least £75 millions a year to these and our other creditors in each of the years 1947 and 1948, leaving a net gain of £150 millions over the period as a whole. These two sources together bring the cumulative deficit down to £1,250 millions, i.e., $5 billions.

18. The conclusion is inescapable that there is no source from which we can raise sufficient funds to enable us to live and spend on the scale we contemplate except the United States. It is true that there are sundry resources which have not been taken into account in the above. For example, we still have some capital assets which could be gradually realised; and we have an expectation of some further aid from Canada. But the above calculation assumes that we have reached equilibrium by the end of 1948 which we have no convincing reason to expect, and also that we have by that date drawn down our ultimate reserves to the minimum. Moreover, the reader may have noticed that I have almost altogether omitted any reference to the vast debt of between £3,000 and £4,000 millions which we shall be owing to almost every country in the world. In other words, it has been tacitly assumed that we have found some way of dealing with this which allows us to discharge nothing in the three years 1946–1948 taken together, and, in fact, to add £150 millions to it. Moreover, the assumed rate of growth of exports is wildly optimistic, unless our methods change considerably. The conclusion holds, therefore, in so far as any firm conclusion can be based on such precarious material, that there remains a deficit of the order of $5 billions which can be met from no other source but the United States.

19. It is sometimes suggested that we can avoid dependence on the United States by a system of semi-barter arrangements with the countries from which we buy. This, however, assumes that the limiting factor lies in the willingness of overseas markets to take our goods. Whatever may be the truth a few years hence, this will not be the position in the early post-war period which we have in view here. The limiting factor will be our physical capacity to develop a sufficient supply of export goods. Barter arrangements assume that we have goods to offer in exchange; and that is precisely what we shall lack in the next two years. At present the

boot is on, and pinching, the other leg—the countries from which we buy are trying to make their sales to us contingent on our accepting barter terms, under which we supply goods which they want but which we unfortunately are unable to provide.

20. What it does lie in our power to do in mitigation falls under two headings. Even to attain the assumed expansion of exports, and certainly if we are to improve on it, we must stop forthwith making munitions which are not wanted and reconvert industry to peace-time production at a much greater pace than is at present in view. Hitherto, the assumed continuance of the Japanese war until the end of 1946 has provided a magnificent camouflage for carrying on as though the end of the German war did not make all that difference. To suggest acting on the assumption that we might beat the Japs before 1947 has been regarded by all the major-generals as a brand of defeatism. Perhaps the time has now come when we can reconvert ruthlessly and with no regard to anything but speed and economy. It is not sensible either to keep men idle at the works or to use up valuable raw materials on producing useless objects merely to avoid statistical unemployment.

21. The second heading probably presents much greater difficulty. We still have a vast number of men in the three Services overseas, and the Government cash expenditure outside this country, which this involves, is still costing more than the value of our total exports. It might be supposed that the defeat of Japan would bring most of this rapidly to an end, subject, of course, to the inevitable time-lags. Unfortunately, that is a long way from the truth. Out of the £425 millions cost of the Services overseas in the current year the South-East Asia Command is responsible for only £100 millions. We have got into the habit of maintaining large and expensive establishments all over the Mediterranean, Africa and Asia to cover communications, to provide reserves for unnamed contingencies and to police vast areas eastwards from Tunis to Burma and northwards from East Africa to Germany. None of these establishments will disappear unless and until they are ordered home; and many of them have pretexts for existence which have nothing to do with Japan. Furthermore, we are still making loans to Allies and are incurring very large liabilities for relief out of money we have not got.

22. Broken up broadly between purposes, I believe that the 1945 expenditure outside North America is distributed as follows:

	£ millions
The Services	425
War Supplies and Munitions (mainly India, South Africa and Australia)	300
Reciprocal Aid, Loans to Allies, Relief, Foreign Office, &c.	75
	800

Of this total about £450 millions was incurred in the first half of the year before V-E and £350 millions was expected in the second half after V-E. The effect of V-J on the rate of expenditure in the last quarter of 1945 has not yet been estimated.

23. Broken up between areas, the expenditure of £725 millions on the Services and War Supplies is made up broadly as follows:

	£ millions
India, Burma and Ceylon	410
Middle East	110
South Africa, Australia and New Zealand ...	110
British Western, British Eastern and Central Africa	20
Malta and Cyprus	10
Europe	40
Other	25
	725

24. To an innocent observer in the Treasury very early and very drastic economies in this huge cash expenditure overseas seem an absolute condition of maintaining our solvency. There is no possibility of our obtaining from others for more than a brief period the means of maintaining any significant part of these establishments, in addition to what we shall require to meet our running excess of imports over exports and to sustain the financial system of the Sterling Area. These are burdens which there is no reasonable expectation of our being able to carry. Yet there are substantial items within the £800 millions which will not be automatically cut out merely as a result of the defeat of Japan.

25. Even assuming a fair measure of success in rapidly expanding exports and curtailing Government expenditure overseas, it still remains that aid of the order of $5 billions is required from the United States. We have reason to believe that those members of the American Administration who are in touch with our financial position are already aware that we shall be in Queer Street without aid of somewhere between $3 and $5 billions and contemplate aid on this scale as not outside practical politics. But this does not mean that difficult and awkward problems of terms and conditions do not remain to be solved. The chief points likely to arise are the following:

(i) They will wish the assistance to be described as a *credit*. If this means payment of interest and stipulated terms of repayment, it is something we cannot undertake in addition to our existing obligations with any confidence that we can fulfil the obligations. It would be a repetition of what happened after the last war and a cause of further humiliation and Anglo-American friction, which we should firmly resist. If, however, the term *credit* is no more than a camouflage for what would be in effect a grant-in-aid, that is another matter.

(ii) The Americans will almost certainly insist upon our acceptance of a monetary and commercial foreign policy along the general lines on which they have set their hearts.[4] But it is possible that they will exercise moderation and will not overlook the impropriety of using financial pressure on us to make us submit to what we believe is to our grave disadvantage. In fact the most persuasive argument we can use for obtaining the desired aid is that only by this means will it lie within our power to enter into international co-operation in the economic field on the general principle of non-discrimination. We should not seek to escape our obligations under Article VII of the Mutual Aid Agreement, but should, rather, ask for the material basis without which it will not lie in our power to fulfil them. In my opinion we need not despair of obtaining an agreement which provides sufficient safeguards and will not seriously hamper the future development of our economy along lines freely determined by our own policies.

(iii) Bases, islands, air facilities and the like may conceivably come into the picture.

26. Nor must we build too much on the sympathy and knowledge of the members of the American Administration with whom we are in touch. It will be a tough proposition, perhaps an impossible one, to sell a sufficiently satisfactory plan to Congress and the American people who are unacquainted with, and are never likely to understand, the true force of our case, not only in our own interests but in the interests of the United States and the whole world. For the time being Ministers would do well to assume that no arrangement which we can properly accept is yet in sight; and that, until such an arrangement is in sight, we are, with the imminent cessation of Lend-Lease, virtually bankrupt, and the economic basis for the hopes of the public non-existent.

27. It seems, then, that there are three essential conditions without which we have not a hope of escaping what might be described, without exaggeration and without implying that we should not eventually recover from it, a financial Dunkirk. These conditions are (a) an intense concentration on the expansion of exports, (b) drastic and immediate

---

[4] In a letter of 13 August to Mr. Dalton (T 236/439) Sir S. Cripps, referring to their meeting with Mr. Bevin on 10 August (see note 3), wrote in particular: 'I regard it as practically certain that they [the Americans] will want the main principles of commercial policy discussed and probably accepted in substance by us before they would be prepared to offer us adequate financial assistance. However well it might suit us to divorce the discussions on finance from those on commercial policy, I think you may already have reached the conclusion that they cannot in fact be kept separate. It would probably help . . . if I were to submit a paper on the commercial policy aspects at the same time as you submit yours on the financial policy aspects, and I propose to have such a paper prepared at once.' Sir S. Cripps' memorandum on 'Article VII of the Mutual Aid Agreement: Commercial Policy', circulated as C.P.(45)116, is reproduced at ii below.

economies in our overseas expenditure, and (c) substantial aid from the United States on terms which we can accept. They can only be fulfilled by a combination of the greatest enterprise, ruthlessness and tact.

28. What does one mean in this context by 'a financial Dunkirk'? What would happen in the event of insufficient success? That is not easily foreseen. Abroad it would require a sudden and humiliating withdrawal from our onerous responsibilities with great loss of prestige and an acceptance for the time being of the position of a second-class Power, rather like the present position of France. From the Dominions and elsewhere we should seek what charity we could obtain. At home a greater degree of austerity would be necessary than we have experienced at any time during the war. And there would have to be an indefinite postponement of the realisation of the best hopes of the new Government. It is probable that after five years the difficulties would have been largely overcome.

29. But in practice one will be surprised if it ever comes to this. In practice, of course, we shall in the end accept the best terms we can get. And that may be the beginning of later trouble and bitter feelings. That is why it is so important to grasp the reality of our position and to mitigate its potentialities by energy, ingenuity and foresight.

30. Shortage of material goods is not going to be the real problem of the post-war world for more than a brief period. Beyond question we are entering into the age of abundance. All the more reason not to mess things up and endanger the prizes of victory and the fruits of peace whilst crossing the threshold. The time may well come—and sooner than we yet have any right to assume—when the sums which now overwhelm us may seem chicken-feed, and an opportunity to get rid of stuff without payment a positive convenience.

KEYNES

CALENDARS TO No. 6

i *17 Aug.–12 Sept. 1945* (a) '*Proposals to the United States for Financial Assistance to follow after Lend Lease*' (see note 2 above) with (b) *comments on Nos. 6 and 6.i(a)* by Mr. J.E. Coulson (Acting Head of Economic Relations Dept. of F.O.), Mr. J.M. Fleming (of Cabinet Offices Economic Section) and Sir D. Waley (Under Secretary in H.M. Treasury) [UE 3837/32/71, CAB 124/913, T 247/50].

ii *16 Aug. 1945* C.P.(45)116 *Memo. by Sir S. Cripps on Article VII of Mutual Aid Agreement and Commercial Policy* [UE 3692/113/53].

No. 7

RAFDEL (Washington) to Air Ministry[1] (Received 15 August)

MIN 325 Telegraphic[2] [UE 3708/32/71]

Immediate. Top secret   WASHINGTON, 15 August 1945, 4.32 a.m.

Sinclair[3] from Self. Refer PROD 311.[4]

1. As advised in para. 1 [2] USLON 115[5] we had meeting yesterday[6] of BSC with JSM and later the P[rincipal] C[ommonwealth] S[upply] C[ommittee] also met. Minutes of BSC meeting are being airbagged today.[7] They contain summary of review of position here at the moment. You will also have received USLONS 116 to 119[8] sent yesterday after the meetings.

2. Your para. 2. Freezing orders are operative in U[nited] S[tates] W[ar] D[epartment] for supplies generally. These have been issued on departmental level and are we surmise merely precautionary pending clarification of situation. This freezing applies to current assignments but not to production lines exclusively for? United Kingdom account e.g. Merlin engines. In these latter cases we are in danger of getting

---

[1] Cf. No. 4, note 13.

[2] Telegrams to the Ministry of Production were designated MIN: telegrams from the Ministry, PROD. The original text of this telegram was in capital letters: the appropriate alterations have been made and some punctuation marks inserted editorially.

[3] Sir R.J. Sinclair had been Chief Executive of the Ministry of Production since June 1943.

[4] Untraced in Foreign Office archives.

[5] This telegram of 11 August reported that the meeting with Mr. Patterson (see No. 4.i) had been postponed until Friday 17 August 'to permit of clarification of situation in light of international developments'. It further reported that on 13 August the B.S.C. would hold a meeting with the Joint Staff Mission (the representative body in Washington of the British Chiefs of Staff, headed by Field Marshal Sir H. Maitland Wilson, with Admiral of the Fleet Sir J.F. Somerville, Lt. General Sir G.N. Macready and Air Marshal D. Colyer, members) to take stock of the situation, with a similar meeting in the afternoon of the Principal Commonwealth Supply Committee.

[6] This telegram was drafted on 14 August.

[7] Untraced in Foreign Office archives: cf. Duncan Hall, *op. cit.*, p. 460.

[8] For USLON telegrams 116–118 see i below. USLON 119 of 14 August transmitted the text of the following letter of 8 August from Mr. Crowley to Mr. Brand: 'On July 24 Ambrose Cramer of our British Empire and Middle East Branch wrote to you concerning certain statistical data regarding stocks to be furnished on requisitions. The point was emphasized that the Foreign Economic Administration with the approach of Japanese defeat wished to avoid any undue accumulation of Lend-Lease stocks in the British Commonwealth. It is equally the wish of the U.S. Government to have throughout the world the minimum possible surpluses after the end of the Japanese war.

'In the absence of any agreement with the British Government at the present time as to any method of financing the pipeline and stocks of Lend-Lease articles after the termination of Lend-Lease the providing of supplies under Lend-Lease will therefore and of necessity be continued on a more restrictive basis as to stocks than would otherwise be the case' (U 3637/32/71).

Lend-Lease debits for items which we may not be allowed to take under Lend-Lease (in view of date [?late] delivery dates involved) and which moreover we presumably shall not require. This is a danger against which we should as soon as possible advise where the production lines can be stopped.

3. We are not clear what USWD intentions are. General expectation is that an attempt will be made to stop all supplies as from V-J day. In this connection adverse effect is feared from report received yesterday that Canada intends to stop Mutual Aid as from V-J day.[9] We are banking on meeting with Patterson next Friday[10] to keep door open and prevent any premature decision to stop Lend-Lease. There is the further danger that Congress may by resolution declare emergency ended in which case Lend-Lease would automatically stop. We are anxious that USWD should recognise continuing need for certain munition supplies and thereby (a) stop any such premature action by Congress and (b) by implication (?) keep the door similarly open for non-munitions supplies.

4. We shall seek to explore USWD intentions with Patterson and urge need for further supplies taking typical examples such as requirements for supplies servicing and civil affairs for further operations involved in occupying present Jap-held areas as also for redeployment of troops and similar projects. These would be given as illustrations of typical needs pending a categorisation by you of what you will need.

5. Pending outcome of meeting with Patterson it is premature to attempt further forecast. We recognise position as stated in your para. 3 and will carefully safeguard it. On the other hand we must keep door open for supplies genuinely required over and above using up pipeline availabilities as also for certain critical supplies.

6. This involves the important question of continuance of Reciprocal Aid. You will no doubt have in mind the danger that Australia and New Zealand may not be anxious to continue Reciprocal Aid when their Lend-Lease needs may fall below Reciprocal Aid levels. We must

[9] The formal termination of Mutual Aid from Canada took place on 15 August 1945. In a personal message of 17 August to the Canadian Prime Minister, Mr. W. Mackenzie King, Mr. Attlee expressed his surprise and disappointment at the Canadian decision and asked him to 'relieve us of this additional anxiety, which of all those we feared is the least expected' (PREM 8/35). Mr. Mackenzie King's reaction was sympathetic, and he agreed to delay any public statement and continue the flow of supplies. He informed Mr. Attlee in a personal message of 8 September that on the previous day the Canadian Minister of Finance, Mr. J.L. Ilsley, had advised the House of Commons 'that the date of the termination of the transfer of supplies as Mutual Aid has been taken as midnight September 1st and that the Canadian Government has waived any rights to take title or ask an accounting for Mutual Aid supplies loaded or in ocean transit up to midnight September 1st', and that discussion of financing arrangements would be deferred pending the outcome of the Keynes mission (telegram No. 209 from Canadian Government to Dominions Office, PREM 8/35).

For the Canadian attitude to the end of Lend-Lease and post-war financial aid to the U.K., and for Lord Keynes' discussions in Ottawa 2–6 September, see Pressnell, *op. cit.*, Chapter 11.(1)–(3), and Duncan Hall, *op. cit.*, pp. 482–8.

[10] See note 5.

therefore avoid on Friday committing the Dominion Governments pending instructions from you.

7. There is the further need for being able to tell USWD as soon as possible what we can cancel off current assignments off current requisitions and off projected programmes. They will want to cancel production lines as quickly as possible. I very much doubt whether they will want to keep production lines running merely for the sake of employment. They certainly are planning for wholesale cancellations of their own orders and ours could not make any substantial difference. On the other hand presumption in your para. 4 is probably correct. The Americans may want to finish such items off but they would not be willing for us to take deliveries unless the Lend-Lease legislative position permits them to do so. If Congress has barred the way they will charge the cost of completion to Lend-Lease account whilst refusing us deliveries. I think our line must be to keep the door open for Lend-Lease eligibility to continue so that we can take all such deliveries where we need them. At the same time we must for unwanted supplies tell Americans quickly where production should be stopped.

8. On the Navy side there has been no concrete evidence of their intentions. At B.S.C. meeting it was thought best to regard that as a reasonably fluid situation under which the contact between the two Naval Departments would ensure the continued flow of essential supplies so long as the legislative position permits.

9. On the non-munitions side we are hoping to be able to hold F.E.A. to previous indications of a breathing space of 30 or 60 days or even possibly longer. They have previously said that Lend-Lease supplies would have to stop after some such breathing space. Obviously their power to give even a concession of this character would be seriously embarrassed if the military door is arbitrarily closed. The 2 things must go together. Nevertheless Crowley had written last week before current events as in USLON 119. I have used this as peg for a reply to enable us to [s]ound the position informally with F.E.A. This it seems better to do quote cautiously on the departmental level rather than have a top hat approach to Crowley himself. In this way we hope to play the situation along pending your instructions as to the preparatory treatment assuming the Keynes mission will materialise. In the meantime United Kingdom and Dominion Missions all agree they can keep matters moving inasmuch as actual movements of current assignments are proceeding and the only freezing is on new requisitions. For any of these which must be cleared all will try to work on a common formula accepting financial liability if eligibility for Lend-Lease is finally ruled out.

10. I am bound to say however that the ability to hold F.E.A. in along these lines will depend very much on the prospect of some clearance of principle in the early future. They will be very insistent on acceptance of credit arrangements or cash payments after a specified date. If the former is unacceptable cash payments to my mind must prejudge the later

arrangements. This is however a matter on which we must await your guidance.

11. You will no doubt appreciate the basic difficulty is legislative authority. For example continued shipments of prefabricated houses cease to rank for support of the war once the war is ended and there is no authority for free supply on humanitarian grounds. Again machinery for opencast mining helps supply of coal for European relief but that is no ground for free issue of the equipment by U.S.A. to U.K. I mention these 2 cases to illustrate overriding difficulty of constitutional authority. We can we hope keep current clearances flowing for a breathing space but the arrangements thereafter will depend on negotiation of new arrangements and supplementary Congressional approval unless they fall within the existing Lend-Lease credit arrangements.

12. The foregoing is my personal answer to your enquiries. I have not delayed to send a reply agreed with Missions but you will have the USLON telegrams and the minutes of the meetings to provide the supporting picture. We can scarcely say more until after (a) the meeting with Patterson and USWD people on Friday and (b) the preliminary sounding with FEA. On the latter I would stress that it must be no more than a sounding lest we precipitate some premature discussions of questions which must wait on London guidance. In this connection please refer to REMAC 61?8[11] giving outcome of first talks with FEA. This emerged after I had written the above and gives inner thinking of FEA but cannot of course be taken for more than Cramer's own ideas. They may not go very far.

13. In the meantime I think it would be wise for departments in London to consider (a) what production lines on United Kingdom account can be stopped at the earliest possible moment (b) what categories of munitions supplies can justifiably be pressed as eligible for Lend-Lease always allowing for taking into use stock and pipeline availabilities (c) what of existing assignments for outstanding requisitions can be cancelled as no longer required (d) what of current requisitions and assignments you would wish to acquire for cash on the assumption that they become ineligible for Lend-Lease as falling outside the categories specified in (b) above.

14. The foregoing suggestions concern the immediate future. You will no doubt be dealing separately with the longer term requirements in connection with the approach to the best arrangements which can be sought with the United States to cover their supply.

15. Assuming V-J day is close at hand I fear we shall not make much progress this week. Washington intends to celebrate V-J day to compensate for V-E day. Indeed I fear our meeting with Patterson may suffer a further postponement under pressure of events. But I will keep you advised.

[11] Not printed. The reference was evidently to REMAC 608, printed as No. 5.

i *14 & 16 Aug. 1945 RAFDEL (Washington) Tels. USLON 116–118, Tel. LONUS 80 to Washington* B.S.C. meeting on 13 Aug. took stock of lend-lease position and prepared for meeting with Mr. Patterson on 17 Aug. LONUS 77 (No. 4.ii) considered. Difficulties of forecasting further requirements [UE 3665, 3637/32/71].

ii *18 Aug. 1945 RAFDEL (Washington) Tel. USLON 120* Case for continuation of Lend-Lease made on 17 Aug. to Mr. Patterson, who was non-committal but would put British case to American Joint Chiefs of Staff who were circulating recommendations to President (UE 3713/32/71].

No. 8

Mr. Bevin to Mr. Balfour (Washington)

CAMER 562 Telegraphic [UE 3633/32/71]

Immediate. Secret   FOREIGN OFFICE, *15 August 1945, 8.49 p.m.*

Your telegram No. 603.[1]

1. Meeting that was postponed was the final one on Middle East Disposals.[2] Postponement was a tactical move though we had good reason to want time to consider Remac 596.[3] There was no disclosure of source of information in Remac 596.

2. We have since received Uslon 118[4] which takes story a stage further. What follows brings you up-to-date and is a comment on Remac 603 and Uslon 118.

3. At meeting with Clayton yesterday (Tuesday)[5] we pressed him strongly to advise Washington that there should be no sudden or unilateral modification in the existing Lend-Lease arrangements and procedure until after we had had time to sit round a table and discuss the appropriate means of winding up the system and what should follow after. He replied sympathetically and promised to advise Washington along these lines.[6]

4. We put to him emphatically that it was not merely a question of

---

[1] See No. 5, note 7.

[2] For the interim agreement reached between the United States and United Kingdom Governments to govern the disposal of U.S. surplus property in the sterling area countries of the Middle East (the 'Eady-Clayton' agreement), see Sir W. Eady's letter of 16 August to Mr. Clayton and the latter's reply printed in *F.R.U.S. 1945*, vol. viii, pp. 82–3. For further details of the arrangements to implement the agreement see iii below.

[3] No. 4.   [4] See No. 7.i.

[5] 14 August. An American record of this meeting is printed in *F.R.U.S. 1945*, vol. vi, pp. 97–101, but no British record has been traced. A record of a meeting between Lord Keynes, Mr. Clayton and others at the Board of Trade, also on 14 August (A.S.(U.S.)(45)11th meeting, cf. No. 2, note 11) is reproduced at ii below. The American record of this meeting, wrongly dated 15 August, is printed in *F.R.U.S., ibid.*, pp. 94–7: cf. also note 72 on p. 92.

[6] See *F.R.U.S., ibid.*, pp. 93–4, and cf. pp. 103–5.

holding up a high-up decision until after there had been opportunity for a proper consultation, but also of issuing positive instructions all down the line that there was to be no change whatever in current practice at the operative level meanwhile. To this he assented.

5. We added that on the above assumptions Reciprocal Aid would, of course, also go on without any modification whatever pending the above conversations.

6. Whilst he did not commit himself precisely in the following sense, we believe that Clayton will advise the President to invite a small Mission to Washington to discuss the wind-up of Lend-Lease and what is to follow after, to start conversations, if possible, in the first week of September.[7]

CALENDARS TO NO. 8

i   *13 Aug. 1945   (a) Note by Lord Keynes* on lines of approach to Mr. Clayton: important to establish global value of lend-lease stocks and implications of sudden cut-off; *(b) Note from Mr. Grant (Treasury) to Lord Keynes* commenting on *(a)* with respect to military supplies, raw materials, oil and shipping [T 236/1684].

ii   *14 Aug. 1945   A.S.(U.S.)(45) 11th meeting* Lord Keynes, Mr. Clayton and officials discuss Article VII of Mutual Aid Agreement and commercial policy; (Annex) Board of Trade summary of Mr. Clayton's I.T.O. proposal (see No. 2, note 11) [UE 3830/113/53].

iii *11 Aug.–9 Sept. 1945   Eady-Clayton agreement on Middle East surplus disposals* Tels. CAMER 554 & 555 to Washington asking for comments on draft agreement, and tel. REMAC 597 in reply; Cairo tel. REMAC 156 regarding communication of agreement to Egyptian & Iraqi Govts., and tel. CAMER 207 to Cairo in reply, rejecting idea of joint Anglo-American approach [UE 3528, 3582, 3958/146/71].

[7] The wording of paras. 3–6 of this telegram was suggested by Lord Keynes in a note of 14 August addressed to Sir W. Eady and Mr. A.T.K. Grant, an Assistant Secretary in the Treasury. The note began: 'I feel that we ought probably to tell Washington the upshot of our morning's conversation with Clayton so far as it related to Lend-Lease ... They are naturally very much preoccupied and should not be left to suppose that we are entirely inactive and uninterested on this side' (T 236/1684).

No. 9

Memorandum by Lord Keynes[1]

[T 236/439]

15 August 1945[2]

I.

My conversation with the Foreign Secretary[3] led me to think that the policy he would prefer, left to himself, would be somewhat as follows:

We should ask the Americans for financial facilities to cover the transitional period, but we should not agree to commit ourselves to any monetary or commercial arrangements, not even Bretton Woods, until we could see our way more clearly. The matter would be kept under continuous review during the transitional period, and we should decide later, in the light of experience, how far it would be safe and advisable for us to commit ourselves along the multilateral and free trade lines upon which the Americans have set their hearts. A recent conversation with Mr. Aldrich[4] had encouraged him in the idea that such a policy might not be unacceptable to American opinion.

Obviously there are many advantages in such a plan, if there were good reason to believe that it is practicable. I told him that Mr. Aldrich would naturally sympathise with such suggestions, since he had been fighting the American Administration on these lines for the past twelve months. But, not only had Mr. Aldrich been thoroughly defeated, but in the course of the campaign, which for some six months had been a nation-wide effort, the Administration had committed themselves absolutely to the view that Mr. Aldrich's policy was mistaken and that it was essential to reach definitive understandings forthwith, not indeed as to what would happen

---

[1] This memorandum was addressed to Sir W. Eady, Sir E. Bridges (Permanent Secretary to H.M. Treasury and Secretary to the Cabinet), and Mr. T. Padmore (Principal Private Secretary to Mr. Dalton) and was copied to Mr. Brand. It is also printed in Moggridge, *op. cit.*, pp. 412–19.

[2] After his signature at foot Lord Keynes wrote '16.8.45'.

[3] According to Mr. Bevin's Appointments Diary his conversation with Lord Keynes took place at 6 p.m. on 14 August. No record of their discussion has been traced in Foreign Office archives.

[4] The American businessman, Mr. Winthrop Aldrich, who was in London in his capacity as President of the International Chamber of Commerce, had an interview with Mr. Bevin at 3.40 p.m. on 14 August. Mr. Bevin recorded that he asked Mr. Aldrich 'à propos of Bretton Woods and Article 7, what he thought of the chances of our two Governments giving to a picked, joint economic Staff (which would ultimately work into the Economic and Social Council [of the United Nations Organisation]) terms of reference as follows:

' "to consider how best to keep our two Economies sound and out of them to contribute to the reconstruction of the economy of the world."

'The intention would not be to prejudice Lease-Lend, but to arrange for constant consultation, which would help both Congress and Parliament.

'2. Mr. Aldrich expressed himself as being fully in favour of this idea. E.B. 14 August 1945' (UE 3684/823/53).

during the transitional period itself, when there will be safeguards, but as to what was to happen when the transitional period was at an end. To retreat from Bretton Woods at this stage would involve such terrific loss of face for the Administration that the idea is, I am sure, altogether untenable. Commercial conversations have, of course, not reached anything like such a degree of crystallisation, and we have much more room for manœuvre there. Nevertheless, in this field also I do not think there would be any chance whatever of persuading the State Department that they should abandon their present ideas *in toto* and should just sit by like good children to see what the future brings. Moreover, it is asking too much of human nature, and certainly of American nature, to suppose that the United States would give us large-scale financial assistance without any present commitments on our part whether, having escaped from our immediate difficulties through this aid, we should or should not walk in step with them so far as international economic policies are concerned for the future.

Nevertheless, I found myself in complete sympathy with what was in the Foreign Secretary's mind and what lay behind his attitude. He is rightly convinced that we must exercise the utmost caution in the giving of commitments, which might limit our autonomy in domestic economic policy and force us into courses we thought mistaken or disastrous, as the result of international engagements entered into as the price of obtaining enough cash to escape from our immediate embarrassments.

This seems to me, however, not to be a sufficient reason for rejecting all commitments, but only for examining them with considerable care. I feel this all the more because a very large part of the American policy is, I believe, in our own interests as much as in theirs and that they are urging it on us sincerely and believing that we also have much to gain from it. We can safely walk with them a very long way. There are only a few elements in their projected policies which are dangerous to us. On those we should stand firm, but there is no need as yet to abandon hope of persuading the Americans to be moderate. I think they are quite genuinely anxious not to use financial pressure to force us into policies which we believe to be to our disadvantage, and, whilst not necessarily able to avoid altogether temptation along these lines, know well enough that to use such pressure would be wrong.

Turning to the principal points of policy concerned, I am quite satisfied that Bretton Woods contains sufficient safeguards to be safe. If America embarrasses the rest of the world by running into a slump, I am confident that the Bretton Woods Plan will improve, and not worsen, a bad situation. We have effective autonomy over our rate of exchange; we can walk out of the Plan at an hour's notice; the basic obligation we are undertaking under the Plan is one which we have believed it to our advantage to maintain, even during the war, namely, that whenever we allow an import into this country we allow it to be paid for in the currency of the vendor. Not even during the war have we blocked dollars in the

45

sense of refusing convertibility for dollar credits arising out of the value of what we have imported from the United States.

Turning to the Commercial Agreements, I admit there is more difficulty. But here also more than three-quarters of the proposals the Americans have put before us[5] seem to me to be, not only acceptable, but helpful. The only matters which are not acceptable in their present form are the following:

(1) *The treatment of preferences*: Nevertheless, if the Americans will allow the preference negotiations to be brought in exactly on all fours with the tariff negotiations, there is no present reason to think that we cannot arrive at a mutually satisfactory result.

(2) *State trading*: Even the present wording is not unsatisfactory. The Americans recognise that they have to make a draft which the Russians can accept. I have little doubt, therefore, that no obstacle of principle will be placed in the way of State trading. The discussions will turn only on the question what safeguards are required to ensure that State trading should be of a non-discriminatory character.

(3) As regards *Exchange Control*, the State Department would like to improve on Bretton Woods and deprive us of some of the safeguards we have obtained under Bretton Woods. We shall have the full support of the American Treasury in resisting this. I feel confident that these ideas will be dropped.

(4) We are not adequately protected against unfair American competition through dumping, export subsidies and, more particularly, shipping subsidies. Here it is a question of finding the right technical protection. On the question of principle the State Department are on our side.

(5) Finally, there remains the biggest snag of all, namely, the objection on the part of the Americans to the continuance of import programming or quantitative restriction or quota regulation, or whatever name one chooses to call it by, after the end of the transitional period. At present the Americans are only prepared to accept the re-imposition of such controls after the transitional period, if an international body has satisfied itself that there exist balance of trade difficulties which cannot be solved otherwise. To accept any such arrangement would be, in my judgment, to incur the Foreign Secretary's just censure on the grounds indicated above. Neither in our case, nor in that of any other country, is it consonant with the present progress of thought and policy on these matters for us to commit ourselves to a return to nineteenth century *laissez-faire* in import programming. This is where we should dig ourselves in. If we have a right to restrict the volume of imports, then it is quite safe under the Bretton Woods Plan to agree to pay in the appropriate currency for those imports which we have voluntarily accepted. If the control of imports is taken entirely out of our hands,

[5] See No. 2, note 11, and cf. No. 8.ii.

then I should agree that the Bretton Woods commitments might be dangerous. To secure what we want here will undoubtedly mean a stiff tussle with the Americans. But, in very truth, they are talking nonsense, and out-of-date nonsense. Moreover, there is scarcely any other country in the world which would be more ready than we to accept the American conditions. I believe, therefore, that we can win that battle. The only point which we might have to yield would be that import programming should be on non-discriminatory lines. It is not easy to implement that in practice, but in principle a non-discriminatory commitment is probably to our own interest, provided other countries enter into a similar engagement.

Our right policy is, therefore, I suggest, not to refuse to walk with the Americans in these matters, but to walk, though willingly, carefully. We must dig in in the right place and choose the right issues for resistance. The right issues are, of course, those that are fundamental to our future position and where we have an irresistibly strong case. If we stick to those, we shall win.

II.

I would, however, urge most strongly on the Chancellor and on his colleagues that it is not necessary to have cut-and-dried Cabinet conclusions on these matters at the present stage. Unless we enter into financial negotiations with the Americans forthwith, we cannot certainly rely on the continuance of Lend-Lease for above another thirty days at most. But, if we enter into conversations, it would be reasonable to expect that there should be an opportunity for the conversations to make progress before the axe falls. These negotiations need not, however, involve any of the above matters in their initial stages. We should begin by discussing the terms and technique for winding up the Lend-Lease and Reciprocal Aid systems. We should then expound in considerable detail the facts of our existing financial and economic position and prospects. Thirdly, we should seek to engage the Americans in discussions of the solution, and we should begin by putting forward proposals which were self-contained and did not offer any premature commitments concerning future commercial policy.

At that stage, if not at an earlier stage, in the discussions we must take it as certain that the Americans will raise, on their side, our acceptance of Bretton Woods and of certain general principles relating to commercial policy. Some further discussion at the official level may serve to narrow the area of difference of opinion. It is at that stage that the Cabinet will have to make up their minds. It would be a great convenience if the matters could have been given attention during the intervening period, so that by the time these matters are coming to a definite head it will be possible for a representative of the the Board of Trade to join the talks at Washington with a fairly clear idea of what the sticking points are so far as

47

the Cabinet is concerned. But it is neither possible nor necessary to delay the opening of the financial discussions until after a provisional decision has been reached as to exactly how far we are prepared to meet the Americans about the conditions.

Apart from the monetary and commercial understandings, which the Americans will seek as a condition of assistance, there remains one matter of extreme difficulty, namely, the form which the assistance shall take. The Americans will certainly begin by offering us something in the nature of a credit, no doubt on generous terms, which is repayable at due dates and ranks, to a considerable extent, ahead of our other creditors. They will not readily understand the honourable character of our obligations to many of the Sterling Area countries. There will be the utmost difficulty in persuading them to agree to a form of credit or grant-in-aid of a kind which we can safely accept. I think there may be more difficulty about the form of the credit than its amount. They will begin by offering $3 billion, whereas we need $5 billion. But, if everything else can be settled satisfactorily, it may be not much more difficult to get $5 billion than $3 billion.

The first stage of the negotiations should, I suggest, be conducted on conditions which allow the negotiator a considerable elasticity of thought and conversation, in the light of the situation as it develops, but extremely little latitude to give way on those matters which are regarded as fundamental to our future position and to our ability to meet our commitments. He must, therefore, to quote the Foreign Secretary, 'have the gift of breaking off' and be ready, if necessary, to come home unsuccessful. That means that the Chancellor of the Exchequer must be prepared, if necessary, to draw on our gold reserves for what one hopes would be a brief period. If it proves impossible to get a sufficiently satisfactory solution, that would be the time for the Cabinet to consider with anxiety and concentration of mind the exact character of the alternative to giving way. We should not yield on any of the basic points until these matters have been meditated upon with that concentration of attention which is possible only when we are right up against it. It would then be for Ministers to visit Washington, in the light of the final decisions reached, with a view to discovering whether we cannot, at the last lap, get sufficient of what we want. It is very possible indeed that at this last lap success would be achieved.

III.

Meanwhile time presses, and it is essential to begin the first stage immediately. I repeat that that needs no more immediate decision on the part of Ministers than that they view with sympathy the nature of our opening bid. There [?Then] we ought to make up our minds in the next few days whether it is in any respects a little too generous and should be

48

further refined.[6] But, broadly speaking, almost everyone would agree, I think, that its chief fault is that it is too good to be true. It certainly would not involve dangerous commitments for the future on the commercial side. Nevertheless, it would be very advisable, if Ministers could reach a conclusion at as early as possible a date in the negotiations whether they agree with the view that the Bretton Woods Plan contains sufficient safeguards. And it would also be useful if, with the least possible delay, certain broad conclusions could be reached as to what our sticking points are in commercial policy.

KEYNES

CALENDAR TO NO. 9

i *16 Aug. 1945 Memo. from Sir W. Eady to Sir E. Bridges* expressing general agreement with Lord Keynes but more pessimism: 'we are at present in the realm of conjecture, either pessimistic or optimistic, about the ultimate American attitude' [T 236/439].

[6] See No. 6, note 2, and No. 17.

No. 10

Foreign Office Memorandum on Anglo-American relations[1]

[*UE 3702/1094/53*]

FOREIGN OFFICE, *16 August 1945*

1. *Financial Support from the U.S.A.*

Far the most important issue in Anglo-American relations at the moment is whether or not we can obtain financial support from the U.S.A. and, if so, on what terms. Lend-Lease, with the end of the Japanese war, may cease at any moment. We have devoted our whole available productive resources to war and counted on Lend-Lease to bridge the gap in our balance of payments. We have been told that the U.S. Government will give us no financial support unless its repayment comes ahead of the

[1] This memorandum was submitted by Mr. J.E. Coulson as agreed with Mr. Butler, Mr. Hall-Patch and Mr. N.B. Ronald, an Assistant Under-Secretary of State superintending General and Reconstruction Departments in particular, in view of a forthcoming meeting between Mr. Bevin, Mr. Dalton and Sir S. Cripps on 17 August. Mr. Coulson's covering note was initialled by Mr. Bevin. The proposed meeting was intended to be the second in the series of tripartite discussions suggested by Mr. Bevin on 10 August (see No. 6, note 3), but the meeting held at the Foreign Office on the morning of 17 August was not attended by Sir S. Cripps or any Board of Trade official. In addition to Mr. Bevin and Mr. Dalton, Sir W. Eady, Mr. Hall-Patch and Mr. Dixon were present: a record of the discussion as it concerned Lend-Lease is reproduced at i below.

repayment of our debts to the sterling area and unless we accept their proposals in regard to commercial and commodity policy, as well as ratifying the Bretton Woods Agreements.

If we get no support from the U.S. until our balance of payments has once more become normal, we shall be faced with the following consequences:

(a) Trade with the U.S.A. would practically cease in a short time. Our gold and dollar balances are only sufficient to cover our immediate requirements in the next few months. It is more than doubtful whether we could find an alternative source of supply to the U.S.A. for many of our essential requirements. The effect on our internal economy would be very serious. The housing programme would be endangered, rations would probably have to drop, cigarettes almost disappear and industry find it even harder to reconvert.

(b) In order to readjust our external trade, we should have to have recourse to all kinds of expedients in order to obtain supplies from elsewhere. The result would be a very specialised system of bilateral deals which would exclude any possibility of our joining an International Trade Organisation, based on general principles of non-discrimination, of the kind hitherto under discussion.[2]

(c) Sterling could not, in the foreseeable future, become convertible into dollars, and in these circumstances it would be difficult for us, in good faith, to enter into the commitments of Bretton Woods. The effect of this on American opinion might be very grave. President Truman's attitude to Bretton Woods and commercial policy is no new departure. It is a policy repeatedly enunciated by Mr. Cordell Hull and sanctified in American eyes by its association with him and with the late President Roosevelt.

(d) There would be a great strain on the mechanism of the sterling area. We could not give the sterling area countries the dollars they need; the Crown Colonies, whose currency reserves we have taken, would be in a serious position; and trading interests in America would attempt every means of disrupting the sterling area.

(e) We should have many minor causes of friction with the Americans. Our exchange control would have to be so strict as to discriminate against them in various ways. For instance, no dollars could be found for purchasing surplus stores of American origin (which they do not wish to recover and are extremely anxious to sell) nor could we allow them to dispose of receipts in local currency in such a measure as to deprive the sterling area of dollar income.

(f) Our commitments to U.N.R.R.A. (which represent exports from which we get no return) would impose a greater strain on our resources. We should be in a precarious position for maintaining our obligations to control Germany and Austria; our ability to do so would

---

[2] Cf. No. 2.

depend entirely on the external expenditure involved being quickly repaid to us in one way or another.

(g) Our economic relations with the U.S. would inevitably deteriorate rapidly and there would be a tendency for cut-throat competition in all the export markets of the world. Nor could we maintain any form of economic collaboration with the Americans on the lines of the Combined Boards.[3] And the Combined Food Board is our principal safeguard against the inflation of the prices of the foods we most require.

2. *Consideration for Lend Lease*

H.M.G. have obtained lend-lease on certain terms and conditions. This 'consideration' is defined in the Mutual Aid Agreement of 1942. Basing ourselves on this document we have taken the line that any such 'consideration' must either

(a) be in the mutual interests of the U.S.A. and the U.K. and promote and maintain world peace. We consider that our obligations under this heading are met by our membership of the World Security Organisation and by the assumption of such responsibilities as may arise out of it.

or

(b) not be burdensome to commerce between the two countries and be such as to promote mutually advantageous economic relations and the betterment of world economic relations, i.e. Article VII. On this point we have, moreover, entered into an obligation to have conversations with the U.S. Government directed to agreed methods of obtaining economic expansion, the elimination of discriminatory treatment and the reduction of tariffs and other trade barriers. It has generally been understood between us that these talks would cover monetary, commercial and commodity policy; the Americans have also wished to include cartels; and have given some signs of regarding civil aviation, oil and telecommunications as being other subjects to be dealt with in the same context. Most important of these subjects are monetary policy, which has already been the subject of agreements ad referendum concluded at Bretton Woods, and commercial and commodity policy which are dealt with below.

3. *Commercial and Commodity Policy*

The U.S. have presented to us certain documents setting out their ideas on commercial and commodity policy in the form of a proposal to

---

[3] For the Combined Boards, their establishment and winding up see Duncan Hall, *op. cit.*, Chapters IX and XI.v, and H. Duncan Hall and C.C. Wrigley, *Studies of Overseas Supply* (London, 1956), Chapters V–VI. Following the Japanese surrender President Truman, Mr. Attlee and the Canadian Prime Minister, Mr. Mackenzie King, announced on 29 August that the Combined Production and Resources Board, the Combined Raw Materials Board and the Combined Food Board (C.F.B.) would continue to operate for the time being: cf. No. 50.i, and see *Public Papers: Truman 1945*, p. 234, note 1, and Eric Roll, *The Combined Food Board* (Stanford, 1956), p. 245.

establish an International Trade Organisation.[4] The main points which are in dispute between us can be summarised as follows:

(a) We disagree about the method of approach. The Americans wish to start with a medley of bilateral negotiations between eight to twelve countries, while we favour a multilateral approach, including the immediate and substantial reduction of the American and other tariffs.

(b) Certain of the specific American proposals are unacceptable to us. Broadly speaking, they might prevent our giving adequate protection to agriculture and generally hamper the execution of the internal programme which H.M.G. would wish to pursue.

(c) We are not prepared to go so far as the Americans expect and desire in eliminating Imperial Preference.

(d) We do not see eye to eye on the application of commodity policy. At the moment only two commodities have been discussed. The first is wheat which forms the subject of the International Wheat Agreement.[5] We have always disliked this Agreement as being an arrangement which guaranteed a high price of wheat to the producers. Latterly there has been a Conference on cotton at which the U.S. Government produced proposals of the same nature which were quite unacceptable to us. In the latter case they admit privately that their cotton proposals are at variance with the general principles on commodity policy which they have always professed, but maintain that their own political situation makes this inevitable. It is unlikely that they would be prepared to accept in regard to tin and rubber the proposals they have made for cotton.[6]

4. *Conclusions*

It is clear from the foregoing that these different questions are all closely connected. The broad position seems to be as follows:

(a) If we do not get from the U.S. the financial assistance we need, we shall be in a very serious economic position ourselves and shall be forced to take measures which would result in a serious deterioration of our relations with the U.S.

[4] See No. 2, note 11 and i, and No. 8.ii: cf. No. 6.ii.

[5] i.e. the Memorandum of Agreement drafted during the International Wheat Meeting at Washington July 1941–April 1942, and initialled on 22 April 1942 by the governments of Argentina, Australia, Canada, United Kingdom and United States. See R.J. Hammond, *Food*, vol. i, Chapter XXVII, and cf. *F.R.U.S. 1942*, vol. i, pp. 501–13.

[6] On 11 September the Ministry of Supply informed the British Raw Materials Mission in Washington in their telegram TAMAR 4823 that the American proposals did not seem 'to provide an effective means either of disposing of the existing cotton surplus or of securing a long-term adjustment of supply to demand'. The Ministry thought that cotton prices were high in relation to those of other textiles and that surplus stocks could not be absorbed nor consumption balanced with production without a 'substantial reduction' (UE 6252/67/53). Subsequently British counter proposals were prepared and, despite some doubts as to the advisability of discussing them with the Americans during the impending debates in Congress on the proposed American loan to the United Kingdom, H.M. Embassy in Washington recommended on 15 December that they should be proceeded with (UE 4122, 6224/67/53).

(*b*) We shall not get financial assistance unless we agree to Bretton Woods, and something on the lines of the U.S. proposals covering commercial and commodity policy.

(*c*) If on the other hand the U.S. do not give us financial assistance, they must renounce the hope of the sort of world economy they have at heart.

(*d*) We are not however entirely free to say, 'You can only have the sort of world you want if you give us financial assistance' because we are already committed to giving consideration for lend-lease and to that extent bound to try to reach agreement with the U.S. on measures leading to the removal of trade restrictions. We can however, refuse to consider, as part of such arrangements, anything that could be demonstrated as burdensome to our commerce or which would make it impossible for us to take part in the economic system which the U.S. are aiming at.

(*e*) We should therefore do our utmost to reach agreement with them on commercial and commodity policy, making it clear that it would be impossible for us to meet them at all on their proposals unless they give us financial assistance on terms which will help rather than burden us in promoting the sort of economic and political condition in the world which they profess to desire.

(*f*) Our immediate objective must be to obtain a breathing space, before the Americans take any final decisions, in which to develop orally the arguments in support of our case. Our case is a good one and we must have the opportunity to convince the Americans that what we regard as essential for our prosperity is also therefore in their own interests.

CALENDAR TO NO. 10

i *17 Aug. 1945 Extract from Note by Mr. Dixon of a discussion between Mr. Bevin and Mr. Dalton: Item III Lend-Lease* Mr. Dalton suggests early return of Lord Halifax and Mr. Brand to Washington in preparation for Keynes Mission 'early in September': Mr. Bevin will decide when he has examined Chancellor's proposals (No. 6.i) [UE 3689/3683/53].

No. 11

RAFDEL (Washington) to Air Ministry (Received 19 August)

USLON *125 Telegraphic*[1] [*UE 3724/32/71*]

Most immediate. Top secret   WASHINGTON, *19 August 1945, 3.25 a.m.*

New York Times reported this morning[2] that President held a conference with Byrnes, Vinson, Snyder,[3] Crowley and Leaky [*sic*][4] about future of Lend-Lease at which plans were discussed for an early liquidation of Lend-Lease programme.[5]

This afternoon Food Mission ascertained from Dept. of Agriculture that orders had been issued by F.E.A. to stop all food shipments to U.K. as from today.

Embassy at once approached State Dept. and informed them [of] this, protesting strongly that order of this kind should be issued without any warning or notice to us. State Dept. said that they knew nothing of any order of this kind which was probably premature and that they would make immediate enquiries. But they confirmed that (?) . . .[6] on termination of Lend-Lease are in the making and would shortly be communicated to us. State Dept. and F.E.A. have now both told Embassy that no repeat no instructions have been issued and that no action will be put in hand without consultation with us which is likely to take place early next week. Although we have managed to stop any immediate action we are clearly not far off end of Lend-Lease and it would not be wise to resist this provided it is done in good order and with reasonable breathing space for non munitions and an appropriate tapering off for munitions.

There might be some advantage, as Clayton has apparently not repeat not been able to hold up decision, in Prime Minister's telegraphing or speaking to President.

He might say that he understands that President is now considering the future [of] Lend-Lease and might ask him that there may be sufficient opportunity given for a full discussion between people concerned on both sides before any decisions which may have been reached are actually implemented.

This telegram is agreed with the Embassy.

Duty Officer please pass copy immediately to A.T.K. Grant Treasury.

---

[1] The original text of this telegram was in capital letters: the appropriate alterations have been made and some punctuation marks inserted editorially.

[2] This telegram was drafted on 18 August.

[3] Mr. F.M. Vinson and Mr. J.W. Snyder were respectively U.S. Secretary of the Treasury and Director of the Office of War Mobilization and Reconversion.

[4] Admiral W.D. Leahy was Chief of Staff to the President as Commander-in-Chief of the Army and Navy.

[5] For this conference on 17 August see *F.R.U.S. 1945*, vol. vi, pp. 102–3.

[6] The text is here uncertain.

i *18 & 19 Aug. 1945   Mr. Balfour (Washington) Tel. REMAC 616* in reply to No. 8. F.E.A. sources say President is under political pressure to discontinue Lend-Lease, but amount of Reciprocal Aid may affect decision; *CAMER 570 to Washington* estimated rate of Reciprocal Aid for second half of 1945 [UE 3697/32/71].

No. 12

Note of a meeting held at 6.30 p.m. on 20 August in the Foreign Secretary's Room at the House of Commons

[*UE 3762/32/71*]

Secret   FOREIGN OFFICE, *21 August 1945*

Present:

Secretary of State for Foreign Affairs (*in the Chair*), Chancellor of the Exchequer, Minister of State,[1] Sir Alexander Cadogan, The Honourable R.H. Brand, Sir Wilfrid Eady, Lord Keynes, Mr. E.L. Hall-Patch, Mr. A.D. Marris,[2] Mr. J.E. Coulson.

Lend-Lease

MR. BRAND reported that he had now received by telephone from Washington the United States communication about the end of lend-lease in the form of a letter from Mr. Crowley. The substance of the new arrangements was as follows:

(1) There were to be no new contracts on lend-lease.

(2) Supplies in process of manufacture or awaiting shipment could be received only against payment or on appropriate conditions.

(3) All existing supplies which had already been transferred could be retained against payment.

(4) Requisitions on terms of cash reimbursement could still be made during the next sixty days after which they would cease.

(5) We were asked to make an inventory of the lend-lease supplies still under our control including all items which had not been lost, destroyed or consumed.[3]

---

[1] Mr. P. Noel-Baker.

[2] Mr. Marris, an Economic Adviser attached to H.M. Embassy in Washington, was a member of the U.K. Delegation to the U.N.R.R.A. Council meeting.

[3] The text of the letter to Mr. Brand, dated 18 August, but not delivered to H.M. Embassy at Washington till 20 August, was transmitted to London in telegram USLON 122 of that day. In the letter, printed in *F.R.U.S. 1945*, vol. vi, pp. 107–8, Mr. Crowley suggested that the above five points should apply in discussions and negotiations, which the F.E.A. desired to enter into immediately with the B.S.C., relating to 'the discontinuance of its lend-lease aid to the British Commonwealth in an expeditious manner which will best promote our mutual interests and which will be consistent with the provisions of the Lend-Lease Act'. See further the White House press release of 21 August, printed *ibid.*, p. 109.

THE CHANCELLOR OF THE EXCHEQUER said that his preliminary view was that now nothing would be gained by further delay and that we should open discussions at once.

In the discussion which followed it was pointed out that the only new factor in the situation was that we had not expected the end of lend-lease to come so soon. It was important that we should obtain a breathing-space of two or three months during which His Majesty's Government could fully examine their position and the Americans could be made aware of our financial situation. The chief dangers were

(a) that we would not be able to use the lend-lease machine after the prescribed sixty days and would have to obtain our requirements through private trade channels. This would be almost an impossibility especially in the case of food.

(b) that the Americans would offer us some accommodation on conditions which we could not accept. They would want us to put our name to some obligation whether we could honour it or not.

There was also some discussion as to whether we should make clear to the people of this country the shabby fashion in which we were being treated by the Americans. On the one hand it was urged that the Americans showed every signs of washing their hands of Europe. On the other hand, it was pointed out that the attitude of Congress made it inevitable that lend-lease should be terminated as early as possible after the Japanese war and that the present action of the United States Government merely amounted to clearing the decks for new arrangements.

It was agreed that, before any final decisions were taken, the Foreign Secretary and the Chancellor of the Exchequer would see Mr. Clayton and discuss the position with him as he might be in possession of further information.

United Nations Relief and Rehabilitation Administration

THE CHANCELLOR OF THE EXCHEQUER said it was clear that, in present circumstances, His Majesty's Government could not undertake any further commitment to U.N.R.R.A. It would be necessary for the Minister of State to stall as best he could at the Council Meeting.[4]

---

[4] The third U.N.R.R.A. Council had opened in London on 7 August with a speech of welcome by Mr. Bevin (see *The Times*, 8 August 1945, p. 2). The main subject for discussion was the provision of further funds for U.N.R.R.A. At a series of meetings between the American Delegation and Mr. Noel-Baker, Lord Keynes and Sir W. Eady concerning a draft resolution that the Council should recommend that contributing members should increase their subscriptions by 1 per cent. of national income, it was made clear that the United Kingdom would have great difficulty in increasing her contribution.

At a meeting on 12 August Mr. Clayton also introduced the question of the Soviet request for U.N.R.R.A. relief to the value of $700 million (cf. Volume I, Nos. 97, 384 and 404, and v below). Despite objections made by Mr. Noel-Baker and Mr. Marris that the proposed 1 per cent increase in the contribution was insufficient even to allow for Mr. Clayton's alternative proposal that $350 million should be given to the Republics of White Russia and the

THE SECRETARY OF STATE FOR FOREIGN AFFAIRS said that, in his speech that afternoon,[5] he had made it clear that we would do our best to help other countries but only so long as we ourselves were treated fairly and that our economic situation remained such that we could see ourselves safely through the transitional period. The Minister of State might take the same line.

MR. MARRIS pointed out that the question of timing was important. During the next two days it seemed likely that statements would have to be made about the future of U.N.R.R.A. If the United States said they were prepared to recommend to Congress that the United States should pay an additional one percent of United States national income, we, too, might have to take up a position as Congress would certainly not vote this money unless others showed willingness to do the same. U.N.R.R.A. would have to wind up between March and June unless it received further funds. In that event, we might well have to take on the support of Greece and also incur some expenditure in Italy. The total might be as great as if we had made a further contribution to U.N.R.R.A.

As against this view, it was strongly urged that there was no need for us to take any commitment at present; that Congress might in any case not vote the necessary funds this year, and that it might well be possible to adjourn the Council meeting without taking any decision on this point.

Various suggestions were then considered in regard to the line to be taken by the Minister of State in the U.N.R.R.A. Council, but it was agreed

Ukraine, without seriously affecting the degree of relief for Eastern Europe and supplies for Displaced Persons in the British Zone of Germany, Mr. Clayton was clearly determined to link the issues of the Soviet request and U.N.R.R.A. financing. The U.K. Delegation accordingly prepared a list of seven conditions which the Americans should be asked to accept before the United Kingdom would agree to put up a further 1 per cent contribution (meeting of 12 August with annexed 'conditions', vi below).

Meanwhile Mr. Clayton introduced a new factor into the negotiations. On 12 August he told M. Sergeev of the Soviet Delegation that if the Council approved a resolution extending the scope of U.N.R.R.A. to Italy and Austria 'he would seek the authority of Congress for a further American contribution of 1%', and that if the Russians agreed to this and other American desiderata he would be ready to try to persuade Mr. Byrnes to agree that $250 million 'might be found for the White Russian or Ukrainian Republics out of the new contribution to U.N.R.R.A'. Mr. Clayton reported this conversation to Mr. Noel-Baker and Sir W. Eady on 14 August, and although the latter tried to explain the difficulties of the British position, with special reference to British commitments to relief for British territories in the Far East, Mr. Clayton only replied that he 'would not himself be able to approach Congress with any hope of success unless he could say that the United Kingdom was also putting up its share' (meeting of 14 August, vii below). On 16 August Mr. Noel-Baker wrote to Mr. Dalton (see viii) enclosing a draft resolution discussed with the Americans, and after further discussion with the Chancellor and with Mr. Bevin he delivered a letter (x) on 18 August to Mr. Clayton and Mr. Pearson (Canadian Ambassador at Washington, leading the Canadian delegation to the U.N.R.R.A. Council) and made a statement on the lines of a note by Sir W. Eady. Mr. Clayton's reply was that he did not think he could get the 1 per cent. from Congress on this basis, and that he wished to discuss the matter further with Mr. Bevin.

[5] See Parl. Debs., 5th ser., H. of C., vol. 413, cols. 283–300.

that, before taking a final decision, the Foreign Secretary and the Chancellor of the Exchequer would discuss the matter on the following morning with Mr. Clayton.

CALENDARS TO NO. 12

i *21–22 Aug. 1945   Mr. Balfour (Washington) Tels. REMAC 623 & 626, RAFDEL (Washington) Tel. USLON 123* Decisions in USLON 122 (see note 3 above) to come into force at midnight on VJ day: discussion of line to take in forthcoming interview with Mr. Crowley and necessity for using cash requisitions to keep supplies moving [UE 3724, 3728, 3735/32/71].

ii *21–22 Aug. 1945   Treasury meeting on termination of Lend-Lease* Lord Keynes outlines financial implications: cash dollar position of U.K. may be 'down to a rock-bottom emergency minimum by the end of the year'; *Mr. Hall-Patch to Mr. H. Broadley (Ministry of Food)* on possibility of bread rationing [UE 3784, 3877/32/71].

iii *Undated   Third Session of U.N.R.R.A. Council* opening in London on 7 Aug. 1945: F.O. background brief [UR 2859/114/850].

iv *6 & 11 Aug. 1945   U.N.R.R.A. relief for Displaced Persons: (a) U.C. (45)11 Record of discussion on 3 Aug.* between U.K. and U.S. delegations on Soviet desire to use withholding of relief to enforce repatriation; *(b) Tel. No. 8290 to Washington* Brief report on progress of U.N.R.R.A. Council: inconclusive discussion on Displaced Persons; cf. *F.R.U.S. 1945*, vol. ii, pp. 1021–2 [CAB 133/92, UR 3122/114/850].

v *11 & 15 Aug. 1945   Soviet application for U.N.R.R.A. aid of $700 millions* Memo. C.P.(45)108 by Mr. Noel-Baker suggests supporting American compromise (see note 4): marginal note on draft by Mr. Bevin: 'Is it proposed to make this offer before you know what the attitude is likely to be to Italy, etc. Will the Russians get this grant and then oppose all else. Remember Russia at Potsdam was trying to get reparations from Italy. I should like to be clear. E.B.' On 15 Aug. Mr. Noel-Baker considered meeting with Soviet delegation revealed readiness to compromise but not if aid for Austria and Italy were agreed while 'Russian application was rejected' (UR 2926, 2967/9/850].

vi *13 Aug. 1945   U.C.(45)30 Note by Mr. Marris of meeting with Mr. Clayton on 12 Aug.* with (Annex) list of U.K. desiderata before agreeing to 1% increase in U.N.R.R.A. contribution [CAB 133/92].

vii *14 Aug. 1945   Record by Mr. W. Hasler (Head of Supply and Relief Dept.) of Meeting with Mr. Clayton:* see note 4 [UR 3004/30/852].

viii *16 Aug. 1945   British policy on proposed further contribution to U.N.R.R.A.* Minute from Mr. Noel-Baker to Mr. Bevin covering letter of 16 Aug. to Mr. Dalton (without attached draft resolution: cf. x below) and memo. of 15 Aug. by Mr. Marris and Mr. Hasler indicating further British subscription of 1% would cost £80 million, but if U.N.R.R.A. ceased to operate non-repayable loans to Greece, Yugoslavia, Poland, Italy and Austria might cost £87 million plus £25 million repayable loans to China and Czechoslovakia [UR 2952/30/852].

ix *17 Aug. 1945   Tel. No. 8475 to Washington* Further report on progress at U.N.R.R.A. Council [UR 3122/114/850].

x *19 Aug. 1945   Further contribution to U.N.R.R.A.* Minute from Mr. Hasler to Mr. Bevin recording conversation of 18 Aug. when Mr. Noel-Baker indicated in letter and oral communication to Mr. Clayton British conditions for supporting attached draft resolution [UR 3012/30/850].

No. 13

Note of a meeting held in the Secretary of State's Room on 21 August at 10 a.m.

[*UR 3033/30/852*]

FOREIGN OFFICE, *21 August 1945*

Further Contribution to U.N.R.R.A.

Present:
The Secretary of State, the Chancellor of the Exchequer, the Minister of State, Sir Wilfred [*sic*] Eady, Mr. Hasler, Mr. W. Clayton, Mr. E.G. Collado

THE SECRETARY OF STATE said that the main problem on the United Kingdom side was to know how we stood financially. We did not wish to enter into a commitment to U.N.R.R.A. or anybody else which we could not meet. We wanted to go along with the United States in this matter, but if we were to do so we needed to know a little more of where we were going. There was another thing which bothered him, namely the fact that the Russians had introduced an element of a political bargain into the deliberations of U.N.R.R.A.[1]

MR. CLAYTON said he quite understood the United Kingdom position, and it was unfortunate that so many developments had taken place at the same time. As regards the Russians, he agreed that great pressure was being exercised to conclude a bargain. He thought it was generally realised that we could not contemplate a contribution of more than one per cent of the national income. It was also clear that if Congress were to appropriate the money, this one per cent would have to cover the needs of Italy, Austria and China. This being so, there was no room to include 700,000,000 dollars for Russia. He had explained this to the Russians, but had added that he was anxious to help (and this ought to have been clear from the way in which the Russians had been given exceptional treatment on lend-lease matters up to date) and therefore he was prepared personally to recommend that support should be given by the United States for 250,000,000 for Byelo Russia and the Ukraine from U.N.R.R.A. The Russian delegation was still, however, pressing for their 700,000,000 dollars, and were trying to block the passage of the resolution about Italy. Mr. Clayton felt that the Russians could be voted down at any time, but if they asked for a further twenty-four hours delay he was disposed to agree

[1] See No. 12, note 4 and iv–v.

to it, on the understanding that this was the last postponement, and a vote were taken on the following day.

THE SECRETARY OF STATE said he agreed with what Mr. Clayton had said about the Russian application. Would this involve a one per cent contribution from us?

MR. CLAYTON said that this must be a decision for the United Kingdom Government to take. He thought, however, that U.N.R.R.A., as the first United Nations organisation, should be held together. He was not certain that this could be done even with a one per cent contribution in view of the Russian attitude, but he hoped so. It was possible that the Russian face might be saved by the inclusion of a formula in one of the resolutions. He was doubtful about this, however, because he thought that if the Russians got the sort of formula they wanted this would enable them to force other applicants for U.N.R.R.A. to agree to surrender some of the assistance they were due to get to the Russians or to give the Russians other concessions as the price for the Russians agreeing to the programmes for the other applicants not being reduced.

THE SECRETARY OF STATE asked Mr. Clayton how he thought the United Kingdom could meet an extra one per cent contribution.

MR. CLAYTON said that this was connected with the discussions he had been having with Lord Keynes.[2] He had suggested that a British representative should go to Washington about the 1st September to discuss lend-lease, financial policy and commercial policy.

THE SECRETARY OF STATE asked Mr. Clayton whether he regarded these three questions as being tied to one another. MR. CLAYTON said he thought it would be necessary for his Government to get a fairly complete idea of our commercial policy since they would find it necessary to try and work out a world commercial policy which would be such as to make the credits which they were ready to grant collectable; if the world went back to autarchy, which was the only alternative to a multilateral system, credits would not be collectable.

THE SECRETARY OF STATE said he thought that it would be very difficult to make any commitment on these questions until we could see our way through the transition period. He thought that it would be necessary for us to continue a strict control of imports for some time.

MR. CLAYTON said he quite realised the necessity for a period of controlled imports and would not seek to make any unreasonable conditions. The only point which the United States would press for was that the controls should not be discriminatory. He realised that for three or four years the Government would have to be in a position to say what people could import. He concluded: 'You will have no trouble from us on that'.

THE SECRETARY OF STATE said he wondered whether three or four years would be sufficient. He would be prepared to take a risk on U.N.R.R.A. or

---

[2] See No. 1, note 2, No. 2, and No. 8, note 5 and ii.

other questions if he could see his way through the transition. He would like five years for this. It would take a year or eighteen months to get the labour back from war industry and from the Services and then there would be a retooling period, so that there would be a long time before there could be a return to peace-time production. In cotton, for instance, the labour was down to 145,000, whereas normally it was 340,000. It would take six months at least to get this labour back. We were suffering over our reconversion now because of the great success we had had in securing complete mobilisation. The aim of all parties in the United Kingdom was to get back to a situation in which we were not financially dependent upon the United States, and to honour our obligations. It was for this reason that we were a little reluctant to go along with the United States on the further contribution to U.N.R.R.A. It was not due to any lack of will on our part. He asked whether, if we were to contribute our one per cent, this would have a beneficial effect upon other negotiations.

Mr. Clayton said it was difficult to answer the Secretary of State's question. He was not sure whether his colleagues in Washington realised the connection. They might not see U.N.R.R.A. as occupying such a large part in the general picture.

The Secretary of State referred to what he had said in the House of Commons on the previous day on U.N.R.R.A.[3] He had emphasised that what Europe needed was to get back to work. U.N.R.R.A. was a kind of dole and it must be used as a means of getting people back to work rather than merely keeping them alive in idleness. Mr. Clayton said he agreed with this. He would like the Secretary of State's advice on the Russian problem, however.

The Secretary of State said that before the difficulty had arisen over lend lease, he would have been prepared to agree to the 250,000,000 dollar arrangement, provided that the Italian and Austrian proposals were accepted and provided that sufficient control was secured over the money voted to U.N.R.R.A. Now that difficulties had arisen over lend-lease, however, he felt he must hesitate. He would be prepared to stand on what he had just said, if only he could see what this involved so far as the United Kingdom were concerned.

Sir Wilfrid Eady said that the problem which was most worrying the Treasury was the shipments which had to be made in the immediate future and the liabilities which matured quickly. Could Mr. Clayton give any information about these? Until we knew what the position was as regards the supplies which we must have to keep the population alive in the next few months, it was very difficult to make any commitment to U.N.R.R.A.

Mr. Clayton said he had discussed the matter with Mr. Byrnes on the telephone.[4] He was afraid the situation was not altogether clear. The

---
[3] See No. 12, note 5.
[4] The record of this conversation on the morning of 20 August is untraced by the editors of F.R.U.S.: see F.R.U.S. *1945*, vol. vi, p. 106, note 99.

President seemed to be worried about a commitment he had made to Congress[5] and Mr. Clayton had not the exact words which had been used. It was possible that because of this commitment shipments would be stopped, but he had pressed strongly that this should not be so and he hoped that the President would agree with the case he had made. The trouble was the United Kingdom had no agreement under Section III C of the Lease-Lend Act.[6] France, Belgium and Holland had made these agreements, which involved repayment over thirty years and interest at two and three eighths per cent. He hoped that it would be possible for the United Kingdom to negotiate some such credit to cover the supplies in the pipe line and thus to preserve the current flow.

SIR WILFRID EADY pointed out that the three countries mentioned had ample exchange and were financially in a much better position than we were. (MR. CLAYTON interrupted to say that he agreed with this.) Should we be expected to make the same terms or should we get terms which were more suitable to our position?

MR. COLLADO said that the interest rate fixed was the average of what the United States Government itself paid on the money it borrowed. He added that the credits carried no amortisation for the first five years and included clauses by which repayment could be adjusted if difficulties arose over the balance of payments. The wording of the latter clause was similar to that in the Bretton Woods monetary fund.

SIR WILFRID EADY said that if these were the terms on which we would have to cover the 500,000,000 dollars in the pipe line, he did not see how he could recommend that we should take on extra liability to U.N.R.R.A. If the 500,000,000 dollars was sufficient to prime the pipe it would be all very well, but we should need very much more than that.

THE SECRETARY OF STATE said that one of our main difficulties was that in 1939 and 1940 we had had to bear the cost of the war single-handed and this had cost us something like six thousand million dollars in exchange. President Roosevelt had often referred to the war as being a common effort and if in some way recognition could be given to the fact that in those early years we had stood alone without the arrangements which had been made in later years to share the burden, he thought this would have a tremendous effect in this country not only morally but psychologically as well. People in this country considered that they had taken it in 1940 and a recognition of this fact would do a tremendous amount of good. He thought it was also in United States interests to help this country on to its feet since they had so much to gain from having us as a partner in a healthy economic condition in peacetime.

[5] The reference was to the promise Mr. Truman had made to Congress as Vice-President before the extension of the Lend-Lease Act which he signed as President on 16 April 1945, that Lend-Lease was a weapon of war and would cease to be necessary when the war ended: see Volume I, No. 255, for his explanation to Mr. Churchill on 24 July, and *Public Papers: Truman 1945*, p. 235, for a subsequent press statement of 23 August.

[6] See No. 4, note 7.

Mr. Clayton said he did not believe that public opinion in the States would support retroactive measures to compensate the United Kingdom for expenditure in 1940. He thought that the most that could be got would be credit on very liberal terms.

The Secretary of State asked whether it would be possible to continue the flow of supplies for the present without prejudice to the terms of the settlement.

Mr. Clayton said that he hoped that this could be done. He had certainly pressed hard enough for it on the telephone to Mr. Byrnes. He thought we could only wait for the decison which would be coming from Washington. In his view the flow must be continued.

The Secretary of State asked whether, in considering the terms of any credit to this country, it would not be possible to make the terms more favourable than those given to France, Belgium and Holland, on account of the part which the United Kingdom had played in 1940.

Mr. Clayton said that he thought a formula could be found which would fit the financial and exchange position of the United Kingdom. He felt that there would be no point in trying to discuss terms now and that it would be better to wait till the British representatives reached Washington.[7]

After Mr. Clayton and Mr. Collado had left, it was agreed that no decision should be taken on the United Kingdom contribution for twenty four hours. This would give time for Mr. Clayton to secure his reply from Washington. In the meantime the Secretary of State said that he would see Mr. Winant[8] and would put to him some political considerations affecting

---

[7] Later on 21 August Mr. Hasler minuted to Mr. Bevin: 'Since this meeting there have been several further developments:

'(a) The Americans have received a message from Mr. Byrnes to say that the flow of Lend Lease supplies to us can be continued, leaving the credit terms upon which these are to be obtained to be mutually agreed [cf. *F.R.U.S. ibid.*, p. 106, for this message and below No. 20, para. 5, for the operative passage of Mr. Clayton's ensuing letter to Sir W. Eady, transmitted to Washington in LONUS 83 of 22 August].

'(b) The proposals to extend U.N.R.R.A. operations to Italy and Austria have been agreed with Russian concurrence [ii].

'(c) The Russians have agreed to withdraw their application to U.N.R.R.A. for 700 million dollars and to substitute applications on behalf of White Russia and the Ukraine, leaving the amounts which these Republics are to receive for subsequent discussion [ii].'

On 22 August Mr. Bevin minuted (P.M./45/9) to Mr. Attlee, who approved: 'The Chancellor of the Excehquer and I have authorised the Minister of State to inform the Council of UNRRA that if the other principal contributing countries (the U.S.A. and Canada) put up a further 1% contribution to UNRRA we will ask Parliament to do the same. We did this after long discussion and in view of the fact (a) that the Americans have now agreed to continue the flow of supplies to us on terms to be negotiated (b) that UNRRA is ready to take over Italy and Austria, thus saving us nearly half of the money we are asked to put up (c) the Russians have agreed to withdraw their request in favour of a much smaller sum for the Ukraine and White Russia.'

[8] The American Ambassador in London had an interview with Mr. Bevin at 3.30 p.m. on 21 August: see No. 14.

the issue. He would inform the Minister of State of what passed with Mr. Winant before the 4.30 U.N.R.R.A. meeting.

CALENDARS TO NO. 13

i *20 Aug. 1945 Sir E. Bridges to Mr. Dalton* Minute on line for Mr. Bevin to take with Mr. Clayton on 21 Aug. [T 236/437].

ii *21 Aug. 1945 U.C.(45)33 Record of discussions between U.K., U.S., Canadian and Soviet delegations on 20 Aug.* on Soviet application for assistance and U.S. proposal to extend U.N.R.R.A. to Italy [CAB 133/92].

iii *23–30 Aug. 1945 Developments in U.N.R.R.A. Council proceedings, Tels. 8704, 8849 and 8934 to Mr. Balfour (Washington)* Council business successfully concluded on 24 Aug. following agreement with Russians on Italy, Austria and contributions (cf. G. Woodbridge, *UNRRA, The History of the United Nations Relief and Rehabilitation Administration*, vol. iii (New York, 1950), pp. 143–4 and 146–7); minute by Mr. Hasler and record of conversation between Mr. Clayton and Mr. Noel-Baker on implications of increased contributions (UR 3122, 3169/114/850].

iv *5 Sept. 1945 Mr. Hasler to Mr. Makins (Washington)* Refers to No. 12.x: further letter for Mr. Clayton and Mr. Pearson on contributions to U.N.R.R.A. and need for tighter control on their use [UR 3012/30/852].

v *6 Sept. 1945 Sir G. Rendel (U.K. member of U.N.R.R.A. Council for Europe) to Mr. Makins (Washington)* on developments concerning proposal for relief for Ukrainian and Byelorussian Republics (cf. *F.R.U.S. 1945*, vol. ii, pp. 1042–3) [UR 3144/3144/852].

No. 14

Brief for Secretary of State's talk to Mr. Winant about Argentina on 21 August 1945

[*AS 4331/12/2*]

FOREIGN OFFICE, *21 August 1945*

The Secretary of State has suggested that he might send, through Mr. Winant, a message to Mr. Byrnes, to the effect that we look to the Americans, for at least the next twelve months, when we (i.e. ourselves and the rest of Europe) shall be short of food, to see to it that political conditions in the Argentine remain stable. The Department agree that this would be valuable, especially if effect could be given to it *soon* so as to forestall any approach from Mr. Byrnes himself about Argentina.

The Secretary of State would no doubt wish to emphasize the predominant importance at this juncture of supplies (stress was laid, in a statement communicated on August 7th by the Combined Food Board to the Council of the United Nations Relief and Rehabilitation Administration (relevant extract attached)[1] on the marked deterioration in the World food situation); and to point out that the existence, where Argentina is concerned, of an atmosphere of strife and turmoil, external and internal, is not likely to be propitious to the maintenance and increase of the supply of raw materials so necessary to the welfare of countries on this side of the Atlantic.[2]

As an illustration, the recent embargo on the export of United States coal to Argentina[3] militates against the achievement of these objectives since it must lead to restriction of railway and frigorifico services, and to the burning of badly needed foodstuffs, e.g. maize and linseed oil, as substitutes.

It may be doubted whether Mr. Winant would wish to embark on any detailed discussion. As regards political stability we, like the Americans, would be glad to see the back of Vice-President Peron[4] and are fully prepared, despite the possibility of injury to British material interests, to maintain an aloof attitude towards the Government of which he is a member e.g. by continuing, if the Americans also adopt a similar self-denying policy, to refrain from selling Argentina armaments.[5] N.B. The exact interpretation which we should desire to give to this term is still under discussion between the interested Government Departments in London. But open interference would seem to us to militate against the

[1] Not printed: cf. i below. [2] Cf. Volume I, Nos. 98 and 135.
[3] See *F.R.U.S. 1945*, vol. ix, pp. 547–8.
[4] Colonel Juan Perón was also Minister of War and Minister of Labour in the Government of President E.J. Farrell.
[5] In response to a series of requests from the U.S. Government during July 1945 that His Majesty's Government should refuse to export any armaments to Argentina and should delegate responsibility for authorising exports to Argentina to H.M. Ambassador at Buenos Aires, Sir D. Kelly (see ii below), the British Government had made no formal statement but informed the State Department on 9 August that for the present they 'were not proceeding with exports coming under Group 17 of the Export Control List, namely, the group relating to armaments' (AS 4270/159/2, cf. *F.R.U.S., op cit.*, p. 546). In a statement of His Majesty's Government's attitude transmitted for the confidential information of H.M. Embassy in Washington in telegram No. 8557 of 19 August, Mr. Butler set out the lines on which Mr. Bevin proposed to speak to Mr. Winant on 21 August and concluded: 'We are not (repeat not) prepared to give these powers to Sir D. Kelly. Terms in which our refusal can most suitably be expressed to Americans are under discussion with other Departments. 'Do you think that end of Japanese war, and resultant American pre-occupation with internal labour situation, are likely to affect American attitude as regards exports to Argentina? If so, it would be useful to have your views in time for Secretary of State's interview with Mr. Winant on August 21st. Is it probable that no more will be heard of these suggestions?' (AS 4271/159/2).
In his telegram No. 5762 of 21 August Mr. Balfour replied that the question of a new American directive concerning arms sales to Latin America had not yet been submitted to the President or Mr. Byrnes, and that 'officials concerned are still divided between those who wish to avoid a race to arm Latin America, and advocates of a "free for all". Even if co-operative group wins they may suggest our leaving to United States Government the re-armament of Latin America on a basis commensurate with internal and hemispheric defence only. In return they are thinking of similar United States self-denial in the Middle and Near East' (AS 4282/48/51).

political stability that is our requirement, and we do not see how it would square either with the 'non-intervention' principle agreed under the Final Act of the Mexico City Conference[6] last March, or with Mr. Byrnes' own statement, in his acceptance speech,[7] about his desire to 'promote toleration and avoid major crises.'[8]

CALENDARS TO NO. 14

i *11–24 Aug. 1945 (a) U.N.R.R.A. request for guidance from Combined Boards on availability of supplies and shipping: Mr. Balfour (Washington) Tels. Nos. 5442 & 5443* on need for caution in view of potentially larger relief responsibilities in 1946, *Tel. No. 8479 to Washington* Boards need not reply but should examine effect of V.J. day on supply question; *(b) Extract from Conclusions of 29th Meeting of Lord President's Committee on 24 Aug.* on present food position and prospects for winter of 1945/6 [UR 2837, 2842, 2846/114/850; CAB 71/19].

ii *7 Aug. 1945 Note by S. American Dept. on U.S. suggestions for control of exports to Argentina*: see note 5 above [AS 4064/159/2].

iii *21 Aug. 1945 Mr. Balfour (Washington) Tel. No. 5761* Refers to his tel. 5762 (see note 5 above): Mr. Rockefeller (Assistant Secretary of State for American Republic Affairs) has submitted his policy for Latin America to the President and Mr. Byrnes [AS 4281/48/51].

iv *28 Aug. 1945 To Sir D. Kelly (Buenos Aires) No. 204* Subjects discussed by Argentine Ambassador, Señor Cárcano, and Mr. Bevin included U.S. intervention, meat exports, Argentine political situation, and Falkland Islands, claim to which, Ambassador said, 'would present itself periodically to Argentine public opinion as a national aspiration', but he believed it 'capable of solution' [AS 4611/12/2].

v *6–27 Sept. 1945 Fuel for Argentina: Tels. Nos. 9202 to Washington and 461 to Buenos Aires, and memo. by Mr. J. V. Perowne (head of S. American Dept.)* As U.S. Govt.

[6] For the Inter-American Conference on Problems of War and Peace held at Mexico City 21 February–8 March 1945 see *F.R.U.S., op. cit.*, pp. 1–153 *passim*. The Final Act (Act of Chapultepec) was published by the Pan-American Union, Washington, 1945: cf. Volume I, No. 42, note 26.,

In a letter of 28 August to South American Department Mr. R.H. Hadow, Counsellor in H.M. Embassy at Washington, referred to a letter of 5 August addressed to Mr. Byrnes by the senior Republican Member of the Senate Foreign Relations Committee: see *The Times*, 7 August 1945, p. 3. Mr. Hadow quoted Senator Vandenberg's statement that in the Act of Chapultepec the United States might well accept 'the exclusive responsibility for any armed forces required to maintain peace and security in the Western Hemisphere. *I doubt whether we shall ever want any other armed forces to enter this area*' [Mr. Hadow's italics], and commented: 'I doubt if the Senator had the Belize dispute [cf. No. 79] in mind; but more and more I find a tendency in this country to wish all "Colonial Powers" out of this hemisphere ... Vandenberg's phraseology is open to the interpretation that no British troops would, in the event of a sudden crisis, be allowed to enter this hemisphere; which again might encourage Guatemala to fake an incident and appeal against British "aggression".'

[7] On 3 July 1945: see *D.S.B.*, vol. xiii, p. 45.

[8] Mr. Bevin minuted on this brief: 'I asked Mr. Winant to endeavour to assist us by leaving political [word illegible] for the moment in view of our great shortage of meat. He agreed to take it up. E.B.' A brief account of the interview was transmitted to Washington in telegram No. 8276 of 23 August (AS 4331/12/2).

have not kept their promise to facilitate Anglo-Argentine meat contract by keeping Argentina supplied with fuels it will be necessary to supply heavy oils from British resources to keep British-owned railways in Argentina running [AS 4626, 5062/189/2].

No. 15

Mr. Balfour (Washington) to Mr. Bevin
(Received 22 August, 6.10 a.m.)

No. 5757 Telegraphic [*UE 3737/32/71*]

Immediate. Top secret   WASHINGTON, *22 August 1945, 12.14 a.m.*

It may useful for you to have some appreciation of the political and personal background of the developments in regard to Lend Lease ending in the letter from Crowley reported in USLON 122.[1]

2. There is little doubt that the proposals in this letter are less favourable than those which had been discussed earlier on the American side and that they represent a hardening of attitude after a conference held at the White House on August 17th.[2] Although President is generally well disposed towards us he lacks the broad, imaginative grasp of Mr. Roosevelt and sees the Lend Lease problem in simple and elementary terms. His reasoning appears to be that as the war is over Lend Lease automatically comes to an end. Congress has been assured of this so it becomes a mere matter of business and accounting.

3. President has been advised in this question by Vinson, Byrnes, Leahy, Crowley and Snyder. Of these probably only Vinson takes a broad and generous view. Leahy and Crowley certainly encourage the President to take a hard-boiled line because they are not being friendly to us.[3] Crowley in particular is probably anxious to make a clean cut end of Lend Lease business before he goes out himself. He is not in any case a man to stand up for a point of view. Byrnes is very much overlorded [*sic*] and is

---

[1] See No. 12, note 3.   [2] See No. 11.

[3] In REMAC 631 of 23 August giving further background to the conference on 17 August (see note 2) Mr. Balfour reported that Mr. Crowley had apparently produced a memorandum at the meeting suggesting action on more drastic lines than the recommendations in REMAC 608 (No. 5), and that he and Admiral Leahy had persuaded the President and 'obtained latter's signature to drastic decision to terminate lend-lease on VJ' day, despite the fact that 'Vinson and Snyder and to a lesser degree Byrnes argued against this course' (UE 3778/32/71).

In a letter to Sir W. Eady of 30 August Mr. Brand, who had returned to Washington on 27 August, added the following comments 'which you may take as more or less correct': 'At the fateful meeting at the White House, Vinson and others left before the end and the final decision was taken by the President with, I believe, Byrnes present. Vinson had, I understand, argued at length and strongly that notice should be given to each country and that there should be discussion with each as to the exact procedure according to their circumstances. When he left the meeting he believed that this course had been accepted by the President. It turned out, however, otherwise' (T 236/1685).

temporarily without Chesnon[4] to advise him whilst Clayton can exert little influence at the end of a trans-Atlantic telephone. Moreover Byrnes is, as you know, not a very forceful personality and may, in this affair have some temperamental affinity with his fellow Irish American, Crowley. Snyder is rather an unknown quality but from his background he will probably share Mr. Truman's views.

4. The conclusions which this picture suggest[s] are first that Clayton should come back as soon as possible and use his influence to stiffen Byrnes, if as I hope he has now fully grasped views of His Majesty's Government.

5. Secondly it seems important that the main discussions on stage III should be opened here as soon as possible.

6. Thirdly as regards tactics, it is evident that from the point of view of personalities, the worst position for us is to have Crowley in sole charge of negotiations about Lend Lease on the American side, and therefore principal adviser to the President with Leahy in attendance. It might be preferable either

(a) to try and settle Lend Lease issue separately, perhaps by some interim credit arrangement, thus eliminating Crowley and Leahy at an early stage and giving a clear run to the stage III talks or

(b) alternatively to bring Lend Lease question into the general negotiations on stage III.

This latter course may be ruled out for reasons of time.

7. I am not of course informed of how your mind is moving on this important matter or how the discussions with Mr. Clayton in London are going. You should however be aware that with the passing of time and the changes of personnel here, there is a certain contraction of view in administration on some of the broad issues affecting our relationship. The dollar sign is back in the Anglo-American equation and the ghost of Mr. Coolidge[5] seems to be hovering near the White House. It is not that Mr. Truman is at all unsympathetic to our cause but he (like many of his entourage) comes from Missouri where they are apt to take a rather narrow and economical view of business transactions. It appears unlikely that the situation either in the Administration or in Congress will improve in this respect. It follows therefore that we ought to try for a broad settlement before the position crystal[l]ises here and while the emotions and experiences of the war are still fresh in the Americans' mind.[6]

[4] A marginal note suggested that the reference was to Mr. Dean Acheson, Assistant Secretary of State.

[5] President of the United States 1923–9.

[6] Mr. Butler minuted: 'I think this is a fair appreciation, and even when Pres. Roosevelt was alive we anticipated a contraction of outlook in the U.S.G. when he was replaced. We are now up against the Congress mentality, but not an unfriendly one. Mr. Acheson has imagination and persuasiveness, but he represents no political force. Mr. Clayton, on the other hand, who also has a broad outlook, carries a good deal of influence with the Southern Senators – and others. N.M. Butler 23.viii.'

In telegram No. 5796 of 24 August Mr. Balfour reported: 'There is evidence that the way in which the lend-lease affair has been handled is regarded as most unfortunate by many United States officials, and regrets, which I believe to be sincere, have been expressed to members of the Embassy staff. It is thought that the President took his decision in view of the commitment which he considers he made to Congress at the time of the renewal of the lend-lease act [cf. No. 13, note 5]. The most charitable explanation we have heard in friendly United States official circles is that he acted as he did in order to clear the political decks for wider financial proposals. Generally speaking the diagnosis in my telegram under reference [No. 15] seems to be fully confirmed. There is much good will towards us both in and out of the administration, but as time passes and the problems of the transition accumulate, this may well become somewhat dissipated' (UE 3791/32/71).

No. 16

RAFDEL (Washington) to Air Ministry (Received 23 August)

USLON *130 Telegraphic*[1] [*UE 3807/32/71*]

Secret   WASHINGTON, *23 August 1945, 5 a.m.*

1. My immediately preceding telegram.[2] Following points were clarified at meeting with Crowley today. He said (*a*) that all new procurement should be discontinued. (*b*) That as far as concerns goods in the course of manufacture and in the pipe line (including food allocated by U.S. Dept. of Agriculture) we could select what we require. However contracts for goods in the course of manufacture might be cancelled after we had had reasonable time to give our decisions as to what we wanted. He overruled his advisers and said we must have a reasonable time but urged need for

---

[1] The original text of this telegram, which was drafted on 22 August, was in capital letters: the appropriate alterations have been made and some punctuation marks inserted editorially.

[2] USLON 129 of 22 August, presumably from Sir H. Self, contained a general report on the discussion with Mr. Crowley that morning. Sir H. Self had pointed out that the suddenness of the decision to terminate Lend-Lease had created great difficulties for the British Government: 'We had deranged our whole economy to produce the maximum war effort and it was impossible for us to reverse the process without a reasonable breathing space . . . Whereas Crowley's letter [see No. 12, note 3] had talked of having discussions in our mutual interests it now appeared that we were faced with a unilateral decision.'

Mr. Crowley replied that 'we should have been aware that Lend-Lease would end on V.J. day as all the evidence that had been given pointed that way', and said 'we were really making a mountain out of a mole-hill. The small amount which we would require under 3(*c*) arrangement would make no difference to the much larger figure which we would have to consider in the longer term arrangements.' When the British representatives 'emphasised strongly the embarrassment and possible prejudice created for the Stage III talks by this sudden stoppage of Lend-Lease', Mr. Crowley 'reacted enigmatically but agreed that we must not repeat not be deemed to have prejudiced the Stage III talks in any way by these interim arrangements.'

The report concluded: 'Our impression was that FEA were slightly ashamed and were endeavouring to soften the blow as much as possible by administrative concessions. If you regard details in my immediately following telegram as reasonably satisfactory (bearing in mind the apparently irrevocable decision in principle) it may be wise to take advantage of present mood of FEA to try and pin them down as soon as possible' (T 236/1685).

speed. You will no doubt see that departments are advised of this immediately so that they can review their programs accordingly. (c) Inventories and goods transferred as of VJ day both in the U.S. and abroad i.e. items coming under paragraph (c) of Crowley's letter,[3] may similarly be selected by U.S. for retention. He agreed that stocks included only those under central government control e.g. stocks in hands of distributors would not repeat not rank against inventory. (d) The obligation that he was asking U.S. to assume for whatever we select under (b) and (c) above would be under $3(c)^4$ and the terms suggested were payment over 30 years in equal annual instalments with interest at 2⅜% per annum. (e) Present machinery for calling forward loading and shipping would continue unchanged until VJ day. Goods consumed and services rendered up till that time would be on straight Lend-Lease. (f) If we require to enter into new contracts we can do so by cash reimbursable requisitions (see para. (d) of Crowley's letter). He would be pleased to make arrangements for credits to be opened to cover these through the Export Import Bank. Such contracts would be accepted if delivery could be given within 6 months.

2. On the question of prices it seems clear that we shall be able to negotiate settlement for goods already transferred as of VJ day (i.e. anything which is at or beyond the stage of actual shipment) and would not necessarily be expected to pay contract prices. We envisage for this some 'machine tool' settlement. (Note – we are arranging for missions to secure maximum shipment by VJ day of all *wanted* supplies to take advantage of this formula. However for goods in the pipe line in U.S.A. which we select and for all new procurement under cash reimbursable requisitions we shall have to pay contract prices.)[5]

3. Following are subsidiary points: (a) Food etc. for military purposes. Crowley said he thought Army would take care of this on presumably War Department appropriations and we had the impression that a limited continuation of Lend-Lease might be arranged probably on basis of our continuing some Reciprocal Aid. We pointed out that since our Reciprocal Aid was very largely military this would not repeat not be a very satisfactory arrangement so far as we were concerned. (b) Crowley and others confirmed inventory would cover only those goods under central government control. We would be allowed to draw from Government held stocks in anticipation of early submission of lists of our requirements provided a record was kept of amounts taken out. This would be without prejudice to price discussions. (c) Prefabricated houses. We pointed out that a good deal of publicity had been given to fact that generous American nation were providing these houses as a gift. Had we now to say they were not repeat not to be a gift after all? Crowley said he had no repeat no powers to provide these on Lend Lease after VJ day. We

---

[3] i.e. point 3 made by Mr. Brand in No. 12.
[5] Cf. No. 13, note 7.

[4] See No. 4, note 7.

understand that this is incorrect constitutionally but he obviously had in mind President's statements that nothing would go after VJ day for rehabilitation.[6] He urged that anyhow he would face political difficulties if they went on providing 'houses for war workers' when there was no war. Venning[7] said he would have to obtain instructions from London whether we could afford to pay cash for these houses which had not yet been shipped. Meanwhile shipment proceeds up to VJ day. Crowley said they would be open to a price offer for such pre (?) shipments and part of inventory stocks, together with houses already en route and not turned over to the local authorities. (d) Bulk procurement of items in short supply. Crowley said if we wished that there would be no objection to procurement through Government channels for delivery periods up to say 6 months from date of orders provided requisitions were filed within 60 days of VJ day.[8]

CALENDARS TO No. 16

i   *22 Aug. 1945   Tel. LONUS 82 to Washington* comments on USLON 123 (No. 12.i) [UE 3706/32/71].

ii *24 & 25 Aug. 1945   Mr. Balfour (Washington) Tels. REMAC 637, 639, 643* concerning implications of offer in Mr. Clayton's letter (see No. 13, note 7) with particular reference to Dominions and non-military supplies [UE 3794, 3813, 3814/32/71].

[6] Cf. on this point Mr. Crowley's statement at a press conference on 24 August, quoting from his testimony before the Senate Committee on Banking and Currency in July 1945: see *The Times*, 25 August 1945, p. 4.

[7] General Sir W. Venning was Director General of the British Supply Mission in Washington.

[8] In his letter of 30 August to Sir W. Eady (see No. 15, note 3), Mr. Brand also reported an 'off the record' conversation with Dr. Harry White, Assistant Secretary in the U.S. Treasury, who made it clear that 'the Treasury at least had no sympathy with the action about Lend-Lease. They feel that it has added to their difficulties. He went so far as to say that in his opinion there was no real political difficulty of extending Lend-Lease to us for, say, 2, 4, 6, 8 or even 12 months longer. It would never do for this expression from him to get outside the Treasury. Therefore, please be very careful how you use it. He said that he was engaged at that very moment in concocting possible plans for meeting our problems' (T 236/1685).

No. 17

Record of a meeting of Ministers held at No. 10 Downing Street, on Thursday, 23 August 1945, at 10.15 p.m.[1]

[UE 3839/3683/53]

Secret

Forthcoming discussions with the United States

THE PRIME MINISTER invited Lord Keynes to make a statement as to the lines on which he thought the negotiations should be handled.

LORD KEYNES said that his first point was that he thought that our negotiators should be given no discretion on the main issues and that everything they did should be ad referendum.

Some questions would have to be settled about *cleaning up Lend/Lease.* He thought that we ought to try and persuade the Americans to agree that Lend/Lease and Mutual Aid should continue for military supplies for a limited period. Nearly half of the food which we were at present receiving from American Lend/Lease was in fact being sent to our troops. He thought that we should also stipulate that the terms of credit on which we continued to receive Lend/Lease supplies should be left to be dealt with as part of the general Stage III negotiations. On this part of the negotiations he thought that points of detail were more likely to arise than points of principle.

In reply to a question he said that Australia had a separate agreement with the United States, and it would probably pay her to cut clear altogether at once.

Stage III Negotiations. On what terms would the Americans offer us help?[2] The terms offered might vary from an out and out grant in aid,

[1] This meeting was called by Mr. Attlee on 18 August to discuss the proposals to the United States for financial assistance to follow after Lend Lease, contained in Mr. Dalton's paper of 17 August: see No. 6.i. Those present were Mr. Attlee, Mr. Morrison, Mr. Bevin, Mr. Dalton, Sir S. Cripps, Lord Pethick-Lawrence (Secretary of State for India), Lord Halifax, Lord Keynes, Sir E. Bridges, Sir R. Sinclair, Sir W. Eady, Mr. Brand and Mr. Hall-Patch. This record is also printed in Moggridge, *op. cit.*, pp. 420–5.

[2] On 22 August Mr. Bevin, Mr. Dalton and Sir S. Cripps had addressed a joint minute to Mr. Attlee stating that 'it is quite clear that what the United States will ask us for is a credit with a fairly high rate of interest and also acquiescence in Bretton Woods and their commercial policy. This presents us in dealing with the economy of this country with very grave difficulties and it may be that in the end we may have to come to some arrangement with the United States. At present, however, we have no bargaining counter because there does not appear to have been a careful study of alternative sources of supply both in food and raw materials, and while we should hate being driven to adopt an exclusive policy or what is sometimes described as an autarchy within the Empire and our immediate friends yet if the United States seeks to drive such a bargain that will embarrass us in the normal development of our economy and our social plans, there appears to be no alternative' (T 230/142).

The Ministers concluded by asking that the Cabinet Secretariat be directed to 'proceed

to a commercial credit. He thought that he should not be authorised to agree to anything except an out and out grant. Help on any less favourable terms should not be accepted except after very long thought on the part of Ministers in London. He thought that the first American proposal would be quite inacceptable from our point of view. We would then give our point of view and they would make counter-proposals and the discussion would so continue. Lord Keynes thought that this point, namely the nature and financial terms of any help to be afforded to us, would constitute the greatest stumbling block.

The next point concerned the *amount of the credit*. We wanted 5 billion dollars (including whatever was necessary to clean up Lend/Lease) in order to put us in a comfortable position. The Americans were thinking in terms of 3 billion dollars, rising possibly to 5. It was fairly clear that Mr. Clayton had come over here instructed to talk in terms of 3 billion dollars, but was now becoming sympathetic to a higher figure. It was just possible that we could manage on 4 billion dollars, but 3 billion would not enable us to make any commitments as to how we should use the help given to us.

This led to the question of what we should give as *quid pro quo* for this help. On this, the first point was a *settlement of our indebtedness to the sterling area*. If the Americans gave us 4 or 5 billion dollars, we could then go to the sterling area countries, and ask them to cancel part of our indebtedness to them and agree that the remainder should be made fully convertible by instalments. This point was of great importance, both to ourselves and the United States, and would be so regarded by the United States State Department and the United States Treasury. Lord Keynes thought that this was the only constructive proposal which he should put forward at the outset.

The United States Authorities would certainly ask about *Bretton Woods*. He would start by pointing out that the Chancellor of the Exchequer had recently re-affirmed the pledge given by his predecessor that we would enter into no commitments before Parliament had considered the matter in the Autumn.[3]

They would then ask what the Government proposed to advise Parliament to do. His own view was that Bretton Woods was a carefully prepared document which contained adequate safeguards and that we could undertake the obligations contained in it, provided they were not coupled with dangerous concessions under the heading of commercial policy.

Commercial Policy. Lord Keynes emphasised that there was no question of our being asked to agree to a detailed commercial treaty at this stage.[4]

with an urgent and immediate study' on these lines. A preliminary note of 22 August by Sir W. Eady in response, and a memorandum of 31 August prepared in the Treasury (GEN 83/1), are filed in T 236/437 and T 230/142 respectively.
[3] See Mr. Dalton's parliamentary answer on 21 August in *Parl. Debs., 5th ser., H. of C.,* vol. 413, col. 450.
[4] Lord Keynes' view on this point was restated by Sir W. Eady in a letter of 25 August to

What we should be asked to do would be to sign a joint invitation with the United States to 15 other countries to attend an international conference next year, on the understanding that the terms of the invitation represented the policy of our two countries.

Most of the United States document[5] was acceptable to us and indeed valuable. There remained, however, four points of specific difficulty which he would refer to. Provided however, that the Americans felt that we were substantially in agreement with them, he thought that they might give us reasonable satisfaction on these points.

The first of the four points concerned *preferences*. On this our line should be that this was inseparable from tariffs and could not be handled on an a priori basis before the tariffs talks started. We should not yield an inch from this attitude.

The second point concerned *state trading*. The document on this point was innocent, but not unambiguous. Since the document had to be acceptable to Russia, there should not be any serious difficulty under this head. The Americans would make the point that state trading should be non-discriminatory. This suited us quite well.

The third point concerned the *programme of imports*. Here we must stand on the ground that we must be able to programme imports, not merely as a temporary expedient in times of difficulty, but as a normal part of our policy. He thought that Mr. Clayton would be prepared to agree on this

Sir J. Woods, Permanent Secretary to the Board of Trade, concerning the arrangements for the forthcoming discussions in Washington. Sir W. Eady concluded: 'In order to avoid any chance of a head-on collision on any question of Commercial Policy while the difficult financial negotiations are still in their early stages, we have thought it right not to have the delegation increased by Board of Trade representatives who would obviously be qualified to enter into the concurrent talks on commercial policy.

'I hope you will agree with this. If we succeed in imposing our tactics on the approach to the whole subject, commercial policy will only arise after the initial rounds on Item 2 [of the agenda: see ii below], and there will be plenty of time for Board of Trade representatives to go out to Washington' (T 236/437).

On 30 August, however, Mr. Hawkins called at the Foreign Office 'in considerable distress' at this decision, to say that Mr. Clayton and the State Department 'felt that it was most desirable that Keynes' team should include from the outset persons fully qualified in commercial policy' (letter from Mr. Ronald to Sir J. Woods and Sir W. Eady, UE 3995/1094/53). A memorandum on this question prepared by the Treasury and Board of Trade was considered at a meeting of Ministers on 31 August, when it was agreed 'that the Foreign Office should explain to Mr. Hawkins.

'(1) that, while developments in the Lend-Lease field compelled us to discuss financial policy as an issue of the greatest urgency, we were, of course, willing to discuss commercial policy and were therefore undertaking the necessary preparation in London so that fully qualified representatives could be sent to Washington as soon as practicable. Ministers, however, must have an opportunity to form considered views on the complex issues involved.

'(2) In the meantime, in order to facilitate matters before fully qualified representatives could go out, Mr. Helmore of the Board of Trade (who was familiar with the issues involved) would go to Washington to act as an observer to keep London informed of any points bearing on commercial policy' (UE 4080/1094/53).

[5] See No. 2, note 11.

point, subject to such programming being non-discriminatory. It was also worth bearing in mind that most of the other 15 countries to be invited to the conference would share our views on this matter.

The fourth and last point of difficulty on the commercial side concerned the *Bretton Woods provisions about exchange control*. Here the United States Department thought that the United States Treasury had conceded too much to us at Bretton Woods and wanted to recover part of the concessions then made as part of the commercial agreement. To this we should not agree.

Finally, Lord Keynes referred to a number of *other questions* which might arise in the discussion. He said that Mr. Harry White in their talks a year or so back had asked whether it would not be possible to throw something into the negotiations which was incapable of monetary measurement. This necessarily led to the question whether we had not some island or islands which we could make over as part of the deal. Lord Keynes added that he thought that a settlement of this matter would require a Bill in Congress and that the United States might well wish to deal in the same Bill with consideration under Lend/Lease and also of formal cancellation of the old debt.

Discussion followed.

THE PRESIDENT OF THE BOARD OF TRADE raised the question whether it would not be best to go straight for a grant in aid, and to do our best to dress it up effectively, and to stand on this line. LORD KEYNES said that this had been his first instinct, but that he had been rather pushed off this in the course of discussion. Thus Mr. Clayton was clearly not thinking on these lines.

SIR ROBERT SINCLAIR favoured the grant in aid as the one solution which was really right on merits and made good sense; but he agreed that means would have to be found to dress it up in such a way as to make it acceptable.

MR. BRAND said that he agreed with Lord Keynes, but perhaps was rather less hopeful. He thought, however, that it would be undesirable that the United Kingdom representatives should ask for a grant in aid. There was the danger that if we did, there would be a leakage and that it would be stated in the United States Press that we had made such a request. This might well be represented to our disadvantage. He thought that we should let it appear from the strength of our case, as we developed it, that this was the one really satisfactory way of dealing with the situation, but that we should let the Americans come to this, rather than make the suggestion ourselves.

This met with general approval.

LORD HALIFAX agreed with this view, and made three further points.
  (i) That Mr. Cordell Hull was still very influential in the background,
  (ii) That the chance of our getting a large sum from the Americans depended less on the size of the sum, than on its being wrapped up in attractive appurtenances,

(iii) That it was important that we should be able to concede some points, and take up an attitude which would strike some spark of enthusiasm or emotion from the Americans. He mentioned the suggestion that he had made some time back that we should say that at the peace conference we would take an unselfish attitude about bases. He also mentioned the suggestion that we should make a gift of the island of Tarawa to the United States in recognition of the noble feat of arms there of the United States Marines.[6] THE FOREIGN SECRETARY said that he would like to follow up this suggestion.[7]

THE PRIME MINISTER asked with whom the negotiations would be carried on. LORD KEYNES thought that they would be carried on by a Committee of the United States Cabinet presided over by Mr. Vinson, but it would be very helpful if Lord Halifax would at an early stage ask the President to designate a specific body with whom we should negotiate on this matter.

Discussions followed as to whether it would be appropriate for us, when the Bretton Woods Agreement came before Parliament, to follow the Congress procedure and to signify our assent subject to an interpretation of one or two points by the governing body organisation. It was generally felt that although the Americans would not welcome this, they could hardly object to it.[8]

THE PRIME MINISTER summing up the meeting said that he thought that the general conclusion of his colleagues was that the matter should be handled by Lord Keynes and his colleagues on the basis that he had outlined that evening; and that the negotiations should be ad referendum, reports being made to Ministers in London as and when necessary.

The question was then raised whether the Prime Minister should make a statement in Parliament on the following day on Lend/Lease and Reciprocal Aid. A copy of a draft statement had been circulated to the Ministers present at the meeting.[9] The great importance of such a statement for United States opinion was stressed.

On the other hand it was felt that a debate on this matter on the adjournment might be embarrassing.

The conclusion of Ministers after discussion was that the statement should be made subject to one or two drafting amendments, but that the Leader of the Opposition[10] should be approached and informed of the

---

[6] The island of Tarawa in the British Colony of the Gilbert and Ellice Islands was recaptured by U.S. Marines from the Japanese after a fierce battle on 23–4 November 1943.

[7] In a minute of 28 August headed 'Tarawa' Mr. Bevin wrote: 'It is clear that we cannot use this in connexion with Lend Lease; it is too obvious. But it should be re-examined and at a suitable moment, perhaps when we know U.S. claims in the Pacific, we can at that time probably find a way to make the gesture. E.B. 28.8.45' (AN 2831/355/45). Cf. iii below.

[8] Mr. W.E. Beckett, Legal Adviser to the Foreign Office, noted against this sentence: 'I am not so sure about this. W.E.B.'

[9] Not attached to filed copy.

[10] i.e. Mr. Churchill.

Prime Minister's intention to make this statement and asked to do his best to handle the matter in such a way as to avoid debate.[11]

[11] The text of Mr. Attlee's statement of 24 August (see *Parl. Debs., 5th ser., H. of C.*, vol. 413, cols. 955–7) was transmitted to Washington in telegram No. 8780 of 24 August. Mr. Attlee expressed regret at the sudden termination of Lend-Lease, pointing out that while it had made it possible 'for us in this island to mobilise our domestic manpower for war with an intensity unsurpassed elsewhere, and at the same time to undertake expenditure abroad on the support of military operations over a widely extended area, without having to produce exports to pay for our imports of food and raw materials or to provide the cash we were spending abroad', this meant that the United Kingdom was 'far worse off, when the sources of assistance dry up, than it leaves those who have been affording us the assistance'. In his letter to Sir W. Eady of 30 August (see No. 15, note 3, and No. 16, note 8) Mr. Brand reported that President Truman and Mr. Byrnes were 'furious at the Prime Minister's statement. If so, their fury must have arisen very largely from a bad conscience. One must, however, remember that they are both probably entirely without understanding of the true difficulties of the U.K. position.'

No. 18

Letter[1] *from Mr. Brand to Mr. Crowley (Washington)*

[*UE 3995/1094/53*][2]

WASHINGTON, *30 August 1945*

Dear Mr. Crowley:

I refer to your letter to me of the 18th August[3] and to the discussions which Sir Henry Self and others had with you on the 22nd August concerning the decision of the U.S. Administration in regard to the termination of Lend-Lease supplies to the U.K.[4] Sir Henry Self has since sent to you a copy of the general statement on this subject made by the Prime Minister in the House of Commons on the 24th August.[5]

The special mission to which the Prime Minister referred are now on their way to the U.S.A. and following their arrival will enter upon general discussions with F.E.A. and the other U.S. Departments concerned in accordance with your invitation.

The Mission will not, however, arrive in the U.S.A. before V-J Day, assuming that that day is on the 31st August or very shortly afterwards. In order, however, that there shall be no interruption in the flow of supplies needed in the U.K., I am authorised to say that the U.K. Government will be prepared to purchase, on terms to be mutually agreed upon following discussion with the mission referred to above, the U.K. requirements falling under (*b*) of your letter of the 18th August.

I hope that on the above basis supplies designated by the various U.K. Missions as required for the U.K. will continue to move forward after V-J Day. The Missions concerned are being asked to advise you at the earliest possible moment as to these requirements.

The U.K. Government will arrange to keep a record of the extent to

---

[1] For the drafting of this letter see i below. The arguments in CAMER 593 (see i), in the light of which the first draft (NABOB 2, see i) was amended, were based on a note of 26 August by Lord Keynes on 'The Interim Credit', addressed to Sir W. Eady and Mr. Grant (T 236/1685). A special telegraphic series was established for the Keynes Mission. Telegrams were despatched through J.A.S. channels to the J.S.M. in Washington (cf. No. 4, note 13), with the prefix BABOON for outward telegrams from London, and NABOB for inward telegrams. According to Pressnell, *op. cit.*, Chapter 10(4), Mr. Crowley was 'known amongst the British as "the Baboon" ' and was thus the inspiration for these designations.

[2] This letter is printed from the text circulated by the J.A.S. on 11 September in GEN 80/5. GEN 80 was a Cabinet Office series used for papers relating to the work of the Keynes Mission. The distribution list for GEN 80 papers, which included officials from all interested Ministries, was headed by Mr. Attlee, Mr. Bevin, Mr. Dalton, Sir S. Cripps and Mr. Morrison, and these Ministers, joined by Sir E. Bridges and Sir W. Eady, held regular meetings, usually on weekday evenings at No. 10 Downing Street, to discuss the Anglo-American financial negotiations. See Douglas Jay, *Change and Fortune* (London, 1980), pp. 136–7: Mr. Jay, as Mr. Attlee's personal adviser on economic matters, also attended the meetings.

[3] See No. 12, note 3.   [4] See No. 16.   [5] Cf. No. 17, note 11.

which use is made after V-J Day of stocks of lend-lease materials in their hands. The terms of settlement in respect of such user will, we assume, be the subject of discussion with the mission after their arrival.

In accordance with the Prime Minister's statement, the U.K. Government will apply procedures similar to those followed in the case of Lend-Lease supplies to the U.K. in the period after V-J Day to U.S. requirements of Reciprocal Aid foodstuffs and raw materials from the U.K. and the Colonies in the period following the general withdrawal on V-J Day of Reciprocal Aid for such supplies.

The foregoing paragraphs relate to all supplies received by the U.K. through F.E.A. other than those obtained for the use of the armed forces—e.g. certain food supplies. In the case of these latter supplies it is hoped that, having regard to the passage concerning military lend-lease needs in the statement issued at the President's press conference on the 21st August,[3] arrangements will be made to ensure the continued movement of supplies after V-J Day without prejudice to consideration of the definitive proposals which will, it is understood, be put forward by the War Department. I am, of course, at your service if you would wish to discuss anything arising out of this letter.[6]

Yours sincerely,

R. H. Brand

CALENDARS TO NO. 18

i *28–9 Aug. 1945* Tel. *CAMER 593 to Washington (also sent as BABOON 1)* Lord Keynes' views on acceptable credit terms if an agreement to purchase pipeline supplies must be negotiated before arrival of Mission: in the light of this *BABOON 2 to Washington* suggests amendments to *NABOBS 1 & 2* which are based on principle that 'we cannot contemplate acceptance of credit'; *NABOB 7* Mr. Brand to Sir W. Eady expressing surprise at CAMER 593 and proposing to press Mr. Crowley for a limited arrangement [UE 3814, 3903, 3904, 3979/32/71].

ii *29 & 31 Aug. 1945* British Missions (Washington) Tel. *NABOB 4* Gives text of letter from Mr. Patterson to Sir H. Self deferring decision on military lend-lease, and proposes addition to draft in NABOB 2 (see i) on food for armed forces; *NABOB 10* refers to draft presidential directive on military lend-lease: 'such indications as we have had do not lead us to expect any generous or far-reaching offer' [UE 3906, 3957/32/71].

iii *29 Aug. – 15 Sept. 1945* (a) British Missions (Washington) Tels. *NABOB 3 & 6* Freedom of Dominion and Indian representatives to negotiate separate credit arrangements with F.E.A. if they wish, but at meeting of P.C.S.C. on 29 Aug.

[6] In a further letter to Mr. Crowley of the same date, also circulated in GEN 80/5, Mr. Brand stated: 'I think that it may be desirable to make clear that in the letter which I sent to you this morning, I was speaking only on behalf of the Government of the U.K. and in regard to U.K. requirements. I understand that the representatives in Washington of the Dominion Governments concerned and of the Government of India will be communicating separately with F.E.A. in regard to their requirements after V-J Day.' Cf. iii below.

they express opinion that their governments will not seek credits but may try to obtain payment for Reciprocal Aid supplies 'by making appropriate abatement in any settlement for lend lease inventories': H.M.G.'s views on these questions are given in BABOON 7; *(b) Letters from Mr. B. Cockram (of D.O., Counsellor in H.M. Embassy in Washington) to Mr. P.A. Clutterbuck (D.O.), and from Mr. A.W. Snelling (D.O.) to Mr. Cockram* on implications for Dominions of financial negotiations in Washington [UE 3905, 3910/32/71, D.O. 35/1216].

No. 19

British Missions (Washington) to Cabinet Offices
(Received 31 August, 9.22 p.m.)

NABOB *11* Telegraphic [*UE 3990/32/71*]

WASHINGTON, *31 August 1945, 7.41 p.m.*

Most immediate. Top secret.

For Eady from Brand.
Your telegram BABOON No. 5.[1]

1. Crowley saw Brand, Self, and Lee this morning and stated that letter written by Brand[2] was not satisfactory to him. He had to deal with 16 or more Governments which had been in receipt of Lend Lease. As soon as it became known that settlement of terms for U.K. requirements for pipeline was being deferred for separate and later negotiations, all other Governments would at once seek to reopen their acceptance of FEA terms of 30 years credit at $2\frac{3}{8}$ per cent. He urged that our ultimate position would not be prejudiced if we accepted terms forthwith since acceptance could always be given on understanding that arrangement and conditions would be subject to review in light of overall financial negotiations. Indeed, both the Russians and Chinese had already indicated that while they were prepared to accept Crowley's terms for their pipe line supplies, they would expect that arrangements would be reviewed in more general financial negotiations.

[1] This telegram of 30 August referred to NABOB 7 (see No. 18.i) and instructed Mr. Brand as follows: 'Please refer back and give us opportunity for further consideration if, after you have been in touch with Crowley, there is any question of paying cash' (T 236/465). BABOON 5 was drafted by Mr. Grant, who later that day addressed a minute (T 236/1685) to Sir E. Bridges suggesting that 'as a matter of courtesy we should give Brand a further answer to NABOB 7', and enclosing a draft. BABOON 9 of 31 August from Sir W. Eady to Mr. Brand referred to Lord Keynes' note on the Interim Credit (see No. 18, note 1) and stated: 'The obvious danger about starting to pay dollars for pipeline supplies is that once we have started to pay it may be very difficult to stop. Indeed, those on the American side who are more hostile to us may try to bleed us of dollar reserves in the hope of making us more amenable in negotiation . . . Even if in the end we do pay cash it may be better that we should do that on an American demand for it rather than as an offer against an American offer of a short interim credit' (T 236/465).

[2] See No. 18.

2. Crowley added (what we find hard to believe) that we are the *only* country which is refusing to take the whole of its pipe line supplies but is making a selection from them. This meant that we were already placed in a more advantageous position than, say, the French who by reason of having signed a 3 (*c*) agreement were being obliged to take the whole of their pipe line supplies, some of which they do not now really want. Thus any separate deal with FEA on terms was impossible.

3. Brand urged that we were in entirely different position from other nations having regard both to the magnitude of our requirements and to the fact that a special mission was on its way to the U.S.A. in accordance with Mr. Crowley's invitation to discuss the winding-up of Lend-Lease. In the circumstances it seemed only reasonable to ask that consideration of terms to be applied to the pipe line supplies should wait until the arrival of this special mission.

4. When Crowley said that he was unable to modify his attitude, we suggested that we should agree to accept his terms for deliveries of our requirements from the pipe line in September or alternatively for deliveries up to a given sum, say, $50–100 million. Crowley said that this would not be acceptable since it would definitely differentiate us from other recipients of Lend Lease and would leave open the problem of what terms were to be applied to our requirements after September.

5. Thayer,[3] who was with Crowley, thereupon suggested that our interests would be safeguarded if our undertaking to accept Crowley's terms was accompanied by specific reservation to effect that this was an interim arrangement and that terms and conditions would be subject to review in course of forthcoming general negotiations. Crowley said that he would be prepared to accept such a stipulation whereupon Thayer hurriedly drafted proposed passage to be inserted in our letter of which text is given in following para. You will appreciate that we may be able to get minor drafting changes accepted in this so long as general substance is not changed.

Proposed passage is as follows:

'I am authorised to say that the U.K. Government will be prepared to purchase the U.K. requirements falling under (*b*) of your letter of 18th August[4] (as designated by U.K. missions) on the terms which were stated by you in the discussion with Sir Henry Self on the 22nd August[5]—i.e. under a credit arrangement providing for repayment by equal annual instalments over a period of 30 years plus interest at the rate of 2⅜ per cent per annum. This agreement is however, given on the clear understanding that the above terms and conditions will be reviewed in the overall financial discussions which are about to be undertaken with the U.S. Government. We, therefore, consider the present arrangement to be an interim one and without prejudice to the general financial discussions

---

[3] Mr. W.N.T. Thayer was General Counsel to the F.E.A.
[4] i.e. point (2) in Mr. Brand's statement in No. 12.   [5] See No. 16.

with the U.S. Government in the sense that the interim agreement would be merged in any overall agreement reached with the U.S. Government and made subject to the same terms and conditions as may be mutually agreed thereunder.'

6. We can see no hope of securing better terms from Crowley or of a successful appeal over his head to the State Department or Treasury. We have some reason to believe that his proposals have been discussed with Clayton and Dean Acheson. Although we are not sure about this, we are convinced that it would be a waste of time to attempt an appeal to Clayton.

7. In the circumstances, if we are to avoid a hold-up from V-J Day, the alternatives before us are:
   (i) to agree to pay cash
   (ii) to accept 3 (c) credit as an interim arrangement subject to the insertion of the proviso as in paragraph 5 above.

Our recommendation is that we should accept latter course since period over which we might have to pay cash might run to several months, whereas under proposed Thayer formula we can secure modification of present 3 (c) terms to bring them in line with terms of any general understanding reached as result of negotiations with missions.

8. Although Crowley did not himself raise the point, we understand that FEA will not accept our proposed paragraph concerning food for military forces.[6] They will want us to say that we will apply terms accepted for our general requirements from the pipe line to food for armed forces on understanding that if agreement is subsequently reached with War Department for bringing such supplies within the ambit of an agreed continuance of straight military Lend Lease, such an arrangement would supersede with retrospective effect agreement to take these supplies on Crowley's terms. We recommend that we should be authorised to accept this.

9. Please let us have immediate guidance at the latest by 10 a.m. Washington time tomorrow (September 1st). We are already in difficulties owing to fact that many U.S. agencies will not be working tomorrow as well as Monday,[7] while notice has already been sent to inland transportation authorities not to load any more supplies.[8]

CALENDAR TO NO. 19

i *31 Aug. –1 Sept. 1945 British Missions (Washington) Tels. NABOB 16–18* Mr. Clayton agrees with Mr. Crowley on interim financing and would be reluctant to refer British views to President; further letter to Mr. Brand from Mr. Crowley rejects arguments in No. 18 but agrees right can be reserved to review terms of pipeline agreement in accordance with forthcoming financial negotiations [UE 3989, 4008/32/71; T 236/453].

[6] See No. 18.ii.   [7] 3 September 1945.

[8] In BABOON 10 of 1 September Mr. Brand was instructed not to reply to Mr. Crowley's proposals in the light of No. 20.

No. 20

Mr. Bevin to Mr. Balfour (Washington)

No. 9086 Telegraphic [UE 3990/32/71]

Most immediate. Secret   FOREIGN OFFICE, 1 September 1945, 4.50 p.m.

Following is text referred to in my immediately preceding telegram.[1] From Prime Minister to President.

We received early this morning (Saturday) from the representatives of the British Treasury in Washington a report[2] of a discussion they had had with Mr. Crowley, the Foreign Economic Administrator, yesterday, 31st August, on the arrangements to be made for Lend-Lease supplies in the immediate future.

2. I am informed that Mr. Crowley has made it plain that any supplies which we need from the pipeline should be taken up either on payment of cash or on credit terms which he had already indicated, that is credit for 30 years at 2⅜ths%. I understand that he was not prepared to await the settlement of the terms of payment until our special Mission had arrived in Washington within the next few days or to agree that we should consider these credit terms as an interim arrangement[3] applying to the supplies coming forward within the next few weeks. He was willing however to agree that if we accepted the credit on the terms and conditions he had indicated this would be on the understanding that these conditions should be reviewed in the over-all financial discussions which were about to be undertaken with the United States Government.[4]

Our representatives requested a reply from us within a few hours and informed us that notice had been given by the United States Administration to the Inland Transport Authorities not to load any more supplies for the United Kingdom meanwhile.

3. You will remember that at Potsdam on 24th July Mr. Churchill wrote to you that very important questions affecting Lend-Lease and the

---

[1] Not printed. This telegram of 1 September informed Mr. Balfour that unless he had very strong reasons for not wishing the message in telegram No. 9086 to be sent at this stage it should be delivered promptly to Mr. Truman. 'The whole situation has been carefully considered by the Prime Minister and we should want some very convincing reason to ask him to reconsider his view.'

[2] No. 19.

[3] Washington telegram No. 5982 of 1 September reported that the preceding three words were omitted from the text communicated to Mr. Truman that afternoon (printed in F.R.U.S. 1945, vol. vi, pp. 113–15) since 'Crowley was prepared to agree that if we accepted his terms we could describe that arrangement as an interim one'. See also notes 4 and 11 below.

[4] The following passage was here added to the final text by Mr. Balfour: 'and, if deemed desirable, might be brought into line with the decisions resulting from those discussions'. According to Washington telegram No. 5982 this phraseology was 'taken from letter sent by Crowley to Brand today and we have thought it advisable to include this statement in description of terms actually offered by Crowley'. See No. 19.i.

financial arrangements to be made after Lend-lease would be coming up and that we wanted to send an authoritative Mission to Washington early in September to discuss the matter with your representatives.[5] You agreed to this and informed Mr. Churchill that you were sending Mr. Clayton, an Assistant Secretary of the State Department, to London to discuss the position with us and to make a report to you.[5]

4. Mr. Clayton came to London and had several discussions both with my Ministerial colleagues and with senior officials.[6] An agenda for the discussions in Washington was worked out in agreement with Mr. Clayton and his colleagues.[7] This agenda covered in the first place Lend-Lease, the financial arrangements after Lend-Lease, and also the lines upon which further developments on commercial policy could be worked out on the principles which we have been discussing with representatives of the United States Administration over the last year or so. One of the items included under the heading Lend-Lease was 'Terms for continued delivery of non-munitions pipeline'.

5. During the progress of those discussions we were advised that the Foreign Economic Administrator had indicated that Lend-Lease supplies coming forward must be accepted on terms to be determined by the United States Administration.[8] As this was contrary to the expectations we had formed from the correspondence between you and Mr. Churchill in Potsdam, representations were made by our Embassy in Washington and we also raised the matter direct with Mr. Clayton.[9] On the 21st August Mr. Clayton wrote to us in the following terms:

'The Secretary of State has informed me that the President has approved an amendment to the August 17th Lend-Lease Directive whereby countries such as the United Kingdom which have not entered into 3 (c) agreements, may obtain delivery of goods in the pipeline upon agreement to pay for them on terms to be mutually agreed on'.[10]

6. I must make it plain to you that none of us here had understood that letter to imply that within a few days we should be informed of the terms under which the supplies in the pipe-line could go forward to us and that meanwhile orders had been[11] given to the Inland Transport Authorities to suspend the loading of supplies for the United Kingdom. Nor can I believe that this action by F.E.A. was in your mind when you authorised the Secretary of State to send us the communication of the 21st August.

7. You are aware that in the immediate future the maintenance of the physical flow of supplies from the United States, both of food and of certain essential raw materials, is necessary for the maintenance of the living conditions in this country. You have probably also been informed by

[5] See No. 1, note 4.   [6] See Nos. 1, note 2, 2, 8 and 13.   [7] See No. 17.ii.
[8] Cf. Section 1(c) of Mr. Crowley's directive to American Diplomatic Missions, F.R.U.S. op. cit., p. 107, and ibid., note 4.
[9] See No. 13.   [10] V. ibid., note 7.
[11] In the final text the two preceding words were changed by Mr. Balfour to read 'would be'.

Mr. Clayton of the general financial position in which we find ourselves because our war effort took a certain shape as part of the combined war plans. I referred to this matter in my statement to Parliament on Friday, August 24th.[12]

8. It is impossible for our Government to give an answer to the proposals of the Foreign Economic Administrator within a matter of a few hours, and you will not misunderstand me if I say that the preparation of a suitable answer would not be made easier for me by the knowledge that instructions had been given to suspend the loading of supplies for the United Kingdom.

9. I hope therefore that you may feel able to give an urgent directive that supplies in the pipeline coming forward for shipment, say within the next month, may proceed to the United Kingdom and that the terms and conditions of payment for such supplies will be discussed and agreed between the United States Administration and the Special Mission which has been sent to Washington for this purpose. We have recognised that with V.J. Day Lend-Lease as we have known it, and as you have described it in your recent striking report to Congress,[13] is at an end. We have realised that in some form or other we shall henceforward have to pay for the urgent supplies that we need from the United States. Therefore it is hardly necessary for me to assure you that if these supplies for the next month come forward to us as I have suggested, they will be paid for.

[12] Cf. No. 17, note 11.

[13] In his letter to Congress of 30 August 1945, transmitting the 20th Quarterly Report on Lend-Lease, President Truman stated that the 'great task of lend-lease has now ended': see D.S.B.., vol. xiii, p. 332.

No. 21

Notes by Mr. Gallop[1]

[W 14447/19/58]

FOREIGN OFFICE, September 1945

United States Surplus Shipping

As a result of the war there has been a serious maldistribution of shipping. Our shipping problems with the United States fall under two headings (1) our own requirements and (2) the disposal of the United States surplus shipping. These two problems are interconnected.

[1] These notes by the Head of the General Department of the Foreign Office were prepared, according to his minute of 20 October, 'at the beginning of September to form part of a paper which it was intended to prepare for the Secretary of State on economic and technical questions at issue with the U.S.'

(1) *British Shipping*

Gross tonnage on the United Kingdom register is now 22% below the 1939 figure and will take some years to make good. We cannot afford to accept any reductions in the amount of tonnage we are able to keep at sea. To maintain this we require to retain under our flag some 2½ million tons of chartered shipping. Of this 1.9 million tons has been lent to us by the United States on lease-lend terms. These ships are chartered to us for a period not extending beyond six months after the cessation of hostilities. As our own new construction proceeds, we may be able to surrender these ships. Ministry of War Transport would like to charter for a period of three years with, if possible, an option to return a proportion of the ships at an earlier date. The United States may wish to make us accept a longer period of charter or even refuse to charter to us. To purchase this shipping would (1) involve a formidable expenditure of dollars (2) increase the proportion of our fleet not best adapted for future trading and (3) limit our ability to place orders in our own ship yards.

(2) *United States Surplus Shipping*

The United States now have six times as much dry cargo tonnage as before the war. They realise that most of this, amounting to at least 2,000 [ships] will have to be laid up or scrapped. They have recently suggested that we and the other maritime Allies should agree to lay up some of our own older tonnage. This proposal is completely unacceptable to the Ministry of War Transport. While regarding the United States problem as essentially a United States liability we must discuss remedial steps sympathetically with them while insisting (1) that the problem of disposing of the surplus cannot be dissociated from the problem of redistribution, (2) that we cannot reduce the total tonnage we can keep at sea and (3) that we cannot commit ourselves to guarantee to the United States a particular share of the world's tonnage.

There is considerable opposition in the United States to the charter of the United States surplus shipping to foreign countries on the ground that the latter, having had the temporary benefit of it to reestablish their trade will then replace it by home built shipping and throw the burden of the obsolete American ships back on the American tax payer. Some of those currents of American opinion which favour sale demand that American operators should receive first choice and more favourable terms than foreign competitors. There is a general feeling that a higher proportion of American trade ought to be carried in American bottoms than before the war.

It does not look therefore as though our objectives will be easy to secure. We have a little breathing space however. The Agreement on Principles establishing the United Maritime Authority remains in force till February 1946, and might conceivably be prolonged.[2] It binds the United States to give shipping help to the contracting Governments where it is required.

---

[2] The International Agreement on Principles having reference to the Continuance of

Oil, Telecommunications and Civil Aviation

These three subjects have been described by H.M. Embassy Washington as 'highly charged with political significance' in the United States and unrivalled as 'subjects of passionate and publicly expressed feeling'. Their world wide exploitation has a triple appeal to the American public; to the imagination of the pioneer, the self-interest of the business man and, since the last two can be presented as vehicles of democratic ways of thought, the moral sense of the self-righteous. Relations with the United States Government over all three are thus apt to be peculiarly delicate. During the war establishments under all three headings have been set up by the United States for war purposes in many parts of the world. Many Americans feel strongly that they should have the right to continue to use them after the war. This applies particularly to telecommunications and air transport. In these two fields it is their ambition to be able to 'telegraph American' and 'fly American' all over the globe. Moreover they wish these services to pay their way without subventions. These conceptions are not easily reconcilable except at the expense of other nations.

Oil

There are at the moment no highly controversial points at issue between the United States and ourselves over oil, and during the war there has been wholehearted cooperation. Nevertheless, there has in the past been some mutual suspicion, particularly on the part of the United States. Faced with a possible domestic shrinkage of subsoil resources they have felt that we control too large a proportion of world's oil and exercise our control in too restrictive a manner. Particularly in the Middle East they thought that our general policy aimed at their ex[c]lusion. During the last ten to fifteen years however, they have obtained a substantial share of Middle Eastern oil. They have not liked our policy in Iran where we have persuaded the Iranian Government to suspend the grant of new oil concessions so long as their country is occupied by foreign troops.[3] While this policy was directed against the extortion by the Soviet of concessions under pressure it also closed the door to the grant of concessions to American oil companies.

Such suspicion as may have existed was mainly dissipated by our readiness to negotiate petroleum agreements with the United States last year. The agreement was concluded on August 8th 1944.[4] It provided for

Co-ordinated Control of Merchant Shipping, signed on 5 August 1944 by the governments of Belgium, Canada, Greece, the Netherlands, Norway, Poland, United Kingdom, United States and the French Provisional Government, was published as Cmd. 6556 of 1944. It provided for the establishment of a central authority, consisting of the United Maritime Council and United Maritime Executive Board, to ensure the supply of shipping necessary for the completion of the war in Europe and the Far East. The Agreement expired on 2 March 1946, but at its final meeting on 14 February the U.M.E.B. recommended arrangements (published in Cmd. 6754 of 1946) for the continuation of some forms of control.

[3] See Sir L. Woodward, *op. cit.*, vol. iv, Chapter LVIII.   [4] V. *ibid.*, pp. 401–2.

the development of petroleum resources in an orderly manner on a worldwide basis so as to make them available in international trade at fair prices on a nondiscriminatory basis. The two Governments undertook to establish an International Petroleum Agreement and the setting up of an International Petroleum Council

The Agreement aroused opposition among American oil interests, though on domestic rather than external grounds. Instead of ratifying it the United States Government have expressed their wish to negotiate certain modifications of it. They have not told us what these are but describe them as points of drafting rather than of substance, except that they want to provide for the extension of the Agreement into a multilateral instrument being made more imminent. The negotiations will begin here on September 17th.

We have reason to believe the Americans may want to drop the preamble setting forth the principles on which the two Governments should work, including one of importance to us viz. that supplies to meet world needs would be derived from various producing areas with due consideration in inter-alia 'relevant economic factors'. This point covers our possible need to conserve dollars by increasing our dependence on sterling sources of supply.

In oil matters we are not at present vitally dependent on the Americans but our position is not so strong that, other factors apart, we could contemplate with equanimity any serious dispute with them.

Telecommunications

The Americans have suggested a World Telecommunications Conference in 1946. We agreed in principle last year to their proposal for preliminary Commonwealth–United States conversations but the uncertainty regarding the future of Cable and Wireless Limited has made us responsible for a delay until November next when it is proposed to hold a United States–Commonwealth Conference at Bermuda. The principal points under discussion will be:— (*a*) rates, (*b*) direct radio circuits, (*c*) allocation of radio wavelengths and (*d*) the re-organisation of the International Telecommunications Union. On a long view the third of these points may be expected to prove the most difficult. The radio frequency spectrum is overcrowded, and our wavelength requirements may prove difficult to reconcile with those of the United States. The detailed allocation of wavelengths as distinct from the principles on which their distribution is based may not, however, come up just yet. At Bermuda the burning question is likely to be that of rates. On this the Commonwealth Telecommunications Conference put forward two alternative sets of proposals. The first constitutes the best offer we can made [*sic*] if we have to carry the consent of Cable and Wireless Limited. We do not think it would be acceptable to the Americans. The second would not be acceptable to Cable and Wireless Limited but could be put to the Americans if the Government have by then decided to purchase the

88

Company's shares and put into effect the Conference's proposals for the reorganisation of the Commonwealth telecommunications services. It presents reasonable prospects of agreement with the Americans. Our joint aim is the regulated reduction of rates throughout the world.

The Americans will have to be allowed to retain the direct circuits which they have opened for war purposes with some of the Dominions. On the general question, however, there is a conflict between the American desire to open direct circuits all over the world (e.g. in the Middle East) and thus create a United States net-work which will compete seriously with the Commonwealth telecommunications net-work, and our view that direct circuits should only be opened where the traffic justifies them and should be confined to terminal as distinct from transit traffic. Our aim is to avoid a wasteful multiplication of redundant installations. We can only hope to obtain some part of our desiderata by negotiation since we are unable to impose our views on the Americans. Only in Saudi Arabia where Cable and Wireless have a monopoly are we in direct conflict with the Americans under this head.

Civil Aviation

The International Conference on Civil Aviation at Chicago last November broke down largely on the conflict of views between the Americans and ourselves over the so-called 'fifth freedom' of the air.[5] This is the freedom to pick up passengers, mail and cargo in a second country and set them down in a third. Our proposals were regulatory rather than restrictive. They were designed to maintain a balance between the carrying capacity available and the traffic offering; and to divide the latter equitably between the countries operating on any given route, thus eliminating wasteful competition. Formally, the points at issue were referred to the Council of the Interim Civil Aviation Organisation at Montreal.[6] No great hopes were placed in this procedure, however, and in practice the way was left open for the conclusion by individual countries of bilateral civil aviation agreements, pending some further effort to bridge the gap and reach agreement on proposals which could be incorporated in a multilateral convention.

Since the Chicago Conference the Americans have energetically tried to negotiate bilateral agreements under which United States airlines would

[5] The Chicago Conference resulted on 7 December 1944 in four main agreements: the Interim Agreement on International Civil Aviation (which set up the Provisional International Civil Aviation Organization (P.I.C.A.O.)), the International Convention on Civil Aviation and the International Air Services Transit ('Two Freedoms') Agreement, signed by the United Kingdom and printed in B.F.S.P., vol. 148, pp. 20–38, 38–73 and 73–9, and the International Air Transport ('Five Freedoms') Agreement printed in Cmd. 6614 of 1945, International Civil Aviation Conference . . . Final Act and Appendices I–IV, Chicago, 7th December, 1944, pp. 57–60. For the British position on the fifth freedom see Parl. Debs., 5th ser., H. of L., vol. cxxxiv, cols. 565–74 passim, Volume I of this Series, No. 394, and the British aide-mémoire of 26 July 1945 printed in F.R.U.S. 1945, vol. viii, pp. 73–5.
[6] i.e. the Interim Council of P.I.C.A.O.

be accorded the unrestricted exercise of the fifth freedom. To this end they have appeared to subordinate more important political and strategic considerations. Beginning with the European neutrals they have concluded such agreements with Spain, Sweden, Switzerland, Eire and Iceland. They are pressing other countries in Europe and the Middle East to sign similar agreements.

Meanwhile, we ourselves have been in consultation with a large number of European and Middle Eastern Governments some of which share our views while others are wavering in the face of United States pressure. We have suggested to them that in negotiating with the Americans they should take into account not only their own interests but those of all present and potential operators, both long distance and regional. We have furnished them with draft standard clauses regulating fifth freedom traffic which we hope to incorporate in such agreements as we may conclude with other countries. We have recommended that they too should insist, when negotiating with the Americans or other countries, on the inclusion of similar provisions. It should be emphasised that we are not trying to resist the mutual extension of fifth freedom rights altogether. We are trying to ensure that they are accompanied by conditions that will protect those countries (particularly European and Middle Eastern) which, owing to the war and the arrangement by which the United States undertook the major construction of transport aircraft for war purposes, are handicapped in the development of their airlines, against cut-throat competition from the United States.

Inevitably the Americans have come to suspect that their failure to make progress has been due at least in part to our intervention. In April they asked for assurances that we would not oppose their efforts to acquire landing rights in the Near and Middle East for commercial air services, including the right to use suitable airports, especially those constructed or improved by the United States Government. To this we replied, after careful consideration by Ministers, that we have no intention of opposing the acquisition by the United States or any other Government of landing rights for civil aircraft in any country, in accordance with the Interim Agreement reached at Chicago, but that when we are consulted by other Governments regarding the negotiation of bilateral civil aviation agreements we naturally tender advice based on our own policy as expressed at Chicago.[7]

This policy has so far proved successful. Without straining our relations with the United States unduly we have maintained a front unbroken except by the neutrals listed in paragraph [sic] above. The position is precarious, however, and if we do not soon exchange a negative policy for a more positive one, we must expect to be charged with a 'dog in the manger' attitude by the United States and faced with the defection of some of the smaller countries under heavy United States pressure. Here,

[7] See *F.R.U.S. ibid.*, pp. 65–7 and 71–2, and cf. iv below.

however, we are severely handicapped by the policy of the Ministry of Civil Aviation. The latter are acutely under-staffed. They are behindhand with the formation of British European Airways and British Latin American Air Lines, the companies to which the operation of our services to Europe and South America have been allocated. They are short of even the minimum of aircraft with which to open commercial services even to the nearest European countries. This all leads them to prefer for the present a continuation of the arrangement by which services are operated by [U.S.] Air Transport Command on a military basis. (Lease-lend considerations and R.A.F. needs prevent the use of these same aircraft for civil purposes.) Some of the smaller countries have urged that it would make it easier for them to resist American pressure if we would conclude bilateral agreements with them. We are endeavouring to induce the Ministry of Civil Aviation to conclude bilateral agreements on their standard model with a number of countries, if necessary in advance of opening actual services. Unless we are successful in this, we appear unlikely to be able to hold the position as long as may be necessary.

It is particularly important that it should be held for the present. For there are signs in the United States of a dawning understanding of our viewpoint. For instance both the Chairman of the Civil Aeronautics Administration and the Chairman of the Civil Aeronautics Board have admitted the reasonableness of our proposals. The State Department, however, have not yet seen the light. Recent informal conversations with them have narrowed the gap but not closed it. They still claim the right to regard e.g. the New York–London service as the first 'leg' of a New York–Calcutta service and to fill up with 'fifth freedom' traffic any capacity which may be unfilled beyond London. In the present state of air transport this would skim off the cream—and more than the cream—from our air services. Moreover, by introducing an incalculable extraneous factor into traffic calculations it would hinder our own bilateral negotiations with other countries. Our own counter-proposals are flexible enough to safeguard reasonable American claims, and if we can hold the diehards off a little longer there is a good chance that reason may prevail.

R.A. GALLOP

CALENDARS TO NO. 21

i *28 Aug. 1945   RAFDEL (Washington) Tel. USLON 137* Text of letter from Mr. Crowley extending Lend-Lease in respect of shipping for 30 days after VJ day: cf. *F.R.U.S. 1945*, vol. vi, pp. 111–12 [UE 3760/32/71].

ii *31 Aug. – 11 Sept. 1945   Correspondence on reconsideration of Anglo–U.S. Petroleum Agreement* Exchange of letters between Mr. Bevin and Mr. Winant on forthcoming visit to London of Mr. H.L. Ickes (U.S. Secretary of Interior) for discussions on oil agreement; *Washington Tel. No. 6149* Mr. Ickes states changes proposed by U.S. are 'principally questions of wording and designed to avoid misunderstandings' [W 11774, 11905, 12149/12/76].

iii *20 Aug. – 14 Sept. 1945 Correspondence on Anglo–U.S. negotiations on civil aviation:* visit to London of Mr. Stokeley Morgan, Chief of Aviation Division of State Department; first meeting of Cabinet Committee on Civil Aviation on 14 Sept. considers memoranda C.A.C. (45)3, 4, 5; F.O. views on 'Order in the Air' [W 11174, 12092, 12234-5, 12285, 12574/24/802].

iv *5 Sept.–7 Oct. 1945 Civil Aviation in Saudi Arabia* Saudi Arabian Govt. informed that T.W.A.'s application to fly through Saudi Arabia is 'highly objectionable' to H.M.G.: Mr. Bevin is 'gravely concerned with our lack of enterprise in the air'; King Ibn Saud, although grateful for plain speaking, would appreciate constructive alternatives from H.M.G.; U.S. argument that they already enjoy fifth freedom rights is without foundation [W 11592, 12017, 12158, 13171, 13283/52/802; W 12856/24/802].

No. 22

Minute from Lord Keynes (Ottawa) to Sir W. Eady[1]

[T 236/437]

Top secret. Immediate   OTTAWA, *4 September 1945*

I attach, in duplicate, a revised version, prepared on the boat, of the draft[2] you saw before I left. There has been no important change of substance, but the form has been touched up throughout. The most significant changes are the following:

1. The preliminary matter has been re-written and the prospective adverse balance of trade presented in a more tentative form.

2. The third section presenting 'the first alternative' has been re-introduced.

3. The concluding section concerning the terms of the 'Credit' has gone over more completely to Brand's preference,[3] and virtually nothing is said about the terms at this stage. On further reflection the choice seemed to me to be between saying more or saying less and that the latter was the preferable alternative.

Nevertheless, although even vague references to the terms of credit have been omitted I gave a good deal of reflection to this matter whilst on the boat. I am increasingly doubtful about the prospects of a straight Grant-in-Aid. There will have to be some camouflage. Moreover, the best

[1] Lord Keynes visited Ottawa from 2 to 6 September: cf. No. 7, note 9, and see further No. 26. This minute was also addressed to Sir E. Bridges and the Chancellor of the Exchequer, and with the enclosed memorandum is printed in Moggridge, *op. cit.*, pp. 425–51.
[2] The memorandum printed below is a revised version of Lord Keynes' papers in Nos. 6 and 6.i(*a*) above: see No. 6, note 2, and cf. i below. Paras. 6–14 below correspond generally to paras. 9–18 of No. 6: Parts II, IV and V are the same as parts I, II and III of No. 6.i(*a*) with some verbal and statistical variation; Part III corresponds to Part III of the draft of 13 August (see No. 6, note 2), which was not included in the revised version in No. 6.i(*a*).
[3] Cf. No. 1.i and No. 17.

way of introducing this question now seems to me to be on the lines that our aggregate undertakings to all our creditors as a whole will be as high as we can safely promise. If, therefore, the U.S.A. want to share in priority to the Sterling Area creditors this means that the latter will get that much less. In the extreme limit where the U.S.A. has complete priority the whole scheme for releasing the Sterling Area balances would be frustrated. It is therefore in the general interests to go as near as is politically practicable to the opposite extreme.

I have been working at a short paper on a version of what could represent a 'credit' but on lines which it would not be unsafe for us to accept. I will send this shortly for your comments. There is, of course, no question at present of going beyond what is in the attached paper.

Moreover, I am still quite uncertain whether it will be advisable to present this document, at any rate until the discussions have made some progress. My feeling is now rather in favour of trying to get the Americans to show their hand before we attempt to be constructive. It may be politic that as many as possible of the points on which we can yield should appear to have been given away under a good deal of pressure rather than that they should be voluntarily preferred [*sic*] at the start.

As you will have gathered from recent telegrams the atmosphere is not particularly good at the moment. I am therefore keeping a very open mind as to the best means of approach until we have actually gone into the talks.

KEYNES

ENCLOSURE IN No. 22

Proposals for financial arrangements in the Sterling Area and between the U.S. and the U.K. to follow after Lend-Lease

GEN 89/1 [UE 4260/1094/53]⁴

Secret

I. *The present overseas financial position and prospects of the U.K.*

1. *Gold and Dollar Reserves.* Before making allowance for any additional cash outgoings in the last four months of 1945 as a result of the partial or complete suspension of Lend-Lease assistance and Canadian Mutual Aid, recent estimates indicate that the British net gold and dollar reserves at the end of 1945 might be of the order of $1.9 billions. The movement of these reserves since the beginning of the war and their composition are shown in detail in Appendix A.[5]

---

[4] The text here printed is that circulated on 12 September as GEN 89/1 to the members of a Ministerial Committee on Financial and Commercial Policy which had its first meeting on 14 September: see No. 32, and cf. Pressnell, *op. cit.*, Chapter 10(4).
[5] Not attached to filed copy.

2. The gold and dollar reserves of other parts of the Sterling Area are also shown in Appendix A. It will be seen that the dollar reserves are insignificant and present no more than a daily working balance. Gold reserves, apart from the substantial holding of South Africa and an amount held by India which is slightly in excess of the statutory minimum, are also insignificant. Thus, in the main, the gold and dollar reserves of the U.K. are the reserves of the whole of the Sterling Area (except South Africa) in the sense that it is only out of these reserves that the rest of the Area can be provided with dollars to meet purchases in excess of their current dollar earnings.

3. *British liabilities to overseas creditors* at the end of June 1945 stood at $13.4 billions. They are likely to approach $14.5 billions by the end of 1945, apart from any consequences of the end of Lend-Lease. In this event, the estimated net reserves of $1.9 billions at the same date will represent about 13 per cent of the liabilities. The distribution and composition of the liabilities are given in Appendix B.[5]

4. *The current adverse balance of the U.K.* In 1945 prior to V-J day the annual rate of overseas expenditure and income was running as follows, exclusive of munitions received under Lend-Lease and Canadian Mutual Aid:

$ Million

Import[s] excluding Munitions	5,000	Exports	1,400
Government expenditure Overseas	3,200	Net invisible Income and Sundry Repayments etc.	400
		Government receipts from U.S. and Dominions for their forces and munitions	1,400
	8,200		3,200
		Deficit	5,000
			8,200

This deficit was being covered roughly, as follows:

	$ Million
Lend-Lease (non-munitions)	2,000
Sterling Area credits, etc. (Net)	3,000
	5,000

The Mutual Aid accorded by the U.K. which might either be entered on both sides of the above account or, alternatively, like the volume of the munitions received under Lend-Lease and Mutual Aid, excluded from both, was running at the rate of about $2,000 million a year. The net effect of the termination of Lend-Lease (non-munitions) on the prospects of the last four months of 1945 has not yet been worked out with sufficient accuracy to be worth quoting.

5. *The prospective current adverse balance of the U.K. in 1946.* There are far too many uncertainties in this picture to allow any close estimates. But the broad results of our preliminary study of the prospects are given in the following paragraphs.

6. In the cost of imports of food and raw materials etc. an increase, rather than a reduction, is in sight compared with 1945, if the public are to be fed reasonably and employed fully, taking account of the fact that stocks are being currently drawn upon and that prices will be somewhat higher. The raw materials required to provide employment, though not always the same in character as those we now import, are unlikely to be reduced in aggregate, since the numbers to be employed in industry will be increased as a result of demobilisation. On the other hand some miscellaneous economies should be possible. One way and another our import programme (c.i.f.[6]) might be kept down to £1,300 millions which would be much the same volume as in 1945, excluding munitions and allowing for some rise in prices. Even this, with sterling prices at double pre-war, means considerable austerity. For our pre-war imports were £850 millions, that is (say) £1,700 millions at the assumed post-war price level. Thus the above figure assumes a reduction of 23 per cent below the volume of our pre-war imports and therefore presumes strict controls, in the absence of which an appreciably higher figure is to be expected as soon as supplies are available.

7. There will, of course, be a substantial economy in Government expenditure overseas but there is likely to be a considerable time-lag in reducing such expenditure for three reasons. In the first place, bills for much of the expenditure are received considerably in arrear, and we are responsible in India and Australia for winding up our munition contracts and for meeting cancellation charges. In the second place the withdrawal of our forces will be protracted on account both of lack of transport and of the slowness of the administrative machine. In the third place a substantial part of our existing Government expenditure overseas is concerned with policing and occupation tasks and the protection of lines of communication over a wide area, some of which is likely to continue throughout the year. It should, however, be possible to bring the annual rate of cost down to $1,200 millions or less before the end of 1946, although the cost during that year as a whole may be not much less than $1,800 millions. The cost of U.N.R.R.A. and other relief and rehabilitation overseas is included in these figures.

[6] Cost, insurance, and freight.

8. There are also certain items of *income* which arise out of the war and will fade away with it. In reckoning the current overseas balance, credit has been taken for income of $1,400 millions a year arising partly out of the personal expenditure of the American forces in this country ($460 millions in 1944 and probably as much as $240 millions in 1945) and mainly out of the contributions made by the Dominions towards the equipment and maintenance of their own divisions which has been provided by us in the first instance. These sources of income will have disappeared almost entirely by the end of 1945, but, allowing for time-lags in meeting old bills, and for possible repayments from the North-Western European Allies, they may amount, on optimistic assumptions, to as much as $600 millions in the year following V-J. Thus we put the net Government expenditure overseas in 1946 at (say) $1,200 millions. But this estimate is very uncertain.

9. Turning to exports there seems a reasonable hope of increasing these from an aggregate of $1,400 millions in 1945 to at least $2,400 millions in 1946. It is dangerous to exaggerate the probable rate of recovery. The processes of demobilisation and reconversion will present acute difficulties. The demands of civilian consumption will be pressing and must be met in some measure. Two industries, cotton textiles and coal mining, which made large contributions to the volume of our pre-war exports, will meet many obstacles in regaining their pre-war level and cannot be expected even to approach this level for some time to come. We must also allow for the time-lag in actual receipts from exports. Extreme energy and concentration on the objective of exports might succeed in bringing our receipts to double the 1945 figure which would be $2,800 millions. It will be safer, however, to base our present estimates on a figure of $2,600 millions whilst aiming at the higher figure as a target area [*sic* ?and] hoping to do even better.

10. We also hope for a considerable increase in the net income from our shipping and also for some steady improvement in other items of invisible income. It will be seen that the cost of imports has been reckoned above c.i.f. It follows that the earnings of our own shipping in bringing in our own imports has to be taken into account in assessing our invisible income. We are inclined therefore to put our net invisible income at the increased figure of $600 million.

11. On the assumption of an export and import price level double pre-war in terms of sterling, the prospects of 1946 can be summed up, subject to every possible reserve, as follows:—

$ Millions

Imports	5,200	Exports	2,600
Govt. expenditure		Invisible	
overseas (net)	1,200	Income (net)	600
			3,200
		Deficit	3,200
	6,400		6,400

12. The precariousness of this estimate must be again emphasised. If we are sufficiently hard pressed, we can do better. For this does not reflect the maximum possible austerity in domestic consumption or the maximum possible reduction in Government expenditure overseas by limiting, or contracting out of, our international commitments. Also it is extremely difficult to predict the rate of export recovery. Perhaps the minimum deficit in 1946 which it would be possible to organise is $2,500 millions and the maximum we need fear is $3,500 millions.

13. *The later years of the transition.* When we look beyond 1946 we are in the region of pure guess work. If by 1949 we can reach the goal of a volume of exports 50 per cent above pre-war, they will be worth $5,800 millions in that year. Assuming that we can combine this state of export business with keeping the volume of imports comfortably below the pre-war level, and that we can gradually curtail Government expenditure overseas, we shall about break even in that year. But this still makes no provision for any repayment of debts.

14. Assuming this result by 1949, which is, it should be emphasised, a hypothesis and not a forecast, and a gradual progress towards this from the 1946 deficit in the intermediate years 1947 and 1948, we are left with a cumulative deficit from the end of the war of (say) $4 billions as a (most unlikely) minimum and (say) $6 billions as a maximum which we ought not to allow ourselves to exceed. More probably the transitional period will be drawn out over a longer period than three years without the cumulative deficit, however, being necessarily outside the above range of figures though longer drawn out.

II. *The Character of the Problem*

15. It will be seen that the financial problem falls into two parts (*a*) the treatment of the sterling balances accumulated during the war and (*b*) our running adverse balance after the war and before we have fully restored our domestic economy.

16. The former is the less urgent problem if we consider only ourselves. For no one can make us release these balances faster than is

materially possible. Nevertheless, they directly react on the latter problem in two ways.

17. In the first place, our existing debts affect what additional amounts we can borrow to help the current position. Our considered view is that we cannot be expected, and will not agree, to pay a commercial rate of interest on the sterling war-debts incurred in the common cause. Nor shall we undertake to repay the capital sums at a greater rate than lies within our reasonable capacity. But we are not prepared to repudiate by unilateral action any part of our capital liability to those who came to our financial assistance without security and on a vast scale when we were in dire straits, or to subordinate them entirely to debts incurred subsequently.

18. We ask our American friends to agree that this is a proper attitude and that they will not ask us, or seek to induce us, to depart from it.

19. In the second place, it would cause very great disturbance to the national economies of some of our Sterling Area creditors and especially to their trade relations with the United States, if we could not begin from the start to release a marginal instalment of their sterling balances. For many countries in the Sterling Area will have a dollar deficit on current account as soon as supplies and transport are available. Since the Union of South Africa holds a large independent gold reserve, what follows does not apply to her. Nor does it apply to our creditors outside the Area. But the rest of the Area, as we have already explained have no significant gold or dollar reserves available either in their Currency Reserves or Central Banks. Their sterling balances in London comprise substantially the whole of the ultimate external reserves of their banking systems and of their note issues, which, more perhaps from habit and good will than from prudent calculation, they have been willing to entrust to us during the war. If in the early years we block these balances entirely within the Sterling Area, we shall throw their trade relations with countries outside the Area into serious confusion and will have been guilty, if there is any means of avoidance, of an abuse of confidence. This applies more particularly to the currency reserves of the Crown Colonies, which have not been entirely free agents in this matter. We have obtained their produce during the war, for our own use or (in some cases) to present it as reciprocal aid to the United States, largely in return for bits of paper, i.e., by expanding their note issues. The expectation has been that after the war, when supplies and shipping are again available, some at least of these bits of paper can be used to pay for essential imports.

20. Thus there is a certain marginal part of the sterling balances which we are under an honourable obligation to treat in the same way, and *pari passu*, with our own current adverse balance. There must be from the outset, that is to say, some minimum addition to our own current requirements to provide for the essential needs of certain Sterling Area countries, the financial systems of which are wholly centred on London.

21. Nevertheless it is our own running adverse balance in the period of

98

three to five years after the war which constitutes the major part of the urgent problem. This is greatly aggravated in the first year or two after victory in Asia by the fact that our military expenditure overseas will not sink to nothing at the hour of Japan's defeat, but must unavoidably continue at a heavy rate for an appreciable period thereafter; and also by the fact that we have incurred obligations to U.N.R.R.A., to our own liberated territories in the Far East, and arising out of the occupation of Germany and the pacification of Europe and Asia.

III. *The First of the Alternative Solutions*

22. It appears to us, after the most earnest study, that we are confronted, broadly speaking, with two alternative courses of action, both of which would require the good will of the rest of the world, but one of which we can carry out or attempt to carry out chiefly on our own initiative, whilst the other would only be possible by a general plan on the part of all the chief countries concerned and could not be executed without the aid of the U.S. There are, of course, certain compromises which are possible between the two alternatives set out below, partaking more of the one or more of the other but for clarity of exposition it will be better to stick at the start to the clear-cut alternatives.

23. The first alternative is to develop, and modify according to circumstances, the system of the Sterling Area as it has been evolved during the war, supported by Payments Agreements (on the model now existing with several European and South American countries) with countries outside the Area. It should be explained that under Payments Agreements a country agrees to hold in sterling, with or without limit, any favourable current balance it may accumulate with the Sterling Area, whilst we enter into corresponding obligations to it if the balance proves out to be the other way. Under such a system all sterling balances would enjoy full convertibility of exchange for current payments within the Sterling Area and between the Sterling Area and those outside countries accepting unrestricted Payments Agreements. Imports into the Area from countries, setting a strict limit to the maximum amount of sterling which they are willing to accumulate or requiring some proportion of such accumulations to be paid or guaranteed in gold or dollars, would have to be more strictly controlled and limited so far as possible to essentials, except to the extent that they were covered by exports to such countries from the Area. With a country declining a Payments Agreement altogether trade would have to be still more restricted; and the excess of imports from it into the Area over exports to it from the Area would have to be limited, necessarily, to what could be paid for by drawing on our gold and dollar reserves. A Payments Agreement along the above lines would be offered to every country including the U.S.

24. If the U.S. were to stay outside such a system, we could not rely on maintaining the Sterling Area Dollar Pool as it has existed during the war.

Sterling Area countries having a favourable current balance with the U.S. or some of them at least, would very likely insist on retaining their dollar surplus for their own use and would not agree to hand it over to the Pool, as they have done hitherto. The partial break-down of the Dollar Pool, with the Sterling Area arrangements continuing unchanged in other respects, would not, however, be to the general advantage and would certainly operate to the disadvantage of the United States. For it would not increase the dollars available to pay for American exports and would merely mean that the Sterling Area countries having a running deficit with the U.S. would be forced to limit their purchases still more strictly. The maintenance of the Dollar Pool is a way of ensuring that all the available dollars are in fact spent within the dollar area with the minimum of discrimination.

25. For this and other reasons such a system would have to be more rigid in relation to a country unwilling to enter into a Payments Agreement than it has been during the war. Hitherto (apart from certain very recent exceptions) the Exchange Control of any member of the Sterling Area has been entitled to obtain from the Central Pool any dollars required for imports considered essential and not obtainable within the Sterling Area. This measure of liberality was, however, only made practicable through the limitations set by difficulties of supply and transport. In peace-time conditions the above practice would have to be replaced by an annual dollar ration (as is already the case with Egypt). Individual members of the Area would, of course, be free to supplement their ration by borrowing from dollar sources though without any guarantee of the availability of their sterling resources for eventual repayment of such dollar liabilities. The principle underlying this procedure is simple and inevitable. All the dollars available from American imports and loans and from drawing within the limits of safety on the central reserves, would be made available in payment for American exports, and no more than all is possible.

26. This system, especially if the United States would accept a Payments Agreement, has certain advantages. The war-time system could slide off into it without any break in continuity. It might provide a highly elastic instrument for dealing with the unpredictable quantities of credit which will be required during the transitional period. It would offer some initial help to British exports which might accelerate the date at which equilibrium in the balance of payments could be achieved. Nor would it be essential, though highly convenient to the trade of both parties, that the U.S. should accept a Payments Agreement without limit of amount.

27. Moreover there would be no intention of maintaining such a system in its full rigour indefinitely. It is obvious that any system must break down eventually unless those concerned (more particularly the United Kingdom in this instance) can find means of reaching equilibrium in their balance of payments within a reasonably short period. When this equilibrium has been achieved, the transitional period will have to come to

an end and there will be no longer any obstacle to the adoption of general multilateral convertibility in respect of the proceeds of future current trade. There is nothing in the above arrangements, provided they are limited to a transitional period, which would prevent the U.K. from accepting forthwith the obligations of the International Monetary Fund. The possibility of a trans[i]tional period having the above character has been strictly preserved in Article XIV,[7] as indeed was essential pending the definite provision of any practicable alternative. Furthermore under the Bretton Woods Plan we should be entitled to put special restrictions on the subsequent use of the sterling balances accumulated before the end of the transitional period.

28. It would also be our intention to follow faithfully the provision of the Bretton Woods Plan that during the transitional period 'members shall have continuous regard in their foreign exchange policies to the purposes of the Fund, and, as soon as conditions permit, they shall take all possible measures to develop such commercial and financial arrangements with other members as will facilitiate [sic] international payments and the maintenance of exchange stability'. It would be our purpose to allow and arrange as free an exchange of sterling between Special Accounts under Payments Agreements as was mutually acceptable to the other countries concerned. And with the improving trend towards equilibrium, the necessary degree of restriction would be progressively reduced. If we have to adopt this system we should hope that it would be with the good will and close collaboration of all concerned. We on our part would do our utmost to minimise causes of friction and to use no more discrimination than is inherent in a system where trade is limited and conditioned by the separate availability of payment facilities.

29. Nevertheless on closer examination this alternative is seen to involve some serious difficulties. It is probably the best we can do if we have to solve the problem by ourselves and on our own initiative. It is not, in our judgment, impracticable for us to make the attempt to enter on the post-war period along those lines. But candour forces the admission that it is not as good as it has been made to look in the preceding paragraphs.

30. It will almost inevitably lead, in practice, though that would not be our deliberate intention, to a greater degree of bilateral trade negotiations than is in theory inherent in it. For countries, whether inside or outside the Area, having a favourable balance of trade with the rest of the Sterling Area, would be reluctant to receive payment in terms of sterling, the future availability of which would be uncertain. They would, therefore, attempt (signs of this are already apparent) to link their sales to us with a definite undertaking as to the scale on which we would export to them. The paradoxical situation would arise that our customers would tumble over one another to obtain as large as possible a quota of our limited supply of desired exports;—obviously a situation in some ways highly

[7] See No. 1, note 11.

attractive to us, yet no less obviously capable of producing very great frictions in international trading relations. The allocation of the dollar quota in the absence of an unrestricted Payments Agreement with the United States would provide another scramble. The whole object of the system would be to make the rest of the world lend us more money than they were inclined to lend and sometimes more than they possessed as a voluntary surplus; and the whole object of each other country, whether inside or outside the Sterling Area, would be to try to distort its operation so that they in particular carried as little of the aggregate burden as possible.

31. In short, the system would be forcing an unnatural pattern on international trading relations, though perhaps one advantageous to British short-term interests, over the whole of the formative post-war period, when as rapid a return as possible to normality is in the permanent interest of peaceful and profitable trade between nations. Moreover, we might reach an equilibrium in the balance of payments in these hot-house conditions in ways which we should be incapable of sustaining when we were deprived of them.

32. Above all, this alternative is open to the major objection that it is merely postponing the solution of the intrinsic problem to the end of the transitional period, without there being any reason to suppose, indeed the contrary that it would be any easier to solve then than it is now. By the end of the transitional period the British overseas sterling debt would have risen under these arrangements to $20 billions or more; and, for reasons already explained, many of the countries concerned would be in serious straits if the whole of their sterling resources became frozen. Yet this is how it would have to be. At the end of the transitional period the trade of a considerable part of the world would be thrown into sudden disorder. For it must be remembered that *during* the transitional period members of the Sterling Area and countries having Payments Agreements with it would have the free disposal over a wide area of their accumulated, and not merely their currently acquired, sterling balances. It is only at the end of the transitional period that they would suddenly lose any effective use of their standing sterling reserves.

33. In fact, when the transitional period came to an end (meaning by this the period before the U.K. had obtained equilibrium in its own balance of current payments), there would be, as there are now, only two alternatives, and they would be the *same* two. Either it would be necessary to continue more or less permanently the Sterling Area system supported by Payments Agreements as heretofore (though in the much more favourable conditions for its operation which would exist when the U.K.'s own balance was in equilibrium). In this case the zero-hour overseas holdings of sterling would become a sort of international fiduciary currency, the amount of which outstanding would remain more or less constant, slowly declining in so far as we became capable of repayment, though the holders of it would change in accordance with the fluctuations

of international surpluses and deficits, a state of affairs better for the holders than freezing;—in short a grand verification of the Law of Sir Thomas Gresham[8] (the first British Treasury official who played with the management of foreign exchanges), the very inferiority of sterling having ensured its final triumph. Or, alternatively, we should have to fall back on the second alternative, the explanation of which is about to follow. When this explanation has been read, it will be clear enough that, if something of this kind is desirable in the long run, it will be vastly easier to put it through now, than when the common emotions and close collaboration of the war are five years behind us in the valley of forgetfulness.

34. This is not to say that we should not decidedly prefer an essay in cunctation, which is what this first alternative really is, to accepting an unsatisfactory expedient or putting our name to what we have no sufficient confidence that we can honour.

IV. *The Second Alternative*

35. The peculiar war-time system of the Sterling Area has been a great success; for one may doubt whether the war would have been won without it. But it has resulted in the economic and financial affairs of half the world becoming inextricably intertwined with our own. Thus, unless means can be found to bring our burden within the limits of what is practicable, immeasurable and lasting confusion to the world's international economy cannot be avoided. The other alternative is therefore to organise, so far as may be, as being in the general interest and not only in our own, a liquidation of the financial consequences of the War amongst all those chiefly concerned who have won a common victory by a common effort. Not a complete liquidation—that would be asking too much. The British people are prepared to accept for themselves and their posterity as the price of deliverance, a burden of external indebtedness to their Allies which no one else will be expected to carry, not even the defeated enemy.

36. We ask our American friends, therefore, to join us in a realistic appraisal of the facts and to aid the acceptance of what, sooner or later, inevitably arises from them.

37. Including some allowance for overseas expenditure arising out of the war after the war is over, the actual and prospective indebtedness of the United Kingdom to the other countries in the Sterling Area[9] will be of the order of $12,000 to $14,000 millions. We think that it is right and

[8] The term 'Gresham's Law' was coined in 1857 by the Scottish economist H.D. Macleod for the principle that the worst form of currency in circulation regulates the value of the whole ('bad money drives out good'): Mr. Macleod attributed the first explanation of this principle to the Founder of the Royal Exchange, Sir Thomas Gresham (1519–1579), in 1558.

[9] *Note in original*: 'Debts outside the sterling area which will have to be dealt with separately, amount to nearly $4,000 millions making $16,000 to $18,000 millions altogether.'

proper and advisable to divide this aggregate in two parts. One part say $4 billions, would be on one ground or another, written off; the other part, say $8 billions would be made available to the holders by instalments for current purchases in any country without discrimination. To make this practicable in addition to our meeting our own running adverse balance in the early post-war period, we estimate that it would be necessary for the United States to provide a sum of $5 billions as an addition to our resources. The plan would enter into force as soon as possible after the end of the war, say at the end of 1946. By this means, whilst the Bretton Woods transitional period could not be formally terminated so soon, we should dispense immediately with any element of discrimination in the use of available sterling balances as between the other countries of the Area and countries outside the Area. Whilst the sterling balances accumulated before the end of the war could be made available to the holders only by instalments, whatever was made available from time to time would be available without discrimination, though this would not preclude additional special arrangements under 39 (viii) below. In particular, the existing arrangements governing the Sterling Area Dollar Pool would be entirely withdrawn.

38. This would afford a total relief of (say) $9 billions, provided to the extent of (say) $4 billions by our sterling creditors and of $5 billions by the United States. We also hope for some aid from Canada. The relief allowed by the sterling creditors would take the form of writing off of a part of their sterling balances. The relief afforded by the United States would be in the shape of a dollar credit which could be called upon, partly to finance our own dollar purchases during the transitional period and partly to give us the resources to implement our offer of general availability by instalments to the remaining uncancelled portion of the sterling balances and also to the current earnings of sterling by the Sterling Area countries after the end of 1946.

39. Before returning to the nature of the proposal as affecting the United States, it will be convenient to develop in greater detail the character of the plan which would be offered to the members of the Sterling Area, as follows:

(i)   A figure would be established for each Sterling Area country which fairly represented its cumulative war-time gains. The amount of its purchases or repatriations of sterling securities and of any gold supplied to it during the war would be added to its sterling balances at the end of the war, and also an estimated figure for net war receipts from the British Government accruing after the end of the war as a result of clearing up war accounts, movements of troops and demobilisation; whilst its pre-war sterling balances and any special receipts of a capital character would be deducted.

(ii)   We have already made a sufficient study of the particular cases to convince us that a uniform all-round formula would not work out fairly. There would, therefore, be separate discussions with each country concerned.

(iii)   We should set out from the starting point that an average writing off of rather more than one-third of their net war gains as estimated above would be generally appropriate except in so far as there were sufficient reasons for a different figure. Account would be taken of the local price-level at which the expenditure had been incurred, of the burden of war expenditure and war strain which they had undertaken in other ways, how far the accumulated sterling balances represent the surplus of normal trade due to war-time impediments to normal importing and how far they are due to special receipts from overseas which would have never accrued apart from the war, and any other relevant circumstances. It might be appropriate to bring various assets and counter-claims of our own into the settlement with certain countries. We think that after making allowance for exceptional treatment, justifiable and necessary in some cases, there would remain an amount approaching $4 billions appropriate for writing off.

(iv)   The negotiations with those concerned would be on a voluntary and agreed basis in the following sense. There would be no unilateral writing off of debt. It would, however, be represented that the possibility of freeing in the near future any significant portion of the sterling balances wholly depended on some measure of agreed general liquidation of the financial consequences of the war and in particular on assistance from the United States. Those countries which were not prepared to take a fair share of the burden could not expect to benefit from the facilities afforded by the United States for freeing sterling balances. That is to say, countries unwilling to come into the general scheme (after receiving all proper allowances under (iii) above) could not participate in its full benefits.

(v)   Let us assume that the plan proves generally acceptable and that the aggregate appropriate writing-off add[s] up to $4 billions out of an initial Sterling Area aggregate of $13 billions, leaving $9 billions still owing to the Sterling Area, apart from our debts outside the Area. We would then propose to free sterling to the equivalent of (say) $800 millions, divided between all the holders of sterling, to be available forthwith to meet their current adverse balances of trade without discrimination. It is obvious that this also could not be shared on a general formula—the amount of the immediately available proportion would have to depend *inter alia* on the proportion cancelled, on the scale of the country's external requirements and on the size of the country's pre-war sterling balances.

(vii [*sic*])   The balance of about $8 billions would be similarly released by instalments over a period not exceeding 50 years. Such subsequent releases (in addition to the initial $800 millions and the whole of net current earnings after the plan comes into effect) might commence in the fifth year at a rate of (say) $100 millions a year with the faithful intention, though without a premature obligation, gradually to step up the rate of releases as time and opportunity permit.

(viii)   In addition to these normal arrangements, if in subsequent years it were to suit us for any purpose or in any context to make the equivalent of loans overseas, including loans through the International Bank for Reconstruction of [and] Development, we should be free to offer a holder of unreleased sterling to release instalments in advance of any due date suitably discounted; so that in this case earlier agreed releases of this character might come to play the same part in our economy as, for example, the Export-Import Bank or loans to the International Bank in the case of the United States. As in the case of the Export-Import Bank such additional releases might be for the purpose of financing British contracts, but in so far as they were for use overseas they would be available without discrimination. The effect of such releases on the British economy will be much the same as our former regular foreign investment, and the time may come when it will prove a useful help to our policy of full employment to have the equivalent of such foreign investment always at hand without having to trouble about the credit of the borrower or the problem of subsequent payment of interest and capital. In fact we should be obtaining at some future date the same kind of advantage as the United States will be obtaining now if they fall in with this plan.

(ix)   It is not proposed that the unreleased portion should carry interest. The more rapid ultimate liquidation made possible by the complete elimination of interest on the portion temporarily frozen seems better in result and more appropriate to the character of loans which have not gone to the creation of commercial assets capable of earning interest. On the available sterling balances interest could, of course, be earned by the holders at (say) Treasury Bill rate, if they were retained in a liquid form, or at a higher rate, if they were to be invested in the United Kingdom, becoming liable in this case to any restrictions in force on capital withdrawals.

(x)   It should be made clear that this offer to the Sterling Area holders of sterling balances would have to be made contingent, for the time being at least, on their remaining members of the Area for certain purposes. We could not safely afford to undertake the releases of the balances on the scale indicated above if we had to assume that the whole of the amounts so released would be immediately withdrawn. Thus there would have to be an understanding that the releases of the war-time accumulations of sterling were to be used solely to meet adverse balances of trade on current account accumulating after the plan comes into operation and not to acquire gold or foreign assets; but when required, they would be available to pay for imports from any source without discrimination. Thus we should be accepting this part of our post-transitional obligations under the International Monetary Fund as soon as the proposed plan came into operation. Furthermore, even when we were retaining the ultimate discretion in our hands, we should endeavour to interpret the rules in any particular case in as free and liberal a manner as the state of our over-all resources permitted; and we believe that the recent experience of the members of the Sterling Area of the way in which we have handled our relations with them even in times when we were in the greatest possible difficulties will have given them confidence in the value of such a general understanding. In particular we should consider it our duty to release sterling balances in advance of the due date, to the full extent that our own resources and other liabilities would permit, to any member of the Sterling Area finding itself in temporary, unforeseen difficulties. Our object throughout is to avoid any absolute obligations beyond what we have confidence we can carry, with the full intention of being better than our word whenever our resources allow and the other party has need.

(xi)   Any favourable Sterling balance arising out of current trade which a Sterling Area country might earn after the plan comes into operation would be similarly available, on the same conditions, without discrimination.

(xii)   The arrangements outlined above are given as a specimen of what the separate negotiations might provide. They are not intended as a binding model in matters of detail. We should endeavour to work out separately in collaboration with each particular country a technique which involved the least possible interference with their normal banking arrangements and the interests of private persons. Here again we believe that we can operate in practice a much better and freer system than any to which it would be safe for us to commit ourselves as a binding obligation.

(xiii)   We believe that the other countries in the Sterling Area can be made to see that their acceptance of this general scheme is as much in their interest as in ours. This does not mean that each will not strive to the utmost to get out of it as much as possible for themselves and it will need resolute diplomacy and great determination on our part to achieve a fair and balanced all round settlement. Nevertheless they are all of them keenly aware of the limitations on what is within our power, and that there is no means on earth by which they can get more than is within our power. If, therefore, the United States is prepared greatly to increase our capacity on condition that the Sterling Area countries also play their fair part in liquidating the financial consequences of the war so as to bring the burden which we (and we alone) will continue to carry within tolerance, they will understand that the choice for them can only lie in the last resort between coming into the plan and sharing its benefits or staying out and foregoing them.

(xiv)   If, nevertheless, there are any countries in the Sterling Area which finally reject a settlement which seems fair in relation to ourselves and to the other participants and to the ultimate governing conditions of the whole plan, we should invite them to withdraw from the Area. Henceforward they would be entirely free to make their own arrangements. But their existing sterling balances would not share in the initial release of available sterling, nor would they carry interest. It would be our purpose and intention to discharge them in due course, but they would have, necessarily, to rank behind our other commitments, and we could give no prior undertakings as to the dates or terms of release.

V. The Proposed Plan in Relation to the United States

40. Our gold and dollar reserves of $2 billions, of which not more than $1 billion could be drawn upon except in the gravest emergency, are so small in relation to the other quantities in the picture that no plan can be built upon them otherwise than as a minor and secondary support. In the absence of any other support we should run through the whole of our available gold and dollar reserves within less than a year after the end of the war.

41.[10] Our suggestion is, therefore, that, to help to solve the international problem of the liquidation of war-time indebtedness, the United States should place at our disposal a sum of $5 billions in three instalments, $2 billions in the first year and $1.5 billions in each of the next two years. This figure has not been arrived at, and cannot be justified by, any exact calculation, and is based on a broad judgment of the necessities of the case. It has to cover four distinct liabilities:

(a) our own running adverse balance during the transition apart from what we can [obtain] from other sources, (b) the obligation to release instalments of their sterling balances to members of the Sterling Area, (c) the settlement of our war-time debts outside the Area and (d) any liabilities to the U.S. arising out of war disposals and the final wind-up of lend-lease. We should have liked to have kept to a lower figure of (say) $3–4 billions, but the magnitude of the various obligations now facing us lead[s] us to feel that with less than $5 billions we could not accept the responsibility of the obligation to make sterling available on the scale suggested above or of relaxing the existing Sterling Area arrangements so soon as the end of 1946. If this proves insufficient, as it possibly may, we must meet the resulting problem in the light of the surrounding facts as and when it arises. On the basis of $5 billions we should be ready to face the risks and responsibilities of a settlement on the general lines indicated above.

42. On what grounds can we make such an unprecedented suggestion to the Administration of the United States?

---

[10] Mr. T.L. Rowan, Principal Private Secretary to Mr. Attlee, attached the following note for the Prime Minister to this paper in preparation for the meeting of Ministers on 14 September (see note 4): 'P.M. This interminable paper is summarised—or rather comes to a conclusion—in para. 41. T.L.R. 13/9' (PREM 8/35).

43. Under Lend-Lease we have already enjoyed an extraordinary measure of liberality. Moreover, our difficulties insofar as they arise out of war-time accumulations of sterling and not out of our running deficit immediately after the war, are precisely due to the fact that we have not had the benefit of similar lend-lease arrangements with other countries; though we must remember that most of these other countries are poor countries or undeveloped countries and countries not so rich as ourselves and, in some cases, hitherto heavily indebted to us, and that they have in fact given us invaluable and even decisive assistance in the war through their having been willing to entrust all their resources to us without security or guarantee, including in some cases their net dollar earnings and to continue doing so after their sterling balances had vastly exceeded any figure even in the remotest anticipation when the arrangements were first made. Moreover, the proposed plan would in fact require of them contributions to the common cause not disproportionate to the contributions of others, if regard is had to their relative wealth and real resources in proportion to their population.

44. In the first place, we can commend these suggestions to the United States in that they may be a sufficient, and perhaps an indispensable, condition of establishing after the war, the type of commercial and financial relations between nations which they wish to see established, and which we, too wish if it can be managed. The object is, as already stated, to facilitate the liquidation of indebtedness arising out of the war on a scale sufficient to allow a return to normal practices at an early date. Not ourselves only are concerned in all this. The financial arrangements of half the world are so entangled with our own, that the pattern of world trade and finance as a whole is deeply involved.

45. But there is also an immaterial element. For nearly two years the United Kingdom with her small population having no support except the steadfastness of the distant members of the British Commonwealth, held the fort alone. Everything we had in energy, man-power and possessions was thrown into the furnace, with an intensity of purpose and eager willingness on the part of all our people. The effort and sacrifices were successful. It cannot then appear to those who have borne the burden of many days that it is a just and seemly conclusion of this sacrifice to be left, as the price of what has happened, with a burden of future tribute to the rest of the world, and mainly to our own Allies, beyond tolerable bearing. Our people would not accept with a quiet mind what was coming to them, when the full meaning of all this came to be felt in the burdens and privations of daily life for many years after the war, and it is by man's feelings, and only so, that the stable foundations of society within and without countries are disturbed. Moreover, we should be prevented from sharing, as we wish and intend, in the responsibility for the reconstruction of the ravaged world and in affording material support for the economic international institutions which are the best hope of a new order of peaceful intercourse between nations.

46. On what terms do we hope or expect such assistance? We would prefer to place our position without reserve before the Administration of the United States and discuss frankly what is right and reasonable without attempting to make any definite proposal in advance of such discussions. We do not yet know whether or how far the United States will favour the general principles outlined above for partially liquidating the financial consequences of the war in the interests of an early return to normal conditions on terms which, in the phrase of Article VII of the Mutual Aid Agreement, will not unduly burden international commerce.

47. Some further figures relating to the war effort of the United Kingdom and on the relation of Mutual Aid to lend-lease are given in Appendix C.[5] If it is thought useful to analyse more deeply how the post-war financial problem has arisen, all possible data will, of course, be made available. But the explanation can be summed up very completely in a few sentences. The financial difficulties of the United Kingdom during and immediately after the war are more than fully accounted for by three factors:

(i) In the period before Lend-Lease, or rather before Lend-Lease came into full effect $3 billions, which constituted almost the whole of the British gold and other reserves, was expended in the United States to pay for munitions (which involved the building up of a largely new munitions industry in the United States) and other purchases required for the war.

(ii) Throughout the war the United Kingdom has been mainly responsible, without any significant assistance from any other quarter except the Government of India, for the local cash expenditure required for military operations over a wide area of Africa and Asia, extending from Tunis to Burma through Egypt, the Middle East and India, which has amounted to some $10 billions and may be higher before the last bills have been paid. Yet it was this expenditure which threw one enemy back at the gates of Egypt and the other at the gates of India.

(iii) It was the very fact of Lend-Lease from the United States, Mutual Aid from Canada and the arrangements with the Sterling Area which made it possible for us to abandon our foreign trade and support a total concentration into the war industries and the armed forces which would otherwise have been impracticable. If it had been our role to maintain and expand our foreign trade with a view to the assistance of others, we should find ourselves in a vastly better position to-day to recover post-war equilibrium, even if we had given away the whole of the net proceeds of our war-time exports.[11]

[11] In the Foreign Office Mr. Coulson minuted on 14 September that this was 'an admirable document', and explained the following connexion between it and commercial policy. 'We know the U.S. are anxious for multilateral trade conditions to be established as early as possible. Lord Keynes' paper shows that this is only possible if the settlement of our sterling area debts and our current deficit on normal trade is solved in a big way including

i *11 Sept. 1945   Memo. by Mr. Grant (Treasury) on Lord Keynes' memo. in No. 22,*
comparing proposals with those in Nos. 6 and 6.i(a) [T 236/439].

the provision of an American credit.' On the same day Lord Keynes was informed in
BABOON 32 that Mr. Dalton had read the paper 'with great interest . . . He agrees with the
view expressed in your covering minute that it would be inadvisable to hand in this
document. It is his strong view in present circumstances that it would be much better to
confine discussions to your great powers of oral exposition, in which he has supreme
confidence.'

No. 23

British Missions (Washington) to Cabinet Offices[1]
(Received 6 September, 1.40 a.m.)

NABOB 26 *Telegraphic* [UE 4109/32/71]

Immediate. Secret   WASHINGTON, *5 September 1945, 11.51 p.m.*

Reference NABOB No. 24.[2]

1. Clayton told Brand that he understood that draft telegram had now
been put before President but he did not know whether President had
approved nor did he reveal its contents. In a private conversation Thayer
and Cramer told Lee that telegram would probably be a short one to the
effect that President agreed that consideration of terms for pipeline
supplies should await arrival here of Keynes Mission and that our
requirements from the pipeline should continue to move in the
meantime.[3] On this latter point we were told this morning by FEA that
order stopping movement had been rescinded. At the time of telegraphing this action has apparently not taken effect down the line and

[1] Also sent to Ottawa for the information of Lord Keynes.
[2] This telegram of 4 September referred to NABOB 21 of 3 September in which Mr.
Brand had informed Sir W. Eady that Mr. Clayton, to whom he had given a copy of Mr.
Attlee's message to President Truman (No. 20), 'had agreed that ample opportunity should
be afforded to U.K. Mission to discuss the terms and that there would be no break in
supplies', although this must be regarded as unofficial as he had not yet spoken to Mr.
Byrnes or Mr. Truman. 'Clayton urged it was highly desirable every effort should be made
to prevent supplies coming forward which we did not need. I assured him all missions were
already under urgent instructions in this respect' (UE 4019/32/71).
NABOB 24 stated that no decision had apparently yet been taken by the President, but
meanwhile there were 'rumours that Crowley is causing difficulties while order freezing
movement of supplies has not yet been rescinded . . . In general we feel that we would be
ill-advised to press Clayton or our other friends strongly at present juncture. In other words
we must leave Prime Minister's message to have its own effect but rely on Clayton to keep us
in touch and do his best to help us' (UE 4065/32/71).
[3] The text of a message to this effect from President Truman to Mr. Attlee, printed in
F.R.U.S. 1945, vol. vi, p. 117, was transmitted to the Foreign Office in Mr. Balfour's telegram
No. 6075 of 6 September (UE 3990/32/71).

supplies are still being held up. We are however pursuing question vigorously with FEA and other agencies concerned.

2. In private talk referred to, Thayer and Cramer told Lee in confidence that according to Crowley he had never been consulted about Clayton letter[4] nor indeed heard of it until recently. Without saying so directly they made it clear that they doubted the validity of Crowley's statement but said that even if Crowley had seen the letter beforehand he clearly interpreted it in quite different manner from Authorities in London. They added that in any event question was only of academic interest now since they wished to make it clear to Lee that following on consultations in the last two days between White House, State Department and FEA (at which Byrnes, Clayton and Crowley had all been present) United States Administration were agreed 'from top to bottom' that only terms which United States Administration could accept were cash payment in full or Crowley Credit Terms.[5] It had been decided that any other course would raise such difficulties for United States Administration vis-à-vis other lend lease countries taking requirements from the pipe line (e.g. the Russians and the Chinese, both of whom had tried hard to obtain concessions on 3 (c) terms) that it would be essential to clear this matter up with Keynes Mission before any general negotiations began by securing agreement of United Kingdom Government to adoption of one of above courses. Matter could not be 'left in the air' or otherwise other countries would run out of their acceptance of Crowley terms. They expressed private view that full payment in cash might conceivably look rather queer as a prelude to negotiations for extensive financial assistance, but they agreed that if we decided in favour of this alternative that would clear position that if Crowley Terms were accepted acceptance could be made subject to formula as in paragraph 6 of NABOB 11.[6] When Lee asked why payments for supplies from pipeline should be singled out from other financial problems connected with winding up of lend lease and should alone be made subject to settlement on pre-ordaine[d] terms, answer was that this was considered standpoint of United States Government and that in any event other problems (e.g. payment in respect of stocks, fixed lend lease assets, etc) varied very widely between lend lease countries.

3. Thayer expressed hope that we would discuss problem with Keynes immediately on latter's arrival and if possible be prepared at once to intimate acceptance of Crowley's terms or pay cash so as to get this troublesome question out of the way before main negotiations were begun. Otherwise atmosphere would undoubtedly be difficult. Their main purpose was to make it clear that White House, State Department and FEA were all united in attitude summarised in preceding paragraph and that this would at once become apparent as soon as discussions with Keynes opened. Apart from asking questions Lee did not attempt to argue merits of matter directly with them. Neither did he explore possibility

[4] See No. 20, para. 5.   [5] See No. 16.   [6] No. 19.

(which in any event now seems pretty hopeless) of their being willing to let supplies move forward 'on the cuff' leaving settlement to be determined later in light of outcome of overall discussions.

4. Foregoing was communicated to Lee in strict confidence and should not be quoted or referred to in any communication with Americans. Thayer is very close to Crowley in these discussions and we see no reason to doubt truth of his statements as to attitude of United States Administration.

CALENDAR TO No. 23

i *3 Sept. 1945 British Missions (Washington) Tel. NABOB 22* Proposes to include Dominions' requirements in any understanding reached with F.E.A. on pipeline supplies, but if U.K. agreement forms part of a total financial settlement Dominions will have to negotiate their own terms [UE 4025/32/71].

No. 24

British Missions (Washington) to Cabinet Offices
(Received 8 September, 2.15 a.m.)

NABOB *32* Telegraphic [UE *4137/32/71*]

Most immediate. Secret　　　　WASHINGTON, *8 September 1945, 12.23 a.m.*

From Keynes.[1]

1. In view of the much more important main negotiations we are anxious not to start off by making unduly heavy weather about issues arising from the termination of lend lease especially in cases where even if we could extort some concessions we have no reason to hope for much. I have two particular issues in mind.

2. The first relates to the terms on which we agree to receive what we require from pipeline. The Prime Minister's intervention[2] secured for us a resumption of loadings coupled with agreement that the settlement of terms should be deferred for discussion with my mission. But in view of what is reported in NABOB 26[3] we think it may be wise to accept Crowley's proposal with the proviso in paragraph 6 of NABOB 11[4] perhaps expressed more definitely. This does not mean that we should wish to act until the information in NABOB 26 is clearly confirmed. But we should like to have authority to yield very early in the discussions if this seems to all of us here the best course.

3. I was at one time much attracted to the alternative of paying cash. I agree with you that Davidson's estimate of 900 million dollars in the

---

[1] Lord Keynes had arrived in Washington on 7 September.　　　[2] See No. 20.
[3] No. 23.　　　　　　　　　　　　　　　　　　　　　　　　　　　　　[4] No. 19.

pipeline reported in BABOON 17[5] is much too high. But the estimates of the missions here of their requirements appear to add up to 500 to 600 million dollars. We shall hope for some significant economy on this after further discussion with them and screening by you. But even so the total seems much too high for it to be worth while to offer cash merely as a demonstration. After all Crowley is prepared to agree that the credit terms he now asks for will be superseded by whatever terms emerge out of the main negotiations.

4. The next point relates to the question whether we should struggle to obtain a continuation of military lend lease within a limited range. The President's directive report[ed] in NABOB 34[6] means that we cannot get a settlement on the lines contemplated before I left London without making much [sic] fuss and trouble than seems desirable. In spite of BABOON 14[i] recent calculations made here convince us that even if we were to succeed, the excess of what we should get on lend lease over what we should have to provide on reciprocal aid would be very small. All here would therefore like to abandon the effort to get the President's directive re-written and extended.

5. On the other hand it does seem worth while to us here to accept the President's directive for what it is worth provided that it is clear that this does not involve a continuation of reciprocal aid or at any rate subject only to the same limitations as the proposed very trifling continuation of lend lease. Reciprocal aid on the same conditions could not amount to more than a trifle. Our proposal is therefore that we terminate reciprocal aid for U.K. account as from September 2nd over the whole field subject to the above possible insignificant exception and accept the President's limited offer which indeed it would be rather churlish to refuse.

6. Moreover, the President's directive is capable either of a strict or a liberal interpretation. I am aware that the service departments attach importance to their continuing to acquire from the American forces in the Far East certain facilities previously arranged. Some of these at least might be brought within the terms of the President's directive by a commander on the spot who was ready to interpret them with reasonable liberality. Thus we think that the President's directive, though disappointing, is worth having provided it carries with it no implication of a disproportionate continuance of reciprocal aid.

7. It would be very helpful to have a reply reaching me by Monday[7]

---

[5] This telegram of 6 September is not printed. Mr. A.E. Davidson was a General Counsel to the F.E.A.

[6] This telegram of 8 September (see i below) transmitted the text of a directive to the American Joint Chiefs of Staff on military lend-lease policy approved by President Truman on 5 September: cf. *F.R.U.S. 1945*, vol. vi, pp. 129–30. The directive constituted the formal termination of military lend-lease, confirmed in a letter of 10 September from Mr. Patterson to Sir H. Self, the text of which was transmitted in NABOB 41 of that date, not printed (UE 4177/32/71).

[7] 10 September 1945.

evening Washington time as the talks are likely to begin on Tuesday and it may be a good plan to start off by making promptly any concessions which we feel to be inevitable sooner or later.[8]

CALENDAR TO NO. 24

i *5–8 Sept. 1945   Termination of Military Lend-Lease: Tels. BABOON 14 & 15 to Washington* giving estimates of value of military Reciprocal Aid and essential munitions requirements from U.S.A.; *Meeting of British War Supplies Committee (B.W.S.C.)* takes note of BABOON 15 and agrees 'that subject to further examination of the figures and to consultation with London it would appear not to be to our advantage to continue military lend-lease and reciprocal aid if food for British forces were not eligible for the former'; *NABOB 33* refers to B.W.S.C. meeting and to President's Directive in NABOB 34 (see note 6) [T 236/465; CAB 122/1471; UE 4138, 4139/32/71].

[8] Mr. Grant sent copies of this telegram and of NABOB 33 and 34 (see i) to Sir E. Bridges on 8 September with a note that he agreed with Lord Keynes' proposals on pipeline financing and military lend-lease: 'On the first point, the Prime Minister having secured the essential question of principle which was that we were not to be bounced unilaterally before Keynes' arrival, it seems to me that honour is satisfied. I should feel most unhappy about going on to a cash basis, since it gives such an opportunity to the Americans to bleed us during the course of protracted negotiations. If we accept the credit provisionally we are in a much stronger position. The second point may have minor administrative inconveniences, but given the fact that a Presidential directive has been issued, I think it would be a great mistake to fight it' (T 236/1685).

In BABOON 23 of 10 September Lord Keynes was informed that his suggestions were agreed. On pipeline financing it was assumed that he would 'impress on the Americans our extreme reluctance to enter into any arrangement so inappropriate to our general economic position, and that this concession in no way commits us on the main issue. We assume also that there will be no question of applying this to stocks in the U.K.' Lord Keynes was further instructed to secure that U.S. Commanders were notified that Reciprocal Aid had also ended on 2 September and that payment should therefore be made for military supplies (UE 4137/32/71).

No. 25

Dominions Office to the Governments of Canada, Australia, New Zealand and South Africa

D. No. 1657 Telegraphic [AS 4640/40/2]

Secret   DOMINIONS OFFICE, *8 September 1945, 6.50 p.m.*

Meat negotiations with the Argentine.

As you will be aware, the United Kingdom authorities have for considerable time past been anxious, in view of serious meat supply position, to negotiate with Argentine Government a meat contract to replace former annual or biennial contracts. Last of these expired towards

115

end of 1944, since when supplies have been obtained on month to month basis.

2. The view taken in Washington of the Argentine Government, from which international recognition had, at the American instance, been withheld, led United States Government last year to apply to United Kingdom Government the strongest pressure to conclude no long-term meat contract. To this pressure we reluctantly yielded in interests of preservation of Anglo-United States collaboration in a wider sphere. When normal relations were, by international agreement, resumed with Argentina last April, political reasons for refraining from concluding such a contract lapsed, and it was with explicit United States approval that negotiations with this object were at once reopened in London.[1]

3. Subsequently, arrangements were made for Mr. Turner, the Director of Meat in Ministry of Food, to proceed to Argentine, where, for past two months he has been engaged in negotiations with a view to conclusion of a contract for the purchase of meat by United Kingdom on behalf of the United Nations.

4. On 21st August Turner reached agreement in principle with Argentine authorities on prices for the main classes of meat for shipment to United Kingdom and other United Nations, in accordance with allocations made by Combined Food Board.[2] Although, however, agreement has been reached in principle on main items, there remain a number of details which it is proposed to endeavour to settle in consultation with Argentine Embassy in London after Turner's return. Intention is that, in interests of maintenance of production and supplies, contract should run for four years from end of 1944 contract (with price revision clause to operate at end of two years).

5. Argentine authorities have not, meantime, guaranteed to ship any specific quantity of meat, but will continue, as they have done since termination of previous contract, to keep Ministry of Food informed of quantities available for shipment each month.

6. Meanwhile, however, United States objections to the contract have been revived, not now, at any rate ostensibly, on political grounds, but on ground that long-term arrangements of this kind are opposed to conception of non-discrimination, which it is hoped will be one of guiding principles of post-war commercial policy. This aspect has been discussed with United States authorities in Washington, where Turner has broken his return journey to this country, and it has been pointed out to them (a) that proposed agreement is of special nature arising out of wartime conditions and vital needs of United Kingdom and other countries, (b) that United Kingdom is buying not merely for itself, but also for liberated

---

[1] See Sir L. Woodward, *op. cit.*, vol. iv, pp. 75–80, and the British *Aide-Mémoire* of 2 June printed in *F.R.U.S. 1945*, vol. ix, pp. 538–9. Cf. also Volume I of this Series, No. 290, note 3.

[2] On 21 August the Argentine Government also presented a note denouncing the Anglo-Argentine Trade Agreement of 1 December 1936 (printed in *B.F.S.P.*, vol. 147, pp 610–45) with effect from 21 February 1946.

countries, and (c) that shipments would be in accordance with C.F.B. allocations. We have not yet received the further views of United States in light of this discussion.

7. A further telegram will be sent when fuller details become available after Turner's arrival in this country.

CALENDARS TO NO. 25

i *14 Aug. 1945 Argentine meat contract: letter from Mr. Hadow (Washington) to Mr. Perowne* Conversations with Mr. Rockefeller and Mr. Avra Warren (Director of Office of American Republic Affairs, Dept. of State) on U.S. objections to a four-year contract [AS 4273/40/2].

ii *2 & 17 Sept. 1945 Mr. Balfour (Washington) Tel. No. 5975* Discussions on Argentine meat contract between Mr. Turner and State Dept. officials, who feel obliged to object on grounds of principle; *Washington Despatch No. 1187 enclosing State Dept. Aide-Mémoire of 13 Sept.* welcoming British assurances that meat contract is a 'special case during the transitional period and that it does not reflect the long-run commercial policy of the United Kingdom', and giving information on U.S. provision of fuels for Argentina (cf. No. 14.v) [AS 4560, 4942/40/2].

No. 26

Letter from Mr. Hall-Patch (Washington)[1] *to Sir A. Cadogan*

[*UE 4370/1094/53*]

WASHINGTON, *8 September 1945*

Dear Cadogan,

The visit to Canada was more successful than we had dared to hope. By various methods of financial jugglery (to which the Canadians have been willing partners) we are almost certainly $300 million dollars better off than we thought we were when we left London: if all goes well we may possible [*sic*] be better off by $500 millions. This has only been possible by the Canadians conceding all the points they possible could in our favour. The helpful and generous attitude of the Canadian officials has been quite outstanding. They have carried their Ministers with them with possibly one exception, i.e. Mr. Saint Laurent, the Minister of Justice, who represents Quebec. He made some rather tiresome reserves but finally accepted the proposals put forward by his minist[e]rial colleagues with whom we had been dealing. The net result is that supplies will come forward from Canada without financial hindrance until the end of the year. This is all very satisfactory and I only wish I could feel sure that we

---

[1] Mr. Hall-Patch, together with Mr. Harmer of the Treasury, had accompanied Lord Keynes on his visit to Ottawa and thence to Washington.

will be treated here in the same generous manner. On present indications this seems unlikely. But usually in this country first appearances tend to be deceptive and when it comes to the point our American friends may be more generous than they seem disposed to be now. In any event it will be of great help in presenting our case here to be able to cite the very generous treatment we have received at the hands of the Canadians.

The announcement made in the Canadian House of Commons[2] does not give the impression that the settlement is as satisfactory as it is in fact likely to be. This is because the present Canadian Government relies to a great extent on a French Canadian bloc in the House of Commons which is not very anxious to meet us, and does not wish, in any circumstances, to appear more generous to us than the Americans. The public announcement will, therefore, read as if we were being treated exactly as all the other recipients of Mutual Aid from Canada, whereas we are being treated much more handsomely. If cash can be considered as the substance, and fair words the shadow, we have succeeded in seizing the substance and the shadow has eluded us. I see no reason to quarrel with this outcome.

The above applies only to the winding up of Lease Lend which is the most immediate problem. We could not, naturally, go very far with the Canadians on our larger financial requirements until we had spoken with the Americans. We confined ourselves therefore to explaining our plight in detail, and we received some very useful hints from Towers (the Governor of the Bank of Canada) as to how to present our case in the most palatable form to the Americans. We are assured of sympathetic treatment from the Canadians when we have cleared the ground with the Americans. So far so good.

The meetings with the Americans are scheduled to commence on September 11th or 12th. We hope between now and then to go over the ground fully with Lord Halifax and to decide with him the tactical scheme to be employed. Meanwhile we have prepared various papers covering the main questions: these will be revised in the light of the discussions on tactics which we are to have with the Ambassador.

I attach a tentative list[3] of the British Members of the Committees which

[2] See No. 7, note 9.
[3] Not printed. The following U.K. members were proposed for the Top Committee and Committees i–iii:

Top Committee: Lord Halifax, Lord Keynes, Mr. Brand, Sir H. Self, Mr. Hall-Patch;
i (Finance): Lord Halifax, Lord Keynes, Mr. Brand, Mr. Harmer, Mr. Hall-Patch;
ii (Lend-Lease): (Lord Keynes), Mr. Brand, Sir H. Self, Mr. M.I. Hutton (Senior Officer of the British Food Mission in Washington), Mr. Harmer;
ii(a) (Military Sub-Committee): Sir H. Self, Lt.-Gen. Macready, Air Marshal Colyer, Rear Admiral J.W.A. Waller (British Admiralty Delegation), General Sir W. Venning, Mr H.O.R. Hindley (British Air Commission);
iii (Commercial Policy): Lord Halifax, Lord Keynes, Mr. Brand, Mr. J.H. Magowan (Minister (Commercial) in H.M. Embassy in Washington), Mr. Hall-Patch, Mr. Helmore
The Secretariat for the various committees included Mr. Lee, Mr. R.B. Stevens (Secretar

have been set up to parallel the American Committees which have been proposed by the State Department. I have specified that the approval of the Ambassador to this list will be necessary before it is communicated to the Americans. The crucial Committees from our point of view are the Top Committee, and Committees (i) and (iii). The Top Committee will act as Steering Committee and meet relatively infrequently, but I hope the Ambassador will feel able to attend Committees (i) and (iii) (particularly the former) as frequently as possible because it is in those Committees that the large issues will be crystallised, and delicate negotiations will be necessary.

Committee (i) is the hub around which everything else will revolve. Makins will act as the Ambassador's alternate, and I have also arranged to attend regularly. There may be a little feeling in the Treasury Delegation that there should not be two Foreign Office representatives on this purely financial Committee, but I have said that I propose to attend anyway and they can disguise me as an observer if they wish. It is important that there should be a F.O. representative who follows *all* the discussions on the Finance Committee, so that if anything goes wrong it can be picked up at the Top Committee. The Ambassador and Makins have many other calls on their time and may not be able to attend regularly when the discussions enter the active stage.

Committee (iii) which deals with Commercial Policy may well also be very important if the Americans wish to tie us down tightly as the price of financial assistance. In that event we may require reinforcements from London. Should things develop in this way, Helmore, (of the Board of Trade) and Magowan, will be able to advise as to the nature of the reinforcements required. In any case if important questions arise for discussion in this Committee I will endeavour to ensure that the Ambassador attends and that things are kept in their right prospective [*sic*]. As things stand, at present, we cannot really go very deeply into Commercial Policy questions until we have further guidance from Ministers who, we understand from Helmore, are now giving serious attention to this subject.

Yours sincerely,
E.L. HALL-PATCH

General of the British Civil Secretariat in Washington), Mr. Goschen, Mr. J.P. Summerscale (Commercial Counsellor in H.M. Embassy in Washington), and Mr. C.R. Woodyard (British Civil Secretariat).

No. 27

Cabinet Offices to British Missions (Washington)

BABOON *21* Telegraphic [*UE 4142/1094/53*]

Secret   CABINET OFFICES, *9 September 1945, 12.15 p.m.*

Hawkins saw Liesching and Magowan on Saturday[1] about resumption of discussions on commercial policy. He read a cable from Clayton[2] to the effect that it was imperative that talks on commercial policy should proceed simultaneously with the financial discussions and that in his view the complexity of the commercial policy questions made it essential that a United Kingdom team of equal standing to that engaged on financial policy should be in Washington if the financial discussions were not to be delayed.

2. Hawkins, speaking for himself, said that it would be most unfortunate if the impression gained ground that the U.S. Administration intended to link financial and commercial discussions tactically in a spirit which would exploit the U.K. financial situation in order to secure our acquiescence to commercial arrangements which would not be advantageous to us. This was not the motive in pressing for very early progress on commercial policy. It was Clayton's view, no less than his own, that the commercial arrangements must be negotiated on their own merits and must produce results which were advantageous to us no less than to the U.S. (Liesching agreed emphatically and referred to the words 'mutually advantageous' which appeared in Article VII)[3]. Hawkins was anxious that his message should not be taken amiss as an attempt to tell H.M.G. when and by what persons these questions should be handled. The motive was to take advantage in the U.S. of the short period—not more than six months—during which really substantial reductions of the U.S. tariff would be politically possible and to press on with discussion of some difficult points on which a reconciliation of U.S. and U.K. views had still to be made. The American proposals handed to us by Clayton[4] should not be regarded as representing a final American attitude but a 'negotiating attitude' as agreed so far between U.S. Departments and, speaking personally, he hoped that some of them would be substantially modified.

3. Hawkins was informed that we were aware of the similar representations which he had made previously to the Foreign Office[5] and which Clayton had made to the President of the Board of Trade. He was reminded of the reply which he had received explaining the reasons for

---

[1] 8 September 1945. Mr. Magowan was in London to participate in the Anglo-American commercial negotiations.
[2] Printed in *F.R.U.S. 1945*, vol. vi, pp. 116–17.
[3] Of the Mutual Aid Agreement: see No. 1, note 5.
[4] See No. 2, note 11 and i.   [5] See No. 17, note 4.

giving priority to urgent financial questions.[6] He was given no ground to think that his present representations would alter what he was then told.

4. Hawkins is due to leave for Washington by air on Sunday, 9th September, where he will be associated with Clayton's team. He was obviously disappointed that we could not give him any encouragement at the moment, and he left us with the firm impression that the Ambassador may hear more of this from Clayton in the near future.

CALENDAR TO NO. 27

i *10 Sept. 1945 Minutes of 1st Meeting of U.K. Steering Committee in Washington (circulated on 20 Sept. as GEN 80/8)* discussion of: (*a*) publicity and procedural arrangements for Keynes Mission; (*b*) BABOON 21 (Committee agreed 'in general it would be desirable to do everything possible to reassure the Americans regarding our willingness to discuss commercial policy'); (*c*) NABOB 32 (No. 24) and draft letter to Mr. Byrnes on mutual termination of Lend-Lease and Reciprocal Aid; (*d*) Lord Keynes' view, which Committee approved, that 'it would be advisable to let suggestions for financial assistance to the U.K. emanate from the American side' [UE 4435/1094/53].

[6] Cf. *F.R.U.S., ibid.,* note 21 on p. 116. Mr. Brand was informed in CAMER 615 of 7 September that an explanation had been given to the Americans in the terms agreed by Ministers on 31 August: see No. 17, note 4 and ii.

No. 28

Letter from Lord Keynes (Washington) to Sir W. Eady (Treasury)[1]

[*T 236/438*]

WASHINGTON, *10 September 1945*

My dear Wilfrid,

Very rashly, but so as to put you in as close touch as possible at as early a date as possible, I have prepared the attached note. It is based on a [*sic*] fairly long talks separately with Vinson and with Harry White. But I shall not have seen Clayton until this afternoon.[2] When I do I am hopeful that I can comfort him on the difficulty discussed in Baboon 21.[3] I am assiduously sticking to the existing arrangements and at present feel some confidence that this is the right start, though quite possibly strengthening the team will be necessary a little later on.

The top copy of this is intended for you, Bridges and the Chancellor. I am also enclosing a duplicate in case you may care to pass one on to the Bank for Catto and Cobbold.[4]

[1] This letter is also printed, with its enclosure, in Moggridge, *op. cit.,* pp. 452–8.
[2] Cf. i below.   [3] No. 27.
[4] Lord Catto and Mr. C.F. Cobbold, respectively Governor and Deputy Governor of the Bank of England.

As you may imagine, we had a pretty strenuous time in Ottawa to get through in three days and I had not a minute away from official or semi-official business. All the same, they were once again so jolly and truly warm in their approach that it was a pleasure from start to finish. And, once again, Gordon Munro[5] was infallibly efficient and helpful.

About the position here, the only thing I would add to the attached note is that the atmosphere is perhaps rather too good. One's experience in Washington has always been that when things look beastliest all will be glowing three months hence, and vice versa. So perhaps it is dangerous for the Press to be starting off so forthcoming. There will, however, I think, remain the solid gain that the public will have got thoroughly used to the idea before we have to break it to them in concrete terms.

Yours ever,
MAYNARD KEYNES

ENCLOSURE IN NO. 28

Some highly preliminary notes on the forthcoming conversations

9 September 1945

I. *General atmosphere*

It is absurd to presume to make any comments so soon; but as one's first impressions are often more clear cut and for that reason sometimes more serviceable than the more complicated and hazier view that one reaches later, I may as well record at once the first impact of Washington on my mind.

In my judgment the result of the Prime Minister's statement about the way in which lend-lease was terminated[6] and the dramatisation of this in the House of Commons and in the Press has been wholly good and tremendously effective. We have seldom, if ever, in my experience, had such publicity on a financial and economic matter. There is something interesting and responsible on the matter in the newspapers every day, and most of it very favourable.

There is general approval for the underlying policy of the President in bringing lend-lease to an early and clear cut conclusion, but the way the thing was done is very unpopular and has caused a noticeable reaction in our favour of doing something for us at any rate in the Eastern Press, as well as giving opportunity for the publicity just referred to.

Crowley's position with his colleagues and people of influence with the Administration seems to be poor and deteriorating; probably much poorer than he himself realises since he believes, probably with good reason, that he has been carrying out the President's present intentions

---

[5] Financial Adviser to the United Kingdom High Commissioner in Canada, Mr. Malcolm MacDonald.
[6] See No. 17, note 11.

122

and he does not yet realise the impending strength of the influences which are exceedingly likely to change this as soon as the President becomes better informed about what is at issue. Crowley's line is that the U.K. must get the same terms as all the other countries who are on the doorstep, that is to say, a 3C credit for what is in the pipe line and an Export-Import Bank credit on the same (or worse) terms for anything else; no more than that and no special cases. The Treasury and the State Department, on the other hand, are perfectly clear that we are a special case which the above provisions go nowhere in meeting. It is also relevant that both Vinson and Clayton are believed to feel that he has recently double crossed each of them on separate occasions in matters arising out of our affairs. He secured the abrupt termination of lend-lease contrary to Vinson's advice after Vinson had left the President's room under the impression that no such decision was going to be made[7]; and in the matter of Clayton's letter to us,[8] Crowley's disregard of it[9] has put Clayton in a position which the latter feels to be rather humiliating and lays him open to having his good faith doubted by us (which would, in fact, be most unjust). White was emphatic that in the long run it would be the advice of Clayton and Vinson which would determine the President's action.

II. *The Machinery of the Conversations*

The nature of the Committees to be set up has been explained by telegram.[10] I gather that it is the intention both of Clayton and Vinson to sit in fairly continuously on the main Committees in a way in which their predecessors never would. Vinson explained to me, on my first courtesy visit to him, that he wants to give close attention to the factual presentation of our case so that he feels he is thoroughly soaked in it. As a lawyer, he added, he felt that the judgment which must follow should be dictated by the facts. I told him that this was exactly what we looked for and would welcome. Vinson also clearly advised me, though not in quite so many words, that we should from now on cease to have any direct or separate contact with Crowley in any matters of principle relating to the winding-up of lend-lease. He indicated that as soon as the conversations had started, the top Committee would have full powers over all lend-lease questions as over anything else and that any decisions should be handed down by the top Committee and not separately discussed at any lower level. We shall certainly not give way at the start on the question of accepting Crowley's terms subject to the proviso.[11] My telegram asking for

---

[7] Cf. No. 15, note 3.   [8] See No. 20, para. 5.   [9] Cf. No. 23.

[10] Information concerning the U.S. proposals for the organisation of committees in the forthcoming negotiations had been given informally to Mr. Brand by Mr. Collado, and was transmitted to London in NABOB 28 of 6 September, not printed. For the U.K. arrangements see No. 26, note 3.

[11] Cf. No. 24, para 2. On the filed copy three lines beginning above at 'discussed' and ending overleaf 'sent off before my', were sidelined. In sending the letter and enclosure to Mr. Burke Trend (who had succeeded Mr. Padmore as Private Secretary to Mr. Dalton on 1

discretion to give way, if necessary,[12] was sent off before my conversation with Vinson and, in any case, was only intended to make provision so that we could act quickly on this point if a stand about it seemed likely to be futile and make unnecessary trouble, thus prejudicing the main negotiations. Our previous information was that on this particular matter Vinson and Clayton would support Crowley. If they do this I think that we should give way, but certainly not until the position is clear cut.

III. *The Possible Substance of the American Plan*

It is evident that an elaborate plan has been or is being worked out in the U.S. Treasury. This is primarily White's plan with, I think, a good deal of assistance from Bernstein.[13] When I saw him White was obviously burning to show it to me and only just managed to restrain himself from doing so. But reading between the lines of what he said and piecing things together, I should infer that the general lines of what they are thinking about are likely to be as follows:

(*a*) I think that White himself has now come round to the view that we need something in the order of $3 billion rather than $3 billion. This was helpful since there was an earlier rumour that White was in favour of too low a figure. He added, however, that he thought the amount might prove a matter of some difficulty with the Committee. The inference certainly was that he would support us in asking for the higher figure.

(*b*) The U.S. Treasury are thinking in terms of a 50 year loan without interest. But here again, White thinks that it will not be easy to get the 'no interest' principle through the Committee. Whether a 50 year loan means a loan in which the capital is repayable by 50 annual instalments or whether nothing is due until 50 years hence, I have no indication, but I should imagine the former. If so, a $5 billion loan without interest would mean an annual service of $100 million a year.

(*c*) The tendency of White's thought which I found most disturbing was that he seems to have returned to an earlier idea by which the U.S. would take over as their liability a certain part of the sterling balances. We must, of course, press them very hard that the right way is to strengthen us so as to liberate some part of the sterling balances and that their plan, instead of assisting multilateral convertibility, would in fact impede it since, if the assistance to each Sterling Area country is segregated, this would be incompatible with rendering their remaining

September), Sir E. Bridges minuted: 'The Chancellor should see this letter from Lord Keynes, which is distinctly promising. You will see from the passage sidelined on page 2 that Lord Keynes has *not* used the discretion [cf. No.24, note 8] given him to accept Crowley's terms, subject to the proviso . E.E.B. 14th September, 1945.' Mr. Dalton minuted on this note: 'Read with interest. H.D. 18/9.'

[12] No. 24.

[13] Mr. E.M. Bernstein was Assistant Director of Monetary Research in the U.S. Treasury.

sterling balances either wholly free or wholly blocked. Our latest plan is so much better than this that we should have hopes of getting it through. Nevertheless, White's line of thinking on this matter is dangerous, since once he associates himself with a general proposition, he is not easily shaken from it.

IV. *Our Initial Tactics*

On this matter I had a very interesting and helpful conversation with Towers during my stop in Ottawa. He was emphatic in preferring our old plan of $3 billion grant-in-aid plus an additional option of $5 billion credit, with the intention of drawing on the $5 billion credit to the least possible extent. He is, of course, anxious that we should arrange a non-discriminatory use of sterling balances on the lines which we discussed with him in Cambridge and which is still part of the plan; and he thinks that this would be enormously attractive to the Americans. But he says that, if he were in our place, he would hesitate greatly before conceding this except in return for assistance which took the form of a grant-in-aid at least in substantial part. He thought that we ought to present our case at the start on something like the following lines.

We should say that one alternative would be to receive a dollar loan on semi-commercial terms. In this case we should try to keep the size of it down to the absolute minimum and in order to do this we should inevitably have to enforce a restrictive policy with regard to imports so far as we and the rest of the Sterling Area are concerned and also, in all probability, a discriminatory one. The alternative plan would be a substantial grant-in-aid which would leave us with at least some potential borrowing power still in hand in the event of the grant-in-aid proving inadequate to our needs. But in this event we could take far greater risks. If we had a substantial grant-in-aid it might go a very long way in seeing us through the transitional period. Thus we could safely promise a far less restrictive policy and could accept the obligation of non-discrimination.[14] To repeat the point, if our potential borrowing power is used up at the start so that we have nothing to fall back upon, we can take no risks and must be restrictive. We can only take the chance of a liberal and expansive policy if our immediate necessities are covered by a grant-in-aid so that we can still have some potential borrowing power in hand against contingencies. The ideal plan would therefore be my original proposal for a grant-in-aid for a substantial, nevertheless moderate, amount such as $3 billion with an option of $5 billion on generous credit terms in hand against contingencies. I should add that Towers was rather disturbed by the low level of imports which I told him we contemplated if we were to have any hope of breaking even within three to five years. He thought that such a low level of imports on our part must have a seriously restrictive influence on world trade as a whole and that we should certainly aim at a

[14] Cf. No. 1, note 11.

settlement which would not force on us such severe and lasting austerity. How far the above advice can be made compatible with the line of thought of the U.S. Treasury as indicated above, remains to be seen. But I feel that basically Towers' advice is very good indeed. (I fancy that Canada will not be less liberal in principle than the U.S.A. and might very likely follow the American model on the above lines, if we can secure it.)

KEYNES

CALENDAR TO NO. 28

i *10 Sept. 1945   British Missions (Washington) Tels. NABOB 38 & 42* Results of discussion in No. 27.i(*b*) on commercial policy tactics are explained to London, and later that afternoon by Lord Keynes to Mr. Clayton, who seemed 'quite satisfied' [UE 4174, 4178/32/71].

CHAPTER II

Preliminary consideration of terms of U.S. loan: Imperial Preference

11 September – 21 October 1945

No. 29

British Missions (Washington) to Cabinet Offices
(Received 12 September, 12.20 a.m.)

NABOB 45 Telegraphic [UE 4193/1094/53]

Immediate. Secret   WASHINGTON, 11 September 1945, 11.41 p.m.

1. Opening meeting of Top Committee took place this afternoon.[1] Proceedings were largely formal. Main subject of discussion was future organisation of meetings of committees and sub-committees.

2. We intimated that we had in mind to communicate forthwith formal withdrawal of Reciprocal Aid as from VJ Day except to extent which would be involved by adoption on a mutual basis of arrangements proposed in Patterson's letter quoted in NABOB 41.[2] We said that we assumed

(a) That the U.S. Administration did *not* propose to suggest that their decision to give a temporary extension of Lend Lease for certain shipping costs and services involved our maintaining similar degree of Reciprocal Aid.

(b) That interpretation of Patterson's letter would be referred to Military Subcommittee of Lend Lease Committee. Crowley however asked that question (a) should be considered at meeting of Lend Lease

---

[1] The agreed minutes of this meeting (COM/TOP 1st Meeting, circulated as GEN 80/9 on 20 September, UE 4436/1094/53) are printed in *F.R.U.S. 1945*, vol. vi, pp. 122–6. The U.K. members of the Committee were as set out in No. 26, note 3. On the American side were Mr. Clayton (Chairman, representing Mr. Byrnes, who had gone to London to attend the C.F.M. (see Volume II, Chapter I)), Mr. Crowley, Mr. Vinson, Mr. Wallace, Mr. T.B. McCabe (Army-Navy Liquidation Commissioner) and Mr. M.S. Eccles (Chairman of the Board of Governors of the Federal Reserve System).
[2] See No. 24, note 6.

Committee on 13 September when it would also be possible to agree on formation of Military Subcommittee. We felt that we could not object to this and are deferring proposed communication on Reciprocal Aid[3] in the meantime.[4]

CALENDAR TO No. 29

i *11 Sept. 1945* Earl of Halifax *(Washington) Tel. No. 6150 to Mr. Bevin* Considers it 'inadvisable at this stage to link in any way these negotiations with those at your meeting of Foreign Ministers': see Vol. II, Chapter I [UE 4206/1094/53].

[3] Cf. No. 27.i(c).

[4] The agreed minutes of the 2nd, 3rd and 4th meetings of the Top Committee on 13, 14 and 17 September, at which Lord Keynes gave an exposition of the British financial position, are printed in Moggridge, *op. cit.*, pp. 466–84, and are not reprinted here. Copies of these minutes, circulated in the GEN 80 series, can be found in file UE 1094/53. At the 2nd Meeting Lord Keynes also presented a document (COM/TOP 3) containing tables of figures relating to the U.K. financial position. COM/TOP 3 was not circulated in London, but proof copies of the statistical tables were circulated in GEN 89/3 on 25 September (UE 4514/1094/53). At the 4th Meeting he presented a further document (COM/TOP 4) containing statistical tables relating to the U.K. war effort and Mutual Aid, which was circulated in GEN 80/19 on 26 September (UE 4514/1094/53).

Some of the figures presented by Lord Keynes were published in Cmd. 6707 of 1945, *Statistical Material presented during the Washington Negotiations.*

No. 30

British Missions (Washington) to Cabinet Offices
(Received 14 September, 1.14 a.m.)

NABOB 49 Telegraphic [UE 4238/1094/53]

Most immediate. Secret   WASHINGTON, *13 September 1945, 11.13 p.m.*

Following for Chancellor of Exchequer and President of the Board of Trade from Keynes.

1. We are not clear how far BABOON 29[1] is intended to modify

[1] This telegram of 11 September referred to NABOB 38 and 42 (No. 28.i) and pointed out that as 'commercial policy questions are now likely to come up sooner and in greater detail than was anticipated when the matter was discussed at the meeting of Ministers on 31 August' (see No. 17, note 4), Ministers would probably desire to postpone a meeting of the Commercial Policy Committee until the arrival of further British representatives, who would leave as soon as possible (UE 4174/1094/53).

In a minute of 12 September Sir E. Bridges informed Mr. Attlee that BABOON 29 had been despatched 'with the approval of Sir Stafford Cripps and Dr. Dalton', as the Board of Trade and Ministry of Agriculture were 'uneasy at the thought of these Commercial Policy questions being handled in Washington in the absence of those who have handled these issues throughout'. The position had been discussed by the Departments concerned at a meeting on the afternoon of 12 September presided over by Sir E. Bridges, when it was agreed that 'the right course would be: (*a*) to send out our Commercial Policy first eleven,

previous arrangements. But as a preliminary to a comment on this telegram by the Ambassador[2] and the Mission as a whole, I should like to analyse the alternative lines of conducting the Commercial negotiations as they present themselves at this stage.

2. During the London conversations Clayton's proposal was that we should agree with him the general headings of an invitation to be issued to a group of other powers to meet early next year to discuss partly together and partly in separate parts the creation of the proposed International Trade Organisation and the negotiation of a new set of commercial treaties within the framework of this institution. He was not asking us to enter here and now into the details appropriate to the negotiation of a commercial treaty. He was only concerned at this stage with the general principles to be embodied in the invitation to the proposed conference. He attached importance to our agreeing the terms of this with the Americans beforehand over as wide a field as possible and to our backing them up at the conference along the agreed lines. He presented a first draft of the principles[3] and we are expecting him to hand us a revised version of it shortly.

3. This line of approach gives us a good chance of reaching within a reasonable time sufficient agreement on the commercial side to allow the financial settlement to go through.

4. For three reasons in particular this approach is promising

(i) Where we are not yet able to reach a firm agreement with the Americans, and I am hopeful that these cases will be few in number, it may be possible to defer a final solution to the main conference with a view to discovering whether our view or the American view is the one more generally shared. On some points of special difficulty we may find that others feel the same difficulty and the Americans may be inclined to give way when they appreciate that particular proposal is widely impracticable.

(ii) By avoiding at this stage the details appropriate to a commercial treaty, a great deal of time can be saved and the multiplication of occasions of difference avoided.

(iii) Ministers at home will find it much easier to accept certain general principles than to agree the exact details of the way in which they are to be carried out at a time when we still know so little about the exact character of our post-war foreign trade problems.

headed by Sir Percival[e] Liesching; (b) that the Delegation, before they leave, should have an opportunity of a general discussion on Commercial Policy with Ministers.' Sir E. Bridges accordingly asked the Prime Minister if it would be possible to arrange a meeting of Ministers on Friday afternoon, 14 September, when Mr. Bevin would be free until 4 p.m. when he had to attend a meeting of the Council of Foreign Ministers: cf. Volume II, No. 53. Mr. Attlee minuted: 'Any time after 2 o'c. C.R.A. 12.9.45' (PREM 8/35). The meeting was arranged for 3 p.m.: see No. 32.i.

[2] See No. 31: NABOB 49 was despatched after NABOB 50, but the telegrams have been printed in numerical order.

[3] See No. 2, note 11, and No. 8.ii.

5. The other line of approach would be to allow ourselves to be drawn into much more detail. I believe that this would be dangerous and premature for reasons which the previous paragraph will have made obvious.

6. If so the small size of our Mission as at present constituted and the fact that it is only equipped to deal with broad principles is a positive safeguard.

7. We believe that the pressure for making the Mission more expert comes from Hawkins and that Clayton is thinking along the lines indicated above and will be satisfied with conversations so limited. But Hawkins looks forward to a resumption of the official conversations in which he has been participating for more than a year. These were attempting to go into much greater detail. Ministers would have to give immediate attention to very difficult matters of detail when the data for a clear cut decision are still largely lacking. Yet without further ministerial clearcut instructions Board of Trade officials would I feel sure think it vain to reopen the former conversations at the former level of detail.

8. This does not mean that we shall not need or will not greatly welcome more expert assistance before we are finished. It is intended as an argument for starting the negotiations on the broader lines indicated above and discouraging the more detailed approach. If we put off beginning until a larger body has arrived armed with more detailed ministerial instructions, I fear that we may find it very difficult not to lapse in practice into the second alternative. If so, I should rate considerably lower the chances of sufficient measure of agreement at an early date. For a much larger surface of possible differences will become exposed.

9. My advice is, therefore, that we be allowed to start forthwith as we are and see how we get on for a week or two; and that the Americans be not encouraged to expect anything different at the initial stage. If we once get well launched on the broader lines we shall be able to get the advantage of more expert assistance without running the risk indicated above.

10. There are two points to which we should like to see further thought given in London at once and on which we should welcome early instructions:

(i) Are ministers ready to agree, before the detailed bargaining about the levels of preferences and tariffs begin[s], that we will waive the obligation as between members of the Commonwealth to maintain bound preferences.

Please see my letter of 4th September to Liesching reporting Norman Robertson's suggestion about this made in Ottawa.[4] This seems a logical consequence of bilateral tariff and preference discussions. A concession on this might help the Americans to accept our fundamental point on which the Canadians will support us that preferences as such are not to be

---

[4] See i below. Mr N. Robertson was Canadian Under Secretary for External Affairs.

yielded in advance but must come into the general horse trade so that any reductions in preferences would be handled pari passu with reductions in tariffs.

(ii) We should like to know more about how far ministers are prepared to go in meeting the American ideas about Cartels and more particularly their reaction to the reply to our previous observations on this matter handed by Hawkins to Shackle on August 30th[5] after I had left.

CALENDAR TO NO. 30

i *4 & 14 Sept. 1945 Exchange of letters between Sir P. Liesching and Lord Keynes* concerning the latter's talks in Ottawa: Mr. Robertson suggested Commonwealth members should be released from existing bound preference obligations as a preliminary to bilateral negotiations with Americans [T 247/2].

[5] The reference was to a note on 'Reactions of U.S. experts to United Kingdom Proposals on Cartels and Combines in International Trade', handed to Mr. Shackle by Mr. Hawkins on 30 August and sent to the Foreign Office with a covering note by Mr. Shackle on 4 September (UE 4021/113/53). Mr. Hawkins had explained that 'he thought it might be useful for us to have a note of the American points in writing, even though they had already been made orally at the last meeting with Mr. Clayton': see No. 8.ii.

No. 31

British Missions (Washington) to Cabinet Offices
(Received 14 September, 12.20 a.m.)

NABOB 50 Telegraphic [UE 4239/1094/53]

Most immediate. Secret   WASHINGTON, *13 September 1945, 11.11 p.m.*

Following for Chancellor of the Exchequer and President of the Board of Trade from Ambassador.

1. I agree generally with Keynes appreciation in NABOB 49.[1] I think it is important to avoid conversations becoming bogged down in detail.

2. Yesterday, before I had seen BABOON 29,[2] Clayton spoke to me following upon a conversation he had had with Hawkins and said that he was anxious to start Commercial policy discussions at an early date but doubted whether any useful progress could be made until enlargement of Mission had arrived. I spoke on lines of NABOB 38[3] and said that I thought a preliminary meeting of the Commercial Policy Committee dealing with the agenda in general terms would show whether useful results could be achieved. Clayton did not demur at this suggestion.

[1] No. 30.   [2] *V. ibid.*, note 1.   [3] See No. 28.i.

181

3. Clayton has since responded to what I said by agreement to have first meeting on Commercial Policy probably on Monday.[4]

4. I anticipate that this talk will be pretty general. Clayton may perhaps be preparing to hand to us a revised paper showing any changes made by the U.S. side since the London talks.[5] If so, we should propose to go through it with him in an endeavour to establish broadly agreed points and points which we know are unacceptable. We should hope in this way to avoid delay and to postpone as long as possible consideration of the sticking points, thus facilitating financial talks and possibly leaving over to the Conference in the Spring points on which we should hope to bring the U.S.A. up against opinions of other countries. In any such talks, we shall of course keep BABOON 29 in mind and report fully.

5. We therefore feel that the best course is for us to see where we get to in Commercial Policy Committee here and, meanwhile, for preparations to go ahead in London so that further team can be ready on short call to come to join in when the right moment arrives.

CALENDAR TO No. 31

i *12 Sept. 1945 Minutes of 2nd Meeting of U.K. Steering Committee in Washington* (*circulated on 3 Oct. as GEN 80/27*) Discussion of: (*a*) commercial policy negotiations, resulting in despatch of Nos. 30 & 31; (*b*) forthcoming meeting of Lend-Lease Committee, where American tendency to request exceptions to ending of Reciprocal Aid should be resisted; (*c*) forthcoming meeting of Surplus Disposals Committee, where 'we should listen to an exposition of the American proposals without making any commitment at this stage' [UE 4622/1094/53].

[4] 17 September 1945.　　　　　　　　　　　[5] See No. 2, note 11, and No. 8.ii.

No. 32

Cabinet Offices to British Missions (Washington)

BABOON 33 *Telegraphic* [*UE 4239/1094/53*]

Immediate. Secret　　　　　　　CABINET OFFICES, *14 September 1945, 9.50 p.m.*

For Ambassador and Keynes.

Ministers met this afternoon and had before them NABOB Nos. 49 and 50.[1]

Ministers were very sensible of the advantages of not getting bogged down in detail or of reaching final conclusions at this stage on Commercial Policy. Nevertheless, they felt that the course which events are taking, including in particular the setting up of the Committee on Commercial

[1] Nos. 30 and 31. The minutes of this Ministerial meeting are reproduced at i below.

132

Policy, have in effect brought about a situation in which the negotiations on Commercial Policy should be conducted principally by the team who have handled the Commercial Policy questions throughout from the earliest stages.

Ministers therefore decided that on balance it would be right that, in accordance with the original plan, you should keep discussion for the present to the deployment of the financial arguments and not enter on discussions on Commercial Policy until the arrival of Liesching and his colleagues.[2] It would follow that the meeting on Commercial Policy arranged for Monday next[3] should be postponed.[4]

As regards the two questions posed in paragraph 10 to NABOB 49, Liesching will be bringing instructions. In the meantime I should let you know that Ministers' reaction to Norman Robertson's proposal about Imperial preference[5] was not favourable, it being held to be unwise to make any such concession at the outset.

CALENDARS TO NO. 32

i *14 Sept. 1945 Record of meeting of Ministers (GEN 89/1st meeting)* Discussion of Nos. 30 & 31, memo. by Sir S. Cripps (GEN 89/2, ii below) and GEN 89/1 (Enclosure in No. 22), in regard to which it was agreed that Lord Keynes should for the present 'confine himself to developing these proposals orally' (cf. No. 22, note 11) [UE 4326/1094/53].

ii *13–14 Sept. 1945 GEN 89/2 Memo. by Sir S. Cripps on Commercial Policy and the Lend-Lease Negotiations at Washington*, with comments by Mr. Coulson (referring also to C.P. (45)116, No. 6.ii) and Mr. Butler [UE 4353/1094/53].

[2] Cf. No. 30, note 1. Professor L. Robbins and Mr. Shackle were to accompany Sir P. Liesching to Washington, together with representatives from the Ministry of Agriculture, Colonial Office and Ministry of Food.

[3] 17 September 1945.

[4] In a personal telegram (NABOB 57 of 15 September) to Mr. Bevin in reply to BABOON 33 Lord Halifax argued that he and Lord Keynes felt that it would be unwise to postpone the meeting of the Commercial Policy Committee: 'If we create fresh suspicions on this subject my own feeling is that we run grave risk of an unfavourable change in the atmosphere of the financial discussions' (UE 4254/1094/53). Lord Halifax had already argued against a suggestion by Mr. Clayton that meetings of the Commercial Policy Committee should be postponed until the arrival of the British experts: see No. 31, and cf. No. 31.i(a). BABOON 34 of 15 September, however, rejected Lord Halifax's arguments on the grounds that 'continuance of meetings on commercial policy before the arrival of Liesching and his colleagues will inevitably make it very difficult for the latter to handle the negotiations on this matter when he arrives', and confirmed that he should suggest a postponement to the Americans. In NABOB 59 of 15 September Lord Halifax reported that he had spoken as instructed to Mr. Clayton, who seemed 'quite happy' about the postponement and expressed the hope that 'we could now make early and rapid progress towards broad decisions' (UE 4273/1094/53).

[5] See No. 30.i.

No. 33

British Missions (Washington) to Cabinet Offices
(Received 15 September, 9.57 a.m.)

NABOB 56 Telegraphic [UE 4251/1094/53]

Secret   WASHINGTON, *14 September 1945, 11.5 p.m.*

Personal for Sinclair from Keynes.
BABOON 26 para 3 and para 4 NABOB 53 and associated matters.[1]

1. Private conversation with McCloy[2] after dinner leads me to think that re-capture ideas of War Department as distinguished from F.E.A. are very moderate. In particular, I agree with NABOB 53 that Lend-Lease equipment actually in use by British Forces will not be re-captured in the present phase. Please treat what follows as mere gossip and not to be taken otherwise than you would have taken it if you had been one of the party.

2. Thinking out loud and without any commitment McCloy was talking in terms of re-capture only of equipment actually needed by War Department to meet certain South American commitments or for European relief.

3. I urged him if possible to confine his re-capture to supplies not yet issued from U.S. Depots.

4. In reply to his question about practical possibilities of our providing an inventory I replied that I thought we could quickly supply inventories of supplies not issued and we could also supply gradually over a considerable period estimates of Lend-Lease material released by units on being disbanded partly as identifiables and partly as an overall percentage of dumps of unidentifiables but it will be difficult if not impossible to furnish an inventory of supplies actually in use by our Forces since both situation and unexhausted quantity would be constantly shifting.

5. When I tentatively suggested the possibility of an overall deal by which in lieu of re-capture we were assessed at a moderate global figure in terms of money neither he nor Dean Acheson who was present thought this politically advisable owing to the difficulty of justifying any global

---

[1] BABOON 26 of 11 September referred to NABOB 32 and BABOON 23 (see No. 24 and *ibid.*, note 8). Para. 3 stated: 'Question of retention of American equipment by British Forces on Lend-Lease terms is so important to us that we cannot afford not to have a clear understanding. We cannot face either expense of purchasing what we need to retain or military inconvenience of doing without it and in some cases planned production in U.K. could be reduced if it were clear that we did not have to return U.S. equipment before we wished to' (UE 4137/32/71). NABOB 53 of 14 September gave the preliminary views of the Keynes Mission on BABOON 26: para. 4 stated that with regard to military lend-lease stocks it was proposed 'to assume it is axiomatic that we are allowed to retain what is needed, whilst being prepared to allow Americans to recapture balance of availabilities over actual needs, this balance being treated as surplus. We think it highly probable that the Americans will wish to scrutinize carefully our justifications for what we wish to retain, but feel strongly that this is an issue which they should raise rather than we' (UE 4251/1094/53).

[2] U.S. Assistant Secretary of War.

figure we might fix on. Their first impression which we must not take too seriously was that it would be easier to defend before Congress a plan by which they exercise physical re-capture in the case of supplies for which they genuinely had a use and beyond that do nothing to disturb our existing uses. No doubt it would not be as good as this in practice. But it is a much better first line of approach than some overall Presidential Directive to start by re-capturing everything and then consider on what terms if any the re-captured material is to be returned to us which judging from your telegrams you in London may have been thinking of as the more probable course.

6. I am convinced that this is not a matter on which we should take any initiative at present but should leave well alone. Americans are not likely to do anything sudden calculated to upset our present use of material and we should do much better to leave it to them to take the initiative.

CALENDARS TO NO. 33

i *14–15 Sept. 1945 British Missions (Washington) Tel. NABOB 52.* At 1st meeting of Lend-Lease Committee on 13 Sept. (cf. No. 31.i(*b*)) Mr. Crowley agreed that U.S. would expect no further Reciprocal Aid after 2 Sept. and said 'it would be more convenient for them not to pay us in cash for supplies or services formerly on reciprocal aid but to treat the cash which would become due to us as a setoff against amounts due from us for pipeline supplies or requirements from stocks'; *NABOB unnumbered,* amending para. 3 of NABOB 52; *NABOB 54* Lord Keynes suggests that neither cash nor credit should be used in payment for pipeline supplies, but Americans should be persuaded to accept 'offsets of an approximately equal value' [UE 4250, 4252/1094/53].

ii *17–26 Sept. 1945 Tels. BABOON 36 & 37 to British Missions (Washington)* Comments on i: Lord Keynes' proposal is attractive but must be on broad lines, while similar negotiations with Russians on miscellaneous claims might be borne in mind; *Washington Tel. REMAC 728* possible American counter-claims against Reciprocal Aid [UE 4252, 4468/1094/53].

iii *19 Sept. 1945 Tel. BABOON 44 to British Missions (Washington)* In reply to No. 33 Sir R. Sinclair agrees with proposed tactics but doubts wisdom of formal valuation of equipment: preparation of pipeline inventories is proceeding [UE 4251/1094/53].

No. 34

Letter from Mr. Hall-Patch (Washington) to Mr. Butler

[UE 4412/1094/53]

WASHINGTON, 15 September 1945

Dear Butler,

I am sending you herewith copies of what the Ambassador and Keynes had to say at the Press Conference held on September 12.[1]

The Ambassador opened the Conference himself. In a masterly way he outlined developments in England since he had left Washington and then led on to the objects of the Keynes Mission. It was an admirable performance and certainly gave Keynes a good kick-off.

A good deal of thought had been given by the Treasury Delegation to the statement to be made by Keynes but at the last minute, when the final text was being prepared, there was a typing crisis, and the Ambassador was not given the time to consider it which I should have liked. However Balfour, Makins and I ran over the paper with him just before the Conference and he approved generally.

Makins thought, and I agreed, that it was perhaps inadvisable to set out quite so boldly the two alternatives shown on Page 3.[2] Keynes was, however, very insistant [sic] that they should remain. In the event, Makins turned out to be right, and it was these alternatives which gave rise to practically the only embarrassing questions at the Conference.

The Keynes talk, as you will see, was rather specialised material and I was a little apprehensive, at one time, that he was talking over the heads of his audience. But from the very intelligent and well informed questions which followed I think my fears were unjustified.

On the whole, I think the first big talk with the Press has gone off quite successfully. The reactions have not been unsatisfactory; the quarters from which criticism has come are those we expected, and the criticism is nothing like as violent as we thought it would be.

I am arranging to see regularly the various Press Relations Officers and to keep them fully posted on developments. It will be their job to keep the Press straight until we have another general Press conference.

[1] Not printed. Lord Keynes' statement is printed in Moggridge, op. cit., pp. 460–6.

[2] V. ibid., p. 463. The 'two alternatives' as set out by Lord Keynes were for the United Kingdom to 'do the best we can with the resources we still command and aim at emerging slowly from our temporary difficulties with as little outside aid as possible', or to work out with American aid 'some means of returning at the earliest possible date to normal trade practices without discrimination and to increased freedom and liberality in commercial and tariff policies': cf. Sections III and IV of No. 22. Mr. R. Ashton of the Economic Relations Department noted on 28 September that Mr. Hall-Patch's point regarding these alternatives was a sound one: 'We shall have to maintain the sterling area whatever happens. The question is rather what degree of relaxation can we attain in dealings between members of the sterling and the dollar areas'.

I am sending you photostats of the more important articles which have so far appeared in the Press,[3] and will continue to do so if it is of any use. On this point perhaps you would let me know?

I would draw your attention particularly to the article headed 'In the Nation' from the *New York Times* of September 14th which appears in the photostats. The 'eminent citizen' referred to therein is Barnie Baruch.[4] This article looks the most unhealthy that has appeared so far from our point of view. There are indications that the Republican Party may take this sort of line, and make the grant of assistance to us a first class issue of party politics. Unfortunately the next elections are already casting their shadow before them.

We had on September 13th and 14th our first 'Business' meetings of the Top Committee of which you will receive the minutes in due course.[5] I was very much struck at the keen interest shown by the Americans in our vast Middle East expenditure. It was quite clear that they had not appreciated this aspect of our financial difficulties, and they were surprised at the extent of our commitments. This may help us to cut down the establishment of Major Generals in Cairo which will be all to the good. There is however, another aspect which clearly interested the Americans and that is whether it is to their advantage to provide the cash to enable us to cut any sort of figure in the Middle East. This may be an important political point. We have long-standing commitments in that area which, if not discharged by us, will have to be undertaken by somebody else. The Americans will have to be brought to realise that unless they are prepared to provide the wherewithal to set us on our feet as worthy partners in world affairs, they will find themselves obliged to step in and take our place with all the expenditure of man-power and cash which that entails. The alternative will be disorder on a grand scale. I think this aspect of the discussions will have to be watched rather carefully.

One further point which has not yet emerged in official discussions, but which seems likely to be brought to the fore very soon, is our position vis à vis our creditors in the Commonwealth and Empire.

As you know our tactical plan was to reach a settlement with the Americans and then to deal with our Sterling Area Creditors. This approach does not appeal to the Americans who are inclined to look at these matters as commercial bankers. They may well propose that this whole problem should be treated in the same way as the reconstruction of a company which has got into difficulties. This would mean that they, as the people who are expected to provide the money, would summon in Washington a general meeting of all the creditors with a view to scaling down by direct negotiations with them their debts to us before lending us

[3] Not printed.
[4] Mr. Bernard M. Baruch had been advising the U.S. Government in various capacities since the First World War, and was economic adviser to Mr. Byrnes during the Second World War.
[5] See No. 29, note 4.

new money. And for this new money they would expect priority both as to interest and amortization over all other creditors. If things develop in this way my own view, for what it is worth, is that we would be well advised to break off negotiations. I hope my fears on this point are unjustified but the straws in the wind are rather ominous. Unfortunately, proposals such as these would be just the sort of settlement which would appeal to the numskulls in Congress.

Please pass on this letter to Charles Stirling[6] or John Coulson.

Yours ever,

E.L. Hall-Patch

Please forgive the appearance of this letter, but I dictated to a strange typist and this is what has been produced!

E.L.H.P. 15/9

CALENDAR TO No. 34

i *13 Sept. 1945 RAFDEL (Washington) to J.A.S. Tel. SEVER 1384* General impression of press coverage is that 'pressmen of all colours were sufficiently impressed by sincerity and logic of Ambassador's and Keynes' statements to avoid facile or sensational deductions not warranted by the information provided' [UE 4255/1094/53].

[6] Mr C.N. Stirling was an Acting Counsellor in the Foreign Office.

No. 35

Mr. Bevin to the Earl of Halifax (Washington)

No. 9527 Telegraphic [Z 10744/28/36]

Important   FOREIGN OFFICE, *18 September 1945, 8 p.m.*

My telegram No. 665 to Lisbon (of 4th September: Facilities in the Azores).[1]

Please inform State Department that we have had under consideration the question of the withdrawal of the British forces which have been established in the islands of Terceira and Fayal in accordance with the facilities granted under the Azores Agreement of 1943.[2] In that agreement (unlike the United States Portuguese Agreement relating to the island of Santa Maria[3] which provides for a maximum period of 9

[1] Not printed: the reference should apparently be to telegram No. 664 of 5 September, not printed (Z 9932/28/36).

[2] This exchange of letters of 17 August 1943 is printed in *B.F.S.P.*, vol. 146, pp. 447–52. The facilities granted included the construction and use of an airfield at Lagens on the island of Terceira and naval facilities at Horta in the island of Fayal. Cf. Sir L. Woodward, *op. cit.*, vol. iv, pp. 52–7.

[3] For details of this agreement of 28 November 1944 and its negotiation see *F.R.U.S. 1944*, vol. iv, pp. 1–84.

months within which United States forces must be withdrawn) no time limit was laid down for the duration of the facilities granted to us, but when we originally approached the Portuguese Government on the matter in June 1943, we gave the assurance that our forces would be withdrawn 'at the end of hostilities'. We are in fact now anxious to withdraw our forces as soon as practicable and estimate that the process should be completed within six months from the date of the end of the war (i.e. September 2nd). We propose, therefore, to inform the Portuguese Government accordingly, adding that we would hope thereafter to enjoy emergency and diversionary rights in the Azores.

2. In view of the share which the United States forces have had in the facilities accorded to us by the Portuguese, and as we understand that the United States forces established in the Azores may be hoping to continue to enjoy the alternative facilities they now possess on the island of Terceira for as long as they themselves remain established at Santa Maria (i.e. possibly for as long as nine months after the end of hostilities and thus 3 months after the outside date for our withdrawal from Terceira), we feel we should inform the United States Government beforehand of our intention.

3. We are, however, anxious to make our communication to the Portuguese Government as soon as practicable.[4] Unless, therefore, we hear from you to the contrary by September 29th, we shall assume that our proposed arrangements are quite convenient to the United States Government and we shall instruct Sir Owen O'Malley accordingly.

4. You should make it clear in your communication to the State Department that the withdrawal of the British forces will of course involve the termination of British responsibility for the Air-Sea rescue service in the Azores, and enquire whether, and if so when, the United States authorities will be able to take over this service. Nor should you hold out any hope that we would be able to prolong our occupation of Terceira beyond a maximum of six months. If the United States Government wish to enjoy facilities there after our departure they will no doubt take this point up direct with the Portuguese Government.[5]

---

[4] Foreign Office telegram No. 700 to Lisbon of 18 September instructed H.M. Ambassador, Sir O. O'Malley, to inform the Portuguese Government that His Majesty's Government were examining the question of early withdrawal of their forces from the Azores and hoped to approach the Portuguese Government on the subject 'shortly'. The Ambassador was also instructed, 'without pressing the matter', to 'express the hope that in view of the operational importance attached to the matter by the Service authorities . . . the Portuguese Government will feel able to grant the facilities for the erection of the additional wireless masts etc. at Vila Nova required by the United States Forces in Terceira under British command, more especially since, now that the departure of the British Forces is impending, these facilities will only be needed for a short time' (Z 10744/28/36). The Portuguese Government gave their consent in an *Aide-Mémoire* of 25 September to the extension of the wireless installations 'for the short period during which they are still necessary' (Z 11366/28/36). Cf. Volume I of this Series, No. 570.iii.

[5] The *Aide-mémoire* of 19 September sent to the State Department in execution of these

i *21–28 Sept. 1945 American plans in the Azores:* H.M. Consul in Ponta Delgada reports rumours of secret U.S.–Portuguese negotiations for American lease of Santa Maria, borne out by noticeably more accommodating attitude of Portuguese Govt. towards Americans; Sir O. O'Malley, however, does not consider facts sinister [Z 10898, 11090, 11420/28/36].

instructions is printed in *F.R.U.S. 1945,* vol. vi, pp. 204–5. In Washington telegram No. 6468 of 27 September Lord Halifax reported that the State Department urgently requested that the British Government postpone their approach to the Portuguese Government so that the U.S. War Department would have time to draw up the necessary plans: 'Moreover they indicate that they would approach His Majesty's Government formally within the next two or three weeks with proposals for establishment of a security base in the Azores which would either be under tripartite Anglo-United States-Portuguese control or under Security Council of the United Nations Organisation . . . State Department emphasise that United States Government attach the highest importance from the point of view of security and defence of Atlantic sea routes to establishment of a base in the Azores' (Z 11137/28/36). Cf. i below, and No. 61.

No. 36

Mr. Bevin to the Earl of Halifax (Washington)

CAMER 650 *Telegraphic* [*UE 4367/1094/53*]

Most immediate   FOREIGN OFFICE, *19 September 1945, 12.8 p.m.*

For Keynes from Eady.

1. We have examined Departmental requirements from United States of America for rest of year summarised in Camer 643 [i]. Details in my following telegram [i].

2. The total excluding munitions and including pipeline is about 640 million dollars. This is larger than expected but contains certainly excessive requirements for food for overseas Services and also some items in which there may be shortfall on supply grounds.

3. It is clear that we can achieve substantial reduction only by drastic cuts in food consumption, and by other measures which would prejudice rapid reconversion. At this stage of your negotiations we do not think we could justifiably urge Ministers to cut the present level of rations. We should keep heroic limitation of dollar expenditure in reserve and embark upon it only when its necessity can be clearly demonstrated to public.

4. We have made minor cuts and could make others at the cost of squeezing end-year stocks but we are not forcing this to the limit where there will be continuing demand from United States of America in the first quarter of 1946 in any case, and where we should run risk of ultimately having to pay more for the same supplies. If we have to take heroic action in early 1946 we need to secure some elbow-room.

5. We are therefore instructing Departments on the following lines:

(a) *Food for United Kingdom* We are authorising programme to the end of 1945 excluding proposed 7 for easements and subject to further questions about flour and certain other items. We are requiring understanding that any excessive supplies which may result, e.g. from over-estimation of Service requirements in United Kingdom will be used to strengthen stocks and not to increase consumption.

(b) *Food for Services overseas* We are withholding all authority until we get revised statement of requirements.

(c) *Raw Materials* We are authorising programme to the end of 1945 subject to certain detailed points.

(d) *Petroleum* Ministry of Fuel and Power requires only monthly authorisation. We shall give October authorisation and are examining Service element in requirements.

(e) *Tobacco* Already settled by Ministers.

(f) *Other requirements* We are examining further with Departments but we do not expect much reduction. This is nearly all machinery, and we should be very unwilling to cut it.

6. We are giving no authorisations for the first quarter of 1946. Departments requirements total about 500 million dollars, including pipeline where this is not exhausted by our requirements to end of 1945. Our first impression of the figures is that the total can be reduced significantly.

7. We are asking Departments to instruct their Missions to consult you before proceeding to procurement. They have pressed us for urgent authorisation as they believe some of their supplies might be endangered by delay and we thought this method of securing your concurrence against the general background of the position would be most expeditious.

CALENDARS TO NO. 36

i   *18–21 Sept. 1945   Tels. CAMER 643 & 651, REMAC 708 to and from Washington*
Details of dollar requirements from U.S. until end of 1945 based on figures from (a) Departments, (b) Missions [UE 4252, 4367, 4376/1094/53].

ii   *21 Sept. 1945   Washington Tel. REMAC 715* Comments on general policy issues raised in No. 36: 'we agree that the aggregate should be cut where possible' [UE 4377/1094/53].

iii   *22 Sept.–7 Oct. 1945   Tels. CAMER 658 & 711, REMAC 724 to and from Washington*
Food: large orders may be embarrassing in context of financial negotiations, but 'if we do not place orders we run a risk of losing supplies altogether'; Lord Keynes and Mr. Brand feel tight control should be maintained in order 'not to deplete our reserves prematurely', but special cases may be considered; after discussions with Ministry of Food authority given for pipeline purchases up to end of March 1946 sufficient to 'maintain existing standards of consumption' [UE 4377, 4479, 4583/1094/53].

No. 37

British Missions (Washington) to Cabinet Offices
(Received 21 September, 7.15 p.m.)

NABOB 68 Telegraphic [UE 4403/1094/53]

Immediate. Secret WASHINGTON, 21 September 1945, 5.49 p.m.

1. Keynes discussed in private talk with Crowley yesterday what general basis of financing should be applied to our requirements from pipeline. Crowley began as usual by stressing that he could not be represented as agreeing to more favourable terms in case of U.K. than for others, especially as Russians were watching developments closely. Keynes urged that we ought not to be asked to commit ourselves at this stage to acceptance of commercial credit arrangement, even on basis that this could be subsumed in later general arrangements, particularly as agreement on our part to quasi-commercial terms of credit might well give rise to considerable misunderstanding in the U.K.

2. After further discussion Crowley suggested that satisfactory compromise might be found by agreement on following lines:

(*a*) payment for U.K. requirements from the pipeline and the inventory would in effect be regarded as one problem.

(*b*) there would be no basis of financing agreed upon for the present

(*c*) supplies would continue to move forward from pipeline in accordance with our requirements and we would continue to draw supplies as necessary from Lend Lease stocks.

(*d*) discussions would proceed in meantime to determine (i) value of supplies to be drawn from pipeline (ii) amount of our requirements from inventories and price valuation to be attached to them (iii) amounts due from U.S., say to end of December, in respect of goods and services previously supplied on Reciprocal Aid and Reciprocal Aid goods in inventory[1] (iv) sums due between U.K. and U.S. on various claims and counter claims (i.e. the dead cats[2] and their opposite numbers)

(*e*) we would agree what is indeed unavoidable in view of the terms of the act (see below) that in principle our requirements would be taken by us in pursuance of an agreement made under section 3(*c*) of Lend Lease Act[3] but that final decision as to means of financing would be deferred until it had been possible to determine more precisely the amounts likely to be involved. We should however agree now that in due course settlement would take form either of cash payment, after

[1] A collection of telegrams on Reciprocal Aid and estimates of the amounts due from the United States, leading up to the note (not printed) sent to the State Department on 10 October formally announcing the termination of Reciprocal Aid from 2 September 1945 (cf. No. 24, note 8, No. 27.i(*c*), and No. 33.i and ii), is filed at UE 4508/1094/53.
[2] A term used for claims and counter-claims arising out of the war.
[3] See No. 4, note 7.

account had been taken of offsets and claims on both sides, or of a credit arrangement on standard 'Crowley' terms[4] (30 years and 2⅜ percent) which could be merged in ultimate settlement if desired.

3. Keynes indicated that in his view compromise arrangement on above lines would be acceptable, subject to your approval. Matter was left on basis that draft exchange of letters would be prepared for consideration.[5] Hannaford and Lee are now preparing such drafts.

4. We recommend that provided satisfactory and water-tight drafts emerge, you should authorise us to accept arrangements on above lines. It will have great advantage of avoiding immediate and public commitment on our part to accept credit basis on quasi-commercial terms while giving Crowley adequate protection vis-à-vis Congress and other countries. It is true that we shall probably not be able to hold position indefinitely (e.g. to hold over settlement so that it becomes part of any general arrangement concluded with U.S. Government) and that in, say, two or three months time we may be obliged definitely to opt for one of solutions mentioned at (e) above. But by that time we should know better where we stand as regards possibility of and timetable for any general arrangement and even if we felt obliged then to accept interim credit arrangement effect of doing so might be much less objectionable then than now. One possible disadvantage is that by linking our requirements from inventory with those from pipeline we might conceivably weaken our bargaining position as regards prices of former category. But we doubt whether there is much in this and we should of course take particular care to ensure that exchange of letters safeguards our position in this respect—i.e. by use of words in referring to inventory requirements such as 'at prices to be agreed'. It should be noted that reference in proposed formula at beginning of (e) above to 'agreement made under section 3(c) of Lend Lease Act' is necessary since only legal basis upon which supplies can continue to move to us is in pursuance of agreement made under that section. It does not connote acceptance of credit terms.

5. Americans have indicated that they will wish to include in letter statement setting October 2nd as terminal date by which we must tell them what we require from pipeline. We are checking with Missions but *prima facie* see no objection to this reasonable request.

---

[4] Cf. No. 16.

[5] NABOB 92 of 26 September reported that a misunderstanding had arisen during discussions with the Americans on the proposed exchange of letters: 'It transpired that Americans were asking us to accept wording which committed us to taking the *whole* of both civilian and military inventories . . . They attempted to argue that Crowley had always taken position that whereas we could select from the pipeline we were to be obligated to take whole of inventories. We protested that Crowley had never made this clear or indeed raised the point either on the Lend Lease Committee or in his talk with Keynes . . .' (UE 4507/1094/53). No agreement had been reached on this point or on the draft letters when Lord Keynes reviewed the position of the Lend-Lease Committees on 2 October: see No. 53.

6. We should be grateful for very early indication of your views.
7. See my immediately following telegram.[6]

[6] No. 38.

No. 38

British Missions (Washington) to Cabinet Offices
(Received 21 September, 6.40 p.m.)

NABOB 69 Telegraphic [UE 4404/1094/53]

Immediate. Secret   WASHINGTON, *21 September 1945, 5.55 p.m.*

For Treasury from Keynes.

1. My immediately preceding telegram[1] on talk with Crowley about finance of our pipeline and inventory requirements.

2. Great advantage of this proposal is that it enables us for the time being to avoid a commercial credit agreement without finally pledging ourselves to payment of cash at a time when the future is obscure. It seems to me to get as near as possible to what we were aiming at before I left London. I think Crowley was on this occasion doing his best to be helpful after I had expressed in the most emphatic terms the almost insuperable objection which I thought that the Cabinet and Parliament and public opinion in England would feel to our being forced to accept commercial terms of credit at this stage of the negotiations.

3. Nevertheless you must appreciate that this does not mean a moratorium of an indefinite term or one which will necessarily last until an overall satisfactory financial arrangement has been finally concluded. What it does is to delay matters until we are likely to have a clearer idea about what is to follow after. Paragraph 1(e) of the preceding telegram means that when the time comes we can meet the bill either out of our own cash or out of the actual or prospective cash of the final settlement or by a temporary Crowley credit made with reasonable certainty that we shall discharge it out of the overall settlement within a month or two. I feel that there will be much less objection to a credit arrangement, should the timetable make that inevitable, if we accept it after the main discussions and as an arrangement which is not merely temporary but one which we can reasonably expect to subsume under other arrangements.

4. I emphasise the timetable because my belief is that even if we reach a satisfactory agreement with the Administration this year the necessary legislation will not have passed Congress before February or March of next year. If it works out like this we have to face the fact that we may possibly have to take some interim credit under existing legislation as the only alternative to allowing our cash reserves to fall excessively. I hope

[1] No. 37.

that this uncertainty about the timetable will also be regarded as a reason for the utmost economy meanwhile and for not committing in advance what is still a long way out of sight.

No. 39

British Missions (Washington) to Cabinet Offices
(Received 22 September, 3.45 a.m.)

NABOB 70 Telegraphic[1] [UE 4460/1094/53]

Immediate. Top secret   WASHINGTON, *21 September 1945, 9.35 p.m.*

For Chancellor of the Exchequer from Keynes.

1. At our fifth session yesterday I completed the series of my opening discourses in which I have set forth the facts of our problem and the alternatives before us. The first three meetings[2] were devoted to the statement of the facts of our position. The next two[3] to the substance of paragraphs 22 to 39 of the revised version of my memorandum which I sent to you from Canada.[4]

2. In the first of these last two meetings I refrained from giving figures of the amount of assistance we shall require and the scale on which we might hope to release sterling area balances assuming sufficient assistance. But I was strongly pressed by Vinson at the end of the meeting to come down to brass tacks and it was generally agreed on our side that this had become the right course.

3. In the second of these meetings therefore I stated the amount of assistance required as five billion dollars plus such amount as turns out to be due from us to pay for the cleaning up of Lend Lease. No reference has yet been made on either side to the terms of such assistance.

4. We have been given a patient and attentive hearing but, apart from a number of questions on points of detail, the Americans have refrained from comment except as reported in the next paragraph and have made no constructive proposals of their own. I fear that the delay in opening the commercial talks may mean that a considerable time may now pass before we receive any concrete reaction from the Americans. Nevertheless our impression is that they were satisfied with the proposals for liberalising the sterling area and were not shocked by the size of the sums mentioned.[5]

5. Clayton and other members of the Committee have repeatedly emphasised the importance they attach to the other members of the sterling area making a substantial contribution to the final solution. We

[1] This telegram is also printed in Moggridge, *op. cit.*, pp. 499–501.
[2] i.e. the second, third and fourth meetings of the Top Committee: see No. 29, note 4.
[3] i.e. the first and second meetings of the Finance Committee on 19 and 20 September (COM/FIN 1st and 2nd meetings, minutes circulated on 3 October as Gen 80/28 and 29, UE 4601, 4602/1094/53). Records of these meetings are printed *op. cit.*, pp. 484–98.
[4] No. 22.   [5] Cf. *F.R.U.S. 1945*, vol. vi, pp. 132–4.

are given to understand that this will be an indispensable condition of American assistance without which they could not hope to approach Congress successfully. They wish to represent the plan as one to which all parties concerned are prepared to make appropriate contributions. We have not disputed the fairness of this approach but have urged them not to underestimate the practical and political difficulties of going too far in this direction and have emphasised the importance of our treating each case individually on its merits and the unfairness of any uniform solution. We have also argued that several of the countries affected, especially India, have made larger contributions to the common effort in proportion to their wealth than appears on the surface. Nevertheless a certain amount of pressure from the Americans in the direction indicated and the fact that they insist on associating jam for the sterling area with the pill may help us in the end to achieve a fair settlement all round.

6. Acting in accordance with your instructions we have handed over to them in writing nothing but the tables of figures of which copies have been sent to London.[6] The proposals relating to the sterling area have been confined to oral exposition. The Ambassador and Brand and all of us here are very strongly of the opinion that the time has come when we should do well to give them in writing a statement more or less on the lines of paras. 22 to 39 of my memorandum referred to above. Excellent minutes of the meetings have been prepared which have or will reach you. But these minutes have deliberately avoided giving any such details as would make them equivalent of a written statement. The result is that much of the detail including some of the safeguards we are preparing for ourselves have probably entered the minds of some or all of the listeners in a vague and inaccurate form: since they have already been given the substance it is better that they should have it before them accurately in a form which they can think over at leisure. May I now prepare a version of the above paras for them which may need a little editing here and there in the light of discussions we have had with the Americans but would not depart in substance from what you already know?

7. The *New York Times* stated today that it has obtained a copy of the statistical tables we presented to the Top Committee some days ago and proves the accuracy of its statement by copious and exact quotations though these are all taken from COM/TOP 4[6] and not from COM/TOP 3[6] which is a much more confidential paper. I have pointed out to the State Department that this does not encourage us to let them have anything further in writing but they assure me that as a result of the Ambassador's having called attention to the excessive size of the gathering at the first three meetings very special precautions have been taken to guard the secrecy of the proceedings at the last two meetings which were with the Finance Committee and not the Top Committee. The papers of the Finance Committee will be treated as Top Secret and given a very

[6] See No. 29, note 4.

146

restricted circulation. At the end of each meeting we called Mr. Vinson's attention to the special need for keeping secret at this stage any discussions affecting other members of the sterling area and at each meeting he has given direct instructions to this effect to all present. Anyhow oral discussions are no more protected from disclosure than written papers and merely render one liable to disclosure in a less accurate form.

8. The Canadian Minister in Washington told Brand last night that Mr. Clayton had mentioned to him in conversation that the American members of the Committee were well satisfied with the statements we made in our first five meetings and considered that we had proved our case but whether Congress would be similarly convinced was another matter. He also told Brand that according to Clayton the President had asked for a full statement of requests to the U.S. for assistance from all applicants including UNRRA and will take no decision until he has the complete picture.

CALENDARS TO NO. 39

i *26 Sept. 1945 British Missions (Washington) Tel. NABOB 91* Statement for President (cf. para. 8 above) likely to show requests for U.S. aid total $20 billion: 'the huge figures . . . are a very real impediment to our own negotiations' [UE 4615/1094/53].

ii *27 Sept. 1945 Lord Keynes to Sir W. Eady, enclosing memo. by Mr. Lee of conversation with Mr. J.W. Angell (Assistant Administrator, F.E.A.)* Americans impressed by exposition of British problems but resent comparison between U.K. and U.S. war efforts [T 236/438].

No. 40

Cabinet Offices to British Missions (Washington)

BABOON 54 Telegraphic [UE 4404/1094/53]

Secret   CABINET OFFICES, *22 September 1945, 7 p.m.*

Reference NABOB 68 and 69.[1]

1. We are grateful for this report of talks. Obviously you must play along with Crowley while you can and therefore we agree that you should make arrangements on general lines proposed.

2. We recognise that idea of separating inventories from pipeline and treating inventories as part of longer term settlement is not now practicable. This increases importance of some aspects of inventories. Most important is the safeguard in paragraph 4 of NABOB 68 about

[1] Nos. 37 and 38.

147

agreement on pricing of stocks. Second, although we have thrown out of the inventory useless surpluses, we should certainly wish to throw further items out if the cost of inventories was raised against us, while we might wish to retain some of those items if we had the prospect of reasonable terms in the long run. Lastly, we do not want to exclude the possibility of your using the argument that a part of these inventories should be deemed replenishments of normal working stocks to correspond to the position at the very beginning of Lend/Lease.[2]

3. It is not unreasonable of the Americans to put in October 2nd as the deadline date for the pipeline decisions. We think we can determine by that date but one difficulty will be food for overseas services in the pipeline. We shall do our best to clear this up in time. We are trying to reduce effective demand for services to very small proportions. This is so important in cost that we still need a few days for softening up.

4. All these questions of keeping down the overall cost of inventories are of special importance to us because the probable time-table in paragraph 4 of NABOB 69 means that our liabilities on standard Crowley terms may amount to large sums before Congress has approved a more satisfactory basis for meeting our needs. Indeed this postponement of the Congressional decision and the doubts about its ultimate shape will give us great anxiety meanwhile in view of our dependence on United States supplies.

[2] In BABOON 120 of 15 October the Treasury stated that figures comparing certain stocks in March 1941 with those in 1945 were not helpful to this argument, since mid-1945 stocks were considerably higher: 'Apologies for a red herring' (UE 4404/1094/53).

No. 41

Mr. Bevin to the Earl of Halifax (Washington)

CAMER 673 Telegraphic [UE 4505/1094/53]

Immediate. Top secret   FOREIGN OFFICE, 26 September 1945, 11.25 a.m

For Keynes.
Reference paragraph 6 of NABOB 70.[1]
Full minutes of meetings have not yet reached us but we infer from paragraphs 2 and 3 of your telegram that you have clearly indicated idea of voluntary scaling down of Sterling obligations and have quantified proposal along the lines of paragraphs 38 and 39 of your memorandum. What you now seek is authority to put forward these proposals in writing on behalf of the Government in detail.

2. We appreciate that you are all agreed time has now come to do this and that in this matter detail is important. We also recognise importance of ensuring that all members of Administration, including Vinson who i

[1] No. 39.   [2] No. 22.

148

not familiar with the whole story, may see exactly what we have in mind and how financial proposals will lead to earlier reopening of certain markets to United States. We also admit risk that unless Administration have before them concrete proposals they may design their own proposals, including ideas of Harry White for taking over part of Sterling Balances,[3] and it may be more difficult to push these ideas out of their heads once they have been formed. All these considerations would lead us to agree to what you ask.

3. Nevertheless, we have serious grounds for hesitation at this stage.[4] Your memorandum will be written proposals formally submitted on behalf of United Kingdom Government. They contain:
1. Indication of size of assistance we want,
2. proposals about Sterling Area which will be represented as virtually abandonment of Sterling bloc,
3. specific proposals for writing down Sterling indebtedness.
In present temper of United States all these points are big news and we would have gravest fear of leakage – whether out of malice or friendliness.

4. The first two we could look after. But we should expect serious trouble with Dominions and India and some other Sterling creditors if it were announced that British Government had made to American Government proposals for significant scaling down of Sterling obligations without the faintest consultation beforehand with the holders of those Balances. To any complaint about our behaviour we should have inadequate defence, and our action would be seized upon by influential critics of our whole plan. The plan might be in danger of being wrecked on this uncomfortable dispute over procedure.

5. In fact it has been the Americans who have publicly suggested that our creditors owe it to us to adjust their Balances to realities of position. Press comments from America have elaborated this theme. In discussions over here with Clayton our memory is that he made two somewhat inconsistent comments on this matter. At one time he said that United States Government would regard our handling of Sterling creditors as a matter with which they were not directly concerned. At another talk he indicated that if American assistance was to serve its purpose some adjustment of our Sterling indebtedness would be necessary.

6. It was in your mind and in ours that it would help us if American Administration could indicate that their assistance on a large scale would in some sense be conditional upon our coming to terms with each of our

---

[3] Cf. Enclosure in No. 28, para. III (c).
[4] In a minute of 25 September to Mr. Attlee seeking approval for the draft of this telegram Sir E. Bridges stated in particular: ' . . . the really big point is, as we see it, that Lord Keynes should not go on written record, in a document submitted on behalf of the British Government, as taking the initiative in proposing a scaling down of our obligations to other countries, including the Dominions, India and some troublesome countries in the Middle East (Egypt and Iraq) who have not been consulted beforehand by us'. Mr. Attlee minuted: 'I agree & approve draft reply. C.R.A. 25.9.45' (PREM 8/35).

main creditors for an adjustment of the debt. Such a condition fits very reasonably into the pattern of the second alternative in your memorandum and it would enable us to enter upon realistic discussions with our Sterling creditors without compelling us to find some other and possibly disputable moral or financial ground for seeking adjustment of total indebtedness. You will appreciate importance of this point in regard to India, also probably Egypt, and indeed Iraq. We should like to avoid this financial issue being linked with the important political issues arising between us and India or Egypt or the other Middle East countries.

7. Tactically therefore we should very much like you to try to get some indication from American Administration in a form which could be used if necessary, that they would expect an adjustment of our Sterling indebtedness and the release of some part of the Sterling Balances after the adjustment to be ingredients in any scheme to which they would be expected to make a very large financial contribution. In speaking of use if necessary we have in mind that if subject leaked in Washington and we received complaints we should be able to say that the suggestion had come to us from the American Administration. We should not excuse ourselves for we would maintain that it was a suggestion which in our opinion also was in accordance with realities of position. But important political point would have been gained that initiative appeared to be that of American Government.

8. We should be glad to have your urgent views whether this can be obtained and how you would propose to set about it. We are not sure that you need press for a written statement from them. It would be enough if you obtained it in sufficiently clear terms at a sufficiently high level for us to be able to say that during the discussions the American Administration at a high level had raised the matter with us.

Prime Minister agrees.

CALENDARS TO NO. 41

i *17 Sept. 1945 British Missions (Washington) Tel. NABOB 63* Proposed meeting of Lord Halifax and Lord Keynes with Dominions Ministers, who would be informed about opening phase of negotiations and that 'question of the sterling balances would undoubtedly be raised by the Americans', but that 'we should not commit ourselves with Americans to any particular arrangements affecting their interests' (full record of meeting on 18 Sept. in D.O. 35/1216, not printed) [UE 4302/1094/53].

ii *22 Sept. 1945 Extract from letter from Mr. Cockram (Washington) to Mr. Snelling (D.O.)* Fears Lord Keynes may be 'over-optimistic about securing the co-operation of the Dominions in scaling down the sterling debts' [D.O. 35/1216].

iii *24 Sept.–5 Oct. 1945 Tels. CAMER 662–4 & REMAC 752 to and from Washington* Possible need to issue statement that any agreement reached in Washington on scaling down of U.K. sterling debt would not commit India [UE 4377, 4640/1094/53].

No. 42

The Earl of Halifax (Washington) to Mr. Bevin
(Received 26 September, 8.11 a.m.)

No. 6439 Telegraphic [W 12858/19/58]

Important   WASHINGTON, 26 September 1945, 2.28 a.m.

Following from Hall Patch.

Reference NABOB No. 80 [ii], final paragraph.

1. It seems most desirable that the question of shipping, civil aviation, telecommunications and perhaps oil should be looked at as a whole and appropriate decisions taken to enable a consistent policy to be pursued with the Americans.

2. From here it looks clear that we should seek to obtain the greatest possible freedom for our shipping to earn in all markets as one of our greatest sources of foreign exchange.

3. Where we are able to stick clearly to the principle of non-discrimination we seem reasonably certain to have, *a priori*, the full support of the State Department, whatever the difficulties with other agencies, and that Department is more and more reasserting its dominance in foreign economic policy.

4. The question of shipping may loom so large later on in the general discussions and seems relatively so much more important that I submit it would be desirable for the Foreign Office to concert with ministers concerned over the whole field mentioned in paragraph 1 so that we may pursue a firm and consistent line here.

5. Ambassador has seen and concurs.

CALENDARS TO No. 42

i *24 Sept.–3 Nov. 1945 Shipping:* letter of 20 Sept. from Mr. Crowley to Mr Brand further extending Lend-Lease on certain British shipping (*NABOB 79*, cf. No. 21.i), and clarification of terms of this extension in Mr. Brand's reply of 18 Oct. (*NABOB Saving 19*), confirmed by Mr. Clayton on 3 Nov. (*NABOB Saving 26*); cf. *F.R.U.S. 1945*, vol. vi, p. 124 and note 39 [UE 4461, 5027, 5415/1094/53].

ii *24 Sept. & 1 Oct. 1945 Tels. NABOB 80 and BABOON 71 from and to Washington* American shipping and shipping subsidies in relation to commercial negotiations: importance of clear undertaking against discrimination; 'we should not accept as a condition either of shipping assistance or of financial assistance any arrangement to guarantee American flag ships a proportion of trade' [W 12833/19/58].

iii   *9 Oct. 1945   Earl of Halifax (Washington) Tel. REMAC 765* Keynes Mission is attempting to obtain greater security for British use of American boats chartered on bareboat terms (i.e. whereby the charterer provides the crew and is responsible for running expenses, insurance and repairs) [UE 4712/1094/53].

No. 43

Mr. Bevin to the Earl of Halifax (Washington)

No. 9741 Telegraphic [W 12795/24/802]

Immediate. Secret   FOREIGN OFFICE, *26 September 1945, 2 p.m.*

My telegram No. 9707 [i] (of September 25th: co-ordination of lease-lend and civil aviation discussions with the United States).

United States Ambassador called on September 25th and left with me note by his Civil Air Attaché[1] stating that Mr. Byrnes had received a telegram from Mr. Clayton urging that Minister of Civil Aviation if possible and Sir W. Hildred[2] should proceed to United States at the earliest opportunity in order that financial and trade problems now under discussion should be co-ordinated with pending civil aviation matters. Mr. Clayton had hoped to continue at the end of the month discussions he had recently had with Sir W. Hildred[3] but 'it was now imperative that Sir William's trip be made at once'.

2. I told United States Ambassador that constant pressure to get people out from this country at the time of lease-lend talks was causing great hostility. We resented anything in the nature of blackmail. Between us we had successfully dealt with oil matters by getting Mr. Ickes over here quite apart from lend-lease and had settled them.[4] I suggested that someone should come over here from United States discreetly to try to arrange a settlement. Meanwhile, I told Ambassador I should like him to get the facts of the civil aviation case from Minister of Civil Aviation and Sir W. Hildred. I asked him, however, not to put on the screw. The British people would go down rather than be clubbed.

3. United States Ambassador did not express entire agreement with me but proclaimed his readiness to see Minister of Civil Aviation as soon as possible.

---

[1] Mr. L. Satterthwaite's note is not printed.
[2] Director-General of Civil Aviation.
[3] These discussions were summarized by the Minister of Civil Aviation in his memorandum C.A.C. (45)4 (No. 21.iii).
[4] See No. 21.ii, and iii below.

i *21 & 25 Sept. 1945* (*a*) *Minutes from Mr. Gallop to Mr. Bevin* for interview with Lord Winster (Minister of Civil Aviation) and Sir W. Hildred: American pressure for agreement on fifth freedom rights (cf. No. 21) cannot be resisted indefinitely by diplomatic means alone; (*b*) *Tel. No. 9707 to Washington* American approach on correlation of civil aviation and financial negotiations may be a bluff, but 'we should strongly object to any attempt to couple such talks' [W 12489, 12795/24/802].

ii *1 & 3 Oct. 1945* *Correspondence between Ministry of Civil Aviation and F.O.* on exchanges with Mr. Winant concerning possible Anglo-U.S. civil aviation agreement: cf. No 58 [W 13295, 13382/24/802].

iii *19 & 26 Sept. 1945* *Minute from Mr. Gallop to Mr. Bevin* for interview with Mr. Ickes: *Report (C.P. (45) 194) to Cabinet by Mr. E. Shinwell* (Minister of Fuel & Power) on negotiations which opened on 18 Sept. between Mr. Ickes and Mr. Shinwell and culminated on 24 Sept. in Anglo-U.S. Agreement on Petroleum (published as Cmd. 6683 of 1945) [W 12780,13147/12/76].

No. 44

The Earl of Halifax (Washington) to Mr. Bevin
(*Received 26 September, 11.17 p.m.*)

No. 6444[1] *Telegraphic* [*UE 4478/1094/53*]

Immediate   WASHINGTON, *26 September 1945, 5.35 p.m.*

Personal and Top Secret for yourself and Chancellor of the Exchequer.

1. At their invitation Keynes and I have had a private talk behind the scenes with Clayton and Vinson to take stock of the situation and explore some of the more delicate matters upon which we have not yet ventured in open committee.

2. The conversation began with a ready admission by them that our proposals for liberalising the Sterling area and scaling down the Sterling debts are acceptable. Assuming therefore no hitch in the commercial talks Clayton thought we might set 25th October as the dead line for finishing. In that case if his advice was accepted they would go at once to Congress. They would think it dangerous to wait lest the matter should go stale. For us avoidance of delay would have great advantage. They accepted our position that the settlement with the Sterling creditors should be our affair, and thought that our mutual understanding about how this would be carried out could be expressed in some contingent way which would allow Congress to act without waiting for our having finalised the details with the sterling area countries, which could be summoned to London for this purpose in November or December.

---

[1] In his telegram No. 6422 of 25 September, printed as No. 125 in Volume II, Lord Halifax had mentioned that he had had 'a little general talk' about the financial negotiations with Mr. Truman that morning.

3. They were emphatic that their case with Congress must depend on the advantages to the United States of liberalising and facilitating international trade. They thought that arguments based on our past sacrifices and especially on comparisons between ourselves and the United States would do no good and should be advanced if at all from the American side.

4. Keynes then sounded them on the amount of assistance they thought we had justified. We understood that some amount in the neighbourhood of \$5 billion was in their minds as well as in ours. So far so good. But when Keynes turned to the question of the terms on which such aid should be granted we ran into difficulties. Not only did they consider a grant-in-aid out of the question but both of them argued strongly that there was no prospect of their being able to persuade Congress to accept a loan without interest, though the rate of interest would be kept as low as possible. They would also accept some escape clause in the event of our inability to pay. They particularly emphasised the difficulty into which any other arrangement would put them with other foreign applicants for financial aid. They are at present discussing with Russians on the basis of 3 per cent interest.

5. We yielded no ground on this issue. Keynes explained that you were thinking in terms of a grant-in-aid. As for discussing a loan at interest I confirmed his insistence that there was no prospect of a proposal on these lines proving acceptable to you.

6. The argument continued some time without visible progress and without either side yielding ground. But they were left in no doubt as to how any such proposals would be viewed in London. The conversations were friendly and good tempered throughout. The matter was left that we would all think over what had been said and meet again on Thursday[2] morning, it being understood on both sides that this exchange of view had been exploratory and non-committal.

7. In answer to my question whether any other conditions were in their mind they did not indicate any.

8. Bad as the above may sound and indeed is, we do not think you need take the position too tragically. Although Clayton and Vinson took so firm a line there is reason to think that their experts are carefully examining the question of a loan without interest. Several kites along these lines are being flown in the American press, probably under the inspiration of the United States Treasury, which do not appear to be arousing seriously unfavourable reaction except in quarters which are always hostile. A proposal for a loan free of interest would not take the American public by surprise. We think that they would be only too glad to meet us if they could see a way of dressing the matter up in a manner which would help them to overcome their genuine political difficulties and also avoid an inconvenient precedent for other countries.

[2] 27 September 1945.

9. Keynes is sending you by air bag a memorandum[3] exploring possible terms of a loan without interest. We think that the chances of a grant-in-aid are remote and that you should examine carefully the acceptability of a loan without interest. He has added to this memorandum which was drafted previously a final paragraph in the light of the above conversation which also deserves your urgent consideration.[4]

[3] The reference was to the memorandum of 26 September, 'The Terms of Assistance', printed with Lord Keynes' covering letter of the same date to Mr. Dalton in Moggridge, *op. cit.*, pp. 502–8, and discussed in Pressnell, *op. cit.*, Chapter 10(11). The last two paragraphs of this memorandum set out alternatives for consideration in the light of the conversation with Mr. Clayton and Mr. Vinson, based on terms of $5 billion and incorporating an 'escape clause', explained earlier in the memorandum, to the effect that 'no creditor country, whether a Sterling Area country or the United States or Canada, would be entitled to draw an instalment in repayment of the service of our War debts now under consideration in any year in which its monetary reserves (as defined by the Bretton Woods Plan) stood above its Bretton Woods quota and *were increasing*, the instalments in question being deferred in this event to the latter end of the period of amortisation which would be correspondingly extended'.

The alternatives were:

'(i) That we still seek to obtain a part, say $2 billions, as a grant-in-aid (which would be much facilitated if we would agree to earmark it to the Sterling Area), and $3 billions repayable as to capital but free of interest. Probably not a starter.

'(ii) A grant-in-aid for $2 billions as above, with the balance of $3 billions at 2 per cent interest repayable over 50 years, beginning 10 years hence. An equal annual service for this of $100,000,000 would pay it off in about 45 years.

'(iii) A non-interest loan repayable over 50 years, beginning 10 years hence, of which the annual service would be $100,000,000. It might take the form of ear-marking gold for us to this extent, this justifying no interest. The gold would never leave their hands since they would only release it as we needed it and as soon as we needed it we would return it to them.

'(iv) A loan at 1 per cent repayable by an equal annual service of $100,000,000 beginning 10 years hence, which would pay it off in about 70 years.

'(v) A perpetual loan at 2 per cent, free of interest for the first ten years, of which the service would cost $100,000,000.

'(vi) A loan at 2 per cent, free of interest for the first 10 years, with an annual service commencing at $100,000,000 and gradually rising by (say) $5,000,000 a year to a ceiling of $200,000,000 a year, which would pay it off in about 45 years.

'14. It will be seen that the proposal is (except in the case of (i) and (vi)) that the annual cost should be kept at $100,000,000. (ii) and (iii) are my own preferences. Failing these, is (v) or (vi), which would probably be more acceptable out of the question? (vi) would probably be acceptable to the Americans but seems to us definitely too expensive' (T236/439).

[4] A letter of 28 September from Sir W. Eady to Lord Keynes regarding this telegram is printed in Moggridge, *op. cit.*, pp. 520–23.

No. 45

Letter from Mr. Hall-Patch (Washington) to Mr. Butler

[*UE 4585/1094/53*]

WASHINGTON, *26 September 1945*

Dear Butler,

Herewith the latest batch of photostats.[1]

We ran into dirty weather yesterday. In a very hole in the corner talk at Blair Lee House (convened there to avoid the officials at the Treasury & the State Dept. knowing anything about it) Clayton & Vinson gave the Ambassador and Keynes to understand:

(*a*) *no* grant in aid

(*b*) no loan *without* interest.[2]

This led to some rather tense exchanges of views and the parties concerned are to meet together again on Thursday[3] (in the same locale) to consider the situation. Meanwhile H.E. & K. are chewing the cud on what to say to London.

I am not at all surprised at this outcome. It is quite obvious that the Administration is only now commencing faintly to appreciate the difficulties of our situation, and that the general public have no conception at all. This is hardly the atmosphere in which to expect large concessions from Congress, and it is from Congress that the concessions must come. Unless the President will come out on our side with a dynamic & forceful appeal our chances are very poor. As I read the situation that is the last thing *this* President will do. Consequently I think you people in London will very soon have to put your thinking cap on and deside [*sic*] whether we should remain here, or whether it is not better tactics for us to withdraw, make all preparations to tighten our belts, & then see in, say, three or four months time, whether the hard facts of life have penetrated sufficiently the crust of ignorance here to permit fruitful discussions to be resumed.

I hope I am not being unduly pessimistic, but on present form I really do not see daylight. The people we are in daily touch with are commencing to see things in their right perspective; Congress & the outside world are blanketed in an impenetrable fog of ignorance & prejudice lit by fitful flickers (too frequent to be pleasant) of downright hostility.

The only good thing from our point of view is that the exporting interests are commencing to sit up and take notice. The Cunard-White Star, for example, have just served notice on the Standard Oil that they may not be able to continue a profitable connexion which has lasted upwards of thirty years. This has brought a couple of New York swells

---

[1] The enclosed copies of articles from the American press are not printed.

[2] See No. 44.

[3] 27 September 1945.

from Standard Oil up to Washington to sit on Clayton's doorstep. This is all to the good, but it will have to go a great deal further before the general public commence to see a glimmer of sense in helping us out of our difficulties.

I hope Thursday's discussion will dispel my doubts. Meanwhile I thought you should know how things stand now.

Please pass on to Coulson or Charles Stirling.

Yours ever,
E.L. HALL-PATCH

No. 46

The Earl of Halifax (Washington) to Mr. Bevin
(Received 28 September, 3.10 a.m.)

No. 6490 Telegraphic [UE 4502/1094/53]

WASHINGTON, *27 September 1945, 9.26 p.m.*
Most immediate. Top secret. Personal

For Secretary of State and Chancellor of the Exchequer from Keynes. Ambassador and I continued today our talk with Vinson and Clayton reported in Ambassador's telegram No. 6444.[1] Since the Ambassador had to leave shortly after the meeting, he asked me to report on his behalf in this and the next following telegram.[2]

2. We re-stated the position that unless they are prepared to treat us as a special case for which financial terms are thought appropriate quite different from those contemplated for other borrowers no solution seemed to us to be in sight. This they eventually conceded. They agreed that special financial terms could be included as part of a general Anglo-American economic concordat. This was at least some progress.

3. At this point the Ambassador raised the question whether there was anything further we or they could suggest which could help to bring the type of solution we desired within practical politics. See my immediately following telegram.

4. They went on to say that, so far as they personally were concerned, and on this Vinson was particular[ly] emphatic, the amount of dollars at issue was not in their opinion important for the United States and they would gladly make any reasonable concession in the financial terms which they thought they could sell to Congress and public opinion. But they repeated in unison that neither a grant-in-aid nor an interest-free loan was practical politics.

5. We then pressed the question whether any financial formula could be devised which was capable of meeting our divergent standpoints. Clayton repeated, what he has said before, that in his opinion we were too

---

[1] No. 44. [2] No. 47.

gloomy about our future prospects. In a few years the sums now troubling us might seem small. He was ready to consider an escape clause which would protect us in the event of his forecast proving wrong. I replied that I hoped he would prove right and thought it quite possible he would. But we required certainty and after much reflection I could discover no satisfactory formula of the kind he wanted. The search for any such formula was faced with the dilemma that it would lay us open either to the charge of so arranging our affairs as to avoid payment or to inquisition about how we did our own business, thus putting us in a condition of semi-servitude. This plan might also lead to continual friction and disputes as to whether we could or could not meet our full obligations. We did not think that this would be in the interests of either country. I agreed however that in the case of any obligation we had accepted we should wish in practice to improve on the minimum rate of repayment in the case both of sterling and of dollar creditors if this should turn out to be within our capacity. If his optimism proved justified we should then hope to discharge our obligations more rapidly and they must trust our good faith to act in this way. We should think it to be in our own interest to escape from debt as soon as possible and this would be the right way of using any surplus we might develop hereafter but it should be at our own discretion.

6. I took this opportunity to outline an escape clause of another type, namely that explained in paragraph 9 of my memorandum of 26th September already sent to London,[3] which I thought should accompany any obligation we might accept. But this dealt with the willingness of the creditor to receive not with the capacity of the debtor to pay. They agreed that it deserved examination and I shall mention it to White.

7. I then explored with them the possibility of combining a grant-in-aid up to a certain amount with a credit at a low rate of interest in addition which could be called on as required up to a further amount. They were obviously interested and attracted by this idea though they thought it prudent to declare that this also was outside practical politics. At the conclusion of our talk however the Ambassador returned to this proposal and asked again whether they ruled out some kind of combination on these lines. Vinson immediately replied that they did not wish to rule it out.

8. In conclusion the Ambassador undertook to report fully to London and we made provisional arrangements to meet again next Thursday, October 4th in the hope that by then we should have further instructions from you.

9. We both think as the result of these talks and also of all other currents of opinion reaching us from various quarters that a straight grant-in-aid of five billions is not on the map, but that the equivalent of an interest free loan[4] of that amount may in the end prove possible if it can be

[3] See No. 44, note 3.
[4] In Washington telegram No. 6528 of 30 September Lord Keynes sent the following message for Mr. Bevin and Mr. Dalton in amplification of this paragraph: 'In speaking of

incorporated as part of a general Anglo-American economic concordat. May we discuss tentatively and of course without any premature commitment on the lines of a formula which would not involve us in an annual liability for debt service exceeding $100 million?[5]

the equivalent of an interest-free loan I had in mind for example a combination of a grant-in-aid with a credit on the lines suggested in paragraph 7. A non-interest bearing loan repayable over 50 years would cost us for debt service $100 million a year from the year in which the repayment commenced. Paragraph 9 is intended to cover any other method of arriving at the same result to us at the same cost' (F.O. 800/512).

[5] On 28 September Mr. Dixon recorded that Mr. Bevin's 'preliminary observation was that he personally had never been persuaded that we should stand out for a grant-in-aid and considered that the right solution was for us to ask for an interest-free credit, say of five million dollars, on which we should draw if our need were imperative . . . Meanwhile the Secretary of State tells me that he expressed the same view to Mr. Byrnes in conversation this evening, and Mr. Byrnes seemed much attracted by the idea' (UE 4582/1094/53). In response to a request from Sir W. Eady to find out more about this conversation, Mr. Grant minuted on 2 October that in the Foreign Office it was 'not clear whether this was a passing thought in conversation with Mr. Byrnes or part of a discussion directed specifically to the point' (T 236/439).

No. 47

The Earl of Halifax (Washington) to Mr. Bevin
(Received 28 September, 2.20 a.m.)

No. 6491 Telegraphic [UE 4502/1094/53]

WASHINGTON, 27 September 1945, 10.55 p.m.
Most immediate. Top secret. Personal

For Secretary of State and Chancellor of the Exchequer from Keynes. Paragraph 3 of my preceding telegram.[1]

1. In course of conversation Ambassador, making plain that he was speaking entirely personally and without any instructions, asked whether from point of view of general presentation of the case at a later stage, it might help the American Administration to include some sweetener that might have public appeal. He had wondered for example whether conversion of the 99 year leases for West Indian bases[2] into 999 years would have any public value. Both Clayton and Vinson at once welcomed

[1] No. 46.
[2] The Exchange of Notes of 2 September 1940 and the ensuing Agreement signed on 27 March 1941 for the lease by the United Kingdom to the United States of naval and air bases in Antigua, the Bahamas, Bermuda, British Guiana, Jamaica, St. Lucia, Trinidad and Newfoundland are printed in B.F.S.P., vol. 144, pp. 180–1 and 645–83. In return for the leases the U.K. received military and naval equipment, including surplus destroyers held in reserve by the U.S. Navy. For the negotiation of the agreement see W.S. Churchill, The Second World War, vol. ii (London, 1949), pp. 353–68.
On 8 September 1945 the U.S. Government had stated that it was prepared to agree, on certain conditions, to the use of military airfields in these bases by commercial aircraft (Washington telegram No. 6147, W 12105/182/802): see F.R.U.S. 1946, vol. i, p. 1455, note 13, and also p. 1454, note 12.

such an idea warmly, judging that it would have considerable popular appeal quite disproportionate to its practical significance. Pursuing the same line of thought, Clayton then said that it would be valuable if, as part of any general settlement at which we might arrive, such questions as telecommunications and civil aviation could be cleared between us.[3]

2. Ambassador replied that while he appreciated their desire to make the general case as attractive as possible to United States Congress and public, great care would have to be taken to avoid the impression – either in the minds of the British Government or public – that the Americans were seeking to blackmail us into settling in their interest a number of totally disconnected matters. Both Clayton and Vinson were emphatic in disclaiming any such intention and made it plain that their thought was rather to cash in on the value of any agreements which we might on merits be willing to make by including these as an integral part of an overall Anglo-American concordat, thus enabling them to put over a satisfactory financial arrangement as a part of it.[4]

3. Your telegrams Nos. 9707 and 9741.[5] Our comments will follow as soon as possible in the light of the above.

CALENDARS TO NO. 47

i *27 Aug. –15 Oct. 1945 Correspondence on possible rewriting of certain Articles of Bases Agreement (see note 2)*: State Dept. feel that present wording makes it 'impossible to stretch interpretation to cover agreed intent' [AN 2615, 2676, 3125/3/45].

ii *29 Sept. 1945 Minute by Mr. P.M. Broadmead (Head of North American Dept.)*

[3] Mr. Gallop suggested in a minute of 29 September that in the field of telecommunications a direct American wireless circuit with Saudi Arabia might be accepted, and other proposals likely to be satisfactory to the United States would be made at the forthcoming conference (cf. No. 21). 'As regards *civil aviation* there is no concession we can make, short of sacrificing our entire position in regard to the orderly regulation of air services with particular reference to Fifth Freedom traffic. If we were to do this we might, by the end of next year, have enough aircraft of our own to compete with the U.S. on more or less equal terms, but we should meanwhile have given them such a start in securing world traffic that we could never hope to recover the ground lost.'

[4] In a minute of 29 September Mr. Ashton recorded that Sir W. Eady's first reaction to Nos. 44, 46 and 47 was that 'the immediate thing to do is to warn Lord Keynes not to show his hand. On principle the Treasury are opposed to granting concessions which are not justified on their merits and indeed would much prefer to use "sweet[e]ners" to round off negotiations that had succeeded than to offer them up piecemeal as instalments of payments on blackmail . . .' Later that day, however, Sir W. Eady sent a minute to Mr. Dalton stating that on reflection he 'thought it might be convenient to include the general arguments in a draft reply [not printed] to the Ambassador'. He suggested that the Chancellor should circulate the three telegrams and the draft reply to Mr. Attlee, Mr. Bevin, Sir S. Cripps and Mr. Morrison, indicating that 'the draft was prepared in this way so that they could see the whole argument, and without prejudice to a decision to send a shorter reply'. Mr. Dalton noted: 'Yes, & say it's a draft prepared by my advisers as a "basis of discussion". H.D. 1/10' (T 247/47). See No. 56, note 5.

[5] Nos. 43.i (*b*) and 43 respectively.

Doubts value to U.S. of extending Bases' leases, which Colonial Govts. are unlikely to welcome [UE 4582/1094/53].

iii *3–7 Oct. 1945   Earl of Halifax (Washington) Tels. Nos. 6568 & 6569, Letter from Mr. N.J.A. Cheetham (General Dept.) to Sir W. Hildred* Implications of possible Anglo-American agreement on transatlantic air services: F.O. feel further negotiations 'should take place in London and should be connected as little as possible with financial and economic negotiations in Washington' [W 13150/24/802].

No. 48

Minute from Mr. Bevin to Mr. Attlee

P.M./45/21 [N 12927/1004/27]

FOREIGN OFFICE, *27 September 1945*

American desire for Bases in Iceland

The United States Government have officially notified His Majesty's Government and the Soviet Government that they intend to propose to the Government of Iceland the conclusion of an arrangement which would give the United States forces permanent sea and air bases in Iceland, subject to the proviso that when Iceland becomes a member of the United Nations, the United States Government would give sympathetic consideration to a request from the Icelandic Government that these military facilities should be made available to the Security Council as Iceland's contribution to the maintenance of international peace and security[i].[1]

2. When I first heard of this matter I persuaded Mr. Byrnes to try to defer the presentation of the American note to the Soviet Government, as I feared its effect upon the Council of Foreign Ministers and upon the chances of the security system for which the Charter provides. But this was too late.

3. I have now considered what action we should take in these circumstances. The Chiefs of Staff have advised[2] that on balance the military advantage lies in not resisting the American desire for bases in Iceland, subject to our obtaining an assurance that in no circumstances would the presence of United States forces in Iceland be allowed to compromise the security of our own communications in the North Atlantic, (e.g. in the event of the United States remaining neutral when we were at war).

[1] In a letter of 18 September Sir O. Sargent had informed Major-General L.C. Hollis, Secretary to the Chiefs of Staff Committee, that during a recent conversation in London Mr. Byrnes had told Mr. Bevin that 'the United States Government were becoming convinced of the need to maintain bases. He mentioned Iceland and Greenland in particular. He said that he proposed to communicate a list of the bases which the Americans had in mind' (N 12432/1004/27). Cf. *F.R.U.S. 1945*, vol. vi, pp. 206–10.

[2] In C.O.S.(45)591(o) of 26 September, not printed.

4. From the point of view of our political relations with the United States, I feel sure that we ought to welcome their assumption of responsibility for the defence of Iceland. But there is obviously a serious risk that the American proposal will give the Soviet Government a pretext for seeking similar bilateral arrangements with Denmark and Norway. The Russians already occupy the Danish Island of Bornholm and this American proposal may induce them to stay in Northern Norway. We might thus get straight back to the worst form of power politics and armed neutrality. The chances of organising world security on an international basis through the Security Council would be gravely prejudiced and the relevant provisions of the Charter might remain a dead letter.

5. However, we can now only make the best of the difficult situation created by this precipitate American action. In my view the proper course would be for the Americans to put their demands on Iceland in the form of a request for a temporary lease of the bases, pending the coming into force of the security procedure laid down in the Charter and the admission of Iceland to the United Nations.

6. I have put my idea in the form of a suggestion to Mr. Byrnes in the attached draft letter[3]. In view of our unfortunate experience in the past with leakages from the State Department into the American press I have confined the letter to the point about the effect on the United Nations Organisation. I would propose to supplement the letter by informing Mr. Byrnes orally (i) that His Majesty's Government would, for their part, be glad to see United States forces permanently established in Iceland (subject to the Chiefs of Staff's proviso mentioned in paragraph 3 above); and, (ii) that my suggestion in the letter is intended not only to avoid an apparent vote of no confidence in the United Nations Organisation but also to deny to the Soviet Government an excuse for demanding Russian bases in Denmark and Norway, both of whom are already members of the United Nations Organisation.

7. The Chiefs of Staff Committee have concurred in the draft letter to Mr. Byrnes, on the understanding that it would be supplemented by oral explanations, as suggested above.[4]

8. I should be grateful to know whether you approve of my proposed action.

ERNEST BEVIN

P.S. The report to the Cabinet will be my letter to Byrnes.

---

[3] The text printed as the Annex to this document is that of the letter as sent to Mr. Byrnes after the Cabinet approved the draft without amendment on 28 September.

[4] The oral communication made by Mr. Dixon when he handed Mr. Bevin's letter to Mr J.C. Dunn (U.S. Assistant Secretary of State, Deputy to Mr. Byrnes at the C.F.M.) on 29 September is summarized in paragraph 3 of the Annex to No. 90 below. Mr. Dunn informed Mr. Dixon that 'speaking personally he thought that there would be constitutional difficulties in the way of giving us the assurance we suggested in the event of the U.S. being neutral in a war in which we were belligerent, although if that event actually arose there would clearly be no difficulty'.

Letter from Mr. Bevin to Mr. Byrnes

[*N 13062/1004/27*]

28 September 1945

When we spoke on the 25th September about the desire of your Government to maintain bases in Iceland you agreed to my suggestion that it would be wise to defer presenting to the Soviet Government your proposed note. I have now learned, however, that the United States Embassy at Moscow had already made the communication.

I know that you share my anxiety that nothing should be done in this difficult period before the United Nations Organisation has got under way to prejudice the successful working of the provisions in the Charter for preserving world security in the future. I hope, therefore, that you will allow me to make the following suggestion, which I believe would help to avoid any impression that this action in respect of Iceland implied a lack of confidence in the machinery laid down in the Charter.

My proposal is that the United States Government might ask the Icelandic Government for a lease of the bases in question for a limited period, as a temporary measure pending the coming into force of the security provisions of the Charter (particularly Article 43) and the admission of Iceland to the United Nations Organisation. It would be understood that when these two conditions had been fulfilled the whole question of military facilities in Iceland for the maintenance of world security would come before the Security Council in connexion with the agreement about Iceland's contribution which the Icelandic Government would have to conclude with the Security Council under Article 43.

I believe that if your proposal were presented in this way to the Governments concerned, and in the public communiqué which will presumably have to be released in due course, it would greatly help to avoid misapprehension and the risk of damage to the United Nations Organisation.

ERNEST BEVIN

CALENDAR TO NO. 48

i *21–25 Sept. 1945   Earl of Halifax (Washington) Tels. Nos. 6329 & 6330* Comments on State Dept. memo. informing H.M.G. of proposed request for Iceland bases: *Tel. No. 9683 to Washington* asks Americans to delay action, but *Reykjavik Tel. No. 144* reports rumours of U.S. pressure on Iceland Govt. and *Washington Tel. No. 6407* states U.S. Govt. feel obliged to proceed at once [N 12597, 12799, 12800/1004/27].

No. 49

The Earl of Halifax (Washington) to Mr. Bevin
(Received 29 September, 8.25 p.m.)

REMAC 738 Telegraphic [UE 4518/1094/53]

Top secret   WASHINGTON, 29 September 1945, 4.26 a.m.

Your CAMER 673 and 674.[1] From Keynes.

1. We fully agree with the procedure you recommend in 673. I will prepare a revision of the draft written from this point of view.

2. The Ambassador and I have already taken an opportunity to approach Vinson and Clayton on the lines indicated in paragraphs 6 and 7 of 673. I read out to them the substance of these paragraphs. They readily appreciated your reasons and expressed themselves as quite willing to fall in with this line of approach. Thus you can assume that we have already reached the necessary understanding with the American administration. The line you suggest is in fact in strict accordance with the facts. We produced no proposal as to the sterling area until Clayton had stated emphatically that we must expect special treatment of the sterling balances to be part of any settlement[2] and that he would like us to communicate at once the lines that a possible solution might take.

3. Clayton told us very confidentially that he had been visited a day or two ago by the Egyptian representative who had asked whether there was any foundation for the rumour that the State Department was pressing us to scale down the sterling balances. Clayton replied cautiously fully protecting our position in the matter but leaving the Egyptian, so we understand, under no misapprehension about the feeling of the State Department that Egypt should make some appropriate contribution to any scheme from which they were to benefit. The Egyptian representative will doubtless have sent home to his Government a message on these lines.

4. I will reply to CAMER 674 in larger detail when I have made progress with the re-draft. I agree with your paragraph 2, but rather a different lead-on to that you propose in paragraph 3 will be advisable. We are told five times a day by everyone we meet that any suggestion that Great Britain has borne an excessive financial burden or has made any efforts or sacrifices which compare favourably with the United States seriously prejudices our case, and if the comparisons are valid that makes it all the worse.

5. I am not sure that I agree with the view that money released should not be free to earn interest. I should have thought that releases ought to be merged in any other free cash they have and that the Bank of England doctrine against there being two kinds of money would hold good. I agree however that there is no need to commit ourselves too deeply upon a point of this kind in a document for the Americans and before we get down to details with the sterling area creditors.

---

[1] Nos. 41 and 41.iv respectively.   [2] See No. 39.

6. I have indicated to the Americans that the new system would come into operation not later than the end of 1946 which would I think allow a sufficient winding-up period in all cases. I have been vague as to whether we could anticipate this date in any cases or what would happen in the meanwhile though I have indicated that in the event of sufficient financial assistance we could administer the sterling area during the twilight on more liberal lines.

No. 50

The Earl of Halifax (Washington) to Mr. Bevin
(Received 30 September, 8.35 a.m.)

No. 6536 Telegraphic [UR 3495/1857/851]

Important. Comply[1]   WASHINGTON, 30 September 1945, 1.56 a.m.

Repeated to Ottawa.

Your telegram No. 9690 Comply.[2]

We have considered your proposals urgently in consultation with Keynes Mission and B.F.M.

2. We trust that you will now have received the text of the statement referred to in my telegram No. 6311 Comply[3] which was despatched as my telegram No. 467 Saving Comply.[4] You will note that this White House release states categorically that

(1) United States Government is taking the necessary measures to ensure a flow of supplies which it is anticipated will be required in addition to requisitions already received and that one purpose is to prevent dissipation in non-essential domestic channels;

[1] Telegrams on matters concerning general economic, supply or relief questions were designated COMPLY.

[2] This telegram of 24 September referred to recent indications 'that United States Administration is considering the abolition of meat rationing in the near future', and expressed concern at the effect such a move might have on the availability of meat supplies for liberated Europe. It further asked the Ambassador's views on the advisability of an approach from Mr. Attlee to President Truman expressing the hope that 'no decision to de-ration meat will be taken at the present time or without full consultation among the appropriate food authorities of our two countries and Canada ... if, as we all hope, the United States are willing to make generous financial arrangements with the United Kingdom and with European countries which will enable them to purchase what they need from the United States, then the problem will again become a supply one. If, by that date, rationing has been removed and if home consumption has been stimulated, there may at that date be little meat available for export. It would therefore be regrettable if de-rationing were adopted now when the future is still uncertain and the needs of Europe so serious' (UR 3342/1857/851).

[3] This telegram of 20 September referred to the statement of 17 September by President Truman on relief and rehabilitation, printed in Public Papers: Truman 1945, pp. 321–4.

[4] Not printed.

(2) that the President's pledge made on his return from Potsdam[5] to help from Europe from going cold and hungry must be kept and that relaxation of rationing in the United States is not a factor in the allocation of relief supplies.

3. In face of this White House statement which was made a week ago at the instance of the State Department we fear that any message from the Prime Minister to the President on the lines of paragraphs 3 and 4 of your telegram under reference might be misinterpreted by the President as casting doubts both on the sincerity of his recent statements and on his ability to make effective his undertakings. Whatever our own doubts on this score may be, this is not in our judgement a good moment to run any risk of either result. That risk is enhanced by our feeling that the United States Administration is at this moment exceedingly sensitive about any suggestion that they are failing or are apt to fail, in the discharge of their international duties.

4. In any event we feel strongly that a message at such a level on this matter is both inappropriate and dangerous. Since the President has stated his intention of seeing that essential food requirements placed on United States are met, a message from the Prime Minister on the meat rationing might appear to him and his advisers as an attempt to interfere in—to them—the purely domestic question of whether maintenance or abandonment of internal rationing will affect their declared purpose. This in itself might engender a resentment which would hardly be helpful at present. Furthermore the possibility—almost, on past form, the likelihood—of a leakage must be recognised, which would present those ill-disposed to us with an excellent opportunity to broadcast accusations that we are attempting not only to take money out of United States pockets but also meat out of United States larders and tell the President how to run the country into the bargain.

5. We have, however, considered an alternative course which we think can be adopted with less risk and perhaps more advantage. We suggest that at the next meeting of the Combined Food Board the United Kingdom member should raise formally the question of possible consequences of a removal of consumer restrictions on any essential food in short supply and remind the members of the Board of (? C.F.)B. resolution No. 104[6] which provided for mutual discussion on the Board before any action was taken by any member of the [sic] country which would result in important changes in the relative consumption levels. United Kingdom member would then ask that there should be annexed to the minute a statement which would set out recommendation No. 104 and then develop the argument of consultation before rationing relaxation on the lines of paragraphs 3 and 4 of your telegram under reference but

[5] The reference was to President Truman's broadcast of 9 August, printed *op. cit.*, pp. 203–14: cf. Volume II, No. 188.
[6] A copy of this Resolution, 'Notice of Intention to Alter Consumption Policy', dated 10 February 1944, is filed with this telegram.

widening the argument to apply to all commodities in short supply and not meat alone. Statement would point out that increased consumption in exporting countries might affect the United Kingdom in either or both of two ways: (? supplies) available to the United Kingdom might themselves be restricted or deficits elsewhere might result in pressure on the United Kingdom still further to reduce its existing consumption. Statement would add that further reductions are not possible in the United Kingdom especially if extensive improvements are taking place elsewhere and would end up with the following sentence: 'On the other hand I can assure you that so far as the United Kingdom is concerned there will be no relaxation in our controls of consumption even in respect of those commodities which we can draw in large measure from sterling sources without full consideration being given to the position of other countries whose needs we know to be great'.

6. There can be no question of our right to raise this matter in the Combined Food Board which is the appropriate channel and if there should be a leakage (which is much less likely in our view than in the case of a message at the highest level) its consequences are less likely to be embarrassing. We feel bound however to warn you that in our judgement no approach is likely to achieve more than a moderate and perhaps temporary success. Nevertheless we believe the gambit is worth playing particularly since we would expect to have the Canadians on our side.

7. I should be grateful for your instructions.[7]

CALENDAR TO NO. 50

i 6 Oct.–5 Dec. 1945 Correspondence on dissolution of Combined Boards (cf. No. 10, note 3), and establishment of international commodity committees for cotton textiles, tin, rubber, hides and leather: meetings with State Dept. on 3 and 9 Oct. on American proposals for above; British desire to continue Combined Food Board until 30 June 1946; doubts about efficiency of proposed committees, and consideration of Soviet membership; resulting announcement of dissolution on 10 Dec. 1945 (see Duncan Hall and Wrigley, Studies of Overseas Supply, pp. 302–3 and 503–4); British consideration of combined Anglo–American unit for collaboration on economic information (cf. No. 9, note 4) [UE 4828–9, 4872, 5142, 5179, 5230, 5450, 5787–8, 5852–3, 5947, 5995/73/71].

[7] Foreign Office telegram No. 9953 to Washington of 4 October agreed that 'it would be preferable not to make approach at level proposed but to adopt alternative suggested in your paragraph 5', but suggested that the sentence at the end of that paragraph should be redrafted to read: 'On the other hand, I can assure you that so far as the United Kingdom is concerned even in respect of those commodities which we can draw in large measure from sterling sources, we should not enter upon major changes in consumption without giving the fullest opportunity for consultation with the other members of the Board' (UR 3495/1857/857). Lord Halifax was also instructed to ensure that the proposed statement covered the protection of the position of liberated areas.

No. 51

The Earl of Halifax (Washington) to Mr. Bevin
(Received 2 October, 6.5 a.m.)

No. 6549 Telegraphic [UE 4568/1094/53]

Immediate. Top secret   WASHINGTON, *1 October 1945, 10.54 p.m.*

From Lord Halifax to Secretary of State.
Personal for Eady from Keynes.
With reference to our telephone conversation.[1]

1. What the Ambassador and I chiefly need at this stage is general guidance rather than authority to act on cut and dried instructions.

2. Our belief is that we shall not get a straight grant-in-aid for the whole amount in any likely circumstances. If we were to press them at this stage to give us their proposals in black and white the indications are that they would take the form of a loan at 2 per cent interest repayable over say 50 years. If we get them to the position of accepting a non-interest bearing loan for the huge amount of five billions, which they are still firmly refusing, they would feel that everything had been done to meet our special circumstances and that if we refused it we must take the responsibility.

3. We could discuss all this more freely if we knew that a non-interest bearing loan might be ultimately acceptable to the Chancellor. This does not mean that we want to commit you to such a solution immediately. But if Ministers feel that we can be content with nothing less than a grant-in-aid it may well be necessary for me to return home having chosen the right moment to break off negotiations, though the public impression produced by this would be serious. In any case it would not be advisable to do this until the commercial talks have made some progress. For otherwise

---

[1] Mr. Lee recorded on 2 October that in the course of a telephone conversation on 1 October Sir W. Eady told Lord Keynes that his memorandum of 26 September (see No. 44, note 3) had only just been received in London, and that he 'doubted whether Ministers would be able to send any definitive advice by the 3rd October': cf. No. 46. Sir W. Eady added that 'Ministers were still very firm on the principle that no commitments should be accepted which the U.K. might subsequently find itself unable to fulfil', and asked Lord Keynes whether he 'now regarded as dead the proposal that the U.K. should, in effect, receive as a grant-in-aid a refund of its pre-Lend Lease war expenditure in the U.S.A. Lord Keynes said that he did regard this proposal as dead in the sense of something which could be put forward by the U.K.: it was, however, conceivable that if the Americans were prepared to contemplate a grant-in-aid they might themselves adopt this proposal as at any rate partial justification for such assistance.'

When Sir W. Eady suggested that Ministers might wish to discuss these matters personally with Lord Keynes and asked 'whether the delay which would be involved by a visit to England would be likely to have an unfortunate effect in "cooling off" the discussions', Lord Keynes replied 'that this might well be the case and he suggested that, in all events for the present, it would be best to continue to exchange telegrams, even if these had to be lengthy' (T 247/47).

it would be supposed that the object of breaking off was to side-step the commercial talks.

4. As a further mitigation in the event of their agreeing to the principle of no interest we might ask that the first instalment of repayment be deferred for ten years. All of us here believe that a non-interest loan, repayment of which begins ten years hence, represents the very best terms we have any hope of getting. We hope therefore that you will consider urgently whether an ultimate burden of 25 million pounds a year is acceptable in addition to a repayment of sterling area debts which may cost us 37 million pounds a year. My own feeling is that this should be within our capacity unless we fail altogether in expanding our exports sufficiently to break even, in which event we shall have to fall back on new and drastic methods of a kind not yet in view, e.g. if we can break even on the basis of a grant-in-aid then we could almost meet the 100 million dollars required to repay a non-interest loan merely by ceasing to take American films. As I have pointed out in my memorandum[2] one hundred million dollars would be only two per cent on the external earnings we require to break even without any repayment at all.

5. I repeat that what we need is general guidance. You can rely on us to be very slow in making any concrete proposition. There will be at least another week or two poker play. We have reason to expect that they will make a request for a complete elimination of preferences a condition of financial assistance. They know that we shall check at this severely. It may be therefore that they will only produce their final terms as an inducement to us to accept this condition. Provided that the commercial talks do not run up against any other snag the crucial questions we shall have to face ultimately are likely to be, on the one hand, the terms of financial assistance and on the other hand, the treatment of preferences. Neither side, therefore, is likely to come clean about their ultimate position until these two issues have been brought to a head. What we should like to know is whether some solution which may be a composite plan but does not involve an annual burden of more than $100 million is a burden you think we could support provided that the negotiations do not break down on any other issue.

6. Ambassador and Brand concur in the above. We have now put off our next meeting behind the scenes until Friday, October 5th. We much hope we can have some guidance by that date.[3]

[2] See No. 44, note 3.

[3] Mr. Dalton informed Lord Keynes in a letter of 2 October that his memorandum of 26 September and his three telegrams (Nos. 44, 46 and 47) were to be considered by Ministers (see No. 62.i) 'and we will do our best to give you some further guidance as soon as we can. We all most highly appreciate the very skilful way in which you have presented our case to the Americans. My present inclination is to decline any loan which carries interest, however it is dressed up, because I do not believe that that principle is appropriate to the circumstances. If we have to borrow from the Americans to buy necessary supplies, then we must expect something like commercial terms. It may be that the cost of borrowing for

i *1 Oct. 1945 Letter from Lord Keynes to Mr. Dalton:* discussion of present state of negotiations and 'some gossip about the atmosphere'; does not agree that failure of C.F.M. (cf. Volume II, No. 159) will drive Americans into isolationism [T 236/438].

American supplies would be about as expensive as a non-interest bearing loan which is designed, not so much for the purchase of supplies, as to modify the sterling area arrangements. But, if the American intention is to help us to modify those arrangements, then I don't see why we should recognise a commercial principle as the price of their help' (T 247/47).

No. 52

British Missions (Washington) to Cabinet Offices
(Received 2 October, 3.15 a.m.)

NABOB 107 Telegraphic [UE 4570/1094/53]

Immediate. Secret   WASHINGTON, 2 October 1945, 1.15 a.m.

For Treasury from Keynes.[1]

1. Our many telegrams show the sub-committees concerned with winding up Lend/Lease are at present engaged in a mass of troublesome detail which suggests great loss of time and considerable friction ending up in an enormous bill. Taken at its face value this would be very depressing. But it is better regarded as a process we must go through rather than a true pointer to the ultimate conclusion, and you should not be unduly alarmed.

2. Time is not being wasted because the itemised and audited method of settlement is being shown to be impracticable and because both sides are becoming better acquainted with what it is all about and with the orders of magnitude involved.

3. In informal conversation with members of the top committee I find some reason to think that a global settlement of a reasonable amount is probably what they would like to end up with if possible. And indeed it is evident that any other method must occupy many months and perhaps years before finality is reached. The difficulty of a global settlement is of course the question how to reach a figure within our means which could be justified to Congress. For this reason Crowley was bent on what he called a business-like settlement. With his departure[2] it is possible that more elastic principles may find favour.

---

[1] This telegram is printed in Moggridge, *op. cit.*, pp. 517–19.

[2] On 27 September the Foreign Economic Administration had been dissolved by executive order of the President. The Lend-Lease functions of the F.E.A. were transferred on 19 October to an Office of Foreign Liquidation in the State Department, under Mr. T. McCabe. See *D.S.B.*, vol. xiii, pp. 491–2 and 703–5.

NABOB 94 of 27 September reported that President Truman had accepted Mr.

4. I think of this settlement as covering:

(a) Requirements from the pipeline.

(b) Food and material end stocks.

(c) Military Lend Lease inventories having a civilian end-use, subject to any items recaptured.[3]

(d) Durable goods and capital installations.

(e) Transport aircraft.

(f) Ships.

(g) United States military surpluses lying in the United Kingdom, and possibly those in some other parts of the sterling area.

5. The aggregate figure for which the Americans might be prepared to settle for all of these might be between 750 and 1000 million dollars. Against this our offset for mutual aid inventory and in the pipeline up to February 28 next, and the various back claims which we should seek to keep alive might be worth at most 400 to 500 million dollars and at worst 200 to 250.

6. I am not including in this the amounts due to us for Lend-Lease shipping and oil reimbursements worth about 150 million dollars. We are aiming to collect these in cash in accordance with the normal procedure which has existed hitherto, thus keeping them out of an overall settlement. But if we do not succeed in this they will presumably have to be brought into the settlement.

7. I do not propose at this stage to discuss in detail the possible scope of the offsetting arrangement or the manner in which it might be dressed up as a question of presentation. Ideas are not yet sufficiently crystal[l]ised on the United States side for this to be profitable. But I think we must proceed on the assumption that the ultimate outcome will be that we shall be asked to accept a commitment for a specific dollar amount which has to be added to the sum of the assistance which we require from the U.S.A.

8. For this reason I think it is not too soon for you to give thought to the question of what global settlement will be acceptable if we can get the principle adopted. My present impression is that the smallest amount covering all the categories mentioned above, of which there is any hope, is

Crowley's resignation as Administrator of the F.E.A. and as Chairman of the Federal Deposit Insurance Corporation with effect from 15 October, although 'we understand that for all practical purposes Crowley has now disappeared from the administrative scene and that we shall see very little more of him in the current negotiations . . . we gather that effect of this change is likely to be that on major policy issues we shall deal with Clayton . . .' (UE 4515/1094/53). Letters of 28 and 29 September from Lord Keynes to Sir W. Eady commenting on these events, are printed in Moggridge, op. cit., pp. 509–12. The opening sentence of the first letter began: 'As you will already have learned by telegram, the Baboon is dead, deader than the cats we were trying to revive and he to bury . . .' (cf. Nos. 18, note 1, and 37, note 2).

[3] BABOON 81 of 5 October stated that the Treasury assumed that this point 'refers only to those military stores which are going to be used for civilian purposes. It is most important that we should not give way on the question of paying for stores with a potential civilian end-use which are still being used for military purposes' (UE 4570/1094/53).

250 to 300 million dollars; that a settlement on these terms would be a very good bargain, but this is considerably better than what we at present have any reason to expect. On the basis of present estimates I should regard 500 million dollars as the highest we should be willing to contemplate, but their starting figure is likely to be higher than this.[4]

9. All this is half-baked and, as the Americans say, thinking out loud. But it would help us to have your first reactions.

10. We are sending by Saving a report on how the work of the Lend-Lease sub-committees stands up to date, with a covering letter from me to Clayton summarising the points of principle on which we need to reach early decision with the United States side.[5]

---

[4] BABOON 81 (see note 3) stated that the Treasury were attracted by the approach suggested by Lord Keynes, 'although if we are to say something between 300 and 500 millions [sic] dollars it is clearly dependent on us having satisfactory financial assistance from the U.S. We do not think there is much which we can add by way of comment at the present stage, more especially as the telegrams . . . make depressing reading and are very remote from the line which you discussed.'

[5] See No. 53.

No. 53

British Missions (Washington) to Cabinet Offices
(Received 8 October)

NABOB Saving 11 Telegraphic [UE 4711/1094/53]

Secret   WASHINGTON, 2 October 1945

Following are texts of (a) Letter to Clayton dated October 1, 1945, (b) Report on position as at 1st October, 1945 of discussions on Lend-Lease Sub Committees, referred to in paragraph 10 of NABOB 107.[1]

(a) Letter to Clayton

Dear Mr. Clayton,

You asked me[2] last week whether I thought that the Lend-Lease Sub-Committees were making sufficiently good progress. In reply I said I thought they had been accomplishing very useful and essential spade work but there might be some decisions of principle which we ought to try to settle shortly in one of the higher Committees.

So that we can take stock of the position more completely I asked for a report from the British members of the Sub-Committees on how matters now stand. I enclose a copy of this which you will no doubt check with your own people.[3] As, however, this is rather a lengthy document and not

---

[1] No. 52.   [2] Lord Keynes.

[3] A report of 15 October from Mr. Crowley to Mr. Clayton on the activities of the Lend-Lease Committees is printed in F.R.U.S. 1945, vol. vi, pp. 149–51.

perhaps very easily intelligible to those who have not taken part in the technical discussions of the Sub-Committees, perhaps I might sum up the position as I see it.

There has been, as you will be aware, only one meeting of the Lend-Lease Committee itself[4] which was at the very beginning of our proceedings. But certain questions of principle which are still unresolved are now, or will shortly be, ready to be brought up for decisions. The most important are the following: 1. At the first meeting of the Lend-Lease Committee it was agreed in principle that reciprocal aid would terminate as from September 2nd 1945. We were asked, however, to postpone formal notification to the State Department to this effect until certain subsidiary matters had been considered. We should like now to be free to make the formal communication.[5]

2. On the 20th September I had a discussion with Mr. Crowley personally in the course of which we reached an agreement[6] which, as I understood it, was on the lines set forth in paragraph 10(a) of the attached paper. Subsequently, however, Mr. Crowley wished to make it a condition of this agreement that we should undertake to accept the whole of the inventory including items which we might wish to discard as being of no use[7]: and secondly, he thought that the offset should apply only to pipeline and inventory claims arising subsequent to V-J Day without taking account of unsettled claims between the two Governments prior to that date. As regards the first point we are, I hope, in sight of an agreement. But as a result of some doubt as to what the inventory would cover in this connection, we have not yet finally cleared the matter with London. On the second point we are not yet quite satisfied as to the object of Mr. Crowley's proposal or its consequences. We should like, therefore, to hear more about it. Meanwhile, could not the arrangement in paragraph 10 (a) be agreed between us so that we could discuss separately the above two points which do not seem to us to be necessarily bound up with it?

3. We are still rather in the dark about how it is proposed to deal with the military inventories. Meanwhile, London is rather disturbed on a matter where we have tried to assure them that there is no serious ground for their concern. They want to feel sure that there will be no question of their having to give up any Lend Lease material which is actually in use by our military forces to aid them in carrying out their responsibilities in the maintenance of world order. If this could be definitely assured, it would, we know, relieve their minds.

4. There has been no significant progress or even much discussion on how the prices to be placed on items in the inventories are to be determined.

5. I should very much welcome, if you could spare the time, the chance of a personal talk with you as to possible ways of expediting and

---

[4] See No. 33.i.   [5] See No. 37, note 1.   [6] See No. 37.   [7] V. ibid., note 5.

simplifying these proceedings, so that we can reach a definite conclusion within a reasonable period of time.

Very sincerely yours,[8]

(b) *Report on Lend/Lease Discussions*

Position as at 1st October, 1945 with regard to winding-up of Lend-Lease &
Reciprocal Aid

Introduction

1. The following statement is in six parts. The first indicates the general position of Lend Lease and Reciprocal Aid arrangements after V-J Day. The second summarises the position reached as regards the definition of the Lend Lease and Reciprocal Aid Pipelines and inventories. There follows a section concerning such discussions as have taken place in regard to the form of the financial settlement in respect, *inter alia*, of pipeline and inventory requirements on both sides. The fourth part consists of a statement of certain special problems which arise in connection with military Lend Lease supplies at present held by the U.K. There follows a short section concerning Lend Lease capital installations, oil and shipping matters, and finally there is a summary setting out those questions upon which decisions of principle by the Top Committee or the Lend Lease Committee may be required.

I

General Position of Lend Lease and Reciprocal Aid Arrangements after V-J Day

2. *General position*

Subject to the minor exceptions referred to in the following paragraph, straight Lend Lease and straight Reciprocal Aid both terminated with effect from the 2nd September, 1945. The formal notification as regards the termination of Lend Lease was contained in Mr. Crowley's letter of the 18th August.[9] Hitherto, however, the communication to the State Department of a formal notification of the termination of Reciprocal Aid has been deferred, at the request of the FEA. The U.K. representatives hope that no objection will now be seen to the immediate communication of such a notification.[5]

3. *Continuation of military Lend Lease and Reciprocal Aid after V-J Day*

It is hoped to reach early agreement concerning the scope of continuing straight Lend Lease and Reciprocal Aid in the military and naval fields after V-J day, in accordance with the President's directive of the 2nd [*sic*] September.[10] A report on the arrangements as agreed will be submitted to the Lend Lease Committee. Briefly, the proposal is that Lend Lease and Reciprocal Aid should be continued up to a maximum of 6 months at the discretion of theatre commanders in respect of certain specified intra-theatre services and transfers in the Far Eastern operational areas, while

[8] Signature lacking from this copy.   [9] See No. 12, note 3.   [10] See No. 24, note 6 and i.

174

certain specified supplies and services made available by the U.S. Navy to the British Navy and *vice versa* in all theatres will pass on straight Lend Lease and Reciprocal Aid for a period of 30 days after V-J day and possibly longer at discretion. U.S. military commanders, at their discretion, may similarly continue to provide supplies and services on straight Lend Lease in cases of hardship in areas other than the Far Eastern operational theatre, but the U.K. representatives have made it clear that it is not intended to give straight Reciprocal Aid in those areas.

4. *Provision of supplies and services previously given on Lend Lease and Reciprocal Aid*
It is contemplated that the machinery under which supplies and services were furnished prior to V-J Day on straight Lend Lease and Reciprocal Aid will continue to be available and that supplies and services may continue to be provided, upon request, without any immediate payment being required. Under this arrangement—which so far as supplies procured in the U.S.A. are concerned will apply only to the Lend Lease pipeline—the amounts due on either side will be recorded and will be brought to account in the overall offsetting arrangement referred to in paragraph 10(*a*) below.

II
Definition of Pipeline and Inventories

5. U.K. requirements from the Lend Lease pipeline
U.K. Missions will have indicated by the 2nd October all their requirements from the Lend Lease pipeline, so that on that date U.S. procurement agencies will be free to cancel any contracts for goods not included in the lists of U.K. requirements.
It has been agreed that military supplies still needed by the U.K. from items in procurement at V-J Day should be treated on the same general basis as U.K. requirements from the civilian pipeline, and that the terminal date of the 2nd October will apply to those requirements also.

6. *Definition of civilian inventory*
The U.S. representatives circulated a paper[11] containing a statement of principles to be followed in the compilation of the Lend Lease inventories as at V-J Day. There has been considerable discussion of this document.[12] As a result, general agreement has been reached as to the basis upon which the inventory of civilian goods should be compiled, and work on the preparation of such an inventory is in active progress in London. Briefly this will comprise (i) a list of undistributed consumable and durable goods

[11] The reference was to an F.E.A. memorandum of 5 September on 'Principles for the Determination of Inventories of Lend-Lease Articles Transferred to Foreign Governments' (COM/LEASE 1), circulated on 25 September as GEN 80/17 (UE 4546/1094/53).
[12] A collection of telegrams on the interpretation and clarification of COM/LEASE 1 is filed at UE 4598/1094/53.

of Lend Lease origin under the control of the Central Government at V-J Day (ii) a separate list of (*a*) durable goods received under Lend Lease which had been distributed before V-J Day (*b*) capital installations financed on Lend Lease.

The paper by the U.S. representatives proposed that military supplies of Lend Lease origin should be included in the same inventory as civilian goods. The U.K. representatives have, however, urged that such special considerations arise in connection with the inventory of military Lend Lease supplies that this should be regarded as a matter for separate discussion and treatment. It is believed that the U.S. representatives will agree to this course, but definite confirmation of this has not been received.

7. *Definition of the Military inventory*

Discussions are still proceeding as to the basis upon which an inventory of military supplies of Lend Lease origin should be taken. The U.K. representatives have expressed the view that practically such an inventory ought to be confined to those supplies of Lend Lease origin which are no longer required for retention by the military forces. The U.S. representatives have indicated that for legal reasons they must have an inventory covering the full range of all military holdings of Lend Lease supplies as at V-J Day, but it has still to be decided whether the inventory should take account of supplies which have been distributed beyond the stage of base depots. In the view of the U.K. representatives, any attempt to carry the inventory beyond such a stage would involve very great complications and delays.

It has been proposed by the U.S. representatives that the inventory of military supplies to be furnished by the U.K. should comprise all military supplies of Lend Lease origin held by the forces of Australia, New Zealand, South Africa, India and the Colonies. The U.K. representatives take the view, however, that where Lend Lease retransfers have been made to Dominion or Indian forces, such supplies should form part of the separate inventories to be furnished by the Governments concerned: the U.K. inventory should comprise only supplies remaining on the charge of the U.K. Government.

8. *Aircraft in the inventory*

The U.S. representatives intend to communicate separate proposals concerning the treatment of Lend Lease aircraft in the inventory. Until these proposals have been received it is not possible to say whether any difficulties will arise on this account.

9. *Reciprocal Aid pipeline and inventory*

It is agreed that whatever arrangements are arrived at as regards the civilian and military Lend Lease pipeline and inventories will be applied *mutatis mutandis* to the Reciprocal Aid pipeline and inventories.

III
Form of Financial Settlement in Respect of the Pipeline and Inventory

10. (*a*) On the 20th September an agreement in principle was reached in discussion between Lord Keynes and Mr. Crowley whereby any immediate financial settlement in respect of U.S. and U.K. requirements from the Lend Lease and Reciprocal Aid pipelines and inventories would be deferred for the present until the amounts at issue on both sides of the account were more clearly known, it being agreed that supplies would continue to move in the meantime as necessary. Lord Keynes agreed that the U.K. would settle any amount due either by a cash payment or by taking an interim credit on the terms originally proposed by Mr. Crowley: subject to the understanding that any credit arrangements could, if mutually agreed, be merged in any overall financial settlement reached with the U.S. Government and made subject to the same terms and conditions as might be agreed thereunder. It was, however, agreed that the sum in respect of which a settlement would be made would be the net amount after a balance had been struck between (*a*) the amounts due from the U.K. to the U.S.A. in respect of requirements from the Lend Lease pipeline and the civilian inventory (*b*) the amounts due from the U.S.A. to the U.K. in respect of U.S. requirements from the Reciprocal Aid inventory and in respect of the cost of former Reciprocal Aid supplies and services furnished in the period 2nd September 1945—28th February 1946 inclusive; and (*c*) any net amount payable to either side in respect of other claims and counter-claims between the two Governments, which might be brought into the settlement by mutual agreement.

(*b*) This agreement in principle has not yet been incorporated, as was intended, in an exchange of letters, since certain questions of interpretation have arisen which have still to be cleared. These are:

(i) The U.K. proposal was that the offsetting arrangement should extend to cover as wide a range of accounts as possible, comprising the claims and counter-claims referred to at (*c*) above and also any amounts which may be due from the U.K. in respect of the military inventories and of Lend Lease capital installations; but it is understood that Mr. Crowley has taken the view that it should cover on the one side only the U.K. requirements from the undistributed goods in the civilian pipeline and inventories plus any amounts due in respect of services given after V-J Day which were formerly provided on Lend Lease, and on the other side corresponding amounts due from the U.S.A. to the U.K.

(ii) The U.K. representatives have been informed that Mr. Crowley was contemplating, as a condition, an arrangement whereby the U.K. would acquire, at prices to be agreed, the *whole* of the goods in the civilian inventory and also all items in the military inventory having a civilian end-use. The U.K. representatives have argued that their understanding had been that they would be free to select their requirements from both inventories and to offer for recapture by the

U.S. authorities items which would be useless to them. They would not be prepared to commit themselves to any undertaking in regard to the military inventory: but on the assumption that the U.S. representatives will agree to regard that as set aside for separate discussion and treatment, it is possible that—subject to approval from London—they will be able to agree to acquire the whole of the civilian inventory (i.e. the undistributed consumable and durable goods referred to in para. 6 (i)) provided that it is understood that no more than a token price would be paid for items within the inventory which are useless to them.

11. *Prices for pipeline and inventory requirements*

There has been some preliminary discussions [*sic*] concerning the prices to be put on the U.K. requirements from the Lend Lease pipeline, but no decisions have been reached. There has been as yet no discussion concerning the prices to be put on requirements from the inventories.

IV

Special Problems Connected with the Military Inventory

12. There are certain special questions connected with the military inventory which involve important points of principle to which the U.K. representatives attach particular significance. These have not as yet been discussed in detail with the U.S. representatives, but it will be desirable to indicate the more important of them here.

13. *Extent of exercise of power of recapture*

The U.K. representatives recognise the right of the U.S. Administration to ask for the return of Lend Lease equipment and supplies in accordance with Article V of the Lend Lease Agreement. But in their view it will be important, as a matter of practical administration, that it should be agreed that the U.S. Administration will not withdraw equipment essential for U.K. military commitments without due consultation and that they will in any event give within a reasonable period of time a definitive indication of the equipment and supplies which it will wish to have returned to the U.S.A., and to agree that thereafter the right of recapture will not be exercised. Otherwise it would be very difficult indeed to make proper arrangements for the maintenance of the British armed forces since there will be constant uncertainty about the extent to which the U.S. Administration might take away equipment in exercise of the right of recapture. It is hoped that the U.S. Administration will give as long notice as possible of any equipment which it may wish to recapture in order to give the U.K. opportunity to discuss any particular proposals which might involve the risk of serious dislocation and time to provide substitute material for equipment actually withdrawn.

14. *Retention by British Armed Forces of Lend Lease equipment etc. essential for military needs*

The U.K. representatives hope that, subject to any exercise by the U.S.

Administration of the right of recapture in accordance with the procedure suggested in the preceding paragraph, there will be formal recognition of the basic principle that the military forces of the U.K. will be free to retain, without any question of payment, equipment and supplies of Lend Lease origin (comprising not only weapons of war in the narrow sense but other essential equipment—e.g. trucks—which might have a civilian end-use) on the scale necessary in order to enable those forces to carry out their responsibilities in the maintenance of world order. It would of course be incumbent upon the U.K. authorities to show, if necessary, that their continued holdings of Lend Lease equipment were reasonable in size.

If the proposals in the above paragraph and the preceding one are accepted the problem of the military inventory (apart from questions of definition) will be narrowed to reaching agreement on arrangements to deal with former Lend Lease items of civilian end-use which are found to be surplus to military requirements at the present time, or which are declared surplus in the future.

V
Miscellaneous Questions

15. *Capital Installations*
There have as yet been no discussions on this subject. The U.K. representatives are obtaining detailed information from London concerning such installations in the U.K. and the Colonies [iv].

16. *Oil Questions*
As special considerations arise in regard to oil in both the Lend Lease and Reciprocal Aid inventories, a separate sub-committee has been appointed to consider oil questions. No difficult questions of principle are likely to arise.

17. *Ships*
Discussions concerning future arrangements in regard to the shipping made available to the U.K. on Lend Lease have not yet begun with the U.S. representatives. There is to be a separate sub-committee on this subject.

18. *Committee to deal with miscellaneous claims*
A separate combined sub-committee has been appointed to sift and consider the financial claims and counter-claims referred to at the end of the opening sub-paragraph of paragraph 10. This sub-committee will also be responsible for collecting the statistics required to give effect to the proposed offsetting arrangement referred to in paragraph 10.

VI
Summary: Questions Requiring Decisions of Principle

19. It appears likely that decisions of principle by the Top Committee

or the Lend Lease Committee may be required on the following questions:
(*a*) The proposed formal communication of the termination of Reciprocal Aid with effect from 2nd September 1945 (paragraph 2 above)
(*b*) The scope of the inventory of military supplies (paragraph 7 above)
(*c*) The scope of the proposed offsetting arrangement (paragraph 10 [6] above)
(*d*) The separation of the military from the civilian inventory as a matter for separate negotiation and treatment (paragraph 10 [6] above)
(*e*) The scope and limitation of time of the exercise of the power of recapturing military supplies (paragraph 13 above)
(*f*) Recognition of the freedom of the U.K. to retain military supplies on the scale required for the maintenance of its armed forces (paragraph 14 above)
(*g*) The general price basis to be applied in respect of the Lend Lease and Reciprocal Aid pipelines and inventories (paragraphs 11 and 18 above).[13]

CALENDARS TO NO. 53

i *15 Oct. 1945 Note of informal discussion between Lord Keynes and Mr. Clayton* (circulated as GEN 80/51 on 30 Oct.) on winding up of Lend-Lease and Reciprocal Aid [UE 5288/1094/53].

ii *2–15 Oct. 1945 Military Lend-Lease and Reciprocal Aid*: agreement reached in military sub-group on exchange of supplies, text (COM/LEASE 6) in *NABOB 112*, approved by Service Depts. (*BABOON 85*); British proposals on scope of military Lend-Lease; State Dept. memo. of 12 Oct. advises that military equipment may be supplied to H.M.G. on cash terms (cf. *F.R.U.S. 1945*, vol. vi, pp. 129–30) [UE 4525, 4598, 5095/1094/53].

iii *20 Sept.–19 Oct. 1945 U.S. policy on aircraft supplied to U.K. under Lend-Lease* and British desire to retain aircraft for military use: U.S. proposals (COM/LEASE 8, text in *NABOB 171*) and U.K. observations thereon [UE 4394, 4421/1094/ 53, T 236/466].

iv *16 Oct. 1945 To British Missions (Washington) Tel. BABOON Saving 4* U.K. views on disposal of American-built installations on British soil [W 13498/10058/ 76].

[13] NABOB 151 of 11 October stated: 'High level discussions on winding up of Lend-Lease and Reciprocal Aid have been in suspense since resignation of Crowley, due to difficulties experienced by Americans in allocating his former responsibilities and in reshuffling their team . . . It is now clear however that responsibility for dealing with policy questions in this field will fall on Clayton who will become head of Lend Lease Committee. Americans propose to amalgamate this committee with Surplus Disposals Committee . . . Owing to jurisdictional difficulties Clayton has so far felt precluded from dealing with questions referred to in NABOB Saving 11 but we are now hopeful that he will take up outstanding questions energetically' (UE 4524/1094/53).

No. 54

British Missions (Washington) to Cabinet Offices
(Received 3 October, 5.35 a.m.)

NABOB *114 Telegraphic* [*UE 4708/1094/53*]

Secret   WASHINGTON, *3 October 1945, 1.15 a.m.*

1. Second meeting of Commercial Policy Committee[1] which took place this morning was devoted to discussion of imperial preference.[2]

2. Discussion was opened on our side by Liesching who passed in review the history of the signature of the mutual aid agreement seeking to establish thereby that the phrase 'towards the elimination of discrimination'[3] implied no simple automatic and instantaneous cut but

[1] The draft combined minutes of the first meeting of the Commercial Policy Committee held at 11 a.m. on 1 October (COM/TRADE 1st meeting) were circulated on 15 October as GEN 80/41 (UE 4889/1094/53). A summary account of the meeting is printed in *F.R.U.S. 1945*, vol. vi, p. 137. In NABOB 106 of 2 October the British Delegation reported that 'discussion was focussed on American programme of stages leading up to International Conference embodied in COM/TRADE 3 and 4': the texts of these two papers circulated by the U.S. Delegation, which concerned the implementation of their proposal for an International Trade Organisation (as set out in COM/TRADE 1, which was identical to the paper communicated on 4 August: see No. 2, note 11), were transmitted in NABOB 103 of 29 September (T 236/453).

NABOB 106 further reported that the British Delegation had challenged the omission of India from the list of countries participating in the nuclear negotiating group (cf. No. 2.i), and stated (para. 3(*d*)) that it became clear 'that the Americans have not abandoned the attempt to secure in the convention provision for the elimination of preference. They have met us to the extent that they now contemplate that, in that part of the negotiations which deals with tariff barriers, the extent of reductions to be made in preferences shall be related to reductions of tariffs secured in bilateral bargain. But they stated that it was their view that when this had taken place, there must further be a provision in that part of the agreement which deals with non-tariff barriers for a formula under which residual preferences would be eliminated. This in their view should take place irrespective of further tariff reductions. Clayton indicated that they were conscious of the difficulties which this would create for us but stated that they would regard it as virtually impossible to secure Congressional approval for extension of further financial aid without some such provision. We naturally at once stated baldly that this was not a position which we could accept' (UE 4708/1094/53).

[2] The second meeting of the Commercial Policy Committee, held at 11 a.m. on 2 October, first considered a memorandum (COM/TRADE 5, circulated on 9 October in GEN 80/38) which had been agreed at a combined sub-group meeting on the afternoon of 1 October, proposing that COM/TRADE 3 and 4 (see note 1) should be amended by '(*a*) including India among the principal trading nations which would conduct trade-barrier negotiations at the meeting in March 1946 and (*b*) revising the provisions of paragraph 12 of COM/TRADE 3 so that new members adhering to the proposed multilateral arrangements on trade barriers would be required to make adequate tariff reductions in order to receive the benefits of the arrangements' (draft combined minutes of COM/TRADE 2nd meeting, circulated on 18 October in GEN 80/44, UE 5023/1094/53). A summary account of the meeting is printed in *F.R.U.S., ibid.*, p. 138.

[3] Sir P. Liesching was quoting from Article VII of the Mutual Aid Agreement of 1942: see No. 1, note 5. He went on to refer in this connexion to Anglo-American discussions in Washington in October 1943 on commercial policy: see Pressnell, *op. cit.*, Chapter 5(2).

rather a process which might develop as the result of a bargain taking into account the simultaneous lowering of a tariff and all the condition of the post-war scene. This was not seriously countered by the Americans.

3. Liesching then went on to examine the consequences to our bargaining position of acceptance of the American view of procedure. We could conceive that as part of genuine bargain in which preferences were considered in relation to tariffs, substantial modification of the system might emerge which would not be adverse to our interest. But what could be expected of a process of bargaining in which one party was publicly committed in advance to surrender within some measurable and perhaps brief period everything in the shape of preference whatever the *quid pro quo*.

4. Liesching concluded by emphasi[zi]ng the political difficulties. If as now appeared to be the case the Americans contemplated asking for elimination not as consequence of Article VII but as price for financial assistance, there were possibilities of dangerous embitterment of political relations.

Americans might say economic sacrifice was small. This itself was highly disputable. But British public in grim mood and in circumstances of continuing hardships after six years of intensive war effort, would say that at this moment of weakness we were being forced to abandon traditional habits by ruthless exercise of economic power.

5. Americans then produced a new document which embodied an expansion of sections C and D of the long statement of principles handed to us by Clayton in July.[4] (For full text see our immediately following telegram [ii]) this they said they hoped would help us.

6. On examination, however, this document revealed no approach to our minimum requirements, the procedure envisaged still treated preferences as an almost purely passive element in a process of bargaining destined to lead to their extinction. We made considerable play with logical inconsistencies of this approach, Keynes posing the question 'what do you expect to get out of horse trading if it [is] known by the other chap that own horse is going to drop dead in three months?'

7. As the discussion proceeded, Americans seemed to become increasingly aware of logical weaknesses of their position. Clayton indeed admitted that some of our arguments had great force. But this produced no modification of their demand which they frankly defended on grounds of the political atmosphere of the American scene. To this of course we retorted that our own political difficulties were no less great and our economic position one of much greater difficulty.

8. Vinson summed up his impression of the position that U.S. administration were faced with insuperable political difficulties in giving financial aid unless it could remove the bogey of imperial preferences, just as he imagined we were faced with the same kind of difficulty in

---

[4] See No. 2, note 11, and No. 8.ii.

abolishing preferences. The meeting, therefore brought no closing of the gulf which at present divides us. Though the Americans will undoubtedly continue to press us to the limit on this point, it is evident that they would greatly welcome discovery of some alternative which would solve the political difficulties. So far, however, no such alternative is apparent.[5]

CALENDARS TO NO. 54

i   *29 Sept. 1945   Minutes of 3rd Meeting of U.K. Steering Committee in Washington* (circulated on 10 Oct. in GEN 80/39) discussion of (*a*) organisational arrangements and (*b*) subject matter, for forthcoming commercial policy negotiations [UE 4865/1094/53].

ii *3 Oct. 1945   British Missions (Washington) Tel. NABOB 115* text of U.S. draft amending proposals for I.T.O. (see No. 2, note 11) in respect of Tariffs and Equality of Treatment [UE 4708/1094/53].

[5] The draft combined minutes of the 3rd, 4th, 5th and 6th meetings of the Commercial Policy Committee held on 4, 5, 8 and 11 October were circulated in GEN 80/45, 47, 48 and 49 (UE 5023, 5054, 5112 and 5110/1094/53). The minutes of all six meetings were subsequently approved without amendment by the Americans.
    At the 6th meeting Mr. Hawkins reviewed the progress of the commercial negotiations. Agreed drafts on the procedural question of participation in the proposed conference on an I.T.O., export taxes, state trading and subsidies had been prepared by sub-committees for consideration in plenary committee that day, and work was proceeding on exchange controls and cartels. 'The subject of preferences would be taken up at a later stage' (UE 5110/1094/53): cf. No. 64. For a general account of the discussions on commercial policy at this time see Pressnell, *op. cit.*, Chapter 10(8).

No. 55

Mr. Bevin to the Earl of Halifax (Washington)

No. 9908 Telegraphic [F.O. 800/512]

FOREIGN OFFICE, *3 October 1945, 2.22 p.m.*

Immediate. Personal and top secret

Following sent by Prime Minister to President telegram No. 15 of 3rd October.
(Begins)
    The British Cabinet have recently given the most urgent and earnest consideration to the need to speed up the return of British Service men from overseas in the period before Christmas of this year. Many of these men have been on active service and away from their homes for five or more years, and the demand by the people of this country for their early return now that hostilities are over has become loud and insistent.
    2. Even after eliminating or deferring movements which would normally command a high priority, we cannot with our present allocation

of personnel shipping, achieve the minimum repatriation programme at which we have hitherto aimed, let alone achieve any acceleration.

3. In these circumstances, I have no alternative but to remind you that the arrangement to loan you the two *Queens*[1] and the *Aquitania* until the end of 1945[2] was conditioned solely by the urgency of redeploying American forces for the war against Japan. With the unexpectedly early termination of the Japanese war, these conditions have for some time now ceased to exist.

4. It is our desire that the two *Queens* and *Aquitania* should continue in your service for a period, and we fully realise the desire on the part of the United States to welcome back their soldiers and airmen who have been fighting in Europe. Our own urgent necessities, however, have compelled us to request that you should loan us in return for the *Queens* and *Aquitania* an equivalent personnel lift in American-controlled troop ships with a view to their being used on the main British trooping routes, i.e. from India and Australia to the United Kingdom. It will be understood that help on the North Atlantic route would not solve our problem.

5. Our Combined Chiefs of Staff have discussed this question between them but have failed to reach agreement. Your Chiefs of Staff 'Regret that the necessity to return United States forces from Europe as expeditiously as possible requires all lifts scheduled under present agreements to December 1945, and that therefore they are unable to provide assistance in United States-controlled troop shipping before the end of 1945'. Your Chiefs of Staff go on to say that 'Action on certain of the captured German passenger ships will, in part, fulfil the need for additional troop lift as expressed by the British Chiefs of Staff'.[3] This latter statement may be true for some time in early 1946, but the captured German passenger ships will not alleviate the position in the all important period before the end of this year.

6. Your Chiefs of Staff seem to think that this question, which is absolutely vital to us, can await discussion at an overall personnel shipping review to be held some time this month, the results of which could not possibly take effect till very nearly the end of the year.

7. I shall speak with the utmost frankness. While so many of our troops overseas are awaiting repatriation after nearly six years of war and of separation from their families, I cannot continue to justify to the British public the use of our three biggest ships in the American service. I am reluctant to suggest the return of the *Queens* and *Aquitania*. I must,

---

[1] i.e. the *Queen Mary* and the *Queen Elizabeth*.
[2] See *F.R.U.S. 1945, The Conference of Berlin*, vol.ii, No. 1191–4.
[3] The decision of the U.S. Chiefs of Staff was transmitted in Washington telegram JSM 67 of 28 September, with the following comment by the British Joint Staff Mission: 'It is evident . . . that the United States Chiefs of Staff do not appreciate the important political and military factors which go to make up our case. We agree therefore that the only satisfactory way of obtaining a reversal of American views will be to take up the matter on the highest level with the strongest possible supporting arguments' (F.O. 800/473).

however, ask you most earnestly, Mr. President, to provide us in the immediate future with an equivalent lift for these three ships.[4]

CALENDAR TO NO. 55

i *13–27 Oct. 1945   Adverse reaction in U.S. to announcement regarding return of liners to U.K.* blamed on lack of advance publicity: *letter from Mr. Butler to Sir G. Jenkins (Deputy Director General of M.W.T.)* expresses regret that 'our expensive fire-brigades should not have been prepared to smother quickly this flare-up at a time when our financial and commercial delegations in Washington are telling us that their success or failure will be affected appreciably by the good-will and mood of Congress'; Mr. W.P.N. Edwards (Joint Head of Industrial Information Division, Ministry of Production) agrees that 'rebuke is fully justified' and points out it was not realised in U.S. that transportation of U.S. troops was paid for 'by the British tax payer under Reverse Lend-Lease' [AN 3152, 3326/22/45].

[4] This telegram is printed in *F.R.U.S. 1945*, vol.vi, pp.139–40. In a personal telegram No.9 of 5 October President Truman informed Mr. Attlee that he had 'directed the Joint Chiefs of Staff to return to you the two "Queens" and the "Aquitania" or to provide equivalent personnel lift, the details to be worked out with your Staff Representatives here' (F.O. 800/512). The Minister of War Transport, Mr. A. Barnes, announced in the House of Commons on 12 October that the *Queen Elizabeth* and the *Aquitania* would in future be used for the carriage of British Troops, while the *Queen Mary* was 'to remain at the disposal of the American authorities for the present, but the Americans are placing at our disposal a number of smaller ships' (*Parl. Debs., 5th ser., H. of C.*, vol. 414, cols. 545–6). For misunderstandings arising from this announcement, leading to the issue of an explanatory statement by General D.D. Eisenhower, Military Governor of the U.S. Occupied Zone in Germany (see *The Times*, 27 October 1945, p. 3), see i below.

No. 56

Mr. Bevin to the Earl of Halifax (Washington)

No. 9913 Telegraphic [UE 4568/1094/53]

Immediate. Top secret   FOREIGN OFFICE, *3 October 1945, 7.45 p.m.*

Personal for Keynes from Eady.[1]
Your telegram No. 6549.[2]

1. It may not be possible to give you considered guidance of Ministers in time for meeting on Friday.[3] Your memorandum of 26th September[4] which is important comment on discussions only arrived Monday and

[1] In a minute of 2 October to Mr. Trend covering the draft of this telegram Sir W. Eady commented that he was 'always a bit anxious about K. when he is being idle and ingenious – & I should therefore like the Chancellor's concurrence to the despatch of this personal telegram which is clearly only at the official level. It will put some ideas in K.'s head' (T 236/439). Mr Dalton minuted his approval on 2 October.
[2] No. 51.   [3] 5 October 1945: cf. No. 51, para. 6.   [4] See No. 44, note 3.

Ministers, despite other urgent preoccupations, will be considering it together with the Prisec telegrams sent at the end of last week[5] as rapidly as possible. At present I can only give you preliminary departmental view.

2. We should not think it reasonable to advise Ministers to insist upon a grant-in-aid or nothing.

3. But we could not recommend acceptance of any commercial principle such as interest even at low rates in a loan designed in great part to modify working of the Sterling Area. The position of the Sterling Area as it is after the war is not a commercial situation and application to its solution of commercial principle would be, we believe, entirely unacceptable over here. We must I suggest consider two per cent interest as commercial principle.

4. We note your view that a non-interest loan whose repayment begins after ten years represents the very best terms you have hope of getting. Departmentally, we are doubtful whether we can see certainty of transferring $100 million (hundred million dollars) annually even after ten years. Fuller explanation of our doubts will follow. Doubts would be still more acute if we are not free to restrict United States imports both into the United Kingdom and also those parts of Sterling Area dependent for external finance on United Kingdom. Power to restrict might be limited in time but might well be needed for five years. Is this necessity understood by Americans?

5. If, in the end, final American offer is $5 billion (five billion dollars) on those terms and without strings, Ministers will obviously have to consider it with our comments upon possible difficulties of undertaking regular repayment.

6. Meanwhile, we are more attracted to earlier version of your ideas. Most attractive proposition would divide assistance into two parts. First part, whether described as grant-in-aid, or preferably, repayment of part of our expenditure in United States of America during cash and carry period,[6] would be devoted to modifying restrictions in Sterling Area. How much modification would depend on size of gift. Even $2 billion (two billion dollars) would take us some distance along lines which Americans desire. If Americans realise, as Harry White probably does, that part of American assistance must in fact be a gift, however wrapped up, we do not see why repayment of cash and carry expenditure should prove more difficult to Congress than other propositions.

7. We should need further assistance and should of course prefer not

[5] i.e. Nos. 44, 46 and 47. These three telegrams and the draft reply to them (see No. 47, note 4), together with Lord Keynes' memorandum of 26 September, had been circulated with a covering note by Mr. Dalton on 2 October as GEN 89/4.

[6] The reference was to a clause of the U.S. Neutrality Act of 1 May 1937: see *D.B.F.P.*, Series II, Volume XVIII, No. 332. For the operation of the Act until its revision by an amendment of 17 November 1941, and the development of the concepts of both 'cash' and 'carry' during the course of the Second World War see Duncan Hall, *North American Supply*, pp. 46–54.

to have to pay interest. But it might on the whole suit us to have drawing rights up to a further $4 billion (four billion dollars) or so of untied credit as we require it and without any enquiries. It might be practicable to arrange 1 per cent interest on the credit in use. Such arrangement would keep visibly before us urgent need for securing all round equilibrium at earliest moment and might check too frequent application to the credit.

8. This is variation on (i) and (ii) of paragraph 13 of your memorandum. Would it not be practicable to try this out further?

9. I make no comment upon Imperial Preference issue. You can understand reaction over here if the abolition of Preference is taken out of tariff settlement and made condition of financial assistance.

10. We hesitate to advise you from here on present tactics. But general reading of your communications suggests that after your exposition of our case and your indication of general lines upon which we would propose to use American help, it might be convenient for you to seek indication from Americans how their mind is running. That does not mean black and white proposals as suggested in paragraph 2, and certainly they probably realise by now that 2 per cent interest on a loan of $5 billion (five billion dollars) for 50 years is likely to be regarded as unmanageable, and therefore contrary to principle that Ministers will not undertake obligations which they do not see a reasonable certainty of fulfilling. Apart from difficulty that at present we should hesitate to advise Ministers that $100 million (hundred million dollars) annually is manageable, we fear that if you now suggest that kind of figure it might be regarded as a first bid, and this might embarrass both you and us. If you judge that you should keep ball in play for the moment, we offer paragraphs 6 and 7 of this telegram as a suggestion.[7]

CALENDARS TO No. 56

i *3 Oct. 1945 Minute from Mr. R.W.B. Clarke (Assistant Secretary in H.M. Treasury)* to Sir W. Eady on possible terms of a U.S. loan [T 236/438].

ii *4 Oct. 1945 Memo. from Sir W. Eady to Mr. Dalton on GEN 89/4* (see note 5), questions and answers on U.S. loan in preparation for Ministers' meeting [T 230/142].

iii *4 Oct. 1945 Note from Mr. Brook to Mr. Attlee* enclosing memo. by Mr. J. Meade (Economic Section, Cabinet Offices) on the end of Lend-Lease and GEN 89/4 [PREM 8/35].

[7] Lord Keynes' letter of 4 October in reply to Sir W. Eady is printed in Moggridge, *op. cit.*, pp. 528–31.

No. 57

The Earl of Halifax (Washington) to Mr. Bevin
(Received 5 October, 5.5 a.m.)

No. 6610 Telegraphic [UE 4613/1094/53]

Immediate. Top secret   WASHINGTON, 4 October 1945, 9.30 p.m.

For Chancellor of Exchequer from Keynes.[1]

Since I understand that Ministers will be considering shortly telegrams Nos. 6444 and 6490[2] and my memorandum of September 27th [26th][3] I should like to add following further observations:

2. As we have already indicated a non-interest loan of five billion dollars repayable over fifty years and therefore costing twenty-five million pounds a year during the period of repayment represents the best terms of which we here see any serious prospect. And of course nothing nearly so good as this is yet in sight. Nevertheless doubts will naturally be felt by all of us whether this is a burden we can safely accept. To point out that it is only an additional two per cent of the external income we shall need anyhow and is only a little more than what we spend on American films may be some comfort but it is not conclusive.

3. In weighing the alternative risks we have to run we have therefore to consider whether there is any other course open to us which will cost us less. Take for example the three following suggestions:

(a) a grant-in-aid of two billion dollars with a right to a further three or four billions credit at one per cent interest. This is an attractive alternative well worth considering but it will cost us nearly as much.

(b) Temporary arrangements with United States to carry us through next year with a postponement of the main settlement until we see our way clear. In effect this will cost us a good deal more without settling anything. For we should need as a minimum five hundred million dollars to clean up Lend-Lease on 3C terms and another one thousand million on Export-Import Bank terms to see us to the end of 1946. On the terms at present standard for other borrowers, such as France, this would cost us more than one hundred million dollars a year in the early years beginning at once. It is therefore a far inferior and uneconomic expedient.

(c) To borrow what we need from the sterling area and other countries apart from United States. No one can suppose that they would continue to lend us on the same terms as during the war without security of any defined prospect of repayment vast sums they have not got and cannot spare except at crushing cost to their own post-war reconstruction. Before we had borrowed more than one-third or one-half of what we need we should have incurred a heavier burden than the equivalent of

---

[1] This telegram is printed in Moggridge, op. cit., pp. 525–8.
[2] Nos. 44 and 46.   [3] See No. 44, note 3.

one hundred million dollars. It must be remembered that under a multilateral currency system one hundred million dollars due to the United States is no greater burden than a similar sum due to any other country.

4. I conclude that there is no means open to us of securing a sum of the order of five billion dollars at a lesser cost than one hundred million dollars a year. Thus, if it is true that this with or without a moratorium is the best that we can get from the United States, the only genuine alternative to accepting this commitment is to do without imports and curtail domestic consumption so as to spare more for exports and cut down our military expenditure overseas and political commitments abroad so as to avoid altogether expenditure equivalent to the greater part of five billion dollars.

5. It would be a brave man who says we can face this. It would mean that we should decline for the time being to the position of a second rate power abroad and we should not only have to postpone for at least five years any improvement in the standard of living at home but would have to ask the public to accept greater sacrifices than at any time during the war, and it would be a foolish man who says that this would be an easier and safer plan than to find ways of making a comparatively small economy five or ten years hence after we have got ourselves straight. To run tomorrow or the next day into major economic and political trouble of this order of magnitude with all its implications for the future of Anglo-American relations is surely a greater risk to the future of the country than to commit ourselves to make economies hereafter equivalent to two percent of our future imports.

6. This does not mean that we can get the non-interest bearing loan which is the basis of the above argument; only that it would be worth having on a balance of considerations if we could get it. Nor does it mean that we should not try to do better still if we see the smallest chance of success. The question of what political price it is worth our while to pay is another matter which this telegram of course has made no attempt to assess.[4]

[4] Sir W. Eady sent this telegram to Mr. Trend on 5 October with a note that Mr. Dalton should see it: 'Personally I believe that 3(a) would suit us best. So do the Bank of England. I should personally prefer it even to a loan of $5 billion free of interest. It costs about the same but for a number of reasons it has both political and economic attractions, and I am glad to see that Keynes has responded to the specific proposal which I put to him [see No. 56].' He added that the 'adjustment of our relations with the Sterling Area is going to be very much more difficult than Keynes has ever been willing to admit. We do not want to be tied to a particular form because many of them would justifiably resent the fact that we had apparently fixed up a deal at their expense with the Americans and then asked them to sign it. What we want is, say, $2 billion with an understanding between us and the Americans that we shall use that for the purpose of modifying restrictions in the Sterling Area' (T 236/439).

No. 58

The Earl of Halifax (Washington) to Mr. Bevin
(Received 6 October, 11.30 p.m.)

No. 6658 Telegraphic [W 13436/24/802]

Immediate. Secret   WASHINGTON, 6 October 1945, 5.6 p.m.

Following Personal for Secretary of State and Chancellor of Exchequer from Lord Halifax.

1. Keynes and I met Vinson and Clayton yesterday October 5th. The conversation was useful but not very conclusive, and to avoid crossing wires we will await your comments on my telegrams Nos. 6549 and 6610.[1]

2. At the beginning of our talk Clayton told us that he had met a day or two ago the representatives of three principal American transatlantic civil aviation operators. They had emphasised necessity of reaching agreement with us, and had asked whether State Department would make agreement on civil aviation a condition of financial assistance. Clayton, while expressing his desire to see an agreement reached, had naturally been unwilling to give any such undertaking. On this the representatives of the air lines had stated with extreme clarity their intention to run this idea as hard as they could in Congress.

3. I said that while I appreciated the fact of his having given us this information, I hoped he was as shocked with it as I was. For outside interests to attempt to force the judgment of Congress or Parliament by what was nothing less than naked blackmail, was thoroughly indefensible wherever it might be attempted.[2] Both Clayton and Vinson agreed with this, sorrowfully admitting that that was what happened all too often in politics.

4. Keynes chipped in at this point with a valuable comment that as against this background and assuming the desirability of reaching agreement on civil aviation if this could be achieved on merits, it would be likely to produce exactly the wrong impression if the British Government sent representatives here at this time.[3] His Majesty's Government would in any case probably find it difficult to send representatives at a very early date and accordingly both on this last practical ground as for the reason of avoiding misunderstanding it was very desirable that United States Government should be prepared, if prospects of agreement were reasonably promising, themselves to send representatives to London.

5. Americans profess hope of finishing main talks this month and being in position to go to Congress next month. When they do this they are very anxious that if possible all outstanding economic matters should have been settled. We emphasised that there was no hope of this on civil aviation unless they could send people to London at once.

[1] Nos. 51 and 57.   [2] Cf. No. 43.i(b).
[3] The preceding clause, beginning 'it would', was underlined in red on the filed copy of this telegram.

190

6. Both Clayton and Vinson were impressed with these arguments and said they would consider as a matter of urgency whether they could not after all send representatives over to London very shortly.

CALENDAR TO No. 58

i *14–21 Oct. 1945   Earl of Halifax (Washington) Tels. Nos. 6850–1 & 6863* message from Mr. Clayton to Lord Winster asking for early discussions on civil aviation in Washington: Lord Halifax considers despite threatening nature of message it may be better to get agreement 'into the kitty this month'; Mr. H. McNeil (Parliamentary Under Secretary of State for Foreign Affairs) agrees, but talks should be in London (cf. No. 47.iii) [W 13584, 13618/24/802].

No. 59

*The Earl of Halifax (Washington) to Mr. Bevin
(Received 7 October, 9.40 p.m.)*

No. 6684 Telegraphic [UE 4654/1094/53]

Immediate   WASHINGTON, 7 *October 1945, 4.12 p.m.*

Following for Clutterbuck, Dominions Office, from Cockram. No. 6. (Begins)

Liesching gathers from Board of Trade that Dominion representatives in London are enquiring about progress of the discussions here.[1]

2. A meeting with Dominion Ministers and officials was held on evening of 4th October at which Keynes explained that the financial discussions were proceeding for the time being only on the expert level, partly to enable progress to be made in the commercial talks, and partly to permit the Americans to check the United Kingdom figures. He then outlined the progress of the talks on the Lend/Lease pipeline and inventories, and stated that a meeting of the P.C.S.C. had been arranged for Tuesday next (9th October)[2] in order that the details might be

---

[1] In a personal telegram to Sir P. Liesching of 6 October (ASKEW 220) Mr. Helmore, who had now returned to London, stated: 'The Dominion High Commissioners are showing great interest in the Washington talks and the Secretary of State [presumably for the Dominions, Lord Addison] has pressed the President [of the Board of Trade] to have something said to them in London at once. We have said that this cannot be done until we know what you have said to Dominion representatives in Washington but it would greatly help if we had an early telegram explaining how far you have gone in giving them the ins and outs.' He added that Dr. Evatt in particular had 'insisted that he should have some information at once', and a memorandum was to be handed to him that day which 'recites the substance of COM/TRADE 3 [see No. 54, note 1] and makes clear the American position on residual preferences. It concludes by saying that you made it clear that elimination of residual preferences irrespective of further tariff reductions was not (repeat not) acceptable . . .' (DO 35/1216).
[2] A record of this meeting, circulated on 24 October as C.S.C.(45)74, is filed in T 230/142.

191

discussed with their experts in order to facilitate their own discussions with the Americans on these subjects.

3. Liesching continued the discussion by explaining the object of the commercial discussions and the procedure envisaged for them (including the United States timetable for discussions with the more important commercial countries, for a meeting of the latter in March next and for a full conference of the United Nations in June).[3] He went on to give an account, omitting technical details except where necessary, of the first three meetings of the Commercial Committee on the lines of the Nabob telegrams summarising them, but it is most important to note that he did not (repeat not) divulge sentences 4, 5 and 6 of paragraph 3(d) of Nabob 106 or paragraph 4 of Nabob 114.[4] Suppression of this point at present stage is justified by fact that it may still prove to be an opening move which Americans can be dissuaded from following up. It was the Ambassador's view that on this issue, it was undesirable to create premature alarm among Dominion representatives, or to run larger risk or [sic? of] leakage. Preferences were thereafter dealt with by Liesching on basis of relevant paragraph quoted in Nabob 115[5] and entirely within framework of Article VII on basis of paragraphs 2 and 3 of Nabob 114. Liesching suggests that as Helmore was here up to end of second meeting, it would be wise to get him to give an oral account. No conference documents have been handed to Dominion representatives here, up to the present. He indicated his desire for further meetings with the Dominion representatives at frequent intervals and as developments made them desirable.[6]

4. Keynes, Liesching and Sir Cyril Hurcomb[7] followed up this meeting by speaking at the Ambassador's meeting this morning, at which all Dominion Ministers were present. Keynes went at some length into the type of settlement which the United Kingdom hoped to obtain for military Lend/Lease supplies and indicated the extent of the credit required by the United Kingdom, and his hope that the United States experts were coming to accept the United Kingdom estimate. Hurcomb gave a review

---

[3] Cf. No. 54, note 1.

[4] See No. 54, and *ibid.*, note 1. In a private letter of 10 October to Mr. Clutterbuck Mr. Cockram commented: 'You will also have appreciated that Liesching kept one skeleton in the cupboard so far as the Dominion representatives here are concerned, namely Clayton's original ultimatum that if we did not agree to the abolition of preferences, no financial assistance would be forthcoming. We are hopeful of getting the Americans away from this position and Liesching shared Keynes' view on this that to go further would be certain to alarm the Dominions and might produce, on their part, premature public statements which would prejudice the whole position here. Again, I did not feel that I was justified in insisting on it being mentioned, since, in view of the assurances of advance consultation to which the whole United Kingdom Delegation are now committed [cf. No.18.iii], the time was a matter of tactics rather than of principle. You may, however, wish to have the point in mind in connection with any telegram which you may eventually decide to send to the Dominion Governments' (D.O. 35/1216).

[5] No. 54.ii.

[6] Full minutes of this meeting are filed in T 236/1657.

[7] Director General of the Ministry of War Transport.

of his negotiations this week on the question of continued charter of United States shipping to the United Kingdom and the United Nations: Liesching repeated his promise to keep the Dominion representatives informed and in reply to an enquiry, said that the question of when any more formal Commonwealth discussions that might be required, could be fitted into American timetable, would be carefully borne in mind.

5. After this morning's meeting, Keynes saw Dunk[8] at the latter's request and gave him for his own information and that of Mr. Chiffley [sic][9] and Mr. McLaren,[10] from whom Dunk brought messages to Keynes, a very frank summary of his ideas as to the possible implications for Australia of the financial settlement at which he was aiming. Dunk told me afterwards that he was most grateful to Keynes and very well satisfied with the frankness with which Keynes had spoken to him. They are to have a further talk before Dunk leaves Washington.

6. My immediately following telegram[11] contains personal message for you from Keynes.

7. I have made notes of the meetings referred to above and copies are being sent to you by the next air-mail.

8. Liesching would be grateful if a copy of this telegram could be passed immediately to Helmore, Board of Trade.

9. Since we must keep in step on information communicated to Dominions please keep us urgently informed of what passes in London.

CALENDAR TO No. 59

i *10 & 12 October 1945 Letters from Mr. Cockram (Washington) to Mr. Clutterbuck (D.O.) on meetings with Dominion representatives and Lord Keynes' conversations with Mr. Dunk [D.O. 35/1216].*

[8] Secretary of the Australian Department of External Affairs: see i below.
[9] Mr. J.B. Chifley, Australian Prime Minister.
[10] The reference should apparently be to Mr. S.G. McFarlane, Secretary of the Commonwealth Treasury and Director of the Commonwealth Bank.
[11] See No. 60.

No. 60

The Earl of Halifax (Washington) to Mr. Bevin
(Received 7 October, 11.59 p.m.)

No. 6685 Telegraphic [UE 4654/1094/53]

Immediate   WASHINGTON, 7 October 1945, 8.45 p.m.

Following for Clutterbuck, Dominions Office, from Cockram. No. 7. Following is message for you from Lord Keynes referred to in my immediately preceeding [sic] telegram.[1]

[1] No. 59.

Begins:

At a meeting behind the scenes last Friday[2] at which only Clayton, Vinson, the Ambassador and I were present, I took the opportunity to emphasise the insuperable political, parliamentary and constitutional difficulties of our agreeing here and now any proposition which went beyond our undertaking to go into next years conference for the purpose of trading reductions of tariffs and preferences with the bona fide intention on our part of going a long way in the matter of preferences provided the tariff concessions were adequate and the whole scheme proved acceptable amongst the countries participating. I said that obviously we could not make concessions which affected our existing commitments to other members of the Commonwealth without a Dominions conference. A public and parliamentary discussion of the American demand for the absolute elimination of preferences in the framework of an unsettled financial offer and without any knowledge of what tariff concessions were to be made in recompense must provoke the most dangerous emotions and controversies.

Clayton had just previously mentioned the great importance he attached to a quick conclusion of these talks which would enable the Administration to go to Congress next month whilst the atmosphere is still good and before interest which is at present intense had cooled off. He therefore seemed much impressed by my arguments, the full force of which in relation to the time table he had not previously appreciated, and he promised to think again. This, in combination with other information, leaves us reasonably hopeful that the situation may become easier. It is very noticeable that the half-truths about our discussions with which the Americans are feeding their own press withhold in every case any mention whatever of Clayton's objectionable proposal about residual preferences. We are therefore most anxious not to alarm the Dominions prematurely and perhaps unnecessarily.

Liesching has seen and concurs. Ends.

[2] 5 October 1945: see No. 58.

No. 61

Mr. Bevin to the Earl of Halifax (Washington)

No. *10086 Telegraphic [AN 3121/3121/45]*

Immediate   FOREIGN OFFICE, *8 October 1945, 8.35 p.m.*

Personal for Ambassador from the Secretary of State.

Mr. Byrnes mentioned to me the question of certain bases, including the one you mentioned when in London,[1] and rather hinted that if anything arose on this problem it might assist us in connection with Lease-Lend.

[1] See No. 17.

194

2. I told him that we could not discuss this problem further until we could see the picture as a whole of what America really wanted, and to check it up in connexion with our commercial aviation plans and our defence plans. I indicated that it was very difficult for me to discuss these matters when only dealing with one base at a time.[2]

3. Later he sent me a memorandum [i] (copy by bag) listing Ascension Island, Tarawa and Christmas Island. There is nothing to show that this is the complete list and I want the United States Government to table all their proposals. I have no intention of being faced with piece-meal demands by the United States Government nor, for that matter, by the Soviet Government. It is unfortunately too late to consider the disposal of any of these possessions from the point of view of a gesture that might have favourable effect on the American attitude towards Lend-Lease.

4. Mr. Byrnes also raised the question of the Azores.[3] He undertook to consult the Chiefs of Staff of the United States and to see if he could give to us the complete and final scheme which the United States had in mind, and I undertook to consider it when I got his communication. He may mention this to you.[4]

CALENDARS TO No. 61

i *30 Sept.–3 Oct. 1945* (a) *Memo. by Mr. Broadmead on Clipperton, Christmas and Ascension Islands* with comments by Mr O. C. Harvey (Assistant Under Secretary of State) and Sir O. Sargent on serious disadvantage to H.M.G. of dealing with bases question piecemeal; (b) *Memo. on bases by Mr. Byrnes* with comments by Mr. Broadmead [AN 3121/3121/45].

[2] According to a minute by Mr. Dixon, in this conversation on 28 September Mr. Byrnes mentioned Clipperton Island, Christmas Island, Ascension Island and Tarawa (see i below) and argued that 'we could surely afford to make a gesture in regard to islands in that part of the world since it was inconceivable that we and the United States should find ourselves at war together there'. Mr. Bevin minuted: 'I have finally asked Mr. Byrnes for a *complete* list. I propose to write him but I want to consult the P.M. E.B.'

[3] See No. 35.

[4] In telegram No. 6727 of 10 October Lord Halifax, after stating that Mr. Byrnes had not mentioned bases during a conversation that day, urged that he should be authorised to take the question up and ask Mr. Byrnes 'to give us the whole picture of what they might have in mind in order that if possible we might bring it out as part of the whole business. If something like this could be done and if we could get agreement on civil aviation and telecommunications and assuming that financial and commercial talks get through the whole picture would not look too bad and could be dressed up as a really large agreement . . .'.

In telegram No. 10241 to Washington of 12 October Mr. Bevin stressed the need to ask Mr. Byrnes for a complete list of bases in which the United States were interested: 'We hope that you will be able to ascertain United States Government's over-all desiderata as regards bases in British Empire without exposing us later to reproaches from any of the Dominions.' Lord Halifax reported on 17 October in telegram No. 6912 that he had asked for such a list, but that Mr. Byrnes was 'still waiting for final view of service departments, who had wished to revise their earlier conclusions in the light of San Francisco and atomic bomb' (AN 3122/3121/45).

No. 62

Mr. Bevin to the Earl of Halifax (Washington)

No. *10094 Telegraphic [UE 4670/1094/53]*

Immediate. Top secret   FOREIGN OFFICE, *8 October 1945, 10.28 p.m.*

From Chancellor of the Exchequer.

Ministers have now considered the personal telegrams from you and Keynes on the financial talks.[1] We admire the forceful way in which our case has been presented and also your patience. We do not give you final decisions here but general guidance for the discussions as they stand.

2. If best American offer is large loan at 2 per cent interest we would not accept it. We remain firm that we will not accept obligations which we do not see reasonable certainty of discharging. Also such a commercial settlement would be regarded here as an inequitable conclusion to our mutual effort with United States during the war, especially as a substantial part of the loan is to be devoted to modifying restrictions of Sterling Area because of American objections.

3. If this is all we are offered we should have to content ourselves with borrowing for necessary purchases in United States and possibly for cleaning up Lend-lease. Borrowing would presumably be on Export Import Bank terms, but we would face that. We should also have to restrict Dollar expenditure to the utmost wherever we could and would have to turn to other sources of supply and other channels of trade.

4. On the other hand, in view of all your reports we clearly cannot attempt to insist that adequate assistance must be given to us as a

---

[1] At their meeting on 5 October (GEN 89/2nd meeting, i below) Ministers considered GEN 89/4: see No. 56, note 5, and Pressnell, *op. cit.*, Chapter 10(11). In a letter of 6 October to Lord Keynes (printed in Moggridge, *op. cit.*, p. 536) Sir W. Eady described the meeting as 'not altogether an easy one. They are very tired and the Foreign Secretary is of course really preoccupied with the results of the Foreign Ministers Conference [see Volume II, Chapter I]. There is rather a natural resentment that in our external affairs we seem to be bullied in turn by the Russians and the Americans, and a certain emotional wish to say "plague on both your houses".'

In accordance with the conclusions of the meeting Sir W. Eady submitted the drafts of Nos. 62–3 to Mr. Dalton on 6 October, commenting that the former 'cuts out all the long argumentative paragraphs in the draft which was circulated' in GEN 89/4 (T 236/439). After approval by Mr. Dalton Sir W. Eady sent the two telegrams to Mr. Coulson for despatch with a note that the former (No. 62) was the more urgent, but No. 63 was in fact despatched first.

grant-in-aid or gift. You will have noticed that within the last few days Aldrich has repeated his view of necessity that American assistance to us should be free of obligation of repayment.[2] But we assume that Administration could not face this politically.

5. If this is impossible the settlement that we should all prefer is a grant of, say, two billion dollars, together with drawing rights on an untied credit up to, say, three or four billion dollars. With the grant we could begin almost immediately on modifications of Sterling Area which would open markets to American exports. If we received grant we should be willing to pay interest of 1 per cent on amount of credit in use. We should do all possible to restrict need for drawing on credit after necessities of next 18 months have been cleared.

6. Do you consider it impossible to persuade Americans to accept argument that grant of, say, two billion dollars could be given as partial repayment of what we had to spend in America during cash and carry period[3]? Aldrich's recent statement repeated suggestion of retroactive Lend-Lease payment and if grant is possible this reason for it might commend it to Congress.

7. But if settlement on such lines is impracticable then we are clear that we could not accept any alternative form of settlement involving us in a liability to pay more than hundred million dollars in any year.

8. Acceptability of offer, say of five billion dollars interest free, repayable over fifty years, depends ultimately upon background conditions. To service the loan we must arrive at a favourable and secure over-all balance of payments and as soon as possible. For our economic independence that is necessary in any case. In order to achieve that we must have an undisputed right to restrict our total imports until we have achieved it. We should be willing to agree to a non-discriminatory restriction of imports on the understanding that non-discrimination means the test of commercial consideration only, that we are free to make long-term contracts with regular suppliers, and that subject to the principle of commercial considerations we can have as much State purchasing of imports as we wish.

9. Even when we achieve a favourable balance of payments it does not follow that we shall be long of dollars. Therefore convertibility of those currencies which are significant to us must be a condition.

10. But fundamental conditions for regular service are (i) that there is no general and obstinate deflationary position possibly originating from American policy which might make weight of annual payment intolerable, (ii) that United States is in general balance either by imports or by suitable

---

[2] In the course of a speech in New York on 4 October Mr. Aldrich had said that he believed that the U.S. 'should give financial aid to England not only on moral grounds, but on the conviction that the restoration of multilateral trade in great volume is essential to the economic well-being of ourselves, England and all the British Commonwealth': see *The Times*, 5 October 1945, p. 3.
[3] Cf. No. 56, note 6.

lending policy so that there is no world shortage of dollars. If there is in fact deflation or a shortage of dollars we must be free to suspend service or if necessary to proceed to discriminate against American imports. In judging whether a shortage of dollars had arrived we must not be required to have exhausted all our dollar loan or credit. Because the United Kingdom is such a large importer of United States goods, it is upon us that the impact of a world shortage of dollars falls most immediately. We must therefore be permitted to take a prospective view of the trade facts as they are manifestly developing, and to arrive at our own judgment of the existence of a shortage of dollars after consultation with the United States. Finally, for the purpose of all our rights the currency unit must be the United Kingdom together with the Colonies.

11. If a situation has arrived at which we cannot service the loan the whole period of the loan must be shifted on to cover the years during which service is not possible so that in no year are we obliged to pay more than hundred million dollars.

12. Subject to your views we think it essential that Clayton and others should understand the importance of these conditions which in some form will have to be written into any agreement made on a loan. We need not elaborate to you our doubts about the real policy that American Administration may follow in the next few years.

13. Has there been any discussion with Americans how we should receive a loan? Is it certain that Congress will vote one Appropriation for the whole sum which will then be put at our free disposal so that we shall not be required to come annually to Americans justifying our need for the tranche or explaining the trading policies which we have been following?

14. We cannot reach even any provisional conclusion about acceptability of the kind of offer that may be forth-coming until we know the whole background and we should therefore like your comments on this telegram as soon as possible.

15. We do not think that Keynes should make any further suggestions at this moment on nature of financial settlement. Problem has been fully stated to Americans and we are entitled to expect that they should soon show their hand. Otherwise everything we suggest will be taken as opening bid.

16. We should like you to consider timing of progress in financial and commercial talks respectively. We see possible dangers if financial talks proceed too far without knowledge of what is practicable in commercial policy or without assurance from Clayton that he recognises importance of background conditions in connexion with service of loan. We do not want financial talks to get bogged down in detail of commercial talks but you will have seen from paragraphs 8 to 11 above that we must have proper picture of prospective trade background. Opposition will certainly press this in Parliamentary discussion.

17. We think it is essential that any arrangement about Sterling Area, and particularly scaling down of Sterling debts, should not (repeat not) be

formalised in America. We should have no answer to criticism that we had arrived at a deal with the Americans at the expense of our Sterling creditors. This view is confirmed by Keynes' telegram, Remac 752[4] about India. We should like understanding with Americans that appropriate part of assistance given to us will be devoted by us to modifications in Sterling Area arrangements to remove chief objections existing now. Americans might quite well urge that in return for their contribution to cleaning up of total situation, they would expect Sterling creditors also to make contributions. But we should like to have greatest possible freedom to settle appropriate nature of contribution from each Sterling creditor. Dominions will be particularly sensitive on the point whether we have already fixed up everything without considering or consulting them.

18. Washington No. 6491.[5] As you know arrangements are being made for conference on telecommunications. We should be willing to discuss civil aviation with Americans at any mutually convenient time, and should of course like to reach agreements on both matters with them. But agreements must be on their merits and not under the pressure of the financial talks, and we should strongly object to any attempt to connect these subjects with financial talks. On bases Foreign Secretary has asked Byrnes to let you know what Americans want.[6] It may be that what they really want is not outrageous but here also matter must be considered on its merits, and not as a possible bribe to get a financial contract. This applies equally to sentimental islands. If everything went well in the financial and economic talks we should certainly wish to try and find a way of tying an agreeable ribbon round the gift.

CALENDARS TO No. 62

i *5 Oct. 1945 Record of meeting of Ministers (GEN 89/2nd Meeting)* discussion of GEN 89/4 (see note 1 above): in response to Mr. Bevin's enquiry 'about the possibility of a more modest proposal by which we should avoid any conditions and borrow what we needed over the next two years until we could stand on our own feet' it was explained 'that even this would involve some $1½ to $2 billion' [UE 4670/1094/53].

ii *6 Oct. 1945 Correspondence regarding forthcoming Telecommunications Conference* (see No. 21): H.M.G. wish to discuss general international agreement and are disappointed by U.S. proposal to restrict scope of Conference [W 13069, 13254/46/801].

[4] No. 41.iii.   [5] No. 47.   [6] See No. 61.

No. 63

Mr. Bevin to the Earl of Halifax (Washington)

No. *10095 Telegraphic* [*UE 4670/1094/53*]

Important. Secret   FOREIGN OFFICE, *8 October 1945, 9.45 p.m.*

Personal for Keynes from Chancellor of the Exchequer.

It is not entirely clear from NABOB telegrams and Press reports whether Americans really have the intention to make elimination of Imperial Preference a condition of financial assistance.[1]

2. We have repeatedly expressed our willingness to consider preferences as part of a satisfactory tariff settlement, but not to treat them separately. Certainly there will be very violent reaction here if preference issue is formally linked, not with commercial talks, but with financial deal. Indeed, a financial settlement otherwise acceptable might be wrecked on this issue.

3. Therefore, if you have real apprehension that American tactics are going to make this mistake will you consider in consultation with Ambassador and Liesching, whether you or Brand should not see Vinson personally as from me and speak to him in the sense of this telegram? You can explain that it is not too easy for me to find a basis of financial settlement acceptable to my colleagues and Parliament, and that my task would be made hopeless if anyone can represent that a financial pistol has been held at our head on subject of Imperial Preference.

4. This is a matter in which all parties in Parliament feel the same. Moreover, Australian and New Zealand Governments are attached to preference system and our present Government has political affiliations with them. Therefore Dominions aspect of American attempt to trade horses at the wrong fair would add to difficulties.

[1] Cf. Nos. 54 and 59–60. In his covering note to the draft of this telegram (see No. 62, note 1) Sir W. Eady commented with regard to Imperial Preference that Mr. Dalton 'may think it best to leave the matter alone until the Americans show their hand on the subject. Personally I believe that a telegram of this kind which puts you, so to speak, in personal touch with Vinson may be wise' (T 236/439).

No. 64

British Missions (Washington) to Cabinet Offices
(Received 9 October, 7.45 a.m.)

NABOB *132 Telegraphic* [*UE 4720/1094/53*]

Most immediate. Top secret   WASHINGTON, *9 October 1945, 4.25 a.m.*

Following for Chancellor of the Exchequer, President of the Board of Trade from Ambassador, Keynes and Liesching.

1. This telegram contains a general survey of the present position in regard to Imperial preference and the nature of the problems arising therefrom. In our next following telegram[1] we ask for guidance on certain specific points. Stated in its most simple form our problem lies in the fact that the Americans are demanding firm assurances from us regarding the reduction and elimination of preferences before they will promise further financial aid. We have told them that their demand in its present form is unacceptable; and at the moment debate has been suspended. But this state of affairs cannot last. Events may well take a turn in the next three or four days which if we are in a position to use our opportunities may enable us to find a way out of the deadlock.

2. This problem with which we are confronted has various aspects:

(A) As regards content.

(I) The Americans may seek to insist that the treatment of preferences be agreed to irrespective of the conditions which govern the treatment of Imperial preference in article VII[2] itself.

(II) They may modify this ruthless attitude. They may agree that preferences should be dealt with in the article VII context. But within that context they may press that the conditions applicable in that article be interpreted in their least acceptable form.

(B) As regards the degree of commitment.

In selecting the item of preference from among all other barriers to trade as a subject of separate assurances from us they may disregard the fact that it is as yet impossible to make a reasonable estimate of the outcome of the proposed international conference, and they may demand from us assurances concerning our attitude in the event of the failure of that conference.

(C) As regards our relations with the Dominions.

Under the constitutional conventions of the British Commonwealth it is impossible for the United Kingdom to take an entirely unilateral action in a matter which involves the Dominions so deeply.

3. The broad argument underlying the American attitude is roughly as follows. The economic sacrifice involved, they contend, is small. A great deal of the preferential system will tend to disappear in the course of the bilateral negotiations contemplated under the proposed convention, as indeed they would disappear in any normal process of commercial negotiation. This process of concession on preferences would be associated with a solid economic *quid pro quo* in the shape of tariff concessions by other parties. What remains they argue, will have comparatively little economic significance. To abandon it therefore as the price of easier financial assistance would be a very good bargain. At the same time, it would be a gesture which would be of immense value in enabling them to get their proposal through Congress. Unless some such gesture is forthcoming, they fear that Congress will be very difficult to manage.

[1] No. 65.　　　　　　　　　　　　　　　　[2] See No. 1, note 5.

4. We are quite convinced that it [if] the American demand is pressed as in the form of alternative (A)(I) above, it is fundamentally unacceptable. There is doubtless some force in their insistence that the economic price is not great. But this is not a matter of a pure economic calculus. We do not doubt that Ministers would feel the strongest repugnance to the idea of our being forced, by reason of financial weakness, to abandon even the residual tokens of habits which for many, symbolise membership of a common community. We have therefore emphasised to the Americans, both in plenary session and in private conversation, that if they file their demand in this way, they are likely to produce a breakdown of the negotiations.

5. In saying this, we do not wish to overstate the difficulties of the position though they are as yet unresolved. Many of the Americans with whom we are dealing are as convinced as we are that further financial aid is essential to us and to their own welfare too. They know that they have much to gain from a restoration of our economic strength and much to lose from a rupture in circumstances in which the rest of the world would tend to regard us as the injured party. The State Department contemplate with real apprehension the prospect of our turning aside to bilateralism. They know too that if the negotiation broke down on this point, we should tend to secure much support from the Dominions who, however lukewarm some of them may be regarding present preferential arrangements, would certainly rally to our support if we were threatened in this particular way. We believe too that Mr. Clayton who is conducting the negotiations and who, it is understood, is a leading exponent of the more extreme form of the American demand is an upright and honourable man; and we do not despair of persuading him that his insistence on this point is open to grave criticism from the moral point of view. But to do this we must be in a position to persuade him that another approach is available.

6. It follows from what has been said already that a solution must be sought which keeps the subject of preferences within the framework of the other obligations accepted by all signatories of article VII, and that its treatment in that context should not be exceptional but strictly compatible with the general process of bilateral bargaining which the Americans themselves propose. Under such a process it should be possible, though it may be difficult to agree with the Americans upon a form of obligation which will produce results that are economically advantageous and politically manageable on both sides of the Atlantic. There is nothing contrary to existing precedent, or indeed necessarily disadvantageous in the idea of an elimination of preferences against a sufficient reduction of tariffs; this is a process which has already taken effect in selected items in the 1938 agreement with the Americans.[3]

7. It does not seem probable that working within this framework the

[3] On the Anglo-American Trade Agreement of 17 November 1938 (printed in *B.F.S.P.*, vol. 142, pp. 183–298) see *D.B.F.P.*, Second Series, Volume XIX, No. 25, note 3.

Americans would be able to make offers of tariff concessions which would constitute a sufficient offset for an immediate elimination of all preferences. Under the Doughton Act[4] the downward limit of the tariff reduction is 50%, and it is not to be expected that all the reductions offered will be of that order of magnitude.

8. But action directed towards the reductions of tariffs and the elimination of discrimination—the obligation under article VII—is not necessarily to be interpretated as an obligation to eliminate preferences here and now against one cut in tariffs. The requirement may be met equally logically by reduction of preferences now against reduction of tariffs, coupled with an undertaking that at a future date, determined by governing economic conditions there should be summoned by the International Trade Organisation, a further conference at which in return for further reductions of tariffs there would be further reductions of preferences and so on into the future, until at some indefinite date the final stage was reached with preferences eliminated but tariffs, although greatly reduced, still perhaps above zero.

9. A solution on these lines has always been contemplated as the most sensible interpretation to be placed on article VII. It was implied in the questions which we have already addressed to the Americans in the course of debate and we should like to continue to press it explicitly upon their attention when discussion is resumed.

10. Assuming that agreement could be reached on this broad line of procedure, there would still remain the question how the reduction of preference contemplated at this first stage should be carried into effect. The following formula would ensure that tariffs and preferences are dealt with by the same process of negotiation and that the system of private consultation between the partners in the Commonwealth was preserved during the process.

(A) Margins of preference on any products should in no case be increased and no new preferences should be introduced.

(B) Whenever general rates of duty are reduced, such reductions should operate automatically to reduce or to eliminate margins of preference.

(C) All margins of preference should be regarded as open to negotiation subject to any necessary modifications of existing commitments to maintain such margins being agreed between the parties thereto before the convention enters into force.

11. (A) and (B) in this formula seem reasonable from our point of view and likely to be acceptable both to the Americans and the Canadians. (C) will probably cause difficulty to the Americans whose own proposal has been that 'all preferences should be unbound' prior to the bilateral tariff negotiations. But this would in effect cancel the Ottawa agreement[5] before

---

[4] i.e. the Act renewing the U.S. Trade Agreements Act of 1934: see No. 1, note 8.

[5] The Act of Parliament of 15 November 1932 giving effect to the agreements made at the Imperial Economic Conference in Ottawa in August 1932 for the extension of Imperial

any alternative tariff regime has been negotiated to take its place and clearly goes too far. The version given at (C) goes some way to meet them without sacrificing a procedure which is important to us both in principle and practice.

12. It is possible that such an offer might be made more attractive to the Americans if there were coupled with it an offer to abolish all preferences on commodities where the proportion of the supplies coming from Commonwealth source is small in relation to the total import of such commodities say 5 per cent. A concession on this basis would cost very little but it would affect a substantial area of trade. (An analysis of the statistics is contained in a following telegram [i].) It is not suggested that this offer should be made immediately but it is conceivable that a point might be reached in which such a comparatively small concession would be found to turn the scale.

13. A difficulty of another kind may arise in regard to the nature of the assurance which the Americans will demand at this stage. On the assumption that the Americans have agreed that preferences are to be dealt with within the framework of the article VII obligation, it is to be presumed that the main assurance which they would require at this stage would be an undertaking that we would support proposals of these lines at the International conference. But it may be doubted whether they would regard this as sufficient. The success of any International conference is not yet guaranteed, and it would be only natural for them to enquire what our position would be if the conference as at present planned were to fail to reach agreement. To this enquiry a possible answer would be that together with the Dominions, we should be willing to enter into negotiation regarding tariffs and preferences with the United States on the lines which we had sponsored at the conference. But we should be bound to point out that if the negotiations were thus restricted in area the degree of reduction of preference which we could contemplate against a given reduction of tariffs would inevitably be smaller.

14. The character of our assurances and conditions to be attached to them present sufficient difficulties in themselves. The situation, however, is still further complicated by the urgency with which some assurances may have to be provided if financial assistance is not to be unduly delayed. We do not think that it would be necessary to consult the Dominions on the broad interpretation of article VII which we have suggested in para 8. But clearly both on the formulae of preference reduction and on the nature of the commitment to the United States in the event of the International conference breaking down, consultation with the Dominions must precede a final commitment to the United States. We are advised that the ability of H.M.G. to commit the Colonies is not uniform but we assume that with so much at stake means can be found of

Preference and the imposition of customs duties is printed in *B.F.S.P.*, vol. 135, pp. 151–61. The tariff schedules agreed between Great Britain and individual members of the Empire are printed *ibid.*, pp. 161–231.

preventing difficulty or delay from arising under this head. If therefore it is decided to proceed upon the lines suggested in this survey it is a matter for urgent consideration what steps should be taken to secure a speedy exchange of views with the Dominions, by paving the way with information both on this matter and on such other aspects of the financial and commercial settlement as may be desirable for them to know. It is certainly our view that, considering the issues involved in a commitment on Imperial preference, the usual requirements as to consultation could not be regarded as satisfied by anything we could do with the Dominion representatives of varying calibre available here. Nevertheless the success of our financial talks could be hopelessly prejudiced if we were obliged to tell the Americans that no answer could be given except after the long period which would intervene if anything in the nature of a formal Imperial conference had to be held.

CALENDAR TO NO. 64

i *9 Oct. 1945 British Missions (Washington) Tel. NABOB 134* analysis of statistics on Imperial Preference: see para. 12 above [UE 4720/1094/53].

No. 65

British Missions (Washington) to Cabinet Offices
(Received 9 October, 8.30 a.m.)

NABOB 133 Telegraphic [UE 4720/1094/53]

Most immediate. Top secret   WASHINGTON, *9 October 1945, 4.41 a.m.*

Following from Ambassador, Keynes and Liesching for Chancellor of Exchequer and President of the Board of Trade.

1. In the light of our NABOB 132[1] we ask for authority to proceed on the following lines.

(A) To tell the Americans that we consider that the obligations of Article VII as regards tariffs and preferences should be dealt with in stages. That is to say that, although we should not be prepared to see all preferences eliminated against the kind of offer which they are likely to make in the first round, we should be willing to agree that at a future date, determined by governing economic conditions, there should be summoned by the International Trading Organisation a further conference at which, in return for further reductions of tariffs or other form of concession which we could regard as adequate there would be further reductions in preferences.

(B) To suggest to the Americans that, subject to the views of the Dominions, we would be prepared to accept the following draft for

[1] No. 64.

205

inclusion in their statement of principles under the heading 'Import Tariffs and Preferences', as an indication of the method by which we would proceed to deal with preferences within the framework of Article VII.

Members should undertake to take effective and expeditious measures, in accordance with methods to be agreed upon, directed to the substantial reduction of tariffs and the elimination of tariff preferences. In the light of the principles associating the two which are set forth in Article VII of the Mutual Aid Agreements the rule should be that tariffs and tariff preferences should be dealt with together, as follows:

(I) Margins of preference on any product should in no case be increased, and no new preferences should be introduced.

(II) Whenever general tariffs are reduced, such reductions should operate automatically to reduce or eliminate margins of preference.

(III) All margins of preference should be regarded as open to negotiation, subject to any necessary modifications of existing commitments to maintain such margins being agreed between the parties thereto before the convention enters into force.

(IV) If there remain preferences not eliminated by the application of the foregoing principles, it should be competent for the International trade organization at a date determined by governing economic conditions to convene a conference to consider whether further tariff reductions could be agreed sufficient to justify further steps towards the elimination of preferences.

(C) To be prepared, if the developments of the situation appear to warrant it, to clinch the bargain by offering to add to the draft statement of principles a provision abolishing all preferences on commodities where the proportion coming from preferred sources to the total import of such commodities is 5 percent or less of the total import of such commodities.

(D) If the Americans, having received an assurance that we would support proposals on these lines at the International Conference, then ask what our action would be in the event of the proposed conference failing to achieve its object, to give them the assurance (subject to the concurrence of the Dominions) that we and the Dominions would enter into negotiations regarding tariffs and preferences on the lines indicated above. It would be understood, however, that, since the area of possible gain from our point of view was narrowed, the degree of concession that we should be prepared to offer in regard to preferences would also of necessity be proportionately restricted.

2. In addition we are anxious to be assured that we are not expected to obtain the necessary clearance with the Dominions concurrently at Washington, and that this part of the business will be handled (presumably by direct exchanges) with the Dominion Governments conducted from London. It is not possible for us here to know the extent and nature of the consultation required in a case of this kind or to conduct a

consultation in the midst of our present negotiations with representative[s] of the varying calibre available here.

3. It is understood, of course, that any discussions with the Americans,
on the lines indicated above, would be non-commit[t]al in the sense that
no definite commitments would be made until the position as a whole had
been reviewed. It would be clearly pointed out that any suggestions we put
forward in connexion with imperial preference could not be regarded as
receiving ultimate ministerial sanction until there had been an opportunity of final reference to London on this and on the other salient questions
raised by the general proposals of the Americans.

4. In addition to this we should point out that a further short interval
would have to elapse before we could be assured of concurrence of
Dominion Governments.

5. An answer by Thursday[2] evening would greatly help us.

[2] 11 October 1945.

No. 66

Mr. Bevin to the Earl of Halifax (Washington)

No. *10100* Telegraphic [AS *5263/12/2*]

Immediate   FOREIGN OFFICE, *9 October 1945, 2.20 p.m.*

Repeated to Buenos Aires No. 514.

Buenos Aires telegram to Foreign Office No. 711[1] and my telegram No.
9832[2] (of October 1st and September 29th Argentina).

As you know, I asked Mr. Winant on August 21st to convey a personal

[1] This telegram of 2 October (i below), in which Sir D. Kelly reviewed the effects on
Argentine politics of Mr. Spruille Braden's four months as U.S. Ambassador in Buenos
Aires, was despatched following an abortive coup of 25 September by General Rawson
against the Argentine Government, which reacted by declaring a state of siege. General
discontent with Colonel Perón's conduct of the emergency, however, led to a military revolt
against him and to his resignation from all public office on 9 October, and to that of the
majority of the Government on 12 October. Continuing unrest and widespread strikes both
in support of and against Colonel Perón prevented Dr. Alvarez, Attorney General attached
to the Supreme Court, from forming a new government until 17 October. Colonel Perón
was not a member of the administration but remained an important figure and seemed a
strong candidate for the elections planned for early 1946: see No. 92.

Meanwhile Mr. Braden, whose appointment as Assistant Secretary of State for Latin
American Affairs in succession to Mr. Rockefeller had been announced on 25 August, had
left Argentina on 23 September. Washington telegram No. 6616 of 5 October reported that
this appointment had 'touched off a debate in the Senate Foreign Relations Committee at
which pointed questions were asked about United States foreign policy in Latin America'
(AS 5165/12/2). The appointment was, however, confirmed by the Senate on 22 October.

[2] This telegram recorded Mr. Bevin's conversation with Mr. Byrnes on 28 September
concerning Argentina: see para. 1 below.

message to Mr. Byrnes expressing the strong hope that he would be able to give us a year's stability in Argentina and to leave political considerations aside for the time being,[3] and on September 28th I emphasised to Mr. Byrnes personally the essentiality to ourselves and others of supplies from that country. Just before leaving London, however, Mr. Byrnes pressed upon me[4] the desirability of refusing to take shipments for [? from] Argentina for say a fortnight, arguing that this would be sufficient to bring the Argentine Government down. I replied that we had only two weeks meat supply; what would be our position? There was no guarantee that the Americans would fill the gap with shipments of wheat or maize. We could not afford to have our meat supplies interrupted. The standard of meat consumption in this country was already far too low. Mr. Byrnes said that he would review the whole problem when he returned to Washington. For your information, I think that the action suggested by Mr. Byrnes is impossible, and in view of the situation developing in the Argentine it has become urgently necessary that the United States Government should be [in] possession of views on the subject generally. I should be glad, therefore, if you would speak to Mr. Byrnes or to Mr. Acheson as soon as possible in the following sense.

2. When I appealed to Mr. Byrnes in August for a year's stability, I had reason to suppose that this would be consonant with his ideas in view of his acceptance statement in July[5] that his general desire was to avoid crises and promote toleration. Since then, however, the very active line taken by Mr. Braden in Buenos Aires has unquestionably contributed to the present state of great turmoil in Argentina, and the latest move of the United States Government as regards the Rio Conference[6] will have done nothing to allay it.

3. Apart from this, the reversal of the State Department's decision (which we had greatly welcomed) to help us to get our meat contract by supplying rubber, oil and coal to the Argentine in sufficient quantities to enable our essential supplies to come forward, has most serious

---

[3] See No. 14, note 8.

[4] Mr. Bevin recorded this further conversation with Mr. Byrnes in despatch No. 1754 to Washington of 5 October (AS 5198/12/2).

[5] See No. 14, note 7.

[6] On 3 October Mr. Acheson had issued a statement that 'in view of recent developments in Argentina, the United States Government does not feel that it can properly negotiate or sign with the present Argentine regime a treaty of military assistance', and suggested the postponement of the Inter American Conference for the Maintenance of Peace and Security due to be convened at Rio de Janeiro on 20 October: cf. *F.R.U.S. 1945*, vol. ix, pp. 159–65. In response to questions Mr. Acheson also stated that a decision on sending a new American Ambassador to Buenos Aires must wait until Mr. Byrnes' return from London: 'Asked if the United States was also having separate consult[ations] with the British Government on this question, Mr Acheson replied in the negative.'

In a minute of 4 October Mr. Broadmead commented that Mr. Acheson's statement had been 'pretty stiff. Whether Mr. Acheson knew what had passed between the S. of S. and Mr. Byrnes is at least open to doubt and there is therefore the possibility that when Mr. Byrnes gets back he may tone down things a bit.'

implications.[7] We appreciate the reluctance of the United States Government to send these supplies and for the time being we might be able to make them good from sources of our own. But the existing lack of fuel in Argentina not only makes it increasingly difficult for the Frigorificos to prepare for despatch of meat which we all in Europe need so much, but has already created a serious transport crisis there, so that essential supplies of food, etc., are not being transported and loaded, and the Argentines themselves are being obliged to burn in large quantities products such as maize and linseed, for which there is desperate need in Europe. They have, in fact, announced that the entire 1944/45 maize crop must be used for fuel to maintain the electricity supply, and that other grains may also have to be used for this purpose unless coal and oil are forthcoming. Fuel shortages are already seriously affecting exports of foodstuffs to Europe, and the first consequence of a complete denial of imported fuel would be that the Argentine Government would use home produced fuel (i.e. maize and linseed needed here) to move supplies needed for the Argentine people, leaving exports to take their chance.

5. [*sic*] This situation is precisely that which my conversations first with Mr. Winant and then with Mr. Byrnes were designed to avert, and it is exceedingly disquieting to us in present circumstances. I most earnestly hope therefore that now that the United States Government have administered their signal rebuff to the present Argentine Government by postponing the Rio Conference, they will take into account that other than purely political issues are here at stake and let the supplies of rubber, oil and coal go forward in the required quantities. I feel bound to add my conviction that affairs in Argentina will not quiet down until that country is left to settle her own affairs. I realise that the Americans may quote against us that non-intervention by the democracies enabled the dictators in Germany and Italy and Spain to place themselves in impregnable positions *vis à vis* their own people. I can only reply that the best information that reaches me, coming in many cases from persons of distinction and of liberal views in countries neighbouring Argentina, is to the effect that Argentina psychologically requires a cessation of intervention from outside, and that she is in no position to be aggressive.[8]

[7] Cf. No. 14.v.

[8] In a minute to Mr. Perowne of 4 October Mr. Butler had expressed doubts, in the light of Mr. Acheson's statement (see note 6), 'about urging the U.S. Government to a political truce or non-intervention – things have gone too far. If we had to say anything of that kind to them my inclination would be [to] ask them, in the interest of restoring stability in Argentina, either to do that which they intend to do quickly, i.e. to take more effective action to get rid of Vice-President Peron [cf. note 1]; or to keep their hands off. But I realise that to speak to them on this line would be dangerous, and on the whole I incline to confine anything from the Secretary of State to Mr. Byrnes pretty well to the necessity of obtaining supplies from Argentina.'

Mr. Perowne, however, replied on 4 October: 'I don't feel it will pay to let Mr. Byrnes – or Mr. Winant – off their having ignored the S/S's message of 21/8. We have been very badly treated over Argentina throughout—we have never been consulted properly, altho' the

6. I would add one further point. Argentina for a number of practical and straightforward reasons is a country in which Great Britain is keenly interested. At various times during these last years the United States Government has taken important steps which have affected our interests without prior consultation with us. We attach great importance to such consultation and believe that things would have gone more satisfactorily in Argentina had it been more consistently forthcoming.[9]

CALENDARS TO NO. 66

i *28 Sept. & 2 Oct. 1945* (a) Memo. by Mr. Hadow on recent U.S. policy towards Argentina (b) Sir D. Kelly (Buenos Aires) Tel. No. 711: 'dramatic and repeated publicity' of Mr. Braden's campaign against Argentine Govt. was 'direct cause' of Gen. Rawson's abortive revolt; U.S. Govt. should be told that H.M.G. cannot support their policy 'unless we are effectively consulted about it in advance' [AS 5110, 5117/12/2].

ii *15 Sept.–31 Oct. 1945* Wheat and maize from Argentina: acute shortage of maize in S. Africa will only be met by Argentina in return for coal (cf. No. 14. v), and Sir D. Kelly is instructed to assist negotiations; Ministry of Food are anxious to obtain delivery of flour and grain [AS 4845, 4868, 5750/189/2].

expense of the whole policy has rested entirely on us—and we ought to make it clear that we can't contemplate a continuation of the process. If we omit all reference to politics the letter is hardly worth sending. As the dft. [of the present telegram] indicates, without political stability *and* fuel the food we need will not be obtained—one is no good without the other.'
[9] Lord Halifax's *aide-mémoire* of 12 October to Mr. Byrnes in accordance with the instructions in this telegram is filed at AS 5507/12/2.

No. 67

The Earl of Halifax (Washington) to Mr. Bevin
(Received 10 October, 5.55 a.m.)

No. 6733 Telegraphic [UE 4718/1094/53]

Immediate. Top secret   WASHINGTON, 9 October 1945, 11.3 p.m.

Following personal for Chancellor of the Exchequer from Keynes.

Ambassador and I saw Vinson and Clayton again this morning. Your telegram No. 10094[1] gave us just the guidance we hoped for and we were able to lead the conversation closely along the lines indicated.

2. Ambassador and I advanced a renewed plea in the very strongest terms why both on financial and on political or psychological grounds at least a part of the assistance say two billions should take the form of a grant. On the surface we failed to shift them from their stand that even a partial grant-in-aid was not politically possible for them. But personally

[1] No. 62.

neither the Ambassador nor I feel certain that this scheme is quite dead or that they have finally (repeat finally) rejected it in their own minds though it may be unlikely that we can ever get it quite in the desired form. I am therefore in favour of still keeping it in reserve as the right plan for meeting the necessities and the justice of the case.

3. Both Vinson and Clayton remained outwardly adamant that neither a grant nor a loan free of interest was practical politics for them. But Vinson added with some vehemence that so far as he personally was concerned, and he called on Clayton to agree with him, he was not worried about the financial concession involved by what we were asking which was, he said with truth, only peanuts to him as Secretary of the Treasury. He was solely moved by the judgement of what was politically possible in the present mood of Congress and the public.[2] The result of the London Conference had caused, he said, a considerable recurrence of Isolationist sentiment and in favour of pulling out from further commitments.[3] Both of them agreed however when challenged by the Ambassador that the feeling for Anglo-American cooperation has also been greatly strengthened.

4. In response to your feeling that the time had now come when the Americans should tell us more clearly what they were prepared to do, we elicited from Clayton a proposal which was not perfectly clear in detail but is we think fairly summarised in the next paragraph. This was an amplification of hints Clayton had already given us last Friday[4].

5. Clayton's proposal is for an untied loan of five billions repayable in fifty annual instalments commencing five years hence, that is by an annuity of one hundred million dollars a year. In addition a further annuity of fifty million dollars a year would be payable by way of interest. This would work out actuarially at a rate of more than one per cent, since as a result of the annual amortisation the average annual amount of the loan outstanding during the currency of the loan would be only half the

[2] In his telegram REMAC 770 of 11 October also referring to this conversation Lord Keynes reported that 'Vinson volunteered the remark that in his opinion there is not a doggone chance that Congress would vote the additional one per cent to U.N.R.R.A. [cf. Nos. 12 and 13] and invited Clayton to agree with him. Clayton was not so explicit but admitted that it had now become exceedingly unlikely.' Lord Keynes therefore suggested that it was 'essential that we should refrain for the present from making any further commitment in Parliament and should take steps to prevent U.N.R.R.A. from overdrawing the amount of our initial one per cent ... There is all the more reason for this action because the winding up of U.N.R.R.A. at an earlier date than would have occurred otherwise will not necessarily relieve us from all further relief expenditure ... apart from our general financial predicament, there is good reason for keeping our ammunition in hand' (UR 3670/30/852).

Mr. Dalton's telegram CAMER 772 to Washington of 21 October in reply commented that Mr. Vinson's view was 'not altogether a surprise, but I hope intervention by the President or in some other form may still be possible ... We took the lead in getting Parliamentary approval to the first 1% contribution [see No. 13, note 7] and it is my firm intention that we should let the United States take the lead this time' (UR 3670/30/852).

[3] Cf. Volume II, No. 174, note 6.   [4] 5 October 1945: see Nos. 58 and 60.

initial amount. But it would be less than two per cent because in proportion to the capital outstanding at various dates a substantial part of the interest would be paid in the latter part of the period. I think he might consider a scheme by which the annual instalments began at one hundred million dollars a year gradually rising to two hundred millions so as to average one hundred and fifty millions over the fifty year period. But I purposely refrained from taking the proposal sufficiently seriously at this stage to wish to go into such details. Furthermore he offered some liberal test of our capacity to pay, which he invited me to try my hand at drafting, so that in years in which this test was not satisfied the instalment of interest would be finally waived (repeat waived) and not deferred. There were also hints of a possible arrangement for dividing the total annuity between interest and capital repayment on exactly the opposite principle to that mentioned above, namely, a larger proportion attributed to interest in the early years so that a larger proportion could be finally waived in the event of our capacity to pay disappointing the more optimistic assumptions.

6. Clayton himself holds very optimistic views both about our capacity to pay and about America's capacity to receive. He wagers that ten years hence our overseas income visible and invisible will reach ten billion dollars and that America's over-seas expenditure visible and invisible will overtake her exports. He sees no argument he can offer Congress why we should escape interest irrespective of what our capacity to pay may prove to be in later years, but realises the risk to us of rigid commitment entered into now and therefore offers us almost any escape clause within reason that we choose to draft provided it leaves him free to say that America will receive interest eventually, if any, [*sic* ? and] when it lies within our plain capacity to meet it. Indeed he pressed me to produce an appropriate clause, to which I replied that I had already given much thought to this but we did not want to have the bailiffs in the house for two generations sizing up the position and I had not yet found a formula which was free from this objection.

7. I doubt if the time has yet arrived when it is advisable to discuss with him in detail on the basis of an annuity of one hundred and fifty millions however carefully safeguarded by waiver provisions. But unless you reject Clayton's line of thought out of hand which we would not yet advise, we might prepare ourselves with a possible formula. What would you say to an annuity of one hundred and fifty millions divided into two equal portions of seventy five millions, the second portion being waived in years in which our visible exports failed to reach six billion dollars reckoned at present prices? Clayton was thinking in terms of our total overseas income visible and invisible, and might press for this. But this is difficult to define statistically and I should therefore prefer the quite definite criterion of the Board of Trade return of our home produced exports as calculated by them in terms of a constant price level. If you think something on these lines is worth pursuing, I could sound him generally without getting into too much detail.

8. We then proceeded to develop at some length the anxieties to which you gave expression in paragraphs 8, 9 and 10 of your telegram. The conditions in paragraph 8 are consistent with the lines of the commercial proposals under discussion and should not present much difficulty. Clayton checked a little at the reference to long-term contracts but we hope he will not press this point. To all the rest in that paragraph he readily agreed.

9. Our exposition of the currency difficulties in your paragraphs 9 and 10 was first met by the statement on Clayton's part, less confidently on Vinson's, that these things would not happen. But they had to admit that they might. They did not reject the principle of escape clauses on these lines and asked me to give them a draft in writing of what would satisfy us. I am sending you a version for your approval in a separate telegram.[5] Since these would be required under any arrangement except a straight grant-in-aid for the whole amount, I see no reason why we should not give them this as soon as you have considered it.

10. I read out the substance of your paragraph 17 relating to sterling area arrangements. They appreciate our difficulties and agree that the arrangements must be made direct between ourselves and the other countries concerned. The only points of doubt which may arise at a later stage are the question of the degree of our commitment as to the exact overall amount of the writing down to be expected from the sterling area as a whole and the position of subsequent instalments of repayment due to the sterling area in relation to similar instalment due to United States.[6] But I hope that these are points which we can handle successfully when we get down to the drafting of details.

11. In conclusion we returned to the proposal of the partial grant-in-aid with which we had started and urged that whilst this might be politically inacceptable as an isolated financial transaction, it might be otherwise when presented as an integral part of a far-reaching Anglo-American economic concordat covering a wide field and perhaps even including strategical bases. They replied that such a presentation would be absolutely necessary anyhow if the sympathy of Congress is to be successfully engaged.

12. We had not seen the recent repetition by Aldrich of his grant-in-aid

[5] No. 68.
[6] In a letter of 5 October to Sir W. Eady (printed in Moggridge, *op. cit.*, pp. 531–5) Lord Keynes had discussed a scheme proposed by Dr. Harry White to finance a reduction of the sterling balances: cf. No. 28, para. III(*c*). The scheme involved the unblocking of a proportion of the balances, the writing off of a further proportion, and the funding of the remainder, to be repayable without interest over a period of years. The U.S. would then buy the funded portion of the debt from the sterling area countries at a discounted value, thus reducing the overall figure owed by the United Kingdom. The plan also obliged the sterling area countries to make a loan to the U.K. to cover the difference between the sterling balances as at 30 June 1945 and 31 December 1946. Lord Keynes also referred to the scheme in a further letter to Sir W. Eady of 12 October, printed *ibid.*, pp. 538–43. For a discussion of the White Plan see Pressnell, *op. cit.*, Chapter 10(13).

proposal which you mention.[7] It has not received prominence in the American press. You must remember that he is an extreme political opponent of the present administration whose remarks carry no weight with them and are indeed apt to be made with the object of embarrassing them. None of our best friends here are encouraging us to pursue the straight grant-in-aid approach.

13. They pressed us for a further meeting as soon as possible. We promised to let them know as soon as we were ready. May we have further guidance at the very earliest you can manage what reply to make to Clayton's proposal.

CALENDAR TO NO. 67

i *15 Oct. 1945   Memo. by Mr. E. Rowe-Dutton (Under Secretary in H.M. Treasury) on the White plan* (note 6 above), questioning its practicability and warning that non-cooperation of sterling countries would lead to chaos [T 236/438].

[7]See No. 62, note 2.

No. 68

The Earl of Halifax (Washington) to Mr. Bevin
(Received 11 October, 10.3 p.m.)

No. 6772 Telegraphic [UE 4778/1094/53]

WASHINGTON, *11 October 1945, 4.30 p.m.*
Immediate. Top secret and personal

Following for Chancellor of the Exchequer from Keynes.

1. In paragraph 9 of my telegram No. 6733[1] I promised a draft of escape clauses to carry out the purpose of paragraphs 9 and 10 of your telegram No. 10094.[2] I submit the following paragraph for approval before giving it to Clayton.

2. The Government of the United Kingdom shall be entitled to approach the Government of the United States for a deferment of the annual instalment of payment due in any year in any of the following circumstances. In the event of deferment the amount due in respect of amortisation shall be postponed so as not to increase the amount due in the years immediately following but by an appropriate extension of the period of repayment.

(a) A breakdown of multilateral clearing.

In the event of less than 75% of the foreign currencies earned by British trade being freely convertible into dollars.

(b) An international depression of trade.

[1] No. 67.

[2] No. 62.

In the event of general and prolonged depression of world trade acknowledged by the International Monetary Fund as constituting a serious disturbance of the equilibrium of international payments.

(c) Scarcity of dollars.

In the event of the International Monetary Fund having notified under Article VII(I) of the International Monetary Fund[3] that a general scarcity of dollars is developing.

3. It will be observed that the above clauses keep strictly to the conditions mentioned in your paragraphs 9 and 10. That is to say they relate primarily to circumstances affecting the inability of the United States to accept payment rather than to an inability on our part to make payment. This seems to me to be wise. I have been shy of offering any escape clause which depends on a criterion of our inability to pay since a future appeal to such an escape clause clearly impugns our credit and even our solvency. Moreover, the offer of such a clause greatly weakens our argument for limiting the amount of the annual burden. If we prepare an escape clause which seems to us reasonably watertight then the Americans will feel no reason why the nominal burden should not be increased subject to the protection of this clause. If, as it may easily turn out, the escape clause is not watertight it would be dangerous and even if it is watertight our credit may be involved.

4. This does not mean that I would reject an escape clause at the appropriate stage. Indeed in paragraph 7 of my telegram No. 6733 I have suggested one which on further reflection still seems to me the best possible inasmuch as it is a real protection and yet seems to me freer than most such clauses from any injury to our credit. But even this clause one would be reluctant to produce until there was no risk of the annual burden to which it related being increased as a result.

5. Indeed at the right time I think some such escape clause should be produced in any case. That is why I am anxious to have guidance as to how you feel about the particular version proposed in my previous telegram.

6. The question of an escape clause may get uncomfortably bound up with the escape clause which the members of the Mission specially concerned with the commercial talks are working out as to the criterion of our being allowed to retain or reimpose import restrictions. If they succeed in producing an acceptable draft the Americans will naturally ask why this should not be applied on the financial side also. They will ask whether we should not feel able to accept a larger nominal annual burden subject to the same escape clause as that which is provided as a criterion of our need for import restrictions. The criteria under their examination are

[3] Article VII of the Articles of Agreement of the International Monetary Fund concerned scarce currencies: Section I provided that if the I.M.F. found that 'a general scarcity of a particular currency is developing, the Fund may so inform members and may issue a report setting forth the causes of the scarcity and containing recommendations designed to bring it to an end'.

taken from A.S.D.(44)16 paragraph 41[4]. We are however discussing this further before putting it forward to the Americans.

7. I should be grateful for an early reply about the acceptability of the proposals in paragraph 2 above.[5]

[4] A.S.D.(44)16 of 21 March 1944 was the Agreed Summary of Discussions on Article VII of the Mutual Aid Agreement (see No. 1, note 5) which took place between United Kingdom, Dominion and Indian representatives in London from 23 February to 21 March 1944. Para. 41 set out a possible objective criterion, based on a country's monetary reserves, which would entitle that country to impose a quantitative regulation of its imports on a non-discriminatory basis (CAB 123/96). Cf. also Pressnell, *op. cit.*, Chapter 6(4).

[5] In telegram No. 10473 to Washington of 17 October Mr. Dalton informed Lord Keynes that the escape clauses in para. 2 above 'appear to protect us adequately against inability of United States to accept payment, and against general breakdown of multilateral clearing or deflationary depression of trade. We suggest however that it would be clearer if your clause 2(*a*) were redrafted to read as follows: "In event of less than 75 per cent of U.K. exports being sold to countries whose currencies are freely convertible into Dollars" [.] Visibles are easier than invisibles' (UE 4778/1094/53).

No. 69

The Earl of Halifax (Washington) to Mr. Bevin
(Received 12 October, 5.5 a.m.)

No. 6798 Telegraphic [*UE 4779/1094/53*]

Most immediate   WASHINGTON, *12 October 1945, 12 a.m.*

Following secret and personal for Chancellor of Exchequer from Keynes.

Your telegram 10095.[1]

1. With approval of Ambassador and Liesching I have shown this telegram to Vinson who received your message with warm sympathy and understanding. He asked me to tell you that so far as he was concerned he repudiated the idea of using a financial pistol to obtain preference concessions against our will. He said that English blood flowed in his own veins and he knew exactly how we should feel about it. He believed that if the idea got abroad that such concessions had been forced from us in this way the harm thus done to the feeling of confidence between our two countries would undo all the lasting good he hopes to achieve from this Conference. The notion of a trade between financial advantages to us and commercial and other concessions unwillingly conceded by us was contrary in his opinion to the spirit of these talks.

2. He continued that he was solely concerned with the problem of framing the administration's ultimate proposals in a way which would make a sufficient appeal to Congress. It was a problem of presentation. He

[1] No. 63.

216

considers that he and Clayton have a very tough assignment in getting Congress to accept anything which approaches what he personally believes to be the right solution. He begs you to believe that any apparent pressure on us has no other object in view than to secure a conclusion which will be fully satisfactory to the public opinion of both countries.

3. Vinson was evidently moved by your message and I am sure that its communication has done good.

4. I feel some confidence that at the last lap we can rely on his aid in working out a form of presentation which will be mutually satisfactory on the basis of your paragraph 2. This does not mean that the State Department does not hold strong doctrinaire views or that it will be easy for us to carry a satisfactory formula. But it does mean that the spirit and purpose of the principal negotiators on the American side are far removed from threats and that in the last resort they will try hard to meet us on any point which they believe we genuinely regard as vital.[2]

[2] In his economic survey for the week ending 13 October 1945 Lord Halifax commented that 'as regards Imperial preference there has been some evidence in inspired articles in the press, notably one in the New York *Journal of Commerce*, that the United States Delegation has withdrawn from its original attitude that preferences would have to be abolished as a condition of financial assistance, and that they have gone a long way towards accepting the British view that these preferences should be regarded jointly with tariffs as barriers to international trade for the reduction and ultimate elimination of which the International Trade Organisation should work' (Washington telegram No. 510 Saving of 14 October, UE 4901/42/53).

No. 70

Cabinet Offices to British Missions (Washington)

BABOON *102 Telegraphic [T 236/465]*

Most immediate. Top secret   CABINET OFFICES, *12 October 1945, 10.10 p.m.*

Reference NABOB 132, 133, 134.[1]

1. We admire the skill with which you have sought to resolve the deadlock on Imperial preference. Our comments on your formula are given in our immediately following telegram [ii]. This telegram deals with the tactical position.

2. The main point about which we are concerned is whether the Americans are likely to agree to the proposals we make, or will only look on them as our bargaining approach to more specific and unconditional

[1] Nos. 64, 65 and 64.i respectively. These telegrams, together with No. 67 and draft replies circulated by Sir E. Bridges on 11 October (GEN 89/5, not printed), were discussed at a Ministerial meeting on the afternoon of 12 October (GEN 89/3rd Meeting, i below). Mr. Bevin, who was taking a short holiday, was not on the list of those invited to the meeting by Mr. Attlee, nor was any Foreign Office representative present at the meeting. For the replies, as despatched after some amendment by Ministers, see Nos. 70, 70.ii and 71.

assurances. We realise that it may be difficult for you to find out in advance whether they will accept certain proposals before they are in fact put forward. But we feel that if you can talk informally on the line that you want some indication of their reaction before you can fairly ask London for directions, you will be able to do something to avoid a situation in which we put in the proposals in question only to find them treated as an opening bid to be raised on the next round. If, after preliminary soundings, you come to the conclusion that something on these lines will not do we want to be free to think again.

3. A further point is to make clear the exact relationship between these proposals and the commercial policy and financial talks. We take it for granted that a move on preferences, even in the terms which you suggest, will not be regarded as the *quid pro quo* for financial aid. On the contrary, if we move on preferences now it is in the expectation that the Americans will meet our point of view on other aspects of commercial policy so that Commercial Policy discussions as a whole may move to a satisfactory conclusion. We recognise that without agreement on Commercial Policy we cannot expect U.S. to get financial aid past Congress. But the U.S. side in their turn must realise that without satisfactory financial aid it would be entirely out of our power to follow a Commercial Policy bearing any resemblance to the proposals now under discussion. On present showing as regards the financial offer we are inclined to think that the Americans realise all this, but we mention the point because it may lead to real difficulty if they do not.

4. There is furthermore very much present to our minds the problem of the public presentation in both countries of a settlement of the preferences issue. If the U.S. Administration were to represent the proposed settlement as an undertaking by us to abandon preferences in return for financial aid, the political repercussions here might be very serious. Due emphasis will have to be given to compensating commercial advantages which we shall receive by way of reduction of other trade barriers. We equally appreciate that it will be incumbent on us to make clear in Parliament the commitment into which we shall have entered. We must therefore have it clear with the Administration that both they and we will use language to the effect that the Commercial Policy discussions have resulted in a mutually acceptable understanding on the lines of paras. 1 (A) and (B) of NABOB 133 as far as tariffs and preferences are concerned. A statement on these lines would not of course appear in isolation but in the context of statements covering the discussions both on trade and on finance.

5. We therefore propose that in the light of the above you explore informally the prospects of making progress on the basis of the views in your telegram, as amended by comments in our following telegram. It would of course be understood that discussions regarding these suggestions would be non-committal in the sense that no definite commitments would be made until the outcome of the negotiations as a whole had been

reviewed here in consultation with Dominion and Indian Governments.

6. This and immediately following telegram have been approved by Ministers.

CALENDARS TO NO. 70

i *12 Oct. 1945 Record of Meeting of Ministers (GEN 89/3rd meeting)* Discussion of Nos. 64, 64.i, 65 and 67: Mr. Dalton's view that tactically 'it would be well for the present to take the line of asking the Americans to think again'; cf. Pressnell, *op. cit.*, Chapter 10(11). [CAB 78/37].

ii *12 Oct. 1945 Cabinet Offices to British Missions (Washington) Tel. BABOON 103* comments on specific proposals in No. 65 [T 236/465].

iii *16 Oct. 1945 British Missions (Washington) to Cabinet Offices Tel. NABOB 174* Meeting on 15 Oct. with Mr. Clayton and Mr. Vinson on Imperial Preference: Mr. Clayton rejected British counter-proposals but 'was not wholly negative' [T 236/454].

iv *12–15 Oct. 1945 D.O. Tel. No. 1909 to Dominion Govts.* summarizes commercial policy negotiations and asks for views on proposals regarding preferences: Board of Trade anxiety 'lest we appear to be pressing Dominions overmuch' by summoning meeting of Dominion Ministers in London (cf. *The Mackenzie King Record*, ed. J.W. Pickersgill & D.F. Forster (Toronto, 1970) vol. iii, pp. 62–3) leads to despatch of further explanatory telegram *No. 1920 to Dominion Govts.* [UE 5212/1094/53, T 236/388, PREM 8/35].

No. 71

Mr. Bevin to the Earl of Halifax (Washington)

No. 10274 Telegraphic [UE 4803/1094/53]

Immediate. Top secret   FOREIGN OFFICE, *13 October 1945, 12.40 a.m.*

From Chancellor of the Exchequer.

1. We[1] have read with great interest your telegram No. 6733.[2] It is a tribute to the work you and Keynes and Brand and your team have done that Clayton should authoritatively indicate willingness of the Administration to lend us five billion dollars and the possible terms suggested are at least an advance upon what you previously expected.

2. We have earnestly considered whether a loan on such terms should be accepted if it is formally offered to you. The Americans probably regard its size and terms as a signal recognition of our special case and rejection of it might set back progress in the discussion. It would in the immediate future fortify our financial position and would lighten some of our present anxieties. It would help us to enter upon profitable negotiations for easing the sterling area and so would reduce a cause of

---

[1] i.e. the Ministers who approved the despatch of this telegram: see No. 70, note 1.

[2] No. 67.

constant misunderstanding and friction. Not least it would enable us, without imprudence, to improve somewhat the consumption levels of our own people in the next twelve months.

3. But we should mislead you if we left you in doubt about the way we judge it. In the circumstances in which our need to borrow has arisen, we do not find a loan on these terms acceptable.

4. In the form in which the proposal has been made to you it fails on the two tests of principle we have applied from the beginning. The first is that the form and terms of assistance from America should be such that we can without reserve present it to all parties in Parliament and to our people as an equitable settlement, that, in Keynes' phrase, it has in it the sweet breath of justice. Both for the immediate impact upon opinion here, and for the basis of Anglo-American relations we believe that this condition is essential.

5. Clayton and Vinson have repeatedly assured you that they are convinced by our case and that they know what they ought to do but they have to think of Congress. We have equally to think of Parliament. At the end of a joint war we are to become a debtor on a vast scale to our richest ally. Our indebtedness did not arise from any attempt on our part to live comfortably or from any withholding of sacrifice. We parted with all our reserves and much of our foreign assets when we were fighting alone so that we could continue fighting for a cause which the Americans subsequently made their own. Our financial difficulties began when we had to make those huge cash payments for munitions and food from the United States and despite Lend-Lease and the substantial but temporary income from American troops we have never been able to recover from this initial burden. Our debts to the sterling area arose directly from the shape and width of our war effort and we owe them also to those with whom and for whom we fought. You have said all this and we repeat it because it will be said again and remains true.

6. The result is that we are gravely short of dollars to buy the food and raw materials which at present the United States is alone able to supply, and that the trade of a large part of the world is clogged by our indebtedness which affects American exporters who are fortunate in being ready to export to markets from which in the past we made much of our foreign income, but who cannot be paid in dollars.

7. To clear this up we are offered still further indebtedness and in the case of the sterling area the partial conversion of a widely distributed sterling debt owed to those who normally trade with us both ways into a canalised dollar debt, to a country whose visible balance of trade with us is so onesided. It is true that we may have the prospects of an expanding world economy for which we also shall work and from which we should benefit. But as will be seen from our brief comment in paragraph 11, to us who stand rather nearer to the economic destruction and political confusion in many of our most important markets the prospects of rapid recovery on a sufficient scale must seem more distant.

8. That we believe is how Parliament would see the proposal in its present form, and they could not fail to note the contrast between the kind of life which our people, after all their sacrifices, have to face for some years, and that which the people of the United States can immediately enjoy. The judgment might not be wholly fair any more than Clayton expects the judgment of Congress to be wholly fair. But it is these feelings which will affect the relations between our two peoples during the coming years. Remembering the last American debt settlement and its sequel[3] we do not wish to expose those relations to the risk of such controversy.

9. Let us consider the stages in the development of this affair. We had hoped that the Administration might have seen that their own real interests as well as ours would be best served by a sufficient grant-in-aid. Indeed we understand that this proposition has been accepted as logically correct. That hope we are told we must now abandon. Next we thought that repayment of what we had spent on the war in the United States while they were still neutral might not unreasonably be given to us. Or if that also was impossible because of Congress we had suggested a partial repayment say of two billion dollars which we should use primarily for the sterling area and to the benefit of United States trade while we contented ourselves with meeting our own immediate needs through a credit on which we should pay a nominal interest. Failing a grant-in-aid we still prefer this solution and we are glad to see from paragraph 2 of your telegram that you do not believe it is wholly dead. We would like Keynes to consider possible ways of bringing it on to the stage again. Finally if no repayment or no gift was to be considered as appropriate between us we would consider the acceptance of a loan whose capital we should repay over 50 years. Interest on a loan made in such circumstances we did not consider appropriate. Now we are offered a loan larger than our own needs require because it also has to look after the easing of the sterling area, and we are to pay interest on it, even though the interest is represented as low and there are provisions for respectable default.

10. The second test we have applied is that unless some economic catastrophe overtook us all or American trading policy made the normal repayment of debts impossible, we should see a reasonable certainty of being able to discharge any obligation we entered upon. We do not think that any informed commentator in this country would agree that there is a reasonable certainty of servicing the loan on the terms proposed by Clayton.

11. Clayton's figures in paragraph 6 of your telegram are based upon

---

[3] For this settlement of 1923 see *B.F.S.P.*, vol. 126, pp. 307–17. For correspondence leading up to the British note of 4 June 1934 suspending payments in respect of war debts to the United States, including consideration of the Johnson Act of April 1934 prohibiting loans to foreign governments which were in default in regard to debt payments to the U.S. Government, see *D.B.F.P.*, Second Series, Volume V, Chapter IX, and Volume VI, Chapter IX. For difficulties caused by the Johnson Act between 1938 and 1941 see Duncan Hall, *North American Supply*, pp. 46, 55–68 and 243f.

the magnitude of American productive economy and neither upon the smaller scales upon which we inevitably must make our plans nor upon an informed experience of the problems of markets in a world largely shattered by the war. It is not upon guesses of what the world will be like in ten years that we can undertake obligations of this kind. Taking a realistic view of prospects including our own efforts, and bearing in mind Keynes' view, we indicated in paragraph 7 of Foreign Office telegram No. 10094[4] that we could not accept an annual liability of more than 100 million dollars a year. This would have serviced over 50 years a loan of five billions which was interest free. This we considered as the maximum liability we could manage with reasonable certainty, and if the loan were interest free we might in the end have regarded that as a settlement to be presented to Parliament.

12. To Clayton and Vinson the difference between one hundred million dollars and one hundred and fifty million dollars a year is no doubt peanuts. But unfortunately it cannot be so to us. It is always difficult for the Americans to adjust their figures to the comparative size of ours as the reception of your paper showing the comparative size of the efforts of the two countries[5] has made clear. When we add that annual liability to the repayment liability which we shall have to undertake towards the sterling area as part of the deal, we come to what we must regard as the last straw.

13. We recognise the breadth of outlook in Clayton's suggestions about escape clauses or default provisions. There are several variants of such provisions which could be suggested and would statistically reflect our annual capacity to pay. But we believe that Congress would not understand their appearance in a scheme which ostensibly ensures that Britain pays the United States what she owes. Moreover even if, as the result of the education you have given to American opinion, the provisions were acceptable at the moment, we strongly dislike provisions for continual adjustments between our two countries on a matter of this kind which is to stretch over 50 years. Every time the escape ladder was used there would be recrimination in both countries. We do not want high liabilities with ample escape clauses. We are sure that manageable liabilities can be our only safe guide, subject to the general conditions in paragraphs 8 to 11 in Foreign Office telegram No. 10094.

14. Summing up, if a grant-in-aid is really impossible we should still prefer a settlement on the lines of paragraph 5 of No. 10094. If in the end even this is found impossible, we would consider an interest free loan for 50 years with a liability not exceeding one hundred million dollars in any year. We should like repayment to begin after 10 years and not after five in order that we might if necessary make use of the dollars available when the R.F.C. loan[6] has been paid off. We believe it would be wise to give

---

[4] No. 62.　　　　　　　　　　　　　　[5] i.e. COM/TOP 4: see No. 29, note 4.
[6] The Agreement signed on 21 July 1941 between the United Kingdom and the U.S. Reconstruction Finance Corporation for a loan of $425 millions was published in Cmd.

Clayton this further indication of our views and allow him an opportunity of improving on the present proposal.[7]

6295 of 1941. For the negotiation of the loan, conducted for the U.K. by Lord Keynes, see Sayers, *op. cit.*, pp. 392–5.

[7] In a letter of 12 October (printed in Moggridge, *op. cit.*, pp. 544–6) Sir W. Eady gave Lord Keynes 'a snapshot of the Ministerial background' behind this telegram, stressing Ministers' 'deep feelings' on the loan. They were 'reluctant to admit that we are in any sense dependent upon the U.S. to get ourselves out of our present difficulties. There is no question that there is more reason for their attitude than there was during the previous five or six months, for they are much firmer on the subject of control of imports and foreign expenditure than were the Coalition or the Caretaker Government . . . Therefore, although at the Treasury we know that we cannot get out of the next eighteen months without incurring a substantial debt to the U.S. probably of two billion dollars, there is rather more prospect that we shall work our own passage home than there was a few months ago.'

No. 72

The Earl of Halifax (Washington) to Mr. Bevin
(Received 16 October, 10.20 p.m.)

No. 6884 Telegraphic [UE 4875/1094/53]

Immediate. Top secret WASHINGTON, *16 October 1945, 4.50 p.m.*

Following personal for Chancellor of the Exchequer from Ambassador and Keynes.

1. At yesterday's meeting with Clayton and Vinson[1] we expounded in detail the argument of your telegram No. 10274.[2] In particular we again emphasised the advantages of splitting the aid into two billions grant and three billions credit. After some hesitation we thought it advisable to put all our cards on the table and therefore indicated that whilst an annual future burden of $150 million was inacceptable we believed that you would in the last resort accept an arrangement involving a burden of $100 million.

2. We made no progress whatever. They repeated their firm conviction that their previous offer is the best they can hope to put through Congress and that a settlement on the terms we suggest is not practicable. They attached importance to a recent statement by the influential Senator George[3] deprecating loans to foreign countries in general at the present time.

3. The atmosphere was gloomy and unconstructive. We are to resume

[1] See No. 70.iii for a record of the part of this meeting concerning Imperial Preference and commercial policy.

[2] No. 71.

[3] Senator W.F. George of Georgia was Chairman of the Senate Finance Committee.

this afternoon with Harry White added to the party.[4] The ball is now with them.

4. Clayton seemed at one moment to allow his mind to return to the idea of two billions grant and three billions credit and pointed out that a service of $100 millions applied to a three billions credit, though we had not offered this would be equivalent to interest at better than two per cent. His mind is also moving in the unpleasant direction of proposing a reduction of the credit below 5 billion whilst keeping the annual service at $100 million.

5. We are not inclined to move ourselves at this moment with any new suggestion to break the jam. It would be as awkward for them to break off as for us.[5]

[4] No record of this meeting on 16 October has been traced: cf. Pressnell, *op. cit.*, Chapter 10(12).

[5] Mr. Dalton replied in Foreign Office telegram No. 10444 of 18 October to Washington: 'We are entirely in agreement with the tactical line you propose for the present in paragraph 5' (UE 4875/1094/53).

In a personal telegram to Mr. Attlee of 18 October Lord Halifax suggested, in connection with arrangements for the Prime Minister's forthcoming visit to Washington for discussions with President Truman on atomic energy (see Volume II, Nos. 202–4), that 'you might think it well to bring Bridges. Presence of the Secretary of the Cabinet . . . would seem natural enough and it might be easy way for Chancellor to send over Treasury representative. If this idea [is] smiled on [by] Dalton and yourself, Keynes would welcome it' (Washington telegram No. 6927, PREM 8/116). Lord Keynes urged in telegram No. 6950 of 19 October to Sir E. Bridges: 'It will be invaluable if the proposed visit could come next week and that you should be in the party. Cabinet will have to make decisions shortly. It will be difficult or impossible for me to come back for consultation. It could therefore be of the utmost help if you could be in a position to size up the general atmosphere here and advise them in the light of it. I beg you to come. Indeed to come anyhow whether the proposed visit is put off or not' (F.O. 800/512). Mr. Attlee, however, wrote on the filed copy of telegram No. 6927: 'No, I don't want to cross wires on finance. C.R.A. 18.10', and he had in any case decided to arrange his visit for November: see Volume II, No. 204.

No. 73

Memorandum by Mr. Gallop

[*W 14144/19/58*]

FOREIGN OFFICE, *16 October 1945*

In Washington 6491 (September 27th)[1] Lord Halifax suggested the possibility of a 'sweetener' to the Keynes talks such as might be provided by the prolongation of the leases for West Indian bases.

In Washington 6439 (September 25th)[2] Mr. Hall Patch suggested that shipping, civil aviation, telecommunications and perhaps oil should be looked at as a whole so that we might follow a consistent policy.

His reference to the importance of shipping and to Nabob 80[3]

[1] No. 47.   [2] No. 42.   [3] See No. 42.ii.

(September 24th) shows that what was uppermost in his mind was the importance of clearing our minds as regards discrimination. Nabob 80 shows that the W.S.A.[4] are pressing for 50% of the U.S. foreign trade to be carried in U.S. bottoms.[5] Our interest lies in seeking clear undertakings against subsidies and discrimination in shipping. In this we might expect the assistance of the State Department. But we might land ourselves in trouble if we argued for the utmost freedom for shipping and at the same time endeavoured to defend what the Americans might regard as restrictive or discriminatory practices in other fields.

The following is the position in the other fields within the province of General Department:

Oil. We have signed an agreement[6] which gives the Americans what they want, viz. equality of opportunity particularly in the Middle East. The Americans recognized in the extract from the minutes of the Discussions annexed to the agreement that under the terms of the Agreement H.M.G. were free to arrange imports as they saw fit, but expressed the view that if H.M.G. restricted the import of dollar oil to safeguard their exchange resources this would operate destructively both to British and U.S. interests. They hoped that in such circumstances H.M.G. would consult with them and explore the possibility of an alternative. It is therefore clear that in the sphere of oil we can offer no further sweetener but shall not expose ourselves to charges of discrimination unless we are forced to do so by shortage of dollars.

Telecommunications. We have at present a telegraph rate system which provides very much higher rates outside the Empire than inside it and is regarded by the U.S. as discriminatory. They would also regard as discrimination any cessation of the direct radio circuits permitted for the duration of the war plus six months between the U.S. and certain Dominions. We have agreed to discuss all outstanding telecommunications matters with the U.S. and Dominions at Bermuda in mid-November.

[4] War Shipping Administration.

[5] Cf. *F.R.U.S. 1945*, vol. vi, pp. 110–12. In a memorandum of 19 October to Lord Keynes Mr. Lee stated in particular: 'We must make it clear from the start that we can accept *no* conditions about shipping . . . an A.P. article in the *Washington Star* of the 14th October referred to the likelihood of a condition that all goods from the U.S. financed by the credit must be transported in U.S. ships. I should not wish such a condition to be sprung on us later when we might have little or no freedom of manoeuver' (T 247/45).

Referring to a similar article in the *Journal of Commerce* of 20 October, Mr. Hall-Patch wrote to Mr. Butler on 22 October: 'This is a good example of sectional interest which makes rational negotiation very difficult. One of the shipowners the other day had the nerve to tell me that the shipping interests were bringing pressure to bear through their lobby to ensure that all UNRRA shipments were made in American bottoms. As shipping is one of the few means by which we can meet our share of UNRRA's activities without too much hardship for our own people, my reactions were, naturally, rather strong. It was news to this man (a very prominent ship-owner) that UNRRA was *not* an American organisation & that American legislation could not be applied to it. This in spite of the name! The fog of ignorance which has to be dispelled here is really very discouraging' (UE 5294/1094/53).

[6] See No. 43.iii.

We expect to be able to meet them over direct circuits to the Dominions and to propose a world ceiling telegraph rate which would exceed the Empire rate only by a margin of tolerance of about 25% which can be justified under Empire preference. There is clearly a certain amount of sweetening here and subject to the results of the Keynes talks we feel that this Empire preference ought to be acceptable to the United States and should not be regarded as discrimination (see Baboon 113[7] of 13th October). As a further measure of sweetening we can throw in the complicated question of the Saudi Arabian direct circuit on which the Americans feel strongly if unreasonably.[8]

Civil Aviation. The Americans are urging us to conclude a bilateral agreement with them but there is a clear clash of philosophies between us. We aim at securing ordered regulation in the air and they are inclined to argue that all such regulation is restrictive and therefore objectionable. They have turned on the heat, urging the Minister and Sir W. Hildred to go to Washington for immediate negotiations.[9] We have declined to be 'clubbed' and have submitted proposals from here. These proposals appear to be unacceptable, and the Americans, while disclaiming any intention of blackmailing us are still pressing us to go to Washington. Lord Halifax suggests at one moment that the negotiations should be disconnected in time and space from the Keynes talks and at the next that we should meet the American wish.[10] The Ministry of Civil Aviation are now considering the possibility of reviving 'escalation' (rewarding the efficient operator by increased frequencies). They think it would bridge the gap with the Americans. It would require the consent of the Ministerial Committee and probably consultation with the Dominions. An agreement would be a useful sweetener. From the discrimination point of view as compared with shipping, the Ministry of Civil Aviation think that our present policy would make it hard to defend us from a charge of inconsistency. They would however be prepared to defend our policy with confidence if it includes escalation.

It seems clear that if there is to be a sweetener, the most effective one would be in the field of civil aviation, and that it is between our shipping and civil aviation desiderata that inconsistency may lie in regard to discrimination and restrictive practices. We are trying, with other departments to get out an agreed paper for submission to Ministers but

[7] Cf. i below.
[8] See i below. In Washington telegram No. 6941 of 19 October Lord Halifax reported that Mr. L.W. Henderson, Director of the Office of Near Eastern and African Affairs in the State Department, had told Mr. M.R. Wright, Counsellor in H.M. Embassy in Washington, that the two questions of civil aviation and telecommunications were creating 'very considerable friction' between the U.S. and U.K. in the Middle East: 'Disproportionate resentment was being caused by the question of Saudi Arabian wireless circuit and he again begged that we should do something quickly' (E 7901/175/65). For an account of negotiations regarding the proposed establishment of a direct radio telegraph circuit between the U.S. and Saudi Arabia see *F.R.U.S. 1945*, vol. viii, pp. 1009–31.
[9] See No. 43.
[10] See Nos. 47 and 58.i.

are at present held up by uncertainty in regard to civil aviation policy. Meanwhile a Baboon telegram is being sent to Washington stressing the danger of using arguments over shipping which might be turned against us on civil aviation.[11]

R.A. GALLOP

CALENDARS TO NO. 73

i *13–26 Oct. 1945 Correspondence relating to Telecommunications*: U.S. attempts to 'extract from us in advance of the Bermuda Conference not only all the concessions which we anticipated might be made there . . . but a great deal more'; negotiations on Saudi Arabian wireless circuit (see note 8) lead to a measure of agreement on 17 Oct. [W 14144/19/58, W 13579, 13585, 13674–5, 13785–6, 13859, 14153/46/801].

ii *23 Nov. 1945 C.P.(45)99 Memo. on Shipping Policy: Part I* Minister of War Transport's account of negotiations in Washington in Sept.–Oct. at meeting of U.M.E.B. [W 15395/19/58].

[11] This telegram, BABOON 125 of 16 October, is not printed.

No. 74

British Missions (Washington) to Cabinet Offices
(Received 18 October, 6.35 a.m.)

NABOB *177* Telegraphic [UE *4920/1094/53*]

Immediate. Top secret   WASHINGTON, *18 October 1945, 1.3 a.m.*

For Chancellor of Exchequer from Keynes.[1]

1. After five meetings on form of financial aid between Vinson and Clayton on their side and Ambassador and myself on ours,[2] it may be useful to take stock. This telegram is after consultation with Ambassador, Brand, Self, Liesching, Robbins and Hall Patch and represents our collective opinion.[3]

2. We came here in hope that we could persuade the U.S. to accept a

[1] This telegram is printed in Moggridge, *op. cit.*, pp. 547–55: see also Pressnell, *op. cit.*, Chapter 10(12). In a personal telegram of 17 October Mr. Stevens of the British Civil Secretariat had informed Sir E. Bridges that 'Keynes is sending long and important NABOB telegram (No. 177 with appendix No. 178 [No. 75]) summing up position of financial negotiations. Ambassador and Keynes are anxious that this should have reasonably wide circulation at both Ministerial and high official levels, and with this in view telegram deliberately goes over a good deal of ground already covered in earlier personal telegrams sent in Embassy-Foreign Office channels' (CAB 122/1471).

[2] See Nos. 44–7, 49, 58, 60, 67 and 72.

[3] In a letter to Mr. Butler of 17 October Mr. Hall-Patch had remarked: 'The going from now on is going to be tougher. The Presidential honeymoon is over & the opposition to the Administration is becoming more vocal & better organised, and say what you will, Truman has not the political skill in handling international affairs which distinguished Roosevelt. We have spent a gloomy afternoon reviewing the situation and, as a result, a rather gloomy telegram has just been agreed for despatch to London' (UE 5162/1094/53).

broad and generous solution which took account of our financial sacrifices before U.S. entered the war and of President Roosevelt's principle of equality of sacrifice as well as of the post-war advantages to the U.S. of a settlement with us which would enable us to share world responsibilities with them free from undue financial pre-occupation and to join them in shaping the pattern of world commerce and currency on lines which would favour expansion and general prosperity.

3. We thought of such aid as being at the best a free grant, failing that a partial grant, and at the worst an interest free loan. A settlement on any of these lines would be intelligible to the British public as being free from commercial considerations and a grand gesture of unforgetting regard to us from a partner with whom our comradeship in the war has been of a very special intimacy. The difference between a settlement on any of these lines and one which tries to imitate however feebly, a normal banker's investment is much greater than is represented by any increase in our future financial burden.

4. If we are to believe what we are told by Vinson and Clayton repeatedly and with great emphasis the American administration has rejected any such settlement. They have done this not because they themselves would resist but because of their honest and considered judgement that Congress and the public are not in the mood to stand for it. No one pretends that public opinion is well informed about the real issues. But public opinion with the usual exceptions is not hostile. There is widespread goodwill and a desire to help. But in this business country where it is a moral duty and not merely a self-regarding act to make any money which the traffic will bear and the law allow, some imitation of a normal banking transaction is necessary if the moral principles of the country are not to be affronted. If the elements of a trade are present, the American way of life requires that at least the appearance of a trade should emerge. Thus precisely those elements which will spoil the flavour to us are necessary to make the result palatable here. At the moment, moreover, there is a phase of withdrawal from the large-scale assistance all-round which was under discussion only a short time ago. Retrenchment is in the air. Congress is also occupied with Vinson's proposals for tax reduction and, as it happens, the total cost of the relief to the general tax-payer now under discussion, namely five billions, is the same size as the aid for which we ask, so that the latter seems much larger than it would in other contexts.

5. There is so much goodwill in most quarters and such wide appreciation of the larger issues in all responsible quarters that it is difficult to believe they do not under-rate what bold and eloquent leadership could do. But you must understand that such leadership is just what is lacking in this present administration from the President downwards. Their policy is to keep in close touch with the opinion and desires of Congress, following rather than leading, and flavouring to taste any pill which it is indispensable to administer.

6. We cannot demand what they tell us it does not lie within their power to give. It may be that the type of settlement which the late President would have delighted to invent and to put through is altogether out of character with the general lines which the present administration feels compelled to follow. We must not be misled by hopes which only the gay, generous and brilliant spirit could have realised for us.

7. If this diagnosis is correct we must think again substituting prose for poetry. Our disappointment does not justify us in doing perhaps irreparable injury to our own body politic and economic or in shattering the basis of day-to-day Anglo-American co-operation. We must do the best we can.

8. Before turning to the possibilities of prose, it may be well to break off to insert a necessary qualifications [sic] to all the foregoing. In this country nothing is certain until the very last moment. We know that Clayton and Vinson and other leaders of the Administration are determined to bring these negotiations to a successful conclusion. The public is being deliberately fed through the press with the expectation of success. Even a delay in settlement would seriously disturb their time-table and upset the Treasury Department policy of Bretton Woods and the State Department policy of a commercial conference on which each has set its heart. To satisfy us may lay them open to criticism. But if they fail to satisfy us they may encounter even more criticism. If we stand our ground to the last, [it] is not impossible that we may not [sic] yet get an offer which at present does not appear to be in sight. Do not, therefore, suppose that there is any defeatism in your mission here. But we have to be prepared for either alternative. Time is now running short and all is set for a conclusion within about a fortnight. It will be useless and injurious to drag on much longer than that. It is, therefore, important that we should have your early guidance on whether prose will be acceptable in the last resort.

9. Clayton frankly admits the force of our case. His point is that he must dress the thing up to look as ordinary as possible, to escape notice wearing a business suit. Subject to this necessity he appeals to us to help him in finding a way which is as acceptable to us as possible. When we remark as we are constantly forced to do, that nothing will induce us to repeat the experience of last time's War debts and sign an obligation we have no confidence we can meet, he accepts our position and offers us any escape clause in reason to provide against this risk.

10. When we try to make precise the burden we think we can support we find ourselves on treacherous ground. We have been again pressed recently to explain exactly how we arrive at five billions as the measure of what we need and what sort of balance of trade we expect to emerge with at the end of five years or whenever it is that the transitional period terminates. An outline of our answer is given in my next following telegram.[4] It will be seen from this that an eventual balance requires that

[4] No. 75, which was however despatched before the present telegram.

our external income from exports and net invisibles shall be of the order of nearly seven billion dollars or say six and a half billion at the very lowest. We say that we are able to assume a debt liability of 100 millions which is 1½ per cent of this but see no reasonable hope of being able to meet 150 millions which would require a further expansion of our overseas income or curtailment of our overseas expenditure by less than another 1 per cent. This obviously lays us open to the accusation of possessing extensive and peculiar information about the future.

11. Our best answer is, of course, that what really scares us is the possibility of owing to the U.S. an amount of money which is enormous in relation to our prospective exports to them in conditions where, for all we know now, multilateral clearings may have broken down, Very well, says Clayton, draft a clause to protect yourselves against this possibility. We admit that commerce in the post-war world either goes all right from our point of view or it does not. In the first case 150 millions may be practicable and in the second case 100 millions may be scarcely possible. Nevertheless failing the solution of a free grant one has to draw the line somewhere and they must not try to involve us in the fallacy of sorites.[5] Very well says Clayton, draft a clause under which your liability will be related to your capacity. We do not want to embarrass you, he adds, but we want to be able to say that we have reached an elastic arrangement which duly protects the interests of both sides.

12. You will be aware how reluctant I have been to enter on the slippery path of escape clauses. But we all think that the time has come when we cannot reasonably excuse ourselves from making some response to Clayton's generous and not unreasonable suggestions. In refusing to do so we are in truth still grasping at the ineluctable poetry and refusing to come to earth in well-reasoned prose. Yet from his own point of view and from ours too when once we have accepted the inevitability of prose, Clayton is generous and is not unreasonable. If you had sat as many hours as the Ambassador and I have sat declaiming all our best poetry before an audience, not indeed unresponsive to those strains in their own hearts, but never deviating from the rejoinder that Congress, they feel quite sure, will be deaf to the[m], you would see our difficulty in persisting with a refusal to come down to earth.

13. Against the risk of a breakdown in multilateral arrangements and the scarcity of dollars, I have already sent a suggestion in paragraph 2 of telegram 6772[6] which for convenience of reference I repeat in the next paragraph . . .

15. As a measure of our capacity to pay more than 100 millions I can think of nothing better than some version of what I have already suggested in paragraph 7 of telegram 6733.[7] The terms might then be as in the next paragraph. I should add that Clayton has not yet seen this

[5] i.e. a 'form of sophism leading by gradual steps from truth to absurdity' (Concise Oxford Dictionary).

[6] No. 68. The repeated text in para. 14 below is omitted.   [7] No. 67.

suggestion but we could offer it in response to his request that we should propose a suitable safe-guard.

16. A loan of five billions of which the capital and interest would be repaid in 50 instalments of 150 millions a year commencing five years hence of which 100 millions in each year would be attributed to capital repayment and 50 millions to interest. Assuming that all fifty instalments of interest are paid this would work out actuarially at the equivalent of about 1.7 per cent interest per annum. But in addition we should receive the advantage of a waiver clause by which the 50 millions representing an instalment of interest would be finally waived in any year in which the volume of our visible home-produced exports did not reach a level of 750 million pounds in terms of pre-war prices. Alternatively and much better if they would accept it, the contract might say that the 50 millions for interest would only become payable in years when the critical figure had been reached.

17. Since we could in this case almost certainly afford the extra 50 millions, the plan is on the face of it reasonable as well as generous. When our exports did not reach the critical figure the loan would become interest-free. Moreover the criterion is definite and is not really open to the criticism of paragraph 13 of your telegram 10274.[8] Can anyone honestly argue that the difference between this and a loan which is interest free in all circumstances is so material that even in the last resort we should prefer a breakdown of the present discussions with all that means to our standard of life, to our hopes of recovery, to our position in the world and to Anglo-American friendship?

18. The only alternatives which may still be worth considering are mentioned in the next two paragraphs. The first of these is before the Americans and has probably been finally rejected but we are not quite sure that it has been. The second is a new idea, not yet put forward.

19. A grant of 2 billions and a credit up to 3 billions at 2 per cent. interest, instalments of capital repayment and of interest beginning five years hence.

20. A loan of 4 billions repayable by fifty five annual instalments of 100 millions beginning five years hence which would cost, allowing for deferment, the equivalent of about 1 per cent. interest, supplemented by a ten years' option on a banking credit of a further 1 (or 2) billion at 2 per cent. interest.

21. The ball now lies with the Americans and they may make a counter-proposal shortly. We do not look forward to it with much hope. We fear that it may take the form of a reduction in the amount of the aid whilst keeping the annual service at 100 millions. But it is just possible that we shall be agreeably disappointed. We repeat that the American side are just as keen as we are to reach a satisfactory conclusion and are as depressed as we are at the deadlock.

[8] No. 71.

22. In conclusion we have naturally given some thought to the question whether there is a way out for us by obtaining a moderate amount here and now to meet our immediate necessities on commercial terms without any commitment about Bretton Woods, commercial policy and sterling area. I have little to add on this to what I have said in my telegram 6610.[9] Those of us here who in recent weeks have been studying intensively our balance of trade prospects believe:

(a) That we cannot reduce our cumulative balance of trade deficit below 3 or 4 billions at the very lowest without great and almost insupportable sacrifices at home and abroad.

(b) That it is an illusion to suppose that the sterling area can carry on as in time of war.

(c) That we cannot hope, therefore, to get a net contribution on capital account much exceeding, say, 1 billion dollars at the utmost from all other outside sources put together.

(d) That our prospects are poor of even a small Government loan here without any commitment about Bretton Woods, commercial policy or the sterling area.

(e) That we should soon have involved ourselves in as heavy a debt charge as what we are now boggling at.

(f) That the measure of disruption of our economic life at home and of our external relations, which would be inevitable if a comprehensive settlement with America fails, can hardly be exaggerated.

23. An agreement for 5 billions would not in fact involve us in any excessive future burden if in practice we can get on with much less. For we should be under no compulsion to draw it all. Yet it would have given us the confidence and security which is indispensable if we are to restore our position in the world.

24. If our present friendly and intimate relations with the American side are brought to an end and we announce that we are tired of being pushed about and would prefer to stand by ourselves without the entanglements of Anglo-American partnership or agreement in the economic field, so much will be disastrously changed over so wide a field and for a period to which no-one can set a term, that we cannot bring ourselves to contemplate it. It may be as difficult to convey to you the complex atmosphere of Washington as it is to make vivid to the administration here the disappointment of London. But the Americans would remain convinced that they had offered us aid on a scale and on terms which they would not dream of offering to anyone else, and which was only possible in remembrance of past comradeship and common sacrifice and in hope of furthering common aims in future. Our rejection of it would undoubtedly be felt here as just one more reason for yielding to the temptation to withdraw into themselves with all the incalculable consequences of that to the future of the world.[10]

[9] No. 57.
[10] Sir W. Eady informed Lord Keynes in BABOON 135 of 19 October referring to

i *16–24 Oct. 1945* (a) *Memo. by N. American and Research Depts. on Congress and the Economic Negotiations*, with minutes by Mr. Butler and Mr. Ronald, and initialled 'Agreed' by Mr. Bevin: (b) *Memo. by Mr. Redvers Opie (Economic Adviser to H.M. Embassy in Washington) on conversation with Mr. H. White concerning financial negotiations and 'Washington official atmosphere in general'* [UE 5221/1094/53, T 236/440].

ii *20 Oct. 1945* *To Earl of Halifax (Washington) Tel. No. 10530* Personal message from Lord Catto to Lord Keynes suggesting financial agreement based on interest free credit in return for settlement of old war debts: for Lord Keynes' reply of 22 Oct. see Moggridge, *op. cit.*, pp. 565–7, and cf. No. 116 below [UE 4803/1094/53].

NABOB 177 that 'Chancellor opens Budget on Tuesday [23 October] so you will understand that situation described by you cannot be considered immediately. But arrangements will be made for study at once and reply as soon after Wednesday as possible' (T 236/440).

On 19 October Mr. Jay sent the following minute to Mr. Attlee: 'You will no doubt have seen the latest long and eloquent telegram from Keynes (NABOB No. 177). In advance of further detailed discussions on this problem, it seems worth noting the following points now emerging: (1) The optimistic reports in the Press of progress towards agreement are evidently rather wide of the mark. There is still a wide gap to be bridged, even between the negotiators; and whether Congress would accept any agreement that was reached, is from all evidence a very open question. (2) Perhaps therefore we should soon begin to consider, simultaneously with the negotiations, what action would have to be taken here if Congress should veto any sort of loan in the course of the Winter. As yet Departments have merely made estimates of their minimum dollar requirements on the assumption of maintenance of consumption here [see No. 36], which is a very different thing. (3) After further discussions with the Treasury, I am not altogether convinced that our Delegation is not assuming rather too easily that we must borrow the whole of the suggested 5 billion dollars from the United States, rather than elsewhere, and accept all the conditions attached. At any rate, this will have to be very carefully watched, since our Delegation is evidently rather more willing to commit us to multi-lateral trading principles than public opinion here' (PREM 8/35).

No. 75

British Missions (Washington) to Cabinet Offices
(Received 18 October, 3.20 a.m.)

NABOB *178* Telegraphic [UE 4920/1094/53]

Immediate. Top secret   WASHINGTON, *18 October 1945, 1.1 a.m.*

For Chancellor of Exchequer from Keynes.[1]
My immediately preceding telegram.[2]
1. Following are details referred to in my preceding telegram of the

---

[1] This telegram is printed in Moggridge, *op. cit.*, pp. 555–6.   [2] No. 74.

further revised explanations which we have given to the Americans why we need five billions. All figures in $ million.

2. Our pre-war balance on the average of 1936–8 worked out as follows:

Imports	3,500	Exports	1,950
		Net invisibles	1,350
		Deficit	200
			3,500

3. Our target is a hypothetical post-war balance in the year immediately after the transition as follows:

Imports	6,500	Exports	5,750
Overseas Govt. Expenditure	250	Net Invisibles	1,250
Available to pay Sterling area and U.S.	250		
	7,000		7,000

Imports, Exports and freights are at an assumed price-level double pre-war.

4. Our estimate for 1946 also at prices assumed approximately double pre-war as follows:

Imports	5,200	Exports	2,600
Overseas War Expenditure (Net)	1,200	Net Invisibles	800
		Deficit	3,000
	6,400		6,400

5. On this basis our deficit may work out as follows:

1946	3,000
1947	1,250
1948	500
1949 } 1950 }	250
	5,000

6. In addition to the above we have a liability for the settlements of Lend Lease etc. to the United States say 500 and a net release of sterling balances to the sterling area 1946–50 of say 800 to 1,000, making grand total of say 6,500. Towards this we can perhaps look to Canada for 500

and 800 to 1,000 of the adverse balance in 1946 might be added to the aggregate of sterling area balances brought into the general settlement.

7. There remains the possible use of our gold and dollar reserves and our remaining capital assets. Also perhaps some small loans from Sweden etc. We argued, however, that we need all these to cover withdrawals of sterling balances held outside the sterling area. In particular withdrawals by European countries during the transition which we can scarcely refuse. Thus we could not reckon on any significant net contribution from these miscellaneous sources.

8. Accordingly our final requirement from the U.S. would be five billions. This represents some reduction on our previous request since we are in effect assuming that it will cover 500 for settlement of Lend-Lease.

9. Admittedly if all goes well we may do better than this. The Americans claim that the final deficit should be at least one billion less. We reply that we hope that they are right and agree they may be. But we cannot enter into commitments about the sterling area etc. without a margin. We shall draw no more than we require but we cannot be expected to enter into the commitments they hope from us unless we have elbow room up to five billions.

CALENDARS TO NO. 75

i *18 Oct.–8 Nov. 1945 Correspondence concerning proposed White Paper on British case for financial assistance* (Cmd. 6707 of 1945, see No. 29, note 4) [UE 4394, 5026/1094/53].

ii *25 Oct.–7 Nov. 1945 To and from British Missions (Washington) Tels. BABOON 150 & 224, NABOB 237* Comments on statistics in No. 75 [UE 4920/1094/53].

iii *30 Oct.–27 Nov. 1945 To and from British Missions (Washington) Tels. BABOON 162, 222–3, NABOB 238, 247, 407* Correspondence concerning estimates of U.K. dollar requirements, on basis of maintaining the sterling area, with reference to ii above [UE 4920, 5305, 5442, 5832/1094/53, T 236/456].

No. 76

Note by Sir G. Rendel of a conversation between Mr. Bevin and Commander Jackson[1]

[UR 3808/24/850]

FOREIGN OFFICE, *18 October 1945*

Following on his long conversation with the Minister of State and myself

[1] Commander R.G.A. Jackson, formerly of the Royal Australian Navy, the Royal Navy, and Director General of the Middle East Supply Centre 1942–5, was Senior Deputy Director General of U.N.R.R.A.

on the evening of October 16th,[2] Commander Jackson had an interview with the Secretary of State this morning at which I was present.

2. Commander Jackson explained that the UNRRA supply machinery was now working well, and had been steadily stepped up. Supplies were coming in and being distributed very satisfactorily, and most of the early faults of UNRRA had already been – or were in process of being – remedied. There was no cause for anxiety on this score.

3. The only trouble now was finance. The balance of 550,000,000 dollars on the original U.S. contribution was most urgently required. Commander Jackson had last night had a message from Governor Lehman,[3] suggesting that the position was not too unfavourable, and although Congress might attach one or two difficult conditions (such as that press correspondents should be allowed to move about freely in any areas receiving help from UNRRA), there was every hope that the necessary appropriation would go through Congress within the next ten days or a fortnight. There was nothing much more that could be done by us over this.

4. A much more serious problem was the further 1% contribution. The President would probably send a satisfactory message to Congress about this,[4] but there would be no punch behind it, as Mr. Truman was now concentrating on internal—rather than international—politics. In the State Department, the only man who could help us was Mr. Clayton, who carried great weight and authority, but he was so overloaded that there was no hope of his getting down to this problem for the present. There were of course snags, especially the strong anti-Russian feeling that was developing in the U.S.A. But Congress itself was not hostile, and would be willing to give the necessary authorisation, if only vigorous publicity on the right lines could be carried through. If the right personality were able to take the lead in this in America, all would be well but there were great difficulties in finding the right man. Governor Lehman, however, was now preparing to fight the issue on a party basis, and might therefore mobilise the Democratic Party machine. Moreover, he had something to give, as he still had great political authority in New York. Commander Jackson was therefore not unhopeful that the contribution might be got through.

[2] In a minute of 17 October recording this conversation Sir G. Rendel had suggested that Mr. Bevin should see Commander Jackson, 'who is the man who is really running UNRRA', and discuss with him in particular the future of U.N.R.R.A., U.N.R.R.A.'s work with Displaced Persons, and supplies for Greece. Sir G. Rendel drew Mr. Bevin's attention to 'some very disturbing telegrams from Washington showing that there may be great difficulty in getting the further United States contribution which will be required if UNRRA is to be able to continue its work after next January': cf. No. 67, note 2. 'Commander Jackson has interesting views on this question, and some useful suggestions to make' (UR 3808/24/850).

[3] Mr. H.H. Lehman, former Governor of New York State, was Director General of U.N.R.R.A.

[4] Mr. Truman's message to Congress of 13 November briefly setting out U.N.R.R.A.' activities and requesting a new appropriation of $1,350,000,000 for U.S. participation in the organisation is printed in *Public Papers: Truman 1945*, pp. 464-7.

5. He realised that there had been a tendency—at one time shared by Lord Halifax and Mr. Makins—to feel that the prospects were so precarious that we ought to start thinking at once about some alternative set up—e.g. transferring the UNRRA machine into the framework of the United Nations Organisation. He did not think this would help. It would be just as difficult to get money from Congress for some new set-up of this kind as for the present set-up, and it would enormously add to the difficulties if we were to try to change horses in midstream.

6. He thought the best hope was that the Minister of State and Mr. Pearson should get into early touch with Mr. Clayton, either at Quebec,[5] or in Washington. The Minister of State was, he believed, proposing to do this.

7. The worst dangers in his view were –

(a) a recrudescence of civil war in Greece;

(b) serious trouble in Italy;

(c) any failure on the part of H.M.G. wholeheartedly to support UNRRA. For instance, if H.M.G. were to allow UNRRA to be placed in a subordinate position for displaced persons work in Germany, as appeared to be suggested by Field-Marshal Montgomery,[6] the effect in the United States would be very bad, and it would be regarded as a

---

[5] See *Food and Agriculture Organisation of the United Nations: Report of the First Session of the Conference held at the City of Quebec, Canada, October 16 to November 1, 1945* (Washington, January 1946). Correspondence relating to the Quebec Conference can be followed on file UE 1/53: documents relating to the Conference, including its resolutions and recommendations and the report of its two commissions, were published in Cmd. 6731 of 1946.

[6] In a letter of 14 October to Mr. Bevin Field Marshal Sir B. Montgomery, Commander-in-Chief of the British Forces of Occupation in Germany, explained that he had 'refused to sign an agreement with UNRRA by which that organisation would take over responsibility for the D.P. camps in the British Zone . . . I must control the British Zone through my Corps District Commanders and they control the D.P. Camps and have them well in hand' (WR 3174/1/48). Mr. P. Mason, Acting Head of Refugee Department, commented in a memorandum of 18 October that Field Marshal Montgomery 'apparently considers that, while he can find a use for U.N.R.R.A. personnel in dealing with the displaced persons problem, they can only be allowed to operate in a completely subordinate manner . . . It is unfortunate that the Field Marshal should choose this moment to condemn U.N.R.R.A. out of hand as a body to whom, or to whose employees, responsibility could be entrusted. U.N.R.R.A. has been planned as a large scale international organisation for the purpose of administering and coordinating relief, which is itself an international problem, on a very wide scale. It is a fundamental misconception to regard it as a supplier of manpower for performing subordinate tasks under purely local control . . .
'If the Field Marshal's view prevails, a general impression will be given that this constitutes a weakening of British support of U.N.R.R.A. This would be most unfortunate at a moment when U.N.R.R.A. is having considerable difficulty in securing from the United States Congress the money necessary if it is to survive at all, since a crack in British support would be seized on as evidence that the British themselves thought U.N.R.R.A. an inferior show. There is some reason to think that news of the Field Marshal's view has already got through to the United States Zone (where U.N.R.R.A. has so far been given increasing authority both as regards administration of camps and as regards coordination of policy) and that it is making the United States military authorities cool off somewhat' (WR 3105/1/48).

weakening of our support, and a sign of lack of confidence on the part of H.M.G.

8. The Secretary of State listened attentively to all that Commander Jackson had to say, and promised him the fullest support. He asked that a note, on the lines on which the kind of publicity Commander Jackson had in mind might be carried out, should be immediately prepared for him,[7] and said he would then like to mobilise American Labour through Mr. Gordon and Mr. Green.[8] He thought he might have an opportunity of doing this unofficially in the near future.

9. The Secretary of State did not believe that there was any immediate danger of a recrudescence of civil war in Greece, but discussed Field-Marshal Montgomery's attitude towards the displaced persons work of UNRRA in some detail (Mr. Mason was present for this part of the discussion). He fully appreciated the unfortunate effect which any weakening in our attitude might have, but asked to be fully briefed in good time before he saw the Field-Marshal. He also asked to be furnished immediately with a copy of the draft Agreement which Field-Marshal Montgomery had refused to sign. Mr. Mason is dealing with these matters.[9]

[7] *Marginal note by Sir G. Rendel*: 'Done. Note sent in to Private Sec. 21. X. 45. G.W.R.' See i below.

[8] Mr. A. McD. Gordon and Mr. W. Green were respectively British Labour Attaché in the U.S., and President of the American Federation of Labour. Mr. Bevin minuted on the filed copy of Sir G. Rendel's note on the future of U.N.R.R.A. (i below: see note 7): 'I think Gordon might have this & ask him in conversation with A[merican] F[ederation of] L[abour] and C[ongress of] I[ndustrial] O[rganisations] leaders in U.S.A. to use it as background & enlist their help discreetly for U.N.[R.]R.A. E.B.' In a message for Sir G. Rendel transmitted in Rome telegram No. 1626 of 20 October Commander Jackson suggested that it might be pointed out to the A.F.L. that there would almost certainly be surplus production capacity in the United States in 1946 'and UNRRA should be a most valuable' means of absorbing surplus production and reducing unemployment' (UR 3809/24/850).

[9] *Marginal note by Sir G. Rendel*: 'Done on WR [Refugee Department] papers on Oct. 19/20. G.W.R.' See note 6 above. A copy of the draft agreement is filed at WR 3105/1/48. In a letter of 19 October Mr. Bevin asked Field Marshal Montgomery 'to consider the question of a reasonable compromise . . . The policy of His Majesty's Government has been to bring UNRRA in wherever possible. Bound up with this question is that of supplies and it is a much wider range problem than the zone under your command. The United States Government is now facing the Congress for a further 1% of the national income in order to provide supplies, and I don't want anything done publicly at this moment which will prejudice that discussion' (WR 3174/1/48). In a minute of 24 October Mr. Bevin recorded an interview with Field Marshal Montgomery that morning: 'As a result of our discussion and my letter to him of the 19th October, the Field Marshal said that he had appointed a committee under a Corps Commander who would meet the UNRRA representatives, his own Staff, and any others who cared to attend . . . to consider whether the UNRRA proposals are practicable . . . I agreed that his was a good method and that UNRRA must cooperate (WR 3176/1/48)'. The text of the *Agreement Relating to the Responsibilities of the Commander-in-Chief of the British Army of the Rhine and Military Governor of the British Zone of Germany and U.N.R.R.A.*, signed on 27 November 1945 by Field Marshal Montgomery and Lt.–Gen. Sir F. E. Morgan, Chief of Operations of the U.N.R.R.A. Displaced Person Operation in Germany, is printed in Woodbridge, *op. cit.*, vol. iii, pp. 194–201. Cf. also M. J

10. Generally, the Secretary of State agreed with Commander Jackson that there would be no advantage in trying to find an alternative to UNRRA, and that the money must be obtained to enable UNRRA to continue to function. He stressed, however, that UNRRA's main concern should be to get the economy of the countries in which it was operating functioning on its own feet. For instance, it would be better to supply tractors and fertilisers than wheat and meat.[10] Commander Jackson showed himself fully alive to this aspect of the question.

11. The Secretary of State also attached great importance to strengthening Italy by bringing adequate relief in time. I am bearing what he said in mind in connection with my own impending journey to Italy.[11]

G. W. RENDEL

CALENDARS TO No. 76

i   *21 Oct. 1945   Memo. by Sir G. Rendel* on the future of U.N.R.R.A. and need for further funds, with minute by Mr. Bevin (see note 8) [UR 3670/30/852].

ii   *27 Oct. 1945   Earl of Halifax (Washington) Tels. Nos. 7123–4* Mr. Noel-Baker's conversations with Mr. Clayton and Mr. Lehman on U.S. additional contribution to U.N.R.R.A. and supplies for Byelo-Russia and Ukraine [UR 3957–8/30/852].

Proudfoot, *European Refugees 1939–52* (London, 1957), Chapter IX.

Mr. Bevin noted on file UR 3940/1246/851 on 24 October that he had also discussed the wheat situation in Germany with Field Marshal Montgomery, and that he was quite satisfied that unless wheat supplies were received urgently 'there will be utter starvation in the Zone'. In conversation with Mr. Winant later that day Mr. Bevin asked 'if he would consult his Government to see whether some temporary arrangement could be made which would provide heavy oil and other fuel for the Argentine, to take from them the maize or any other surplus grain they might have to use it for feeding cattle both in the United States and in Great Britain, and to release the wheat for Europe so as to assist our Commanding Officers in their task of preventing starvation this winter. He undertook to consider the matter and to let me have the view of his Government.' Cf. No. 14.v and No. 66.

[10] In his telegram No. 11559 to Washington of 17 November in relation to reports on the 17th meeting of the Central Committee of U.N.R.R.A. on 2 November (see F.O. 371/51373) Mr. Bevin stated in particular: 'Our essential aim is to assure that the continuance of UNRRA's assistance during 1946 should be made conditional on some real attempt by the beneficiary countries to help themselves and to prepare for the period after 1946. If UNRRA is left to operate as it has done hitherto supplies will reach the beneficiary countries in large volume, but the countries are not likely by the end of 1946 to be in a noticeably better position to face the future by reason of UNRRA's intervention. This is particularly true of Greece (where, however, we readily agree that the fault is not wholly that of UNRRA), but it may be true of other countries also. The arrangements required to meet the case are that the major contributing powers associated in UNRRA should exercise a closer control over the manner in which their contributions are spent, and should assist the Administration, so far as they can, to stimulate the economic recovery of the recipient countries till they are in a position where they can stand on their own feet. This means in the first place that some committee in Washington should make a periodical survey of the supply, distribution and finance aspects of UNRRA's operations in the beneficiary countries' (UR 4083/114/850).

[11] Sir G. Rendel visited Italy from 25 October to 14 November: his report to Mr. Bevin on the relief situation in Italy is filed at UR 4273/365/850.

No. 77

Mr. Bevin to the Earl of Halifax (Washington)

No. 10525 Telegraphic [AS 5207/159/2]

Important   FOREIGN OFFICE, 19 October 1945, 10.10 p.m.

Repeated to Buenos Aires No. 533.

Your telegrams Nos. 6651 and 6652 (of October 6th: control of exports to Argentina).[1]

Reconsideration by Mr. Byrnes of whole Argentine problem in light of developments described in your telegram No. 6616[2] and in my telegrams Nos. 10051[3] (of October 7th) and 10100[4] (of October 9th), leads us to wish to avoid any further delay in explaining to Americans our policy as regards their outstanding requests[5] for the control of exports to

[1] These telegrams of 6 October were in reply to Foreign Office telegram No. 9884 to Washington of 2 October, which referred to Foreign Office telegram No. 8557 (see No. 14, note 5). Telegram No. 9884 contained a statement of 'our considered attitude towards State Department's requests (a) for a refusal of Argentine demands for armaments, (b) for the delegation to His Majesty's Ambassador at Buenos Aires of power to sanction or refuse all exports to Argentina'. With regard to (a), the telegram set out the lines on which His Majesty's Government would be guided (see i below), while expressing 'considerable misgivings as regards the application of any long term programming of imports to Argentina'. On (b), it was felt that it would serve no purpose to delegate such powers to Sir D. Kelly, 'unless it were the intention that the majority at any rate of these applications should be refused' (AS 4634/159/2). Telegram No. 9883 of 1 October instructed Lord Halifax to 'telegraph whether, having regard to current financial talks you or Lord Keynes see any serious objection to reply on these lines . . .' (AS 5056/159/2).

In telegram No. 6651 Lord Halifax stated in particular: '(a) Munitions. It is plain from Acheson's declaration about not making a military pact with the Argentine [see No. 66, note 6] . . . that we should be wise to refrain from sanctioning any British exports to Argentina of munitions, warships, military aircraft or supplies of a direct military or naval character. cannot guarantee that the United States will not eventually scoop the pool; but feel confident that they would regard our entry into the field, whether now or later, as a breach of hemisphere security plans of United States general staff . . . I consider that we should keep out of the munitions field but insist as far as possible upon our need for selling borderline goods and for permitting legitimate trade with interests in Argentina (e.g. the union of industry and Argentine stock exchange) which have shown their hostility to Argentine Government and are in need of support if they are not to be cowed into submission by Peron' (AS 5204/159/2).

In telegram No. 6652 Lord Halifax commented generally that 'it seems evident that the United States Counsellors are to some extent divided, and much may depend upon decisions taken by Byrnes in complicated divergence of views between political theories and defence practice. Congress is also showing signs of becoming restive at the failure to consult them in advance of decisions of policy about Argentina which may retard the programme of full employment in the United States' (AS 5206/159/2). He added that Lord Keynes concurred generally with both telegrams 6651 and 6652.

[2] See No. 66, note 1.

[3] This was a telegraphic version of despatch No. 1754 to Washington of 5 October: see No. 66, note 4.

[4] No. 66.

[5] On 27 and 28 September Mr. W.J. Gallman, Counsellor in the U.S. Embassy in London

240

Argentina. We are, moreover, anxious to forestall further American requests of this kind, and to liberate ourselves as soon as possible from our present embarrassments as regards licensing of exports, in order to develop potentially valuable market to fullest extent possible at present. Present chaos in Buenos Aires[2] need not, in our view, affect principles involved.

2. Please now therefore act as instructed in paragraph 5 of my telegram No. 9884[6] indicating to State Department:

(1) that this is our considered reply to all outstanding requests for the control of exports to Argentina;

(2) that it goes a long way to meet their wishes, and that it is the limit to which we can go, since it involves considerable sacrifice of our interests, having regard to considerations set forth in second sentence of paragraph (b) of your telegram No. 6651[7] and in the second sentence of paragraph 3 of your telegram No. 6652;[8]

had addressed letters to Mr. Perowne concerning Anglo-American policy on the control of exports to Argentina. In the first he referred to the State Department's view that an 'understanding' existed between British and American authorities in Buenos Aires prohibiting the export of any type of aircraft to Argentina, and that a recent contract for the sale of British Sunderland aircraft to Señor Alberto Dodero, a Uruguayan businessman based in Argentina, appeared to contradict this policy. According to a minute of 27 September by Mr. Perowne, it was explained to Mr. Gallman 'that this transaction had specifically been approved by Mr. Braden in conversation with Sir D. Kelly, that the Americans themselves had provided engines and sent them to this country for fitting in the aircraft in question, and that anyhow Sr. Dodero had been here in May and the whole thing completed on our side before we received the American request, early in July, to refuse armaments exports to Argentina' (AS 5015/159/2): cf. No 14, note 5.

Lord Halifax commented on this point in his telegram No. 6651 (see note 1): 'I see no justification for any United States objections to our proceeding with a supply of purely civilian Sunderland aircraft to Dodero, a Uruguayan citizen of recognised integrity with whom ... United States interests are admittedly negotiating for eventual sale on their part of similar aircraft. This deal, obviously one in which Braden has expressly disclaimed American interest, is now in any case in too advanced a stage to be held up without serious loss of prestige'.

Mr. Gallman's second note referred to a report that the Board of Trade, 'unlike the Foreign Economic Administration, is unwilling to put Argentina in the same category with enemy countries as far as trade controls are concerned because the United Kingdom is not in a position to antagonize prospective clients. In Mr. Byrnes' view, if this report is correct, the effect of the Foreign Economic Administration's action in putting Argentina in the same category with Spain and previous Axis satellites will be largely nullified' (AS 5021/159/2).

[6] See note 1: para. 5 instructed Lord Halifax to explain to the State Department that the directive by which His Majesty's Government would be guided (see i) could not be applied unless 'a similar procedure has been put into effective operation by the competent United States authorities'.

[7] This sentence referred to the necessity to insist on the British Government's need to supply 'borderline' goods to Argentina, covered by the definition attached to the directive in below.

[8] This sentence included Lord Halifax's opinion that 'it would seem advisable in any explanations we may have to give to the State Department, to stress our immediate dependence upon Argentine market for raw materials and foodstuffs essential to our economy and that of Europe': cf. No. 66.

(3) that Dodero transaction must stand, for reasons already given (see my telegram No. 10475[9]);

(4) that procedure described in paragraphs 3 and 4 of my telegram No. 9884[10] (which, for your information, does not amount to definite export prohibition) is being put into operation forthwith, and that we shall only consider ourselves bound to the self-denial involved by the above policy for so long as we are satisfied that the Americans are practising a corresponding self-denial.

3. For your information, although in the purely military field we may sympathise with United States views regarding hemisphere defence, we are not disposed to sacrifice these valuable export markets in countries with dollar currencies particularly when we know that many Latin-American countries do not want to become wholly dependent on the United States of America and when if we do not supply they may buy from other countries, e.g. Sweden—see Buenos Aires telegram No. 742.[11] If, therefore, the second sentence of paragraph 1 (a) of your telegram No. 6651[12] means that the United States would claim the permanent right to be the sole suppliers to any or all of the Latin American countries, this is a claim which should be strenuously repudiated if ever it were advanced.

4. You will have noted that some of the points made in your telegram No. 6652 are covered in message to Mr. Byrnes in my telegram No 10100,[4] including point concerning fuels for Argentina.

5. Please telegraph immediately you have acted since we are to our great present embarrassment obliged to hold several borderline case until communication has been made to the State Department.[13]

CALENDARS TO NO. 77

i 23 Oct. 1945 Letter from Lord Halifax to Mr. Byrnes, enclosing aide-mémoir containing directive by which H.M.G. will be guided in their export policy to Argentina: ' "While His Majesty's Government are in the present circum stances opposed to the supply to Argentina or to private Argentine firms o any arms or munitions of war or other goods particularly adapted for warlik uses, they would have no objection to the supply to Argentina of articles such as are generally of a civilian character although they may be capable o military use". This directive covers the supply of aero engines, trainin aircraft, civil aircraft, such as the Sunderlands recently sold to Dodero, and a

[9] This telegram of 18 October referred to the impossibility of rescinding licences alread granted to Señor Dodero: cf. note 5.
[10] i.e. the procedure set out in the aide-mémoire at i below.
[11] Not printed (AS 5296/159/2).   [12] Cited in note 1.
[13] Lord Halifax reported in telegram No. 7018 of 23 October that he had delivered a aide-mémoire in the sense of the present telegram to Mr. Byrnes that day: see i below. M Perowne commented in a minute of 1 November that the aide-mémoire did 'not really compl with the instr[uction]s in our tel. 10525 .. The Embassy have indeed been succinct, but suppose they know their local ground best. It wd. be worse than useless for them now to try unsolicited, to explain matters . . .' (AS 5680/159/2).

aircraft not suitable for combat.' State Dept. *aide-mémoire* of 15 Nov., also in reply to British note of 12 Oct. (see No. 66, note 9), is printed in *F.R.U.S. 1945*, vol. ix, pp. 555–7 [AS 5680/159/2].

ii *31 Oct. 1945 Mr. Hadow (Washington) to Mr. Perowne* expressing concern that 'our assets in Argentina may be thrown into the melting pot of an Anglo-American agreement', and transmitting memo. on British capital in Argentina [AS 5807/12/2].

No. 78

British Missions (Washington) to Cabinet Offices
(Received 20 October, 3.27 a.m.)

NABOB *191* Telegraphic [UE *4994/1094/53*]

Immediate. Top secret   WASHINGTON, *20 October 1945, 12.59 a.m.*

For Chancellor of Exchequer from Keynes.

1. Ambassador, Brand and I have seen Vinson and Clayton again to hear their proposals. These took just the form which in para. 21 of NABOB 177[1] we warned you they might, only worse.

2. Vinson told us rather solemnly that there had been a further meeting of the Top Committee on the American side and also of the National Advisory Council under the Bretton Woods Act, of which the membership largely overlaps, and that both bodies were unanimously of the opinion that the best offer they could make us which they believed Congress would accept was as follows.

3. A loan of three and a half billions at 2 per cent interest plus whatever is required to clean-up Lend-Lease on 3C terms.[2] The first instalment of service on the loan could be deferred five years and subsequent instalments of service could be arranged if we wished on an ascending scale beginning say at 90 millions and not exceeding 110 millions before 25 years, provided the interest worked out in the end to the actuarial equivalent of 2 per cent. The Lend-Lease accommodation on 3C terms would be at 2⅜ per cent, the capital repayable over 30 years beginning next year, that is to say the same as for other people.

4. In reply to my question whether they would expect us on the basis of this limited aid to enter into the same commitments in regard to the sterling area as those we had previously discussed,[3] they answered that they would.

[1] No. 74.   [2] See No. 4, note 7.
[3] In response to a request from Sir W. Eady in BABOON 145 of 23 October to 'telegraph immediately how Vinson and Clayton understand our commitments about sterling area' (T 236/466), Lord Keynes replied in NABOB 209 of 23 October that he had been referring to the proposals discussed at the second meeting of the Finance Committee (see No. 39, note 3), amended in accordance with CAMER 673 and 674 (Nos. 41 and 41.iv) and accepted in

5. Some time was wasted in a confused discussion how they had arrived at three and a half billions as sufficient. The answer seemed to depend partly on sheer confusion in Clayton's mind, partly on double counting and largely on assuming that we could run down our gold and dollar reserves from an assumed figure of one and three quarter billions at the end of this year to the bedrock figure of one billion at the end of the transitional period. Thus we should leave the transitional period stript [sic] and without available resources for the precarious years beyond, but with our commitments unabated.

6. In spite of the air of finality with which this announcement was made I can scarcely believe that they expected us to accept it. I replied that we would of course report this offer to London. But Ambassador and I warned them that there could be only one answer. We could not imagine that an agreement was possible on these lines; yet a failure to reach agreement must have dangerous and even tragic consequences. I asked whether their advice would be that we should adjourn without more said, or that I should prepare for an early return to London or that we should try to think of something quite different. After an anecdote from Vinson about how hosts behaved to guests in his native Kentucky smiles returned to faces and there was a general agreement that we should try to think of something quite different.

7. I ventured therefore, and I hope that in all the circumstances you will not blame me, to return to Clayton's proposal of a five billion loan against a 50 year annuity of 150 millions beginning five years hence with a waiver clause for the interest.[4]

8. As regards the amount I urged that in view of the commitments we are asked to accept we must start with a figure which was adequate in our own judgment. If we did not need so much we certainly should not draw it and they must trust us so to act. They replied that whilst previously they had talked in terms of five billions they were increasingly concerned about the difficulty of putting so high a figure through Congress. This was chiefly due, we think, to the remarks of Senator George already reported to you,[5] who is chairman of the Senate Committee which will deal with the legislation to provide aid to us, though they admitted they themselves were surprised that George had spoken that way. In any case it would help them a little if we could talk in terms of four and a half billions plus whatever is required to clean-up Lend-Lease. No harm in this, provided it is clear that the Lend-Lease addition is on the same terms as, and is

principle by Mr. Clayton and Mr. Vinson (see No. 44). Lord Keynes further explained that he now intended to produce a redraft of these proposals, doing his best 'to preserve for us the necessary latitude[,] I think the Americans appreciate that any uniform or cut and dried commitment is impracticable. Nevertheless as you already know large concessions by the sterling area are of course an absolutely essential and, we think, not unreasonable condition for American assistance. They started this way and are most unlikely to change their position' (UE 5048/1094/53). The draft statement was transmitted in NABOB 215 of 24 October: ii below.

    [4] See No. 67.   [5] Cf. No. 72.

incorporated with, the main loan. I emphasise this because Vinson mentioned that he was now hearing for the first time of any suggestion that the Lend-Lease finance should be handled outside the 3C terms. When we reminded him that this had been already settled in our favour,[6] he said that this was news to him but readily withdrew if the question had been already fixed otherwise. It is not unnatural that Vinson and also Clayton should know very little on the Lend-Lease side. Angell, the last survivor of the Senior F.E.A. Officials who are acquainted with our affairs is leaving next week to replace Pauley[7] on the reparations commission which is good for Waley but bad for us, all the others having resigned in the course of the month since I arrived. On the Lend-Lease end our party faces a new audience every week. In other respects as well as in this you must take it as basic that your negotiators have to do their best in an environment which must be difficult to understand in London and will indeed again become unintelligible to us when we are back, although when one lives in it, deep in the heart of Texas,[8] or rather in this case, half in Texas and half in Kentucky, it comes to seem part of the landscape and even to have some advantages.

9. They urged, therefore, that it would help them very much if we could keep the figure down to say four billions plus the clean-up of Lend-Lease. If you can meet them on this, it will certainly help a good deal. For my part I think we need elbow room and would be reluctant to cut the figure at any rate at this stage. There is also a danger that the service of the lower amount would be kept the same as for the higher, though this risk may become less when we have made more progress with drafting the exact terms. Perhaps in the end we might take an option on the last million on rather different conditions though this might not fit in with the waiver provisions discussed below.

10. We then turned to the nature of the waiver. They said that they had abandoned this line of settlement because I had so firmly rejected the whole idea of an escape clause. I admitted that this was so both on instructions from London and because we all felt a strong moral objection to such clauses if there was any means of avoiding them. I said that I was still under the same instructions. Nevertheless in an effort to break the jam, perhaps we might explore the possibilities a little further quite off the record.

11. First of all, they corrected their previous offer by substituting 159 millions for 150 millions as the fixed annual service on 5 billions. Clayton explained that their actuaries had worked out that this was the correct figure required in order to yield 2 per cent interest after presenting us with five years deferment. When Clayton spoke previously of 150 millions

[6] See Nos. 33.i and 37, and iii below.
[7] Mr. E.W. Pauley had been U.S. Representative on the Allied Reparations Commission since April 1945.
[8] Mr. Clayton's home state was Mississippi, but he had moved his family to Houston, Texas, in 1916.

he warned us that this was subject to calculations on which his actuaries were at work and was his own first shot. Thus in using this figure as the basis of our own calculation, as in paragraph 16 of NABOB 177, we were giving it greater exactitude than has proved to be warranted. On the other hand we did not appreciate or allow in our calculation for the fact that no interest is debited against us in respect of the first five years. In fact, an annual service charge of 159 millions for fifty years, beginning after five years, is actuarially equivalent to an interest rate of 1.6 per cent over the whole term of the loan, which is slightly less than what we told you before.

12. After emphasising that I was going quite beyond my instructions, I then tried on them the type of waiver clause outlined in paragraph 16 of NABOB 177. They immediately expressed a lively interest and said that something on these lines might be acceptable. The reaction against the strain of the first half of the interview seemed by now to be clearing the atmosphere. Having delivered their mouthful, they were now wanting to help if they could.

13. Clayton began by wanting to take our balance of payments as the criterion. But Vinson soon saw the serious objections to this and supported my alternative. Clayton remained emphatic, however, that the criterion of our external income must include our net invisible income. The absence of this item would lead to suspicions. Americans rely greatly on future tourist traffic for filling the gap. They calculate that with 100,000 Americans on the average of the year (presumably in Oxford) each spending at the rate of pounds 500 a year, the whole problem of what we are now discussing is solved with something to spare. I replied that the only real objection to including our net invisible income was the lack of a sound statistical estimate for it but admitted that it might be good for us to have to improve our statistical departments.

14. The upshot was that they might be prepared to recommend and thought they could defend an arrangement by which we should repay the capital of a loan by fifty equal annual instalments, beginning five years hence, and would pay an additional fixed annual sum, by way of interest, over the same fifty years, calculated so as to be equivalent to 2 per cent over the whole period. But the latter sum would be payable in those years only in which our exports and net invisible income exceeded 7 billion dollars at a price level double pre-war, or say pounds 875 million at the pre-war value of money—this part of the annuity being finally waived in years in which this figure was not reached. This is only a way of splitting up a fixed annual service charge, which has the effect of deferring interest and speeding up repayment in the earlier years, and conversely in the later. Actuarially it comes to the same thing in the end as a normal sinking fund table. Perhaps you may think it would suit us better to propose the latter, under which the capital instalment in the first year would be 59 and the interest 100 the former rising and the latter falling as time goes on, since in the earlier and, presumably, more difficult years, we should thus be entitled to waive a greater proportion of the annual payment. If so, I

do not believe that they have yet formed any fixed views on the method to be followed so long as the total annual instalment is the same. On this please see the draft to be telegraphed later.[9]

15. After consideration of the above the ambassador and the others named in paragraph 1 of NABOB 177 have nothing to add to the reasons given in that telegram why we think this proposal deserves your consideration, except that we are now more convinced than before that nothing better than this is on the map. For example the alternatives in paragraphs 19 and 20 of NABOB 177 are now, in our opinion, out. The Americans seem quite convinced that they must offer Congress what purports to be a two per cent loan but think it quite defensible from their angle that the payment of this interest should depend on our full recovery in the sense of our having reached our post-transitional target of external income. Indeed who can argue that the extra amount we are now resisting will not be a very small matter when once we have accomplished the tremendous task of reaching the target. Moreover, we obtain subsequent relief in any year in which our position again deteriorates. I should add that the Americans propose over and above the waiver clause in the contract to take unilateral powers to themselves in the proposed legislation authorising the executive to waive or defer the capital instalments or otherwise modify the terms in our favour in any future circumstances in which they deem this to be advisable.

16. At the end of the meeting reported above Vinson and Clayton asked that we should put our ideas in writing. I said that I could go no further without guidance from London and it was agreed not to meet again until we had heard from you. We recommend that we be authorised to continue discussion on the above lines, except that we shall put the target of our external income at not less than seven and a half millions rather than seven. See my next following telegram.[10] We should make it plain that the more precise version we were giving them in response to their invitation to explore the possibilities of a waiver clause was not a formal proposal from you and was in common with our negotiations on other issues without commitment.[11]

17. A further telegram[9] will contain a draft of our ideas. It will incorporate the escape clauses as in your telegram 10473.[12] There will be no need to wait for this before considering the general principles involved since it will only add technical and more precise details to what you will already know.[13]

[9] See No. 80.   [10] NABOB 192 is printed in Moggridge, *op. cit.*, pp. 563–4.
[11] The preceding part of this telegram is printed *ibid.*, pp. 557–63.
[12] See No. 68, note 5.
[13] In a personal telegram to Lord Halifax, BABOON 146 of 23 October, Mr. Dalton stated: 'You and Keynes were clearly right in telling Vinson and Clayton that there could only be one answer from us to the offer in the form in which it was made in paragraph 3 of NABOB 191. Despite the solemnity of the offer, their readiness to think differently suggested that it may still be a tactical move . . . I am sure that it would be inadvisable for

i *20 Oct. 1945 Brief by Economic Relations Dept.* summarising the financial negotiations so far and speculating on future programme [UE 5043/1094/53].

ii *24 Oct. 1945 British Missions (Washington) Tels. NABOB 214 & 215* Lord Keynes' draft statement on sterling area arrangements (see note 3) [UE 5075/1094/53].

iii *24 Oct. 1945 British Missions (Washington) Tel. NABOB Saving 22* Text of letter from Lord Keynes to Mr. Vinson summarising negotiations leading to agreement on Lend-Lease settlement [UE 5214/1094/53].

Keynes to discuss further, in however non-committal a manner, ways of working out an adjustment of our annual liability by some annual measurement of our capacity to pay until my colleagues and I have examined the latest turn of the situation and we can send you our considered views. If there has been some significant change in the American offer since NABOB 191, please telegraph most immediately so that my colleagues and I can have the latest facts before us' (T 236/466). Lord Keynes replied in NABOB 210 of 23 October that he had not as yet had any further discussion with Mr. Clayton and Mr. Vinson, but 'indirect indications based on Clayton's remarks to third parties which have reached our ears are that he remains considerably attracted by the suggestion in paragraph 12 of NABOB 191 and would almost certainly regard a counter-proposal from us on these lines as constituting very satisfactory progress' (UE 5057/1094/53).

No. 79

Sir D. Kelly (Buenos Aires) to Mr. Bevin
(Received 31 October)

No. 304 [AS 5679/453/2]

BUENOS AIRES, *20 October 1945*

His Majesty's Ambassador at Buenos Aires presents his compliments to His Majesty's Principal Secretary of State for Foreign Affairs and has the honour to transmit to him the under-mentioned documents.

Reference to previous correspondence:

Foreign Office telegram No. 452 of 9th September, 1945 to Buenos Aires.[1]

Name and Date	Subject
Copy of Note No. 230 of 11th September, 1945 to Minister for Foreign Affairs	British Sovereignty in Falkland Islands

[1] This telegram instructed Sir D. Kelly to act on instructions sent in despatch No. 158 of 23 July to present a note to the Argentine Government, the draft of which was enclosed, at 'the first opportune moment after the conclusion of the present meat contract negotiations' (cf. No. 25).

248

Sir D. Kelly to Dr. J. Cooke
No. 230

Copy   BUENOS AIRES, 11 September 1945

Monsieur le Ministre,

I have the honour, on the instructions of His Majesty's Principal Secretary of State for Foreign Affairs, to refer to the action of the Argentine Delegation at San Francisco in formulating a reservation as regards territories which might be placed under trusteeship in language intended apparently to refer to the Falkland Islands.[2] By this action, the

---

[2] See *Documents of the United Nations Conference on International Organization, San Francisco 1945* (London, 1945), vol. x, pp. 469 and 475–6 (cf. *F.R.U.S. 1945*, vol. i, p. 2). In a minute of 27 May Mr. R. Allen of South American Department had explained: 'The Guatemalan Delegation to the San Francisco Conference proposed an amendment to the draft Trusteeship Charter which, after revision, read as follows: "The Trusteeship system shall not be applied to the territories in dispute concerning which there is pending any question, claim, controversy or litigation between states members of the international organisation". They appended to this the following statement of reasons: "The Delegation of Guatemala submits to the consideration of the committee this amendment, which is inspired by the principle of justice that the rights of third parties should be safeguarded in the face of any situations which might derive from the application of the trusteeship system. Thus in so far as concerns the republic of Guatemala, which maintains a controversy with Great Britain in relation to Guatemalan sovereignty over Belize (British Honduras [cf. No. 14, note 6]), it could in no case admit that such territory be placed under the trusteeship system, because this would imply a change in the status of Belize, in such a manner that it might complicate Guatemala's action toward regaining this territory."

'When Guatemala moved this amendment in the Trusteeship Committee, Lord Cranborne [then Secretary of State for Dominion Affairs], after expressing surprise that the circulation of the Guatemalan paper had been permitted, said that the amendment appeared unnecessary and asked that a record should be made in the minutes that the United Kingdom did not admit Guatemala's claims. This request was accepted by the Chairman. The Chinese delegate urged the Guatemalans to withdraw the amendment but they refused to do so. Finally the amendment was put to the vote and defeated by 18 to 13, the United States abstaining . . . As will be seen from the present telegram [San Francisco telegrams Nos. 424–5 of 24 May, not printed] the Argentine Delegation were instructed to put forward a reservation in support of the Guatemalan amendment, the relevant part of which is that the "Argentine Republic in no case accepts that the present system of trusteeships should be applied to or over territories belonging to Argentina, whether they be the subject of a claim or controversy or are in the possession of other states." The Argentine Delegation asked that their reservation should appear in the record. The Chairman of the Committee said that he could not accept reservations but agreed that the Argentine text should be included in the minutes as a statement of the Argentine Government's view. Lord Cranborne made no comment in order to play the matter down and no reference to it has appeared in the Press.'

In a comment on San Francisco telegram No. 424 Sir D. Kelly stated in his telegram No. 358 of 31 May: 'According to my understanding we have to safeguard our legal position in the Falkland Isles and dependencies by keeping it consistently on official record, so that if we . . . [text uncertain] ever had to justify to third parties our dossier would be complete; but at the same time we always endeavour to keep it on academic level and avoid any controversy unless strictly necessary for the above purpose.' He disagreed with the view of

Delegation incurred the risk that there would be raised, at a Conference which was in no way concerned with particular territories, a public dispute on the subject of these Islands. That a dispute was in the event avoided was due solely to the restraint exercised by the United Kingdom Delegation.

2. Such a dispute would have been greatly to be deplored, not only because it would have been unnecessary (the respective standpoints of the interested parties having long been defined and well known) but because it could only be expected to impair the good relations which it is the desire of His Majesty's Government to see maintained between the United Kingdom and Argentina—a desire which His Majesty's Government assume that the Argentine Government reciprocate. I am therefore to express the concern of His Majesty's Government at the despatch to the Argentine Delegation at San Francisco of the instructions which led to the formulation of the reservation referred to above.

3. I am to take the opportunity to recall to Your Excellency the Memorandum which I had the honour to leave with your predecessor on 12th April, 1943[3], and which in part recites His Majesty's title to the Falkland Islands Dependencies and instances a number of infringements of that title by the Argentine Government.

4. After this Memorandum was delivered, His Majesty's Government learnt with surprise of the second voyage of the Argentine naval transport

the British Delegation at San Francisco that 'recent Argentine action is due to the belief that provided they play in with the United States Government they can treat us as they please [cf. Volume I, No. 65]. The fact therefore that the Argentine Delegation's reservation had not been in any way played up in Argentine Press suggests on the contrary that this action was not intended to be provocative but is formal reservation such as no Argentine Government will ever lose an opportunity to make.' Sir D. Kelly thought it important to bear in mind that the previously violent Argentine propaganda about the Falkland Islands had ceased and his representations in 1943 (see para. 3 below) had been kept secret.

With regard to British Honduras Mr. J.R.M. Leake, H.M. Chargé d'Affaires in Guatemala, transmitted in his despatch No. 105 of 1 October a copy of the Guatemalan note of 24 September (printed in L.M. Bloomfield, *The British Honduras-Guatemala Dispute* (Toronto, 1953), pp. 68–9) which expressed 'the wish to initiate negotiations' on the question. The note drew attention to the Motion passed by the Guatemalan Congress on 18 September requesting the Guatemalan Government to end the suspension of its claim to which it had committed itself during the war. In his despatch Mr. Leake stated in particular that the press campaign on the subject had been 'of brief duration and comparatively mild' and that it would be difficult to stir the average Guatemalan into 'genuine enthusiasm' about the claim to British Honduras. Guatemala had however 'reaped considerable prestige by her handling of the dispute' and could 'always count on the support of the Central American Republics who, although they may not want Guatemala in Belize, certainly want Great Britain out, while the growing solidarity of Latin American feeling ensures her of sympathy further afield.' This despatch further transmitted a draft decree declaring void the Anglo-Guatemalan convention of 30 April 1859 on the Boundary of British Honduras (printed in *B.F.S.P.*, vol. 49, pp. 7–13). Subsequently Mr. Leake reported in his telegram No. 271 of 11 October that the Guatemalan Ministry of Foreign Affairs had announced that 'all inhabitants of territory of Belize are to be considered Guatemalans provided they express a desire to become so and renounce previous nationality'.

[3] Not printed.

Primero de Mayo in February–March 1943 and of the activities of the officers of that vessel at Deception Island, Port Lockroy, the Melchior Islands and Neny Fjord.

5. I have the honour to draw Your Excellency's formal attention to the fact that His Majesty's Government must take serious exception to these activities in so far as they imply a denial of British sovereignty over the areas in question, and in particular to the erasure of British emblems at Deception Island and to the surreptitious restoration of Argentine emblems for a second time on this island. His Majesty's Government have also learnt with surprise that an Argentine flag was hoisted at Port Lockroy and that a cylinder was deposited there containing an Argentine claim to sovereignty over the lands between longitudes 25° West and 68°34' West, to the south of latitude 60° South. These further attempted encroachments on the part of the Argentine Government upon territory under His Majesty's sovereignty have not passed unobserved by His Majesty's Government. The Argentine marks have been removed by British administrative officials and I am directed to enter an energetic protest against a course of conduct which cannot but be calculated to injure relations between the Argentine Government and His Majesty's Government.

6. The attention of His Majesty's Government has further been drawn to Chart No.100, published in July 1944 by the Ministerio de Marina at Buenos Aires, with the title 'República Argentina, Océano glacial Antártico, Isla Decepción'. His Majesty's Government can only deplore the publication of this official document, with its implication of Argentine sovereignty over this British possession.

7. Finally, I am instructed to protest against the action of the Argentine Government in continuing to maintain an illegal post office and wireless telegram station in the South Orkney Islands. The international character of the meteorological work which is being performed at the Argentine observatory on Laurie Island in no way justifies an open breach of the regulations in force in the Dependencies relating to the maintenance of such stations.

8. I should recall to your Excellency that the South Shetland Islands, Graham Land and the South Orkney Islands, have the legal status of Dependencies of the Falkland Island[s]. Your Government are doubtless aware that a British Stipendiary Magistrate has been in residence at Deception Island between 1910 and 1930, that a post office and mail service was maintained on the island for eighteen years (1912–30) during the operation of the shore whaling station, and that all the whaling carried on in this region has been done with the permission and licence of His Majesty's Government. Although the residence of a Magistrate at Deception Island ceased to be necessary in 1930, in view of the cessation of shore whaling activities, British vessels have since made frequent use of the island. At various times British installations have also been established and occupied at points along the coast of Graham Land. In addition to

these operations on shore, the ships of the 'Discovery' Committee have for many years past made a long series of visits to the South Shetlands and the coasts and islands of Graham Land, and have carried out a comprehensive programme of surveying, hydrology, sounding and biological work with a view to developing the economic resources of the region. In the Dependency of South Orkney all whaling activities since 1908 have been carried out under the licence and control of His Majesty's Government. Furthermore, land on Signy Island was held during the years 1921 to 1930 on lease to a Norwegian Company from the Falkland Islands Government, under the laws of that Colony, and shore whaling installations were erected on the island. In order to safeguard the due observance of the Falkland Islands Ordinances on the conduct of whaling, a series of visits were made during this period by officials of the Falkland Islands Government. Since 1930, when the need for a shore whaling station in the islands ceased to exist, British sovereign functions have been exercised during the visits of His Majesty's ships and the research ships of the 'Discovery' Committee, which made a thorough survey and scientific investigation of all the islands in the group between 1927 and 1937.

9. Visits to the Dependencies by His Majesty's ships and by ships of the Government of the Dependencies have continued throughout the war, and I now have the honour to inform Your Excellency that in 1943 the work of the 'Discovery' Committee's ships and the land investigations started by the British Graham Land Expedition of 1934–37 were resumed, and to add that an extensive programme of research, exploration and development is now being carried out. New shore establishments, meteorological stations, post offices and wireless telegraph stations have been set up, and Magistrates have been appointed for Graham Land, the South Shetland Islands and the South Orkney Islands.[4]

10. In conclusion I have the honour to emphasize that His Majesty's Government must continue to take all steps necessary to conserve their Sovereign Rights over the Falkland Islands Colony and its Dependencies.

I avail, &c.,

DAVID V. KELLY

CALENDAR TO NO. 79

i *12 Oct. 1945   Colonial Office political instructions to the Commander of the F.I.D.S. 1945–6* (without appendix) British sovereignty to be clearly stated but use of force avoided if Argentine or Chilean parties encountered; foreign emblems to be obliterated [AS 5317/453/2].

[4] For an account by J.M. Wordie, 'The Falkland Islands Dependencies Survey, 1943–46', see *The Polar Record*, vol. 4, July 1946, No. 32, pp. 372–84; also *op. cit.*, vol. 5, pp. 27–39, for an account by Surgeon-Commander E.W. Bingham, leader of the F.I.D.S. 1945–47, 'The Falkland Islands Dependencies Survey, 1946–47'.

No. 80

British Missions (Washington) to Cabinet Offices
(Received 21 October, 2.8 a.m.)

NABOB 200 Telegraphic [UE 5024/1094/53]

Immediate. Top secret   WASHINGTON, 21 October 1945, 1.5 a.m.

For Treasury from Keynes

1. The next four paragraphs contain the text promised in para. 17 of NABOB 191.[1] The critical figure of £875 million in 4(*a*) corresponds to the seven and a half billions at post-war prices suggested in para. 3 of NABOB 192[2] since we now intend to take account in reckoning net invisible income of Government expenditure overseas previously entered separately on the expenditure side of the account. You will see that in 3 we have adopted the formula suggested in the latter part of para. 14 of NABOB 191 which means that in the first year our liability would be only $59 million unless the critical figure has been reached. The draft also regards the period of grace as lasting until the end of 1951 rather than 1950 which might be justified on the ground that credits may not be effectively available by the end of 1945. It is not essential to put forward now all the provisions suggested in para. 2 but it might be well to table them so as to make sure that there is no snag and to indicate the machinery we are contemplating.

2. Credit facilities up to an amount not exceeding $4.5 billion (together with an amount equal to the net sum mutually agreed as due from the U.K. in respect of 'Lend-Lease' supplies furnished after September 2nd 1945 and Lend-Lease inventory and U.S. military surplus after taking account of 'Reciprocal Aid' supplies and services furnished by the U.K. to the U.S. between September 2nd 1945 and February 28th 1946 and Reciprocal Aid inventory and all other accounts between the two Governments otherwise unsettled and arising before September 2nd 1945) will be set up in favour of the U.K. which will be drawn upon in so far as the U.K. may require from time to time to replenish the balances of the U.K. Treasury or Bank of England with the Federal Reserve Bank of New York. Any amount not drawn by December 31st 1951 will be cancelled unless it is mutually agreed otherwise at a later date.

3. The U.K. will repay the principal sum of the net credit drawn upon and outstanding on December 31st 1951 together with interest calculated at 2 percent per annum on the amounts of the credit outstanding in each subsequent year by equal annual instalments of $31,800 for each $1,000,000 outstanding on December 31st 1951, beginning on December 31st 1952 until the capital amount has been repaid. Out of each annual instalment an amount equal to 2 percent of the principal outstanding in

---

[1] No. 78.   [2] V. *ibid.*, note 10.

that year shall be attributed to interest and the balance to capital repayment.

4. The Government of the U.K. having represented to the Government of the U.S.

(a) that the pre-war level of imports into the U.K. on the average of the three pre-war years 1936–1938 amounted to £875 millions at the prices of those years

(b) that the difficulties of the post-war transitional period arising out of the sacrifices and disturbance of the war to the U.K. economy cannot be considered to be at an end until U.K. earnings overseas have been restored to a level at least sufficient to pay for the pre-war volume of imports, and

(c) that a payment of interest on the scale prescribed above would involve a burden on world commerce which could not be met without restrictive measures which it is the purpose of both Governments to avoid, unless conditions exist in which the overseas earnings of the U.K. are sufficient to cover a volume of import not less than the pre-war volume, the Government of U.S. agree that the proportion of the above annuity attributable to interest shall be waived in any year in which the home-produced exports and net invisible income of the year fall short of £875 millions reckoned in terms of money of the same value as in 1936–1938, as calculated by the statistical section of the International Monetary Fund.

5. The Government of the U.K. shall be entitled to approach the Government of the U.S. for a deferment of the annual instalment of payment due in any year in any of the following circumstances. In the event of deferment the amount due will be postponed so as not to increase the amount due in the year immediately following but by a corresponding extension of the period of repayment.

(a) *A breakdown of multilateral clearing*

In the event of less than 75 per cent of U.K. exports being sold to countries of which the currencies are freely convertible into dollars.

(b) *An International depression of trade*

In the event of general and prolonged depression of world trade acknowledged by the International Monetary Fund as constituting a serious disturbance of the equilibrium of International payments.

(c) *Scarcity of dollars*

In the event of the International Monetary Fund having notified under Article VII (I) of the International Monetary Fund that a general scarcity of dollars is developing.

CHAPTER III

Negotiations leading to financial and commercial agreements of 6 December: convertibility of sterling

27 October – 7 December 1945

No. 81

Cabinet Offices to British Missions (Washington)

BABOON 155 Telegraphic [UE 5024/1094/53]

Immediate. Secret CABINET OFFICES, *27 October 1945, 4.47 p.m.*

Personal from Chancellor of the Exchequer.

NABOBS 177, 191 and 200.[1]

1. We[2] have carefully considered these telegrams. In view of the vacillation of the Administration, and of our uncertainty how the real situation is developing, we have come to the conclusion that it may be wise to bring matters to a head by making a definite proposal to the Americans. We should like you to consider an oral communication to them in the sense of the following paragraphs. You should say that these proposals represent what we believe, though not with any certainty, could be recommended to Parliament with prospects of general acceptance. The proposals are alternatives on distinct principles.

2. Alternative A.

(*a*) We should seek a loan now of $2½ billion for 50 years at 1 per cent, repayment beginning after 5 years.

(*b*) We should seek an option on a further $2 billion free of interest as

---

[1] Nos. 74, 78 and 80.

[2] At their meeting on the afternoon of 26 October (GEN 89/4th meeting, ii below) Ministers considered Nos. 74, 78 and 80, together with a draft reply to these telegrams prepared in the Treasury and circulated in GEN 89/7 on 25 October (UE 5134/1094/53): cf. i below. In discussion of the draft reply, it was Mr. Bevin who suggested that it should be amended to form two telegrams (Nos. 81 and 82), the despatch of which the meeting authorised. See further Pressnell, *op. cit.*, Chapter 10(14).

backing for an offer to members of the sterling area to make their sterling as freely available for current expenditure outside the area as inside.

(c) If both these proposals are accepted we should go to our sterling creditors and seek agreement with each of them for an appropriate contribution towards the rehabilitation of the whole situation.

(d) Subject to the commercial discussions reaching a conclusion satisfactory to us, we should be willing to go on sponsoring the International Trade Conference and doing our best to make it a success.

(e) Subject to the acceptance by the Administration of this financial proposal, we should be prepared to recommend to Parliament adherence to the Final Act of Bretton Woods.

(f) This agreement would be subject only to a waiver condition on the lines of paragraph 5 of NABOB 200.

3. Alternative B.

If Alternative A is not acceptable to the Americans then we must borrow on commercial terms and without commitments of any kind except the service of the loan. We expect better than Crowley terms[3] and should seek an open credit up to $2½ billion plus Lend–Lease, at 2 per cent for 50 years, repayment beginning after 5 years.

4. See my immediately following telegram[4] for comments on these alternatives and on question of Waiver Clauses.

CALENDARS TO NO. 81

i *26 Oct. 1945* (a) *Note by Mr. Coulson on GEN 89/7* (see note 2 above) considers 'rather rigid line proposed in the Treasury draft is the right one to take . . . we shall bring home to the Americans what they will lose by going so little distance to meet us': Mr. Ronald minutes his agreement; (b) *Memo. by Mr. Jay for Mr. Attlee* on U.S. loan proposals: 'taking into account all the political and moral advantages of a "general settlement", I think on the whole we should take the risk' [UE 5134/1094/53, PREM 8/35].

ii *26 Oct. 1945* *Record of meeting of Ministers (GEN 89/4th meeting:* see note 2 above and No. 83, note 1) discussion of Nos. 74, 78 and 80: Mr. Bevin feels independence of a commercial loan would be 'worth the increased price', but considers $3 billion should be available [UE 5135/1094/53].

[3] See No. 16.   [4] No. 82.

No. 82

Cabinet Offices to British Missions (Washington)

BABOON 156 Telegraphic [UE 5024/1094/53]

Immediate. Secret   CABINET OFFICES, *27 October 1945, 7 p.m.*

Personal from Chancellor of the Exchequer.
These are explanatory notes on my immediately preceding telegram.[1]
1. We are grateful to Keynes for his appreciation in NABOB 177.[2] It is disappointing that the position seems to have slipped back in NABOB 191.[3]
2. We are fully conscious of the importance of these negotiations for Anglo-American relations and if we appear to be guarding our own vital interests rather cautiously, not least of those interests is a relationship with the United States which will stand the test of the future. It is on this account that we cannot accept obligations which we may not be able to fulfil, or agree to conditions which are capable of double interpretation. We are not negotiating with principals. It is Congress who will decide, particularly on the form of the various conditions which may have to be written in. We have no margin for last-minute concessions and we do not wish to be confronted at short notice by pleas that the whole settlement will be endangered unless we meet Congress on some point which may be of material importance to us. Whatever we agree must demonstrably have the same meaning for Parliament as it has for Congress, both now and in the years over which its fulfilment will take place.
3. You began with the bold constructive idea that the American Government might give us $5 billion free of repayment or at least free of interest. This would enable us to end the transitional period more quickly and to move into a multilateral world, to build up our reserves, to secure a favourable settlement with the sterling creditors, and to strengthen sterling so that it could play its full part quickly in the release of international trade. It seemed to us that you had convinced the Administration of the wisdom of such a settlement in the interests of the United States as well as in our interests.
4. This plan has almost disappeared. We are offered not $5 billion free of interest but perhaps $4 billion as a loan at 2 per cent interest, which we should hold is a commercial rate for our credit. Thus we are offered virtually commercial terms apart from the waiver clause for interest which on principle we dislike. From NABOB 191 we assume that we should be expected still to accept the following conditions:
   (*a*) In addition to accepting a liability of at least $1 billion with interest at 2 per cent for the purpose of enabling countries which are valuable markets of our own to turn to dollar goods in the immediate future, we are apparently to find about another billion dollars out of our reserves

[1] No. 81.   [2] No. 74.   [3] No. 78.

so that the dollars available to the sterling area are to be the same as if the loan were $5 billion.

(b) Probably making sterling convertible earlier than we should like.

(c) If the commercial talks reach some agreement, sponsoring the Commercial Conference, with pressure for some Empire commitment to the United States if the Conference fails.

(d) Presumably abolishing discrimination against U.S. exports even in 1946.

All these might have been safely undertaken with $5 billion grant in cash or possibly on an interest free basis, but they are neither safe nor a good bargain for $4 billion at 2 per cent interest. The difference between that situation and the original plan is in our judgment not one of degree but of kind.

5. *Waiver Clause*

Before discussing the two alternatives in my preceding telegram we think it necessary to set out fully our present views on this.

We have considered again the idea of a Waiver Clause cancelling an annual payment of interest on some index of our capacity to pay. It is not difficult to construct a suitable index such as that suggested by Keynes in paragraph 4 of NABOB 200.[4] But the idea still seems to us open to grave practical objections. The datum figure is clearly a matter of argument both with the Administration and later in Congress, for there is no principle to which we can appeal to decide the appropriate figure objectively. Even if the Administration were to accept a formula from us we cannot see them forcing a British formula through Congress. Congress might conceivably agree that in a defined situation we could apply for deferment or cancellation of the interest payment, but they would retain the decision in their own hands. That is clearly no safeguard for the future. Even if a formula emerged from the present circumstances and present Congress which appeared to safeguard our position, there would be argument in any year in which we appealed to it. We doubt whether this argument would be much reduced even if the figures emanated from the International Monetary Fund for they would still be our figures. If the short-fall in our exports were relatively small we should be expected to pay the $50 m. or $60 m. due for interest. If the short-fall were relatively large, the Administration or Congress of the time might urge that had we disposed of our productive resources more satisfactorily we should have obtained better export figures and that they should not forego their claim to interest because we had pampered the home market, or had lost ground on exports through internal policies which they disliked. My colleagues and I are seriously apprehensive of the future risk of interference by the Americans in our internal affairs as in 1931[5] or worse,

[4] No. 80.

[5] This reference, which did not occur in the original Treasury draft (cf. No. 81, note 2) and may have been added by Mr. Dalton personally, was presumably to the alleged demand by the American bankers J.P. Morgan in August 1931 for a 10% cut in U.K. unemployment

or of acrimonious argument. We would think it very unwise to expose Anglo-American relations to a recurrent strain on such an issue.

The proposals in my preceding telegram do not include a waiver based on our capacity to pay. But if you wish us to consider further the idea of such a waiver we must know whether Clayton has suggested any formula satisfactory to us which he would guarantee to get through Congress and which would work automatically.

We should assume that if Alternative A in my preceding telegram were accepted there would be no waiver clause based on our capacity to pay but the general waiver conditions mentioned in paragraph 5 of NABOB 200 would stand. If Alternative B had to be taken presumably there would be no Waiver Clause at all for it would be for all practical purposes a commercial loan.

6. Turning to Alternative A, this is of course our first preference and we make the following comments on it.

(a) It assumes that Keynes will be able to settle with Clayton that after allowing for all offsets, the net debit against us for the clean-up of Lend–Lease, including ships, will not exceed $500 m. and that we shall have this included in the loan at 1 per cent.

(b) We are reasonably satisfied that with $2 billion we can cover essential imports from the United States in 1946 and 1947 after allowing for vigorous switching during 1946, and in addition can look after the Canadian position to a reasonable degree, and have some Dollars available for immediate easements in the working of the Sterling Area. We could not of course let those easements go far, except as part of a settlement with the Sterling creditors.

7. *Sterling Creditors*

We believe there is risk of deep misunderstanding with the Americans about this.[6] We are not in a position to give any undertaking as to the amount by which the Sterling Balances as a whole will be reduced. Keynes will remember the large contribution that India had to make towards any total which the Americans might regard as respectable. We are advised that we may have the greatest difficulty in persuading India to accept such drastic scaling down, and unless we succeed with India we may expect difficulties with Egypt and Middle East countries. If the Americans attempt to insist upon an agreement by us to secure scaling down to a named figure or proportion, we believe the whole negotiations must break down. It is for this reason that the separation of the Sterling negotiations from the loan for our own purposes is suggested as the only practicable and candid handling of the business. Had the American assistance taken the form which Keynes had suggested, the whole moral impetus of this constructive act would have put the negotiations with the Sterling creditors on an entirely different plane, and although we could not have

benefit as a condition of a loan. For Mr. Dalton's views on this episode see the account in his memoirs, *Call Back Yesterday* (London, 1953), pp. 275–6 and footnote 1.

[6] Cf. No. 78, note 3 and ii.

guaranteed to secure cancellation of one/third of the aggregate Sterling Balances owing to the different circumstances of the creditors, we would certainly have secured a large cancellation, for we could have used the argument that in the light of the bold nature of the American assistance, the Sterling area should freely make a real contribution to the speedier international movement of goods. Even so those negotiations would have been voluntary and free. We could not at any time have been bound by advance arithmetic on this matter.

8. If Alternative A is accepted we should of course use the argument of the interest free Dollar option to its full extent and would vigorously try and secure substantial cancellations. We do not despair of achieving impressive results.

9. It is important for you to know the general lines of the assurance about the Sterling creditors that we think we could give.

(a) We will enter forthwith into negotiations with each of the countries concerned with a view to liberalising as quickly as possible, and to the utmost possible extent, the Sterling Area financial arrangements.

(b) To the extent that we are able to make satisfactory agreements with each of the countries concerned we will arrange that any Sterling Balances made available to each member of the Sterling Area for its current overseas expenditure shall be available for expenditure in any part of the world without discrimination.

(c) In establishing the amount of Sterling Balances to be made available for current overseas expenditure during the next 5 years full account will be taken of the additional purchasing power outside the Sterling Area which is provided by the use of the option.

(d) We understand that the United States Government consider it reasonable and proper that those Sterling Area creditors whose Balances have largely increased as a direct result of the war should discuss with us the cancellation of some of this indebtedness as a contribution to a settlement and to freeing the channels of trade. We will have full regard to this opinion of the United States Government in all our negotiations with the individual countries concerned.

10. *Interests*[7]

We have throughout regarded this assistance from America as an essential part of the war effort, for its necessity arose directly out of the shape and range of our own war effort. For this reason we thought that on merits it should be a grant-in-aid or a loan without interest. But if the Americans regard either a grant-in-aid or a loan without interest as impracticable, we would be willing to agree to pay a nominal rate of interest, say 1 per cent, on the part of the loan which we require for our own purposes. We should not be asked to pay a commercial rate of interest for what was not a commercial transaction.

On the loan which we take up for the purpose of financing American

[7] In the draft telegram circulated to the GEN 89 Committee (see No. 81, note 2) this word read, evidently correctly, 'Interest'.

exports to the Sterling Area we are unwilling to pay interest.

11. We have tried to devise Alternative A within the framework of the broad purposes for which the negotiations began, and if it were accepted we should do all in our power over the whole field of the negotiations now taking place to secure the fulfilment of those purposes as soon as possible.

12. But if a settlement very closely in accordance with the lines of Alternative A is not acceptable, then as at present advised we think that we can only contemplate another form of loan which must be outside the framework of the purposes of the talks. Alternative B represents this loan.

13. Out of the credit in Alternative B we should discharge the $500 million for Lend–Lease and prepare a programme of United States dollar purchases in 1946 of the order of $1 billion. In the circumstances which have compelled us to adopt Alternative B, we might expect that Parliament would press for postponement of adherence to the Final Act[8] until at least the end of 1946. Further, our difficulties with Parliament and the Empire would increase to a point at which further progress on commercial policy might well prove impossible in the immediate future.[9] We should of course have to retain discrimination against United States exports, though it would continue to be our policy, as it always has been, to ease discrimination in the Sterling Area as much as our Dollar position permits. We cannot yet see the form which our negotiations with the Sterling creditors would take. They would probably be on the lines originally discussed with Keynes, that is a continuance broadly of the present position, but allowing countries to spend their current Dollar earnings. Further freeing of the Sterling Balances would depend upon our general position. We would also try to meet Canada's position as best we could. We do not under-estimate all these difficulties, especially the awkward period in the early part of 1946 before the increased flow of our exports has consolidated confidence in Sterling. But as regards our general position in the Sterling Area see BABOON 150.[10]

14. We leave to you the decision on the tactics of presenting these alternatives to the Americans, provided that they realise that there are only two kinds of settlement open which we would take.

15. We do not ask you to approach the Administration on these two telegrams without further comment to us if you wish to make it.[11]

---

[8] i.e. of the Bretton Woods Conference: see No. 1, note 7.

[9] Cf. No. 70. NABOB 225 of 27 October stated with regard to the commercial policy negotiations that in response to an American request 'that if the project for multiple international action on trade barriers should fail . . . we should not exclude the possibility of bilateral discussion with the U.S. . . . we replied that, while we were not authorised to give a formal answer, we thought that it would be possible provided it was understood that on our side the whole circle of Empire countries would participate. We added that in the event of the negotiations being narrowed in this way, the scope of possible concessions on our side would be reduced also' (UE 5144/1094/53). [10] No. 75.ii.

[11] On Lord Keynes' immediate reactions to Nos. 81 and 82 see Pressnell, op. cit., Chapter 10(14).

No. 83

Cabinet Offices to British Missions (Washington)

BABOON 157 Telegraphic [UE 5066/1094/53]

Most immediate   CABINET OFFICES, *27 October 1945, 11.57 p.m.*

For Liesching from President of the Board of Trade.

This telegram gives my appreciation of the preference position as we see it in London.[1] After you have considered it with others in Washington I look forward to a discussion with Robbins as contemplated in the private telegram[2] sent to you yesterday.

2. The development of this question since your arrival in Washington has been that after very gloomy meetings early in October at which Clayton and Vinson took up a determined stand on a doctrinal handling of the matter, you later saw a possibility of moving them to a position at which the parallel approach to tariffs on the one hand and preferences on the other as set out in Article VII,[3] came within sight. NABOB 133[4] contained your draft of a passage for inclusion in the American document.[5] Ministers supported this formula (subject to one or two minor amendments of no great importance in this context) as offering a solution acceptable both to Parliament and, in their view, to the Dominions. A circular telegram was accordingly sent to the Dominions[6] based on NABOB 133 and you were authorised[7] to try to elicit from the Americans a solution based on your proposal.

3. When you saw Clayton and Vinson,[8] they were not hopeful, but in the end agreed that officials should try to draft a formula embodying the principles of NABOB 133 which 'might be capable of successful presentation to Parliament and Congress'. In NABOB 186 and 195[i] you reported great progress in getting the Americans at least at the official

---

[1] This telegram was despatched following discussion at the GEN 89 meeting on 26 October (cf. No. 81.ii), which had before it the Board of Trade memorandum at iii below, together with D.O. telegrams Nos. 352 from the Government of Australia (ii), 1357 from the U.K. High Commissioner there (ii) and Mr. Chifley's unnumbered personal telegram to Mr. Attlee (ii). The memorandum set out the position reached in Anglo-American discussions on Imperial Preference: see No. 70, and i below. Sir S. Cripps stated at this meeting that NABOB 216 (i) revealed 'a substantial difference of opinion' between the United Kingdom and United States on this issue, and he therefore proposed 'to send a telegram to Washington explaining our view of the position, as well as asking for Professor Robbins to return for consultation to see that the views between London and Washington were not too far apart' (UE 5135/1094/53). Mr. Hall-Patch returned to London with Professor Robbins: cf. further No. 125, para. 6.

[2] Not traced in F.O. archives.

[3] Of the Mutual Aid Agreement of 1942: see No. 1, note 5.

[4] No. 65.

[5] i.e. the American proposal for an International Trade Organisation: cf. No. 54, notes 1–2 and ii.

[6] See No. 70.iv.   [7] See No. 70.   [8] See No. 70.iii.

level to try their hands at such a draft. In the explanations of this formula which appeared in paragraph 3 of NABOB 186 it appeared that all the points essential both to the U.K. and the Dominions could be held to be covered. It was not however clear that the formula without such explanations would necessarily be read in this way.

4. You then sent us in NABOB 216[i] a number of answers to probable questions about the formula designed for use here and in America which were intended to clarify points of doubt. It is the answers to these questions which makes [sic] us wonder whether the Americans really have moved as far to meet the fundamentals of our own and Dominion position as appeared at first sight.[9]

5. You have seen copies of the replies to D.O. circular telegram 1909 from the Governments of Australia and New Zealand[6] and also that of the Government of India to a similar telegram.[10] BABOON 115[6] indicated that there will be little difficulty to be expected from Canada. This week Hofmeyr[11] has told the Dominions Secretary that he thought South Africa would be content on the basis of NABOB 133 though in a conversation which I had with him he was less definite and was obviously seeking to establish that in the first round there could be no question of abolishing preferences of key importance to South Africa, e.g. citrus fruits.

6. The Prime Minister has also heard personally from the Prime Minister of Australia [ii] to the effect that while they are fully prepared to join in commercial policy negotiations on a reciprocal basis he sees difficulty in obtaining from the U.S. the concessions which would make it possible for Australia to play. In these circumstances Chiffley [Chifley] feels that he is unwilling to commit himself at this stage on the question of preferences especially as Australia has not been represented in the conversations. It should be noted that all these Empire reactions are on the basis of NABOB 133.

7. I feel that great as your success has been in bringing the Americans to realise that tariffs and preferences must now be dealt with together on a selective and mutually acceptable basis they remain unwilling to face the consequences. They still propose notwithstanding their own attitude in the case of the Philippines to hold out to Congress the hope that the

[9] In Washington telegram No. 7117 of 25 October Mr. Hall-Patch stated that Mr. Bevin had told him that 'we should be guided generally on tariffs and preferences by his speech at Blackpool [cf. No. 1, note 12]. The proposals in NABOB 186 [i] as elaborated in NABOB 216 [i] have only been obtained by very hard bargaining with the Blackpool speech well in mind the whole time . . . I do not think we can hope to obtain better results unless we are prepared to face a breakdown. I am surprised we have been able to get so far with the administration and the present proposals may meet stiff opposition in congress' (UE 5069/1094/53).

[10] BABOON 122 of 16 October had informed the British Mission in Washington that the Indian Government accepted the proposals on Imperial Preference as set out in D.O. telegram No. 1909 (No. 70.iv), subject to 'outcome of talks as a whole being generally satisfactory' (T 236/466).

[11] South African Minister of Finance and Education.

preferential system can be eliminated as a result of the forthcoming negotiations and are unwilling to admit that the complete fulfilment of their desires is an ultimate goal which can at best be reached by stages. (In saying 'by stages' I mean after a period which on any present and realistic estimation of possibilities of action both by other countries and by the Dominions certainly could not be two or three years). You have often reminded the Americans of the actual wording of Article VII and of the fact that the whole article must be read together. At your second meeting with Clayton you made great play with the American Ambassador's explanatory message in 1942,[12] and it is the American attempt to cloak under words capable of a double interpretation the necessity for an approach by stages which gives rise to my particular apprehension. In the light of these considerations Ministers found a striking contrast between NABOB 133 and NABOB 216.

8. There are in fact two fundamental matters which seem to stand out:

(i) Do the Americans realise that their present powers are insufficient to obtain general abolition of preferences (even if they were prepared to use them to the full)?

(ii) Do they realise that even if their present powers were sufficient and they were prepared to use them to the full it would be impossible for the Empire as a whole to contemplate anything but a gradual abolition of the preferential system?

Question (ii) divides into two parts. United Kingdom's position as a trader with all nations would enable us to go very far in giving up preferences which we enjoy in other markets in return for really adequate counter concessions in foreign markets generally. The Dominions could not within the limits of what at present foreign countries could offer in return, go as far in giving up their preferences in our market, since they so largely depend upon it and in some respects have moulded their economies accordingly.

9. In Parliament I believe that we could secure approval for a readiness to contemplate the substantial elimination of the preferences we (United Kingdom) enjoy provided we got in return conditions in foreign countries which would enable us to export to the full. Apart altogether from reasons of sentiment, there are strong reasons of commonwealth policy which would prevent, in my judgement, the acceptance here of a policy which might leave Empire producers open to the full blast of foreign competition before they could reasonably be expected to face it. Some preferences which the Empire enjoys here no doubt could be abolished and many others reduced but Parliament would not be satisfied unless it were clear that the formula on which we are proceeding was not to be understood in a sense that might jeopardise the basis on which Dominions were to go into the March conference. If that were not clear we should

[12] See *F.R.U.S. 1942*, vol. i, pp. 525–37, and cf. Pressnell, *op. cit.*, Chapter 3(5).

inevitably be accused of selling them out in order to obtain financial assistance.

10. Thus it is most material to ascertain the extent to which Dominion Governments would be prepared, *before* we give the Americans a general presumption of success, to concur in the formula (with explanations) which we put to them. It seems likely that we shall have no difficulty on the basis of the NABOB 133 formula (which is all that has so far been put to them on the preference issue) with Canada and India and that the other Empire countries can be persuaded to play subject to the following:

(*a*) South Africa will want to be assured that certain key preferences are not to be abolished

(*b*) Australia will want to be satisfied that her plans for industrialisation (or full employment) will not be jeopardised and that adequate concessions for her primary producers will be forthcoming in the American market in return for any concessions she makes. There will also be certain key preferences which Australia will wish to have agreed with us in advance, e.g. dried and canned fruit,

(*c*) New Zealand is more interested in our plans for State trading including bulk purchase and long term contracts and her own power to use import quotas though here again the treatment accorded to certain primary products in the American market will have considerable weight,

(*d*) S. Rhodesia has not yet been consulted, but will certainly want to be assured about tobacco,

(*e*) In addition the Colonial Office would no doubt expect to be covered in respect of sugar at least.

11. My conclusion from this appreciation is that our own suggested answers to questions 3 and 4 would not satisfy Dominion opinion and would therefore (as explained in para. 9 above) cause great political difficulty here.

12. (This is by way of parenthesis.) If it becomes necessary to express our support of a general formula almost at once, there will be no opportunity before we do so of agreeing with Empire countries the practical effect of this formula when it comes to actual concessions for individual commodities at the March conference. I understand that when you first saw the American proposals on procedure you gave some preliminary consideration to a proposition that Empire consultations would in any case be necessary in February. On the assumption that after further negotiations with Americans we arrive at the position where we feel that from the purely U.K. point of view we could associate ourselves with the American proposals, we should then still have to carry the Dominions with us, and I feel that at that stage to invite the Dominions to have detailed discussions about possible concessions might go far to allay their fears. What do you think of this, and what do you think American reaction would be if we told them that this was our intention?

13. I hope the above paragraphs will have made clear the reasons why

NABOB 216 has not convinced Ministers of the practicability of American Draft VII[i]. The key point to my mind is that these disclose a real difference of interpretation to that expressed in paragraph 3 of NABOB 186.

14. In the light of the foregoing Ministers feel that it is no use continuing to formulate rules which ingeniously cloak the fundamental differences of outlook. They would further like you to consider whether the best chance of arriving at a satisfactory conclusion that will be stable and will not lead to misunderstandings hereafter, would not be to give the Americans (*after* informing the Dominions) a short statement as set out below. This would show them the absolute maximum to which we are prepared to go towards the elimination of preferences. We do not of course suggest that this should be the form of the agreement but that which should form the foundation so far as we are concerned of any arrangement we arrive at.

15. (Statement begins) It is the objective of the U.K. Government to work out in association with the Government of the U.S.A. the policies of Article VII of the Mutual Aid Agreement. The U.K. Government do not understand this Article as laying down self-executing substantive provisions but as pointing a broad course and committing the two countries to collaborating in making headway along that course. In that collaboration the U.K. Government further understands that both Governments will recognise the governing economic conditions in seeking the best means of making the goal attainable. The governing economic conditions so far as the U.K. is concerned at the present make it impracticable to eliminate preferences and reduce trade barriers otherwise than by gradual stages. Under these circumstances the U.K. Government must make it clear that so far as the elimination of preferences is concerned they could not at the present time undertake to proceed further than is set out below.

(i) They are prepared, with the consent of the Dominions, to enter immediately into a conference at which on the basis of adequate reductions in trade barriers by the other nations, there would be open to negotiation the reduction of any margin of preference and the elimination of some.

(ii) The U.K. Government would agree that the International Trade Organisation, at a date determined by governing economic conditions, should convene a conference to consider whether further tariff reductions could be agreed sufficient to justify further steps towards the elimination of preferences.

(iii) The U.K. Government wish to make it clear that they are prepared to work towards the elimination of preferences by gradual steps. But it would not be possible in their view finally to eliminate all preferences for a number of years to come and until there had been an opportunity for the necessary readjustments of the channels of international trade resulting from such action.

If the Americans accepted this statement of our position we could then proceed to collaborate with them in devising the best form in which to incorporate it in the American proposals for setting up an I.T.O.

(Statement ends)

16. I am most anxious that you should let me have the frankest reaction to the above observations from your knowledge of the attitude of mind of the American negotiators. I rely upon Robbins when he arrives to state fully and frankly your reactions to the arguments and views in this telegram.

CALENDARS TO NO. 83

i *19–25 Oct. 1945   British Missions (Washington) Tels. NABOB 186, 195, 216* Further conversations with State Dept. on Imperial Preference lead to new American 'Draft 7': specimen questions and answers on possible interpretations of draft; Board of Trade comments (*ASKEW Tels. 242 & 243*) [UE 4720, 4958, 5066/1094/53].

ii *23 & 24 Oct. 1945   Reactions of Australian and New Zealand Governments to Imperial Preference proposals* (cf. No. 70.iv and note 1 above), including personal message for Mr. Attlee from Mr. Chifley, who appreciated difficulties of U.K. negotiating position but felt that 'the sterling area should surrender its currency and trade defences only in return for fully equivalent action on the part of the United States' [PREM 8/35, T 236/388, T 230/142].

iii *25 Oct. 1945   GEN 89/6 Memo. by Board of Trade on Commercial Policy* NABOB 216 (see i) shows 'Americans have in mind a bargain which Ministers would probably regard as neither equitable nor acceptable' [UE 5133/1094/53].

iv *28 Oct. 1945   British Missions (Washington) Tel. NABOB 229* Further conversation with American officials who are 'in a state of emotional excitement' after persuading Mr. Clayton and Mr. Vinson to accept Draft 7 (see i): Sir P. Liesching and Professor Robbins expressed 'interest but no corresponding elation' in advance of instructions from London [UE 5147/1094/53].

v *28 & 30 Oct. 1945   British Missions (Washington) Tels. NABOB 231 & 242* Comments by Sir P. Liesching on No. 83 [UE 5148, 5225/1094/53].

No. 84

Minute[1] *by Mr. Butler*

[*AN 3820/3121/45*]

FOREIGN OFFICE, *27 October 1945*

I have not been able to follow closely the course of the Halifax–Keynes talks, but Sir W. Eady told me on Thursday[2] that the outlook was poor. A breakdown now would not necessarily, I suppose, be permanent, but the

---

[1] This minute was addressed to Mr. Ronald and Sir A. Cadogan.
[2] 25 October 1945.

breach might make positions harden, and a settlement later impossible. On the assumption that it would be a real disaster, domestic and international, if we had to fall back on the 'other alternative',[3] I am concerned that we sh[oul]d try to forestall a breach by letting the American negotiators know pretty well for certain that they would be able to tie their proposals up with a 'piece of ribbon' to which Treasury have referred, e.g. something in regard to Bases.[4]

The old war debts controversy was treated, I believe, as a purely financial question. Mr. Ramsay MacDonald on his second visit to Washington telegraphed to London some political or military suggestions in regard to Bases in the Caribbean and these were turned down flat by Mr. Snowden and his colleagues.[5] The issue then moved inexorably to a deadlock that nearly had disastrous results in 1940.[6]

Lord Halifax, Mr. Wright and I have consistently believed that no solution will be possible this time if the issue is treated as a purely financial one, which it is not. Lord Halifax recently urged strongly that he might be allowed to explore the Bases aspect confidentially with Mr. Byrnes. The Secretary of State withheld this authority wishing first to see the full picture of American demands.[7]

This would obviously be right and necessary if it were not for the time factor. It may, however, have led Messrs. Vinson and Clayton to believe that there would be no 'piece of ribbon' to tie. The Secretary of State and Ministers contemplate, I believe, making some concessions in the matter of Bases. It would be most unfortunate if an irreparable breakdown now occurred because the Americans were not aware of this. It would ease my conscience if this point could be considered by those more closely concerned than I with the current negotiations.[8]

N. BUTLER

[3] The reference is uncertain, but may be either to para. III of No. 22, or to 'Alternative B' in No. 81.

[4] See No. 47 and No. 62, para. 18.

[5] In October 1929: cf. *D.B.F.P.*, Second Series, Volume I, No. 77, Section 3 and Appendices 1–12. Mr. P. Snowden was Chancellor of the Exchequer January–November 1924 and 1929–1931.

[6] Cf. No. 71, note 3. [7] See No. 61, note 4.

[8] Sir A. Cadogan minuted on 27 October that he was 'afraid I, too, have been unable to follow the Keynes talks'. Mr. Butler's minute was submitted on 30 October to Mr. Bevin, who commented: 'The difficulty is I cannot get from U.S. what they want. Halifax has been trying. I discussed Bases with Byrnes [see Nos. 48 and 61] & told him my difficulty would be to face it piecemeal. E.B.'

Telegram No. 11120 to Washington of 4 November referred to Washington telegram No. 6912 (see No. 61, note 4) and instructed Lord Halifax that, as the final negotiations for the financial and commercial agreements 'may be conducted at a very brisk pace', he should, 'without connecting the two questions', enquire when the list of bases was likely to be furnished (AN 3122/3121/45). Lord Halifax reported in telegram No. 7392 of 5 November that Mr. Byrnes had told him that morning 'that United States Staffs had now completed list and that he would let me have it at once . . . He begged us to exercise particular caution about avoiding any leakage on this matter for fear of obvious repercussions on Russians' (AN 3405/3121/45).

No. 85

British Missions (Washington) to Cabinet Offices
(Received 29 October, 2.30 a.m.)

NABOB 230 Telegraphic [UE 5169/1094/53]

Most immediate. Secret   WASHINGTON, 28 October 1945, 10.55 p.m.

Personal for Chancellor of Exchequer from Ambassador and Keynes. BABOON 155.[1]

1. We are not sure how far the policy of this telegram is governed by the belief that Alternative B will be available if Alternative A fails. If so the realities of the position here are fatally misunderstood in London. All of us are convinced that this alternative has to be ruled out altogether as being quite beyond any practical possibility. The administration have no powers for Lend-Lease finance outside 3C or for other aid outside the Export Import Bank. The minimum Export Import Bank terms are 3 percent and repayment over twenty years starting next year so that the annual service begins at 8 percent. 3C terms are, as you know, slightly better, namely $2\frac{3}{8}$ percent interest and repayment over thirty years also starting next year, so that the annual service begins at 5.67 percent. If we were pursuing our independent course regardless of American feelings there would be no prospect of the administration obtaining from Congress special and more liberal terms for us outside the above.

2. It follows that a credit of $2\frac{1}{2}$ billions on commercial terms and lend–lease finance of $\frac{1}{2}$ billion would cost us an annual service of \$228 million commencing next year. Apart from its prohibitive cost to us $2\frac{1}{2}$ billion would be much beyond the resources of the Export Import Bank having regard to their other actual and prospective commitments. We should be lucky if we got $\frac{1}{2}$ billion with the possibility of another $\frac{1}{2}$ billion later on, in addition to the 3C loan for lend–lease. Thus at the best we should obtain aid by instalments on cat and mouse lines.

3. So much is certain. The above is the best that could happen if our American friends in spite of their disappointment were to try to do their best for us within the limitations of their power. But we are not confident that you can rely on any significant financial assistance on the basis of our standing aside from currency and commercial policy commitments as alternative B contemplates. If we follow this line we must expect a dangerous hardening of opinion in all quarters here. In American eyes we should appear to be deliberately preferring the policy of separate economic blocs. Their first reaction might be just to sit back, content to allow the financial pressure against us to develop under its own steam.

4. Turning to alternative A we see the advantages from your point of view if American aid could be dressed up in this form and we are ready to advocate it to the best of our ability. It might serve as you say to bring

[1] No. 81.

matters to a head. We shall therefore present it to Vinson and Clayton tomorrow, Monday. Unless you telephone otherwise to Lee at Executive 2020 extension 36 between 9 and 10 a.m. Washington time or Morrison[2] sends Stevens a Most Immediate to arrive by 10 a.m. After all we have not yet had any definite proposal from them since the inacceptable scheme reported to you in paragraph 3 of NABOB 191.[3] When therefore we have offered them your counter-proposal, the ball will again lie in their court.

5. At the same time [? in view of] our judgement in paragraphs 1–3 above that alternative B does not in fact exist to fall back upon, we think you should be considering what we do next, if we fail to obtain any response from the Americans along the lines of alternative A. Perhaps however we had better await the reactions of Vinson and Clayton to your proposals before sending you our considered thoughts on this.

6. Running through BABOON 156[4] is the idea that we cannot safely accept even reasonable proposals from Vinson and Clayton because we cannot be sure that Congress will not alter the details to our disadvantage. To act on this would obviously knock the bottom out of any negotiations and lead to the rejection even of a proposal not inacceptable on its merits. Nevertheless the fact that the American administration cannot commit Congress is always in our minds. We think the way to guard against this danger is to make it an absolute condition of our proposals that the final scheme agreed with the administration must be put up to Congress in a form in which it has to be accepted or rejected en bloc and cannot be amended. We believe that there are ways of doing this. We will take up this issue when we next see Vinson and Clayton. We think it unlikely that Congress will in fact throw out in its entirety a comprehensive plan for an Anglo-American economic concordat which the administration presents. But if they do worse things could happen. Our resulting position, having accepted a plan which the American administration had themselves judged fair and reasonable, would be immensely stronger in the eyes of everyone than if we had rejected what would be regarded here as a fair and very liberal arrangement, far better than anyone else is to get. Everyone in America and most people elsewhere would conclude that we thought this a suitable moment to choose, in spite of all the perils of the world, to consolidate an economic bloc from which America would be excluded. No one would believe that our scruples about a waiver clause which on the face of it was greatly to our advantage and was as water-tight as we ourselves were able to make it, could be the real reason.

7. It is important that you should not forget the time table. We believe that it is the resolute intention of Clayton and Vinson, provided we reach agreement in the very near future, to make every possible effort to put the settlement through Congress before Congress adjourns in early December. We will take the opportunity of our next meeting with them to elicit

[2] Mr. R. Morrison was a Principal on the Civil Staff of the Cabinet Office.
[3] No. 78.   [4] No. 82.

their plans more definitely. One cannot be sure that they will succeed. But Congress has a way of acting either suddenly or not at all. If we can secure that the plan cannot be amended, there will be less room for protracted debate in committee. Anyhow, if there is a chance that the administration can pull off quick action, it would be an immense advantage to you to know before the end of the year just where you stand. Much further delay on our part will inevitably mean that you will know nothing for certain before well into the new year. At the moment the administration has a strong motive for early action, since this will fit in with the Bretton Woods time table and will allow the State Department to get on with their commercial policy programme before next autumn's elections are in sight. A postponement until next year having made this impossible their whole time table may suffer some considerable retardation. The effect of prolonged uncertainty on the planning of the Ministry of Food and many other departments, including the Treasury, not least, must be serious.[5]

8. This telegram has been prepared in consultation with Brand, Self, Liesching, Robbins, Hall Patch and the other members of the mission and represents our collective opinion.

CALENDAR TO NO. 85

i *26 Oct. & 2 Nov. 1945 British Missions (Washington) Tel. SEVER 1588* U.S. press treatment of present stage of Anglo–U.S. negotiations: *Earl of Halifax (Washington) Tel. No. 532 Saving, economic summary for week ending 27 Oct.* (Extract) Americans 'continue to work the technique of the calculated press "leak" as an instrument of policy' [CAB 122/1471, UE 5301/42/53].

[5] See further Lord Keynes' letter of 28 October to Mr. Dalton, printed with comments in Hugh Dalton, *High Tide and After*, pp. 76–8.

No. 86

Cabinet Offices to British Missions (Washington)

BABOON 158 *Telegraphic* [*UE 5202/1094/53*]

Most immediate. Secret   CABINET OFFICES, 29 *October 1945, 11.5 a.m.*

Personal from Chancellor of the Exchequer for Ambassador and Keynes.

NABOB 230.[1] Try Alternative A for all you are worth. For a quick firm deal on it I should be prepared to accept a recommendation from you for 2 per cent interest on the 2½ billion dollars for ourselves provided that the 2 billion dollars for the Sterling Area is interest free.[2]

[1] No. 85.
[2] The wording of this paragraph was suggested to Mr. Dalton on 27 October by Sir W. Eady, who then sent the draft for the Prime Minister's early concurrence. Mr. Rowan

2. We reserve further comments on NABOB 230 until hearing from you. You will no doubt ensure that Vinson and Clayton do not treat Alternative A as a first bid from us which they can put on one side and then turn back to their own ideas. Also please guard position of Sterling Area negotiations.[3]

minuted the same day to Mr. Attlee that he assumed that the draft was in accordance with decisions at the meeting in No. 81.ii. Mr. Attlee minuted: 'Agreed. C.R.A. 27.10.45' (PREM 8/35).
[3] Cf. No. 78, note 3.

No. 87

British Missions (Washington) to Cabinet Offices
(Received 30 October, 3.20 a.m.)

NABOB 232 Telegraphic [UE 5202/1094/53]

Most immediate. Secret   WASHINGTON, 29 October 1945, 11.51 p.m.

Personal for Chancellor of Exchequer from Ambassador and Keynes.

1. Paragraph 1 of BABOON 158[1] should help us considerably in our task of urging this plan on the Americans. Nevertheless we have thought it wise to put off seeing them until we had cleared up with you the matters set out in the following paragraphs where we have felt some doubt about your exact intention.

2. Does 2½ billion dollars in paragraph 2A of BABOON 155[2] include the cost of lend–lease clean-up reckoned at a provisional figure of ½ billion? If so, perhaps the proposition is better expressed as 2 billion dollars plus lend–lease.

3. We should like to be sure that we understand correctly the second sentence of paragraph 2 of BABOON 158. We shall assume this to mean that we are not free to discuss any plan except on the general lines of alternative A. We cannot of course dictate to the Americans what they say in reply or prevent them from making a counter-proposal for report to you.

4. We are not clear what is particularly in view in the last sentence of paragraph 2 of BABOON 158 relating to sterling area arrangements. The plan we outlined to the Americans some weeks ago[3] still holds the field and we have not recently discussed it with them or added anything to it. See our next following telegram[4] for our appreciation of the present position.

5. Alternative A of BABOON 155 as modified by paragraph 1 of BABOON 158 comes fairly near the first American proposal[5] in terms of financial burden and chiefly differs from it in form. We shall call attention

[1] No. 86.   [2] No. 81.
[3] See No. 78.ii, and cf. No. 88, para. 1.   [4] No. 88.
[5] See No. 67.

to this and emphasise it in our presentation of alternative A. But we think that the considerations in the following paragraphs deserve your further consideration before we put your terms to the Americans.

6. The Americans originally offered us 5 billion for an annuity of 159 million[6] for 50 years beginning 5 years hence. It follows that 4½ billion on the same terms would cost 143 million. We calculate that the offer you now authorise us to make would cost a similar annuity of 120 million, so that the concession you are asking from them is not very large. The American offer was on the basis of a waiver clause based on an objective criterion of our capacity, which would reduce our unqualified commitment to 53 million or thereabouts in the early years. Your present offer though subject to a waiver based on their willingness to receive payment, will have no waiver based on our capacity to pay. Thus by foregoing this latter waiver we should be taking on an unqualified commitment which might be more than double what is necessary. For the reasons given in the next paragraphs, a waiver of the kind which the Americans offer to us is surely not so objectionable that we should refuse it as a free option if we can get it. We need never avail ourselves of it in a marginal case if we prefer not to do so. We cannot lose by having a possible safeguard against unforeseen difficulties.

7. We do not find the arguments against a waiver in paragraph 5 of BABOON 156[7] conclusive or even very convincing, though, as you know, we are no friends to waivers. We rule out the objection based on a possible alteration of the formula by Congress, because, whether there is a waiver or not, it seems to us essential, as explained in paragraph 6 of NABOB 230,[8] to secure that Congress is not free to amend the agreed arrangements in detail. If the interpretation of the agreed formula is left, as is proposed, to the International Monetary Fund, there can be no excuse for a subsequent dispute or for any responsible American attempt to exercise surveillance over our affairs. If the shortfall in our exports was small we need not use the waiver if we feel able to pay. We think it most unlikely that when the time comes the administration or Congress will want to quarrel with our using the waiver. For if the occasion arises they will be searching round for plausible reasons for escape from a difficult and embarrassing position. In fact the administration prefer a waiver precisely because they are so anxious to avoid the possibility of what might become a default. For this would involve grave embarrassment to both sides as on the previous occasion. They wish, therefore, to have arrangements provided beforehand so that such a situation cannot arise. Indeed we might be able to get them to agree to a deferment of the capital instalment in the same conditions as apply to the waiver of the interest.

8. Anyhow do not all your arguments apply with equal force to the much vaguer waiver on the lines of paragraph 5 of NABOB 200[9] the retention of which is proposed in paragraph 2(F) of BABOON 155. Let us

[6] Cf. No. 78, para. 11.   [7] No. 82.
[8] No. 85.   [9] No. 80.

call this for short the London waiver and that discussed in paragraph 7 above the Washington waiver.

9. We feel therefore very strongly that the introduction into your alternative A of a Washington waiver cannot do us any harm and might conceivably prove to be a safeguard we shall be very glad to have some time in the precarious future. As mentioned in paragraph 7 above, we think it would be worth while, and very much worth having, to try to improve the Washington waiver by making it apply to the deferment of capital as well as to the waiver of interest. A commitment costing 120 million, qualified by a free option to us to fall back on such a waiver in difficult circumstances, seems to us to be immensely more attractive than an unqualified commitment of 120 million.

10. We think that your alternative A thus protected has great attractions and we would try very hard to get the Americans to accept the way you have dressed it up. We hope you will agree to our proceeding on the above lines.

11. We should like to have your authority to proceed at the earliest possible date. When we mentioned to Clayton this morning that we were not yet ready for another meeting with him and Vinson he made no difficulties about a little further delay but called our attention to the time table as he sees it. He thinks that Congress will not adjourn till December 10th or 15th. It is the intention of the administration to take the agreement, if we can reach one, straight to Congress. Clayton said that he regarded the present time as more propitious than any later date was likely to be and left us with the impression that the President, Vinson and he will be able to carry through whatever may be agreed. He warned us, however, that Congress must be allowed about a month for the necessary stages. He therefore regarded November 10th as the dead line for the conclusion of our present talks. Thus it is important to move matters on with as little delay as possible.[10]

---

[10] In NABOB 235 to Sir W. Eady of 30 October Mr. Brand referred to the war debt controversy after the First World War (cf. No. 71, note 3) and expressed strong support for the views in No. 87: 'I cannot believe any trouble arising out of a waiver could possibly equal that which would be caused by another default, if we were ever forced to it . . . From point of view of pride I see no difference between asking for grant-in-aid or interest free loan and accepting waiver. Americans feel obliged to ask for interest, but their readiness to consider waiver is genuine and sincere attempt on their part to meet our views of what is just and fair. It seems to me that this is most reasonable way open for both parties of reconciling very different national sentiments and of securing in early period of loan after five years grace that British people are not too hardly pressed.' Sir W. Eady replied in BABOON 170 of 1 November that he was grateful for Mr. Brand's telegram: 'It is not any feelings of pride that are influencing us on waiver clause. Arguments in paragraph 5 of BABOON 156 [No. 82] are strongly held both in high and middle circles here' (UE 5224/1094/53).

In the Foreign Office Mr. Coulson commented on 2 November with reference to NABOB 235: 'It seems a pity to omit the waiver which might be a very valuable safeguard and which there is no need to avail ourselves of unless we wish. At the tactical stage in the negotiations when the last instructions were sent off [see Nos. 81–3], the advantages in standing firm were very strong. We always knew that the point would come where we had to have a showdown and it was most undesirable to run away at that point. We have yet to know what result this will have on the Americans. If, however, they are still not prepared to give us anything like the terms we need, then I submit that we would be well advised to reconsider the waiver.' Mr. Hall-Patch noted on 3 November that he had discussed this question with Mr. Bevin who 'does not like waivers in principle. Nevertheless if they were necessary in order to enable us to obtain the financial assistance we need he would be prepared to accept them on the distinct understanding that they were drawn in such a manner that they do not admit of any prying into our affairs, or interference with our domestic policy. Moreover if we reached agreement in a text with the American Administration arrangements would have to be made that Congress would not be able to modify them to our disadvantage subsequently' (UE 5224/1094/53).

No. 88

British Missions (Washington) to Cabinet Offices
(Received 30 October, 3.50 a.m.)

NABOB 233 Telegraphic [UE 5202/1094/53]

Most immediate. Secret   WASHINGTON, 29 October 1945, 11.53 p.m.

For Chancellor of Exchequer from Keynes.
Sterling area arrangements.
1. My immediately preceding telegram.[1] Paragraphs 7 to 9 of BABOON 156[2] may have been drafted before there had been time for consideration of my NABOBs 214 and 215.[3] Since these NABOBs follow the version which has been presented to the Americans, it would be convenient if you would take these as the basis of your comment.
2. Two separate points arise. The first relates to the extent of our commitment to secure a writing down of the sterling area balances by a specific amount such as 4 billions. Early in our discussions I mentioned this amount on the lines which you authorised before I left London.[4] The Americans, as you know, have been inclined to argue that it was not enough, but they have not pressed this lately and there has been no further discussion of the matter for some time.
3. When we give them our proposals in writing on the lines of NABOB 215 they may press for something more specific. I was, however careful about this in my original exposition and spoke of the 4 billion as a target rather than a commitment. We have emphasised repeatedly that the arrangements we contemplate with the sterling area are agreed arrangements and not a unilateral imposition of a cut-and-dried settlement. I pointed out over and over again the political difficulties with which we should be faced. Obviously, therefore, we have to provide for the possibility that some sterling area countries will prefer to stand out. What the Americans require, and all that they are entitled to require, is that the accumulated sterling balances of countries standing out of the arrange-

[1] No. 87.   [2] No. 82.
[3] No. 78.ii.   [4] See Nos. 17, 22, 39 and 41.

ments should not benefit from the finance the Americans are putting up.

4. Take India for example. We are not committed to insist on India's acceptance of cancellation. If India prefers to stand out, she would be free hereafter to use at her discretion for current transactions her post-war earnings of sterling and other currencies but her war-time accumulations would only be repaid and become available to her out of any surplus we might be prepared to release to her *after* we had met our obligations to the U.S. and to sterling area countries entering the general scheme.

5. The second point relates to the nature of the future arrangements in the liberalised sterling area. About this there can have been no misunderstanding in the minds of the Americans. My instructions on this aspect had been carefully drafted and approved before I left London and I followed them very closely, as you will have found from the agreed minutes of my discourse[5] which have been in your hands for some time. I have not modified or added to the original outline in the meanwhile.

6. Paragraph 9 of BABOON 156 is too much compressed to be entirely clear but we are assuming that it does not differ materially from what was previously contemplated by you and spelled out at greater length in NABOB 215. On this we are certainly committed up to the hilt and it would be impossible to make any material change now. The Americans were well satisfied with the proposals I had been authorised to make and their satisfaction about this has of course played an essential part in getting them to go along with us to the extent they have. Without this we should have got nowhere.

7. I should therefore be grateful for your comments on NABOB 215 since time now presses for us to give the Americans something in writing along these lines.[6]

CALENDAR TO No. 88

i *30 Oct. & 4 Nov. 1945* (a) *GEN 89/8 Memo. by Secretary of State for India* emphasises 'extreme difficulty' of reaching agreement with India on scaling down sterling credit (b) *GEN 89/9 Memo. by Secretary of State for Colonies* significant scaling down of sterling balances would be 'quite inconsistent' with H.M.G.'s general policy towards colonial Empire [UE 5258, 5348/1094/53].

---

[5] See No. 29, note 4.

[6] In NABOB 236 of 30 October Lord Keynes informed Sir W. Eady that Mr. Harry White 'rang up this morning pressing me to let him have a draft in writing giving precision to the proposed modifications of Sterling Area arrangements which I outlined to the committee on September 20th [see No. 39]. He wanted to be sure there was no misunderstanding and also indicated that his side might have some further points to suggest . . . This reinforces the urgency to which I called attention in paragraph 7 of NABOB 233 . . .' (UE 5075/1094/53).

No. 89

Mr. Bevin to Sir D. Kelly (Buenos Aires)

No. 558 Telegraphic [AS 5636/189/2]

Immediate   FOREIGN OFFICE, 30 October 1945, 11.10 p.m.

My immediately preceding telegram.[1]

His Majesty's Government in the United Kingdom have recently reviewed the general position in regard to world wheat supplies and requirements for the year from 1st July, 1945 to 30th June 1946, in the light of the Memorandum submitted by the Minister of Food. The principal features of the Memorandum, together with certain recommendations adopted by His Majesty's Government to mitigate the serious prospective position disclosed, are contained in subsequent paragraphs of the present Memorandum.

2. *Supplies*

(a) For practical purposes, Canada, the United States, Australia and Argentina can be regarded as the sole sources of supply of export wheat during the period under review. At the time the Minister of Food's Memorandum was submitted, the estimates then available of production and usage in the four main exporting countries indicated that after setting aside the quantities which these countries might wish to hold as 'carryover' at 30th June, 1946, the total quantity of wheat which would be available for export from these four countries (including wheat required for export flour) during the period under review would be[2]

Million long tons

19.68

(b) If, however, the four countries agree to reduce their 'carryovers' at 30th June, 1946 to levels consistent with the minimum end of season 'carryovers' provided for in the International Wheat Agreement,[3] the total quantity which could be made available for export would be increased to

25.63

---

[1] This telegram of 30 October informed Sir D. Kelly that telegram No. 558 contained the text of a Ministry of Food memorandum on the world wheat situation, communicated to the Foreign Office on 22 October. Para. 6 of the memorandum embodied recommendations adopted by Ministers at the 37th meeting of the Lord President's Committee on 12 October, following their consideration of a memorandum of 1 October by the Minister of Food, Sir Ben Smith, on World Wheat Supplies and requirements for the year 1 July 1945 to 30 June 1946 (L.P. (45) 181), not printed.

The Committee also considered a further memorandum of 1 October by the Minister of Food on the World Food Outlook (L.P. (45) 182), reproduced at i below.

[2] A note on the file by Mr. C.T. Crowe of Supply and Relief Department stated that the figures in the Ministry of Food memorandum communicated on 22 October (see note 1) were an amended version of those in L.P. (45) 181 on the basis of later information.

[3] See No. 10, note 5.

(c) It should, however, be noted that crop estimates published since the submission of the Minister of Food's Memorandum have the effect of reducing the assumed export availability of 25.63 million tons at (b) above to   24.16

3. *Requirements*

(a) The total requirements which have been notified by importing countries before the Minister of Food's Memorandum was prepared amounted to   28.15
(of which 5,773,000 would be needed for flour exports)

(b) A careful review of the importing countries claims in relation to their earlier demands and the known facts indicated that certain cuts could possibly be made while still ensuring rough justice as between one country and another and providing imports sufficient with proper use of indigenous supplies to maintain a reasonable standard of nutrition. These cuts, if applied would reduce the total requirements including reasonably adequate provision for Germany[4] and a general contingency reserve of one million tons to   26.03

(c) But since the submission of the Minister of Food's Memorandum certain importing countries have indicated the need for increasing their requirements by over 1½ million tons which, if added to the total at (b) above would make a revised total requirement of   27.05 [*sic*]

4. *Supplies/Requirements Reconciliation*
It will be seen that the revised total requirements figure shown in paragraph 3 (c) above at 27.5 million tons is 7.8 million tons in excess of the available supply calculated as in paragraph 2 (a) at 19.68 million tons and 3.3 million tons in excess of the total availability calculated as in paragraph 2 (c) at 24.16 million tons.

5. It is therefore apparent that even if the four main exporting

---

[4] In L.P. (45) 181 the Minister of Food had stated that the best available estimate of the amount of imported bread grain required for the Western zones of Germany for the year ending 31 August 1946 was '3,110,000 tons on the basis of 1,550 calories daily for normal "non-self-suppliers" and that the amount needed up to the end of June 1946 might be assumed to be 2,600,000 tons'. He added that the 'Allied Control Commission are satisfied that a very substantial import of wheat into Germany is essential if severe malnutrition and possibly starvation are to be averted. Failure to meet this need would result in civil disorder and serious loss of productive effort at a time when it is urgently needed' (UR 3654/1592/851). Cf. No. 76, note 9.

countries are prepared to run down their stocks at the end of June 1946 to levels consistent with the minima set out in the International Wheat Agreement, there would still be a deficit of over 3 million tons if the requirements of importing countries are to be met in full even on the reduced basis indicated at paragraph 3 (c) [3(b)]. This deficit could be met if the four main exporting countries would arrange to restrict their usage of wheat for animal feeding. If this were possible administratively the effect on livestock production should be insignificant.

6. *Recommendations*

His Majesty's Government in the United Kingdom have agreed to adopt the following Recommendations made by the Minister of Food:

(1) that the United Kingdom Member of the Combined Food Board should be instructed to submit to his United States and Canadian colleagues on the Board the appreciation of the world wheat position as set out in this paper and to press for acceptance and application by their Governments of the following principles:

(a) to set aside at the 30th June, 1946, no more wheat than is consistent with the minimum end of season carryover set out in the International Wheat Agreement;

(b) To restrict the use of wheat for animal feeding to the extent necessary to meet essential world requirements for direct human consumption;

(c) to grant the necessary facilities to secure, as a matter of the utmost urgency, the maximum movement of wheat to seaboard;

(d) to enter into no commitments with importing countries independ[en]tly of the Combined Food Board;

(2) that the Governments of Australia and the Argentine[5] should be approached through the appropriate channels and also requested to accept and apply the principles set out in Recommendation 1.

CALENDARS TO NO. 89

i *1 & 11 Oct. 1945   L.P. (45) 182 Memo. by Minister of Food on World Food Outlook* includes recommendation that U.K. food requirements from North America

---

[5] In his telegram No. 801 of 31 October Sir D. Kelly reported that on the previous day the Argentine Minister for Foreign Affairs had referred to a passage in Mr. Bevin's speech in the House of Commons on 26 October (*Parl. Debs.*, 5th ser., H. of C., vol. 414, col. 2379) concerning the political difficulties of supplying fuel to Argentina to enable the release of maize stocks: cf. No. 14.v and No. 66. The Foreign Minister had said that 'Argentina was of course most anxious to help in supply of foodstuffs to Europe but was greatly hampered by shortage of fuel and motor tyres', and Sir D. Kelly warned that 'Minister for Foreign Affairs may be expected to revert to this point when I speak as instructed' (AS 5833/189/2). In his telegram No. 807 of 2 November he reported that when he had presented that morning a 'complete memorandum' laying 'full emphasis on paragraph 2' above, 'Minister for Foreign Affairs, after general assurance of utmost goodwill to cooperate, reverted to the internal transport situation and stated that Argentina was unable at present to fulfil obligations already contracted to Brazil, Spain, France and Italy' (AS 5834/189/2).

should not be reduced: *Minute from Sir W. Eady to Mr. Trend* explains this is unacceptable to Chancellor and encloses note on 'Switches away from U.S.A. for Food' [UR 3650/1592/851, T 236/438].

ii *22 Oct. 1945   C.P. (45) 237 Memo. by Minister of Food on Food for Europe* with comments by Mr. Ronald favouring discussions with sponsors of 'Save Europe Now' campaign [UR 4076/1617/851].

No. 90

Memorandum by Mr. Bevin on United States request for bases in Iceland

C.P. (45) 261 [N 15020/1004/27]

Secret   FOREIGN OFFICE, *30 October 1945*

I circulate to my colleagues the annexed memorandum, prepared in the Foreign Office, outlining the developments that have taken place since the United States Government informed us of their intention to secure a long-term lease of bases in Iceland.

2. It will be seen that the United States Government have decided not to adopt the alternative proposal, which I put to Mr. Byrnes, that they might ask the Icelandic Government for a lease of the bases in question for a limited period, as a temporary measure pending the coming into force of the security provisions of the United Nations Charter (particularly Article 43) and the admission of Iceland to the United Nations Organisation.[1] (Under Article 43 agreements for base facilities are to be negotiated on the initiative of the Security Council and between the Security Council and Members or groups of Members: there is no provision for such negotiations to take place between one nation and another.)

3. As the Icelandic Prime Minister[2] has formally asked for an expression of our views before deciding how to respond to the United States proposal, I have authorised His Majesty's Minister at Reykjavik[3] to speak to him on the following lines:

'This war has shown that the presence of United States forces in the North Atlantic area is essential for the security of that area. We therefore welcome the proposal that United States forces should continue to occupy bases in Iceland. We naturally assume such occupation will be brought in due course under the international security system provided in the United Nations Charter. In the meantime it would seem natural for an arrangement to be made direct between the Icelandic and United States Governments.'

4. I would propose that we should reconsider our attitude in the event of the Russians taking up an openly hostile attitude to the United States initiative or demanding as a counter-move a long-term lease of bases in

---

[1] See Annex to No. 48.   [2] M. Olafur Thors.   [3] Mr. G. Shepherd.

Denmark or Northern Norway. In such circumstances it might be desirable for His Majesty's Government to come forward as a mediator with the proposal that the Americans should have a short-term lease of bases in Iceland. We could then presumably encourage Denmark and Norway, both of whom are members of the United Nations Organisation, to invoke the Security Council's procedure in respect of any Russian demands and to refuse to negotiate bilaterally. The Norwegian Minister for Foreign Affairs[4] has already expressed the fear that the American demands on Iceland may lead to similar Russian demands in connexion with Spitzbergen, about which they had already made approaches to the Norwegian Government a year ago.[5] I have accordingly authorised His Majesty's Ambassador at Oslo[6] to draw M. Lie's attention to the Security Council procedure as laid down in Article 43 of the United Nations Charter. I am also authorising His Majesty's Minister at Copenhagen[7] to take similar action with the Danish Foreign Minister.[8]

5. My reasons for adopting this policy are as follows:

The choice before us was whether to back the Americans in their policy of trying to secure their position now by bilateral arrangements with the Icelandic Government or to insist on the point of view which I had put to Mr. Byrnes. On the one hand the Chiefs of Staff and the Foreign Office agree that the vital interests of the United Kingdom would be served by the retention of United States forces in permanent bases in Iceland. On the other hand, it is a main objective of His Majesty's Government to make a success of the United Nations Organisation. The United States action may, by antagonising the Russians and minimising the rôle of the Security Council, destroy the whole United Nations Organisation system of security before it has been given a chance. The decisive factor, however, seemed to be that the Americans are now committed to their scheme and have refused to accept my alternative suggestion of a short-term lease pending the setting up of the Security Council and the admission of Iceland to the United Nations Organisation.[9]

E.B.

ANNEX TO No. 90

On the 24th September the United States Government informed us officially of their intention to ask the Icelandic Government for a long-term lease of naval and air bases in Iceland. On the next day the United States Chargé d'Affaires in Moscow so informed the Soviet Government.

2. On the 28th September, the Secretary of State wrote to Mr. Byrnes

[4] M. Trygve Lie.   [5] See Volume I, Nos. 162 and 299.
[6] Sir L. Collier.   [7] Mr. A.W.G. Randall.   [8] M. Christmas Möller.
[9] The Cabinet endorsed Mr. Bevin's proposals, as set out in para. 4 above, at their meeting on 1 November (C.M. (45) 48th Conclusions).

suggesting that an American demand for a long-term lease would amount to a vote of no confidence in the United Nations Organisation and that the United States Government might instead ask the Icelandic Government for a lease of the bases in question for a limited period and as a temporary measure pending the coming into force of the Security Provisions of the United Nations Charter and the admission of Iceland to the United Nations Organisation.[1]

3. On the 29th September, a member of the State Department was asked orally for an assurance that the presence of the United States forces in Iceland would in no circumstances be allowed to compromise the security of our own communications in the North Atlantic. The hope was also expressed that the United States Government would agree to grant diversionary and emergency landing rights in their airfields in Iceland for aircraft of the British Commonwealth. It was also explained that the suggestion made in the Secretary of State's letter to Mr. Byrnes was intended not only to avoid an apparent vote of no confidence in the United Nations Organisation, but also to deny the Soviet Government an excuse for demanding Russian bases in Denmark or Norway.[10]

4. Mr. Byrnes replied to the Secretary of State's letter that his suggestion had been communicated to the State Department with the request that the matter should be discussed with the War and Navy Departments and the Chiefs of Staff.

5. The requests made in our oral communication were referred by the State Department to the War and Navy Departments with the State Department's recommendation.

6. The Secretary of State's letter to Mr. Byrnes did not stop the United States Government from making their communication to the Icelandic Government, who were approached on the 1st October by the United States Minister in Reykjavik with a request for the lease of bases.

7. The matter was discussed at a secret session of the Icelandic Parliament on the 2nd October. A Committee of three members of each of the four political parties was appointed to consider the matter and to report. His Majesty's Minister in Reykjavik reported on the 10th October that the majority of opinion in the Committee favoured granting the American request but that a decision was being delayed by uncertainty as to the British attitude. The United States Minister subsequently expressed concern at this delay.

8. On the 12th October, His Majesty's Embassy in Washington were instructed to express the hope to the State Department that the United States Government would seriously and urgently consider the proposal put forward in the Secretary of State's letter to Mr. Byrnes, and, if they were convinced by our arguments, that they would consider amending their demand on the Icelandic Government.

9. On the 25th October His Majesty's Ambassador in Washington

[10] Cf. No. 48, note 4.

reported that he had been informed by the State Department that the United States Government had regretfully decided that they could not do otherwise than adhere to their present course of action.

10. The question of the form in which the assurances we asked for (see paragraph 3 above) should be given has been raised by the State Department. His Majesty's Ambassador in Washington was instructed to press for written assurances in one of various forms. It was, however, decided that in the last resort we should be prepared to content ourselves with an oral communication of which an agreed version would be kept on record. The State Department have been unable to meet us on the point of written assurances, on the grounds that any undertaking which could be construed as having the nature of a treaty would require ratification by two-thirds of the Senate, and any 'executive agreement' would have to be published. An oral reply has been given; a copy has been handed to His Majesty's Ambassador and a copy is to be kept on the files of the State Department. This reply is now being examined by the Foreign Office and the Chiefs of Staff.

11. His Majesty's Minister at Reykjavik has on more than one occasion been sounded unofficially on behalf of the Icelandic Government regarding the attitude of His Majesty's Government, and on the 24th October he reported that the Icelandic Prime Minister had officially asked for an expression of our views. Mr. Shepherd has been instructed to speak in the following sense: . . .[11]

CALENDARS TO NO. 90

i *14–28 Oct. 1945 Correspondence regarding U.S. refusal to give H.M.G. written assurances that occupation of Iceland base will be brought within U.N. Charter,* including text of oral communication from State Dept.: see paras. 9–10 above [N 13886, 14121, 14592, 14606/1004/27].

ii *30 Oct. 1945 To Earl of Halifax (Washington) Tel. No. 10876* Text of message of 27 Oct. from Mr. Byrnes to Mr. Bevin in reply to letter in Annex to No. 48: prompt action by U.S. is essential to secure existing rights in Iceland and will enhance public confidence in U.N. Charter [N 14883/1004/27].

iii *31 Oct. 1945 Letter from Mr. C.H. Waldock (a Principal Assistant Secretary in the Admiralty) to Mr. Beckett* questions interpretation of Article 43 of U.N. Charter in No. 90: Mr. Beckett agrees but considers memo. as a whole is not affected [N 15020/1004/27].

iv *31 Oct.–16 Nov. 1945 Correspondence regarding Icelandic Govt.'s attitude to U.S.* and implications for H.M.G., who must 'not be accused of contributing to the failure of the United States Government's attempt to secure bases in Iceland' [N 14837, 15149, 15249, 15393, 15451/1004/27].

[11] The instruction cited in para. 3 of C.P. (45) 261 is not reprinted.

No. 91

Letter from Mr. Bevin to Lord Winster

[W 14060/24/802]

FOREIGN OFFICE, 31 October 1945[1]

Many thanks for your letter of the 23rd October [i] enclosing notes on the position between the United States and ourselves as regards civil aviation.

2. I agree that for the present at any rate it would be best to continue the civil aviation talks as a separate matter and not as part of a general settlement. At the present juncture you and Sir William Hildred can clearly no more go over to the United States of America than Mr. Clayton can come over here, and I agree that the most suitable next move would be to tell Winant that we were very disappointed to hear from Halifax that our latest proposals were regarded as marking no improvement on our Chicago proposals[2] and that in these circumstances we would be glad to know on what basis the State Department felt that discussions could be renewed.

3. I think that this should be done without waiting for the short term difficulties over the proposed interim agreement and the cut in fares made by Panamerican Airways[3] to be got out of the way. Until progress has been made with these I should certainly not press you to offer the further concessions which you outline in your letter and notes. Much will of course depend on the progress of the financial and economic talks at Washington, but so far, there seems to have been a welcome lack of comment contrasting our shipping and civil aviation policies.[4]

4. At the same time, I ought not to conceal from you my anxiety at the strain which the continued absence of any decision on these questions of principle is imposing on our relations with the United States and with those countries which have consulted us and which we have advised to resist the strong pressure to which they are being subjected from the American side. It is most important that the resulting friction should be reduced to a minimum and I cannot say that I am satisfied that this is being done. I refer particularly to the failure to start or continue negotiations with those countries which have indicated that a bilateral agreement with ourselves, even if it had to precede the actual opening of services, would strengthen them in resisting American pressure.

5. On the 25th October, the Portuguese Ambassador[5] informed Sir Alexander Cadogan that he had now come round to the view that it would be in the interests of his country if the Portuguese Government were to grant unconditional fifth freedom rights. He is evidently disturbed at the

---

[1] Opening and closing salutations omitted from the filed copy.
[2] See No. 73, and i below.
[3] See No. 93.i.
[4] Cf. No. 73, para. 8.
[5] The Duke of Palmella.

284

weight of American pressure being put upon his Government and is advising them to give way. You will recall that after the satisfactory conversations which Mr. Cribbett[6] and Mr. Cheetham had in Lisbon in August it was agreed that Mr. Cribbett should return in October in order to conclude a definite agreement. He has not however done so and it would scarcely be surprising if the Portuguese Government were now swayed by the thought that we had lost interest in the matter.

6. An even more unfortunate consequence of the failure to initiate negotiations has been the decision of the Norwegian Government to conclude an agreement with the Americans according unconditional fifth freedom rights. This they appear to have done under the mis-apprehension that the Danish Government had decided to ratify and implement the agreement which their Minister signed *ad referendum* in December 1944 while Denmark was still occupied. As you are probably aware, the energetic action taken by my department in the first half of this year was successful in restoring the status quo. This was still the position when Mr. Christmas Moeller came here at the end of August although he took the opportunity to advise us not to delay the conclusion of an agreement with the Danish Government much longer since they could not indefinitely resist American pressure. I am convinced that there was a good chance of Denmark and Norway, if properly encouraged, resisting the temptation to follow the example of neutral Sweden, but I am afraid that since the defection of Norway it is unlikely that Denmark will hold out much longer single-handed. In any case, here as in the case of Portugal and also Greece, there is no time at all to be lost.

7. I could contemplate the strain which these matters are placing on our political relations with the countries concerned with more equanimity if I felt that we had at least effectively defended the British interests involved but I fear that on the contrary we may only be making the worst of both worlds. After one or two more defections like that of Norway the position we are defending will clearly have been softened up to the point where it is no longer defensible. Nor, when we abandon its defence, shall we derive any goodwill in the other countries concerned. The Americans will regard us as having conceded late and grudgingly what they would have wished us to give early and willingly. The countries whom we have attempted to weld into the united front will regard us as having once again followed the policy of 'too little and too late' and we shall suffer a corresponding loss of prestige.

8. If therefore you feel that you need my assistance in pursuing your difficult negotiations with the Americans I hope that you in your turn will bear in mind the importance of making my task no more difficult than need be by pursuing with the countries of Europe and Middle East those negotiations which the situation clearly calls for.[7]

ERNEST BEVIN

[6] Mr. W.C.G. Cribbett was Deputy Director General of Civil Aviation.

[7] Lord Winster's reply of 5 November was summarized for Mr. Bevin in a minute of that

i *23 Oct. 1945 Letter from Lord Winster to Mr. Bevin*, without enclosed notes, summarizing Anglo-American position on civil aviation: 'our hopes of an orderly and equitable development of air transport will be prejudiced by concessions to that section of American opinion which is out to hog the air' [W 14060/24/802].

date by Mr. Gallop, in preparation for a discussion that evening with Lord Winster and Sir S. Cripps: 'Lord Winster chiefly argues that even if we had been able to enter into bilateral negotiations with the countries concerned, it does not follow that we should have been successful in stiffening them against American pressure owing to:
   (a) their need of aircraft which we cannot supply,
   (b) their desire to attract traffic to the costly airports they are building, and
   (c) the geographical factors which incline some of them to concede Fifth Freedom rights.
'The fact that we could not have been certain of uniform success does not seem an adequate reason for not doing our best . . . I suggest that your line might be that it is more profitable to see what we can do in the future, than to analyse the reasons of our past shortcomings; that you realise that negotiations with the Americans, and other commitments, place a strain on his depleted staff; but that you hope he will do his best to get negotiations started this month with Portugal at least, and if possible with other countries' (W 14624/24/802).

No. 92

Mr. Bevin to Sir D. Kelly (Buenos Aires)

No. 270 [AS 5776/12/2]

FOREIGN OFFICE, *1 November 1945*

Sir,
   The Argentine Ambassador came to see me to-day. He informed me that he intended to return to his own country but was staying on until December owing to the marriage of his daughter.
   2. The Ambassador raised the question of the upheaval that had taken place in Argentina[1] and asked what was my attitude to the present situation. I answered him that his Government must appreciate that the whole world was sick of Fascism and of military government and there could be no good relations while this continued. On the other hand, the policy of this country had been that, while we made our position quite clear when faced with the kind of action which had taken place in the Argentine, we should intervene as little as possible and leave it to the people of the Argentine to settle their own affairs. Señor Cárcano indicated that if the United States had adopted the same attitude and had left the situation alone for six months a change would have come about and the present difficulties been overcome. On the other hand, he informed me that, owing to wages being so low and conditions so bad in

[1] See No. 66, note 1.

the Argentine, Perón having raised the standard of life for the working people the latter felt that their security depended upon keeping Perón in office, hence the strikes in his support. There was no doubt that he would pursue his policy. The Ambassador admitted that there had been too little consideration given to the grievances and burdens of the ordinary people and this accounted for the present support of Perón.

3. Señor Cárcano then asked what were my views about the United Nations and the reception that Argentina would receive at the [Security] Council.[2] I said I thought that the very fact that these events had taken place would produce a good deal of ill feeling, but I could not say what the result would be. The Ambassador then told me that his Government intended to hold elections in April. Would that have any effect? I answered that I thought it would be far too late as the Council met in January; if the elections could be held earlier and a civil Government established, it might make for a change of view on the part of other nations. He thought this would be impossible, but I reiterated that if arrangements could be made for the elections to be held round about that time and conducted correctly, and a civil Government set up as a result of the free vote of the people, this would create a situation where it might be possible to forget the past.[3]

I am, &c.,

ERNEST BEVIN[4]

CALENDAR TO NO. 92

i *15 Nov. & 5 Dec. 1945 From and to Sir D. Kelly (Buenos Aires) Tels. Nos. 834 and 635* Discussion of advisability of making statement of H.M.G.'s policy towards Argentina to counter rumours that H.M.G. are not interested in fight for constitutional government [AS 5969/12/2].

[2] Cf. Volume I, No. 65.

[3] In a minute of 30 October Mr. Perowne had suggested that Mr. Bevin might take advantage of Señor Cárcano's visit to convey a 'serious warning' to the Argentine Government on three counts: (1) that the Argentine Government, which would be judged by 'acts and not by words', must hold free elections (cf. No. 66, note 1): (2) that His Majesty's Government expected the Argentine Government to take active measures to ensure the production and despatch of urgently needed foodstuffs, and that 'some criticism has been occasioned in this country by the fact that Argentina, a nation of 14 millions, manages to consume three-quarters of its total meat production, and that recent visitors to Buenos Aires have been greatly shocked by the extravagance and waste of food to be seen in that capital'; (3) that His Majesty's Government expected that 'proper treatment' should be accorded to their vested interests in Argentina.

Since Mr. Bevin did not raise points (2) and (3) Mr. V.G. Lawford, an Assistant Private Secretary to Mr. Bevin, enquired in a minute of 27 November whether South American Department should take it that he did not approve the policy in these points, or 'if it is merely that you did not consider the moment opportune'. Mr. Bevin minuted that 'in view of U.S.A. attitude' he doubted the wisdom of pressing these points.

[4] In a letter to Mr. Bevin of 16 November Señor Cárcano stated that he had transmitted a record of their conversation to the Argentine Foreign Ministry, and that the Argentine Cabinet had now decided to advance the date of the general elections to 24 February 1946 (AS 5989/12/2).

No. 93

The Earl of Halifax (Washington) to Mr. Bevin
(Received 3 November, 12.35 a.m.)

No. 7334 Telegraphic [W 14467/24/802]

Immediate   WASHINGTON, 2 November 1945, 6.35 p.m.

My telegrams Nos. 6850, 6851 and 6863.[1]

Clayton telephoned me yesterday on the subject of civil aviation and telecommunications.

2. In further conversation with Keynes, Clayton expressed himself as satisfied to leave telecommunications to the Bermuda Conference.[2] He said that as that was arranged for so early a date it offered him a satisfactory reason to give the enquirers for keeping a settlement of this matter separate from the financial discussions.

3. He then turned to civil aviation and expressed himself as attaching the very greatest importance to a similar arrangement by which a definite and early date is fixed for discussion of that matter also. He said that he was anxious to keep this separate from the financial conversations and certainly did not intend to require our agreement with the American view either on that matter or on telecommunications as a condition of the financial discussions. He repeated however the warning he had given before that the airline operators are lining up to put pressure on Congress when the financial proposals come before them to link the two together.[3] He considers that if he can point to an early forthcoming conference, that may be sufficient answer as in the case of telecommunications but that he will be on the spot if he cannot point to that.

4. Now that the discussions concerning the nationalisation of civil aviation have reached a conclusion[4] I very much hope that you will be able to meet Clayton on this. He mentioned the end of November as suitable

---

[1] See No. 58.i.

[2] Cf. No. 73.i. Foreign Office telegram No. 11235 to Washington of 8 November stated in particular: 'We are glad the Americans agree that telecommunications should be dealt with at Bermuda as a subject separate from the financial and economic talks' (W 14524/46/801). The Report of the U.K. Delegation to the Bermuda Telecommunications Conference, which met from 22 November to 4 December 1945, is filed at W 16692/46/801. Annexed to the Report is the text of the agreement signed on 4 December 1945 by the participating governments (Australia, Canada, India, New Zealand, South Africa, Southern Rhodesia, United Kingdom and United States) concerning radiotelegraph circuits and rates, press communications, cables and standardisation. Also annexed is the text of the protocol signed by the U.K and U.S. delegations on exclusive telecommunications arrangements, which included provision for the erection of a U.S. radiotelegraph station in Saudi Arabia: see No. 73.i, and F.R.U.S. 1945, vol. viii, pp. 1030–1.

[3] See No. 58.

[4] Lord Winster announced in the House of Lords on 1 November that all civil air transport, including airports, was to pass into public ownership: see Parl. Debs., 5th ser., H. of L., vol. cxxxvii, cols. 623–9.

and convenient. Since he will be in charge and indeed from our point of view it is very desirable that he should be in charge and as he cannot leave Washington just when he will be engaged in helping to put the financial proposals through Congress it seems inevitable that the meeting should take place here.[5]

5. The Civil Air Attaché has been discussing informally possible lines for an interim arrangement under which airlines could operate between the United States and the United Kingdom.[6] Some satisfactory progress appears to have been made. Such an interim arrangement could no doubt do something to sweeten the atmosphere but will not (repeat not) meet Clayton's point.

CALENDARS TO NO. 93

i *27 Oct.–8 Dec. 1945 Correspondence concerning negotiation of an interim agreement on commercial air services between U.S. and U.K.* State Dept.'s rejection of British proposals and determination of Pan American Airways to introduce under-cutting transatlantic fare are met by U.K. refusal, despite critical stage of financial and economic negotiations, to increase frequency of American flights unless International Air Transport Association (I.A.T.A.) minimum rates accepted: U.S. airlines' acceptance of higher rate leads to H.M.G.'s agreement to grant landing rights, but State Dept., while recognizing H.M.G.'s right to fix rates, maintain stand on 5 freedoms (cf. *F.R.U.S. 1945*, vol. vi, pp. 228–244); Lord Halifax (*Washington Tel. No. 8095*) urges careful preparation for bilateral talks sought by Americans [W 14119, 14468, 14578, 15041, 15123, 15220, 15229, 15380, 15439, 15451, 15637, 15796, 15858, 16001/24/802].

ii *2 Nov. 1945 British Missions (Washington) Tel. NABOB 258* Sets out American timetable for completion of negotiations and refers to No. 93: Mr. Clayton's sensitivity to suggestions that he is 'using financial pressure to obtain our assent in various other matters' means Bill for financial aid will be 'on the simplest possible lines and will not include any conditions on extraneous matters'; 'shock tactics' may work best with Congress [T 236/456].

[5] For President Truman's suggestion that civil aviation should be discussed with Mr. Attlee during his visit to Washington in November 1945, and their ensuing discussion, see Volume II, Nos. 215 and 234.

[6] See i below.

No. 94

Cabinet Offices to British Missions (Washington)

BABOON 206 Telegraphic [*T 236/466*]

Most immediate. Secret   CABINET OFFICES, *6 November 1945, 5.40 a.m.*

Personal for Ambassador and Keynes from Chancellor of the Exchequer.

1. My colleagues and I have considered the whole situation.[1] We wish you all to know that you have earned our confidence in these long talks by the ingenuity and determination with which you have withstood disappointment there and some vexations from here. We are therefore sending you guidance for the conduct of the negotiations so far as we can foresee their possible developments. Please keep us fully informed and seek our authority when you judge it necessary, or when a reference back would suit your tactics.

2. NABOB 230.[2] Alternative B can be dropped.

3. NABOB 232.[3] Alternative A in BABOON 155[4] is our first choice, especially the principle that we should not pay interest on the \$2 billion option for the Sterling Area. You can use your authority in BABOON 158[5] to recommend payment of 2 per cent on the \$2½ billion at whatever stage you think suitable.

4. NABOB 232. (paragraph 2). If it suits your case you can propose Alternative A as \$2 billion plus Lend–Lease, provided that:

(a) we do not have to pay more than \$½ billion for Lend–Lease and

(b) the separation will not encourage the Americans to press for 3(c) terms on Lend–Lease because that is what other countries have accepted.[6]

---

[1] At a meeting on the evening of 5 November (GEN 89/5th meeting, ii below) Ministers considered a memorandum by Mr. Dalton, circulated on 4 November as GEN 89/10, summarizing the instructions which he proposed should be sent to Lord Keynes. In a minute of 5 November to Mr. Attlee, commenting on GEN 89/10, Sir E. Bridges referred to NABOB 258 (No. 93.ii), which showed that 'time is very short. I feel that the meeting tonight should, if possible, authorise instructions to be sent at once and that the earliest opportunity should be taken of informing the Cabinet, probably by way of oral statements, of the course of negotiations . . . If this seems cavalier treatment of so important an issue, you will no doubt bear in mind how intensely difficult it has always proved to get effective discussion of these matters in any large gathering' (PREM 8/35). An unsigned note on this minute read 'P.M. agrees'.

BABOON 205, despatched at 2.20 a.m. on 6 November, informed Lord Halifax and Lord Keynes that BABOON 206 contained 'text of guidance for you after discussion at Cabinet Committee tonight (Monday [i.e. 5 November]). Matter comes before full Cabinet tomorrow (Tuesday) for final approval of text of guidance. I shall telegraph immediately approval has been given and am sending you the advance text for study meanwhile' (UE 5349/1094/53). Mr. Dalton's proposals, presented to the Cabinet (C.M. (45) 49th Conclusions) in C.P. (45) 270 (iii below) on the morning of 6 November, were approved following a second Cabinet meeting later that day (see No. 95.ii). BABOON 218 to Lord Halifax and Lord Keynes, despatched at 7.56 p.m. on 6 November, stated: 'BABOON 205 and 206. Cabinet have approved. You may go ahead with our blessings' (T 236/467). See further Pressnell, op. cit., Chapter 10(14).

[2] No. 85.   [3] No. 87.   [4] No. 81.   [5] No. 86.

[6] Mr. Hall-Patch had stressed the importance of the points in (a) and (b) in the course of a minute of 5 November commenting on GEN 89/10 (see note 1): 'I suggest we should be clear on these points, as otherwise the Americans, at the official level, may attempt after the main settlement is reached to drag out Lease–Lend discussions and increase the amount due under this head' (UE 5349/1094/53). In his telegram No. 549 Saving of 7 November, however, Lord Halifax reported that 'active discussions have been proceeding in connexion with the evaluation of the civilian inventory and the formulation of outstanding claims and

5. Subject to paragraph 9 below on the condition of a satisfactory Waiver Clause, we leave it to your judgment whether to try for a Washington Waiver,[7] in Alternative A. We made Alternative A simple in form and in the principles it contains for the sake of a quick and firm deal. We should not want to endanger its acceptance by introducing the complication of a Washington Waiver. But if you can secure it without undue difficulty, it would be an additional protection.

6. If Alternative A is unobtainable, our limit is an open credit for $4 billion at 2 per cent on the amount of the credit in use, with an option on a further $1 billion at 2 per cent.

7. Under either Alternative A or paragraph 6, repayment would begin not before 5 years, and would continue over 50 years.

8. Any improvement either in the rate of interest or in the period of repayment or the postponement of the starting date of repayment would of course be welcome as it would ease our burden.

9. Waiver Clause. The basis of the Washington Waiver in paragraph 4 of NABOB 200[8] seems reasonably satisfactory. To be acceptable to us a Washington waiver must fulfil two conditions:

(a) It must be embodied in the agreement in terms which cannot be altered by Congress.

(b) It must apply automatically without any argument or scrutiny of our policies by the United States.

10. We assume that a London waiver[7] would be inserted, either in Alternative A or in a settlement under paragraph 6. We shall be very interested to learn how far Vinson and Clayton would be willing to bind the Administration to the proposal in paragraph 6 of NABOB 230 that the final agreement between us and the Administration should be put to Congress in such a form that Congress could either accept or reject it, but not amend it. A binding agreement with them on this point would obviously help with the Waiver Clause and would be of importance to the whole of the negotiations.

11. I want personally to emphasize to you how strongly we should feel about the proposal if the Americans insist that we should pay 2 per cent interest on the whole of a loan, a large part of which is to be devoted to assisting American exports to the Sterling Area. It is bad enough for us to turn a diffused Sterling indebtedness into a Dollar indebtedness. But to turn the present interest of ½ per cent on the Sterling debt into 2 per cent interest on a Dollar debt would be much more serious. I feel sure that you and Keynes will emphasize this.

12. *Sterling Area arrangements.* We agree to use the assistance for the progressive removal of discrimination, and to seek a contribution to the solution of the whole situation, including writing down of Sterling

counter-claims under lend–lease and reciprocal aid. Their financial timetable has infused American consideration of all outstanding lend–lease questions with a new sense of urgency' (UE 5370/42/53).

[7] See No. 87.   [8] No. 80.

Balances by voluntary agreement with each creditor. The details of this undertaking are sufficiently covered by the recent personal telegrams between Keynes and the Treasury.[9]

CALENDARS TO No. 94

i *2–5 Nov. 1945 Correspondence between Lord Keynes and Sir W. Eady* on sterling area arrangements and amendments to NABOB 215 (No. 78.ii): Sir W. Eady hopes that the draft need not be presented yet, but should follow on an agreement 'reached between you and the administration rather than it should appear as a definition of an offer' (BABOON 189); NABOB 276; 'American obduracy for a quantified commitment on cancellation might bring the talks to a real deadlock' (BABOON 198) [UE 5075, 5308, 5326/1094/53, T 236/456].

ii *5 Nov. 1945 Record of meeting of Ministers (GEN 89/5th meeting)* Discussion of GEN 89/10 (see note 1): Professor Robbins stresses 'complete contrast' between attitudes of U.S. Administration who are anxious to help, and Congress and public opinion who were 'losing interest rapidly in the outside world' (see also No. 95, note 1) [UE 5400/1094/53].

iii *6 Nov. 1945 Memo. by Mr. Dalton (C.P. (45) 270)* on loan proposal to be put before Americans: would include U.K. acceptance of I.T.O. and Bretton Woods, and writing down of sterling balances [UE 5399/1094/53].

[9] Cf. No. 88, note 6. Following the exchange of telegrams between Lord Keynes and Sir W. Eady reproduced at i below, Lord Keynes prepared a revised draft which it was agreed should be shown to Mr. White 'as a draft not yet cleared with London which is in elucidation of your earlier oral communications' (BABOON 198, i below). Lord Keynes' letter of 5 November to Mr. White enclosing the revised draft on sterling area arrangements is printed in Moggridge, *op. cit.*, pp. 570–7. This letter was sent before Lord Keynes received detailed comments from Mr. Rowe-Dutton, including a redraft of paras. 1–10 of NABOB 215 (No. 78.ii), in BABOON 202 and 203 of 5 November, printed *ibid.*, pp. 577–9. A subsequent exchange of telegrams with Sir W. Eady on points of detail, leading to further revision of the draft, is printed *ibid.*, pp. 579–84.

No. 95

Memorandum by Sir S. Cripps on Commercial Policy[1]

C.P. (45) 269 [UE 5398/1094/53]

Secret   BOARD OF TRADE, *6 November 1945*

Discussions with the Americans which have been proceeding side by

[1] This memorandum was presented to the Cabinet on the morning of 6 November in accordance with decisions taken at the meeting of Ministers on 5 November: see No. 94, note 1. At that meeting Ministers had also considered memoranda GEN 89/8 and 89/9 (No. 88.i), and two memoranda of 5 November by the President of the Board of Trade on Commercial Policy and Imperial Preference (GEN 89/11 and 89/12, not printed). In GEN 89/11 Sir S. Cripps summarized the progress of commercial policy negotiations since the first meeting of the GEN 89 Committee (see No. 32). GEN 89/12 contained the revised formula on Imperial Preference and explanation in Annexes A and B below, which had

side with the financial talks have reached an advanced stage, and they now hope to publish on Sunday,[2] as their proposal, the document which has been under discussion.[3] We should hope, with the general support of the Dominions, to be able immediately thereafter to indicate our support of the document as a basis for discussion.[4] Following is a brief indication of the main points, on all of which our negotiators have established our essential point of view where it differed from the original United States proposals.

(1) *Procedure.* (*a*) A conference of fifteen nations (including all the Dominions and India) in, say, March, to consider the document and to initiate bilateral negotiations on tariff matters.

(*b*) A United Nations conference in, say, June, to set up an International Trading Organisation on the basis of the document as revised in March. Nations joining, and thereby subscribing to the general rules in the document, if not in the original fifteen, would be required within a reasonable space of time to make comparable agreements on tariff matters.

(2) *Imperial Preference.* This has been the critical point. At Annex A is the full text of the American proposal on preferences as it has emerged from a long discussion. At first the Americans were inclined to make it a *sine qua non* that we (and therefore the Dominions) should agree to a form of words which would have bound us to do away with preference in a comparatively short space of time. We resisted this.[5] Relying upon

been drawn up as a result of 'further pressure' brought to bear on the Americans to recast their previous formula: cf. No. 83.

Ministers decided to refer both issues to the Cabinet the next day, but meanwhile the text in Annexes A and B was sent to Washington in paras. 2 and 3 of BABOON 207 despatched at 4 a.m. on 6 November, which explained that the concurrence of the Dominions and India in the formula was being sought. The British Delegation was meanwhile instructed to 'show the explanation to U.S. representatives and satisfy yourself that they will not question this explanation of the formula'. BABOON 208, despatched at 4.5 a.m. on 6 November, conveyed the following message from Sir S. Cripps to Lord Halifax and Sir P. Liesching: 'Ministers decided to recommend to Cabinet, subject to Dominion support and to final clearance of one or two minor points, that Commercial Policy proposals as a whole are acceptable. My best thanks to you and your colleagues for your magnificent fight' (UE 5350/1094/53).

[2] 11 November 1945. The document was not in fact made public until 6 December: see *F.R.U.S. 1945*, vol. vi, p. 160, note 8.

[3] i.e. COM/TRADE 1 (see No. 54, notes 1–2 and ii), summarized in revised form in Annex C below.

[4] In a note to Mr. Attlee of 6 November before the Cabinet meeting, Mr. Jay suggested that 'it may be worth emphasizing in particular the fact that, on Commercial Policy, Preferences etc., we are merely undertaking to enter a future Conference on an agreed Agenda, and we are signing nothing now. To agree an Agenda is very different from signing an Agreement. Also with a view to the Debate in the House, it seems worth emphasizing that Article VII binding us to "the elimination of all forms of discriminatory treatment in international commerce" [see No. 1, note 5] was accepted by the Coalition Government, and that the Conservatives are thus bound also to work towards "elimination" of preferences' (PREM 8/35).

[5] See Nos. 54, 60, 63 and 69.

Article VII of the Mutual Aid Agreements, we have brought them round to a formula which, subject to an interpretation which we are seeking to be enabled to give without fear of contradiction, can be accepted. The text of this interpretation is at Annex B.

(3) Apart from the preference issue, the United States proposal (entitled 'Proposal to set up an International [Trade] Organisation') is arranged as shown in Appendix C.

The main points of interest are

(a) *The Preamble*. This emphasises the need for international co-operation on economic matters, requires each member of the Organisation to adopt full employment policies and says that no nation should seek the maintenance of employment through measures that aggravate the problems of other nations.

(b) *State Trading*. Our own policies are safeguarded, but State Trading is not to be used to introduce by a side-wind protection greater than that allowed for as a result of the proposed tariff negotiations. Empire preference and long-term contracts are also safeguarded.

(c) *Subsidies and Export Subsidies*. The former are allowed, the latter are subject to rules which considerably limit the freedom of the United States to force her agricultural products on export markets.

(d) *Transitional Period and Balance of Payments Difficulties*. Our need for Import Regulation and Exchange Control in such circumstances is recognised, but import quotas are not to be used for protective purposes. (This use of quotas by other countries is a potential menace to our exports.)

(e) *International Cartels*. The Americans have been induced to give up their proposal for outlawing certain named practices (e.g., division of markets). Instead there is provision for complaint by a Government, consideration by the Organisation, and recommendation to the Government of the offending concern, the latter Government being then left to act in accordance with its own procedures.

(f) *United Kingdom Agriculture*. Our negotiators were instructed to safeguard the position for a long-term policy of reasonable stabilisation and adequate remuneration for our agriculture. On this point we have had a very frank exchange of views with the Americans, who well understand our position and have made provision in their document which gives us the elbow-room that we need for our policy of State purchase and averaged prices.

R.S.C.

Annex A to No. 95

Revise of Preferences Formula

1. In the light of the principles set forth in Article VII of the Mutual Aid Agreements, members should enter into arrangements for the

substantial reduction of tariffs and for the elimination of tariff preferences, action for the elimination of tariff preferences being taken in conjunction with adequate measures for the substantial reduction of barriers to world trade, as part of the mutually advantageous international arrangements contemplated in this document.

2. As an initial step in the process of eliminating tariff preferences it should be agreed that

(*a*) Existing international commitments will not be permitted to stand in the way of such action as may be agreed upon with respect to tariff preferences.

(*b*) All negotiated reductions in most-favoured-nation tariffs will operate automatically to reduce or eliminate margins of preference.

(*c*) Margins of preference on any product will in no case be increased and no new preferences will be introduced.[6]

Annex B to No. 95

Explanation of Preferences Formula

1. The formula determines the procedure to be followed by common consent in considering, in the context of a general lowering of tariffs and other trade barriers, what contribution can be made from our side by way of reduction or elimination of preferences.

2. The formula makes it clear that, in pursuit of the objectives of Article VII of the Mutual Aid Agreements, we for our part are ready to agree that the existing system of preferences within the British Commonwealth and Empire is capable of contraction *pari passu* with the improvement in trading conditions between Commonwealth and Empire countries and the rest of the world.

3. The formula further provides that in entering negotiations for the reduction of tariffs the parties concerned will not refuse to discuss the modification of particular preferences on the ground that these are the subject of prior commitments; on the contrary, all margins of preference will be regarded as open to negotiation and it will, of course, be for the party negotiating the modification of any margin of preference which it is bound by an existing commitment to give to a third party to obtain the consent of the third party concerned.

4. Further points to be noted are:

(1) The formula makes it clear there is no commitment on any country in advance of negotiations to reduce or eliminate any particular margin of preference. The position is that each country remains free to judge, in the light of the offers made by all the others, the extent of the contribution it can make towards the realisation of the agreed objective.

(2) It is recognised that reduction or elimination of preferences can

---

[6] An expanded version of this formula is printed in *F.R.U.S., op. cit.*, pp. 160–1.

only be considered in relation to and in return for reductions of tariffs and other barriers in the world as a whole which would make for mutually advantageous arrangements for the expansion of trade. There must be adequate compensation for all parties affected.

5. This formula does not in advance of the detailed negotiations lay down how far the process of reduction and elimination of preferences will be carried at this immediate stage. It must be realised that some preferences are of particular importance to the economy of certain parts of the world just as some tariffs are important in others. The immediate elimination of all preferences would be such a step as would require a very drastic clearance of other trade barriers involving substantial and widespread reductions in tariffs and other trade barriers by a large number of countries. All this is well recognised. Thus, the degree to which the final objectives can be reached at the initial stage can only appear at the negotiations themselves and as the result of a mutually advantageous settlement.

Annex C to No. 95

Summary of United States Proposal to Establish an International Trade Organisation

Inter-relation of Trade and Employment Problems and Measures

High and stable levels of employment are essential for an enlarged volume of trade. Prosperity in each nation depends on the prosperity of other nations, the levels of employment in the major industrial nations having an especially important influence in this respect. Accordingly there should be an undertaking that

(1) Each signatory nation will take appropriate action designed to secure full employment within its own jurisdiction.

(2) Maintenance of employment should not be sought through measures which aggravate the trade and employment problems of other nations.

Proposal to establish an International Trade Organisation

Measures designed to expand trade are essential to reach maximum employment, production and consumption. To attain these objects continuous international collaboration will be necessary. It is accordingly proposed to establish an International Trade Organisation of the United Nations, the members of which would undertake to conduct their international commercial policies and relations in accordance with agreed principles to be set forth in the articles of the Organisation.

Chapter I. Purposes and Principles of the Organisation

These would aim at effective expansion of world production, employment, and the exchange and consumption of goods.

Chapter II. Membership

Chapter III. Principles relating to Commercial Policy

A. *General Commercial Provisions*
There would be a body of rules of the kind normally found in Commercial Treaties governing e.g., internal duties, transit duties, anti-dumping duties, tariff valuations, marks of origin, &c. The working-out of these rules in detail would fall to the International Trade Organisation.

B. *Tariffs and Equality of Tariff Treatment*
Countries should take effective and expeditious steps, on lines to be agreed to bring about substantial reductions of tariffs and elimination of tariff preferences. Emergency action to prevent sudden and widespread unemployment would be provided for.

C. *Quantitative Restrictions*
The member countries would undertake in general not to maintain any import or export restrictions, subject to the following main exceptions:
(1) Restrictions required in the early post-war transition period, to economise shipping space, to secure equitable distribution of products in short supply, and for the orderly liquidation of war surplus stocks in the hands of Governments.
(2) Restrictions required to relieve conditions of distress in exporting countries due to shortages of foodstuffs or other essential products.
(3) Import quotas on agricultural products necessary to the enforcement of governmental measures (*a*) restricting marketing or production; or (*b*) intended to dispose of temporary domestic surpluses.
(4) To safeguard the balance of payments.[7]

D. *Subsidies*
1. *General subsidies* would be permitted; but members should inform the Organisation and be prepared to discuss their action if the subsidy increases exports or diminishes imports.
2. *Export subsidies.* These are disapproved. Three years after the end of hostilities, members granting such subsidies would undertake to discuss their action.
3. *Commodities in world surplus.* The provisions of 1 and 2 above would not apply to commodities declared by the Organisation to be in burdensome world surplus if inter-governmental action had failed to

---

[7] In his telegram No. 549 Saving of 7 November (see No. 94, note 6) Lord Halifax reported that there had been 'difficult discussions on the question of quantitative trade restrictions ... considerable difficulties still have to be overcome in reconciling the American dislike of quantitative trade restrictions and of their discriminatory application with our position that such measures should be allowed as a measure of economic defence when all other means for rectifying a disequilibrium in balance of international payments have failed'.

suggest other ways of removing the surplus. Even then the subsidy should not increase the export share of the country concerned.

E. *State Trading*

1. *Equality of Treatment.* Members should accord equality of treatment to other members. For this purpose, their State trading enterprises, in making purchases and sales, should be guided solely by commercial considerations, such as price, quality, terms of sale, &c.[8]

2. *State monopolies of individual products.* State-trading is not to introduce greater protective or preferential margins than would be allowed as a result of tariff negotiations.

3. *Complete State monopolies of foreign trade.* Countries should undertake to purchase from other members, on a non-discriminatory basis, products valued at not less than an aggregate amount to be agreed upon.

F. *Exchange Control*

This is dealt with by reference to the International Monetary Fund Agreement.

CHAPTER IV. PRINCIPLES RELATING TO RESTRICTIVE BUSINESS PRACTICES

This chapter begins by declaring that certain types of business practice (of which examples are given) may impede full employment policies and the objects of the convention.

Any member may bring to the notice of the Organisation a complaint that the objectives of the document are being frustrated by restrictive business practices of international character. The Organisation is then to investigate the matter, and, if the complaint is found justified, may make recommendations to the Governments of the offending business concern for action under their own laws.

CHAPTER V. PRINCIPLES RELATING TO INTERGOVERNMENTAL COMMODITY ARRANGEMENTS

1. Intergovernmental commodity arrangements involving restrictions on production or trade may be desirable to facilitate adjustments and the solution of problems affecting particular commodities, thus avoiding resort to unilateral action by the countries affected.

2. Such arrangements, if they involve limitation of production or exports or allocation of markets, should not be entered into unless and

---

[8] BABOON 219, despatched at 10.15 p.m. on 6 November, stated that the Cabinet had 'approved generally the Commercial Proposals', subject to consultation of the Dominion Governments and to the revision of the second sentence of paragraph E.1 of Chapter III in Annex C to read: '. . . solely by commercial considerations as price . . .'. NABOB 303 of 7 November stated that the American officials had replied that it would be very difficult to make this change, since the whole document had been printed, but that 'it was their clear understanding that the enumeration "such as price, quality, marketability" etc. was intended solely to be by way of example (UE 5326/1094/53).

until the Organisation has (1) investigated the root causes of the problem; and (2) has determined that a burdensome world surplus exists which cannot be corrected by the play of market forces; and unless a programme of adjustment has been prepared and adopted by members, calculated to solve the problem in a reasonable time.

3. *Governing Principles.* The following principles should govern inter-governmental commodity arrangements: (*a*) they should be open on equal terms to all members; (*b*) members substantially dependent on imports of the commodity concerned should have an equal voice with exporting countries; (*c*) they should assure adequate supplies for world consumption at all times at reasonable prices; (*d*) they should provide increasing opportunities for meeting world requirements from sources able to supply them most effectively.

4. Such arrangements should not remain in effect initially for more than five years; if renewed, it must be shown that substantial progress towards solution of the underlying problem has been made or is in prospect.

5. Existing or future intergovernmental commodity arrangements should be submitted to the Organisation for review.

CHAPTER VI.   ORGANISATION

The International Trade Organisation, its functions, organisation, and rules of procedure, and its relation to other international organisations are dealt with in detail.[9]

CALENDARS TO NO. 95

i *5 Nov. 1945   British Missions (Washington) Tels. NABOB 280 & 281* At meeting on 4 Nov. initial reactions of Dominion representatives to U.S. proposals on commercial policy are favourable: cf. note 9 above [UE 5367/1094/53].

ii *6 Nov. 1945   C.M. (45) 50th Conclusions of Cabinet meeting at 4.30 p.m. with Confidential Annex* Discussion of No. 95 and of C.P. (45) 270 (No. 94.iii): Mr. Bevin 'had been forced to the conclusion that we were faced with the hard choice between accepting these terms as the best we could get, or . . . asking the British people to endure for perhaps another three years, standards of living even lower than those to which they had been reduced at the end of six years of war' (cf. Hugh Dalton, *High Tide and After*, p. 79) [PREM 8/35].

iii *6 Nov. 1945   To British Missions (Washington) Tel. BABOON 209* Text of D.O. tel. 2069 informing Dominion Govts. of position on commercial policy negotiations and asking their support [UE 5350/1094/53].

iv *7–10 Nov. 1945   Correspondence concerning further discussion with Americans of explanation of Preferences Formula* (Annex B above) leading to certain amendments [UE 5147, 5350, 5445/1094/53].

[9] Correspondence concerning the reaction of the Dominion and Indian Governments to the proposals for an I.T.O. and on Imperial Preference can be followed on UE 5147, 5479 and 5497–8/1094/53, and on Treasury file T 236/388; see also v below.

v *22 Nov. 1945 C.P. (45) 295 Memo. by Viscount Addison* summarizing Dominion reactions to U.S. commercial policy proposals (see iii above), with: (Appendix A) exchange of personal telegrams between Mr. Chifley and Mr. Attlee, who understood Australian anxieties but stressed his 'strong impression that if you ever hope to secure advantageous concessions from the Americans the proposed negotiations offer a unique opportunity of doing so'; (Appendix B) statement of New Zealand Govt.'s policy on Imperial Preference [UE 5796/1094/53].

No. 96

British Missions (Washington) to Cabinet Offices
(Received 7 November, 4 a.m.)

NABOB 295 Telegraphic [*UE 5401/1094/53*]

Immediate. Secret   WASHINGTON, *7 November 1945, 12.7 a.m.*

For Chancellor of Exchequer from Ambassador, Keynes and Brand.

1. We are very grateful for the terms of your Baboon 206,[1] which have been a great personal encouragement and should help us to reach a reasonably favourable conclusion in an environment which presents very special difficulties in kind as well as in degree.

2. We decided to use the discretion you gave us to put up alternative (a)[2] on the basis of 2 per cent interest, since we believed we should lose any chance of making progress along these lines if we had tried for 1 per cent as well as for the other features of alternative (a). But we have not gone beyond that today and have made no use of the ultimate discretion you allow us in paragraph 6 of Baboon 206. We saw no harm, however, in attaching the Washington waiver[3] to alternative (a) from the start.

3. Since our proposals were too technical to be easily intelligible by merely oral exposition, we prepared a written paper as in NABOB 296.[4]

4. We presented this paper to Vinson and Clayton at a meeting at the Treasury this afternoon[5] at which no others were present, and discussed it clause by clause.

5. On its first paragraph, Vinson reminded us that the formal offer he had made us previously with the approval of his group had not gone beyond 3½ billion. On our emphasising the importance you attached to bringing the cost of Lend–Lease clean-up under the terms of the main loan, Vinson replied that he had studied the letter in Nabob Saving 22,[6] in which the previous history of this controversy is recorded, and claimed

---

[1] No. 94.   [2] See No. 81.   [3] See No. 87.
[4] No. 97, which was however despatched before the present telegram.
[5] This telegram was drafted on 6 November. Mr. Vinson referred to this meeting, of which no other record has been traced, in his statement to the U.S. Top Committee on 7 November: see No. 97, note 3.
[6] No. 78.iii.

that, in the light of this, the U.S. Government were not yet definitely committed to accepting our view of the matter.

6. Its third paragraph was, of course, the heaviest going. I do not think that either you or we have appreciated how violently Clayton and Vinson have reacted against the philosophy of the Harry White plan[7] which expressly associated the credit with the sterling area arrangements. They both declared that this is the opposite of what they now find convenient and that they have been busy denying stories that any part of the proposed credit was for the purpose of bailing out the Sterling area. At the same [? time] that they regard our proposals for liberalising the area as a necessary condition of the credit, they reject the idea of definitely associating the two things. As in the case of the commercial arrangements they prefer to take the line of going no further than that one of the purposes of the credit is to make us feel strong enough to take certain steps towards restoring multilateral clearing. Since the meeting, Keynes has sent Clayton an alternative draft which you will find in Nabob 297.[8]

7. Our version of the Washington waiver in paragraph 4 was well received by both, and Clayton went very near to saying that it was definitely acceptable.

8. The London waiver[3] in paragraph 5 was not so well received. Vinson limited himself to the remark that it would need a lot of selling. Clayton admitted that it was logical.

9. They took the whole paper quietly without giving us any clear indication of their views except in the case of the Washington waiver. They replied that they must take it away for discussion with their own top group, a meeting of which they would summon early tomorrow.

10. Although they did not react strongly against any part of the paper, or reject any clause out of hand, we were left without any confidence that they would accept paragraph 3 or that there might not still be trouble on other paragraphs. However, we yielded no ground and developed the arguments for paragraph 3 in a way which to ourselves at least, sounded fair and reasonable.[9] But the wind was, of course, taken out of some of our sails by their strong reaction against directly associating any part of the credit with the sterling area arrangements.

11. If they make sufficient progress with their own group, they will invite us to a further meeting later tomorrow.

12. We raised the question how they would avoid the possibility of amendments to the agreement by Congress not only in connection with the waiver clause, as you requested in paragraph 9 of Baboon 206, but in general. They confirmed what we had previously reported to you that they contemplated presenting the agreement in an annex which will be incapable of amendment. They reminded us that they could not prevent

[7] See No. 67, note 6. [8] See No. 97, note 2.
[9] Later on 6 November Lord Keynes reinforced his arguments for a $2 billion interest-free loan in a letter to Mr. Vinson, printed in Moggridge, *op. cit.*, pp. 585–6.

Congress from adding riders to the bill, as we have already informed you is the case, but they would resist to the utmost any amendments in conflict with the agreement. Vinson was emphatic that Congress was most unlikely to interest itself in altering such details as the provisions of the waiver clause. They also expressed themselves as emphatically of the opinion that the provision by which the waiver clause will be interpreted by the I.M.F. would avoid any possible argument or scrutiny by the U.S. We were left feeling as comfortable on these particular matters as is compatible with the constitution of the United States.

No. 97

British Missions (Washington) to Cabinet Offices
(Received 7 November, 4.5 a.m.)

NABOB 296 Telegraphic [UE 5401/1094/53]

Immediate. Secret   WASHINGTON, 7 November 1945, 12.5 a.m.

Following is statement referred to in paragraph 3 of NABOB 295.[1]

1. The Government of the U.S. agree to make available to the Government of the U.K. credit facilities up to an amount not exceeding $4 billion (together with an amount equal to the net sum mutually agreed as due from the U.K. in respect of the winding up of lend lease and reciprocal aid and other outstanding accounts).

2. Of the above credit $2 billion and the agreed net additional amount referred to above together with interest calculated at two percent per annum on the amounts outstanding in each year beginning with 1951, shall be repaid by equal annual instalments of $31,800 for each $1,000,000 outstanding on December 31st 1951, beginning on December 31st 1951, until the capital amount has been repaid. Out of each annual instalment an amount equal to two percent of the principal outstanding in that year shall be attributed to interest and the balance to capital repayment.

3. In respect of the remaining credit facilites, namely the $2 billion which it is estimated that the U.K. will require to make the future current earnings of sterling area countries available without discrimination to meet current outgoings in any currency together with such instalments of their accumulated balances as may be made similarly available, the U.K. will repay the principal sum without interest by fifty equal annual instalments, beginning on December 31st 1951, until the capital amount has been repaid.[2]

[1] No. 96.
[2] Lord Keynes' alternative draft of this paragraph, which he sent to Mr. Clayton on 6 November (see No. 96, para. 6), read as follows: '3. In respect of the balance of the credit, namely 2 billion dollars, which it is estimated that the U.K. will require, not for its own direct requirements in the U.S. but in multilateral trading so as to make sterling earned in

302

4. The Government of the U.K. having represented to the Government of the U.S.

(A)   That the pre-war level of imports into the U.K. on the average of the three pre-war years 1936–38 amounted to 875 million pounds (C.I/F.) at the prices of those years.

(B)   That the difficulties of the post-war transitional period arising out of the sacrifices and disturbance of the war to the U.K. economy cannot be considered to be at an end until U.K. earnings overseas have been restored to a level at least sufficient to pay for the pre-war volume of imports, and

(C)   That a payment of interest on the scale prescribed above would involve a burden on World commerce which could not be met without restrictive measures which it is the purpose of both Governments to avoid, unless conditions exist in which the overseas earnings of the U.K. are sufficient to cover a volume of imports not less than the pre-war volume.

The Government of U.S. agree that the proportion of the above annuity attributable to interest shall be waived in any year in which the home-produced exports and net invisible income of the year fall short of 875 million pounds reckoned in terms of the money of the same value as in 1936–38, as calculated by the statistical section of the International Monetary Fund. ('Net invisible income' excludes all receipts and payments of a capital nature, and includes all items of net current income, except receipts in respect of exports, after deduction of outgoings of a similar character including Government expenditure abroad.)

5. The Government of the U.K. shall be entitled to approach the Government of the U.S. for a deferment of the annual instalment of payment due in any year in any of the following circumstances. In the event of deferment the amount due shall be postponed so as not to increase the amount due in the years immediately following but by a corresponding extension of the period of repayment.

(A)   *A breakdown of multilateral clearing.* In the event of less than 75 percent of U.K. exports being sold to countries of which the currencies are freely convertible into dollars.

(B)   *An international depression of trade.* In the event of general and

overseas trade available without discrimination to meet current outgoings in any currency, the U.K. will repay the principal sum without interest by fifty equal annual instalments, beginning on December 31st, 1951, until the capital amount has been repaid' (NABOB 297, UE 5401/1094/53).

In BABOON 229 of 7 November to Lord Keynes the Treasury commented on this telegram: 'The Agreement will be published and as such will be read by Special Account countries such as the Argentine. We do not want to give the Argentine an opportunity to argue that special accounts should be immediately abolished and sterling made convertible. Whatever we may do later on, in the first instance the beneficiaries should be ourselves and the sterling area. We are not suggesting any change in the text in NABOB 297 if it is acceptable to the Americans, but only asking you to bear this point in mind should the Americans in their turn make counter proposals' (UE 5147/1094/53).

303

prolonged depression of World trade acknowledged by the International Monetary Fund as constituting a serious disturbance of the equilibrium of international payments.

(C)   *Scarcity of dollars.* In the event of the International Monetary Fund having given notice under article VII (1) of the International Monetary Fund that a general scarcity of dollars is developing.[3]

[3] The proposals contained in NABOB 296 and presented to Mr. Vinson and Mr. Clayton on 6 November (see No. 96) were discussed by the U.S. Top Committee at their meeting at 10 a.m. on 7 November: see *F.R.U.S. 1945,* vol. vi, pp. 157–62. The amendment to para. 3 contained in NABOB 297 (see note 2) had apparently been incorporated in the draft in time for the meeting: see Pressnell, *op. cit.,* Chapter 10(15). The meeting also discussed the revised formula on sterling area arrangements sent to Mr. White by Lord Keynes on 7 November: see No. 98.

NABOB 304, despatched at 11.29 p.m. on 7 November, stated that Mr. Vinson had told Lord Keynes that 'the Americans have decided that their immediate timetable for the next few days is now impracticable. In particular the publication of the International Trade Organisation Paper scheduled for Sunday [11 November: cf. No. 95, note 2] has been postponed . . . The further meeting on finance with Vinson and Clayton is postponed until tomorrow as their experts are occupied all today examining the papers we have left with them . . .' (T 236/457).

Between 7 and 15 November there appear to have been a number of Anglo-American discussions of which no detailed reports were sent: cf. Nos. 100–1 and 104.

No. 98

British Missions (Washington) to Cabinet Offices
(Received 12 November)

NABOB Saving 32 Telegraphic [*UE 5565/1094/53*]

WASHINGTON, 7 *November 1945*

Reference NABOB 276 and BABOON 198.[1]
Following is text of letter from Keynes to White dated 7th November forwarding a revised text of the proposed statement concerning the sterling area arrangements. The revised statement is also appended.

My dear Harry,

Sterling Area Arrangements

I warned you when giving you the provisional draft of the above on Monday,[2] that the earlier descriptive passages might need revision. I have now received the material for this from London and enclose a dozen copies of the revised draft.

You will find that the changes relate mainly to paragraphs 1 to 7 and none of the substantial matter of the following paragraphs has been altered. Paragraphs 1 to 7 are entirely descriptive. The revised form represents the version London prefers for a document which we must

[1] See No. 94.i.   [2] 5 November 1945: see No. 94, note 9.

assume will be published. I do not think you will find anything in the changes which needs any comment.

This draft as now amended you may take as final from our side.

Yours ever,
KEYNES

Sterling Area Arrangements

1. The Sterling Area is a trading and banking system which had, over a century or more, taken natural growth and shape from the practice of British and other communities overseas to conduct most of their overseas transactions in sterling and to hold in sterling a substantial part of their external monetary reserves. This natural evolution of the Sterling Area involved three practical consequences: first, foreign exchange accruing to banks in the area in the course of their business was normally converted by them into sterling; secondly, as a counterpart of this, the foreign exchange holdings and dealings of the entire area were centred in London; and, thirdly, sterling area countries, inasmuch as they transacted a large part of their business in sterling have always been willing to accept sterling in payment for their exports.

2. Until the outbreak of war in 1939 this system worked with the utmost freedom. Sterling could be used for payment to any country in the world and could be freely converted into any foreign currency.

3. When war broke out there was no change in the three elements of the system mentioned above, and all members of the Area acted on the understanding that these practices should remain unchanged. But under the stress of war time necessity Exchange Controls were introduced throughout the Sterling Area, as in virtually every country in the world outside U.S.A. Individual countries within the area have administered their own Controls independently of London, but with a common concern to reserve scarce currencies for essential expenditure.

4. Under the arrangements now in force the current earnings and accumulated sterling balances of the Sterling Area countries are available to be spent freely within the Sterling Area. But residents in the Sterling Area may only make payments to residents outside the Area with the approval of the Exchange Control of their country of residence. Transfers outside the Area for capital purposes are, generally speaking, disallowed. Personal remittances, including expenses of travel, are scrutinised in respect of their amount and their purpose. Exchange is provided to pay for any imports for which an import license has been obtained, and it is, therefore, through import licensing that control is effectively exercised over purchases abroad. Since some foreign currencies have been in much shorter supply than others, it has been inevitable, if accounts are to be balanced, that the system of import licensing should be exercised so as to discriminate in favour of those currencies which are in free supply and against those which are in scarce supply.

5. Since the members of the sterling area have followed their

305

longstanding practice of carrying out the bulk of their transactions in terms of sterling and of passing over to the London exchange authorities foreign currencies which come into their hands, and drawing their requirements of these currencies from London, thus feeding and drawing upon a 'pool', this system, as it affects the U.S., has come to be described as 'the sterling area dollar pool'.

6. The U.S. Government has represented to the British Government that the administration of this system in present conditions compared with the complete freedom it permitted before the war, is seriously detrimental to the interests of U.S. trade and commerce, since inevitably, there has been introduced an element of discrimination against American exporters.

7. The United Kingdom Government point out, as explained above, that until the outbreak of war in 1939 this system worked with the utmost freedom, and without discrimination. It is not the system as such which is restrictive of international commerce, but the fact that the area as a whole has command over a supply of dollars, and other foreign currencies, which is far from adequate to meet its natural requirements. Liberalisation of the administration of the system can only spring from an increased supply of dollars and other foreign currencies, and in no other way whatever. The strong desire of the United Kingdom to effect such liberalisation will ensure that any such increased supply is utilised to that end.

8. Moreover, there is a further obstacle to complete equality of treatment. At the end of June 1945 the sterling area balances and other liquid resources in London, representing the obligations of the U.K., amounted to $10.9 billion and the total gold and dollar reserves of the U.K. to no more than $1.8 billion, and the position is likely to deteriorate further during the ensuing twelve months with an increase in the sterling area balances to the neighborhood of $12 billion. Thus the reserve resources available to the U.K. exchange authorities are entirely inadequate to allow the sterling balances to be freely withdrawn. The position of the holders of these balances would be seriously worsened if the whole of their accumulated balances were to lose their availability. Indeed this would throw the commerce of a considerable part of the world into confusion and the field over which multilateral trade could be conducted would be greatly curtailed.

9. This does not mean that the Government of the U.K. would not wish, if it lay in their power, to return to the non-discriminatory arrangements which existed before the war, by which the group of countries, using London as the base of their external finance, were able to employ their available external purchasing power in all areas of the world with equal facility. Indeed the primary purpose of the Exchange Control of the U.K. has been to mobilise their resources and use them in the way most suited to war needs, while doing as little damage as possible to the status of sterling.

10. The problem is, therefore, to find a means of making the earnings from all future trade available to be expended without discrimination and, in addition, to free a sufficient portion of the accumulated balances and further portions by stages, so as to provide a sufficient working balance for the restoration of freedom of commerce.

11. The Government of the U.K. would be prepared on the basis of aid on a scale appropriate to the size of the problem, to proceed not later than the end of 1946 to make arrangements under which the current earnings of all sterling area countries would be freely available to make purchases in any currency area without discrimination, apart from any receipts arising out of military expenditure by the U.K. which it may be agreed to treat on the same basis as the balances accumulated during the war; and in addition to treat similarly a portion of the accumulated balances forthwith, and further portions by instalments in future years for the purpose of meeting current needs. This would require that a part of the accumulated balances should be retained until they become similarly available; thus unless the amounts released were reasonable in relation to the requirements of the holders, the position of the holders might be changed for the worse.

12. The result would be that any discrimination arising from the so-called 'dollar pool' would be entirely removed, in the sense that each member of the sterling area would have both its current earnings and its available sterling balances at its free disposition for current transactions anywhere.

13. The representatives of the U.S. Administration agreed that they would regard the carrying into effect of these measures as a matter of great interest and importance to the U.S. They would represent a decisive move towards the liquidation of the financial consequences of the war to commerce, over a wide area. Nevertheless it was the strongly held opinion of the U.S. representatives that they should not be the only contributors to a general settlement of this kind. It seemed to them that the sterling balances had been largely built up during the war and represented gains in external resources which would not have accrued to some of the countries concerned if those countries had contributed to the common costs of the war on the same principles as the aid which the U.S. had afforded to her Allies under the Lend Lease Act. They regarded it, therefore, as an essential condition of such a general settlement, if it were to commend itself as fair and right to the public opinion of the U.S., and indeed of the world at large, that the other countries concerned should also make retrospective contributions in a degree related to the improvement during the war in their external financial position. They were of the opinion that the indirect benefits through freeing their balances which would derive from aid furnished to the U.K. by the U.S. should go only to those countries which were themselves prepared to make an appropriate contribution to the common settlement.

14. The representatives of the U.K. agreed that they would naturally

welcome common action along such lines. At the same time they affirmed that they could not properly press a unilateral settlement on the countries which had shown such great trust in them during the war and had in this way given the U.K. essential support in contributing to the common victory. Any such settlement must be by mutual agreement. Nor would any settlement be a fair one which worked on a rigid formula or on cut-and-dried lines, since other factors ought to be taken into account besides the present size of the accumulated balances. They agreed, however, that the principles underlying the thesis of the U.S. representatives were fair and constructive and in the interests of all parties. They would, therefore, be ready at an early date to discuss a re-settlement with those concerned on the basis of dividing the accumulated sterling balances of each country into three categories, one category being freed at once and becoming convertible into any currency for current transactions, one category being similarly released by instalments over a long period of years, and one category being written off as a contribution to the success of the scheme as a whole and in recognition of the benefits which the countries concerned might be expected to gain from it. For the countries in question would have to recognise that, failing such a settlement as that under discussion and without aid from the U.S., it would be physically impracticable for the U.K. to repay the balances except over a long period of years and at a rate about which it would be impossible to enter into any definite commitment in advance. Thus it might be hoped that the sterling area countries would agree that it was in their own interest, as well as fair and reasonable, to come into such a general settlement, rather than to stay out of it.

15. The U.K. representatives would seek to arrive at voluntary agreements with the sterling area creditors varying according to the circumstances of each case by which each would make an appropriate contribution to the common plan by arrangements which would include a scaling down of the sterling claims. Of the sterling balances scaled down as above a limited part would be released immediately and the remainder by instalments over a period of years. As regards the subsequent releases it would be necessary to protect the position of the U.K. by a clause permitting postponement of releases in certain contingencies. Conversely there might be a provision to the effect that releases could be anticipated in cases where a particular country holding sterling balances was in a position such as might have called for assistance by way of a loan from the U.K. in normal times. More precise arrangements than the above could not be specified in advance of discussion with the countries concerned. The U.K. representatives however, agreed with the view that countries unwilling to enter into an agreement on these lines, which the U.K. would consider satisfactory and fair in relation to the contributions of others, could not expect to participate in the special releases which would become available to participants in the scheme and would have, out of the sheer inescapable necessities of the case, to accept a lower priority of release of

balances than those countries entering into the common scheme and to depend on the U.K.'s future capacity to repay after the U.K.'s obligations under the common scheme had been fully met. Nevertheless all future sterling earned by members of the sterling area, whether participants in the scheme or not, would be freely available for the purpose of current transactions, subject to the qualification relating to military expenditure in paragraph 9 above.

16. The U.K. representatives called attention at the same time to the weight of the commitments into which they would be entering by acceptance of a comprehensive scheme on the above lines. They would be foregoing the advantages to British exports of the large volume of potential purchasing power in overseas countries which would otherwise be available on a discriminatory basis favouring the U.K.: and they would be committing themselves to make substantial future payments in full convertible currency without the assistance to their capacity to liquidate the sterling balances which they would otherwise have retained. They were not prepared to accept commitments which they did not see their way to fulfil on reasonably cautious estimates. Their acceptance of a plan on the general lines indicated above would, therefore, only be possible if the aid contemplated was on a sufficient scale, and of this they must be the final judges, to carry the weight of the commitments they would be expected to undertake.[3]

[3] In a message to Sir W. Eady in Washington telegram No. 7491 of 8 November Lord Keynes reported 'strong rumours' that the Americans were 'most disturbed by what is apparently a sudden discovery so far as they are concerned, of the fact that our sterling area proposals do not cover payments agreements': cf. *F.R.U.S. 1945*, vol. vi, p. 161, and No. 97, note 3. Lord Keynes commented: 'I think I can put up a good case showing that any cut-and-dried commitments by us at this date would be impracticable and might lead to all sorts of difficulties for us. I can also argue that some of the payments agreements are very much of the same character as their own tied loans. If however they raise this issue at the top level in a definite and determined way it will be very difficult to get away with nothing'. He accordingly proposed the following formula: 'As soon as is practicable after completing the proposed arrangements for the liberalisation of the sterling area it will be the policy of the United Kingdom to provide by mutual agreement with countries outside the sterling area adhering to the International Monetary Fund that monetary agreements with them shall not be so operated in practice on either side as to involve discrimination in the use of a favourable balance arising from current transactions.'

Sir W. Eady replied in Foreign Office telegram No. 11322 of 9 November that the Treasury saw 'no special objection to this draft though we should prefer "to seek by mutual agreement" in place of "to provide by mutual agreement"' (UE 5441/1094/53).

No. 99

Memorandum by Mr. Bevin on the Foreign Situation[1]

[*F.O. 800/478*]

Top secret   FOREIGN OFFICE, *8 November 1945*

I think it desirable to circulate an appreciation of the foreign situation and the developments that are taking place as a whole.

2. We are committed to the World Organisation[2] and I have been trying to shape the whole policy of the Foreign Office to work in with this Organisation when it is established, on the assumption that such an Organisation would provide equality of treatment, impartial judgment, and lead to the establishment of a much greater measure of liberty for the people throughout the world.

3. Many organisations are being created, those dealing with food, labour, economics, health, education, &c., and each organisation that is established under this World Organisation must have the right conditions created in the political and territorial field if they are to grow in strength and usefulness and to be able to accomplish the purpose for which they have been established.

4. The whole question of the Security Council is designed by its creation to give relief from fear and aggression or war, or any kind of incidents which would wreck the efforts I have referred to above, and thereby lead to a long period of the progressive raising of the standard of life and liberty. If, of course, the Powers were really committed to it and meant what they are saying, other problems, such as territorial adjustment, could be approached with an entirely different attitude of mind.

5. On the top of this, of course, has come the effect of atomic energy, which has made in many cases territorial adjustment and frontier arrangements of less importance than they used to be, provided you can remove from the different States and people any sense of domination by others. As long as the conception of national sovereignty exists, frontiers will continue to be essential from the ethnic point of view as well as the economic; and very often even these two principles are in violent conflict. But from the point of view of peace the right use of atomic energy both militarily and commercially does in fact minimise the old conceptions of strategy.

6. I should be willing to pursue this policy of working in with the United Nations Organisation on the ground that it gives the best hope for

---

[1] This memorandum on 'three Monroes' (cf. Volume II, No. 294) was given 'a strictly limited' circulation (cf. i. below) and does not appear to have been formally circulated to the Cabinet. Extracts are printed in Alan Bullock, *Ernest Bevin: Foreign Secretary 1945–51* (London, 1983), pp. 193–4. The filed text, marked as 'copy No. 50', is in the form of confidential print, and no other text has been traced.

[2] i.e. the United Nations Organisation: documentation on the first meetings of the General Assembly and Security Council will be included in a future volume of this Series.

the world, if the facts of the situation allowed us to do it. But my colleagues must be made aware of the situation that has arisen and is developing with great rapidity. Instead of world co-operation we are rapidly drifting into spheres of influence or what can be better described as three great Monroes.

7. The United States have long held, with our support, to the Monroe Doctrine for the western hemisphere, and there is no doubt now that notwithstanding all the protestations that have been made they are attempting to extend this principle financially and economically to the Far East to include China and Japan, while the Russians seem to me to have made up their mind that their sphere is going to be from Lubeck to the Adriatic in the west and to Port Arthur in the east. Britain therefore stands between the two with the western world all divided up, with the French and British colonial empire[s] separated and with a very weak position in what is called the western group, and notably the position of Franco is embarrassing. If Spain was settled the western area would be improved, and I do not believe that it is entirely love of democracy that causes Russia to want to keep the Spanish pot boiling. If this sphere of influence business does develop it will leave us and France on the outer circle of Europe with our friends, such as Italy, Greece, Turkey, the Middle East, our Dominions and India, and our colonial empire in Africa: a tremendous area to defend and a responsibility that, if it does develop, would make our position extremely difficult. It will be realised that the continental side of this western sphere would also be influenced and to a very large extent dominated by the colossal military power of Russia and by her political power which she can bring to bear through the Communist parties in the various countries. Meanwhile, France would stand in a kind of intermediate position, balancing herself against the east and out of sheer necessity resting upon us. The future too of the German people is going to be a constant source of insecurity, and every sort of political trick will be resorted to in order to control or eliminate this eventual reservoir of power. The French demands on the Ruhr and the Rhineland,[3] and Russia's action in transferring Eastern Germany to Poland[4] are already examples of this tendency, and when the German people recover consciousness we may be sure they themselves will soon be playing an active part in these highly dangerous manœuvres.

8. But there is another great difference in these spheres of influence from anything that has existed hitherto. If they merely represented three security areas for which the three great Powers took responsibility when any territorial adjustment or claims made one upon another were referred to the international Security Organisation, then they would merely represent three, as it were, police areas for which each of us would accept responsibility for keeping order and preventing the outbreak of aggression. But it is going a great deal further than that. The naked fact is

[3] See Volume II, Nos. 46, 50, 62, 129, 140 and 286.   [4] See Volume I, No. 115.

that, whereas under the old Monroe system economic institutions and the system of government afforded liberty of trade and intercourse to other countries of the world, present tendencies are quite different. If you take Russia, for instance, all the argument and pressure that is going on indicates that in the whole life of the communities concerned there is an attempt to incorporate it into the Russian complete economy, while the United States, notwithstanding their claim to establish multilateral agreements with trade, appear to me to be taking similar steps so far as the Far East and South America are concerned by financial and economic methods. In fact, in all the efforts I have been associated with since I have taken office, in this field it seems to me that we are dealing with power politics naked and unashamed; and that either we have got to confront the world with it and ask if that is their intention or whether the United Nations Organisation and its effectiveness is to be the real goal of international relationship. A favourable opportunity will arise in dealing with problems that arise out of the great secrets developed in the war. Should we share them? On what basis should we share them? Has there got to be a real stand-up challenge for nations to declare whether World Organisation and co-operation is to be their policy with complete liberty of the States to form their own governments so that the peoples may rest on the basis of a real democracy; or is it to be power politics with the sure and certain knowledge that the predominating note is the division of the world into these three great spheres of influence, any one of which could be aggressor at any moment on the other two or vice versa? I cannot believe that foreign affairs can be brought on to a level in which the discussion will be honest and straightforward unless this issue is clearly faced. It seems vital to me not to deceive the peoples of the world by leading them to believe that we are creating a United Nations Organisation which is to protect them from future world wars, in which we share our knowledge, our secrets, and which they will regard as a beneficent protection against war, while at the same time we know, in fact, that nothing of the kind is happening. There are at least two mighty countries in the world which, by the very nature of things, are following the present policy which is bound to see them line up against each other, while we in Great Britain who have had the brunt of two great wars will be left to take sides either with one or the other. Just as there may be a clash between France and Russia over who is to get control of the German people, so there are all the makings of a still more dangerous conflict between the United States and Russia over the body and soul of China. The prospect at the moment is not healthy and not encouraging, and I cannot believe we shall make any real progress until the three of us bluntly and unequivocally ask each other to put on the table clearly and straightforwardly what our real policy is and which road we propose to travel.

9. Finally, there is no more striking illustration of the difficulty that arises from the present position than the terrible situation in Central Europe in which millions of lives could be saved and prosperity brought

back to the territory under peaceful conditions comparatively quickly, certainly within a decade, if the policy of all of us was adjusted in a manner that would assist us in grappling with this terrific problem.

10. I have reviewed the whole position in the light of the above and have reached the conclusion that, with the present deadlock between the Big Three,[5] we shall not accomplish very much. Therefore, I propose, in dealing with all these problems, to proceed in the light of the obligations which will be assumed by all under the United Nations Organisation and to assure myself that the decisions I reach will ultimately fit in with the precedure, constitution and obligations of that body. I consider this course essential, having regard to what I deduce to be Stalin's[6] present position: namely, to create a vast area under Russian control from Lubeck to Port Arthur, and to obtain a position equal with that of the United States in Japan.[7] This interpretation of the Soviet position is reinforced by the speech made by Molotov on the 6th November.[8] In my view, therefore, the only safe course for this country is to stand firm behind the United Nations Organisation and, in carrying out our policy there, to rely on our right to maintain the security of the British Commonwealth on the same terms as other countries are maintaining theirs, and to develop, within the conception of the United Nations, good relations with our near neighbours in the same way as the United States have developed their relations on the continent of America.

E.B.

CALENDAR TO NO. 99

i *12 Dec. 1945 & 13 Jan. 1946*   (a) *Letter from Lord Halifax (Washington) to Mr. Bevin* enclosing his 'reflections' on No. 99: 'from the Washington angle the available evidence does not warrant the pessimistic view that America is pursuing a policy designed to divide the world in the manner described'; (b) *Minute by Mr. Butler* commenting on (a) and incorporating views of Sir H. Seymour (H.M. Ambassador at Chungking) and S. American Dept.: American professions about U.N. should be taken seriously, but 'when the Administration embarks on re-insurance in ways which conflict with their obligations towards U.N.O. then it is for us to stand up for what we consider to be right and not to defer automatically to American wishes' [F.O. 800/478, 513].

[5] Cf. Volume II, No. 171.
[6] Marshal of the Soviet Union J.V. Stalin.   [7] *V. ibid.*, No. 182.
[8] In a survey of international events (see *The Times*, 7 November 1945, p. 4) M. Molotov, Soviet Commissar for Foreign Affairs, had stressed the Soviet contribution to winning the war, referred to the need for 'vigilance concerning possible fresh breakers of the peace' and declared: 'We, too, shall have atomic energy and many other things'.

No. 100

Letter from Mr. Hall-Patch (Washington) to Mr. Coulson

[*UE 5533/1094/53*]

WASHINGTON, *9 November 1945*

Dear Coulson,

In Butler's absence[1] I am sending you these cuttings.[2] Please pass them on to anybody concerned.

The high spot to-day is the open opposition of Baruch and Jesse Jones[3] to any sort of settlement which we would consider reasonable. So much for the press. These two people are names to conjure with and the press gives perhaps undue attention to what they say. Nevertheless they are unpleasant opponents to have in the field.

Keynes has just received the reply to alternative 'A' which we are to discuss in a few minutes.[4] I have not the full details, but the Americans, as we expected here, will simply not look at any portion of the credit being interest free. That cock simply will not fight: I never thought it would. Now we are thrown back on the 'other alternative'.[5] But the field is not so clear as it was. The Americans apparently want us to give sterling full Bretton Woods convertibility by June 1946 as a counterpart of *any* financial assistance.[6] This is a bitter pill, and quite impossible for us to swallow. How they expect us to assume this obligation when they are only prepared (apparently) to give us 3½ billion on practically commercial terms, I simply do not know. It shows such a lack of appreciation of the real issues that I am almost in despair.

We shall probably be telegraphing later in the day. This is just background in case we decide not to telegraph, but simply to tell the Americans to go away and think again. One thing seems certain: the Clayton timetable[7] is down the drain.

Yours ever,

E.L. HALL-PATCH

CALENDAR TO NO. 100

i *11 & 14 Nov. 1945 From and to British Missions (Washington) Tels. NABOB 325 & BABOON 277* In response to Mr. Vinson's enquiry Mr. Dalton informs Lord

[1] Mr. Butler left for Washington on 9 November with Mr. Attlee: see Volume II, No. 216, note 1.
[2] Not printed.
[3] Mr. Jesse H. Jones, prominent Texan public figure and former U.S. Secretary of Commerce, was owner and publisher of the *Houston Chronicle*.
[4] See No. 101.   [5] See No. 94, para. 6, and cf. No. 97, note 2.
[6] Mr. Coulson wrote against this passage: 'This is news'. Cf. No. 98, note 3, and Pressnell, *op. cit.*, Chapter 10(16).
[7] See No. 93.ii.

Keynes of his intention to present Bretton Woods agreement to Parliament as soon as possible: 'If, however, we are refused sufficient dollars we shall have to refuse all Bretton Woods commitments' [UE 5504, 5555/16/53].

No. 101

British Missions (Washington) to Cabinet Offices
(Received 11 November, 8.15 p.m.)

NABOB 324 Telegraphic [UE 5525/1094/53]

Secret   WASHINGTON, 11 November 1945, 6.37 p.m.

For Chancellor of Exchequer from Keynes and Brand.

1. Despite all our efforts Vinson and Clayton have finally rejected alternative A[1] after having put our proposals in NABOB 296[2] before their Top Committee.[3] We have since proceeded tentatively along the lines of paragraph 6 of BABOON 206.[4]

2. They have not yet formally increased the amount of their previous offer but discussions are proceeding on the assumption that the amount will be increased to 4½ billion inclusive of lend–lease clean-up provided that all other outstanding matters are settled satisfactorily.

3. By implication they have dropped the idea of covering lend–lease by a separate 3C loan. We have not yet put your condition that the lend–lease settlement must be kept within ½ billion, since if we set this maximum it would be in danger of becoming a minimum also. We think that this is better handled in direct connection with the lend–lease settlement where we consider your present instructions to be that we are to refuse any aggregate settlement in excess of ½ billion. We hope soon to be in a position to make a definite proposal on this.

4. The terms of the 4½ billions would be a five years moratorium followed by a fifty years annuity of 31,800 dollars for each 1,000,000 dollars of the original amount of the loan. They would describe this as a 2 per cent loan but allowing for the moratorium it works out at 1.6 per cent.

5. We are now engaged on detailed discussion mainly at the technical level, though Vinson and Clayton are sometimes present, about the draft of the financial agreement and more particularly the clauses dealing with the waiver and with the sterling area arrangements.

6. Several tiresome and difficult points have been raised and some matters have been re-opened which we hoped had been settled. We are trying to clear out of the way as many as possible of those of the novel points of the draftsmen which seem to us clearly inacceptable. On Monday or Tuesday[5] we may be able to send for your consideration a revised text

---

[1] See No. 81.   [2] No. 97.
[3] Cf. *F.R.U.S. 1945*, vol. vi, p. 162, note 11.   [4] No. 94: cf. No. 97, note 2.
[5] 12 or 13 November 1945. In NABOB 339 of 14 November Lord Keynes sent the

of the technical clauses which we believe the Americans might accept together with our recommendations.

following message to Sir W. Eady: 'For the whole of today and yesterday the Americans have gone into purdah with their own drafting committee. We are moderately hopeful that what will emerge will not be too different on major matters from what we were discussing with them on the two previous days, though new tiresome details may well come up. Meanwhile we have nothing sufficiently authentic to send you. We expect to be given the semi-final American text on Thursday morning [15 November: see No. 104]' (UE 5566/1094/53).

No. 102

Letter from Mr. Churchill (Paris)[1] to Mr. Bevin

[F.O. 800/512]

Most secret   PARIS, 13 November 1945

Dear Ernest,
Thank you for sending me the telegrams,[2] which I have duly burnt.

[1] Mr. Churchill was paying a private visit to Paris during which he was presented with the Gold Medal of the Académie des Sciences Morales et Politiques: see The Times, 13 November 1945, p. 4.

[2] In a personal letter of 12 November Mr. Bevin sent to Mr. Churchill copies of three telegrams (Washington telegrams Nos. 7470 and 7516, and Foreign Office telegram No. 11298 to Washington) concerning U.S. proposals on bases, and asked for his views. Washington telegram No. 7470 of 8 November contained the text of an aide-mémoire of 6 November which had been enclosed in a letter of 7 November from Mr. Byrnes to Lord Halifax (Washington telegram No. 7469 of 8 November, not printed), listing the bases required by the United States, as promised to Lord Halifax by Mr. Byrnes on 5 November: see No. 84, note 8. The main points of the aide-mémoire were as discussed in No. 135 below: the U.S. Government wished for an assurance that His Majesty's Government would assist them in negotiations for bases in Iceland and the Azores (see Nos. 48, 61 and 90), and listed the territories administered by the U.K., Australia or New Zealand (two of which were under mandate to the latter two countries) where the U.S. wanted long term military base rights. The aide-mémoire also suggested the negotiation of an agreement on certain Pacific Islands claimed by both the U.K. and the U.S., as a result of which the U.K. and New Zealand should withdraw from those islands.

The text of the aide-mémoire and list of bases printed in F.R.U.S. 1945, vol. vi, pp. 206–11, was similar but not identical to that in telegram No. 7470: it also contained a passage concerning the relationship between the bases proposals and the financial negotiations, and the following sentence: 'It would be agreeable to him [Mr. Byrnes] to have no connection established between the lend–lease settlement and the financial talks and negotiations about bases, other than in the matter of timing.' The text in F.R.U.S. also contained two paragraphs concerning the U.S. Government's desire to share with the U.K. permanent rights for the military use of two air bases in India, and suggesting joint negotiations to secure the agreement of the Indian Government.

In response to Mr. Bevin's telegram No. 11298 of 9 November asking Lord Halifax whether the list of bases in telegram No. 7470 was complete, Lord Halifax replied in telegram No. 7516 of 10 November that Mr. Byrnes had spoken to him on 9 November concerning the two Indian air bases which were judged to be 'strategically important and

1. The long-term advantage to Britain and the Commonwealth is to have our affairs so interwoven with those of the United States in external and strategic matters, that any idea of war between the two countries is utterly impossible, and that in fact, however the matter may be worded, we stand or fall together. It does not seem likely that we should have to fall. In a world of measureless perils and anxieties, here is the rock of safety.

2. From this point of view, the more strategic points we hold in Joint occupation, the better. I have not studied particular islands and bases in detail on the map, but in principle there is no doubt that the Joint occupation greatly strengthens the power of the United States and the safety of Britain. Although the United States is far more powerful than the British Commonwealth, we must always insist upon coming in on equal terms. We should press for Joint occupation at all points in question rather than accept the exclusive possession by the United States. We have so much to give that I have little doubt that, for the sake of a general settlement, they would agree to Joint occupation throughout.

3. I do not agree with the characteristic Halifax slant that we should melt it all down into a vague United Nations Trusteeship.[3] This ignores the vital fact that a special and privileged relationship between Great Britain and the United States makes us both safe for ourselves and more influential as regards building up the safety of others through the international machine. The fact that the British Commonwealth and the United States were for strategic purposes one organism, would mean:

(a) that we should be able to achieve more friendly and trustful relations with the Soviet Russia, and

(b) that we could build up the United Nations organization around us and above us with greater speed and success. Whom God hath joined together, let no man put asunder. Our duties to mankind and all States and nations remain paramount, and we shall discharge them all the better hand in hand.

4. As you know, I write as a strong friend of the Russian people, and as one of those responsible for the Twenty Years' Treaty with Soviet Government,[4] to which Treaty I most strongly adhere. The future of the world depends upon the fraternal association of Great Britain and the Commonwealth with the United States. With that, there can be no war. Without it, there can be no peace. The fact that strategically the

which the United States Government would like to see us control. Could we keep or get these under United Kingdom control?' Lord Halifax had explained that His Majesty's Government would find 'great difficulty' with this suggestion, and would feel 'that proper authority United Nations organisation ought in due course to express its interest in these bases, if it felt that way, and that we might at that stage, if His Majesty's Government so desired, work it out in some way to assist India in doing whatever was required'. See No. 103, and cf. *F.R.U.S.*, *ibid.*, p. 209, note 88.

[3] Cf. note 2.

[4] i.e. the Treaty of Alliance between the U.K. and Soviet Union signed on 26 May 1942: see *B.F.S.P.*, vol. 144, pp. 1038–41.

English-speaking world is bound together, will enable us to be all the better friends with Soviet Russia, and will win us the respect of that realistic State. Strategically united, we need have no fear of letting them come out into the great waters and have the fullest efflorescence as their numbers and their bravery deserve.

5. The Joint Association of the Great British Commonwealth and the United States in the large number of islands and bases, will make it indispensable to preserve indefinitely the organization of the Combined Chiefs of Staff Committee. From this should flow the continued interchange of military and scientific information and Intelligence, and also, I hope, similarity and interchangeability of weapons, common manuals of instruction for the Armed Forces, inter-related plans for the war mobilization of civil industry, and finally, interchange of officers at schools and colleges.

6. What we may now be able to achieve is, in fact, Salvation for ourselves, and the means of procuring Salvation for the world.

You are indeed fortunate that this sublime opportunity has fallen to you, and I trust the seizing of it will ever be associated with your name. In all necessary action you should count on me, if I can be of any use.[5]

Yours very sincerely,
WINSTON S. CHURCHILL

[5] In a letter of 17 November Mr. Bevin thanked Mr. Churchill 'for giving me so fully your views. I agree with you about joint bases. But the difficulty is that we have committed ourselves to the United Nations, and I must keep this aspect in mind' (F.O. 800/512). Mr. Bevin had also sent copies of the telegrams in note 2 to Mr. Eden: see Alan Bullock, op. cit., pp. 200–1.

No. 103

Mr. Bevin to the Earl of Halifax (Washington)

No. 11501 Telegraphic [F.O. 800/512]

Immediate. Top secret   FOREIGN OFFICE, *15 November 1945, 11.8 p.m.*

Your telegrams Nos. 7469, 7470 and 7516.[1]

I am glad to have received from Mr. Byrnes the total claims which the United States Government is making on us, but it is obvious that this raises a very difficult problem to decide, and while you in your telegram said it was for me alone it was obvious that I could not deal with it without advice. I therefore privately consulted the Chiefs of Staff and asked them to look into it from the military angle.

2. Meanwhile pending their report there are certain points upon which perhaps Mr. Byrnes can help to clarify my mind.

3. The first—and this rather attracts me—is the proposal to deal with a

[1] See No. 102, note 2.

number or all of these places jointly. To what extent would Mr. Byrnes be willing to reciprocate by allowing a wider area of joint use over some of the already United States owned bases, for instance Manila? It would go better with the British people if it were felt that this was a mutual arrangement.

4. The next thing is, how much of this is wanted for military purposes and how much for civil aviation, because it seems to me that a number of these places have no military value at all. Obviously if a commercial proposition is involved, the question will have to be dealt with on two different grounds.

5. The next thing is, Mr. Byrnes has told us what bases he wants in our own territory and as regards support by us in Iceland (C)[2] and in Portuguese territory. Does he want anything from other countries such as France or Holland?

6. With regard to the Azores, this raises separate problems on which I will telegraph later.

7. With regard to India, it is virtually a sovereign state in all these matters and I really could not handle India in the way suggested.

8. As to the disputed places mentioned in paragraph 3 of your telegram No. 7470, I am having this question examined but could you tell me what is at the back of Byrnes' mind? Are the United States Government thinking of establishing military bases in them (and if so, under the United Nations system) or what is special value attached to them by United States e.g. is civil aviation at the bottom of it?

9. Now I come to the really crucial point. So far as the joint bases are concerned in British territory is it really necessary to formalise existing arrangements in advance of the international system of security under the United Nations Charter? I cannot see that there is any conflict with the United Nations or with Russia so long as in the event of aggression the joint base would be open for use by the Security Council. Surely what we want to do is at the right moment to formalise the existing United States position in the British territories in question, as joint users of the bases, in the United Kingdom's 'special agreement' with the Security Council under Article 43 of the Charter.[3] I am concerned at the risk of harming the United Nations Organisation (and of giving the Russians serious grounds for complaint) by attempting to formalise the existing arrangements in advance, and appearing to face them with a *fait accompli*. The same applies to arrangements about the future of the disputed Pacific islands. I have made a declaration in the House that all my policy must square with the obligations we have entered into,[4] and this preliminary series of deals

[2] In 1941 Mr. Churchill had directed that in official correspondence Iceland should be designated Iceland (C) to avoid confusion with Ireland: the letter (C) was dropped in 1946.

[3] Cf. No. 90, para. 2. Article 43 of the U.N. Charter referred to the obligation of all Members to 'make available to the Security Council, on its call and in accordance with a special agreement or agreements, armed forces, assistance, and facilities, including rights of passage, necessary for the purpose of maintaining international peace and security'.

[4] For Mr. Bevin's statement to this effect during the Foreign Affairs debate on 7 November see *Parl. Debs., 5th ser., H. of C.*, vol. 415, col. 1335.

about bases and territories will look to the world like sharp practice and I do not want my foreign policy to be guilty of that. Therefore it would mean very careful study.

10. There are two places which are mandated territories.[1] Can we fortify mandated territories without the organisation which is taking the place of the League of Nations? That is another worry.

11. I think it is asking me too much to go on and discuss this thing and not to say a word to New Zealand and Australia before the United States approaches them, because both countries will obviously know that we know about it and it will only cause bad blood between the Dominions and ourselves. Is it not better to be frank with them and say that we want to enter into the best possible mutual arrangements for our difficulties and to bring them in at the beginning especially if in all cases it is joint? I beg of you to impress upon Mr. Byrnes that it is difficult for me to lend myself to anything which will produce bad blood between the Dominions and ourselves.

12. Finally, when I have had the thing studied in all its aspects I will communicate with you again, but although I have entered what looks like criticism, again let me thank Mr. Byrnes for being so helpful and letting us see the picture as a whole. If he does not mind my putting a few daubs of paint on it from our angle so as to make it a better picture I will be glad.

13. Please show this telegram to the Prime Minister.[5]

CALENDAR TO NO. 103

i *20–24 Nov. 1945   Correspondence between Mr. Bevin and Lord Halifax* concerning Mr. Byrnes' reaction to No. 103 (cf. *F.R.U.S. 1945*, vol. vi, pp. 214–16): Dominion Prime Ministers informed of expected approach to Australia and New Zealand on mandated territories [F.O. 800/443].

[5] This was evidently the telegram of which Mr. Attlee expressed approval in the letter to Mr. Bevin printed as No. 242 in Volume II.

No. 104

Letter from Mr. Hall-Patch (Washington) to Mr. Coulson

[*UE 5841/1094/53*]

Personal   WASHINGTON, *15 November 1945*

My dear Coulson,

I only wish the situation were as clear and the outlook as promising as this batch of cuttings[1] would lead the reader to suppose.

I am becoming steadily more worried. The 'smoke-filled' room

[1] Not printed.

technique with no witnesses and no record is a form of negotiation which is only possible if you are supremely confident that the people with whom you are dealing are powerful enough to put through what they agree with you as reasonable. With the rabbits with whom we are dealing I am not sure it is the right technique, and I am not at all sure that what will emerge from the smoke-filled room will be at all palatable to London.

Qui vivra verra[2], but my present mood is one of definite pessimism. As an indication of the sort of thing which shakes me to the core let me cite what the Chairman of the Federal Reserve Board said at a Top Finance Committee this very afternoon.[3] Note who he is: one of the key financial figures in the U.S. corresponding to the Governor of the Bank of England. We were discussing 'waivers' and objecting strongly to an American suggestion which tied us down far too tightly. To our objections Marriner Eccles replied: 'But we would then have no safeguards if some of our money was used to raise your standard of living or to meet military expenditure'. That a man in his position should suggest that we would ever accept money from anybody which would give the lender a right to control our standard of living or our defense expenditure is so utterly fantastic that one is almost driven to the conclusion that, work on them as we may, it is impossible to convince them that there are certain things which are just not possible.

I hope I do not take too prejudiced a view, but at present I am very depressed.

Yours ever,
E.L. HALL-PATCH

CALENDARS TO NO. 104

i   *15 Nov. 1945   COM/FIN 3rd Meeting (Washington)*, with annexed U.S. draft memo. of 14 Nov. in reply to No. 97 (cf. Pressnell, *op. cit.*, Chapter 10(17), and *F.R.U.S. 1945*, vol. vi, p. 164, note 16) [UE 6249/1094/53].

ii *16 Nov. 1945   Note by Economic Relations Department* on progress of financial and commercial negotiations [UE 5621/1094/53].

[2] He who lives will see.
[3] See i below for the minutes of this meeting, together with a 'U.S. Draft Memorandum of Understanding on Financial Matters', which was received by the British Delegation on the morning of 15 November: cf. No. 101, note 5. NABOB 342 of 16 November states that it had been intended to forward the American proposals to London, but the U.S. memorandum contained 'certain clauses so clearly inacceptable that we had to warn them [the Americans] that to present it to you could only end in deadlock. They asked, therefore, for time to reconsider the whole of their draft, partly in detail and partly in substance, before we send anything to you as their formal counter-proposal to Alternative A [see No. 97]' (UE 5994/1094/53).

No. 105

The Earl of Halifax (Washington) to Mr. Bevin
(Received 17 November, 4.15 a.m.)

No. 7688 Telegraphic [AN 3708/3121/45]

Immediate. Top secret   WASHINGTON, 16 November 1945, 10.58 p.m.

Personal for Secretary of State from Lord Halifax.
My telegram No. 6491.[1]
I met Vandenberg last night. He began talking to me about the loan negotiations about which he said with some bitterness that the present régime, unlike that of Hull and Stettinius, had kept himself and other Senators in complete ignorance. On the broad question of the loan he did not (repeat not) appear unreceptive of argument but said that the principal difficulty in the Senate would be the feeling that if they made a loan to us they would also have to make other loans to a lot of other people, including Russia. Our problem would therefore be greatly assisted if we could in any way discriminate in the mind of the American public our position from that of others. He asked whether there were not some 'gadgets' that we could attach to make the thing look different. In this connexion, without prompting from me, he asked whether it was not possible to convert the 99 (repeat 99)-year leases in the West Indies into 999 (repeat 999)-year leases. This, he thought, would have a very large effect.[2]

CALENDAR TO No. 105

i 27 Dec. 1945   Letter from Mr. Butler to Lord Halifax (Washington) regarding C.O.S. views on possible extension of base leases (see note 2): 'the verdict is clearly against our making an offer' [AN 3821/3121/45].

[1] No. 47.
[2] Mr. Bevin wrote on the filed copy of this telegram: 'Ask Chiefs of Staff. E.B.' In response to letters from the Foreign Office of 29 November and 5 December (not printed), the Chiefs of Staff, having consulted the Joint Planning Staff (J.P. (45) 302 of 10 December, not printed), expressed the opinion in a letter of 15 December that 'militarily it is undesirable to surrender now our rights to bases at a future date and that there is no worth while military concession which we could hope to obtain from the Americans as a *quid pro quo* for our offer of extended leases' (AN 3821/3121/45).

No. 106

British Missions (Washington) to Cabinet Offices
(Received 18 November, 10.35 p.m.)

NABOB 356 Telegraphic [UE 5629/1094/53]

Immediate. Secret   WASHINGTON, 18 November 1945, 5.17 p.m.

For Treasury from Keynes, Brand, Robbins and all the other members of the Mission.

With reference to NABOB 355[1] this is telegram A. Our immediately following telegram[2] gives the text of the waiver clause as we expect it to emerge from the American top committee. The following are our comments.

1. Clause (1)(a) is now on the general lines about which you were informed some time ago. You should, however, be aware that in the meanwhile several other versions have been proposed on the American side some of which seemed to us so clearly inacceptable that we were unwilling to transmit them to you.

2. In our small committee[3] Clayton began by proposing a version involving a deferment of capital instalments and interest instead of a waiver of interest which in our opinion, [? would] have had certain merits.

3. When, however, Clayton's proposals were transmitted to the other

---

[1] This telegram of 18 November explained that the following 7 telegrams, designated A–G (see Nos. 106 and note 2 below, 107–8, 109 and note 5 and 110 respectively) constituted 'a series of related messages commenting on or reproducing the text of certain sections which we think are likely to be included in the American financial proposals' expected on 19 November. In a personal message to Sir W. Eady in NABOB 354 of 18 November Lord Keynes had stated that these telegrams would deal with 'particular questions that have arisen from our recent discussions with the Americans, partly at the technical level and partly in the main finance committee. Some of them are of very great, some of lesser, importance, but they will all require close technical study. For this reason we feel it desirable to send you this material piecemeal, and not necessarily in systematic order.' He further commented: 'We should warn you that, as you may gather from the contents of our following telegrams, we are having heavy going and there may be further troubles ahead . . .' (T 236/457).

In BABOON 290 of 19 November in reply to all these telegrams the Treasury stated: 'There are quite clearly involved not only matters of great technical complexity, but also major issues which will have to be put to Ministers. We cannot say anything until we have the full text of the American proposal as and when it comes to you, together with your comments' (UE 5629/1094/53).

[2] Not printed. The text in NABOB 357 (Telegram B) was the same as para. 4 of No. 113 below except that: (i) clause I(a) read '. . . from the invisible items in its balance of payments (as defined in Article XIX(i) of the Articles of Agreement of the International Monetary Fund)'; (ii) the concluding phrase of clauses I(a) and (b) read 'from 1950 to the given year'; (iii) the first sentence of clause I(b) did not include the italicized words in the phrase 'less than *the sum of* (1)' nor the concluding words 'as of the end of the preceding calendar year'; (iv) there was no clause corresponding to clause II and clause III was accordingly numbered II.

[3] Cf. No. 104, note 3, for discussions on 15 November.

323

departments, especially the Treasury and the Federal Reserve, the technicians and lawyers got to work, in elaborating complicated provisions which were clearly incompatible with your fundamental conditions for accepting a waiver clause. A very strong effort was made by certain elements on the American side to introduce a discretionary element. When, after prolonged wrangling, we had succeeded in throwing this out, they produced in its place further provisions which would have required just that continuous scrutiny which you had forbidden us to accept.[4] Finally it became necessary for the Ambassador and the rest of us to inform the American top committee in unambiguous language that if they persisted with clauses as drafted we should not be able to continue negotiations along the present lines. We also put it forcibly to Clayton and Vinson in the presence of the other members of the committee that it was only on the basis of certain expectations they had held out to us as to the nature of the waiver that we had been able to overcome your reasonable scruples and your fears, which had now turned out to be only too well founded, as to what a waiver might end up in and what they were now asking us to send you was of a totally different character. If, therefore, they were to press us further on these lines, the negotiations must go right back to the point at which they stood before Clayton made his original suggestion. The result was that at a meeting between the Americans themselves later in the day, many of the most objectionable passages were abandoned by the Americans and the general plan went back more nearly to the form in which Clayton had first put it to us. Unfortunately there was one survival, namely, clause (1)(b) about the state of our reserves, to which we return below. The above struggle was particularly severe and protracted because some of those on the American side who have sometimes come to our support, lent us little aid.

4. The waiver provision in (1)(a) of NABOB 357 differs from what you know already in two particulars, both of which we regard as improvements.

5. The critical figure of our external income relates to a moving average of five years instead of a single year. This is an advantage to the Americans in that we cannot claim deferment as the result of an isolated bad year, and an advantage to us in that the criterion of our position is placed on a broader basis. In particular, we shall not have to pay if a single good year follows a succession of poor years until there have been enough good years to compensate for the bad ones. Perhaps we cannot complain overmuch against the petty meanness of substituting 866 million pounds which is the exact average of the three pre-war years instead of our rounded up figure of 875 million pounds.[5]

6. Secondly, the critical figure of our external income is increased by taking account of the annual repayments of all the war and post-war debts that we have undertaken or shall undertake. Our external income must be sufficient to pay not only for the pre-war war volume of imports but also

[4] Cf. Nos. 82 and 104.   [5] See No. 97.

instalments of interest and capital repayment on the American credit and Canadian credit and any annual amortisation at a reasonable rate to which we may agree in respect of sterling balances held by the sterling area, special account countries, etc. This may have the effect of raising the critical figure by an amount of say 75 million pounds. It is the result of accepting as the definition of net invisible income the Bretton Woods formula which in reckoning net external current income allows the deduction of payments of a moderate amount for the amortisation of loans in addition to the interest on them. A reference to article XIX (1)[6] shows that in other respects also the definition is a generous one. This means, of course, that we must bring into credit normal annual amortisation on our own loans to overseas though not lump sum repayments on maturity. On balance however, we clearly gain substantially. There is no misunderstanding about the intention here since it was at the American suggestion that Bretton Woods definition was brought in precisely in order that the critical figure might be enough to pay for the debt charges as well as pre-war volume of imports.

7. You will appreciate that, since the annual service is to be a fixed sum covering both interest and amortisation the effect of the waiver clause is to give us greater protection in the earlier years when interest constitutes the greater part of the fixed sum that [sic] in the later years when the proportion goes the other way. Thus for every billion of the loan 20 million of the 1951 payment will represent interest and 11.8 million capital.

8. Clause (1)(b) which provides that we cannot avail ourselves of the main waiver clause if our gross reserves exceed a given figure is another matter. As mentioned above, this is the survivor of other and even more objectionable clauses. The Americans claim that the insertion of some such clause is a necessary consequence of making the waiver automatic. We have repeatedly informed them that we cannot regard this clause as acceptable either in principle or in detail and they are under no illusion as to the likelihood of your accepting it.

9. We have argued against this clause on two grounds. In the first place we think it quite wrong in principle and against the interest of both countries. The Bretton Woods plan, the projected provisions of the I.T.O. and the continued liberalisation of the sterling area will be rendered far more likely to endure over a long period of years if we hold substantial reserves than if we are constantly in anxiety and too near to bedrock. It is hardly an exaggeration to say that the whole American scheme essentially depends on our establishing a position which in all normal conditions is a strong one. Thus a provision which attempts to curtail our reserves points to what is the wrong direction in the interests of both countries. The clause is also objectionable because it might easily suggest to the layman that the Americans wish to keep us in as weak a position as possible.

[6] i.e. of the Articles of Agreement of the I.M.F. (see No. 1, note 7): Article XIX(i) defined the scope of 'payments for current transactions'.

10. In the second place, we have pointed out that even if the principle of such a clause is admitted, the numerical values they have adopted, which we heard of for the first time yesterday in its present version, are clearly inacceptable since it is hopelessly inadequate. We told them frankly that we could not regard it otherwise than as a bad joke and we suspect that some of them share our opinion. The difficulty is, as we pointed out, that any such clause is faced with the dilemma that if the figure for our reserves is low it is open to the objections set out above, whilst if it [is] high it will not help them much with their critics in Congress.

11. Nevertheless, they adhere to the position that it will be difficult for them to defend against critics a waiver clause which would enable us to escape payment in circumstances where our accumulated reserves were very high indeed and plainly capable of meeting the payment without any embarrassment. They will not accept our rejoinder that in such circumstances they must trust us not to wish to avail ourselves of the waiver clause.

12. We should add that one of the reasons which the Americans have mentioned to us for wishing to retain a clause on these lines which may bulk more largely in their calculations then they have admitted, is the creation of precedents for other countries. They are very conscious that they will be under pressure to make similar concessions in other cases, for example, France or Russia. With these two countries they may well be justified in insisting on some clause of this kind. They fear that if they let us get away without such a clause, their difficulties in enforcing on other countries will be much increased.

13. It seemed useless to argue the matter further at this stage. We hope you will instruct us to reject the clause as it now stands. We have given the Americans no reason to expect that you will accept any alternative. Nevertheless, we should be grateful if you would consider the possibility of a compromise since undoubtedly the American position is held firmly and with conviction, we shall have the utmost difficulty in persuading them to abandon it unless we can offer some kind of compromise.

14. It seems to us that if there is to be a formula it must take account of our liabilities as well as our gross reserves [and] the best version would entitle us to deduct the whole of our quick external liabilities. The Americans object that it has never been our practice nor is it necessary for us to hold a reserve against 100 percent of our external liabilities. Nor do they like for this purpose the definition of net monetary reserves in article XIX of Bretton Woods because it is too complicated and in some respects a little vague.

15. But we do not see how they can reasonably object to a version under which the waiver can only be exercised if our gross reserves are less than say 25 per cent of our imports plus 50 per cent of convertible sterling balances, restricting the latter to the balances of banks, central banks and central monetary authorities of overseas countries. Our convertible sterling balances immediately after the present plan comes into effect, i.e., at the beginning of 1947 will scarcely be less than 250 million pounds and

a normal figure looking further ahead is hardly likely to be less than 500 million pounds. Taking the smaller of these figures the formula based on a pre-war volume of imports at double pre-war prices would give 563 million pounds as our minimum gross reserve, whilst the larger figure would give 688 million pounds. If we started a depressed period of exports with reserves above this, the formula would of course mean that we should have to meet the instalments out of our reserves to start with, but the waiver would operate as soon as using our reserves in this way had brought them down to the critical figure.

16. An advantage of relating the formula to our net reserves in this way is that this would not seriously prejudice the Americans in discussions with Russia and France since in their case there is no significant difference between gross reserves and net reserves.

17. Another line of thought would be to take our bedrock reserves at 250 million pounds and make the critical figure 25 per cent of imports plus 250 million pounds. This would give a figure exactly the same as the higher of the two figures above namely, 688 million pounds. We mention this because White threw it out at one point.

18. As stated in para. 8 above we have endeavoured to reject the whole principle but nevertheless it is, of course, difficult to produce an entirely convincing answer to the American contention that if our reserves are large enough we should pay. Once we admit that, we are driven to the question of what is large enough. Thus it might be well to have some compromise which we could offer in the last resort.

19. After a prolonged struggle we have failed to retain any part of the London waiver.[7] After purporting to agree to something on these lines the Americans have steadily receded since they saw the terms in black and white. The so-called technicians and Federal Reserve lawyers have swept aside the provisional agreement with Clayton and Vinson to such a clause on which we were relying. The Americans urge in particular that any reference to scarcity of dollars is a red rag to Congress, clause (II) in NABOB 357 is all that remains. We understand that this can only be invoked with the assent of Congress. This is not much use to us in present context and is intended as a provision for exceptional circumstances such as 1929, the war, or the collapse of Bretton Woods. Having regard to the fact that the London waiver was in any case of a discretionary character and is cared for to a certain extent by the Washington waiver[8] which was not on the map when the London waiver was first discussed, we here do not feel very strongly about carrying the dispute any further. If, however, there is some clause with the original purpose in view which you would wish us to press, will you instruct us accordingly?

CALENDAR TO NO. 106

i 22 Nov. 1945   Note by Mr. L.P. Thompson-McCausland (Bank of England) on the Washington Waiver criticizing terms set out in para. 6 of No. 106 [T 236/441].

[7] Cf. Nos. 87 and 96.   [8] See No. 87, and i below.

No. 107

British Missions (Washington) to Cabinet Offices
(Received 18 November, 9.16 p.m.)

NABOB 358 Telegraphic [UE 5629/1094/53]

Immediate. Secret   WASHINGTON, 18 November 1945, 5.21 p.m.

The liberalization of the sterling area and arrangements regarding payments agreements.

Reference NABOB 355.[1] This is telegram C.

1. The position of that part of the proposed terms of agreement which relates to the liberalization of the sterling area is much more satisfactory than at one time we would have ventured to hope. The Americans have agreed to be content with a brief declaratory statement which runs as follows:

The Government of the United Kingdom will complete arrangements as early as practicable and in any case not later than the end of 1946 under which, immediately after the completion of such arrangements the sterling receipts from current transactions of all sterling area countries, apart from any receipts arising out of military expenditure by the United Kingdom prior to December 31, 1948, which it may be agreed to treat on the same basis as the balances accumulated during the war, will be freely available for current transactions in any currency area without discrimination, with the result that any discrimination arising from the so-called dollar sterling pool will be entirely removed and that each member of the sterling area will have its current sterling and dollar receipts at its free disposition for current transactions anywhere.

2. Thus, this statement, which you will recognize as being largely an extract from NABOB 215[2] paragraphs 11 and 12, takes the place of that disputed document.

3. On the question of the payments agreements, as we anticipated, there has been considerable difficulty with the Americans.

4. We put to them the version discussed a little time ago between Keynes and Eady.[3] They objected to this on two grounds—that it was too tentative in nature and that it was not synchronized with the proposed arrangements regarding the sterling area. They have suggested a draft as in the following paragraph.

5. The Governments of the United States and the United Kingdom agree that after December 31st, 1946, or earlier if practicable, they will impose no restrictions on payments and transfers for current international transactions (as defined in the Articles of agreement of the International Monetary Fund) but this obligation shall not apply to foreign-owned balances accumulated prior to December 31 1946 or to foreign-owned

---

[1] See No. 106, note 1.   [2] See No. 78.ii.   [3] See No. 98, note 3.

balances arising from military expenditure prior to December 31 1948.

6. We have told them that this is not acceptable, but that we should be prepared to put up for your consideration without commitment, the following:

Begins: Within the same period (i.e. the period ending December 31 1946) The Governments of the United Kingdom and the United States will negotiate with any countries outside the Sterling area, with which either country has monetary or other agreements, that such agreements shall not be so operated in practice on either side to prevent the free availability for current transactions anywhere of favourable balances arising from current transactions but this obligation shall not apply to non-resident balances accumulated prior to December 31, 1946 or to non-resident balances arising from military expenditures prior to December 31 1948. Ends.

7. You will see that paragraph 5 [6] differs from the version referred to in paragraph 4 above [in] that it is more binding and defines the period within which the negotiations must take place.

8. Our main and indeed insuperab[l]e objection to the American formula in paragraph 5 is that it commits us to grant convertibility to future non-resident balances irrespective of whether the other country accords us reciprocity. For example Argentine could block the receipts from our exports and at the same time convert the sterling proceeds of their exports to us into dollars and then into gold.[4] Our text avoids this and also retains the advantage that it enables us to maintain the existing fabric and mechanics of our monetary agreements and merely modify the existing clauses for extending multilaterality though this might also be possible under the American text.

9. Clayton and the State Department prefer their own text because it enables them to say in plain language that in this respect we give up completely our rights under the Bretton Woods transition[5] not later than the end of 1946. In any case we believe they attach first class importance to some clause of this kind.

10. Will you please let us have your observations.

---

[4] Cf. No. 97, note 2.
[5] i.e. under Article XIV of the Articles of Agreement of the I.M.F.: cf. No. 1, note 11.

No. 108

British Missions (Washington) to Cabinet Offices
(Received 18 November, 11.32 p.m.)

NABOB 359 Telegraphic [UE 5629/1094/53]

Immediate. Secret   WASHINGTON, *18 November 1945, 5.23 p.m.*

Discrimination in the transition period.

Reference NABOB 355.[1] This is telegram D.

1. A message from the Chancellor of the Exchequer of 8th October included the following passage.

'We should be willing to agree to a non-discriminatory restriction of imports on the understanding that non-discrimination means the test of commercial considerations only, that we are free to make long-term contracts with regular suppliers, and that subject to the principle of commercial considerations we can have as much state purchasing of imports as we wish'.[2]

2. Nevertheless we took no initiative in raising this with the Americans, but when they saw our exchange provisions in writing, and realised that they did not cover discriminatory import licensing they immediately pressed for a clause along the above lines. They recognise the exceptional freedoms provided in the transition in this respect both under Bretton Woods and under the draft proposals for a trade convention[3] and also in the Oil Agreement recently concluded in London[4] but they do not feel that they should be necessary if a country is assured of financial support in other ways. They contend that it is one of the main purposes of the loan to us to enable various objectionable features of the transition period to be abbreviated; and they therefore ask that as from the end of December 1946, we should agree to forego the right to discriminate in import licensing. It should be noted that they do *not* question our right to exercise severe quantitative limitation of imports during this period. It is the right to discriminate which is the question.

3. Notwithstanding the authority referred to in paragraph one we thought it best to reserve our position vis-à-vis the Americans until you were in a position to review the proposals as a whole. Meanwhile, however, we tried to work out a draft acceptable to them which fell within the limits of our authority and in addition contained any qualifications the Americans were ready to concede. Without committing you in any way to accept the draft we told them we were willing to put to you what seemed to us to be the least objectionable way of putting their stipulation.

4. The draft which the Americans would be prepared to accept would run as follows:

Begins   Exchange Restrictions and Import Controls
The Governments of the United Kingdom and the United States will impose no exchange restrictions on transactions permitted by the authorities controlling imports. If the Government of either country imposes quantitative import restrictions as an aid to the restoration of equilibrium in the balances of payments, such restrictions shall be administered on a basis which does not discriminate against imports from the other country in respect of any product; provided that this undertaking shall not apply (A) in cases in which its application would have the effect of preventing the country imposing such restrictions

[1] See No. 106, note 1.   [2] See No. 62, para. 8.
[3] See Annex C to No. 95.   [4] See No. 43.iii.

from utilising, for the purchase of needed imports, inconvertible currencies accumulated up to December 31 1946, or (B) in cases in which there may be special necessity for the country imposing such restrictions to assist, by measures not involving a substantial departure from the general rule of non-discrimination, a country whose economy has been disrupted by war. The provisions of this paragraph shall become effective as soon as practicable and in any case not later than the end of 1946.

Ends

5. You will notice that in three respects this is rather better for us than your formula in paragraph one. It relates only to discrimination against the United States and is mutual. Thus we retain a free hand during the transitional period in relation to other countries. It allows us the let-out under (A) above relating to inconvertible currencies which might be useful in the case [? of] certain countries. Finally, after a considerable struggle, we obtained the qualification in (B) above which would enable us, for example, to nurse back the export trade of such countries as France or Greece, by discrimination to a moderate extent in their favour. The phrase 'authorities controlling imports' is chosen so as to cover state trading.

6. Our judgement is that whilst we should have preferred to retain a more comprehensive discretion during the transitional period we should not run too great a risk in accepting the above if the other features of the settlement are satisfactory. And it seems to us that with the above qualifications what we give away by foregoing discrimination in import licensing cannot amount to very much. So far as we know the only important loss of income and increase on our Dollar expenditure resulting from this clause is in the case of oil, on which see Keynes separate telegram to Eaden [*sic*] (NABOB 353) [i], where it will be seen that over a four year period from January 1947 (date at which discrimination must cease) the cumulative loss from not being able to concentrate United Kingdom demand on Sterling oil might amount to 120 million Dollars. Nevertheless on a broad view we do not question the view implicit in your earlier instruction that it may be wise to agree to non-discriminatory restriction of imports.

7. We should be grateful if you would confirm that your instruction of 8th October still stands and if draft in paragraph 4 above is to be regarded as acceptable.

CALENDAR TO No. 108

i *18 & 19 Nov. 1945 British Missions (Washington) Tel. NABOB 353 from Lord Keynes to Sir W. Eady, and Washington Tel. No. 1154 ELFUNOCOP from Mr.* M.R. Bridgeman (Principal Assistant Secretary in Ministry of Fuel and Power) effect of liberalisation of sterling area on U.K. oil exports [T 236/441, 457].

No. 109

British Missions (Washington) to Cabinet Offices
(Received 18 November, 11.34 p.m.)

NABOB 360 Telegraphic [UE 5629/1094/53]

Immediate. Secret WASHINGTON, 18 November 1945, 7.17 p.m.

The settlement of Sterling balances.
Reference NABOB 355.[1] This is telegram E.

1. On the settlement of accumulated Sterling Area balances our difficulties with the Americans have concerned three separate questions:

(a) The extent to which the terms of the loan will include a statement of our intentions in this respect.

(b) The quantification of these intentions and the degree of our prior commitment.

(c) The relative priority of our obligations to the Sterling Area and other creditors in relation to the proposed new American credit.

2. On the first of these questions we believe that our efforts have attained results which you will find satisfactory. The Americans seem likely to agree that any extensive reference to our intentions and procedure will be out of place in the main document and they suggest as sufficient for their purpose a short statement on the lines of the first paragraph of NABOB G.[2] The wording of this is, in certain respects, unsatisfactory, and we recommend that we adhere to our own draft in the second paragraph of NABOB G. You must appreciate that either of these texts will take the place of the much longer story set out in NABOB 215,[3] as subsequently amended.[4]

3. The question of quantification has changed its form but remains one of our chief anxieties. In one respect we have fully met your requirements. For we have entirely got away from any figure for the scaling down of the Sterling Area balances. The Americans have, however, proposed that there shall be a ceiling to the amount of the aggregate annual service of any obligations we assume in the post-war settlement of Sterling Area and other Sterling balances beginning in 1951. They argue on the analogy of putting new money into a concern which is already overloaded with debt, that they have a right to ask that an upper limit be set to the amount which will be paid to old creditors.

4. As you will expect, we have consistently refused to concede the possibility of any provision of this sort. We have told the Americans in so many words that we completely refuse any agreement which is dependent upon our stating in advance of negotiations the amount of the annual

[1] See No. 106, note 1.
[2] No. 110, which was however despatched before the present telegram.
[3] See No. 78.ii.   [4] See No. 98.

332

repayment we make to our Sterling creditors. We have explained that we naturally have no desire to make this amount any more than is absolutely necessary but that the repeated pledges which we have given that there shall be no unilateral settlement, make it quite out of the question for us to consider their suggestion.

5. The Americans would be more within their rights in making the operation of their waiver clause related to a ceiling as the amount of the future annual commitment which ranks pari passu with the American Credit. Whilst rejecting the text of NABOB F,[5] will you consider the compromise suggested in paragraph 7 below?

6. Clayton began by being very insistent that the American credit, being new money, was to have absolute priority over repayment of accumulated Sterling balances. It would, therefore, be a concession from his point of view to agree to what amounts to pari passu conditions up to an amount not exceeding 175 million dollars for the Sterling area and other balances. But this should not mean that we cannot initially undertake to repay Sterling balances at a rate of more than 175 million dollars a year including interest if we choose to do so. It should only mean that the whole of such additional payments must be deferred in any year in which we are exercising the waiver against the Americans.

7. The American proposals as we last heard them are given in NABOB F. The most objectionable features in this, which were introduced by the technicians and lawyers, we heard of for the first time yesterday and might not be sustained against objections at a higher level. On the three points following we see every reason why we should insist on amendments of the draft of NABOB F:

(I) The first clause applies to all new loans after January 1, 1945. It is clear that we cannot apply it retrospectively so as to override existing agreements, and equally clear that no sovereign government can bind itself on such a matter for all future time. 1(a) of NABOB F should therefore, relate only to new loans arranged during 1946.

(II) The last sentence of 2(II) of NABOB F should in any case be deleted. Either it limits the scale of our future settlements in advance or it compels us to increase the rate of repayment to America. We might, however, accept a provision under which contractual annual payments under 1(b) in excess of 175 million dollars would be wholly deferred in the event of our exercising waiver rights against America.

(III) We should insist on an exception in the first sentence of 2(II) in favour of Colonial dependencies.

8. You will appreciate that the clauses in NABOB F are the only clauses in the actual agreement affecting the Sterling balances. Apart from this, we have, by a series of stages, succeeded in eliminating the whole subject

[5] i.e. NABOB 361 of 18 November, which transmitted American proposals in two paragraphs corresponding closely to paras. 4(II) and 5(II) of No. 113.

and in reducing our statement of intention to something on the lines of NABOB G. If, therefore, we can obtain an amendment of NABOB F on the above lines the subject will have been reduced to much smaller dimensions than seemed likely at an earlier stage. As to the unacceptability of F as it stands we have no hesitation.

No. 110

British Missions (Washington) to Cabinet Offices
(Received 18 November, 7.55 p.m.)

NABOB 362 Telegraphic [UE 5629/1094/53]

Secret   WASHINGTON, 18 November 1945, 5.25 p.m.

Reference NABOB 355.[1] This is telegram G.

1. Following is statement proposed by Americans:

The Government of the United Kingdom intends to make an early settlement, varying according to the circumstances of each case, of the sterling balances accumulated by sterling area and other countries prior to such settlement (together with any future receipts arising out of military expenditure by the U.K. which it may be agreed to treat on the same basis). The settlements with the sterling area countries will be on the basis of dividing these accumulated balances into three categories, (A) balances to be released at once and convertible into any currency for current transactions, (B) balances to be similarly released by instalments over a period of years beginning in 1951, and (C) balances to be written off as a contribution to the settlement of war and postwar indebtedness and in recognition of the benefits which the countries concerned might be expected to gain from such a settlement.

2. Following is our draft settlement:

It is the intention of the Government of the U.K. at an early date to discuss with the sterling area countries mutual agreements, varying according to the circumstances of each case, for the settlement of their accumulated sterling balances (together with any future receipts arising out of military expenditure by the U.K. which it may be agreed to treat on the same basis as the balances accumulated during the war) on the basis of dividing these accumulated balances into three categories, (A) balances to be released at once and convertible into any currency for current transactions, (B) balances to be similarly released by instalments over a period of years beginning in 1951 without prejudice to the possible anticipation by the U.K. [? of] releases to a particular country which was in a position such as might otherwise have called for assistance from the U.K. by way of a loan, and (C) balances to be written off as a contribution to the

[1] See No. 106, note 1.

334

settlement of war and postwar indebtedness and in recognition of the benefits which the countries concerned might be expected to gain from such a settlement.

No. 111

British Missions (Washington) to Cabinet Offices
(Received 21 November, 5.17 a.m.)

NABOB 370 Telegraphic [UE 5672/1094/53]

Immediate. Secret   WASHINGTON, 21 November 1945, 2.19 a.m.

For Chancellor of Exchequer from Ambassador, Keynes, Brand, Robbins and all members of the Mission.

1. As explained in NABOB 364[1] the Americans did not present us with formal or complete proposals at yesterday's[2] meeting of the Top Finance Committee. They offered for discussion a provisional text which still included our amendments and proposed omissions within square brackets. It became clear in the course of discussion that their text embodied novel provisions prepared by their experts with the consequences of which not all the American members were yet familiar; that they attached much more importance to some of their proposals than to others; and above all, that they were deliberately allowing both their experts and certain official members of their committee to have a fling at us with the apparently full authority of their Top Committee in cases where the more influential American members had not finally decided against our contentions. As you may suppose, this is an exhausting and exasperating procedure. But you can perhaps take some small comfort from the fact that they obviously hesitated to present you with the text as it now stands on their side.

2. In NABOB 372[3] we transmit for convenience of reference the complete American text in the latest version we possess. Although this is not a final or formal proposal from their side, we think that the only convenient course, in view of the time table, is for you to treat it as if it were. We should be most grateful for your instructions on this basis at the earliest date practicable. Our suggestions on the various points outstanding are given in the following paras.

---

[1] This telegram of 19 November from Lord Keynes briefly reported on the fourth meeting of the Finance Committee (COM/FIN 4th meeting) that day, extracts from the agreed minutes of which are printed in *F.R.U.S. 1945*, vol. vi, pp. 162–7. See further Pressnell, *op. cit.*, Chapter 10(17). Lord Keynes stated in particular: 'we know very little more about the nature of their proposals than is contained in our seven alphabetical telegrams [see No. 106, note 1] . . . The chief value of the meeting was that we were enabled to develop before those who will take the decisions, arguments which had previously risen no higher than the expert level. Some of those present were evidently hearing some of our arguments in their full force for the first time' (UE 5663/1094/53).
[2] This telegram was drafted on 20 November.   [3] No. 113.

3. The amount of the loan is still left blank. We believe that we can obtain 4 billions new money if we stand out firmly and that it is the question of the lend–lease clean-up dealt with in 4 below which is holding them up. We suggest you give us firm instructions that 4 billions is the minimum amount of new money on which you can contemplate the commitments in paras 6, 7 & 8 of their draft.

4. We believe that they are still troubled amongst themselves whether the net sum due in respect of lend–lease etc. should be on the same terms as the main loan or whether Clause 3C of the lend lease Act[4] should again raise its head. The service of this would cost us 5.675 percent in the early years and would not be subject to waiver. To accept it would, therefore, upset the whole financial basis of the compromise settlement. We advise that we should be given no latitude to give way on this, subject only to the possibility of some face-saving arrangement for the sake of the precedent with other Powers which would in fact cost us nothing significant.

5. They are finding it difficult to bring down the net lend–lease bill below $750,000,000 though they are obviously anxious to do so. Our own figures are now nearer $600,000,000 than $500,000,000. Both of the above are before allowing for our claim for diverted aircraft.[5] If only they can bring themselves to admit this, even their own bill would be brought within $500,000,000. Our latest appreciation of this position as a whole is given in NABOB 373.[6] We hope that you will give us here a little latitude for negotiation. We will not, of course, agree to a final figure without further consultation. But we do not think we can stand on any exact figure as a point of principle. If the amount of the credit is fixed at 4½ billions we might find room for lend–lease clean-up within this up to say $600,000,000 or thereabouts.

6. On para (4)(I)(B) of the American Draft, which attaches to the waiver clause a condition as to the state of our reserves, we made some progress in yesterday's discussion towards convincing them of the unsuitability of this clause at any rate in its present form. It may be the right course at the next round when we present your reply to ask for its total deletion. But we are convinced that for them to concede this will present them with genuine difficulty when they come to defend the waiver clause before Congress. We hope, therefore, that consideration will be given to the compromise we suggest in para 15 of NABOB 356.[7] We should like to have authority to offer this in the last resort provided that we were receiving sufficient satisfaction in other respects. We think it quite probable, after yesterday's discussion, that we could get this compromise.

7. For the reasons given in NABOB 360[8] we regard para 4(II) and 5(II) of the American draft to be quite inacceptable. This is a problem of particular difficulty to us and particular importance to the Americans. We explore it further in a separate telegram NABOB 371.[9]

---

[4] See No. 4, note 7. [5] See No. 129, note 5. [6] No. 114.
[7] No. 106. [8] No. 109. [9] No. 112.

8. For the reasons given in NABOB 358 and 359[10] we hope you will authorise us to accept paras 6 & 8 of the American draft. As regards para 7 of their draft on exchange arrangements outside the sterling area we hope you will be prepared to go at least as far as our draft in para 6 of NABOB 358. Para[s] 6, 7 & 8 of their draft are of course central to the American offer and of primary importance in the minds both of the State Dept and of the Treasury. If we cannot give them sufficient satisfaction here, any negotiation on the present lines will fall to the ground.

9. Furthermore, if we can give them full satisfaction within this field, they may be willing to go a long way to meet us on all other matters. We believe, therefore, that the question whether we could not in the last resort accept their draft in para 7 deserves your most earnest consideration. For the reasons we have given in para 8 of NABOB 358 we regard the American draft as open to grave objection in principle and as asking an unreasonable concession. Nevertheless after further reflection and in the light of the enormous importance attached by Clayton to a clean-cut settlement on this issue, we wonder how much of importance to us is really at stake in practice. When the sterling area balances have been liberated, there will no longer be much significance in restricting other currently earned sterling. Indeed it will not be easily practicable to do so. You will know better than we how easily our monetary agreements can be adapted to conform with the American draft. If they can, you will be presenting us with a very powerful inducement to the Americans to fall in with our ideas in other matters. We should like to be in a position at the last lap to go to Clayton with this ultimate concession if he will meet us on any other outstanding matters.[11]

10. In any case we must remedy the inadvertence in our draft by which the balances of any country with which we have no monetary agreement, for example the United States, are left out in the cold.

11. For para 9 of the American draft we think that we should adhere to our text as given in para 2 of NABOB 362.[12]

12. It will help us if you can answer any of the above paras. piece meal on a provisional and non-committal basis in advance of your considered reply to the telegram as a whole.[13]

---

[10] Nos. 107–8.

[11] NABOB 383 of 22 November stated that the Delegation now wished to withdraw the above paragraph: 'We do not think we can accept the American draft as it stands even in the last resort. Not only would this clause compel us, as we have already pointed out, to surrender our Bretton Woods transitional rights without any guarantee of reciprocity. It would also compel us to forgo both forthwith and permanently our rights against non-members of the I.M.F. under article XI(2) of the final act [i.e. the I.M.F. agreement]. We think that the Americans themselves must have overlooked this' (UE 5672/1094/53).

[12] No. 110.

[13] In Washington telegram No. 835 REMAC of 21 November Lord Keynes reinforced his plea for 'as quick a reply to our long series of NABOB telegrams as is practicable for Ministers . . . There can be no doubt that the position here is deteriorating and that any further delay weakens our position. We started in a good atmosphere partly resulting from

reaction of opinion against the sudden termination of Lend–Lease. The effect both of that and of the impact made by our original exposition has now largely passed away as a result of the long drawn out negotiations. The subject has gone stale and critics and sceptics of all kind and from all directions are recovering their courage.' Lord Keynes also stated, with regard to a possible visit to Ottawa after the negotiations were over, that he was 'rather near the end of my physical reserves' (UE 5661/1094/53): cf. Moggridge, *op. cit.*, pp. 591–2.

No. 112

British Missions (Washington) to Cabinet Offices
(Received 21 November, 7.30 a.m.)

NABOB 371 Telegraphic [UE 5672/1094/53]

Immediate. Secret   WASHINGTON, 21 November 1945, 2.21 a.m.

1. This is the telegram on sterling balances arrangements referred in paragraph 7 of NABOB 370.[1]

2. We are much perplexed how best to meet the legitimate requirements of both parties. Clayton is much concerned to be able to tell Congress five conclusions without qualification, namely

(i) That the American credit will be wholly used to meet our adverse balance of trade during the transition and no part of it will be required to bail out the sterling balances. This is spelled out in paragraph 2(ii) of the American draft[2] and is also again repeated in our suggested draft below.

(ii) He wants to be able to say further that after having pleaded that we have no sufficient expectation of convertible exchange to make larger payments to America we should not then obligate ourselves to provide convertible exchange to liquidate old sterling balances without some ceiling to the amount.

(iii) He wishes further to be able to assure critics that if at a later date we invoke the waiver clause, we shall not go on paying other creditors in full whilst escaping in part on our American obligations.

(iv) The above relate to old sterling balances. He also has to be able to say that other loans we may raise for the same general purpose, in particular the Canadian loan, would not be on better terms to the lender than the American.

(v) Finally, he would like to be able to say, but we do not think he attaches so much importance to this, that if at a later date we feel flush enough to anticipate repayments to other creditors, we should at least offer the same treatment to the Americans.

3. It is easy to say that for so rich a country as the United States to insist on these conditions shows some lack of liberality. But they are not in themselves unreasonable and are, we fear, in tune with widespread opinion in this country.

[1] No. 111.   [2] See No. 113.

4. The difficulty is to find any way to make them compatible with the elasticity we must reserve for ourselves and in particular the observance of our principle that we cannot enter into any definite commitment about the treatment of the sterling balances until we have discussed the matter with others concerned.

5. We see no prospect whatever of by-passing this problem altogether. The American solution appears to us to be open to the serious objections we have set out in NABOB 360.[3] To do justice to the American draftsman, however, we should point out that he was genuinely endeavouring to solve this problem in a way which preserved the formal position of the Americans, to satisfy our constitutional scruple that we must not enter into firm commitments in advance of discussion with the sterling area countries, and at the same time to assist us in getting a satisfactory bargain out of the sterling area countries. His proposal amounted, therefore, to leaving us free to settle the sterling balances for a larger amount than 175 million dollars a year so that constitutionally we were perfectly free, but requiring that we should increase our annual repayments to the U.S. by the amount, if any, by which our sterling area settlements in the aggregate exceeded the above figure. This would at the same time protect the position of the U.S. and enable us to put pressure on the holders of sterling balances to be moderate owing to the serious consequences to us, and indeed the practical impossibility, of going beyond the stipulated figure.

6. Perhaps the best hope of a solution is to be found in a fresh draft. Would you consider putting forward a revised proposal on the lines of the next paragraph?
Begins
7. The Government of the U.K. undertake:
(1) That they will not arrange any long-term loans from Governments within the British Commonwealth after the date of this memorandum of understanding and before the end of 1950 on terms more favourable to the lender than the terms of this line of credit.
(2) That any net repayment before the end of 1951 of external sterling balances accumulated before the date of this memorandum of understanding will be covered by resources outside this line of credit.
(3) Further payments after the end of 1951 in respect of external sterling balances accumulated in hands of governments, monetary authorities and banks before the date of this memorandum of understanding will be made subject to the condition (under reserve of any special commitments already attaching to them), that, in any year in which the U.K. Government take advantage of the waiver provision under 4(I) above[2], they shall not exceed in the aggregate the figure which bears the same proportion to $175,000,000 which the repayment to the U.S. Government of the capital instalment due in that year bears

[3] No. 109.

to the total sum which would have been paid to the U.S. Government if the waiver provision had not been invoked.

(4) That if the Government of the U.K. offer to any government which is a creditor in respect of loans contracted under (1) above or in respect of repayments of sterling balances under (3) above (except in the case of Colonial dependencies), to pay future instalments of capital repayments in advance on certain terms, they will offer to the Government of the U.S. on the same terms an advance repayment of an equal amount in respect of the present line of credit.

Ends

8. We think that (I) [of] paragraph 7 above is not unreasonable if it is limited to Commonwealth Governments. We might suggest the end of 1946 rather than the end of 1950. But this would not be nearly so well received by the Americans.

9. We think that (II) of paragraph 7 above is perfectly safe particularly as sterling balances accumulated during 1946 would fall out of the reckoning. The Canadian loan will be included in other resources and thus all this clause means in practice is that if our own over-all adverse balance of current payments with the rest of the world in the six years 1946–1951 inclusive was less than four billions we should not draw the whole of the credit, which, in any case, is the understanding.

10. You should note that under (III) there is no limit to the initial contractual amount we undertake to pay to holders of old sterling balances in years in which we are not exercising the waiver. In that respect it differs fundamentally from the American formula. Moreover even in waiver years, the holders of sterling balances would receive quite a good dividend at least as high as we could expect to afford in such circumstances.

11. You may look with some suspicion on (IV) but we think this is fairly safe in practice. It would mean that if we offered India, for example, to anticipate certain future instalments up to a moderate amount subject to say three or four percent discount, we should have to offer the same to the U.S., and one can probably assume that they would not wish to take advantage of the offer.

12. Thus we should like to be able to offer the counter-proposals in paragraph 7. Nevertheless (III) is almost certain to fail in satisfying Clayton for the reasons given above. Can you think of a way round?

13. Another line of thought would be to ask the Americans to revert to the suggestion made by Clayton at one time, namely, that instead of interest being waived when the waiver conditions are satisfied interest is not waived but both interest and capital are deferred to the end of the series of annuities. Would you prefer this to the present waiver clause? If so, our counter-proposal about the position of other creditors could be much simplified as in the following paragraph.

14. The Government of the U.K. undertake to arrange that

(a) any long term loans from governments within the British Commonwealth after the date of this memorandum of understanding and before the end of 1950, and

(b) payments in respect of external balances accumulated in the hands of governments, monetary authorities and banks before the date of this memorandum of understanding and made after the end of 1951 (with the exception of colonial dependencies) will be subject to conditions (under reserve of any special commitments already attaching to them) that in any year in which the U.K. Government take advantage of the deferment provision all the above annual payments shall be similarly deferred.

15. We are equally divided amongst ourselves about the advisability of a fresh approach on these lines. Those who hesitate do not dislike it in substance, but because they believe that a revival of the deferment idea will bring back a whole batch of exceptionally objectionable proposals about re-examining our economic position year by year in future to see whether we have not become strong enough to repay the deferment. We have not previously reported any of this to you because we eventually got rid of it by their abandoning deferment and returning to waiver. Nor does it help us much on the point in (III) above on setting a ceiling. Nevertheless, if you decidedly prefer this line, we might cautiously explore whether we could safely and usefully raise it.

CALENDAR TO No. 112

i *27 & 28 Nov. 1945* (*a*) *British Missions (Washington) Tel. NABOB 401* explanatory comments on para. 7 of No. 112, urging importance of meeting Americans as far as possible: (*b*) *Letter from Mr. Ashton to Mr. Grant (Treasury)* enclosing alternative draft of para. 7 by Mr. G.G. Fitzmaurice (Assistant Legal Adviser in F.O.) [UE 5784, 5828/1094/53].

No. 113

British Missions (Washington) to Cabinet Offices
(*Received 21 November, 5.30 p.m.*)

NABOB 372 Telegraphic [UE 5672/1094/53]

Immediate. Secret   WASHINGTON, *21 November 1945, 2.23 a.m.*

Following is text of U.S. draft memorandum of understanding on financial matters dated November 18, 1945.

1. *Amount of the Line of Credit*
    (I) The Government of the United States will extend to the Government of the United Kingdom a line of credit of . . .[1] billion.

[1] Omission in filed copy.

(II) This line of credit will be available until December 31, 1945.[2]

2. *Purpose of the Credit*

(I) The purpose of the credit shall be to facilitate purchases by the United Kingdom of goods and services from the United States, to assist the United Kingdom to meet transitional postwar deficits in her current balance of payments, to help the United Kingdom to maintain adequate reserves of gold and dollars and to assist the United Kingdom to assume the obligations of multilateral trade, as defined in this and other agreements.

(II) It is understood that any amounts required to discharge obligations of the United Kingdom to third countries outstanding on the date of this contract will be found from resources other than this line of credit.

3. *Amortization and Interest*

(I) The amount of the credit outstanding on December 31, 1951 shall be repaid in 50 annual instalments, beginning on December 31, 1951, until 50 instalments have been paid, subject to the provisions of (4) below.

(II) The rate of interest shall be 2 percent per annum, computed annually beginning with January 1, 1951, on the amount outstanding each year, and payable in 50 annual instalments, beginning on December 31, 1951, subject to the provisions of (4) below.

(III) The 50 annual instalments of principal repayments and interest shall be equal, amounting to 31.8 million dollars for each 1 billion dollars outstanding on December 31, 1951. Each instalment shall consist of the full amount of the interest due and the remainder of the instalment shall be the principal to be repaid in that year.

4. *Waiver of Interest Payment*

(I) The Government of the United States, at the request of the Government of the United Kingdom, will agree to waive in any year the amount of the interest due in that year if:

(*a*) as certified by the International Monetary Fund, the income of the U.K. from home-produced exports plus its net income from invisible current transactions in its balance of payments (as defined in article XIX(I) of the Final Act of Bretton Woods)[3] was on the average over the five preceding calendar years less than the amount[4] of U.K. imports during 1936–8, fixed at 866 million pounds, as such figure may be adjusted for changes in the price level of these imports. If waiver is requested for an interest payment prior to that due in 1955, the average income shall be computed for the calendar years from 1950 through the year preceding the given year; and

---

[2] This year was in error for 1951: cf. Moggridge, *op. cit.*, pp. 629–32, where the present text is printed in full.

[3] Cf. No. 106, note 6.

[4] i.e. the average amount: cf. No. 106, para. 5.

(*b*) as certified by the International Monetary Fund, the U.K.'s official holdings (gross) of gold and convertible foreign exchange were at the end of the preceding calendar year less than the sum of (1) 15 percent of the average value of the U.K.'s commodity imports over the preceding five calendar years and (2) 25 percent of the current demand and short term liabilities against the U.K.'s official holdings of gold and convertible foreign exchange in favour of other governments and central banks, as of the end of the preceding calendar year. If waiver is requested for an interest payment prior to that due in 1955, the average value of imports shall be computed for the calendar years from 1950 through the year preceding the given year.

(II) Waiver of interest will not be requested or allowed in any year unless the aggregate of the agreed releases or annual payments in respect of the following is reduced, through waivers or deferments during the life of this credit, by an amount proportionate to the reduction in the annual instalment of this credit:

(*a*) new loans to the U.K. Government arranged after January 1, 1945,

(*b*) sterling balances for release subsequent to 1950.

(III) Either Government shall be entitled to approach the other Government for reconsideration of the manner and time of payment, if in its opinion the prevailing conditions of international exchange justify such reconsideration.

5. *Accelerated Repayment*

(I) The Government of the U.K. may accelerate repayment of the line of credit.

(II) If the Government of the U.K. accelerates releases or annual payments as described in 4(II) above in advance of the rate originally agreed, it will make an accelerated payment of an equal amount of the principal repayments in the next instalments due on this line of credit. Releases and annual repayments of more than 175 million dollars per year under 4(II)(*b*) above shall be considered an accelerated payment.

6. *Sterling Area Exchange Arrangements*

The Government of the United Kingdom will complete arrangements as early as practicable and in any case not later than the end of 1946 under which, immediately after the completion of such arrangements the sterling receipts from current transactions of all sterling area countries, apart from any receipts arising out of military expenditure by the United Kingdom prior to December 31, 1948 which it may be agreed to treat on the same basis as the balances accumulated during the war, will be freely available for current transactions in any currency area without discrimination with the result that any discrimination arising from the so-called dollar sterling pool will be entirely removed and that each member of the sterling area will have its current sterling and dollar receipts at its free disposition for current transactions anywhere.

7. *Other Exchange Arrangements*

The Governments of the United States and the United Kingdom agree

343

that after December 31, 1946 or earlier if practicable they will impose no restrictions on payments and transfers for current international transactions, (as defined in the articles of agreement of the International Monetary Fund); but this obligation shall not apply to foreign owned balances accumulated prior to December 31 1946 or to foreign owned balances arising from military expenditure prior to December 31, 1948.

8. *Exchange Restrictions and Import Controls*

The Governments of the U.K. and the U.S. will impose no exchange restrictions on transactions permitted by the authorities controlling imports. If the government of either country imposes quantitative import restrictions as an aid to the restoration of equilibrium in the balances of payments, such restrictions shall be administered on a basis which does not discriminate against imports from the other country in respect of any produc[t]; provided that this undertaking shall not apply (*a*) in cases in which its application would have the effect of preventing the country imposing such restrictions from utilizing, for the purchase of needed imports, inconvertible currencies accumulated up to December 31 1946, or (*b*) in cases in which there may be special necessity for the country imposing such restrictions to assist, by measures not involving a substantial departure from the general rule of non-discrimination, a country whose economy has been disrupted by war. The provisions of this paragraph shall become effective as soon as practicable and in any case not later than the end of 1946.

9. *The Accumulated Sterling Balances*

The Government of the U.K. has communicated its intentions to the Government of the U.S. as follows:

The Government of the United Kingdom intends to make an early settlement, varying according to the circumstances of each case, of the sterling balances accumulated by sterling area and other countries prior to such settlement (together with any future receipts arising out of military expenditure by the U.K. which it may be agreed to treat on the same basis). The settlements with the sterling area countries will be on the basis of dividing these accumulated balances into three categories, (*a*) balances to be released at once and convertible into any currency for current transactions, (*b*) balances to be similarly released by instalments over a period of years beginning in 1951, and (*c*) balances to be written off as a contribution to settlement of war and post-war indebtedness and in recognition of the benefits which the countries concerned might be expected to gain from such a settlement.[5]

[5] The texts in paras. 6–9 were the same as those in Nos. 107, paras. 1 and 5, 108, para. 4, and 110, para. 1, subject to small variations in punctuation.

No. 114

British Missions (Washington) to Cabinet Offices
(Received 21 November, 4.54 a.m.)

NABOB *373 Telegraphic* [*UE 5673/1094/53*]

Immediate. Secret   WASHINGTON, *21 November 1945, 2.25 a.m.*

1. The following paragraphs summarize in general terms the position reached to date as regards a settlement concerning the winding-up of Lend Lease and Reciprocal Aid. All figures are in dollars million.

2. It now seems likely that the Americans will be prepared to accept an immediate settlement on the basis of global figures as being definitive for all items except the lend lease and reciprocal aid pipelines which will have to be settled on the basis of ascertained actuals. We are assuming that for your part you would be prepared to accept settlement on above basis, Lee will write to Treasury Officer of accounts on accounting aspect of arrangement.

3. For convenience of presentation we propose to deal first with all items on lend lease side of account, secondly with reciprocal aid pipeline and inventory and lastly with position concerning claims.

4. Lend lease pipeline.

No difficulties of principle arise here. We have agreed that general basis is to be U.S. contract prices. Americans agree that cotton subsidy should apply. Best estimates we can make at moment are as follows:

   (*a*) civilian pipeline   270
   (*b*) military pipeline   12
   (*c*) shipping services   40

Amount at (*c*) includes services and supplies in respect of October and freights and charter hire on bareboats[1] for December–February inclusive. But figure for latter charge has been included on basis of proposed American hire rates and would be reduced by 2–3 if we secured lower rates which we have proposed.

5. Naval and military items under billing procedure.

Americans have tentatively estimated this at 5 but agree that this is probably too high. No difficulty of principle arises.

6. Lend lease inventory (class I).

On basis which includes (I) military food holding (II) all 'surplus' items and (III) ten percent element for ocean freight, Americans put valuation

---

[1] See No. 42.iii.

345

of this in terms of current U.S. contract prices at 600. Our own calculation on same basis is about 570. Discrepancy mainly concerns valuation of raw materials and is being discussed with Americans.

We are urging that as regards settlement

(a) military food holdings should be treated on same basis as other items in military inventory required for continued use by armed forces and therefore left out of account.

(b) unwanted surpluses must be left out of account.[2]

(c) ocean freight element is inadmissible since delivery of goods is taken at f.o.b.[3] stage.

(d) there should be certain specific deductions (e.g. for cotton subsidy, revised prices for synthetic rubber, 'uneconomic' cost of certain timber (BABOON 213)[4] and some general deduction on account of presence in food inventory of high priced meat and dairy products which we might have drawn from S. dominions except for incidence of reciprocal aid.

We are fairly confident that Americans may be prepared to concede some of above points. We might secure a settlement at say 340–360 but you should take this as optimistic.

7. Oil.

Bridgeman will be able to explain position as he left it.[5] There are still two uncertainties (a) freight element which is in dispute with Americans and we may have to concede their point and (b) extent to which Americans will withdraw 'military' oil from the U.K. is still undetermined and this affects amount which we shall take as part of inventory. We are urging Americans to make definite decision as regards (b). On assumption that we concede freight question and on basis of substantial American withdrawals of 'military' oil, settlement covering claims on both sides of account (but not recovery of sums due in respect of Venezuelan crude oil and royalties which will be cash payment outside settlement) will probably involve payment by U.K. of about 100.

8. Lend lease civilian inventory class II.

This amounts to about 60 on initial cost price basis. Americans agree that question of possible addition of ten percent for ocean freight should

---

[2] BABOON 136 of 19 October had explained that it had emerged from a Departmental meeting on 17 October that 'Acquisition of U.S. surpluses will indeed be an embarrassment to disposal Departments who are under strong pressure to release storage space . . . Conclusion therefore was that an overall deal is desirable provided that the figure fairly represents the value of surpluses to U.K. economy . . . and is also manageable within the framework of the general financial settlement'. BABOON 180 of 2 November added that subsequent reports by Departments 'confirm our provisional conclusion that value to U.K. of United States surpluses in this country are [sic] only a small fraction of the greatly inflated figures put forward by the Americans' (UE 5028, 5027/1094/53).

[3] Free on board.

[4] This telegram of 6 November concerned the considerable difference between the U.K. price and the dollar value of certain types of timber (T 236/467).

[5] Cf. No. 108.i.

be decided in light of general conclusion as regards this element in class I inventory. They have just suggested settlement for twenty-five percent of initial cost which we are considering. We could probably arrange that this covered any payment for lend lease installations as well.

9. Military inventory.

With American concurrence we are proceeding on basis that financial settlement for military inventory will only be on basis of the civilian end-use items. We have calculated that residual value of such items which will become surplus to military requirements might be put at approximately 20. We have tentatively put this to Americans who are examining it. They are likely to press for some increase (especially if military food is taken out of civilian inventory) and also to stipulate that settlement should cover only disposals in U.K. and colonies.

10. Lend lease aircraft.

Except in improbable event of Americans accepting our proposal for free user of transport aircraft for military purposes, we may have to pay about 10–15 under this head.

11. Lend lease installations.

We have not been able to proceed very far with discussions under this head in absence of details concerning such installations in U.K. and colonies. But it is clear that Americans are more concerned with conditions concerning post-war disposition and user of facilities (especially oil installations) than with recovery of any financial sum. For practical purposes therefore they can be neglected in financial calculations.

12. U.S. owned surpluses in the U.K.

Strictly speaking these fall outside the lend lease settlement. Americans are apparently still hoping to get about 100 under this head. We have consistently said that something like 10 is our outside limit. Americans say that deal on this basis is very unlikely.

13. Reciprocal aid pipeline.

No difficulty of principle arises here. Americans will be prepared to agree to cut-off date at 31st December 1945 for bulk commodities. On this basis we estimate amount due to us at 154.

14. Reciprocal aid inventory.

This is now put at about 35. Oil inventory has been netted in arriving at figure of 100 in para. 7.

15. Claims.

Broad position is that balance of claims so far admitted on both sides shows 53 in our favour. We have reserved for separate consideration aircraft claims amounting to over 250.

16. It will be seen that as we see position at present emergeny [sic ?emerging] balance may be as follows:

(a) due from U.K.

pipeline (including military billing)		325
inventory class I		350– 500
oil	say	100
inventory class II and installations	say	15
military inventory		20– 25
aircraft		10– 15
U.S. surpluses		10– 50
		830–1030

(b) due from U.S.

pipeline	154
inventory	35
claims	53

(apart from aircraft claim)

242

This gives a difference of 588–788.

17. We have deliberately inflated the net total both of pipeline and inventory wherever we could gain immediate cash by doing so. We have also left out of the offset our large prospective recoveries for shipping and oil items. Similarly if we take 'military' oil referred to in para. 7 this will put up amount due from us under offsetting arrangement but will be in relief of cash expenditure. Furthermore, above takes no credit for the unsettled aircraft claim. Thus our own revised figure of nearly 600 represents, if we can get it, a real burden not much more than our original idea of 500, in spite of several items against us, not previously within our knowledge, having since come to light.

CALENDARS TO NO. 114

i *30 Oct.–20 Nov. 1945 Correspondence concerning Lend–Lease settlement on aircraft* American refusal of free retention by U.K. of transport aircraft for military use means British Delegation must agree to purchase minimum requirements of Dakotas and Beechcraft [UE 5026, 5616/1094/53].

ii *24 Nov. 1945 Minutes of special Anglo-American meeting in Washington on Lend–Lease Settlement* (circulated as GEN 80/82 on 8 Jan. 1946) with Annexes on overall settlement and surplus property, and balance sheet of claims and counter-claims accepted (cf. *F.R.U.S. 1945*, vol. vi, pp. 168–73) [T 236/1689]

No. 115

Mr. Bevin to the Earl of Halifax (Washington)

No. 11672 Telegraphic [UR 4349/1246/851]

Immediate   FOREIGN OFFICE, *21 November 1945, 12.10 p.m.*

Following is the text of a message from myself[1] to Mr. Byrnes. It is self-explanatory and I would be glad if you would convey it to him unless you see objection or have any improvements to suggest.

Begins.

Recent reports from both Germany and Italy show that the European wheat crisis this winter is going to be even more serious than we had anticipated.[2]

The Emergency Economic Committee for Europe has already telegraphed recommendations to the Combined Food Board for economies by both exporting and importing countries, to which I would like to call your attention as they seem to me to be the only means of averting a terrible disaster in Europe this winter. Public opinion here is becoming acutely aware of the problem and I expect a ready response to the sacrifices which we shall have to ask of our people in an effort to mitigate the starvation developing at our doorstep.

You will, I expect, be receiving the same disturbing reports as have prompted my present message. With such fearful prospects in store, the picture of good human food being burnt as locomotive fuel in the Argentine appals me. Before the human tragedy that threatens, may I express the hope that you will not allow any political factors to deter you from sending promptly to Argentina the coal and fuel oil which are necessary to release these cereals for Europe?[3]

---

[1] i.e. Mr. Bevin, who initialled the draft of this telegram.

[2] Cf. No. 89 and Eric Roll, *The Combined Food Board, op. cit.*, pp. 269–70.

[3] Cf. No. 89, note 5. In Washington telegram No. 7780 of 21 November Lord Halifax stated that Mr. Bevin's message had arrived 'most opportunely' as it constituted a reply to the State Department *aide-mémoires* of 15 November in response to the British *aide-mémoire* of 12 and 23 October: see No. 77.i. Lord Halifax had therefore sent the contents of No. 115 to Mr. Byrnes 'as a personal message; omitting only the word "political" in last sentence as likely to set up resistance in the department which might defeat our object' (UR 4350/1246/851). Mr. J.D. Murray of South American Department pointed out in a minute of 23 November that the State Department *aide-mémoire* of 15 November was 'only incidentally concerned with the present issue, because, in the exchanges leading up to these *aide-mémoires* [cf. Nos. 66 and 77], mention had been made of our compelling necessity to maintain supplies of fuel to Argentina, in order to prevent any diminution in her exports of foodstuffs. In their *aide-mémoire*, the State Department have implied some disappointment that we were not prepared to go further in pressure on Argentina, for example, by refusing export licences for civil aircraft, but it does not affect their decision, taken some weeks ago, not to attempt to impose on Argentina any economic pressure which might tend to diminish the flow of foodstuffs from that country' (cf. *F.R.U.S. 1945*, vol. ix, pp. 555–7). Mr. Murray also noted that recent reports from Buenos Aires indicated that 'the fuel situation and the

i *7 Nov.–7 Dec. 1945 Correspondence with Sir D. Kelly (Buenos Aires)* concerning Argentina's fuel requirements for 1946 and possible reduction of Argentine wheat stocks: in reply to No. 89 Argentine Government say their stocks are already below minimum level, and although fuel problem would 'shortly be solved' transport of wheat is still affected by shortage of tyres, spare parts and railway rolling stock [AS 5834, 5951/189/2, UR 4861/1246/851].

ii *19 Dec. 1945 GEN 108/1st meeting of Cabinet Wheat Committee* Wheat for Germany and world wheat position: overall reductions in requirements must be decided by U.K. and U.S. Governments; matter to be discussed in Washington by Minister of Food (Sir Ben Smith) [UR 4861/1246/851].

rubber situation in Argentina have recently improved considerably, and look like continuing to improve': cf. i below.

No reply had been received to Mr. Bevin's message before the first meeting of the Cabinet Wheat Committee on 19 December: see ii below.

No. 116

The Earl of Halifax (Washington) to Mr. Bevin
(Received 23 November, 3.25 a.m.)

No. 7816 Telegraphic [UE 5676/1094/53]

Immediate   WASHINGTON, *22 November 1945, 10.2 p.m.*

Personal for Catto from Keynes.
Your telegram No. 11653.[1]

1. If there were any chance of settlement on your lines all of us here would welcome it. But it seems to us to be the opposite pole from what is now the American thought.

2. In fact they are at present asking something not less than three quarters of a billion for lend lease alone and some of their side are still advocating that this should not be on as liberal terms as the main loan but at $2\frac{3}{8}$ per cent interest plus capital repayment in thirty equal instalments beginning next year. Throwing in a quarter of a billion, or at best half a billion, of the old war debt would certainly not operate as an inducement to them to accept one per cent interest over all and would we think merely complicate the problem by bringing in the old war debt, which has not been brought so far into the present negotiations.

3. You must appreciate that the long delays have caused a steady deterioration of the position. After I had made my initial exposition of our case[2] the atmosphere both with the American group and with the

[1] Not printed. This telegram of 20 November suggested the revised version, discussed below, of Lord Catto's proposal in No. 74.ii.
[2] See No. 39.

press and Congress was at its best. For more than a fortnight after that we had to mark time waiting for the arrival of the commercial party. And when they arrived we naturally concentrated on their business.[3] You know how quickly things go stale in this country. Then there was another gap of more than a fortnight whilst we were awaiting instructions from the Cabinet.[4] All this was inevitable but the consequences were that the initial atmosphere was completely lost. The American side now seem convinced that they can get nothing past Congress which they cannot represent as hard trading out of which America gets as much future benefit as it concedes. They are also much concerned with the precedent for other countries which your proposal would not meet since other countries also have both old war debts and lend lease settlements. In particular it is because of their obstinacy that two per cent is the minimum rate of interest that half our difficulties have arisen.

4. All the old wiseacres and bogus elder statesmen are now shaking their hoary locks to our disadvantage. Baruch, Jesse Jones, Crowley and the like are inserting insidious words.

5. It is in this atmosphere that we have to consider what we can reasonably and safely concede. The strength of our position is that the other side are convinced that they will get a settlement and will be deeply shocked at the discovery that this is not as easy for them as all that. Our course is therefore to stand firm on essentials but all of us here are strongly of the opinion that it would be wise for our counter-proposals to follow their pattern as they have now presented it in so far as that is possible for us and not to try something brand new.

CALENDAR TO NO. 116

i *27 Nov. 1945   Letter from Mr. Brand (Washington) to Sir W. Eady* enclosing copy of letter of 23 Nov. to Mr. Baruch stating British case for a loan: U.K. will be 'repaying during something like two generations vast debts incurred to the rest of the world for the part we have played in this war'; without U.S. help U.K. will be forced into 'all sorts of trading and financial arrangements with other countries, which are bound to be most distasteful to the United States' [T 236/438].

[3] Cf. No. 54.   [4] Cf. Nos. 78 and 94.

No. 117

Note by Mr. Coulson on GEN 89/13 [ii]

[UE 5770/1094/53]

FOREIGN OFFICE, 23 November 1945

Washington Financial Talks

1. The Chancellor draws attention to three objectionable features of the latest American proposals:[1]

(1) We cannot avail ourselves of the waiver if our monetary reserves are higher than a certain figure.

(2) We are to be tied down to 'convertibility' by the end of 1946, thus making our negotiations with our sterling creditors impossible.

(3) We shall be forced to abandon our Payments Agreements with the Western European countries and Latin America.

There is a fourth serious objection, viz. that the Americans are asking us, if we use the waiver, not to make higher payments to our sterling creditors than we make, proportionately, to America.

2. Though the arguments against accepting these proposals are of a Treasury rather than a Foreign Office kind, they are overwhelmingly strong and, I think, must be supported by the Foreign Office.

3. The American proposals are appallingly complicated and legalistic. Taken as a whole, they could not but give rise to continual dispute. The only possibility is to clear the brushwood away and revert to simple lines. The draft telegram attached to this paper (Annex I)[2] seems to me just right in this respect.

4. Neither the paper nor the telegram go into the question of tactics, if the Americans do not at once accept our new approach. In a private and personal letter to Sir Alexander Cadogan,[3] Mr. Hall-Patch has suggested that it might be a good idea if Lord Keynes were to come home and explain the situation to the Cabinet. Moreover, he thinks that a break in the negotiations might in itself not be a bad thing, since it would give a salutary jolt to American opinion and Congress. In the end, this might produce better results than if the present negotiations were continued

---

[1] See No. 113.　　　　　　　　　　　　　　[2] Not reproduced at ii below.

[3] Untraced in Foreign Office archives. In a subsequent letter of 24 November to Mr. Butler Mr. Hall-Patch commented in particular: 'We are not going to be able to get the wide and generous settlement which, if there were statesmen in charge in this country, we should obtain without too much difficulty, as being the course most in the interest of the United States. This is not possible: we are dealing with small men of narrow vision. The politics of this great country is being conducted on the level of a haberdashery store in Independence Missouri . . . Within the severe limitations imposed on them the Americans with whom we are dealing are anxious to reach a settlement on *their* terms. I feel we can obtain our minimum essential requirements provided that we stand quite firm on what *we* consider to be essential: there must be no wavering. These essentials will be disputed by the Americans on the ground that they will be unpalatable to Congress. I still suggest we stand firm, even at the risk of a temporary break' (UE 6135/1094/53).

352

uninterrupted. Mr. Hall-Patch's letter was, however, admittedly, sent before we had received all the latest telegrams from Washington and at a time when we were completely in the dark in London and explanations were more necessary. Since then, Lord Keynes (Washington telegram No. 7825)[4], apparently with the Ambassador's agreement, has pointed out that any course which involved serious delay would be thought by the Americans to be a menace to the Bretton Woods timetable;[5] and it would, therefore, be a grave mistake to start over again on new lines.

5. In the circumstances the best plan seems to be to try the approach now suggested by the Treasury, namely, a rejection of the American unpalatable proposals and an attempt to revert to an agreement on simple lines. But if this does not meet with anything like American approval, then I submit that we should not be afraid of breaking off the negotiations for a little.[6] I still feel that the prizes which the Americans win if the negotiations succeed, to wit, our acceptance of Bretton Woods, our acceptance of the proposals for an International Trade Organisation and the liberalisation of the sterling area, are so important to them and are such an essential part of their policy, that we can afford to be tough even though this knocks their Bretton Woods timetable out of joint. A break would have the added advantage that both sides, who are exhausted, would have time to recuperate and see the picture with more statesman-like eyes.[7]

CALENDARS TO NO. 117

i *21 Nov. 1945 Note by Mr. Rowe-Dutton for Sir W. Eady* on dangers of convertibility: 'If I were an American deliberately seeking to destroy British financial and economic future, I could choose no better way of setting about it' (cf. Pressnell, *op. cit.*, Chapter 10(18)) [T 236/438].

ii *22 Nov. 1945 GEN 89/13 Memo. by Mr. Dalton on financial talks* (without Annexes): proposals in No. 113 are unacceptable 'both in form and in spirit' (cf. *op. cit.*, Chapter 10(19)) [UE 5770/1094/53].

---

[4] This telegram of 22 November is printed in Moggridge, *op. cit.*, pp. 594–5.

[5] In a letter of 21 November to Mr. Coulson, Mr. Hall-Patch commented that Mr. Harry White, who was 'becoming extremely vocal on Bretton Woods', pointed out that 'the European countries are waiting for us to ratify. And unless the requisite number ratify by Dec. 31st Congress will be free to look at again, with an ever more critical eye, the whole Bretton Woods setup. He warns us in emphatic terms that if this happens the new Bretton Woods will be very much less satisfactory from our point of view than the old . . .' (UE 5907/1094/53).

[6] In a memorandum of 22 November for the Lord President Mr. Fleming had discussed No. 113 in detail and commented: 'Rumours have reached us that the Treasury is highly perturbed about certain features, some of which seem to us harmless, in the American proposals and contemplates asking Ministers to authorise the breaking off of negotiations. This seems crazy: (a) because the American proposals are put forward tentatively and subject to our amendment; (b) because we cannot do without the money; and (c) because no alternative supplies of the necessary finance are in sight' (T 230/142). Mr. Morrison spoke on these lines at the 6th meeting of the GEN 89 Committee on 23 November: see No. 118.i.

[7] This note was minuted as follows by Mr. Ronald and Sir A. Cadogan: 'I agree. N.B. Ronald 23/XI.' 'A.C. Nov. 23, 1945.'

No. 118

Mr. Bevin to the Earl of Halifax (Washington)

No. 11789 Telegraphic [F.O. 800/512]

Most immediate   FOREIGN OFFICE, 24 November 1945, 1.14 a.m.

Personal from Chancellor of the Exchequer for Keynes.

1. Ministers considered the whole position this evening [i]. You will see our views in the telegram No. 11790[1] which the Prime Minister will be sending to the Ambassador.

2. The fact is that we could not stomach much of Nabob 372[2] any more than I suspect you can. That is not the kind of agreement you went out to obtain or would like to bring back with you. We thought it was time we came to your help after all your labours. I hope you will agree that the line proposed to the Ambassador can be profitably followed for in essentials it is what you have been trying to put over those argumentative fellows.

CALENDAR TO NO. 118

i 23 Nov. 1945   Record of meeting of Ministers (GEN 89/6th meeting) Discussion o GEN 89/13 (No. 117.ii): Mr. Dalton felt 'we had to take the risk of a break' in negotiations, but Mr. Bevin suggested personal approach from Mr. Attlee to President Truman, who would 'not wish to jeopardise the whole position . . A breakdown would be misunderstood by the peoples of the two countries, b the Empire, by the rest of the world' (cf. Pressnell, op. cit., Chapter 10(19) [UE 5785/1094/53].

[1] No. 119.   [2] No. 113.

No. 119

Mr. Bevin to the Earl of Halifax (Washington)

No. 11790 Telegraphic [F.O. 800/512]

Most immediate. Top secret   FOREIGN OFFICE, 24 November 1945, 2.4 a.m.

From Prime Minister to Lord Halifax.

1. My colleagues and I have considered the whole position of the financial talks and in particular Nabob 372.[1]

2. We should be prepared to agree with the Americans on the following points:

(a) *Amount of credit* not less than 4 billions including Lend/Lease at 2 per cent, to be repaid over 50 years beginning after 5 years.

(b) Liberalisation of the Sterling Area on the lines in Nabob Saving 32,[2] paragraphs 11 and 12 and 14 and 15.

[1] No. 113.   [2] No. 98.

(c) Recommendation to Parliament of Bretton Woods as soon as we reach a financial agreement.

(d) Commercial policy as in the documents recently agreed.[3]

3. We are not (repeat not) prepared to agree to the following conditions in Nabob 372:

(a) Completion of the negotiations with creditor countries by the end of 1946.

(b) Abrogation at the end of 1946 of our transitional rights under Bretton Woods.

(c) Formally ranking the American debt ahead of all other external obligations.

4. On the *waiver* we should like the Washington waiver and the London waiver in the form in which they were originally presented,[4] in order to ease the heavy liabilities we are accepting for fifty years. We are not prepared to accept the additional test of the state of our reserves now added to the Washington waiver.

If we cannot obtain the two waivers substantially in their original form and free from any risk of intervention in our affairs, we should prefer to content ourselves with a clause to the following effect. 'Either Government shall be entitled to approach the other for review and modification by mutual consent of this agreement if its working has become such as to burden international commerce within the meaning of Article VII of the Mutual Aid agreement of February 23rd 1942[5] or is otherwise contrary to the intention of the two Governments in entering on this agreement.'

5. You will see that although we have not yet formally offered this we are prepared for the sake of an agreement to accept the heavy burden of interest at 2 per cent on the whole of the credit in use.

6. We cannot accept the time limit for the Sterling Area negotiations (a) because it would be regarded by our creditors as a dictation and (b) because it would put us at a serious disadvantage in negotiating. The other party would know we must meet them in order to fulfil our contract with the Americans.

But we could begin negotiations early in 1946 and would carry them on as rapidly as possible. The policy is in our interests and we stand by it.

7. We cannot so prematurely give up our transitional rights. We do not know yet what will be the policy of other countries or what will be the results of the Commercial Conferences planned for 1946. But we should hope to be able to modify our restrictions progressively and our policy would be shaped to this end.

8. A departmental telegram [i] is being sent to you about the priority of the American debt.

9. We expect to have difficulty with Parliament both on Bretton Woods and Commercial policy but if we secured a satisfactory financial agreement we should use every endeavour to secure early approval.

---

[3] See No. 95, and ii below.   [4] See No. 87, paras. 7 and 8.   [5] See No. 1, note 5.

10. I have set this out to show you how near we believe we are to the essentials of the American position. I am therefore all the more dismayed that the financial negotiations should drag on and be cumbered with all kinds of legalistic and controversial conditions which are not necessary to the common purpose of the negotiators on both sides. This situation is having a bad effect on the relations between our two countries and that at a time when there is much other important international business on which we want to work out a common policy.

11. I am therefore contemplating speaking in the next two or three days personally to the President in the sense of this telegram and asking him whether he can intervene to clear the ground so that a simple agreement with only the essential matters in it could be drawn up rapidly. Before I do so I should like to have your views particularly on the proposed procedure. If you think my plan is the best step to take at this juncture you might care to consider explaining the matter to Vinson and Clayton.

CALENDARS TO No. 119

i   *24 & 25 Nov. 1945   To British Missions (Washington) Tel. BABOON 299* Technical commentary from Treasury on No. 113, as background to No. 119 (cf. No. 125): 'The American debt will always be a prior charge on our external resources and reserves'; British Delegation reply in NABOB 395 [UE 5784, 5799/1094/53].

ii   *24 Nov. 1945   Memo. by Sir S. Cripps (C.P. (45) 297)* (circulated in draft form on 22 Nov. as GEN 89/14) with (Annex A) draft statement for use in parliament on U.S. commercial policy proposals (Annexes B & C, summary and full text of U.S. proposals, not reproduced) [UE 5850/1094/53].

iii   *26–28 Nov. 1945   Anglo-American discussions on procedure in connection with results of financial and commercial negotiations* Americans unreceptive to British suggestions (NABOB 390) and propose (NABOB 391) joint communiqué (NABOB 392) and joint statement (text regarding commercial policy in NABOB 393): British revised text of NABOB 393 and comments (NABOB 394 & 398): comments by Sir S. Cripps (BABOON 311) and Mr. Fitzmaurice [UE 5826/1094/53].

No. 120

The Earl of Halifax (Washington) to Mr. Bevin
(Received 26 November, 2.48 a.m.)

No. 7893 Telegraphic [UE 5769/1094/53]

Immediate   WASHINGTON, *25 November 1945, 9.20 p.m.*

Personal for Chancellor of the Exchequer from Keynes.
Your telegram 11789.[1]

[1] No. 118.

356

1. Subject to certain comments below we were well satisfied with the line of instructions in the Prime Minister's telegram.[2]

2. Ambassador and I delivered the substance of these instructions to Vinson and Clayton this morning. In order to be formally on the record and also in order that your position might be clearly understood by all the American group and not merely by the two we were seeing, we decided to deliver your reply in writing. The text of this is being telegraphed separately.[3]

3. Vinson and Clayton were considerably taken aback. Nevertheless they did not react too violently against the change in the general approach for which we were pleading. One lives on a see-saw here and there are several indications recently that we may have reached bottom point. There are quite a few on the American side who sympathise with us and are experiencing some revulsion of feeling against the legalistic binding provisions which they have been pressing on us lately. We had to go through this phase. But there is at least a chance that we shall escape from it. The Prime Minister's instructions gave us a grand chance and I hope you will feel that we have taken good advantage of it.

4. Unfortunately after we had delivered our case with supporting comments, Clayton who has been seedy for some time, had to tell us that he had fever and was not well enough to continue discussion. This is rather a disaster.

5. It will undoubtedly help us at the last lap to have your authority to reduce the figure to 4 billions including Lend–Lease. But as they have not yet proposed a firm figure to us there is no need for us to offer this concession now. Moreover we see some danger in it if it can be avoided. The Americans are still asking $750,000,000 net for Lend–Lease[4] and they can make a case difficult for us to resist on merits up to about $600,000,000. We still hope to settle for the latter figure but scarcely for less. Since we first started, London's estimates of the inventory for which we are liable have steadily increased.

6. All of us here feel that to have no more than $3,400 million new money is to cut things dangerously fine. Certain statistics we have seen which might appear to justify such a figure are, in our opinion, misleading and based on fallacy.

7. As you will see from the text as telegraphed, we are fighting hard to retain a satisfactory waiver on the lines of paragraph 4 of the Prime Minister's telegram.

8. All of us here are greatly disturbed by the relatively small importance London now seems to attach to the waiver. The suggested reduction in the amount of the credit makes matters worse, since this may mean that we shall end the transition with inadequate reserves. In our

[2] No. 119.
[3] See No. 121. The remainder of the present telegram is printed in Moggridge, *op. cit.*, pp. 596–7, where it is wrongly numbered as 7895.
[4] See No. 114.

view a waiver clause has inestimable value both practically and politically. This is especially the case if it creates a precedent for other settlements. We cannot face with equanimity an unqualified liability to external creditors which may reach 75,000,000 pounds sterling a year in the aggregate. We must not overplay immediate technical considerations to the disadvantage of the responsibilities of cautious statesmanship towards the future. We feel that such a settlement, half of which, if Canada gets the same terms, would cost 2 percent interest, would be widely and justly criticised as too nearly a repetition of last time's war debts. I am asked by my colleagues here, and I share their view, to say that we would give up an objective waiver only on the most express instructions and we should ask to be excused from taking any responsibility for it.[5]

[5] In his immediately following telegram No. 7894 of 25 November Lord Halifax sent the following message to Mr. Attlee in reply to para. 11 of No. 119: 'After seeing Vinson and Clayton today and judging their reaction to the message you instructed us to give them, we think we should do well to give the medicine a few days to work before you call in a higher opinion. We should I think get as far as we can on the present basis before invoking the President, though the time may easily come before we are finished when we shall have to ask you to raise the decision to the highest level.' In F.O. telegram No. 11875 to Washington of 26 November, marked 'Personal and Secret' to Lord Halifax, Mr. Attlee agreed to leave it to the Ambassador 'to determine when you want to call me in. A delay of a few days for reflection does not work adversely for us here. But you know that the immediate Parliamentary time-table is becoming jammed, though we are trying to keep time for Bretton Woods during December. On this point, however, the clock is ticking against the Americans at least as much as against us' (UE 5769/1094/53).

No. 121

British Missions (Washington) to Cabinet Offices
(Received 25 November, 11.59 p.m.)

NABOB 396 Telegraphic [UE 5784/1094/53]

Immediate. Secret   WASHINGTON, 25 November 1945, 9.33 p.m.

Following is text[1] begins:
Comments of the UK Government on the provisional American Draft.[2]

1. Certain of the clauses in the draft (which is, they appreciate, of a provisional and tentative character) lately remitted to the Government of the U.K. are, in their view inacceptable, not because they are not pointing in the right direction, but because they attempt to go into more precise details in respect of the time and manner of application of agreed principles, than is either practicable or advisable.

2. The Government of the U.K. desire, therefore, to recall the discussions to their central objects and to emphasise how large a measure

[1] See No. 120. The present text is printed in Moggridge, *op. cit.*, pp. 633–6.
[2] No. 113.

of agreement can be accomplished, if unnecessary points of difference can be avoided on matters of detail not essential to the main purpose.

3. On the assumption that agreement is reached on the measure and terms of the financial aid required to enable the U.K. to surmount the balance of trade difficulties of the transition, and subject always to the views of Parliament on matters which have not yet been submitted, the Government of the U.K. are ready to proceed as follows:

(i) To modify the exchange arrangements of the sterling area as set forth in paragraph 6 of the American draft;

(ii) To recommend to Parliament the ratification of the final act of Bretton Woods as soon as a financial agreement has been reached with the U.S. administration;

(iii) To associate the Government of the U.K. with the proposals on Commercial Policy as in the documents recently drafted;[3]

(iv) To modify progressively and at as early dates as circumstances permit any remaining exchange restrictions and import controls of the character referred to in paragraphs 7 and 8 of the American draft, and to shape their policy to this end;
and

(v) To seek by voluntary agreement with the countries of the sterling area an early settlement of the accumulated sterling balances on terms varying according to the circumstances of each case, on the lines already indicated to the U.S. group.

4. To reach so comprehensive a measure of agreement over so wide and so difficult a field would seem to them to represent enormous progress and to show how close together the American and the British positions are on essentials.

5. They are, therefore, all the more dismayed that the financial negotiations should drag on and be cumbered with over-precise and inevitably controversial conditions which are not necessary to the common purpose of the negotiations on the two sides. Such a situation cannot but have a bad effect on the relations between the two countries, and that at a time when there is so much other important international business on which a common policy has to be worked out.

6. On the contrary, in a position of great complexity, the Government of the U.K. feel that they ought not to be asked to risk success in so difficult an endeavour as that which they are facing, by attempting to move more rapidly than circumstances can safely allow or with less liberty of manoeuvre than is both reasonable and desirable in negotations in prospect with the many other countries concerned. They would remind the U.S. group that the policy of other countries and the results of the Commercial conferences planned for 1946 are not yet known.

7. In particular, they cannot accept a time limit for completing the negotiations on the accumulated sterling area balances, for this would put

[3] See No. 95, and cf. No. 119.ii.

them at a serious disadvantage in negotiating. The other party would know that the U.K. must meet them in order to fulfil its contract with the U.S. The Government of the U.K. intend, however, to begin negotiations early in 1946 and to carry them on as rapidly as possible. The policy is in their interest and they stand by it.

8. Nor, except to the extent indicated above, can they forego prematurely the safeguards of the transitional arrangements provided for in the Bretton Woods plan and in the agreed paper on Commercial Policy,[4] regardless of the course of events in the precarious period ahead and irrespective of reciprocal action by the other countries affected. The U.K. Government would however, consider themselves pledged as already stated to shape their policy so as to terminate these arrangements as soon as practicable.

9. Turning to the terms of the proposed line of credit, the Government of the U.K. greatly regret that there should be a departure from the simplicity and certainty of the Waiver clause based on the volume of the external income of the U.K., as it was originally communicated to them. They see the greatest difficulty in arriving at a suitable and undisputable definition of 'reserves'. They think it is impossible to define the adequacy of reserves at any given figure in a contract for forty-five years when so much may happen, which cannot now be foreseen in the methods and technique of conducting international financial relations. Moreover, any such provision might give rise to the misconception that the U.S. wishes to keep the U.K. reserves in as weak a position as possible. Indeed a clause based on examining the statistical state of reserves must be rejected as quite wrong in principle and against the interest of both countries. The Bretton Woods final act, the projected provisions of the I.T.O. and the lasting liberalisation of the sterling area will be far more likely to endure over a long period of years if the U.K. hold substantial reserves than if they are in anxiety on this score and are liable to be reduced in any temporary adverse circumstances too near to bed-rock.

10. There is a far better solution of the issue which this objectionable provision seeks to solve. The object appears to be to prevent advantage being taken of the waiver rights under the criterion of external income in circumstances when the reserves were strong viewed in the light of the circumstances existing when the occasion arises. But in such circumstances the U.K. would not wish to take advantage of the waiver clause. To do so will always be, in the view of the U.K. Government, a grave matter, never to be acted upon if it is avoidable. Whenever this right is invoked the credit of the U.K. is bound to suffer. To invoke it, except in the case of clear necessity, must necessarily impair the good relations between the U.K. and the U.S. There will be no intention on the part of the U.K. to

[4] i.e. the revised version of COM/TRADE 1, dated 12 November, which was attached as Annex C to C.P.(45)297 but is not reproduced at No. 119.ii. This text was identical to that adopted at the final meeting of the Commercial Policy Committee on 1 December (see No. 163.ii) and printed in Cmd. 6709 of 1945, pp. 2–18.

exercise their rights of waiver in any circumstances in which they see their way to avoid it. A readiness to accept the bona fides and honourable intention of the U.K. not to take advantage of the waiver clause to escape a liability which they are well able to meet, would be worth more than any amount of drafting ingenuity. Nor without such mutual confidence can there be good prospect of an enduring common policy in the wider field and larger hopes which it is the purpose of these discussions to keep in view.

11. The Government of the U.K. are also much disappointed that the U.S. Group have found no means of providing against difficulties arising, not out of the inability of the U.K. to earn an external income, but out of an inability or a reluctance on the part of the U.S. to receive sufficient goods and services from the rest of the world to discharge what the rest of the world owes to them in the balance of payments. They hope that a search for a suitable provision can be resumed. In any case they would suggest the inclusion of a clause to the following effect:

'Either Government shall be entitled to approach the other for a review and modification by mutual consent of this agreement if its working has become such as to burden international commerce within the meaning of Article VII of the mutual aid agreement of February 23rd 1942 or is otherwise contrary to the intention of the two Governments in entering on this agreement'.

12. Finally, the Government of the U.K. regret their inability to accept paragraphs 4(II) and 5(II) of the American draft inasmuch as they limit in advance the freedom of negotiation of the U.K. with sterling area creditors, a limitation which would be bound to carry with it political complications of the gravest nature within the British Commonwealth.

Ends.

No. 122

Letter from Commander Jackson (Washington) to Mr. Noel-Baker

[UR 4638/24/850]

Top secret and personal   WASHINGTON, 25 November 1945

My dear Minister of State,

I am sending you with this letter a survey of the present position in UNRRA. This is the second survey I have written about the Administration and on each of those occasions we faced a crisis.

I hope that this will be my swan-song as far as these surveys are concerned. Perhaps next year I may write a third one making recommendations for the liquidation of the Administration and making proposals for the continuation of particular aspects of its work by other and new international organisations. However, we need to get some dollars from Congress before considering that final stage!

If I get the new money and the additional men pretty quickly, I shall go away and rest from early February onwards. For me to have gone before would possibly have meant the collapse of the Administration. It may be thought that I have cried 'Wolf, wolf' too often about UNRRA, but I do not think that General Gale[1] and General Morgan—both of whom are conservative men—would feel that I have exaggerated the seriousness of the situation during the past few months. Similarly, I do not feel that this present survey is an exaggeration of our present difficulties.

By February we shall have done everything possible to have made a contribution to combat the winter in Europe, for it will take a further three months for supplies to run through the pipelines. Then I shall be able to rest with a clear conscience.

It will have been a tough year, but, if we win this final round, then it will have been worth everything.

Yours very sincerely,
R.G.A. JACKSON

ENCLOSURE IN NO. 122

I. INTRODUCTION

First Crisis In May 1945 I wrote to the Minister of State and reviewed UNRRA.[2] At that time, there were grave doubts as to whether it could ever be made to function efficiently. The war in Europe had ended, but UNRRA was still completely unprepared to carry out the task for which it had been created. No policy for any major aspect of its work had been developed. The organisation was chaotic, and the majority of the staff was demoralised. It was decided, however, to try to save this, the first of the new international organisations. Another decisive reason for making this decision was the fact that time would not have permitted the establishment of a new relief organisation which could have been put into full operation before the winter set in. It was decided, therefore, that UNRRA should be re-organised, first priority being given to cleaning up the mess in Europe (taking a chance that the Headquarters in Washington would hold together for a little while) and then giving attention to the Far East.

Second Crisis At that time it was appreciated that, even if the re-organisation of the Administration was successful, a second crisis would arise about the end of 1945, or early 1946 (depending on the ending of the war with Japan), when it would be necessary for the Administration to receive further funds to carry on its work. We are now in the middle of that second crisis and, in view of His Majesty's Government's active participation in UNRRA, it may be useful for you to have a review of the present situation.

Before dealing with the present crisis in detail, it may be useful to

[1] Lt.-Gen. Sir H. Gale was the Personal Representative of the Director General in the European Regional Office of U.N.R.R.A.

[2] Commander Jackson's letter of 15 May to Mr. Richard Law is not printed (UR 1439/24/850).

summarise the present position of UNRRA both from the point of view of Administration and Operations.

Europe We have surmounted the first crisis by the skin of our teeth. From an administrative point of view it is sufficient to say that the organisation on the Continent has been simplified, that all the Missions in the various countries have been strengthened, and that some exceptionally good men have been appointed to key positions. Much remains to be done before the whole organisation will run really smoothly, but the back of the job has been broken and there is no reason why a constant improvement should not be maintained. I have every confidence that the European Regional Office will function efficiently under the direction of Sir Humfrey Gale. This improvement, however, has just been achieved in time, for already the beginning of winter has begun to test the strength of the organisation.

You know the situation in Europe much better than we do. Generally speaking, UNRRA operations in Central and South Eastern Europe are going well. Greece is an exception, but that is not the fault of UNRRA. The supply lines to all the countries are functioning quite well and, were it not for the financial difficulties—to which reference is made in this paper—I should have confidence that UNRRA could make a substantial contribution to the relief of the various countries in which it is working.

The Displaced Persons Operation in Germany is always going to be a very difficult problem to handle, especially from the point of view of securing the services of really good people for this work, but it is most fortunate for us that a man like General Sir Frederick Morgan has been appointed to take charge. (He badly needs a first-class American Deputy and I refer to this later on.)

Far East Work in the Far East is just beginning and it is too early to comment in detail. Efforts are being made to prevent a repetition of the mistakes made initially in Europe. The staff is being strengthened.

Washington Headquarters The organisation of the Headquarters in Washington will require a very considerable amount of modification and the quality of the top-level personnel is far from satisfactory. This latter problem and the problem of further financial aid are the two elements which constitute the present crisis threatening the future of the Administration.

II. The Financial Crisis

(a) *The $550,000,000 Appropriation* At the present moment, two separate series of Congressional Hearings are in progress. The first relates to the balance of 550 million dollars which is still outstanding from the original 1% contribution from the United States; the second Hearing is concerned with the further 1% contribution which is now needed so urgently from the United States.[3]

Already the Hearings concerned with the 550 million dollars have gone

[3] Cf. No. 76.

on for five weeks. The House of Representatives has approved a Bill for the appropriation of this money, but unfortunately an amendment was included in the legislation by which the Administration would be required to give a certificate to the President, before 1st January, 1946, indicating that representatives of the Press had been given full access to the Administration's work in each of the countries where it is operating. This amendment was accepted during the debate on the floor of the House of Representatives, despite a strong recommendation to the contrary from Mr. Byrnes. It has subsequently become something of a political issue in this country.

The Hearings before the Senate Appropriations Sub-Committee began over a fortnight ago and slowly ended yesterday. The Senate Sub-Committee recommended the appropriation and eliminated the objectionable press amendment. But, alas, a new amendment (and nearly as objectionable as the earlier amendment) was introduced, by which UNRRA would have to pay 'parity prices' for farm products purchased in the United States. The Bill goes to the full Senate Appropriations Committee tomorrow and Mr. Clayton and Senator Vandenburg [Vandenberg] will try to have the latest amendment eliminated. Then, we hope that the Bill will be heard on the floor of the Senate during the coming week. It should pass the Senate successfully, but it will then be necessary for a conference to be held before Representatives of the two Houses to compromise over the press amendment, and any amendments introduced in the Senate. On the assumption that agreement is reached, a fresh Bill, authorising the appropriation, would then come to the floors of both Houses for approval and should be passed very quickly. With luck, this additional 550 million dollars might be made available to UNRRA by the end of the first week in December.

If that happens, it will already have been seven weeks too late for the Administration to have made the best use of the funds. Everything possible has been done to emphasise the urgency of the situation to the President, the State Department and Congress, but only moderate success has been achieved. This situation has caused the Bureau of Supply to freeze requisitions for supplies which could be obtained very easily at the present time in the United States, and which would be invaluable in Europe during the coming winter. Already, requisitions covering 50 million dollars' worth of agricultural machinery, seeds, medical requirements and other supplies, have had to be frozen in order that the minimum supply of food could be shipped in December and January.

It is tragic that this should have happened. There is a very great danger, even if all the additional money is forthcoming within the next few weeks, that a considerable amount of UNRRA supplies will arrive too late to have the best effect in Europe. Of course, these supplies will always be of great value, but if they could have been delivered in accordance with UNRRA's original programme, they would have had a much greater effect on food production, and the distribution systems in the various countries.

In addition, 50 million dollars' worth of orders for surpluses of United States military equipment on the Continent have had to be frozen as well. That, too, is tragic. For example, some of the United States Army transportation equipment which is available to-day in Europe, would be invaluable if it were moved quickly into the countries which depend on UNRRA for assistance. Poland is a particular example. Locomotives and rolling-stock are available which could be used for the internal distribution of indigenous foods from areas which at present can only be approached by railway.

One more example. On 23rd November nearly all foods were finally taken off ration in the United States.[4] We need oils and fats desperately, and this is well known to the Department of Agriculture. As a rather shamefaced gesture, we were offered $12,000,000 worth of oils on the 24th November (yesterday). They would have been worth their weight in gold to us, but—alas—we did not have the dollars.

Never have I seen a better example of a situation where there is every danger of too little being delivered too late. This is a heart-breaking situation when one realises that if we had the necessary dollar resources, we could deliver large quantities of essential supplies at the right time. It will be even more heart-breaking if the money is finally appropriated at a time which makes it impossible for us to remedy the situation in Europe. But, as I have said, we have done everything possible to emphasise the urgency of the situation to the President, to the State Department, and to Members of Congress. Very recently, we have started to go to the American public direct. This is a dangerous policy, but it is now our only hope. I shall refer to this later.

(b) *The Second 1% Appropriation* Whilst the Hearings of the 550 million dollars were still proceeding in the Senate, we succeeded in persuading the House Foreign Affairs Committee to commence Hearings with a view to obtaining *authorisation* for a further 1% of the United States National Income. Everything possible has been done to expedite these Hearings and it is possible that they may be completed in another day. A debate on the floor of the House of Representatives will follow, and our aim is to see that the debate is completed by the end of the first week in December. Again, we are doing everything possible to ensure that Hearings before the Senate Foreign Relations Committee are begun at the earliest possible date, after the Bill has passed the House . . .[5]

[4] The U.S. Secretary of Agriculture, Mr. Clinton Anderson, announced on 23 November that rationing of all meats and fats would end the following day, only sugar remaining rationed (see *The Times*, 24 November 1945, p. 3).

[5] The remainder of this section, and the following sections 'General Comment on the Hearings' and 'Washington Headquarters Staff' which related to American politics and to personalities in U.N.R.R.A. headquarters are omitted. Commander Jackson mentioned in particular that 'there was no clear policy within the Administration itself and little had been done to impress on the President [cf., however, No. 76, note 4], the State Department, and on Congress itself [cf., however, Governor Lehman's letter of 9 November to the President of the Senate, printed in *F.R.U.S. 1945*, vol. ii, pp. 1040–2] the vital need for additional

IV[III]. Note on Headquarters Operations

As far as the supply operations carried out by this Headquarters are concerned, I am reasonably satisfied with the programmes[6] (if it were not for the lack of money), with the exception of industrial rehabilitation supplies. The policy is far too indefinite in dealing with industrial machinery and raw materials and I have already initiated a survey of these operations.

Financial control has been disgracefully lax. The comments of the auditors have been entirely justified. The personnel in that field of work is being strengthened and action is being taken here to introduce new procedures and to tighten up on control in every possible way. Much remains to be done and it is in that field that the need for a new Deputy Director-General in charge of Finance and Administration is so urgent.

There is a complete absence of forward-planning and consideration of means by which UNRRA's job can be terminated. Little has been done in the field of economic and financial analysis and, again, no consideration has been given to the effect of UNRRA's work on the economies of the various countries with which it is concerned and how the Administration can withdraw without creating chaos in those countries. I hope that this deficiency will be remedied at an early date.

Linked with this same subject of medium-term planning, will be the vital need, early in 1946, of co-ordinating the plans for the various international economic organisations which have yet to come to life, but which should certainly overlap the UNRRA period, so that there can be continuity of action, especially in countries such as Greece and Italy. If this work can be started, it will have an excellent effect on the staff of UNRRA who, whilst willing to carry on in this field of work if they can see even a dim future, will most certainly seek other employment if plans are not developed at a fairly early date.

V[IV]. Conclusion

If some means can be found of obtainin[g] the additional United States funds quickly, and if we can obtain the three or four key Americans mentioned above, then I am confident that UNRRA will be able to

funds'. Action by the Roman Catholic Church and testimony by General Eisenhower to the House Foreign Affairs Committee (see *The Times*, 23 November 1945, p. 3) had been helpful, and Commander Jackson hoped to persuade Governor Lehman to secure action by the President.

Commander Jackson further observed: 'Another factor which we are keeping an eye on during our campaign is the possibility of the British loan proposals arriving (perhaps like an atomic bomb!) in the very Committees with which we are now dealing. That would make our battles still harder!' On the U.N.R.R.A. Headquarters Staff Commander Jackson, while pointing to weaknesses in the administration, reported that steps were being taken to make some new appointments and in particular that Major General L. Rooks of the U.S. Army, who had been Deputy Chief of Staff in the Mediterranean Theatre, was to assist him as a Deputy Director General.

[6] Details of the proposed U.N.R.R.A. programmes for 1946 can be found in files UR 114/850 (1945) and UR 1/850 (1946), F.O. 371/51374 and 58005–9, respectively.

perform a good job of work. I am reasonably certain that we can obtain the men. The political battle, however, will continue to be bitter and tough. I do not predict that we shall win both victories. One, I believe, is reasonably certain. But I am by no means admitting the possibility of any defeat at this stage. We shall continue to attack. A great deal will depend on the initiative and the ingenuity with which we handle our case over the next three or four weeks.

The constant Canadian support for the Administration has been a source of satisfaction and strength to us: still more so, the strong and positive attitude adopted by His Majesty's Government has been the decisive factor whether we could have carried on or not. The attitude of the House of Commons during the Debate on the 16th October,[7] when further support for UNRRA was given, has been a source of the greatest encouragement and confidence to the whole staff of the Administration. The comparison between the attitude of the House of Commons and Congress is a sad one. But, as one good member of Congress said rather sorrowfully to me on the following day: 'There you see the difference between responsible Government and the thoroughly irresponsible condition of the United States Government at the present time'.[8]

R.G.A. JACKSON

[7] Corrected, evidently by Mr. Noel-Baker, to read 'November'. For the Minister of State's speech of 16 November in which he announced that H.M. Government would make a further contribution of £75 million to U.N.R.R.A., thus making their total contribution £155 million, equivalent to 2% of the national income for the year 1942–3, see *Parl. Debs., 5th ser., H. of C.*, vol. 415, cols. 2601–15: cf. also i below.

[8] In a further letter to Mr. Noel-Baker of 17 December Commander Jackson stated that the $550 million appropriation had been signed by the President on 13 December, and that 'by the following morning we had committed $435 million of the new funds'. He recounted the successful campaign, in which 'the President helped most effectively', to obtain Congressional approval of the 1% appropriation, which was to be given on 22 December with $750 million available immediately. 'On the operations side, we are signing Agreements with the two Soviet Republics tomorrow [printed in Woodbridge, *op. cit.*, vol. iii, pp. 255–62 and 332–8] after four weeks of ponderous negotiation. I think honour is satisfied on both sides. We are taking over Italy—but ten days later than I should have liked. We are waiting tonight to receive a request from the Allied Council in Vienna—I shall move the moment new funds become available out of the second United States 1%. We are facing a real grain crisis at the present time: that is clearly going to be another presidential party—it is clear that the French are in the same boat! It would be tragic if our first action in giving assistance to Italy and Austria were to fall down on grain deliveries, even if the actual circumstances were not under our control.'

Commander Jackson raised, in particular, two further questions: 'First of all, I am more and more convinced that this 1% approach to relief in Europe is a completely false one. We shall do a moderate job with the available funds, but if we really want to restore some degree of stability in Central and South-Eastern Europe, then we must all be prepared to spend more money (and this quickly) and invest better manpower . . . Herbert Hoover [U.S. President 1929–33, involved in organisation of relief for Europe] clearly appreciates that the job is being done on far too narrow a scale—he is one of the few senior Americans I have found with a real grasp of the size of the job . . . What has really worried Congress and the people of this country as well is whether the administrative machinery of UNRRA is strong enough or efficient enough to make reasonable use of the funds which they are placing at its

i *16 & 22 Nov. 1945 To and from Earl of Halifax (Washington) Tels. Nos. 11504 and 7789* Messages to and from Governor Lehman regarding Mr. Noel-Baker's parliamentary statement on H.M.G.'s contribution to U.N.R.R.A. (see note 7) [UR 4121, 4353/30/852].

ii *27 & 28 Nov. 1945 To and from Earl of Halifax (Washington) Tels. Nos. 11913 and 7948* Lord Halifax considers that 'at the moment it is better to let the American forces behind UNRRA play their hand with Congress' than for Mr. Bevin to take further action [UR 4315, 4452/30/852].

iii *6–8 Dec. 1945 Correspondence concerning supply aspect of U.K. contribution to U.N.R.R.A.* with particular reference to Europe and Far East [UR 4613/65/852, UR 4515, 4614/114/850].

disposal to get food into the mouths of starving people in Europe and China. If they could have been convinced of that earlier, then I believe we could have asked for ten times our present financial requirements—and got it.

'The second particular problem is to consider whether UNRRA is to continue beyond the end of 1946, or whether its functions are to be turned over to some new organisation—presumably under the Social and Economic Council of UNO. An early decision in this field is essential' (UR 4638/24/850).

No. 123

British Missions (Washington) to Cabinet Offices
(Received 27 November, 1.45 a.m.)

NABOB *397* Telegraphic [UE *5827/1094/53*]

Top secret. Immediate   WASHINGTON, *26 November 1945, 8.39 p.m.*

For Bridges and Eady from Ambassador and Keynes.

1. After we had delivered the text of NABOB 396[1] yesterday morning, the American group had a three hour meeting amongst themselves, in the absence of Clayton and of White who is also sick. Much to our surprise Keynes was invited to attend a meeting at the technical level an hour later, indicating intense effort on their part to make rapid progress.

2. No formal proposals were communicated to us at this meeting. But all those present appeared to be under instructions to explore with us means satisfactory to us for meeting all the points where we had raised objections at the first morning meeting. The attitude seemed more conciliatory than at any meeting this delegation have attended since they came to Washington.

3. We believe that there is now a better prospect than at any previous time of our gaining acceptance for a draft prepared within the limitations set by the instructions of the Prime Minister in telegram 11790.[2] We are anxious to move immediately and before the impact of yesterday's

[1] No. 121: see No. 120.   [2] No. 119.

communication has worn off. Nevertheless we have hesitated to give the Americans a further draft from our side until we have cleared it with you. We most earnestly hope that, provided you are satisfied we have preserved our position on essential points, you will allow us a certain latitude in the choice of language which the Americans can find it not too difficult to accept after what has gone before. We may of course, be disappointed in our present hopes. But we should like to be able to exploit, with the least possible delay and in a spirit as conciliatory on our side as theirs now seems to be, the last-minute opportunity which may be now presenting itself.

4. The matters on which we should like to go ahead the moment you can release us are set out in the next following paragraphs. As we have said above, we believe that we have drafted within the Prime Minister's instructions.

5. We have explained in NABOB 371[3] paragraph 2(I) and 9 why we consider paragraph 2 of the American draft in NABOB 372[4] acceptable as it stands. We much hope you will let us take this without any verbal changes. The meaning of American draft 2(II) is spelled out by us in paragraph 7(II) of NABOB 371 and further referred to in paragraph 8 below.

6. Vinson has always had his doubts about attaching a gold reserve clause to the waiver. After our further assaults yesterday, his experts were asked to explore with us the possible terms of some general statement on the lines of paragraph 10 of NABOB 396 to the effect that we should regard our exercise of the waiver under (a) of the American draft[4] as not being automatic but only to be made at our discretion in the light of the adequacy of our reserves and other relevant conditions at the time. We should like to offer a new clause as follows as a substitute for 4(I)(b) of the American draft:

Begins: 4(II) Before making a request to the Government of the United States under (I) above, the Government of the United Kingdom will take due account of the prospective and actual prevailing conditions of international exchange and adequacy of their available reserves. Ends.

7. We have good reason to think that the Americans will accept the terms of the clause of [sic] the end of paragraph 9 [4] of your telegram 11790 in substitution for the existing 4(III) of their draft.

8. We think there is a reasonable chance of getting them to take the text we submitted to you in paragraph 7 of NABOB 371 in substitution for 4(II) and 5(II) of their draft. This sets no ceiling to our settlements in respect of sterling balances. They are within their rights in keeping some vestige of their proposals about priority of pari passu treatment of new American money if they on their side will concede as much as this compromise draft involves. For the reasons already developed in paragraphs 8 to 11 of NABOB 371 we do not believe that we are giving

---

[3] No. 112. [4] No. 113.

away anything here which should embarrass us seriously. If we are to retain the waiver something of this kind is clearly both justifiable and necessary.

9. The objections of the Cabinet to clauses 7 and 8 of the American draft present by far the most serious obstacle in the minds of the Americans, as we always knew would be the case. Nevertheless, they have been instructed to explore with us the possible terms of a clause on the general lines of paragraph 3(IV) of NABOB 396 which would take the place of these two clauses. It will help a good deal if we can add a flat-footed provision about the maintenance of existing arrangements regarding the exchange freedom of the current sterling earnings of Americans. We conceive that there can be no objection to this. In view of the prevailing ignorance here, what is no concession at all nevertheless looks like such. We should like to offer a text as in the next paragraph.

10. *Begins*:

(*a*) Exchange arrangements between the United States and the United Kingdom.

The Government of the United Kingdom agree that after the date of this memorandum of agreement they will apply no exchange restrictions, except in accordance with the articles of agreement of the international monetary fund, so as to prevent payments or transfers in respect of transactions permitted by the authorities controlling imports into the United Kingdom or of other current transactions between the two countries as defined in article XIX(1) of the said articles[5] or on the use of sterling balances in the hands of United States residents arising out of current transactions; and in pursuance of the policy of reducing restrictions on trade between the two countries at the earliest possible date they agree not to avail themselves in respect of the transactions referred to above of article XIV of the articles of agreement of the International Monetary Fund.[6]

(*b*) Other exchange restrictions and import controls.

In relation to other remaining exchange restrictions and to import policy, the Government of the United Kingdom associates itself with the objectives of the Government of the United States as set out in the articles of association of the International Monetary Fund and in the United States proposals for an I.T.O. Their policy in the transitional period will accordingly be directed towards assuring as rapidly and over as wide a field as world economic conditions permit, the free use of sterling accruing to other countries through current transactions; and towards reducing to the greatest extent compatible with the restoration of the United Kingdom's external position, the application of their import controls and the discriminatory use of such controls.

[5] See No. 106, note 6.   [6] Cf. No. 1, note 11.

i *27 Nov. 1945   British Missions (Washington) Tel. NABOB 402* Suggests alternative draft of para. 9 of No. 113 following technical discussion with Americans [UE 5828/1094/53].

No. 124

Cabinet Offices to British Missions (Washington)

BABOON 303 Telegraphic [UE 5672/1094/53]

Most immediate. Secret   CABINET OFFICES, *26 November 1945, 9.20 p.m.*

Personal from Chancellor of the Exchequer for Keynes.

1. I find NABOB 396[1] admirable in tone. It breaks right away from NABOB 372[2] which both in form and spirit was unacceptable and would have been sharply criticised from all quarters in Parliament and outside. These negotiations were designed to conclude the very close financial and economic co-operation between our two countries during the war. In sending you our instructions we were making an effort to ensure that the agreement would retain something of that spirit, and you have supported us just as we wished.

2. I am disturbed only on paragraph 3(I) of NABOB 396. Paragraph 3(*a*) and paragraph 6 of 11790[3] stated that the time limit in paragraph 6 of NABOB 372 was unacceptable for the reasons which we gave and which were elaborated in BABOON 299.[4]

3. I am not sure whether you are promising that we shall release all current earnings throughout the whole of the Sterling Area as from the end of 1946. We do not wish this formal and public promise to be made, for it will certainly create the difficulties for us mentioned in 11790 and BABOON 299. Surely we must treat the clearance of current earnings as part of the general negotiations with each creditor, and until NABOB 372 I always thought that this was the proposal you were discussing with the Americans. See for example paragraph 11 of NABOB Saving 32[5] which covers both current earnings and portions of accumulated balances. We would expect to be able to complete the negotiations in many cases before the end of 1946 and would clear current earnings as well as an agreed proportion of existing balances on the successful conclusion of each agreement at some near date fixed in each agreement. But it is extremely unlikely that we would have been able to complete all our negotiations by the end of 1946. If the Americans have introduced this time limit because of doubts about our bona fides, I am quite confident that you can dispel their doubts. I think we must avoid this formal commitment, for it is of the

[1] No. 121.   [2] No. 113.   [3] No. 119.
[4] No. 119.i.   [5] No. 98.

highest importance to us in relation to the conduct of our very difficult negotiations with the Sterling Area. Surely the Americans will appreciate these difficulties if you put the argument to them.

4. *Waiver Clause* I have carefully noted your views in paragraph 8 of 7893[6] but before raising this matter again with my colleagues I should like to have the American reactions to paragraphs 9 to 11 of NABOB 396.

[6] No. 120.

No. 125

British Missions (Washington) to Cabinet Offices
(Received 27 November, 4.44 a.m.)

NABOB 400 *Telegraphic* [*UE 5828/1094/53*]

Most immediate. Secret   WASHINGTON, *27 November 1945, 1.19 a.m.*

For Chancellor of Exchequer from Ambassador, Keynes, Brand, Liesching, Robbins and all members of the delegation.

1. We are gravely disturbed by paragraphs 2 and 3 of BABOON 303.[1] For reasons set forth below we think it impossible to go back on the offer repeatedly made to the Americans with your full authority that the newly earned Sterling receipts of Sterling area countries would be liberated not later than the end of 1946. This is, of course, quite a separate issue from our having to complete the settlement of the accumulated Sterling balances before that date, where we have always reserved your position and have lately communicated your views to the Americans without qualification as in paragraph 7 of NABOB 396.[2] Perhaps we had better go back somewhat fully on the earlier as well as on the more recent history.

2. These two questions have always been quite separate in our proposals. The first concerns our offer to the Americans to give up the so-called Dollar pool of the current earnings of the Sterling area as at an early defined date, which is much the most attractive offer we were in a position to make in the financial field.

3. After much debate this offer was approved by the Cabinet before we left London.[3] Keynes made it in the course of our opening discussions and reported to you the great satisfaction with which it was received.[4] Subsequently we agreed with you the precise terms in which we could repeat it in writing, namely, as in paragraph[s] 11 and 12 of NABOB Saving 32.[5] That was given to the United States Treasury on November 7th with a covering letter to the effect that this was the form in which you had finally approved it.[5] It has appeared without contradiction in every draft which has been discussed subsequently.

4. To bring the history more up to date, the same provision appeared

[1] No. 124.   [2] No. 121.   [3] See No. 17.
[4] See No. 39, and cf. Nos. 41 and 49.   [5] No. 98.

as paragraph 6 in the American draft NABOB 372.[6] In the Prime Minister's reply to this, telegram 11790,[7] of a few days ago, he categorically reaffirmed our previous instructions and specifically referred with approval to the relevant paragraphs, namely 11 and 12 of NABOB Saving 32. We communicated to the Americans accordingly on November 25th as in paragraph 3(I) of NABOB 396.

5. It never occurred to us that paragraph 3A and paragraph 6 of 11790 were intended to be inconsistent with paragraph 2B of the same telegram. We assumed that these passages were intended to emphasize and explain your refusal to go beyond paragraph 2B by adding a definite time limit to the completion of the negotiations with creditor countries on accumulated balances, which is what the Americans were asking.

6. It is relevant to add that shortly prior to November 7th when we were authorised to communicate our offer in writing, we had an uneasy feeling here that London might be having second thoughts on this vital matter. This was a main purpose of the return of Robbins and Hall-Patch to London[8] so that they could represent to you what a serious and indeed disastrous effect any such backward step must have on the whole negotiations. They received complete assurances which were also telegraphed to us here that there was no thought of walking out on this so definite commitment. See BABOON 189 paragraph[s] 2 and 4, and BABOON 206 paragraph 12 and the personal telegrams referred to therein.[9]

7. We are now told that all the above is undone and the Prime Minister's unambiguous instruction in 2(B) of 11790 is contradicted by later passages in the same telegram which appeared to us to relate to the second and not the first of the two questions distinguished in this telegram and by somewhat confused passages in a personal telegram to Lee, namely BABOON 299,[10] which we assumed in the light of paragraph 2A of the Prime Minister's telegram and the previous clear understandings must relate to the second of the two questions distinguished above. The reversal after all that had happened of the undertaking in para 11 of NABOB Saving 32 would have been a change of front of such magnitude and importance that we could scarcely have been expected to infer that it has been reversed by indirection and obscure implication in a telegram which began by unambiguously reaffirming the former position; and with an apparent complete unawareness of the very serious consequences both to

---

[6] No. 113.   [7] No. 119.   [8] See No. 83, note 1.
[9] See No. 94.i, No. 94 and *ibid.*, note 9. Professor Robbins had recapitulated this correspondence in a message for Sir E. Bridges in J.S.M. telegram LETOD 388 of 26 November, in which he pointed out that on his recent visit to London he had made 'strong representations' on the implications of a withdrawal of the offer to liberalize the Sterling Area by the end of 1946: 'When I told Eady of these fears he assured me with great emphasis that they were ill founded and that his dispute with Keynes related to the quantification of cancellation and not to the offer of liberalization which still stood' (CAB 122/1471). Cf. further in this connexion Pressnell, *op. cit.*, Chapter 10(20).
[10] No. 119.i.

373

our personal position here and to the American reaction. Since the natural interpretation of the words was that they referred to the new demand the Americans were making, we ask to be excused for having so interpreted it.

8. The passage in BABOON 299 so far from clearing up the matter in the sense now suggested seems to confirm our interpretation, since the relevant passage ran as follows:

'If we were to contemplate accepting an early time limit, we could not proceed by voluntary agreement and we are not prepared to block existing balances unilaterally'.

We assumed from this that the objection to an early time limit related, as is stated, to the *existing* balances and referred therefore to our not accepting a definite date for completing our settlements in respect of these. This was consistent with our previous interpretation of the Prime Minister's telegram and merely armed us with an additional argument.

9. The second question relates to our accepting a time limit for settling with the Sterling area about their accumulated balances. This was dealt with in paragraph[s] 14 and 15 of NABOB Saving 32, which carefully avoided any time limit. The last sentence of paragraph 15 underlines their difference in this respect from the definite commitments in paragraphs 11 and 12. On this second question we have never had authority to commit you and have never done so. The Americans put a time limit in their NABOB 372 draft. We have since rejected it on your instructions.[2] We believe they have been moved by your arguments and we have already almost succeeded in getting this obstacle out of the way.

10. It seems to us too late in the day to re-open the argument whether on merits we yielded too much in paragraph 11 of NABOB Saving 32. We, however, do not think we have. It is a valuable weapon in negotiation to say that failing an agreement we will block the balances we already have. This we have retained. It is rather an empty threat to say that we will block the balances which the other party has not yet entrusted to us. Thus what we are giving up could only be of secondary importance as a bargaining inducement.

11. We are unanimously and strongly of the conviction that it is impossible to withdraw our long standing and frequently repeated undertaking to accept clause 6 of the American draft without what the Americans would regard, and in our judgement with full justification, as complete retraction on a vital matter, and that one in regard to which we have with your full authority made a perfectly express commitment.

You will understand our feeling that something like our own bonafides is here involved and accordingly the extreme difficulty in which your telegram has placed us. It would inevitably on the American side destroy the mutual confidence to which with your help we have just made appeal.

Moreover, if you were to insist on these instructions it would certainly be in vain. For in that event you may take it as assured that there will be no financial agreement.[11]

[11] In a personal and private message despatched at 2.15 p.m. on 27 November (telegram No. 11897 to Washington), Sir W. Eady assured Lord Keynes that 'we are not trying to sabotage your efforts or being more stupid than nature has made us. To settle such an important and complex document in a hurry by cable is very difficult for both sides, and we must be patient with each other. We are doing all we can to help you but we have to remember the impact of the document upon opinion here and elsewhere.' Lord Keynes expressed his gratitude for this message in Washington telegram No. 7933, despatched at 8.30 the same evening: 'We thought we were in sight of home and were, and indeed still are, dismayed at the revival of what must wreck things here when we believed it had been disposed of long ago' (UE 5824–5/1094/53).

However, in a note of 1 December attached to a documentary record of the sterling balance question prepared by Mr. Thompson-McCausland of the Bank of England (of 28 November, not printed), Sir W. Eady commented that he could not 'get excited about the controversy—it has obviously always been in all our minds that the £ area negotiations must deal with old & new balances at same time (you can't do otherwise) & the "time limit" has become a question of how much vagueness we can get away with' (T 236/438).

No. 126

British Missions (Washington) to Cabinet Offices
(Received 27 November, 11.30 p.m)

NABOB 404 Telegraphic [UE 5831/1094/53]

Most immediate. Secret   WASHINGTON, 27 November 1945, 8.45 p.m.

For Chancellor of Exchequer from Keynes.

1. There was a further meeting of the Top Finance Committee yesterday with Vinson in the chair at which we tried to explore a little further the outstanding points of difference. We were left with certain strong impressions about which are the points of most and least resistance respectively.

2. The meeting ended in a pronouncement by Vinson couched in the most generous and sympathetic language we have yet heard from him which amounted to a withdrawal by the Americans of their proposal to add a definite criterion of our reserves to the waiver clause. This was probably intended as much for his own people, who have continued to press us hard on this point, as for us. Vinson will be content with some general statement of our intention that, whilst the operation of the waiver is entirely at our discretion, we shall not regard it as automatic.

3. We suggested a text in paragraph 6 of NABOB 397.[1] Perhaps [it] should be slightly re-written to run:

Begins:

4(II) The Government of the United Kingdom will not avail themselves of the provision under (I) above except after taking due account of the prospective and prevailing conditions of international exchange and adequacy of their available reserves. Ends.

[1] No. 123.

375

4. May we have discretion to accept a sub-clause on these general lines? In view of the decisive importance which we here attach to securing a waiver clause in an acceptable form, we regard the above as a very great gain.

5. We think we can get your draft at the end of paragraph 4 of 11790[2] subject perhaps to verbal changes; but we doubt if we can get more of the London waiver[3] than this. May we have authority to accept this as sufficient? The waiver clause would then run as follows:

4(I) As in NABOB 372[4]
4(II) Substantially as in paragraph 3 above
4(III) Substantially as in paragraph 4 of 11790.

6. On the provisions for pari passu treatment of the American credit see NABOB 401[5] and paragraph 7 of NABOB 371.[6] May we have general discretion to settle along these lines?

7. On the form of our statement of intention about the settlement of accumulated sterling balances see NABOB 402.[7] This falls within the authority you have given us previously and we hope it is satisfactory.

8. There remain three central questions not yet resolved corresponding to paragraphs 6, 7 and 8 of NABOB 372. On paragraph 6 please see NABOB 400.[8]

9. On paragraph 7 which deals with exchange arrangements outside the sterling area we think we have made some headway along the lines of paragraph 10 of NABOB 397. We doubt if this is a sticking point on their side. To the best of our belief 10(a) of NABOB 397 merely confirms the maintenance of the existing arrangements, and 10(b) is a statement of intention without time limit along the lines of the Prime Minister's telegram.[2] May we settle on these general lines?

10. Paragraph 8 presents the greatest difficulty since Clayton and all the State Department attach very great and perhaps justifiable importance to it. If we could do something to meet them here, it would do more than anything else to aid us to get satisfaction on other matters, particularly the amount of the loan.

11. To forego the right to discriminate against the United States during the transition[9] will certainly cost us something, particularly in the case of oil. But if it is only the right to discriminate against the United States which we give away we do not believe it will cost us much. Moreover, in view of our statement of policy and intention, we should have to exercise any rights we retained with the utmost moderation, and even that is certain to cause constant friction.

12. Furthermore, it is almost certain that Canada will raise the same point and will attach almost decisive importance to it. Our latest advices from the High Commissioner confirm this. If we refuse this clause to United States as a condition of the loan, how can we grant it to Canada as a condition of their loan? Yet if we refuse it to Canada we shall be in very

[2] No. 119. [3] Cf. No. 87, para. 8. [4] No. 113. [5] No. 112.i.
[6] No. 112. [7] No. 123.i. [8] No. 125. [9] Cf. No. 1, note 11.

great difficulties indeed and may find the amount of the loan considerably reduced as well as relations with Canada impaired.

13. We would, therefore, urge that we have authority to offer something like the following:

Begins:

The Governments of the United Kingdom and United States agree that if either country imposes quantitative import restrictions as an aid to the restoration of equilibrium in the balance of payments, such restrictions shall be administered on a basis which does not discriminate against imports from the other country in respect of any product; provided that this undertaking shall not apply

(a) in cases in which its application would have the effect of preventing the country imposing such restrictions from utilizing, for the purchase of needed imports, inconvertible currencies accumulated up to December 31, 1946 or

(b) in cases in which there may be special necessity for the country imposing such restrictions to assist, by measures not involving a substantial departure from the general rule of non-discrimination a country whose economy has been disrupted by war. The provisions of this paragraph shall become effectve as soon as practicable and in any case not later than the end of 1946. Ends.

14. The above is the same as paragraph 8 of NABOB 372 with the reference to exchange restrictions omitted. Since this question is largely a Board of Trade question, Liesching is sending a separate telegram to his President[i].

15. Our ideas would be to make the above concession, to which, as we have said, the State Department and also Clayton personally attach the greatest importance, contingent on our reaching a satisfactory conclusion on all other outstanding matters. Particularly the amount of the loan. It is logical to associate these two questions. For to give up the right to discriminate against United States will cost us exchange. In recent argument with the State Department we were rather at a loss to find any other ground on which to defend our position.

16. We should propose, therefore, to link up this concession with fixing the amount of the loan at [$]4½ billions including Lend-Lease. We believe that the agreement which might then emerge would be the best possible in the circumstances from both our points of view.

17. We should have to agree that the above figures would include the Lend-Lease settlement whatever the latter worked out at. This now stands as in the next three paragraphs.

18. In effect we have now got rid of the 3C[10] loan bogey. Clayton's proposal to us is that the net pipeline after deduction of our net claims, would be regarded, for the sake of precedent with other countries, as either falling under 3C or paid in cash. The figure is estimated with fair

[10] See No. 4, note 7.

accuracy at 118 to 128 million dollars. The exact outcome would have to be fixed at long last by the accountants. It is assumed that we should opt for cash. In order to give verisimilitude to an otherwise inconvincing narrative, they would appreciate it if we would make a substantial cash payment on account as soon as possible after reaching agreement and before we have actually touched the credit. But it would, of course, be understood that indirectly we should in fact be meeting this out of the credit and account would be taken of this liability in fixing the amount of the credit.

19. We may be asked to treat what is due from us for purchasing the United States military surplus in the same way. As we do not intend to pay more than 10,000,000 dollars this does not matter. But we think that the Americans may, on second thought, prefer to include this in the global settlement referred to in the next paragraph, so as not to highlight the smallness of the sum.

20. For all the rest, namely, inventory, capital installations, military inventory having civilian end-use, aircraft, all other undetermined claims and everything else real or imaginary, we should fix on a global figure and call it a day. This would come straight out of the credit. The Americans have offered us a figure of 750 million dollars inclusive of 118 million dollars under paragraph 18 above and the payment under paragraph 19 above which they have put in provisionally at 50 million dollars. In other words they are asking us 582 million dollars for the global figure under this paragraph. Undoubtedly they can make out a fairly reasonable case for this on paper and any abatement of it would be in the nature of a concession. For the details see NABOB 373.[11] Nevertheless, I would hope to get acceptance for a firm offer of 500 million dollars and would try to get a little less, say 475 million dollars. We are getting a great quantity of real value for this, and once we accept, as we have to, the principle of paying anything at all, it would not be a bad bargain. Nor is it really appreciably worse than the idea we started out with, since it comprehends a good deal more stuff than we knew about when we began. May I do my best along these lines?

21. A quick O.K. to this telegram, and we might be home in both senses of the word.[12]

[11] No. 114.
[12] In NABOB 405 of 27 November Mr. Brand sent the following appreciation of the position to Mr. Dalton: 'I believe we are presented at this moment with most favourable opportunity we can hope for to settle whole business but that this opportunity may well fade away unless we seize it. If, moreover, you were to accept our recommendations in NABOB 404 you will, I also believe, give us best chance we are likely to have of securing full amount of 4½ billions including Lend-Lease. I would strongly urge, therefore, that we should not lose this favourable moment.' Lord Keynes reinforced this opinion in his telegram No. 7933 to Sir W. Eady (see No. 125, note 11). Referring to No. 126 he stated that 'we have a real chance of a settlement in the next few days if you will give us just enough elbow room. If we miss taking advantage of the present mood, my judgement is that things will move backward and not forward. Once granted the inevitable that we have to pay 2 per cent., the rest of what we recommend . . . is not too bad.' See further Pressnell, *op. cit.*, Chapter 10(19).

i *27 Nov. 1945 British Missions (Washington) Tel. NABOB 406* Message for Sir S. Cripps from Sir P. Liesching on refraining from trade discrimination against U.S.: '. . . in return for a satisfactory understanding regarding the size of the loan, we should be prepared to make this offer in order to clinch the final bargain' [UE 5831/1094/53].

ii *29 Nov. 1945 To British Missions (Washington) Tel. BABOON 320* Lend-Lease settlement: $600 million would be acceptable with a loan of not less than $4½ billion, but 'you should have discretion to accept the best terms available in the last resort' [UE 5831/1094/53].

No. 127

Mr. Bevin to the Earl of Halifax (Washington)

No. 11921 Telegraphic [Z 13110/28/36]

Immediate. Top secret   FOREIGN OFFICE, *27 November 1945, 12 midnight.*[1]

Your telegram No. 7759 (of 20th November: Azores).[2]

Please thank Mr. Byrnes for this information and explain that, owing to the special problems which it presents, I think it would be best if we dealt with the question of bases in the Azores and Cape Verde Islands as a separate matter, apart from the other questions about bases which the United States Government have raised with us.

2. Mr. Byrnes will, I am sure, understand that before I can express any opinion on the proposals set out in your telegram under reference, I must consult the Chiefs of Staff and His Majesty's Ambassador in Lisbon. He can be assured, however, that in consulting the latter I will only inform him of the proposals regarding Portuguese territory and not of the wider United States plans.

3. Mr. Byrnes will appreciate that we shall have to give serious consideration to the effect of United States proposals on Anglo-Portuguese Alliance[3] and the responsibilities which devolve on us therefrom. Consideration must also be given to the situation which might arise if United States were neutral in a war in which Great Britain was engaged.

4. Before, however, I can proceed to consult the Chiefs of Staff, it

---

[1] This telegram and No. 128 were despatched in reverse order.

[2] Not printed. This telegram of 20 November transmitted the text of the *aide-mémoire* of 19 November (printed in *F.R.U.S. 1945*, vol. vi, pp. 211–14) in which Mr. Byrnes described the rights which the U.S. Chiefs of Staff desired to obtain in the Azores and Cape Verde Islands. A covering letter from Mr. Byrnes, received by Lord Halifax on 20 November and transmitted in Washington telegram No. 7558 of that date, referred to Mr. Byrnes' *aide-mémoire* of 6 November: see No. 102, note 2.

[3] For British commitments under the Anglo-Portuguese Alliance, dating back to 1373 (see *B.F.S.P.*, vol. 1, pp. 462–8), see *D.B.F.P.*, Series IA, Volume I, pp. 853–4.

seems essential that the United States Government should clear up the following points:—

(a) Are these bases in the Azores and Cape Verde Islands the only bases which United States Government are seeking in that part of the Eastern Atlantic? Or are they also contemplating establishing bases at Dakar and elsewhere in French colonial territory or in Liberia, etc?

(b) In their first proposal (see your telegram No. 6468)[4] United States referred to bases in the Azores 'either under Tripartite Anglo/United States/Portuguese control or under Security Council of United Nations Organisation'. However, present proposals seem to contemplate both in Azores and Cape Verde Islands a predominantly United States base under joint United States/Portuguese control and in which His Majesty's Government would have no part. You were instructed in my telegram No. 10672[5] to make it clear that, in the event of it being decided to proceed with plans for a base on a short-term lease pending the entry into force of World Security Organisation, His Majesty's Government would wish to participate. Subsequently you were instructed in my telegram No. 10781[5] to suggest that possibility of Brazilian participation should be carefully considered. Am I to assume the American proposals set out in your telegram under reference imply that British participation in both bases has been definitely rejected? Or has Mr. Byrnes not been made aware of the substance of my telegram No. 10672? And what is the position as regards Brazil?

As regards the question of British participation, you should emphasise to Mr. Byrnes that, quite apart from His Majesty's Government's vital interest in this part of the world from the strategic angle, their long standing and intimate connexion with Portugal makes it politically essential from their point of view that, if any base is to be set up in the Azores and the Cape Verde Islands before the coming into force of the World Security Organisation, His Majesty's Government should participate in it as an equal partner. Furthermore, on being consulted in the matter a few weeks ago, His Majesty's Ambassador in Lisbon made it clear that, in his view, it was highly unlikely that the Portuguese Government would be willing to agree to the establishment, in advance of the coming into force of the World Security Organisation, of any base in which His Majesty's Government were not actively associated. Sir O. O'Malley felt that the Portuguese would be most unwilling to accept a United States or a United States/Portuguese base. The Portuguese took just such a line in the wartime Azores negotiations and we cannot help feeling, therefore, that if the United States Government were to press for a base with which His Majesty's Government were not associated, they would meet with a refusal from Portugal.

As regards participation of Brazil, Sir Owen O'Malley has advised us strongly that this would be likely to make the project considerably more

---

[4] See No. 35, note 5.   [5] Cf. No. 61.ii.

acceptable to Portugal, more particularly if the Portuguese Government were allowed to take the initiative in approaching the Brazilians. (c) What action does the United States Government contemplate taking vis-à-vis the French Government in respect of their Cape Verde Islands proposals? These islands are not far from Dakar and, apart from their general interest in the security arrangements for that part of the Eastern Atlantic, the French Government would, presumably, be particularly interested in any arrangements for the establishment of bases in the Cape Verde Islands. To ignore this interest might have embarrassing consequences.

Apart, however, from the foregoing considerations, we feel strongly that it would be very much wiser not to proceed with any plans for the establishment of bases in the Azores or the Cape Verde Islands *now*, but to await the coming into force of the World Security system, and the entry of Portugal into the United Nations Organisation. Apart from the obvious objections in principle to doing anything which might be regarded as implying a lack of confidence in the United Nations Organisation or which might encourage the U.S.S.R. to take unilateral action in respect of bases they desire, there would not seem to be any necessity from the military point of view for establishing bases in these Portuguese islands in the immediate future. Nor is there the same need as there is in the case of Iceland, to for[e]stall the Russians. Furthermore, Sir Owen O'Malley has advised us that the chances of Portugal agreeing to the setting up of a base in Portuguese territory would be very greatly increased if these bases were to form part of the general world security system and if the Portuguese action could be represented as a valuable contribution from Portugal to international security. While I am most anxious not to discourage United States active interest in this part of the world, which is clearly in our own long-term interest, I would, therefore, press Mr. Byrnes strongly not to pursue this matter further for the time being.

If, however, the United States Government feel obliged to press on with the matter now, then we will, of course, be very ready to consider to what extent we can assist them in the matter. Before, however, we can proceed to this consideration we should require to know the answers to the points set out above in (a), (b) and (c). It would also, I think, be very difficult for us to take any action in the matter unless we were assured that:

(i) the bases were being sought on a purely short-term basis, pending the coming into force of the world security system;

(ii) His Majesty's Government were associated in both projects as an equal partner. Since any short-term arrangement might in fact last a considerable period, especially if any difficulty was experienced over Portugal's admission to the United Nations Organisation, it is essential that any provisional régime should be entirely satisfactory to us.

(iii) The United States Government would co-ordinate their representations to the Portuguese Government very closely with ourselves. Please make urgent representations to Mr. Byrnes on the foregoing lines. I trust that you can persuade him not to make any approach to the Portuguese Government until we have reached agreement between ourselves as to the best method of proceeding. If approached unilaterally by the United States Government with proposals on the lines set out in your telegram No. 7759, the Portuguese Government is almost certain, I think, to consult His Majesty's Government and might well make some appeal to the Anglo-Portuguese alliance. Mr. Byrnes will appreciate that it would be highly embarrassing for His Majesty's Government to be placed in the position of having to advise Portugal on the United States proposal.

Finally, you should remind Mr. Byrnes that, at the State Department's request, His Majesty's Government postponed, some weeks ago, a communication they were about to make to the Portuguese Government notifying them of the date on which the British forces would evacuate the present British base in the Azores.[4] The Portuguese Government had already, a little time before, been informed that His Majesty's Government were giving consideration to this matter and would shortly be making a further communication to them on the subject. Our delay in making the further communication is becoming increasingly embarrassing to us. Furthermore, the delay is also embarrassing to the British Service authorities who are anxious to start making their plans for evacuating the base and cannot do so until the date has been agreed on with the Portuguese Government. In this connexion Sir O. O'Malley recently advised us that it would be the greatest mistake for either ourselves or the United States to try to blackmail the Portuguese Government into agreeing to proposals for new bases in the Azores by threatening to refuse to carry out our obligations to evacuate the existing bases.

My immediately following telegram[6] contains my own approach to the problem which you should take up with Mr. Byrnes at the same time as you give him the formal reply to his memorandum of 19th November, as set out above.

[6] No. 128.

No. 128

Mr. Bevin to the Earl of Halifax (Washington)

No. 11922 Telegraphic [Z 13110/28/36]

Immediate. Top secret　　　FOREIGN OFFICE, *27 November 1945, 8.47 p.m.*

My immediately preceding telegram.[1]

I have given considerable thought to the question of the Azores. I think it bad in the interests of world peace to talk about the Azores and Cape Verde being military bases. Everybody recognises that the Azores are a

[1] No. 127.

great air communications station, and would it not be better if they were treated as such? Should this view be accepted by the United States it would be preferable that, as a result of our treaty arrangements, we should approach Salazar[2] and induce him to make the proposal that the Azores should be treated as a free-for-all civil aviation station[3] but that the agreement to equip the station should be between Portugal, who would retain sovereignty, Brazil (which would bring in South America and please Portugal) the United States, Canada and ourselves. In the unlikely event of war, if the station were supplied with meteorological equipment and we had again to use it for war-like purposes, it would be very easily convertible; and there could be a declaration that in the event of war it would be available to the Security Council. But in my view it would give great satisfaction in Great Britain and in many other countries in the world if we talked less of bases and more of development along the above lines, and I would like you to approach Mr. Byrnes with this rather bigger view.[4]

For your own information I should like to point out that many people in this country are getting frightfully worried about the push of the United States right around us with bases which, it appears from their claim, are to be a purely United States affair. While I have no fear of any difficulty with the United States in the future yet many thoughtful people are becoming nervous here and I want to avoid that. I want partnership, which will give us a sense of fairness and security.

[2] Dr. A. de L. Salazar was Portuguese President of the Council and Minister for Foreign Affairs.

[3] In a letter of 5 December to Mr. F.R. Hoyer Millar, Head of Western Department, Sir O. O'Malley enquired the exact meaning of the preceding phrase, commenting that if it meant 'that aircraft of any nationality could drop in, refuel, take off and if necessary break bulk, I should think the Portuguese Government would want some concrete inducement to agree to the proposed arrangement . . . the Portuguese realize very well that in the Azores they possess something of great value to the world of civil aviation and I can't see them throwing it into the pool and getting nothing in exchange. I suppose that in our hearts we should all prefer free communications for everybody everywhere, just as many of us would like to see trade and currency and so on free for all in all directions, but the longer we live the further we seem to get from this ideal' (Z 13475/28/36).

[4] Lord Halifax reported in Washington telegram No. 7998 of 29 November that he had acted on Nos. 127–8 that afternoon, reinforcing orally Mr. Bevin's general argument about the greater wisdom of treating these matters if possible through the U.N.O.: Mr. Byrnes listened attentively; see *F.R.U.S. 1945*, vol. vi, pp. 216–20.

No. 129

Cabinet Offices to British Missions (Washington)

BABOON 310 Telegraphic [UE 5673/1094/53]

Immediate. Secret   CABINET OFFICES, 28 November 1945, 5.4 p.m.

Reference NABOB 373.[1]

1. We are grateful for this detailed summary with its account of the real progress which has been made.

2. On your actual figures we have the following comments:

(a) Shipping services 40. We assume that the period for freight and charter hire pipeline should be November—February inclusive and on this assumption we think that your figure is too low owing to increase of requirements for U.S. tanker assistance. We would suggest 50.

(b) Military inventory 20. This seems reasonable if there is included in it the inventory in the hands of British forces in India. We are also not sure whether 'U.K. and Colonies' specifically includes the Middle East countries covered by the Eady-Clayton disposals agreement.[2] We should wish you to press for this, but leave you discretion to compromise on the lines of para. 3 of NABOB 313.[3]

(c) Aircraft. We should regard your figure as a worth while price to pay for the unrestricted use of Lend-Lease aircraft.

3. We agree with the general picture outlined in your paragraphs 16 and 17 and regard 600 as not unreasonable as compared with our original 500, given the fact that the lower figure was based on more generous estimates of the Reciprocal Aid pipeline. While, therefore, in the context of an adequate financial settlement we should not object to 600[4] in view of present uncertainties we feel that we must continue to work to the 500 level for the time being. This figure exceeds by 187 the optimum settlement of 313, being your 588 minus the critical aircraft and Persian railway claims which we put for the moment at 275.[5] No doubt you will

---

[1] No. 114.   [2] See No. 8, note 2.

[3] This telegram of 9 November referred to the desirability of persuading the Americans to accept a global settlement figure for Lend-Lease military surpluses sold for civilian end-use. Para. 3 stated that it might, however, be necessary to agree to make separate arrangements to cover 'sales to civilian users of surpluses counted in third countries such as Egypt, Iraq and India' (UE 4406/1094/53).

[4] Cf. No. 126.ii.

[5] NABOB 345 of 16 November had stated that with regard to claims and counter-claims discussed with the Americans for offsetting arrangements in the Lend-Lease settlement the only outstanding items were: (a) the U.K. claim for dollar refunds in respect of aircraft transferred during the war from U.K. contracts to the U.S. Government for its own use and to fulfil U.S. obligations to the Russians (for a full statement of the British case see NABOB Saving 38 of 14 November, UE 5615/1094/53); (b) the U.K. claim for the U.S. Government to pay freight charges on American supplies carried to Russia on the Iranian Railways.

In NABOB 345 the British Delegation asked for authority to withdraw the Iranian Railway claim if necessary to achieve a settlement, but BABOON 295 of 22 November

continue presenting the problem in such a way that the Americans realise that if they are generous in respect of these claims we, in turn, shall be able to afford concessions in regard to other items such as United States surpluses, or the inventory, where we are on strong ground in keeping the figures low.

4. If, however, the Americans insist on knocking the big cats right out we are in a much more difficult position to make concessions on other heads. We feel that the way in which the Americans could meet us easily would be by reducing the charges in particular for foodstuffs in the Class 1. inventory. Even if the suggestion that the Americans should value foodstuffs at British internal prices is rejected (and if they wish to be helpful we are not convinced that they need turn this down) there is still opportunity for substantial downward decision on this score.

5. Should all this yet prove of little avail, no doubt you will stall for the last lap until you see how things are shaping. In this final round of bargaining there are perhaps certain broader issues which it might be well to call to mind, more especially as they are questions which are likely to be raised by public critics here. Article V of the Lend-Lease Agreement does not say that we should be charged full value for everything which may be useful to us. Indeed, the spirit would suggest that the Americans (if they insist on charging at all) ought only to charge what they could realise net elsewhere if they took the stuff away. Secondly, we have no evidence that the Americans are pressing the Russians in the same sense or are proposing to charge them. Is there any reason why we should be singled out for this treatment notwithstanding the differing contexts of the negotiations? Finally, is it not the case that under the Master Agreement the right to recapture only comes into operation on the termination of the emergency. Are we wrong in thinking that this is a strict legal concept and that the emergency is yet to be terminated by Presidential Proclamation? If so, are we not being asked to waive our strict legal rights for the sake of an early settlement to suit the Americans? On all or any of these general grounds we might reasonably press for an overall abatement which would seem to be quite in keeping with the general conception of Lend-Lease. With such an abatement we have a clear and convincing answer to any criticisms, since we could point to an overall deal in which these aspects have been allowed for. Without it what answer would the Americans have us give?

6. We have given you these background comments, but we must clearly leave the handling of this issue largely to your discretion.

7. Your NABOB 404[6] just received, but we are sending this for what it is worth and will telegraph further at once.

___

objected that the American arguments on this question were unconvincing and the claim should be preserved for the present: 'Of course, if they accept the aircraft claim, it would be a different matter, but until they do so it would seem better not to throw away a good card.'
[6] No. 126.

i *15–22 Nov. 1945* *British Missions (Washington) Tels. NABOB 377 & 378* Proposed statement drafted in Combined Claims Committee providing for mutual waiver of unsettled claims, based on *NABOB Saving 40* [UE 5615–6/1094/53].

No. 130

Cabinet Offices to British Missions (Washington)

BABOON *312 Telegraphic* [UE 5828/1094/53]

Most immediate. Secret   CABINET OFFICES, *28 November 1945, 11.25 p.m.*

Personal from Chancellor of the Exchequer to Ambassador and Keynes.

NABOB 400.[1]

1. Plainly there has been a misunderstanding about our respective positions which I must try to clear up.

2. Paragraph 3(*a*) and paragraph 6 of the Prime Minister's telegram[2] were intended to refer specifically to paragraph 6 of NABOB 372[3] as well as to the other paragraphs containing a final date.

3. I am not going back over all the textual history of the interminable telegrams. I am personally satisfied that this situation has arisen out of a genuine misunderstanding. There is no change of policy on our side on the liberalisation of the Sterling Area.

4. When Keynes explained to my colleagues and myself the line he proposed to follow,[4] he described the proposals for the Sterling Area arrangements as including release of current earnings, together with the release of a portion of the accumulated balances, and in return for that relaxation of war-time arrangements an agreed scaling down of the Sterling accumulations of our creditors. In his paper of the 12th. September[5] the release of current earnings was to take effect after the general plan came into operation.

5. The present issue between us is that when NABOB 372 arrived we learned that we were being asked to surrender publicly, and in advance of our negotiations with the Sterling creditors, the valuable bargaining weapon of relaxing present arrangements running indefinitely, they are still in force, and we would have used the year 1946, when war conditions are still implicitly recognised, as the period for negotiation, though we could not expect to complete the negotiations.

6. If we are forced to surrender this bargaining point in advance, we have scarcely any other, for we are not prepared to enter upon these negotiations with the threat of blocking unilaterally accumulated balances.

[1] No. 125.   [2] No. 119.   [3] No. 113.   [4] Cf. No. 17.
[5] Enclosure in No. 22.

7. I did not know of any long-standing undertaking in the terms of paragraph 6 of NABOB 372, that is with a definite time limit for completion and the separation of the release of current earnings from the release of accumulated balances, and I cannot believe that this is a vital principle to the Americans. I should hope that, if the arguments in my personal telegram BABOON 303[6] were put squarely to them, they would realise that, if they insist upon this formal undertaking in advance, the only result can be gravely to reduce the chances of a wide and successful clear-up of the accumulated balances and the writing down of the debt. We have not only our own position to consider in these negotiations. In the case of several countries the Sterling Balances are not held wholly by the Central Monetary Authority, but represent commercial balances. If the political authorities in those countries can represent to their own legislature and commercial interests that they have secured not only the clearance of current earnings but also the clearance of an agreed proportion of accumulated balances, they are more likely to be able to gain acceptance of the principle of scaling down the total of the debt. I ask you to try these arguments seriously upon the Americans.

8. I am examining NABOB 404 and NABOB 397[7] urgently and sympathetically. They have much hope in them and I think it will be possible to send you a reply early on Thursday.[8] Even on the difficult point about the transitional period, I think we should be prepared to agree, subject to one amendment which will be dealt with in the reply to that telegram. I should find it easier to do this if the Americans can be persuaded to modify paragraph 6 of 372 as suggested above. As you know we should always have preferred a less precise undertaking about the Sterling Area, but the reply to NABOB 404 suggests a draft which I hope will be acceptable to you and to the Americans.

9. If you wish to reply to this I suggest that you might prefer to await the answer to NABOB 404, and I hope you will find that answer really helpful.

[6] No. 124.   [7] Nos. 126 and 123.   [8] 29 November 1945.

No. 131

British Missions (Washington) to Cabinet Offices
(Received 29 November, 6.15 a.m.)

NABOB 412 Telegraphic [UE 5673/1094/53]

Immediate. Secret   WASHINGTON, *29 November 1945, 2.21 a.m.*

For Treasury from Keynes.
1. A brief comment on paragraphs 4 and 5 of BABOON 310.[1]
2. At a recent meeting of the top Lend-Lease Committee[2] I again put

[1] No. 129.   [2] Cf. No. 114.ii.

387

forward the major aircraft claim with as much force as possible. I think some impression may have been made. Opposition, however, on the part of the Treasury based, not on the legal merits of the case, but on all the back history in relation to the size of our dollar balances, will never allow us to get the claim admitted in so many words. All we can get out of it in my opinion is a sufficiently bad conscience on their part to make them a little more willing than they would otherwise be to bring down their present demand for 750 to something more of the order of 600. Ostensibly, however, they will do this on other grounds than the aircraft claim.

3. The considerations you put forward in paragraph 5 have been very much in our minds. It would do our hearts good to be able to attack on these lines. If we thought it would pay us to stand on our strict legal rights we should not have hesitated to do so. But we are quite clear that any such attempt would, in practice, be disastrous and land us in a far worse situation. At a talk very early in the proceedings with McCloy,[3] who was, until he resigned, one of the most friendly and reasonable of the high-up American officials, he made it clear that if there was any attempt on our part to stand on our legal rights, we must expect that they would do the same and take the earliest opportunity to recapture the whole of our military equipment. This was in response to an attempt on my part to state quite moderately our legal rights as I saw them. I might add that Dean Acheson, who was present on the same occasion, entirely supported McCloy, although he also can be relied upon to take a friendly and reasonable line toward us.

4. You must not overlook that there is a great deal of their legal rights which the Americans have conceded. In particular, we are to retain the whole of military Lend-Lease, whether it has civilian end-use or not, the original cost of which was many billions, for a figure which, if we reach the settlement we are talking about, will not rank above twenty to thirty millions.

5. Further, we have not, in fact, departed seriously from the position you put in the paragraph under reference that the Americans should only charge what they could realise net elsewhere. The trouble is that by far the greater part of the value consists of food, materials and oil in the pipeline and inventory which we cannot possibly do without. Thus, if they exercise their right to recapture we shall have immediately to buy it back from them, probably at a higher price.

6. The Lend-Lease pipeline and inventory including oil and military food but excluding surplus articles we can do without, comes to about 850 after making deductions for freight etc. at (c) and (d) of NABOB 373[4] paragraph 6.

Deducting our counter-claims of 242 at most we are left with slightly over 600.

[3] See No. 33.

[4] No. 114.

7. Thus, if we can settle for 600, and the idea that we can do so is no better than a hope at the moment, we should be paying no more than the commercial valuation for unused supplies which we definitely want and we should, in fact, be paying nothing whatever for the whole of military Lend-Lease outside food and oil, the civilian inventory Class II, Lend-Lease installations, such Lend-Lease aircraft as we retain, and U.S.-owned surpluses in the U.K.

8. We will telegraph further if we have any comments on your paragraph 2.

No. 132

Confidential Annex to Cabinet Conclusions C.M. (45) 57 of 29 November 1945, Minute 3[1]

[*PREM 8/35*]

Top secret   CABINET OFFICE, *29 November 1945*

Washington Discussions on Financial Questions and Commercial Policy
(Previous Reference: C.M. (45)50th Conclusions)[2]
    The Cabinet had before them the following memoranda
C.P. (45)312:[3] by the Chancellor of the Exchequer covering the draft of a financial agreement;
C.P. (45)297:[4] by the President of the Board of Trade covering the text of the United States proposals on commercial policy and the draft of a statement which the President proposed to make in Parliament, subject to a satisfactory conclusion of the financial side of the negotiations;
C.P. (45)295:[5] by the Secretary of State for Dominion Affairs, reporting the attitude of Dominion Governments towards the discussions on commercial policy.
    THE CHANCELLOR OF THE EXCHEQUER said that the draft annexed to C.P. (45)312 had not been approved by the United States Government, but represented the best that our negotiators were likely to be able to secure. It would, therefore, be essential to give them freedom to make

---

[1] Minute 3 is not printed. The Cabinet met at 11 a.m.   [2] No. 95.ii.
[3] This memorandum of 28 November by Mr. Dalton is not printed. The annexed draft financial agreement, as sent to Washington after Cabinet consideration, is printed as No. 134. In a note of 29 November, evidently prepared as a brief for the Cabinet meeting, Mr. Coulson commented on specific points in the draft agreement (see notes 6 and 7 below) and concluded: 'Though the points at issue are now all Treasury points, I think there is no objection to them from the Foreign Office point of view. Both Lord Keynes and Mr. Brand have strongly recommended that this is the moment to clinch the affair [see No. 126, note 12] and I think we should support the proposals in the draft agreement in the form in which it now stands' (UE 5967/1094/53).
[4] No. 119.ii: cf. also No. 121, note 4.   [5] No. 95.v.

concessions on particular points, provided that they did not depart substantially from the proposals set out in the draft. He drew particular attention to the following points:

(i) *Amount of the credit*

It was not yet certain that the United States Government would agree to extend to His Majesty's Government a credit of as much as $4½ billions and, although our negotiators would try to obtain the full amount, we might have to be content with $4 billions. It seemed likely that $750 millions of this amount, and not $500 millions, as we had previously hoped, would have to be set aside for the liquidation of Lend-Lease.

(ii) *Purpose of the Credit*

Paragraph 2(II) of the draft agreement, which provided that drawings on the credit should not exceed the United Kingdom overall cumulative adverse balance of current payments, had been proposed by the United States negotiators because of their fear of criticisms in Congress that the sole object of the agreement was to get the sterling area out of its present difficulties. While he would prefer to omit this provision, it was not likely to cause any serious trouble.

(iii) *Waiver and postponement of payment*

There was good reason to hope that the United States Government would agree to paragraph 4(I), which provided for waiving the interest and postponing the repayment of the amount of principal due in any year in which the income of the United Kingdom from home produced exports, together with its net income from invisible current transactions, was less than the amount of United Kingdom imports during 1936/38. Our negotiators had resisted a proposal which would have given the United States Government the right to audit our financial transactions, but had been compelled to agree to paragraph 4(II), which imposed on His Majesty's Government the obligation not to avail themselves of the provision for waiver and postponement except after taking due account of the prospective and actually prevailing conditions of international exchange and the adequacy of their available reserves, as well as of the rate at which obligations to other creditors were to be met. Although this last requirement might conceivably give the United States Government grounds for arguing that we were discharging our obligations to other creditors too quickly, it was much more likely to operate in our favour, since it would enable us to point to obligations already incurred to other creditors as a reason for postponing our payments to the United States.

(iv) *Sterling area exchange arrangements*

Paragraph 6 bound His Majesty's Government to proceed, not later than the end of 1946, to make arrangements under which sterling receipts from current transactions would be freely available in any currency area without discrimination, and at the same time to seek, by voluntary agreement with the countries of the sterling area, a settlement under which the accumulated balances would be disposed of in one or other of the three ways set out in paragraph 6(II). Thus, we were merely undertaking to carry out, without committing ourselves to an absolutely rigid time limit for completion, the negotiations which it had always been our intention to undertake with the sterling area countries.[6]

(v) *Exchange arrangements between the United States and the United Kingdom*

The provisions of paragraph 7 had been carefully designed to enable His Majesty's Government to impose restrictions on the movement of capital and bound the Government only to refrain from imposing restrictions on current transactions.

THE PRESIDENT OF THE BOARD OF TRADE said that a difficult point arose on paragraph 7(II) of the draft agreement, which provided that, if either the United Kingdom or the United States imposed quantitative trade restrictions as an aid to the restoration of equilibrium in the balance of payments, such restrictions should be administered on a basis which did not discriminate against imports from the other country in respect of any product.[7] If this provision were read alone, it might tie our hands too much, and it was, therefore, essential that our negotiators should obtain a written undertaking from the United States Government that paragraph 7(II) was to be interpreted in the light of the provisions with regard to quantitative trade restrictions and to State trading in Sections C and E of the American commercial policy proposals set out in Annex C to C.P. (45)297.[8] If we obtained an undertaking of this kind we should not be precluded from continuing, for example, to purchase particular products from our Dominions or Colonies in accordance with long-standing trade arrangements, even though the United States Government were in a position to make us an occasional offer of supplies of the same products at a lower price.

The following points arose in discussion:

(*a*) Was there not a risk that the undertaking in paragraph 6 that current earnings would be made available in due course for current

---

[6] Mr. Coulson commented (see note 3) with regard to para. 6 of the draft agreement: 'The Delegation have pointed out that we are too far commit[t]ed with the Americans for us to refuse an undertaking that the *current earnings* of the sterling area should be convertible by the end of 1946. They have pointed out that this is quite different from an undertaking to conclude agreements with the sterling area countries by the end of 1946 in regard to their *accumulated sterling balances*. The Chancellor has apparently accepted this view, on the ground that it would only be an undertaking on the latter point which would make our negotiations with the sterling area countries impossible.'

[7] Mr. Coulson commented in particular with regard to para. 7 of the draft agreement: 'The Delegation have pointed out forcibly that we shall have immense disputes with the U.S. if we do discriminate against their imports on exchange grounds and that, although we may lose a certain amount of dollars thereby, it is well worth our entering into this commitment. From experiences we have already had, I am sure this is right.'

[8] Cf. No. 121, note 4.

transactions would be detrimental to this country since it would throw open the United States market to sterling area countries?

THE CHANCELLOR OF THE EXCHEQUER pointed out that, unless we were able to make some relaxation of the restrictions on the use of sterling balances, there was little hope of our being able to maintain the coherence of the sterling group, some of the countries in which were already showing signs of a desire to break away.

(b) THE SECRETARY OF STATE FOR INDIA pointed out that, whereas paragraph 6(I) merely bound His Majesty's Government to proceed to make arrangements for the release of sterling receipts from current transactions not later than the end of 1946, the United Kingdom negotiators were of opinion that we were pledged by earlier undertakings to complete the release of these receipts by the end of 1946. It would, in his view, be unfortunate if, through our insistence on the form of words given in the draft, the chance of reaching agreement at an early date were to be lost.

(c) THE SECRETARY OF STATE FOR THE COLONIES asked whether the proposals in paragraph 6(II)(C) for writing off sterling balances would apply to balances held by Colonies.

THE CHANCELLOR OF THE EXCHEQUER said that such balances would be covered and it would be necessary to enter into negotiations with representatives of the Colonies on this matter in due course.

(d) THE CHANCELLOR OF THE EXCHEQUER undertook to consider whether paragraph 6(II)(C) should not rather refer to an 'adjustment' of balances than to the 'writing off' of balances.[9]

(e) THE MINISTER OF EDUCATION[10] asked whether there was not a danger that the undertaking in paragraph 7 not to apply exchange restrictions to payments or transfers arising out of current transactions between the United Kingdom and the United States would enable capital sums to be sent from this country to the United States under the guise of revenue, e.g. through the payment of excessive salaries to United States residents in this country.

THE PRESIDENT OF THE BOARD OF TRADE said that the risk of any such evasion was negligible.

(f) THE MINISTER OF HEALTH[11] asked whether the provisions of Section E of the American commercial policy proposals would prevent His Majesty's Government from establishing new State monopolies of particular products. Under paragraph 2 of this Section a new State monopoly would be prohibited if it created a greater protective margin

[9] Mr. Jay had drawn Mr. Attlee's attention to this point in a note of 29 November, evidently prepared as a brief for the Cabinet meeting: 'I think we can accept everything in the draft agreement suggested by the Chancellor ... except the inclusion of words in paragraph 6(II) actually mentioning the "writing off" of part of our debts to the sterling area ... I should have thought this would have a bad effect on the Commonwealth' (PREM 8/35).

[10] Miss E. Wilkinson.

[11] Mr. A. Bevan.

than the tariff that might have been negotiated in relation to the product concerned.

THE PRESIDENT OF THE BOARD OF TRADE said that the proposals would not preclude the creation of new State monopolies but were merely designed to prevent Governments from nullifying through the creation of State monopolies reductions in tariffs to which they had agreed in negotiation.

The Cabinet then considered whether the proposals set out in C.P.(45)312 should be generally approved.

THE MINISTER OF FUEL AND POWER said that he was still strongly of opinion that it would be a mistake to accept the proposals, which were, in his view, incompatible with the successful operation of a planned economy in this country and would ruin our export trade. It was wrong to assume that all the advantage lay with the United States Government, since their need to export would place them in an impossible position if we refused to come to an agreement with them on their terms. It would be better for His Majesty's Government to borrow from the United States at 3, 4 or even 5 per cent than to accept the conditions attaching to the credit which had been offered, particularly since this involved His Majesty's Government in supporting commercial policy proposals which were, in his view, objectionable. In any event, it was desirable that those members of the Cabinet who had not been constantly in touch with the progress of the negotiations should have more time in which to assess the effect of the proposed agreements on their Departmental plans. He therefore urged that no decision should be taken until these Ministers had had an opportunity for further consideration of the proposals.

THE MINISTER OF HEALTH supported the Minister of Fuel and Power. In his view, it was a mistake that we should approach the United States as suppliants, since their need to find markets for their exports was just as great as our need for assistance. He was convinced that a firm attitude on our part would produce a good effect on our general relations with the United States. He also urged that a decision on the proposals should be postponed in order to give all members of the Cabinet adequate time to consider them.

THE SECRETARY OF STATE FOR FOREIGN AFFAIRS said that it was essential that a decision should be taken without further delay. He had examined the proposals with great care in order to ensure that they did not constitute an impediment to the Government's internal policy, and he was satisfied that this point had been safeguarded. He had also considered the possibility of obtaining a loan at a higher rate of interest free from conditions, but even if this proved possible (and there was evidence that the United States would not be willing to make us a loan at a higher rate of interest free from conditions) the burden of such a loan would be beyond our capacity. Unless we obtained assistance from the United States, it would be impossible for us to make any progress with the essential task of reviving our trade with European countries. For these reasons he was in favour of giving authority to our negotiators to proceed on the basis of the documents before the Cabinet.

THE LORD PRESIDENT said that he thought it was a mistake to regard the proposals put forward by the United States Government as designed solely to further their interests. He believed that they were genuinely anxious to promote a freer and more ordered world trade, although they were undoubtedly influenced by the largely ill-informed criticisms which they had to meet in Congress. He did not believe that this country could face the privations which it would be necessary to undergo if we failed to obtain assistance from the United States, and he thought that any attempt to postpone the negotiations further would lead to a less satisfactory bargain.

THE CHANCELLOR OF THE EXCHEQUER said that he appreciated the points which had been made by the Minister of Fuel and Power and the Minister of Health, but he was satisfied that failure to reach an agreement with the United States, with the consequent shortages of food and luxuries, such as tobacco, would be disastrous for the Government. He therefore strongly urged the Cabinet, on economic, financial and political grounds, to accept the proposals.

THE PRESIDENT OF THE BOARD OF TRADE supported the Chancellor of the Exchequer. He pointed out that, so far as the commercial policy proposals were concerned, our negotiators had obtained satisfaction on all the points which they had raised.

THE PRIME MINISTER said that it was clear that the preponderant view of the Cabinet was in favour of authorising our negotiators to proceed on the basis of the proposals in the draft annexed to C.P. (45)312 on the understanding that they were free to make concessions on points of detail (e.g. with regard to a time limit for the unfreezing of sterling receipts from current transactions) within the general framework of the draft.

No. 133

Cabinet Offices to British Missions (Washington)

BABOON *314 Telegraphic* [*UE 5879/1094/53*]

Most immediate. Secret   CABINET OFFICES, *29 November 1945, 3.40 p.m.*

From Chancellor of the Exchequer for Ambassador, Keynes and Brand.

My immediately following telegram[1] contains text of suggested financial agreement.[2] My colleagues asked that they should see the form of the agreement they were expected to consider. This text represents conflation of American texts and suggestions from you, together with a few modifications of our own.

[1] No. 134.   [2] See No. 132.

394

2. Ministers would be prepared to accept this text subject to one point. They would strongly prefer that paragraph 2(II) should disappear owing to the difficulty of explaining it to Parliament. They would not press this to breaking point and would accept the principle in the form in the attached text.

3. Ministers ask you to give this text to the Americans as representing what we would be prepared to accept. If it should prove necessary they would be prepared to consider minor modifications.

4. Any further communication from you should refer to the numbered paragraphs in this text.

5. My succeeding telegrams[3] contain explanatory comments in detail.

[3] No. 134.i.

No. 134

Cabinet Offices to British Missions (Washington)

BABOON *315 Telegraphic* [*UE 5879/1094/53*]

Most immediate. Secret   CABINET OFFICES, *29 November 1945, 4.40 p.m.*

From Chancellor of the Exchequer for Ambassador, Keynes and Brand.

My immediately preceding telegram.[1]

1. *Amount of the Line of Credit*

(I) The Government of the United States will extend to the Government of the United Kingdom a line of credit of 4½ billion dollars.

(II) This line of credit will be available until December 31, 1951.

2. *Purpose of the Credit*

(I) The purpose of the credit shall be to facilitate purchases by the United Kingdom of goods and services from the United States, to assist the United Kingdom to meet transitional post-war deficits in her current balance of payments, to help the United Kingdom to maintain adequate reserves of gold and dollars and to assist the United Kingdom to assure the obligations of multilateral trade, as defined in this and other agreements.

(II) It is understood that drawings by the United Kingdom on this line of credit will not be in excess of the United Kingdom overall cumulative adverse balance of current payments during the period of its availability.

3. *Amortisation and Interest*

(I) The amount of the credit outstanding on December 31, 1951, shall be repaid in 50 annual instalments, beginning on December 31,

[1] No. 133.

1951, until 50 instalments have been paid, subject to the provisions of (4) and (5) below.

(II) The rate of interest shall be 2 per cent per annum, computed annually beginning with January 1, 1951, on the amount outstanding each year, and payable in 50 annual instalments, beginning on December 31, 1951, subject to the provisions of (4) and (5) below.

(III) The 50 annual instalments of principal repayments and interest shall be equal, amounting to 31.8 million dollars for each 1 billion dollars outstanding on December 31, 1951. Each instalment shall consist of the full amount of the interest due and the remainder of the instalment shall be the principal to be repaid in that year.

4. *Waiver and Postponement of Payment*

(I) The Government of the United States, at the request of the Government of the United Kingdom, will agree to waive in any year the amount of the interest and postpone to the end of the period of repayment the amount of the principal due in that year if as certified by the International Monetary Fund, the income of the U.K. from home-produced exports plus its net income from invisible current transactions in its balance of payments (as defined in Article XIX (1) of the Final Act of Bretton Woods) was less than the amount of U.K. imports during 1936–8, fixed at 866 million pounds, as such figure may be adjusted for changes in the price level of these imports.

(II) The Government of the United Kingdom will not avail themselves of the provision under (1) above except after taking due account of the prospective and actual prevailing conditions of international exchange and the adequacy of their available reserves, as well as of the rate at which obligations to other creditors are to be met.

5. *Accelerated Repayment*

The Government of the U.K. may accelerate repayment of the line of credit.

6. *Sterling Area Exchange Arrangements*

(I) The Government of the United Kingdom will proceed not later than the end of 1946 to make arrangements under which the sterling receipts from current transactions of all sterling area countries, apart from any receipts arising out of military expenditure by the United Kingdom prior to December 31, 1948, which it may be agreed to treat on the same basis as the balances accumulated during the war, will be freely available for current transactions in any currency area without discrimination.

(II) As an integral part of these arrangements the Government of the U.K. intends to seek by voluntary agreement with the countries of the sterling area an early settlement, varying according to the circumstances of each case, covering their accumulated sterling balances (together with any future receipts arising out of military expenditure by the U.K. which it may be agreed to treat on the same basis as the balances accumulated during the war). The Government of the U.K.

will propose that the settlements with the sterling area countries should be on the basis of dividing these accumulated balances into three categories.

(A) balances to be released at once and convertible into any currency for current transactions, (B) balances to be similarly released by instalments over a period of years beginning in 1951 without prejudice to the possible anticipation by the U.K. [? of] releases to a particular country which was in a position such as might otherwise have called for assistance from the U.K. by way of a loan, and (C) balances to be adjusted as a contribution to the settlement of war and post-war indebtedness and in recognition of the benefits which the countries concerned might be expected to gain from such a settlement.

(III) The effect will be that when the arrangements contemplated above are completed any discrimination arising from the so-called dollar sterling pool will be entirely removed and that each member of the sterling area will have its current sterling and dollar receipts at its free disposition of current transactions anywhere.

7. *Exchange arrangements between the United States and the United Kingdom*

(I) The Government of the United Kingdom agree that after the coming into force of this memorandum of agreement they will apply no exchange restrictions, except in accordance with the articles of agreement of the international monetary fund, so as to prevent payments or transfers in respect of imports from the U.S.A. into the United Kingdom which are permitted by the authorities controlling imports or of other current transactions between the two countries as defined in article XIX (i) of the said articles or on the use of sterling balances in the hands of United States residents arising out of current transactions.

(II) The Governments of the United Kingdom and United States agree that if either country imposes quantitative import restrictions as an aid to the restoration of equilibrium in the balance of payments, such restrictions shall be administered on a basis which does not discriminate against imports from the other country in respect of any product; provided that this undertaking shall not apply

(a) in cases in which its application would have the effect of preventing the country imposing such restrictions from utilizing inconvertible currencies for the purchase of needed imports or

(b) in cases in which there may be special necessity for the country imposing such restrictions to assist, by measures not involving a substantial departure from the general rule of non-discrimination a country whose economy has been disrupted by war.

The provisions of this paragraph shall become effective as soon as practicable and in any case not later than the end of 1946.

(III) Nothing in this paragraph shall be in derogation of Section 5 of

397

Article VII of the Final Act of the Articles of Agreement of the International Monetary Fund.[2]

8. *Other exchange restrictions and import controls*

In relation to other remaining exchange restrictions and to import policy, the Government of the United Kingdom associates itself with the Government of the United States in the objectives set out in the Articles of Association of the International Monetary Fund and in the United States proposals for an I.T.O. Their policy in the transitional period will accordingly be directed towards assuring as rapidly and over as wide a field as world economic conditions permit, the free use of sterling accruing to other countries through current transactions; and towards reducing to the greatest extent compatible with the restoration of the United Kingdom's external position, the application of their import controls and the discriminatory use of such controls.

9. *Provision for Review*

Either Government shall be entitled to approach the other for review and modification by mutual consent of this agreement if its working has become such as to burden international commerce within the meaning of Article VII of the Mutual Aid Agreement of February 23rd 1942, or is otherwise contrary to the intention of the two Governments in entering on this agreement.

10. (Possible paragraph on coming into force)

CALENDARS TO NO. 134

i *29–30 Nov. 1945   To British Missions (Washington) Tels. BABOON 316 & 317 & Unnumbered* Commentary on details of draft agreement in No. 134, and on NABOB 371 (No. 112): alternatives suggested in BABOON 317 for securing agreement that scarce currency would be a valid reason for waiving of non-discrimination requirement (cf. note 2 above) [UE 5879/1094/53].

ii *29–30 Nov. 1945   To British Missions (Washington) Tels. BABOON 321 & 328* Message from Mr. Attlee to Lord Halifax on tightness of parliamentary timetable in relation to conclusion of financial agreement [UE 5831/1094/53].

[2] See No. 68, note 3: Section 5 of Article VII stated that Members agreed 'not to invoke the obligations of any engagements entered into with other Members prior to this Agreement in such a manner as will prevent the operation of the provisions of this Article' with a view to avoiding scarce currencies.

No. 135

Memorandum by Mr. Bevin

D.O. (45)38 [CAB 69/7]

Top secret   FOREIGN OFFICE, 29 November 1945

United States request for Bases

I circulate herewith to my colleagues on the Defence Committee copies of certain documents (a list is given in the Annex)[1] in connection with a request recently made by the United States Secretary of State for assistance in obtaining American requirements as regards military bases in British and other territory.

2. When he was in London for the Council of Foreign Ministers, Mr. Byrnes intimated to me that he had requests of this nature to put forward. I made it clear in return that I could not consider any piece-meal proposals and that I must have a full list of the United States requirements.[2]

3. The requests now received (and Mr. Byrnes has assured me that they comprise all that he has it in mind to ask in so far as either British support for his projects or actual requirements in British territory are concerned) fall into the following categories:

(a) A request for support for United States requirements as regards military bases in Iceland and in the Portuguese Atlantic Islands.

(b) A request for the grant of military bases in 10 islands, all but one (Ascension Island) of which are in the Pacific. Of these 10 islands 4 are indisputably British, one is under Australian mandate, one under New Zealand mandate, one is under Franco-British condominium, one under joint British and United States control, and in the remaining two the United States dispute our sovereignty.

(c) A request that we should abandon our claim to sovereignty over 25 islands in the Pacific in which the United States contest our claim, and that we should recognise United States sovereignty therein.

(d) A request that we should 'keep or get under United Kingdom control' two existing bases in India.[3]

---

[1] The documents in the Annex were as follows: Washington telegrams Nos. 7469–70 and 7516 (see No. 102, note 2); record of discussion on 12 November between Mr. Bevin, the three Service Ministers and the Chiefs of Staff (not printed); telegram No. 11501 to Washington (No. 103); a Chiefs of Staff Report dated 19 November (i below); Washington telegram No. 7742A (cf. No. 103.i); Washington telegrams Nos. 7758–9 (see No. 127, note 2); telegrams Nos. 11681 and 11810 (cf. No. 103.i) and 11921–2 (Nos. 127–8) to Washington.

[2] See No. 61.

[3] Cf. No. 102, note 2. For the Ministerial view that negotiations for the retention of any bases in India would form part of the final political settlement in connexion with the grant of Dominion Status see *Constitutional Relations between Britain and India: The Transfer of Power 1942–7* (London, 1970f.), vol. vi, p. 644.

4. Mr. Byrnes requested that he should be allowed to approach Australia and New Zealand direct in respect of those of the above demands which particularly concern them. I accepted this, but stipulated that I must be allowed to warn them that I knew such an approach was to be made to them. The Prime Ministers of Australia and New Zealand have been informed accordingly in strict secrecy, and we have promised to keep in close touch with them over all this, as also with Canada and South Africa, whose Prime Ministers have similarly been informed.[4]

5. I have kept in touch on this matter on a personal basis with the three Service Ministers and the Chiefs of Staff and with the Secretaries of State for the Dominions and the Colonies. The Chiefs of Staff have, at my request, made a preliminary survey of the United States list of their requirements, and their report [i] is among the documents now circulated to the Committee.

6. The Chiefs of Staff and I are in general agreement at the present stage on the following points:

(a) It is clearly to our advantage, and is indeed on broad grounds of the highest importance, to take advantage of Mr. Byrnes's move to tie up the United States to the maximum extent in the defence of the British Commonwealth. This is of particular importance since, as I understand the American proposals they envisage dealing on a *joint* basis with at least a number of the places in British territory where bases are being sought.

(b) As against this, Mr. Byrnes apparently contemplates concluding arrangements in advance of the international system of security under the United Nations Charter (even though, as I see it, he envisages that all bases acquired thereunder would be made available to the Security Council on its call). This is clearly open to very serious objection. The Chiefs of Staff have pointed out that it is of military importance to us that the United Nations Organisation should be a success, and that any action taken now, which tends to prejudice the establishment or success of the World Organisation must be subject to grave objections—military as well as political. From the political standpoint, I fully agree. I am not convinced of the need for hurried arrangements in advance of the Security Council. They would not easily fit in with my declared intention that all my policy must square with the obligations we have entered into: they might even make us appear guilty of sharp practice: and they would give the Russians gratuitous and justifiable cause for suspicion and ground for making difficulties when we start setting up the Security Council. It might also determine them to exert direct pressure to obtain bases that they may require, e.g., in the Straits.

(c) We should take the opportunity to secure reciprocal support from the United States for our own requirements, including the right of joint user of such American bases as the Chiefs of Staff may think desirable.

[4] See No. 103.i.

(*d*) It is of great importance, particularly in connection with the American requests for our support for bases in third party territories, to know what, if any, demands Mr. Byrnes may intend to make on other countries such as France or Holland.[5]

(*e*) We must make a clear distinction between the granting of rights for military bases and the granting of facilities for civil aviation: and we should bear this particularly in mind when considering the American requests as regards the disputed islands in the Pacific, both from the standpoint of preserving our right to the facilities therein for civil aviation and with a view to obtaining such facilities in territory in the Pacific under United States control.

7. I have put some of these points to Mr. Byrnes in a preliminary way, and have in particular expressed the apprehensions which I feel on point 6 (*b*) above. Until he replies on that particular point it is difficult to go further into the matter with the Americans. My colleagues may, however, agree that in the meantime the considerations given in paragraph 6 should be put to the Dominion Governments as being our first reactions to Mr. Byrnes's approach and as containing the essential points by which we should be guided in giving our further consideration. It seems to me of great importance that we should so concert our policy with that of the Dominions that our eventual replies (since no doubt Australia and New Zealand will have to respond separately to the separate approaches made to them) constitute to the fullest possible extent a proof of the solidarity of the British Commonwealth as a unit.

8. When Mr. Byrnes's further reply comes in I propose to circulate a further paper after consultation with the Chiefs of Staff and others concerned, giving my views as to the lines on which we should seek to reach agreement with the Dominions on the final reply to be sent to Mr. Byrnes as regards each of the categories of the requirements presented by him.

9. I would beg my colleagues to observe the strictest secrecy in regard to this matter and to give the strictest possible limitation to the number of the officials in their departments to whom the knowledge of this paper is disclosed.[6]

E.B.

[5] Lord Halifax subsequently reported in his telegram No. 8689 of 31 December that Mr. J.D. Hickerson, Deputy Director of the Office of European Affairs in the State Department, had told Mr. A.D. McIntosh, Head of the New Zealand Prime Minister's Department and Secretary for External Affairs, that the U.S. Government were 'asking the French Government for a base at Noumea (French Caledonia) and the Netherlands Government for bases at Morotai and Baik' (F.O. 800/512). A record of this conversation was circulated to the Defence Committee on 12 January 1946 as D.O.(46)4 (CAB 131/2).

[6] With reference to Washington telegram No. 7742A (see note 1) Mr. Bevin stated in telegram No. 12315 of 8 December to Lord Halifax: 'As you know, I have had no reply from Mr. Byrnes to a number of points raised in my telegram No. 11501 [No. 103], particularly major points dealt with in paragraphs 5 and 9 thereof. Present situation was considered by Defence Committee on 7th December and conclusion reached that we should

i *19 Nov. 1945   Report by C.O.S. Committee on military implications of U.S. proposals for bases* (see note 1): on consideration of Washington tels. Nos. 7470 & 7516 (see note 1) C.O.S. conclude that if U.S. request is agreed reciprocal facilities should be sought in return; no objection on military grounds to recognising U.S. sovereignty where requested except for Christmas Island, although rights to civil aviation facilities should be reserved [CAB 69/7].

ii *6 & 20 Dec. 1945   (a) Earl of Halifax (Washington) Tel. No. 8138*   In answer to F.O. tel. No. 11529 (No. 90.iv) U.S. Government do not wish to share Iceland bases with H.M.G. as Soviet Government 'would be likely to react still more strongly against joint lease', but if H.M.G. wish to press for joint participation they should make definite approach 'before American agreement with Iceland took definite form'; *(b) Mr. Shepherd (Reykjavik) Tel. No. 210* U.S. desire for negotiations in Iceland in Dec. has met with 'extreme reluctance' on part of Icelandic P.M., who feels 'it would be particularly embarrassing in view of recent public criticism of the idea of leasing bases' [N 16735, 17371/1004/27].

not be anxious to press on with this matter. I do not (repeat not) therefore wish you to try to get an answer out of Mr. Byrnes on outstanding points' (F.O. 800/512).

On 10 December Mr. Byrnes' views (see *F.R.U.S. 1945*, vol. vi, pp. 220–4) on Nos. 103 and 127–8 were transmitted in Washington telegrams Nos. 8254–5, not printed. In particular Mr. Byrnes did not agree that it was undesirable to conclude special agreements in advance of the Security Council arrangements, but accepted that bases could be joint except 'those to which the traditional position of the United States attaches for western hemispheric reasons'. Mr. Byrnes further stated 'as respects the disputed islands in the Pacific, there is a definite program to maintain military bases on three of them, and no definite program now for the improvement of others as commercial airfields. The idea is rather now to settle amicably a dispute and provide this country with added assurances of cooperation by your Government at a time when we seek to extend cooperation to your Government'. In a brief of 12 December for Mr. Bevin Mr. P. Mason, Head of North American Department, further pointed out that 'the Azores have been advanced to the front of Mr. Byrnes' overall picture, and that Iceland has dropped back'. Mr. Mason suggested that Mr. Bevin, who, according to General E.I.C. Jacob, Military Assistant Secretary to the Cabinet, seemed to 'think that it might be advisable to try and get the Americans to agree to bring the Russians in on the current discussions about Bases' (CAB 120/201), might discuss the question of bases with Mr. Byrnes at the forthcoming Moscow Conference of Foreign Ministers (see Volume II, Chapter III).

Subsequently, in connexion with minuting in the Foreign Office on the withdrawal of British forces from the airbase at Lagens on Terceira (see No. 38), Sir A. Cadogan minuted on 30 December: 'Nothing was said about bases, so far as I know, at Moscow. In fact the S. of S. told me he did *not* intend to speak about it. Having let the situation slide for so long, can we not let it be till the Assembly [of the United Nations] meets? I don't quite see what can be done before that, and wd. it not be preferable to discuss it with Mr. Byrnes here? A.C. Dec. 30, 1945' (Z 250/250/36 of 1946). See further Volume IV, No. 18.

No. 136

British Missions (Washington) to Cabinet Offices
(Received 30 November, 4.15 a.m.)

NABOB 417 Telegraphic [UE 5879/1094/53]

Most immediate. Secret   WASHINGTON, *30 November 1945, 3.19 a.m.*

For Chancellor of Exchequer from Ambassador, Keynes, Brand,
Robbins and the rest of the Delegation.

1. We have found much that is helpful in BABOONS 314 to 317[1] but
before going back to the Americans there are certain matters we should
like to clear up. In the next two telegrams[2] we deal with two major points
of difficulty, namely (1) your proposed omission of any pari passu
arrangements for other loans and settlements and (2) the date at which
newly earned sterling will become free, and in a third telegram[3] with
certain details of smaller importance.

2. The concession you authorise us to offer in 7(II) of BABOON 315
should be of great value. We propose, as you suggest in BABOON 316 to
associate this concession closely with the amount of the loan.

3. We will do our best to persuade the Americans to allow postponement of principal as well as waiving of interest. But we think that the
prospects of this at the present stage of the argument are not good, and
that the introduction of deferment would revive certain highly objectionable proposals which are [*sic* ?we] successfully resisted. If as a compromise,
they were to propose to postpone both interest and principal instead of
waiving interest, which would be returning to a position they took up at
one time, would you prefer this to the waiver of interest without
postponement of principal? We infer from your comment in BABOON
316 that this is a point where you want us to do our best but where you are
ready to give away [*sic*] if necessary.

[1] Nos. 133–4 and 134.i.
[2] Nos. 137–8, which were, however, despatched out of order.
[3] No. 139, also despatched out of order.

No. 137

British Missions (Washington) to Cabinet Offices
(Received 30 November, 3.15 a.m.)

NABOB 418 Telegraphic [UE 5879/1094/53]

Most immediate. Secret   WASHINGTON, *30 November 1945, 1.17 a.m.*

(Waiver on other loans).

1. One of the hardest tasks you have set us is to persuade the

Americans to be content with no special provisions for the waiver or deferment of other credits and settlements when we are using the waiver against them. Indeed, we see no chance of getting rid of some such provision altogether.

2. That does not mean that we have not from the start shared your dislike of the elaborate clauses which the Americans have worked out. We are ready to try again to get them to accept something simpler, subject to 9 below.

3. The additional words you have added at the end of paragraph 4(II) of BABOON 315[1] seem to us most unlikely to satisfy them. Indeed, they can be read to work the wrong way, so as to mean that the more fully we are meeting the obligations of others the less is our capacity to pay the Americans and therefore the greater the reason for exercising the waiver. Even if the sentence can be verbally improved in this respect, we believe that we should prejudice the chance of getting an improvement by attempting to shirk the issue so completely.

4. We should therefore like to have your authority to offer in place of the words you have added to paragraph 4(II) an additional sub-clause 4(III) as follows:

5. *Begins*

(III) The Government of the U.K. will not avail themselves of the provision under (I) above unless they are at the same time reducing proportionately the annual payments or releases in respect of any new loans from Commonwealth Governments contracted before the end of 1950 and of settlements of the sterling balance[s] under (vi)[6] below, except in the case of colonial dependencies.

Ends

6. We greatly doubt the advisability of acting on your suggestion in BABOON 316[2] to get some informal opinion from Canada to satisfy the Americans. Munro, who is here, considers that this would be very badly taken in Canada and is, indeed, impracticable.

7. This is a question which we have debated for endless hours and days since, we have said, we have from the start shared your dislike of the whole business. But it is a matter on which Clayton personally is particularly insistent. It would be more liberal on the part of the Americans not to insist. But from a banker's point of view, and that is how Clayton believes Congress will look at it, they are on strong ground.

Clayton considers that he has made a great concession in giving up his original demand that the American credit should have absolute priority. We are most anxious, therefore, to find some way of meeting him which satisfies your conditions.

8. The above would relieve you of your difficulty vis-à-vis other Commonwealth ports [*sic*] since it does not formally compel us to put similar clauses in other agreements. It merely means that if we are so weak

---

[1] No. 134.　　　　　　　　　　　　　　　　[2] No. 134.i.

as not to do so we shall lose the advantage of the American waiver. Surely there must be some provision in all our settlements of a similar character? If there is not, then, in fact, all the other loans and settlements would have priority to the American credit. The likelihood of the Americans agreeing to a form of words which would leave that possible is very small.

9. We all of us reckon the prospects very poor of their taking the formula in paragraph 5 above. Moreover if you press your point too hard, there will be a risk of losing the waiver change [sic ?clause] altogether which, as you know we should consider fatal. May we in the last resort take something on the lines of 7(i) of [sic ?and] (iii) of NABOB 371[3] omitting 7(ii) as [sic ?and] (iv) as we have already suggested in paragraph 10 of NABOB 401?[4]

[3] No. 112.   [4] No. 112.i.

No. 138

British Missions (Washington) to Cabinet Offices
(Received 30 November, 6 a.m.)

NABOB 419 Telegraphic [UE 5879/1094/53]

Most immediate. Secret   WASHINGTON, 30 November 1945, 3.17 a.m.

Reference BABOON 315 para. 6 and 317[1] para. 2.

1. We are still very perturbed about the line you instruct us to take regarding the liberalization of the sterling area.

2. We recognize that in BABOON 315 para. 6 you have retained the wording of NABOB Saving 32[2] with its reference to proceeding to action not later than the end of 1946. But your instruction that we are to construe this in the light of the Chancellor's reply to NABOB 400[3] means, if we are to be frank with the Americans, that the position as we and they have understood it hitherto is fundamentally altered.

3. We do not wish here to indulge in an inquisition into the past save that we must put on record our firm conviction that the authorization to hand NABOB Saving 32 to the Americans read in conjunction with the wording of BABOON 189,[4] which in para. 2 refers to the operation of the scheme at the end of 1946, constituted full warrant for the position we have taken with the Americans.[5]

4. Our concern is with the future. We fear the effect on the negotiations of the steps we are instructed to take, and we do not believe that the policy suggested is one which we can defend in argument.

5. So far as the effect on the negotiations is concerned, we can only repeat our unanimous conviction that the course we are told to take must

[1] Nos. 134 and 134.i.   [2] No. 98.
[3] i.e. BABOON 312 (No. 130), in reply to No. 125.   [4] See No. 94.i.
[5] The remainder of this telegram is printed in Moggridge, op. cit., pp. 600–3.

be disastrous. We wonder whether it is appreciated in London to what extent our offer to liberalize the sterling area by a specific date has been one of the main attractions to the Americans throughout the negotiations. To approach them at this stage and to say that consideration of the difficulties involved compels the U.K. Government regretfully to retract this offer must create the very worst impression. We are all convinced that the Americans would not be prepared to accept a retraction of this kind.

6. We should be in a stronger position for re-opening this question if we believed that it really was important for us and could produce a convincing reason. But all of us here, and we have given considerable attention to the matter, believe that the importance now attached to it by London is not only misplaced but definitely erroneous.

7. In the first place, we do not believe that we can argue that the liberty of action we should now demand to retain is of sufficiently real value to be material to our negotiations with the sterling creditors. We have repeatedly emphasised to the Americans the fact that the sterling area arrangements are informal and voluntary and that there exist no agreements which compel the sterling area countries to surrender to us their current foreign exchange earnings. What is at stake here is whether they will be willing to continue trading with us in sterling which is not freely convertible into other currencies, and this over a period in which we shall not be able to satisfy all their demands for goods. Even apart from the question of settling the accumulated balances it seems to us that convertibility of current earnings is something which for the most part we shall have to give away *de facto* even if it is not given away *de jure*. Indeed it may be that convertibility will be the main inducement to some of the more difficult countries to continue to trade with us in sterling, and to increase their sterling holdings, at a time when such assistance may be of vital importance to us.

8. May we try to disentangle the issues:

(*a*) We are not prepared to cancel any part of the accumulated balances unilaterally. Agreed.

(*b*) No one has ever supposed that we can release these balances except at a very slow rate. The pace of that release has always been our real bargaining weapon. Agreed.

(*c*) Whilst with luck we may persuade the sterling area countries to carry on with the present basis for another year, we have no power to compel them to do so when we have reached a state of disagreement or to use this as a threat to bend them to our will. We cannot force these countries to go on accepting restricted sterling. To forego what is an empty threat would seem, therefore, to be no great matter. Why not agreed?

9. But assume for the sake of argument that we did in fact retain the power to refuse convertibility, might not its exercise give rise to consequences which would be much more embarrassing than the course which we here propose? If it were proposed that release of current

earnings should, in the case of each creditor, only take place from a date to be separately negotiated with each creditor, this would raise the difficult question of differential treatment for different creditor countries. The release date in each case would depend, not merely on the success or otherwise of each particular negotiation, but also on such fortuitous factors as the order in which we negotiated with the different creditors. It seems to us here that such differentiation would be very invidious and difficult to defend. The only way to avoid it (unless a common release date for all sterling countries is adopted) would be to delay release to any one of the creditors. But it would be grossly unfair to impose such delay on the rest of the creditors and would certainly raise serious political difficulties.

10. Moreover, if notwithstanding the foregoing, we proceeded to release each country's earnings as and when we reached agreement, then surely the position would be technically untenable? Australia's earnings for instance might have become convertible through a settlement, but negotiations with India were still hanging fire. Under existing arrangements, which we infer you would continue to apply to India, her sterling would be freely transferable to Australia where it presumably would appear as current earnings. Would not this lead to endless possibilities of evasion, and indeed the complete disruption of the existing sterling area arrangements?

11. Apart from the arguments on merits which we have attempted to set out above, we have to consider what the American attitude would be if we were to put your draft, with the arguments in BABOON 312,[6] to them. In the first place, as we judge, they would ask, as they have repeatedly done before whether we intended to release each country's earnings upon reaching a settlement. In the past we have replied, and successfully, on the lines of paras. 9 and 10 above. If these arguments are sound, they would lead to the conclusion that there could be no releases until we had completed all the settlements, i.e. until some quite indefinite future date. This would at once bring to light the fundamental difference between your attitude, and their and our understanding of the position hitherto. Next they might no doubt enquire what would happen in the event of our failing to reach agreement with any one of the countries concerned. Would this finally nullify the whole of our undertaking? Your draft does not cover this contingency. Again we are forced to the position that either a definite date must be given or the undertaking is of very doubtful value. Thus, even apart from the questions of good faith which we have referred to elsewhere, the position we should have to take up would be one which it would be impossible to defend.

12. There is a final argument which in our opinion deserves full consideration in any practical weighing of alternatives and that is the attitude to this question of Canada. On this point we have had the benefit of consultation with Munro who assures us that the Canadians are highly

[6] See note 3 above.

sensitive on this point and are certain to insist as a price of further assistance, that at an early and named date the current earnings of the sterling group shall be freely convertible. Should we not look very foolish if, having broken with the United States on our refusal to pursue this policy, we find that the Canadians, to whom we turn for aid are insistent on just the same point?

13. We urgently request that this matter be reconsidered. We believe that we are in sight of the goal of a satisfactory settlement. But we believe too that this will be denied us, if our instructions remain as they are at present; and, what is more, the failure of the negotiations on this point would leave a most painful impression and even more important issues would be in jeopardy.

No. 139

British Missions (Washington) to Cabinet Offices
(Received 30 November, 3.12 a.m.)

NABOB 420 Telegraphic [UE 5879/1094/53]

Most immediate. Secret   WASHINGTON, 30 November 1945, 1.15 a.m.

For Treasury.
Reference NABOB 417.[1]
1. This telegram deals with various matters of detail not covered in preceding telegrams.[2]
2. Paragraph 2(II) of BABOON 315.[3] We think we have a good chance of getting your form of words accepted but not much chance of cutting this clause out altogether.
3. We will tell the Americans that you dislike the five year moving average[4] and we do not know how much importance they attach to it. We ourselves think it an improvement and not at all nonsensical. For it is after more than one year of bad times and before increasing prosperity has brought us back again to where we started that we shall be in difficulties. It is also a particular safeguard in the early years. We should also tell you that the original introduction of the five year moving average was with a view to making less necessary the formerly proposed provision about the state of our gold reserves. By making the waiver dependent on the state of affairs over a period and not merely on a purely temporary situation the U.S. Treasury felt that the necessity for the gold reserve clause was diminished. We conclude therefore that it is not a point that we should fight too hard against American resistance.
4. We argued at considerable length against paragraph 7(II)(A) of BABOON 315 being applied only to past accum[u]lations. We concur with

[1] No. 136.   [2] Nos. 137–8.   [3] No. 134.
[4] See para. 4(I)(a) of No. 113.

you that this is not logical. We will therefore try again and may quite well succeed.

5. Now that you have conceded paragraph 7(II) of BABOON 315, paragraph 8 can be considerably simplified and need not refer to import controls. May we use our discretion to make this part of the document tidy?

6. Your addition of paragraph 7(III) of BABOON 315 is of course entirely reasonable. The Americans however are very sensitive to overt reference to the scarce currency clause which they say is a red rag to Congress. We feel sure therefore that they would prefer to have it handled by the alternative which you suggest in paragraph 4(D)(I) of BABOON 317.[5] We do not think there is any serious doubt that you would then be covered on this point.

[5] No. 134.i.

No. 140

Cabinet Offices to British Missions (Washington)

BABOON 323 Telegraphic [*UE 5879/1094/53*]

Most immediate. Top secret   CABINET OFFICES, *30 November 1945, 1.15 p.m.*

Following for Ambassador from Prime Minister and Chancellor of the Exchequer.

1. We have given the very fullest consideration to the points in NABOBS 417 to 419.[1] The Cabinet considered the whole position at great length[2] before sending the text in BABOON 315.[3]

2. It is now our firm opinion that you should put that text to the Americans as soon as possible as from His Majesty's Government with the supporting arguments which we have supplied to you.

3. The Americans must realise that time is running very short if they wish for action on Bretton Woods. They must also be got to understand that we have difficulties on our side, and it has not been easy to get agreement here.

4. When you have seen the Americans we shall of course be ready to consider any representations from them which you wish to transmit to us on particular points. But I should warn you that the Cabinet, when they considered the draft agreement yesterday, were by no means disposed to approve of any agreement less favourable to this country, or containing more specific limitations on our freedom of action.[4]

---

[1] Nos. 136–8.   [2] See No. 132.   [3] No. 134.
[4] See further Pressnell, *op. cit.*, Chapter 10(21).

No. 141

Note by Mr. Coulson

[*UE 5879/1094/53*]

FOREIGN OFFICE, *1 December 1945*

Mr. Hall-Patch rang me up from Washington last night and referred to paragraph 5 of Nabob 419 (Flag A).[1] He said that he and all the members of the Delegation felt that, if we took the line which the Cabinet had suggested, this would have a serious effect on Anglo-American relations. It was not merely a technical point, but one which will involve us in serious accusations of bad faith.

The point at issue, as I understand it, is this. Our draft in regard to the sterling area arrangements (paragraph 6 of Baboon 315: Flag B[2]) says 'The Government of the United Kingdom will proceed not later than the end of 1946 to make arrangements under which the sterling receipts from current transactions of all sterling area countries . . .[3] will be freely available for current transactions in any currency area without discrimination'. The delegation have, on an interpretation of previous instructions, given the Americans to understand that arrangements for the convertibility of receipts of current transactions would be *completed* by the end of 1946. The Cabinet have maintained that they could not tie the hands of our negotiators with the sterling area countries by agreeing to this in advance of the negotiations.

Thus, even if our text is accepted by the Americans, there will be a danger that we and they interpret it in different ways.

Unfortunately, this is a very difficult matter to take up. The telegram to which Mr. Hall-Patch referred has already received a reply yesterday from the Prime Minister and the Chancellor (Baboon No. 323: Flag C[4]), saying that these points have had the fullest consideration, but that 'it is our firm opinion that you should put the text to the Americans as soon as possible, . . .[3] though we shall be ready to consider any representations from them which you wish to transmit to us on particular points'. The Delegation have asked permission not to put the text to the Americans until they have had a chance of discussing the background with Sir. E. Bridges, who is due to arrive this afternoon.[5] But I understand from the

---

[1] No. 138. [2] No. 134. [3] Punctuation as in original. [4] No. 140.

[5] For the decision on 30 November by Mr. Dalton, approved by Mr. Attlee, to send Sir E. Bridges to Washington see Dalton, *High Tide and After*, p. 84, and Pressnell, *op. cit.*, Chapter 10(22). In NABOB 423 of 30 November to the Prime Minister Lord Halifax had explained that he wished 'to await the arrival of Bridges before communicating with Americans' as the Delegation would be in a stronger position 'if he can convey to them the views of the Cabinet first-hand'.

Lord Halifax also pointed out, with reference to BABOON 321 (see No. 134.ii), that an explanation to the Americans of the tight Parliamentary timetable in relation to the Bretton Woods agreement would need careful handling as it might be taken as a sort of

Treasury that he is unlikely to hold out any hope that the Cabinet would be willing to reconsider their attitude on this particular point.[6]

The people on the spot must be the best judges of the effect this will have on relations with the Americans. Mr. Hall-Patch insisted very strongly that this effect would be grave. As against that, must be set whatever view the Cabinet take as to the length to which we can afford to go to meet the Americans. In the circumstances I can only ask for instructions as to whether the Secretary of State is willing to take this up.[7]

J.E. COULSON

blackmailing pressure and provoke very sharp reaction if coupled with the presentation of the text in No. 134. Mr. Attlee replied in BABOON 329 of 1 December that it should be explained to the Americans that there would be criticism if Parliament and public opinion were not given sufficient time to examine the agreement (UE 5879/1094/53).

[6] In a minute of 1 December addressed to Mr. Dalton Sir W. Eady commented as follows on No. 138: 'Sir Edward Bridges knows that if everything else is more or less all right we are not going to break if the Americans insist upon a definite undertaking about current earnings. He also knows that our Delegation are to do their utmost to get the point conceded to us and to make full use of the arguments in BABOON 303 [No. 124] and your answer (BABOON 312) [No. 130] to NABOB 400 [No. 125]. Keynes does not appear to have read 303 properly for we made it plain there that we would release current earnings and an agreed proportion of accumulated balances as we reached agreement with each country, and were not going to wait until we had got everybody into line. Therefore some releases will come into operation at a very early date. It is quite true that that means taking one country before another but that is inevitable anyway [cf. No. 22, para. 39(ii)]. It would suit our tactics, in the very difficult position we shall have, to choose a few "easy" countries and get their agreement so as to create the general impression that the Sterling Area countries are falling in with the plan. Then we can tackle the more difficult ones' (T 236/438).

[7] This minute was countersigned by Mr. Ronald on 1 December and minuted as follows by Mr. Bevin: 'Will speak to Dalton Monday morning [3 December 1945]. E.B.' Mr. Coulson added in a further minute of 6 December: 'N.B. The text in question had already on Sunday been put to the Americans & a compromise reported to the Cabinet by Monday morning.'

No. 142

British Missions (Washington) to Cabinet Offices
(Received 2 December, 7.48 p.m.)

NABOB 435 Telegraphic [UE 5984/1094/53]

Most immediate. Secret   WASHINGTON, *2 December 1945, 7.15 p.m.*

Eady from Bridges.

1. At meeting with the Americans this morning[1] we handed in our

[1] i.e. at the meeting of the Combined Finance Committee at 10.30 a.m. on 2 December (COM/FIN 6th meeting, GEN 80/86): cf. also Nos. 143 and 147, and *F.R.U.S. 1945*, vol. vi, pp. 185–8. In NABOB 432, despatched at 4.17 a.m. on 2 December, Sir E. Bridges had informed Sir W. Eady that following discussions 'all the afternoon and evening' since his arrival in Washington at lunchtime on 1 December, it was proposed to present the 'London

411

draft heads of agreement (NABOB 433[i]) and they handed in a definite draft at which they had been working for the last week. This U.S. draft is set out in my immediately following telegram.[2]

2. We parted this morning with an arrangement to meet again this afternoon when we had studied each other's documents. In the meantime we are reserving comment. But we thought it right to let you have the U.S. draft as soon as possible so that you can start studying it as a technical document.

CALENDAR TO No. 142

i *2 Dec. 1945 British Missions (Washington) Tels. NABOB 433 & 434* Amendments to text of No. 134 as handed to Americans (see note 1) [UE 5984/1094/53].

draft' (No. 134) to the Americans, subject to 'a few quite minor drafting amendments' (see i below), at this meeting.
[2] Not printed. This American draft of 30 November is printed in *F.R.U.S. 1945*, vol. vi, pp. 173–7: see further No. 144, note 1. In a brief of 3 December for Mr. Dalton Sir W. Eady commented that this American text 'follows fairly closely on the lines of the provisional text in NABOB 372 [No. 113] which the Cabinet had said was unacceptable in certain points. It sharpened the case against us, particularly on certain aspects of the Sterling Area arrangements and the transitional period' (T 236/438).

No. 143

British Missions (Washington) to Cabinet Offices
(Received 3 December, 6.50 a.m.)

NABOB 441 Telegraphic [*UE 5984/1094/53*]

Most immediate. Secret   WASHINGTON, *3 December 1945, 5.35 a.m.*

1. The U.S. representatives have proposed[1] that the winding up of Lend Lease and Reciprocal Aid should be settled by a comprehensive global payment which for the purposes of calculation is put at $650 million. This figure is made up of

(*a*) a net sum representing the difference between the Lend Lease and Reciprocal Aid pipelines less the net sum due to the U.K. under the Claims Settlement,

(*b*) a balance of $532 million to cover all other items.

The Americans have estimated the net amount under (*a*) at $118 million, which assumes a net sum due to us under the Claims Settlement of $53 million. We think that this latter figure may in the end work out at nearer $50 than $53 million, whilst our most recent estimates show the Lend Lease pipeline at $322 million and the Reciprocal Aid pipeline at $125 million. This would give a net amount due from the U.K. of $147 million instead of the American estimate of $118 million. The difference

[1] At the 6th meeting of the Combined Finance Committee: see No. 142, note 1.

of about $30 million is due to the reduction in the Reciprocal Aid pipeline estimate owing to

(i) termination on 31st December of arrangements for bringing bulk commodities into the offset,

(ii) exclusion of oil which we understand they are now paying for in cash.

Whilst, however, the total amount due for Lend Lease is increased our overall financial position is not affected since we shall be receiving cash for (i) and (ii) above.

2. You will appreciate that the actual sum due under (*a*) above would be dependent on the ascertained outturn of the Lend Lease and Reciprocal Aid pipelines. In other words if, when all the accounts due on both sides were finalized, it transpired that the net sum due from the U.K. under this head (allowing for the offset on account of the claims) was say $140 million the total settlement would in fact be one for $672 million. Conversely if the net figure under this head turned out to be less than the American estimate of $118 million the total settlement would be correspondingly reduced below $650 million.

3. Americans have dropped any idea of our being required to pay cash or take 3(*c*) credit terms for this settlement. What they contemplate is a separate loan agreement for whatever sum is found to be due from the U.K. on this account, which settlement will be on precisely the same terms as those agreed for the main loan. We see no objection to this procedure.

4. The proposed global payment would cover the financial settlement for the following items.

I *Due from the U.K.*

(*a*) Lend Lease Pipeline.

(*b*) Civilian Inventory Class I (for both the U.K. and Colonies).

(*c*) Civilian Inventory Class II (for both the U.K. and Colonies) (i.e. distributed durables).

(*d*) Net sum in respect of oil.

(*e*) Lend Lease capital installations in the U.K. and Colonies.

(*f*) Military Inventory—Payment for civilian end-use goods (subject to remarks below).

(*g*) Payment for Lend Lease transport aircraft.

(*h*) U.S.-owned surpluses in the U.K. together with capital installations in the U.K. financed by the U.S. from other than Lend Lease funds.

II *Due from the U.S.*

(*a*) Reciprocal Aid pipeline.

(*b*) Balance in respect of claims in Claims Settlement.

(*c*) Reciprocal Aid Inventories.

NOTES

(1) The settlement for the Military Inventory will not cover disposals of identifiable Lend Lease goods in third countries (including India).[2] The

[2] Cf. No. 129, note 3.

local currency proceeds in such cases will have to be paid over to the U.S. Government.

(2) There will be agreed conditions as to user and disposition in respect of item 1(e) and possibly 1(h) also.

(3) There are two uncertainties about above items. We do not yet know the amount of U.S. military oil in the U.K. which we shall be acquiring under this global settlement. We will investigate this as soon as possible. Similarly as regards aircraft we do not know the numbers and prices of aircraft which Americans envisage as covered by the settlement. They have told us that they consider that $15 million out of the $532 million represents the cost of aircraft. But we shall have to investigate how many aircraft they will agree can be brought within this total.

5. Americans have told us that they will wish to regard global settlement on above lines as having in effect subsumed our aircraft and Persian railway claims[3] and their claim for Suez Canal dues. For political reasons they do not want to describe their claim as having been formally abandoned.[4]

6. We believe that this settlement can be justified as a fair one if a computation of this kind is to be made at all. Indeed, as we have already explained, if we valued on a replacement basis the food, oil and raw materials in the pipeline and Inventories, the residual amount to cover all the other items to which we now acquire title is a modest one even on a basis of $650 million.

[3] V. ibid., note 5.

[4] These three claims were dealt with in Agreement II annexed to the Joint Memorandum and Agreements between the United Kingdom and the United States of America regarding Settlement for Lend-Lease, Reciprocal Aid, Surplus War Property and Claims, signed on 27 March 1946 and printed in B.F.S.P., vol. 147, pp. 1123–68.

No. 144

British Missions (Washington) to Cabinet Offices
(Received 3 December, 9.3 a.m.)

NABOB 443 Telegraphic [UE 5984/1094/53]

Most immediate. Secret   WASHINGTON, 3 December 1945, 5.39 a.m.

My immediately preceding telegram.[1]

Begins

(This is designed to serve as the basis for the more detailed Contract,

[1] Not printed. This telegram of 3 December reported the textual alterations to the American draft communicated on the morning of 2 December (see No. 142) which resulted from discussions at the meeting of the Combined Finance Committee at 3.30 p.m. that afternoon (COM/FIN 7th meeting, GEN 80/87): see also No. 146 and F.R.U.S. 1945, vol. vi, pp. 185–8. NABOB 442 further explained that the present telegram contained the 'full text embodying above changes'. The main differences between the two texts are noted below.

Financial Agreement and other documents which may be agreed.)

1. *Amount of the Line of Credit*

(i) The Government of the United States will extend to the Government of the United Kingdom a line of credit of . . . [2] billion.

(ii) This line of credit will be available until December 31st, 1951.

2. *Purpose of the Credit*

The purpose of the credit shall be to facilitate purchases by the United Kingdom of goods and services from the United States, to assist the United Kingdom to meet transitional postwar deficits in her current balance of payments, to help the United Kingdom to maintain adequate reserves of gold and dollars and to assist the United Kingdom to assume the obligations of multilateral trade, as defined in this and other agreements.

3. *Amortization and Interest*

(i) The amount of the credit outstanding on December 31st, 1951, shall be repaid with interest in 50 annual instalments beginning on December 31st, 1951, subject to the provisions of (4) below.

(ii) The rate of interest shall be 2 per cent per annum. For the year 1951 interest shall be computed on the amount outstanding on December 31st, 1951, and for each year thereafter, interest shall be computed on the amount outstanding on January 1st, subject to the provisions of (4) below.

(iii) The 50 annual instalments of principal repayments and interest shall be equal, amounting to $31.8 million for each $1 billion outstanding on December 31st, 1951. Each instalment shall consist of the full amount of the interest due and the remainder of the instalment shall be the principal to be repaid in that year.

(iv) The Government of the United Kingdom may accelerate repayment of this line of credit.[3]

4. *Waiver of Interest Payments*

In any year in which the Government of the United Kingdom requests the Government of the United States to waive the amount of the interest due in that year, the Government of the United States will grant the waiver if:

(*a*) The Government of the U.K. finds that a waiver is necessary in view of the present and prospective conditions of international exchange and the level of its gold and foreign exchange reserves, *and,*

(*b*) As certified by the International Monetary Fund, the income of the U.K. from home-produced exports plus its net income from invisible current transactions in its balance of payments (as defined in Article XIX(I) of the Articles of Agreement of the International Monetary Fund) was on the average over the five preceding calendar years less than the amount of U.K. imports during 1936–38. Fixed at 866 million pounds, as such figure may be adjusted for changes in the price level of

---

[2] Punctuation as in original.   [3] Para. 3(iv) was not in the earlier text.

these imports. Any amount in excess of $175 million released or paid in any year on account of sterling balances accumulated in the hands of overseas Governments, monetary authorities and banks before the date of this Agreement, shall be regarded as a capital transaction and therefore shall not be included in the above calculation of the net income from invisible current transactions for that year. If waiver is requested for an interest payment prior to that due in 1955, the average income shall be computed for the calendar years from 1950 through the year preceding the given year.[4]

5. *Position of this Credit in relation to other obligations*

(i) It is understood that any amounts required to discharge obligations of the U.K. to third countries oustanding on the date of this Agreement will be found from resources other than this line of credit.

(ii) The Government of the United Kingdom will not arrange any long-term loans from Governments within the British Commonwealth after the date of this Agreement and before the end of 1951 on terms more favourable to the lender than the terms of this line of credit.

(iii) Waiver of interest will not be requested or allowed under 4 above in any year unless the aggregate of the releases or payments in that year of sterling balances accumulated in the hands of overseas Governments, monetary authorities and banks except in the case of Colonial dependencies[5] before the date of this agreement, are reduced proportionately, and unless interest payments on loans referred to in (ii) above are waived. The proportionate reduction of the releases, [? or] payments of sterling balances shall be calculated on the basis of the aggregate released in the most recent year in which waiver of interest was not requested.

(iv) The application of the principles set forth in this section shall be the subject of full consultation between the two Governments as occasion may arise.

6. *Sterling Area Exchange Arrangements*

The Government of the United Kingdom will complete arrangements as early as practicable and in any case not later than one year after the effective date of this agreement unless in exceptional cases a later date is agreed upon after consultation. Immediately[6] after completion of such arrangements, the sterling receipts from current transactions of all

---

[4] A 'note on the second half of 4(*b*) of Waiver', transmitted in NABOB 448 of 3 December, read as follows: 'The intention of the Waiver is to cover our imports plus necessary payments. Among those necessary payments must be allowance for payments to our creditors. This item directly affects the figures. Therefore, it is not unreasonable to put some limit on this. Hence the American suggestion.'

[5] The preceding seven words were inserted to meet a point made by the British Delegation.

[6] In the earlier text the preceding passage had read '. . . not later than the end of 1946 under which immediately . . . This amendment was agreed by the Americans after 'a long discussion'.

sterling area countries, apart from any receipts arising out of military expenditure by the United Kingdom prior to December 31, 1948, which it may be agreed to treat on the same basis as the balances accumulated during the war will be freely available for current transactions in any currency area without discrimination; with the result that any discrimination arising from the so-called sterling area Dollar pool will be entirely removed and that each member of the sterling area will have its current sterling and Dollar receipts at its free disposition for current transactions anywhere.

7. *Other Exchange Arrangements*

(i) The Government of the U.K. agrees that after the effective date of this agreement it will apply no exchange restrictions, except in accordance with the articles of agreement of the International Monetary Fund, which will restrict payments or transfers in respect of products permitted to be imported into the U.K. from the U.S., or of other current transactions between the two countries as defined in article xix (i) of the said articles or on the use of sterling balances in the hands of U.S. residents arising out of current transactions; and in pursuance of the policy of reducing restrictions on trade between the two countries at the earliest possible date it agrees not to avail itself in respect of the transactions referred to above, of article xiv of the articles of agreement of the International Monetary Fund.

(ii) The Governments of the U.S. and the U.K. agree that not later than one year after the effective date of this agreement, unless in exceptional cases a later date is agreed upon after consultation, they will impose no restrictions on payments and transfers for current international transactions as defined in the articles of agreement of the International Monetary Fund. The obligations of this paragraph shall not apply:

(*a*) To balances of third countries and their nationals accumulated before this paragraph becomes effective;

(*b*) To restrictions imposed in conformity with the provisions of the articles of agreement of the International Monetary Fund[7] (but the U.K. and the U.S. agree that they will not continue to invoke the provision of article xiv section 2 of the articles of agreement of the International Monetary Fund after this paragraph becomes effective);[8] or

(*c*) To restrictions imposed in connection with measures designed to uncover and dispose of assets of Germany and Japan.[9]

[7] The earlier text had here read '. . . imposed with the approval of the International Monetary Fund'.

[8] In NABOB 449 of 3 December, evidently sent in response to a telephone call from Sir W. Eady, Mr. Lee confirmed that 'words in brackets in para. 7(ii)(*b*) of NABOB 443 are of universal application and are *not* bilateral'.

[9] The earlier text had here included paragraph 7(III) which read: 'The obligations assumed by the Governments of the U.S. and the U.K. under this Section and Section 8 are also assumed by all of their respective colonies, overseas territories, all territories under

8. *Import Arrangements*

If the Government of either country imposes or maintains quantitative import restrictions, such restrictions shall be administered on a basis which does not discriminate against imports from the other country in respect of any product; provided that this undertaking shall not apply (*a*) in cases in which its application would have the effect of preventing the country imposing such restrictions from utilizing, for the purchase of needed imports, inconvertible currencies accumulated up to December 31, 1946, or (*b*) in cases in which there may be special necessity for the country imposing such restrictions to assist, by measures not involving a substantial departure from the general rule of non-discrimination, a country whose economy has been disrupted by war. The provisions of this paragraph should become effective[10] as soon as practicable and in any case not later than 31st December 1946.

9. *Accumulated Sterling Balance[s]*

(i) The Government of the United Kingdom intends to make agreements with the countries concerned, varying according to the circumstances of each case, for an early settlement covering the sterling balances accumulated by sterling area and other countries prior to such settlement (together with any future receipts arising out of military expenditure by the U.K. which it may be agreed to treat on the same basis). The settlements with the sterling area countries will be on the basis of dividing these accumulated balances into three categories, (*a*) balances to be released at once and convertible into any currency for current transactions, (*b*) balances to be similarly released by instalments over a period of years beginning in 1951, and (*c*) balances to be adjusted[11] as a contribution to the settlement of war and post war indebtedness and in recognition of the benefits which the countries concerned might be expected to gain from such a settlement. The Government of the United Kingdom will make every endeavour to secure the early completion of the arrangements contemplated above.

(ii) In[12] consideration of the fact that an important purpose of the present credit is to promote the development of multilateral trade and facilitate its early resumption on a non-discriminatory basis, the Govern-

---

their protection, suzerainty or authority and all territories in respect of which they exercise a mandate.' NABOB 442 explained that the Americans 'agreed to omit this on the understanding that the point should be dealt with outside the Agreement in an exchange of letters. This exchange of letters would indicate the extent to which the Colonies could be committed to acceptance of provisions of Paragraphs 7 and 8 of the Agreement.'

[10] The earlier text here continued 'not later than one year after the effective date of this agreement unless a later date is agreed upon after consultation.'

[11] The earlier text here read 'written off', and did not include the last sentence of this sub-paragraph.

[12] In the earlier text this sub-paragraph began: 'In view of the importance of the interest of the United States in the method of dealing with sterling balances from the standpoint of their relation to non-discriminatory trade policies, and in . . .'.

ment of the United Kingdom agrees[13] that any sterling balances released, or otherwise made available for current payments, whether by arrangements under (i) above or in the event of failure to arrive at such arrangements, will, not later than one year after the effective date of this agreement unless in special cases a later date is agreed after consultation, be freely available for current transactions in any currency area without discrimination.

10. *Consultation on Agreement*
Either Government shall be entitled to approach the other for reconsideration of any of the provisions of this agreement, if in its opinion the prevailing conditions of international exchange justify such reconsideration, with a view to agreeing upon modifications for presentation to their respective legislatures.

CALENDAR TO No. 144

i *3–6 Dec. 1945   From and to British Missions (Washington) Tels. NABOB 454, 475 & 481, BABOON 348 & 356* Correspondence concerning proposed exchange of letters to replace para. 7(III) of earlier American draft (see note 9), and list of Colonial Dependencies asked for by Americans [UE 5984/1094/53].

[13] The earlier text here continued 'that, not later than one year after the effective date of this Agreement unless a later date is agreed upon after consultation, any sterling balances available for payments, whether pursuant to settlement or otherwise, will be available for use in any currency area without discrimination.'

No. 145

British Missions (Washington) to Cabinet Offices
(Received 3 December, 10.16 a.m.)

NABOB 444 Telegraphic [*UE 5984/1094/53*]

Most immediate. Secret   WASHINGTON, *3 December 1945, 9.25 a.m.*

From Ambassador, Delegation and Bridges.
1. In regard to the amount of the Loan the Americans have now made their offer firm, namely, $3,750 million new money and the Lend Lease settlement provisionally estimated at $650 million on the same terms making a total of $4,400 million.
2. As explained in NABOB 441[1] the Americans have dropped their previous suggestion of 3(c) terms[2] or cash for Lend Lease settlement, which is now on exactly the same terms in all respects as the main loan. The Americans will, however, divide the aggregate of $4,400 million as above into new money and the lend lease settlement since the funds will come from different sources and since it suits them to regard the amount

[1] No. 143.   [2] Cf. No. 4, note 7.

419

of new money as the aggregate of the loan for which they will be asking from Congress special appropriation.

3. As explained in NABOB 441 the Lend Lease settlement may come to a little more than the above figure, say another $30 million, which will, in effect, be an increase of the loan by that amount since it will be due to our having put reciprocal aid supplies and services on a cash basis at a rather earlier date than we had originally estimated, so that in that event we shall get an extra $30 million in cash.

4. It will be seen that the above falls short of our own figure of $4,500 million by $100 million or a little less. It also falls short of our own best estimate of the new money we require by a rather larger amount. Nevertheless, the American offer is so near our own demand that we recommend its acceptance.

No. 146

British Missions (Washington) to Cabinet Offices
(Received 3 December, 11.11 a.m.)

NABOB 445 Telegraphic [UE 5984/1094/53]

Most immediate. Secret   WASHINGTON, *3 December 1945, 9.27 a.m.*

Following from Ambassador, Delegation and Bridges.

1. This telegram contains a summary of the main points.[1] References are to the American draft. (NABOB 443).[2]

2. *Amount*

On amount, they will let us have $3,750,000,000 plus $650,000,000 for a clean-up of Lend Lease. The latter sum would be the subject of a separate agreement but on the same basis as the larger amount. See NABOBS 441 and 446[3] on this.

3. *The Waiver*

(a) The Americans pressed us very strongly to maintain the five year moving average which they held will be far more easily defensible for American public opinion. They also reminded us that the substitution of the five year average for a single year was of great help to them in abandoning their proposal to make the waiver subject to the state of our reserves.

(b) They will not accept the proposal that principal should be deferred as well as interest waived. They were not prepared to take this again into consideration at the present stage of the negotiations.

(c) They will also insist on a specific statement on the lines of

---

[1] i.e. the main points discussed at the 7th meeting of the Combined Finance Committee: see No. 144, note 1.

[2] No. 144.

[3] Nos. 143 and 147. The latter reference should, however, probably be to No. 145.

paragraph 5 (III) of their draft, as amended to exclude the Colonies, about proportionate reduction of other external obligations. We pressed them strongly to take 4 (II) of our draft[4] but without success. 5(IV) which is new perhaps helps a little.

4. *Sterling Area Arrangements*

The Americans were clearly disturbed at what they regarded as the re-opening of what they had taken to be the understanding that current earnings should be freed not later than 31st December, 1946. After great insistence we succeeded in getting two concessions inserted in paragraph 6:

(a) That the date when current earnings are to be freed is to be a year from the date when the financial agreement becomes effective. This we are told may be three or four months hence.

(b) That in exceptional cases a later date may be agreed upon after consultation. This last concession was only made with great reluctance.

5. *Other Exchange Arrangements*

The first part of paragraph 7 (I) is on the lines of our draft. The second part must in their view stand in order to ensure that we do not forthwith use Article XIV[5] to escape from the obligation we have just accepted. The point seems to us to be a good one.

We suggested the addition of the following sub-clause to paragraph 7 (II):

'(d) To balances of third countries which do not accord reciprocal treatment in the above respect.'

The Americans resisted but you may wish us to press for its inclusion as above or in the bracket in 7 (II)(b) where it would be less obtrusive. If the Americans can be persuaded to agree this will draw the sting from this paragraph. You will appreciate that 7 (II)(b) as now amended enables us to deal with non-members. Liesching is telegraphing separately to the Board of Trade on this point.[6]

6. *Import Arrangements*

We repeated our arguments why the exception in para 8 (a) should not be limited to balances accumulated before the end of 1946. It appeared, however, that the Americans attach great importance to this limitation in order to be able to say that a definite time limit was set to this particular form of possible discrimination. We consider their attitude unreasonable, but do not believe that in practice anything very substantial from our

[4] Cf. No. 142, note 1.   [5] See No. 1, note 11.

[6] In NABOB 447 of 3 December Sir P. Liesching explained to Sir S. Cripps that the amendment of the text cited in No. 144, note 7, 'preserves our right to apply exchange restrictions against countries not members of the monetary fund . . . it is subject only to the Fund not finding that the restrictions are prejudicial to the interests of members or contrary to the purposes of the Fund. In this way, the point made in paragraph 5 of NABOB 406 [No. 126.i] is substantially met as regards non-members. As regards members which are still applying transitional measures, we propose to press for an amendment which will free us from the obligations of the paragraph against countries which do not reciprocate.'

point of view is at stake. We suggest you instruct us to try again but leave us discretion in the last resort.

7. *Purpose of the Credit*

What previously appeared as paragraph 2 (II)[7] has now reappeared as paragraph 5 (I) of the American draft. We pressed them to withdraw this provision altogether but they are anxious to maintain their draft of this paragraph since they think that this will help them politically with Congress more than our version. They agree, however, (and this will be entered in the Minutes) that if the Chancellor of the Exchequer is asked to explain what this paragraph means he can explain it in terms of the London version of the paragraph. We hope that you may regard this as sufficiently satisfactory.

8. *General*

We agree with the judgment expressed by Bridges[8] that the terms are now clear on which agreement can be reached, and that all relative material for a decision has now been placed before the Cabinet.

[7] See No. 113.   [8] See No. 147.

No. 147

British Missions (Washington) to Cabinet Offices
(Received 3 December, 11.34 a.m.)

NABOB 446 Telegraphic [UE 5984/1094/53]

Most immediate. Secret   WASHINGTON, *3 December 1945, 9.29 a.m.*

Personal for Prime Minister and Chancellor of Exchequer from Bridges.

1. We have spent about six hours today[1] with the Americans. We began by presenting the British Draft.[2] We took the Americans through this and emphasised the points to which you attach importance.

2. The Americans then produced the draft already sent to you in NABOB 436.[3] This also was discussed at length and we took occasion of again raising the various points on which it differed from your draft.

3. The Americans plainly did not view the London draft with any favour. They looked upon it as reopening matter[s] on which they felt that their attitude had for some time been made sufficiently clear, or which they had regarded as settled. It seems clear that if we are to come to terms this will have to be broadly on the basis of the U.S. Draft, modified as may be necessary.

4. You may wish for my personal impressions on the outstanding points. The offer on amount seems to be satisfactory. While it might not

[1] This telegram was evidently drafted on 2 December: cf. No. 142, note 1, and No. 144, note 1.
[2] See No. 142.   [3] V. *ibid.*, note 2.

be impossible to get the 3¾ billion up to 4, I would not recommend trying.

5. I am clear that we cannot secure any improvement in the three U.S. conditions for a waiver as now stated.

6. On the sterling area the compromise we have secured was only won by hard fighting on a point on which the U.S. feel very strongly. I do not think we shall be able to push them any further on this.

7. There remain the questions about exchange arrangements outside the sterling area and accumulated sterling balances. On these two points also the U.S. feel strongly, but they are also a trifle uncertain of their facts. I am not versed in these technicalities, but I judge that if you think the amendments we have secured on these points are not altogether satisfactory, we should stand a chance of gaining some further ground. Anyhow it would be worth trying if you would tell us what you want in very specific terms and provide ammunition. But we should hope that you will feel able to give us discretion to settle on these points without further reference back.

8. As you will see my general conclusion is that we now know pretty well what we can and cannot get, and that there is not much left to argue about.

No. 148

Cabinet Offices to British Missions (Washington)

BABOON 338 Telegraphic [*UE 5984/1094/53*]

Most immediate. Secret   CABINET OFFICES, *3 December 1945, 11.15 p.m.*

For Ambassador from Prime Minister, Chancellor of the Exchequer and President of the Board of Trade.[1]

We have anxiously considered your series of telegrams and the latest revise of the American draft[2] in which you have been able to make notable improvements and we should be prepared to accept the whole of this draft, with one important exception. It seems to us to be quite impossible to gain the acceptance of the Bretton Woods Agreement in Parliament if we are to associate its passage through Parliament with a statement that we are, by the financial agreement, losing the main safeguards of Bretton Woods. As you know, there is already a great deal of hostility against the Bretton Woods scheme on all sides of the House but we believe,

[1] At their meeting at 11 a.m. on 3 December the Cabinet had authorised Mr. Attlee, Mr. Dalton and Sir S. Cripps 'to settle, on their behalf, any necessary modifications of the draft Financial Agreement which could be made without encroaching upon the general principles determined by the Cabinet in their discussions on 6th and 29th November [see Nos. 95.ii and 132]' (Confidential Annex to C.M. (45) 58th Conclusions, UE 6004/1094/53). According to Mr. Dalton, the present telegram, printed in *High Tide and After*, pp. 85–6, was also agreed with Mr. Bevin (*ibid.*, p. 84).

[2] No. 144.

nevertheless, that we could secure its passage on the strength of the safeguards which it contains. We have to bear in mind particularly that it would be necessary for us to secure Parliament's assent to the Bretton Woods Agreement before the Congress has dealt with the financial agreement. Under these circumstances, it seems to us essential that you should inform the Americans of the situation and exert the utmost pressure upon them to leave the Bretton Woods Agreement untouched by the financial agreement. The three essential points where the financial agreement runs counter to the Bretton Woods Agreement are, first, we are deprived of the benefit of the five years transitional period provided at Bretton Woods,[3] which, for us, alone among all the other signatories, is cut down to fifteen months; second, we are deprived, alone of all the other signatories, of the benefit of the scarce currencies clause; third, we are deprived, alone of all the other signatories, of the right, by resigning membership of the fund, to regain freedom of action in matters regulated by the Bretton Woods Agreement. This third freedom, moreover, is withdrawn from us for more than half a century, i.e. during the currency of the loan agreement.

We cannot believe that the U.S. Government will desire to jeopardise the success, which seems so near, of these negotiations, on the ground that we could not consent to strip ourselves of these essential safeguards introduced by the unanimous agreement of forty-four nations into the Bretton Woods Convention.

[3] See No. 1, note 11.

No. 149

Cabinet Offices to British Missions (Washington)

BABOON *339 Telegraphic* [*UE 5984/1094/53*]

Most immediate. Secret   CABINET OFFICES, *3 December 1945, 11.30 p.m.*

Personal for Bridges from Eady.

This in explanation of ministerial message of tonight.[1]

1. American Ambassador has been seen and Ministers have explained the position to him and emphasised the serious view they take of the matter.[2]

2. Transitional period. The major point arises on paragraph 7(II)(*b*) of NABOB 443[3] which commits us, at the end of a year from the effective

[1] No. 148.
[2] For Mr. Winant's account of this interview on 3 December with Mr. Attlee, who was joined by Mr. Dalton and Sir S. Cripps, and of his receipt of a statement based on the last two sentences, beginning 'The three essential points', of the second paragraph of No. 148, see *F.R.U.S. 1945*, vol. vi, pp. 188–9.
[3] No. 144.

date of the agreement, to give up all our rights under Section 2, Article XIV of Bretton Woods.

3. The protection against countries which do not reciprocate suggested in NABOB 447[4] would be useful, but there is no real protection in reciprocity between an international currency and a local currency.

4. If you get rid of the reference to Article XIV in that place, we suggest that the reference at the end of paragraph 7(I) should also disappear. We do not see why the reference should be required in view of the clear meaning of the paragraph without it, and we should only be embarrassed with other countries by this specific reference to Article XIV, even though in this place it is only bilateral.

5. NABOB 443, paragraph 8. Import Arrangements. The disappearance of the safeguards for a scarcity of Dollars which we propose in paragraph 7(III) of BABOON 315[5] and commented on in paragraph 4(d) of BABOON 317[6] has seriously disturbed ministers, NABOB 420,[7] paragraph 6, encouraged us to believe that one of the alternative safeguards suggested in BABOON 317 would be acceptable.

6. There is another important point of difficulty. In paragraph 4 of NABOB 401[8] Keynes stated that it had been explicitly made clear to the Americans that our undertaking about the release of Sterling Balances did not restrict our freedom to make tied loans or to secure such tied loans on future releases of Sterling. We must have this right to finance public works programmes or other capital development from Sterling Balances in the situation contemplated in that paragraph. We should prefer to have this in the text of the agreement either in the form suggested in paragraph 6(II)(b) of BABOON 315 which was taken from paragraph 2 of NABOB 362[9] or in other suitable words. But if inclusion in the agreement would raise difficulties, then we must be on formal record in the sense of the paragraph quoted from NABOB 401.

7. Paragraph 4(b). Could you replace 175 million dollars by 43.75 [million] pounds sterling? The rest of the paragraph is dealing with Sterling and we do not want to create the impression that we are undertaking to release a minimum number of dollars. We are releasing multilateral currency.

8. And soon perhaps *nox una dormienda*.[10]

[4] See No. 146, note 6.   [5] No. 134.   [6] No. 134.i.
[7] No. 139.   [8] No. 112.i.   [9] No. 110.   [10] 'A night's sleep.'

No. 150

British Missions (Washington) to Cabinet Offices
(Received 4 December, 6.45 a.m.)

NABOB 456 Telegraphic [*UE 5984/1094/53*]

Most immediate. Secret   WASHINGTON, *4 December 1945, 6.1 a.m.*

Personal for Eady from Bridges.
Your Baboon 339.[1]
We should be grateful for answers to the following questions:

1. Your paragraph 2. Would this point be met by the deletion of the words in parenthesis at the end of paragraph 7 (II)(B)?[2]

2. Your paragraph 3 noted. Presumably this point would not arise if we secured the deletion suggested above.

3. Your paragraph 4. Is it the view of the ministers that we are authorized to surrender our transitional rights *vis à vis* United States only?

4. Your paragraph 4 seems to imply that the omission of the reference to article XIV in the last five lines of paragraph 7(II) does not alter the meaning of that paragraph on this question. We submit that it does, since in agreeing in the first part of the paragraph, to apply no exchange restrictions except in accordance with the articles of agreement of the I.M.F., we are left at full liberty to avail ourselves of article XIV.

5. Your paragraph 5. We assume that you agree this would be met by the insertion of the words 'except with the authority of the I.M.F.' after 'administered on a basis which'.[3]

6. Your paragraph 6. This point has been made orally to the Americans on many occasions and has never been questioned. We agree, however, that it would be well to have it placed on a formal record in the minutes.

7. Your paragraph 7. We think we can get this.

8. Baboon 338[4] seems corrupt and we have asked for a repeat. One point mentioned in this telegram but not in Baboon 339 is that we alone of all signatories would be deprived of the right, by resigning membership, to regain freedom of action and that we deny ourselves this freedom for 55 years. How do Ministers suggest that the point should be met? One possible suggestion is to provide for consultation between the U.K. and the U.S. Governments about those clauses of the financial agreement which are concerned with the provisions of the I.M.F. in the event of either party ceasing to be a member of that fund? To suggest inclusion of a specific provision to that end seems, however, pretty difficult. Could this point be regarded as already covered by paragraph 19?[5]

---

[1] No. 149.   [2] Of No. 144.   [3] See para. 8 of No. 144.   [4] No. 148.
[5] A record made at 6 a.m. on 4 December by Mr. O.L. Williams, a Principal in H.M. Treasury, of a telephone conversation at 5 a.m. that morning with Mr. Lee and Mr. Harmer, which covered the gist of the present telegram, here referred, evidently correctly, to para. 10 of No. 144.

9. Another view might be that if we resigned from the I.M.F. we should be bound by this agreement to act *vis à vis* the U.S. as if we still belonged, but not *vis à vis* other countries.

10. An answer to these questions is required by 8 a.m. Washington time 4th December.

11. If we can settle with the U.S. Government on the line proposed above, can we conclude the heads of agreement without further reference to London?

No. 151

Cabinet Offices to British Missions (Washington)

BABOON *342 Telegraphic [UE 5984/1094/53]*

Most immediate. Secret   CABINET OFFICES, *4 December 1945, 1.30 p.m.*

Personal for Bridges from Eady.
NABOB 456.[1]
Numbering in accordance with numbers in your telegram under reference.

This telegram has been approved by Prime Minister, Chancellor of the Exchequer and President of the Board of Trade.

1. 7(II(*b*).[2] Yes.

2. We agree.

3. and 4. Paragraph 7(I). The reference to Article XIV[3] must be omitted. We have no intention of using 'full liberty to avail ourselves of Article XIV' in order to escape from the obligation we have just accepted. This additional padlock against bad faith on our part is an example of the last moment difficulties created by NABOB 443.[4] The argument in paragraph 5 of your NABOB 445[5] must be rejected.

5. We would accept insertion of words 'except with the authority of the I.M.F.'

6. Formal record in the minutes of the last full meeting will be sufficient.[6]

7. This small point will be helpful.

8. and 9. If you get the deletions of the references to Article XIV in paragraphs 7(I) and 7(II) we should be content to regard this point as covered by paragraph 10 of NABOB 443.

---

[1] No. 150.   [2] Of No. 144.   [3] See No. 1, note 11.
[4] No. 144.   [5] No. 146.
[6] In NABOB 487 of 6 December Lord Keynes informed the Treasury that it had been agreed at the meeting of the Combined Finance Committee on 4 December (COM/FIN 8th meeting, GEN 80/88), that the following passage should be included in the minutes (printed in *F.R.U.S 1945*, vol. vi, pp. 190–3): 'It has been understood in these discussions that there is nothing in this Agreement which restricts the future freedom of the U.K. to make overseas loans of any character' (*ibid.*, p. 193).

10. No comment.

11. As stated in Ministerial telegram[7] *if* you get the changes requested above, we are prepared to accept text, as thus amended, of NABOB 443 as the formal agreement. We also accept the total of the loan and its division between new money and Lend–Lease on the conditions in NABOB 444.[8] You are authorised to conclude on this basis.

[7] No. 148.   [8] No. 145.

No. 152

British Missions (Washington) to Cabinet Offices
(Received 4 December, 8.30 p.m.)

NABOB *458 Telegraphic* [UE *6044/1094/53*]

Most immediate. Secret   WASHINGTON, *4 December 1945, 7.49 p.m.*

Following for Eady from Bridges.
The U.S. Delegation made it perfectly clear[1] that they would break off the negotiations rather than concede the point about the transitional period. We are all convinced that they meant what they said. They are reinforced in their attitude by the results of their soundings of Congress leaders. They also emphasized that they had met us on all the other points in your last telegram.[2]

[1] At the 8th meeting of the Combined Finance Committee: see No. 151, note 6.
[2] No. 151.

No. 153

Cabinet Offices to British Missions (Washington)

BABOON *349 Telegraphic* [UE *6035/1094/53*]

Most immediate. Secret   CABINET OFFICES, *5 December 1945, 1.56 a.m.*

Personal from Prime Minister for Bridges.
We have considered your telephone messages[1] and your telegram[2] about paragraph 7(II)B.[3] In my view if we tried to get Bretton Woods through Parliament without the transitional period we should probably fail. The odds against success are so great that I should have the greatest hesitation before making the attempt. In every speech advocating Bretton Woods, the five years transitional period has been put forward to justify our acceptance, and by no one more strongly than by Keynes.[4] The

[1] No record of these messages has been traced in Foreign Office archives: cf. Pressnell, *op. cit.*, Chapter 10(23).
[2] No. 152.   [3] Cf. No. 144.   [4] See No. 1, note 11.

abrogation of a solemn undertaking signed at Bretton Woods by forty-four nations would place our Government in an indefensible position.

2. We all appreciate that in other clauses of the draft Financial Agreement we have in fact agreed to give up our transitional rights over a large part of the field, and that the offer by the Americans to concede consultation on exceptional cases might be held to cover the rest of the field. But this leaves the decision in their hands.

3. You will know how anxious I am that these negotiations should have a successful conclusion both for the sake of our general relations with the United States Government and for the economic policies in which we have agreed to co-operate. I am, therefore, anxious to meet your difficulties to the best of my ability.

4. There are two possible ways which we can see out of this difficulty, either of which I am prepared you should put to the American Government.

(i) We will agree to Article 7(II)B if the date on which we voluntarily abandon our transitional rights under Article XIV is December 31, 1948. We shall then have had an opportunity to see the results of the International Trade Conference and of the negotiations with our sterling creditors. We shall also have seen the prospects of economic recovery in Europe upon which much of our export trade must depend.

(ii) If the Americans are unwilling to accept our alternative of December 31, 1948 instead of their present proposal, then I should be prepared to agree that, if the words in parenthesis in 7(ii)B are deleted, the following should be inserted:

'Provided that not later than one year from the effective date of this Agreement the Governments of the United States and the United Kingdom shall consult together to determine by agreement whether or not any such restrictions as either Government has maintained in virtue of Article XIV of the International Monetary Fund shall be continued either generally or in exceptional cases'.

5. The paragraph will then read:

'To restrictions imposed in conformity with the provisions of the Articles of Agreement of the International Monetary Fund provided that not later than one year from the effective date of this Agreement the Governments of the United States and the United Kingdom shall consult together to determine by agreement whether or not any such restrictions as either Government has maintained in virtue of Article XIV of the International Monetary Fund shall be continued either generally or in exceptional cases.'

6. The insertion of the words 'whether or not' means that if there is no agreement, on the facts as they will then have disclosed themselves, we retain our rights under Article XIV in respect of any restrictions still remaining.

7. We have not underrated the gravity of your last telephone message, and this answer is sent after careful consideration of it.

No. 154

British Missions (Washington) to Cabinet Offices
(Received 5 December, 6.32 a.m.)

NABOB 463 Telegraphic [UE 6035/1094/53]

Most immediate. Secret   WASHINGTON, 5 December 1945, 5.41 a.m.

Following for Prime Minister from Bridges.

1. The Ambassador, Brand, Keynes and I put to Judge Vinson tonight[1] the first alternative in BABOON 349.[2] He thought about the matter for a long time and then said that he feared that this proposal was unacceptable. He consulted Acheson whose reaction was even more unfavourable than his own. Clayton was not consulted but Vinson said that he would hold even stronger views as to the impossibility of any concession on this point.

2. Judge Vinson was not in a position to give us a formal decision on behalf of the whole committee but it is, I fear, perfectly clear that this alternative stands no chance of acceptance.

3. We also tried out tentatively with Vinson the possibility of some new formula about consultation. This he rejected even more decisively as having the appearance of a sham.

4. None of us were surprised as we had all felt convinced after this morning's meeting[3] that the point was one on which the Americans had made up their minds. We fear that you must take it that there is no chance of getting the decision reversed and that no appeal to the President would affect this. If we are to reach an agreement we believe that we must accept the American formula which I gave on the telephone and which reads as follows:

Begins

To restrictions imposed in conformity with the Articles of agreement of the International Monetary Fund; provided that the Governments of the United Kingdom and the United States will not continue to invoke the provisions of Article XIV Section 2 of those articles after this paragraph (II) becomes effective, unless in exceptional cases after consultation they agree otherwise;

Ends

5. This telegram has been seen by and has the full agreement of the Ambassador, Brand, and Keynes.

[1] i.e. 4 December: cf. Pressnell, *op. cit.*, Chapter 10(23).
[2] No. 153.
[3] See No. 152.

No. 155

British Missions (Washington) to Cabinet Offices
(Received 5 December, 6.5 a.m.)

NABOB *464 Telegraphic [UE 6035/1094/53]*

Most immediate. Secret   WASHINGTON, *5 December 1945, 5.43 a.m.*

Following personal for Prime Minister and Foreign Secretary from Lord Halifax.

I, of course, appreciate your difficulties and we have all done our level best to move the Americans to meet them. I am sorry we have failed. During this last very sticky week I have been struck by the real friendliness and desire to get over or round difficulties that Americans have shown. But they are, of course painfully conscious of their own. Now, however that issue is completely clear I cannot think the practical disadvantage of accepting American Draft comes anywhere near the grave mischief over many fields of Anglo-American relations that must be the inevitable and enduring consequences of rupture. Most earnestly I trust the Cabinet may take the same view.

No. 156

British Missions (Washington) to Cabinet Offices
(Received 5 December, 6.40 a.m.)

NABOB *465 Telegraphic [UE 6035/1094/53]*

Most immediate. Secret   WASHINGTON, *5 December 1945, 5.45 a.m.*

For Prime Minister and Chancellor of the Exchequer from the Ambassador, Bridges, Keynes and all members of the Delegation.

1. In this telegram we try to explain why the Americans are so insistent on the point and the degree of importance it has for us.

2. The Americans hold that the Bretton Woods transitional period was justified at the time by our prospective lack of resources in the early years. They argue therefore that the proposed loan should surely make enough difference to justify us in giving up a part of what we obtained at a time when we had no assurance of the resources which they now offer us. Indeed, they regard it as one of the most important purposes of the loan from their point of view to get rid of the remnant of discrimination against American exporters which would remain if nothing were done to curtail the present transitional period arrangements. They tell us that this is a point to which powerful commercial influences, which can exert great pressure on opinion in Congress, attach decisive importance.

3. As to what is at stake, it seems to us that the substance of the point

still at issue under Article 7(II) of NABOB 436[1] has now been reduced to the following dimensions. This article has of course no relation to the sterling area, the United States or Canada. As regards other areas:

(a) We are free in all cases up to one year after the effective date of this agreement which probably means at least up to March 1947.

(b) The whole of this clause lapses at the end of 1951.

(c) Subject only to the provisions of Article XI (2) of Bretton Woods[2] we remain completely free in our dealings with non-members of the I.M.F. This covers Argentine, Spain, Turkey, Switzerland, Sweden for example who will be non-members at least for the present.

4. What is [are] left therefore are the surplus earnings of certain South American and European countries, other than those named in (c) above, accruing between March 1947 and December 1951. Even in this respect we shall be left free if on consultation we can satisfy the Americans that the cases are exceptional. Thus, all we are conceding is that, failing our so satisfying them, these earnings must be freely available.

5. We doubt whether in terms of protecting our external resources any significant amount is at stake.

[1] See No. 142, note 2.   [2] Cf. No. 111, note 11.

No. 157

British Missions (Washington) to Cabinet Offices
(Received 5 December, 9.25 a.m.)

NABOB 467 Telegraphic [UE 6080/1094/53]

Most immediate. Secret   WASHINGTON, *5 December 1945, 7.41 a.m.*

Reference NABOB 466[i].

Following is text of Sections 1 to 5 of the finally revised draft agreement.[1] Opening words and Section 1 are new. Other changes in the text are indicated by underlining.[2]

Begins

Financial Agreement between the Governments of the United States and the United Kingdom

It is hereby agreed between the Government of the United States of America and the Government of the United Kingdom of Great Britain and Northern Ireland as follows:

1. *Effective date of the Agreement*

The effective date of this Agreement shall be the date on which the Government of the United States notifies the Government of the United Kingdom that the Congress of the United States has made available the

[1] The final text transmitted in the present telegram and Nos. 158–9 was published in Cmd. 6708 of 1945.   [2] Here italicized.

funds necessary to extend to the Government of the United Kingdom the line of credit in accordance with the provisions of this Agreement.

2. *Line of Credit*

The Government of the United States will extend to the Government of the United Kingdom a line of credit of *$3,750,000,000 which may be drawn upon any time between the effective date of this Agreement and December 31, 1951 inclusive.*

3. *Purpose of the Line of Credit*

The purpose of the line of credit *is* to facilitate purchases by the United Kingdom of goods and services *in* the United States, to assist the United Kingdom to meet transitional postwar deficits in its current balance of payments, to help the United Kingdom to maintain adequate reserves of gold and dollars and to assist *the Government of* the United Kingdom to assume the obligations of multilateral trade, as defined in this and other agreements.

4. *Amortisation and Interest*

(i) The amount of the line of credit *drawn by* December 31 1951 shall be repaid in 50 annual instalments beginning on December 31 1951 *with interest at the rate of 2 per cent per annum.*

Interest for the year 1951 shall be computed on the amount outstanding on December 31 1951 and for each year thereafter, interest shall be computed on the amount outstanding on January 1 *of each such year.*

49 annual instalments of principal repayments and interest shall be equal, calculated at the rate of $31,823,000 for each $1,000,000,000 of the line of credit drawn by December 31 1951, and *the fiftieth annual instalment shall be at the rate of $31,840,736.65 for each such $1,000,000,000.*

Each instalment shall consist of the full amount of the interest due and the remainder of the instalment shall be the principal to be repaid in that year. *Payments required by this section are subject to the provisions of Section 5.*

(ii) The Government of the United Kingdom may accelerate repayment of *the amount drawn under* this line of credit.

5. *Waiver of Interest Payments*

In any year in which the Government of the United Kingdom requests the Government of the United States to waive the amount of the interest due in *the instalment of* that year, the Government of the United States will grant the waiver if:

(*a*) the Government of the United Kingdom finds that a waiver is necessary in view of the present and prospective conditions of international exchange and the level of its gold and foreign exchange reserves *and*

(*b*) *the International Monetary Fund certifies that* the income of the United Kingdom from home-produced exports plus its net income from invisible current transactions in its balance of (words omitted)[3] was on

---

[3] From the text in No. 144. The word 'payments' was omitted in error.

the average over the five preceding calendar years less than the *average annual* amount of United Kingdom imports during 1936–8 fixed at 866 million pounds, as such figure may be adjusted for changes in the price level of these imports. Any amount in excess of 43,750,000 pounds released or paid in any year on account of sterling balances accumulated *to the credit of* overseas governments, monetary authorities and banks before the *effective* date of this Agreement shall be regarded as a capital transaction and therefore shall not be included in the above calculation of the net income from invisible current transactions for that year. If waiver is requested for an interest payment prior to that due in 1955, the average income shall be computed for the calendar years from 1950 through the year preceding *that in which the request is made.*

Ends

CALENDAR TO NO. 157

i *5 Dec. 1945 From and to British Missions (Washington) Tels. NABOB 466 and BABOON 355 concerning procedure for signature and implementation of financial agreement* [UE 6080/1094/53].

No. 158

British Missions (Washington) to Cabinet Offices
(Received 5 December, 10.35 a.m.)

NABOB 468 Telegraphic [*UE 6080/1094/53*]

Most immediate. Secret WASHINGTON, *5 December 1945, 7.43 a.m.*

1. Following are paragraphs 6–10 of the finally revised draft agreement. Changes in the text as compared with that which you have already received (NABOB 443)[1] are indicated by underlining.[2] You will observe that there has been a change in the numbering of the paragraphs.

2. The matter still outstanding regarding transitional arrangements in 7(II)(B)[3] is the American draft as finally left with us this morning.[4]
Begins

6. *Relation of this line of credit to other obligations*

(I) It is understood that any amounts required to discharge obligations of the United Kingdom to third countries outstanding on the *effective* date of this agreement will be found from resources other than this line of credit.

(II) The Government of the United Kingdom will not arrange any long term loans from Governments within the British Commonwealth

---

[1] No. 144. [2] Here italicized.
[3] See 8(II)(B) below. [4] For this draft of 4 December see No. 154.

after *December* [5], *1945* and before the end of 1951 on terms more favourable to the lender than the terms of this line of credit.

(III) Waiver of interest will not be requested or allowed under *Section 5* in any year unless the aggregate of the releases or payments in that year of sterling balances accumulated *to the credit* of overseas Governments, monetary authorities and banks (except in the case of Colonial dependencies) before the *effective* date of this agreement *is* reduced proportionately, and unless interest payments *due in that year* on loans referred to in (II) above are waived. The proportionate reduction of the releases or payments of sterling balances shall be calculated *in relation to* the aggregate released *and paid* in the most recent year in which waiver of interest was not requested.

(IV) The application of the principles set forth in this section shall be the subject of full consultation between the two Governments as occasion may arise.

7. Sterling Area Exchange Arrangements.

The Government of the United Kingdom will complete arrangements as early as practicable and in any case not later than one year after the effective date of this agreement, unless in exceptional cases a later date is agreed upon after consultation, *under which* immediately after the completion of such arrangements the sterling receipts from current transactions of all sterling area countries (apart from any receipts arising out of military expenditure by the *Government of the* United Kingdom prior to December 31, 1948, *to the extent to which they are treated by agreement with the countries concerned* on the same basis as the balances accumulated during the war) will be freely available for current transactions in any currency area without discrimination with the result that any discrimination arising from the so-called sterling area dollar pool will be entirely removed and that each member of the sterling area will have its current sterling and dollar receipts at its free disposition for current transactions anywhere.

8. Other Exchange Arrangements.

(I) The Government of the United Kingdom agrees that after the effective date of this agreement it will *not* apply exchange *controls in such a manner as to* restrict

(A) payments or transfers in respect of products *of the United States* permitted to be imported into the United Kingdom or other current transactions between the two countries (*words omitted*)[6] or

(B) on the use of sterling balances *to the credit* of *residents of the United States* arising out of current transactions. (*Words omitted*).[6] *Nothing in this paragraph (1) shall affect the provisions of Article VII of the Articles of Agreement of the International Monetary Fund when those Articles have come into force.*

(II) The Governments of the United States and the United Kingdom

[5] Omission in original: the final text here read '6th December, 1945'.
[6] From the text in No. 144.

agree that not later than one year after the effective date of this agreement, unless in exceptional cases a later date is agreed upon after consultation, they will impose no restrictions on payments and transfers for current transactions (*words omitted*).[6] The obligations of this paragraph (II) shall not apply:

(A)   To balance[s] of third countries and their nationals accumulated before this para. (II) becomes effective; *or*

(B)   To restrictions imposed in conformity with the Articles of Agreement of the International Monetary Fund; *provided that* the Governments of the United Kingdom and the United States will not continue to invoke the provisions of Article XIV Section 2 of *those Articles* after this para (II) becomes effective *unless in exceptional cases after consultation they agree otherwise*; or

(C)   To restrictions imposed in connection with measures designed to uncover and dispose of assets of Germany and Japan.

(III) *This Section and Section 9 which are in anticipation of more comprehensive arrangements by multilateral agreement, shall operate until December 31, 1951.*

9. Import Arrangements.

If either the Government of the United States or the Government of the United Kingdom imposes or maintains quantitative import restrictions, such restrictions shall be administered on a basis which does not discriminate against imports from the other country in respect of any product; provided that this undertaking shall not apply in cases in which

(A)   its application would have the effect of preventing the country imposing such restrictions from utilizing, for the purchase of needed imports, inconvertible currencies accumulated up to December 31, 1946; or

(B)   there may be special necessity for the country imposing such restrictions to assist, by measures not involving a substantial departure from the general rule of non-discrimination, a country whose economy has been disrupted by war; *or*

(C)   *either Government imposes quantitative restrictions having equivalent effect to any exchange restrictions which that Government is authorised to impose in conformity with Article VII of the Articles of Agreement of the International Monetary Fund.* The provisions of this Section *shall* become effective as soon as practicable but not later than December 31, 1946.[7]

---

[7] In NABOB 470 of 5 December the British Delegation indicated 'the main changes in the American draft which were introduced to-day [4 December: cf. No. 152] in an attempt to meet the requirements' of Nos. 148–9: '2. Paragraph 7, NABOB 443 [No. 144] has been redrafted as paragraph 8, NABOB 468 so as to remove all reference to Article XIV of Bretton Woods. The last sentence of the redrafted paragraph safeguards our scarce currency rights under Article VII.

'3. As you know we have failed to secure deletion of the substance of the parenthesis in 7(II)(*b*) of NABOB 443. But the final version 8(II)(*b*) (NABOB 468) includes explicit provision for consultation in exceptional cases.

10. Accumulated Sterling Balances

(I) The Government of the United Kingdom intends to make agreements with the countries concerned, varying according to the circumstances of each case, for an early settlement covering the sterling balances accumulated by sterling area and other countries prior to such settlement (together with any future receipts arising out of military expenditure by the *Government of the* United Kingdom *to the extent to which they are treated on the same basis by agreement with the countries concerned*.) The settlements with the sterling area countries will be on the basis of dividing these accumulated balances into three categories:

(A) Balances to be released at once and convertible into any currency for current transactions;

(B) Balances to be similarly released by instalments over a period of years beginning in 1951; and

(C) Balances to be adjusted as a contribution to the settlement of war and post war indebtedness and in recognition of the benefits which the countries concerned might be expected to gain from such a settlement. The Government of the United Kingdom will make every endeavour to secure the early completion of *these* arrangements.

(II) In consideration of the fact that an important purpose of the present line of credit is to promote the development of multilateral trade and facilitate its early resumption on a non-discriminatory basis, the Government of the United Kingdom agrees that any sterling balances released or otherwise *available for current payments* will not later than one year after the effective date of this agreement unless in special cases a later date is agreed upon after consultation, be freely available for current transactions in any currency area without discrimination.

Ends.

'4. 8(III) is new and is introduced to limit application in time of undertakings of both paragraphs 8 and 9. This meets the criticism that we should be signing away for 55 years our right to walk out of Bretton Woods.

'5. 9(*c*) safeguards the exceptional provision for the use of discriminatory quantitative restriction where a condition of scarcity of any particular currency has been declared.'

No. 159

British Missions (Washington) to Cabinet Offices
(Received 5 December, 12.46 p.m.)

NABOB 469 Telegraphic [UE 6080/1094/53]

Most immediate. Secret   WASHINGTON, 5 *December 1945, 7.45 a.m.*

Reference NABOB 466.[1]

Following is text of sections 11 and 12.

Section 11 is new and we hope you accept its form. It seems to us reasonable that the sterling area should be defined for the purposes of this documents [*sic*] as it is at present constituted. Please confirm that we have referred to the correct Treasury order. Section 12 is unchanged.

Begins.

11. *Definitions* For the purposes of this agreement:

(I) The term 'current transactions' shall have the meaning pre-scribed in article XIX (I) of the articles of agreement of the International Monetary Fund.

(II) the term 'sterling area' means the United Kingdom and the other territories declared by the Defence (Finance) (definition of sterling area) (no. 2) order, 1944,[2] to be included in the sterling area, namely 'the following Territories excluding Canada and Newfoundland, that is to say:

(*a*) any Dominion,

(*b*) any other part of His Majesty's Dominions,

(*c*) any Territory in respect of which a Mandate on behalf of the League of Nations has been accepted by His Majesty and is being exercised by His Majesty's Government in the United Kingdom, or in any Dominion,

(*d*) any British Protectorate or Protected State,

(*e*) Egypt, the Anglo-Egyptian Sudan and Iraq,

(*f*) Iceland and the Faroe Islands'.

12. *Consultation on Agreement* Either Government shall be entitled to approach the other for a re-consideration of any of the provisions of this agreement, if in its opinion the prevailing conditions of international exchange justify such reconsideration with a view to agreeing upon modifications for presentation to their respective Legislatures.

Signed in duplicate at Washington, District of Columbia this .... [3]
day of December, 1945.

For the Government of the United States
.... [3]

For the Government of the United Kingdom
.... [3]

[1] No. 157.i.

[2] Dated 19 October 1944 and published by H.M.S.O. as *Statutory Rules and Orders 1944*, No. 1185.

[3] Omission in original.

438

No. 160

British Missions (Washington) to Cabinet Offices
(Received 5 December, 12.24 p.m.)

NABOB 471 Telegraphic [UE 6049/1094/53]

Most immediate. Secret   WASHINGTON, 5 December 1945, 7.49 a.m.

Reference your BABOON 345,[1] paragraph 3(e).

1. Immediately following telegram[2] contains text of joint statement on Lend Lease, Reciprocal Aid, surplus property and claims as agreed with Americans at operating level to-night. We are promised clearance at ealiest possible time to-morrow.

2. We have made strenuous efforts to confine this document to essential points. Detailed agreements relating to specific subjects such as surpluses, military inventory, aircraft, nature of items covered by settlement, installations, will certainly be required but these can be drafted next week.

3. There are a number of drafting points in statement, on which, had time allowed, we might have been able to improve. But we have considered it necessary to avoid arguing over minor points particularly as we have succeeded in securing the all-important statement regarding consideration for Lend Lease in the last sentence of paragraph 2. We can only hope that text is self-explanatory.

4. You will see from paragraph 5(d) that we have not found it possible to obtain the right of free disposal of civilian end-use goods in the military inventory in India and Burma,[3] but it has been evident to us for some time that the Americans were not prepared, for political reasons, to grant this concession at any price. In fact we count ourselves fortunate to have retained right of free disposal in the U.K. and the colonies, concerning which the Americans have recently seen great difficulties.[4]

---

[1] Not printed. This telegram of 4 December referred to NABOB 450 of 3 December which reported a meeting with the Americans that morning which discussed a proposal, in the event of a satisfactory outcome of the financial negotiations, for a general communiqué on the lines of NABOB 392 (cf. No. 119.iii) covering joint statements on the I.T.O. proposals (cf. *ibid.* and No. 163.ii), the financial agreement, Lend–Lease (see below) and the further matters discussed in No. 163, note 6. BABOON 345 set out the form and content of the parliamentary statement to be made by Mr. Attlee on 6 December generally covering the points set out in NABOB 450.

[2] Not printed. This telegram transmitted the text of the Joint Statement regarding Settlement for Lend-Lease, Reciprocal Aid, Surplus War Property and Claims printed in Cmd. 6708, pp. 6–8.

[3] Cf. No. 143, Section 4, Note 1.

[4] In BABOON 353 of 5 December the British Delegation were informed that paras. 1 to 4 of the Joint Statement were acceptable but 'great practical difficulties' in implementing para. 5(d) were foreseen. A preferable formulation would be: 'Disposal for military or civilian use, other than in U.K. and Colonies, of Lend–Lease articles held at V.J. Day by the U.K. Armed Forces will be made on conditions to be mutually agreed.' In NABOB 485 of 5

5. This document is of course subject to the same rigours of the timetable as are mentioned in NABOB 460,[5] paragraph 4.

CALENDARS TO NO. 160

i *11 Dec. 1945   British Missions (Washington) Tel. NABOB 499* Agreement reached with Americans on definition of U.S. military surpluses and installations to which the U.K. are entitled under Lend–Lease settlement [UE 6049/1094/53].

ii *12 Dec. 1945   British Missions (Washington) Tel. NABOB 501* List of detailed agreements to be negotiated with Americans (see para. 2 above), which British Delegation wish to press on with while U.S. representatives are still in Washington (see further Duncan Hall, *North American Supply*, pp. 479–82) [UE 6049/1094/53].

iii *12 Dec. 1945   British Missions (Washington) Tels. NABOB 502–4* Comments on discussions with Americans and on text of 'Subsidiary Agreement on Non-Combat Aircraft' (NABOB 503) [UE 6049/1094/53].

December, however, the Delegation expressed the view that the American argument, 'that they do not see why we should have the right to give away Lend–Lease equipment, which was provided for our use, to the armed forces of, e.g., the Union of South Africa', was not unreasonable, and that they did not therefore propose to suggest the amendment to para. 5(*d*). The text in NABOB 472 remained unchanged except for minor verbal amendment.

[5] Not printed. This telegram of 5 December referred to BABOON 345 (see note 1) and explained the latest plans for identical statements by Mr. Attlee and President Truman, to which American agreement had been obtained with 'considerable difficulty'. Para. 4 stated: 'The Americans have told us that all documents must be cleared with you by 11.30 a.m. tomorrow, Wednesday [5 December], Washington time if the time-table for agreed release on Thursday evening is to be adhered to' (UE 6035/1094/53).

No. 161

Cabinet Offices to British Missions (Washington)

BABOON *350 Telegraphic* [UE 6247/1094/53]

Most immediate. Secret   CABINET OFFICES, *5 December 1945, 3.5 p.m.*

From Prime Minister to Ambassador.

1. Ministers have considered the whole position. You have all done your best and we are very grateful to you for your long and arduous efforts.[1] We accept and Ambassador may sign.

2. It would help us considerably if the operative date for 7(II)[2] could be 31st December 1947 instead of one year from the effective date of the agreement.[3] This would particularly help in Parliament and in view of the

[1] See also Mr. Dalton's letter of thanks of the same day to Lord Keynes printed in H. Dalton, *High Tide and After*, p. 87.
[2] i.e. in para. 8(II) in No. 158.
[3] This amendment had been suggested to Mr. Dalton by Sir W. Eady in a note of 5 December (i), evidently in preparation for the Cabinet meeting that day (see ii).

other clauses in the agreement could not materially harm Americans.

3. We should like you to try this but not to press it to a situation creating any more difficulties. If you should succeed please inform us at once.

4. At time of despatch the amended text[4] has not come to the hands of officials concerned. If there are any points to be cleared we will try to do this by telephone.

CALENDARS TO NO. 161

i 5 Dec. 1945 Minute from Sir W. Eady to Mr. Dalton on implications of relinquishing transitional period of Bretton Woods, but 'on the merits of the financial situation as a whole your Treasury officials must advise you that you ought not to break' [T 236/438].

ii 5 Dec. 1945 C.M. (45) 59th Conclusions, Confidential Annex Cabinet discussion of draft financial agreement: general view 'clearly in favour of accepting'; Mr. Bevin felt 'there could be no question of breaking off the negotiations on the narrow issue of the length of the transitional period' [UE 6101/1094/53].

[4] i.e. Nos. 157–9.

No. 162

British Missions (Washington) to Cabinet Offices
(Received 5 December, 6.30 p.m.)

NABOB 474 Telegraphic [UE 6247/1094/53]

Most immediate. Secret   WASHINGTON, 5 December 1945, 6.15 p.m.

To Prime Minister from Ambassador.
Your BABOON 350.[1]

1. We saw Vinson, Clayton, and Acheson this morning,[2] and put to them your proposal that the operative date should be 31st December 1947, stressing how much this would help you in Parliament.

2. It was abundantly clear that the Americans would have liked to have done this to meet you if they had felt that they could do so without real risk of jeopardizing the passage through Congress of the loan arrangements. But reluctantly they felt bound to refuse.

3. The clause must therefore stand as drafted. But the Americans said that our representations would be on record and would certainly weigh with them if and when we consulted them on the lines laid down in the clause.

4. We are going ahead with the programme as planned.

[1] No. 161.
[2] The agreed minutes of the 9th meeting of the Combined Finance Committee (COM/FIN 9th meeting, GEN 80/89) are printed in *F.R.U.S. 1945*, vol. vi, pp. 193–4.

i *5 Dec. 1945 Note of meeting in Washington between British Delegation and Dominion Ministers,* who were given explanation of agreements reached with Americans: 'Their reports to their Governments are likely to be sympathetic and helpful' (*NABOB 484*) [UE 6035/1094/53, T 236/1657].

No. 163

Mr. Bevin to H.M. Representatives Overseas

No. 46/21 Circular Telegraphic[1] *[UE 6086/1094/53]*

Immediate   FOREIGN OFFICE, *7 December 1945, 7.30 a.m.*

My immediately following telegram contains the text of the Financial Agreement[2] which has been signed in Washington to-day.[3] My second following telegram[4] contains a commentary on these proposals, my third following telegram [i] the text of a statement to be made by the Chancellor of the Exchequer tomorrow and my fourth following telegram the text of the Prime Minister's statement in connexion with the commercial proposals[5] which are referred to in paragraph 3 below.

[1] Transmitted to Washington as telegram No. 25 Saving of 7 December.

[2] Not printed: cf. No. 157, note 1.

[3] NABOB 486 of 6 December had reported: 'Financial Agreement was duly signed and other statements initialled at brief ceremony in State Department at 10.30 a.m. Washington time this morning.' Remarks then made by Mr. Byrnes and Lord Halifax are printed in *D.S.B.*, vol. xiii, p. 910: see further *ibid.* pp. 905–29. The other joint statements were those on commercial policy printed in Cmd. 6709 of 1945, p. 18 (cf. No. 121, note 4 and ii below), and on the final settlement of Lend–Lease (cf. para. 5 below and No. 160, note 2). For extracts from press comments see UE 6174/1094/53.

[4] This telegram, No. 48/23 Circular of 7 December, stated: 'The Financial Agreement contains important references to future changes in the Sterling Area arrangements. In my immediately following telegram [see i] is the text of the statement to be made by the Chancellor of the Exchequer explaining the purpose of these arrangements and the intentions of His Majesty's Government in that connexion. As there may be misunderstanding, or even anxiety, about the intentions of His Majesty's Government with regard to the Sterling Area arrangements, you should take an early opportunity of seeing the Government to which you are accredited and leaving with them a copy of the statement.' BABOON 357 of 6 December explained to Lord Keynes that although the 'close substance' of the statement in i (variant text in BABOON 358 not reproduced) would be given at '"off-the-record" background Press Conference' that evening it would not appear textually in the press on 7 December. The statement was 'designed for Sterling Area countries but we believe that we have been scrupulously fair to text and intentions of Financial Agreement'.

The passage on the sterling area (cf. No. 2, note 9) in Mr. Dalton's parliamentary statement on 12 December (*Parl. Debs., 5th ser., H. of C.,* vol. 417, cols. 422–44) was a compressed version of the text in i.

[5] Telegram No. 50 Circular transmitted a slightly variant text of the latter part of Mr. Attlee's statement on 6 December, printed in *Parl. Debs., 5th ser., H. of C.,* vol. 416, beginning 'His Majesty's Government welcome' in col. 2666, and ending 'depends so much' in col. 2670. For the preceding part of Mr. Attlee's statement, relating to the agreement and statements referred to in note 3, *v. ibid.*, cols. 2663–6.

2. His Majesty's Government have at the same time undertaken to adhere to the Bretton Woods Agreements and to lend their support to the United States proposals for an International Trade Organisation in the sense explained in paragraph three below. Both the Financial Agreement and the Bretton Woods Agreements will have to be approved by Parliament, who will also be given an opportunity of debating the International Trade Organisation proposals. Similarly the loan proposals will have to be ratified by Congress.

3. As mentioned above, concurrently with the financial discussions, negotiations on commercial policy have also been taking place. The document under discussion was a proposal for an International Trade Organisation put forward by the Americans in August. Before the talks began we were already in substantial agreement with a good deal of this document. Apart from the constitution of the I.T.O. the proposals deal with general and export subsidies, quantitative restrictions, state trading, restrictive business practices and commodity arrangements. The central feature is however, the proposal for the reciprocal lowering of Tariffs and Preferences. The Americans have conceded the fundamental principle that any steps towards the elimination of preferences must be taken concurrently with steps to reduce tariff barriers. We are accordingly expressing ourselves as in full agreement on all important points in these proposals and accepting them as a basis for international discussion. For your confidential information discussion will in the first place, it is hoped, be held in the spring between the United States, ourselves, the Dominions, India, U.S.S.R., China, Brazil, France, Netherlands, Czechoslovakia, Belgium, and Cuba; the principles of the document will be discussed on a multilateral basis and questions of tariff and preferential reductions on a bilateral basis with a view to paving the way for a full Conference in the summer.

4. In addition, an exchange of letters has taken place between Lord Halifax and the State Department on outstanding matters of economic import, such as civil aviation, shipping, telecommunications and oil, the intention being to record that these matters have not been overlooked and that they will be discussed in the fairly near future.[6]

---

[6] NABOB 409 of 29 November had reported an American proposal that among the 'formal documents to be published recording outcome of present negotiations' should be included an exchange of letters on 'certain economic problems not specifically discussed in course of present negotiations but to the early discussion of which importance is attached by U.S. administration . . . The object is to forestall and frustrate possible criticism to the effect that advantage should have been taken . . . to negotiate agreements over a wide field.' The text of a draft letter by the State Department covering civil aviation, telecommunications, shipping, oil and a possible renegotiation of the Anglo-American commercial treaty of 1815 was transmitted in NABOB 428 of 1 December, but NABOB 450 (cf. No. 160, note 1) of 3 December reported that 'Americans are now rather doubtful about desirability of publishing this exchange of letters this week in view of current civil aviation troubles': cf. No. 93.i. BABOON 345 (cf. No. 160, note 1) of 4 December agreed with this view, and the proposed exchange of letters did not take place. See further note 7 below.

5. Agreement has also been reached for the final settlement of Lend–Lease and Reciprocal Aid, the disposal of surplus war property in the United Kingdom owned by the United States and the final settlement of the claims of each Government against the other arising out of the conduct of the war. All these claims will be met by a payment of $650 millions by the United Kingdom on the same terms and conditions as those applicable to the repayment of the credit of $3750 millions covered by the main agreement.[7]

CALENDARS TO No. 163

i *6–7 Dec. 1945 Press Conferences on Washington Agreement* (*a*) statement on sterling area: see note 4 (Tel. No. 49 circular); (*b*) Notes for statements by Lord Keynes (NABOB 489); (*c*) Comments by Sir W. Eady on preliminary press reactions (BABOON 361) [UE 6086, 6090, 6246/1094/53].

ii *30 Nov.–2 Dec. 1945 Concluding discussions on commercial policy* Discussions with Americans on their draft of joint statement on I.T.O. (cf. No. 119.iii): British objection to special mention of tariffs and preferences, though Sir P. Liesching thought draft 'a token of their genuine goodwill' (NABOB 414–15): problems for British on timetable and Australian sensitivity on preferences. Final meeting of Commercial Policy Committee on 1 Dec. (*F.R.U.S. 1945*, vol. vi, pp. 178–84) adopts COM/TRADE 1 (cf. No. 121, note 4) and 3 (cf. No. 54, notes 1–2). Cf. also No. 160, note 1 [UE 5935, 5985, 6036/1094/53].

[7] In his telegram No. 617 Saving of 17 December, containing an economic summary for the week ending 8 December, Lord Halifax commented that the 'most significant feature of the Lend–Lease agreement was the clause providing that no further benefits would be sought by either Government as a consideration for Lend–Lease and Reciprocal Aid. An American decision not to have an exchange of letters on outstanding problems [see note 6] . . . but to include instead a paragraph in the Lend–Lease agreement on the wider aspects of economic collaboration, with reference to Article VII of the Mutual Aid Agreement, provided an opportunity at the last moment for the inclusion of this quittance clause [see para. 2 of the 'Joint Statement' in Cmd. 6708]. This was not done without some hesitation on the American side, but it speaks well for the American negotiators that, in order to clear away a possible source of friction in the future, they were ready to write *finis* to Lend–Lease clearly in black and white rather than hedge on such a vital issue' (UE 6295/42/53).

Index of Main Subjects and Persons

This straightforward index to document numbers is designed to provide, in conjunction with the Chapter Summaries, a quick finding aid to the main references to the main subjects. Since most documents in the volume refer to aspects of Anglo-American relations, relevant index entries normally come under the main subjects and not under the countries. Similarly entries for the main persons have been limited to items of special interest not otherwise mentioned in the main subject entries or Chapter Summaries. For others, who recur frequently, a reference to the descriptive footnote has been included.

449